Michael Sailstorfer

Till M.

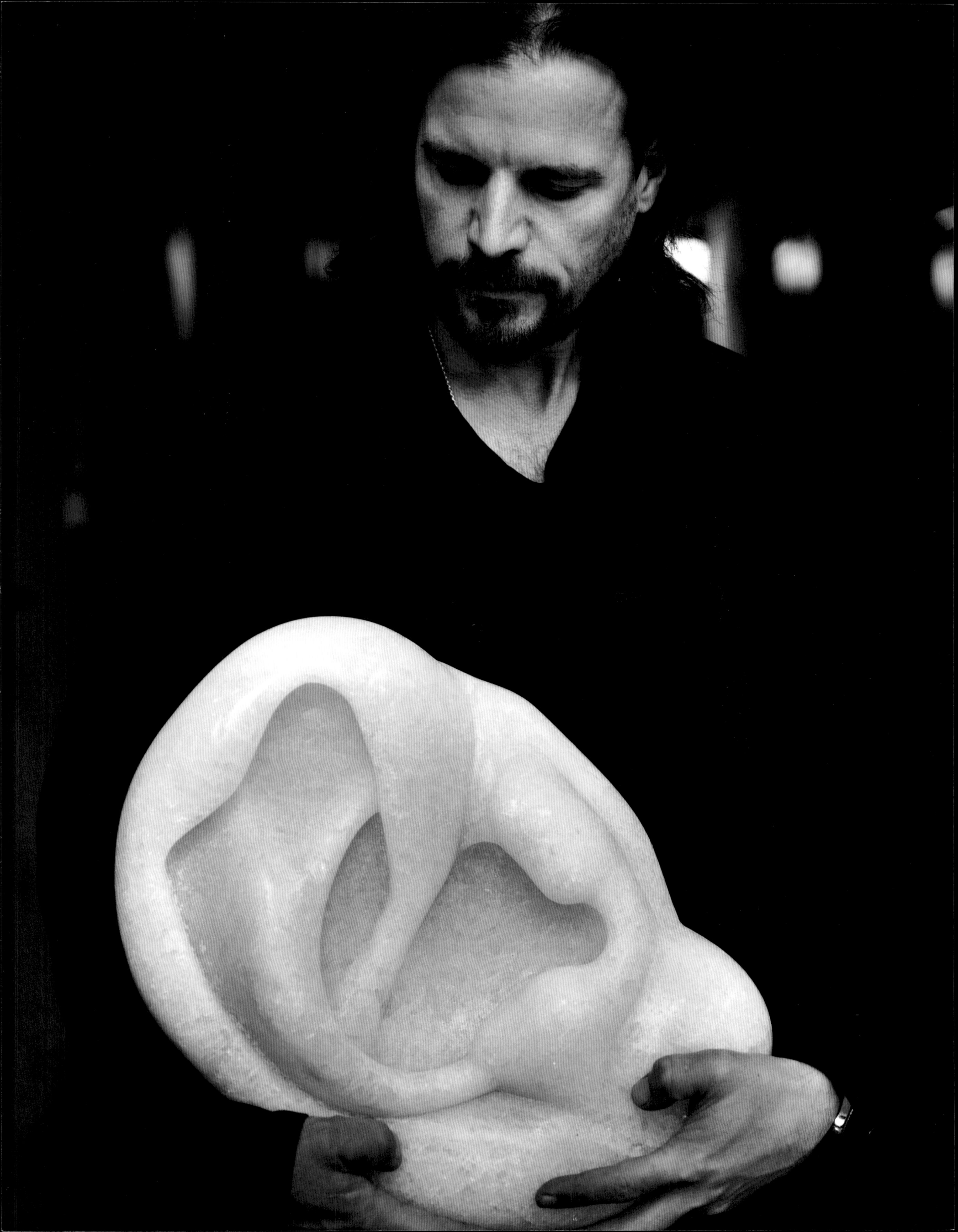

M00
S22

Tearcracker, 2018
C-print, 55 × 42 cm (framed / gerahmt)

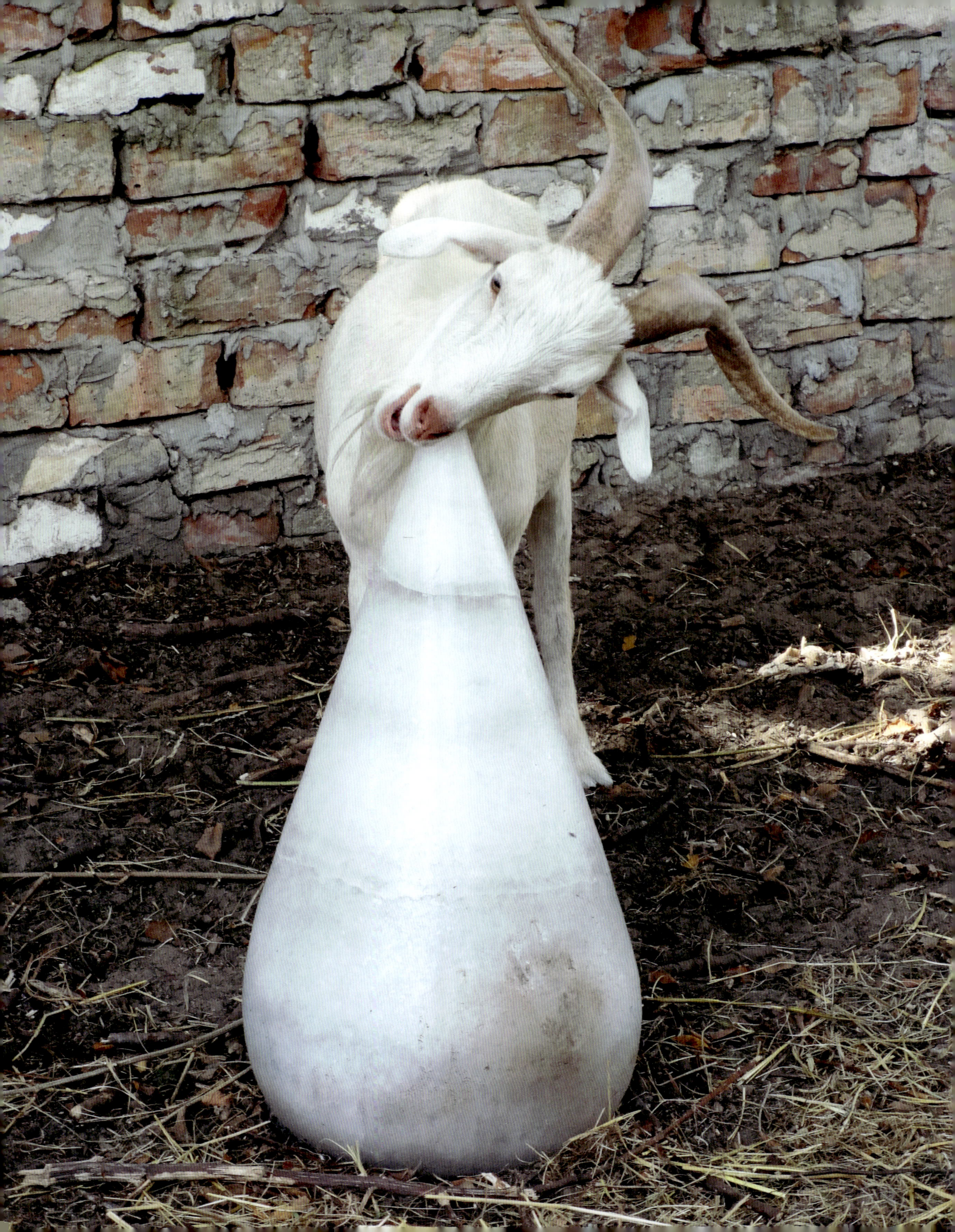

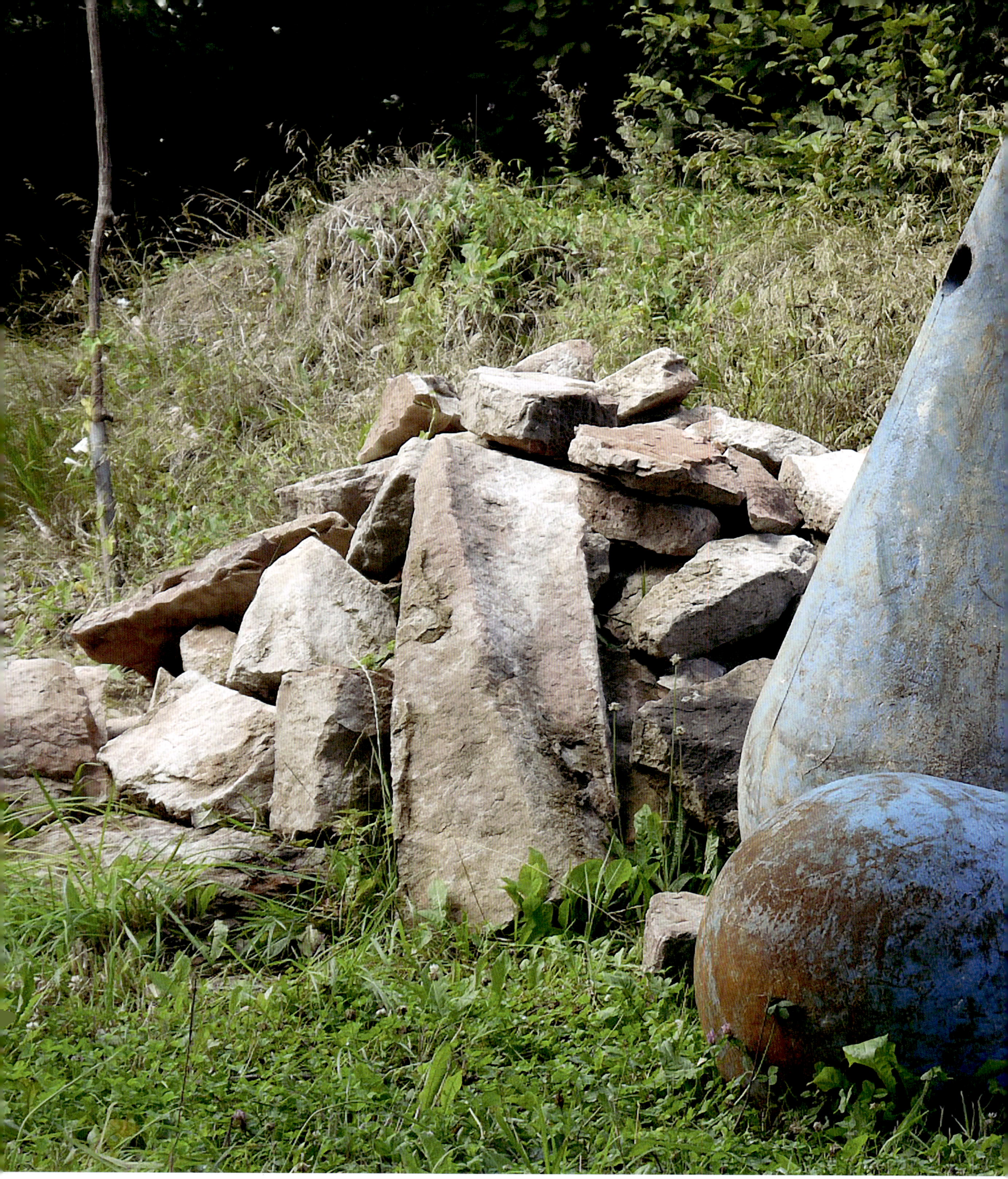

Tränen, 2015

Iron / Eisen, 88 × 47 × 47 cm, 108 × 57 × 57 cm, 128 × 67 × 67 cm

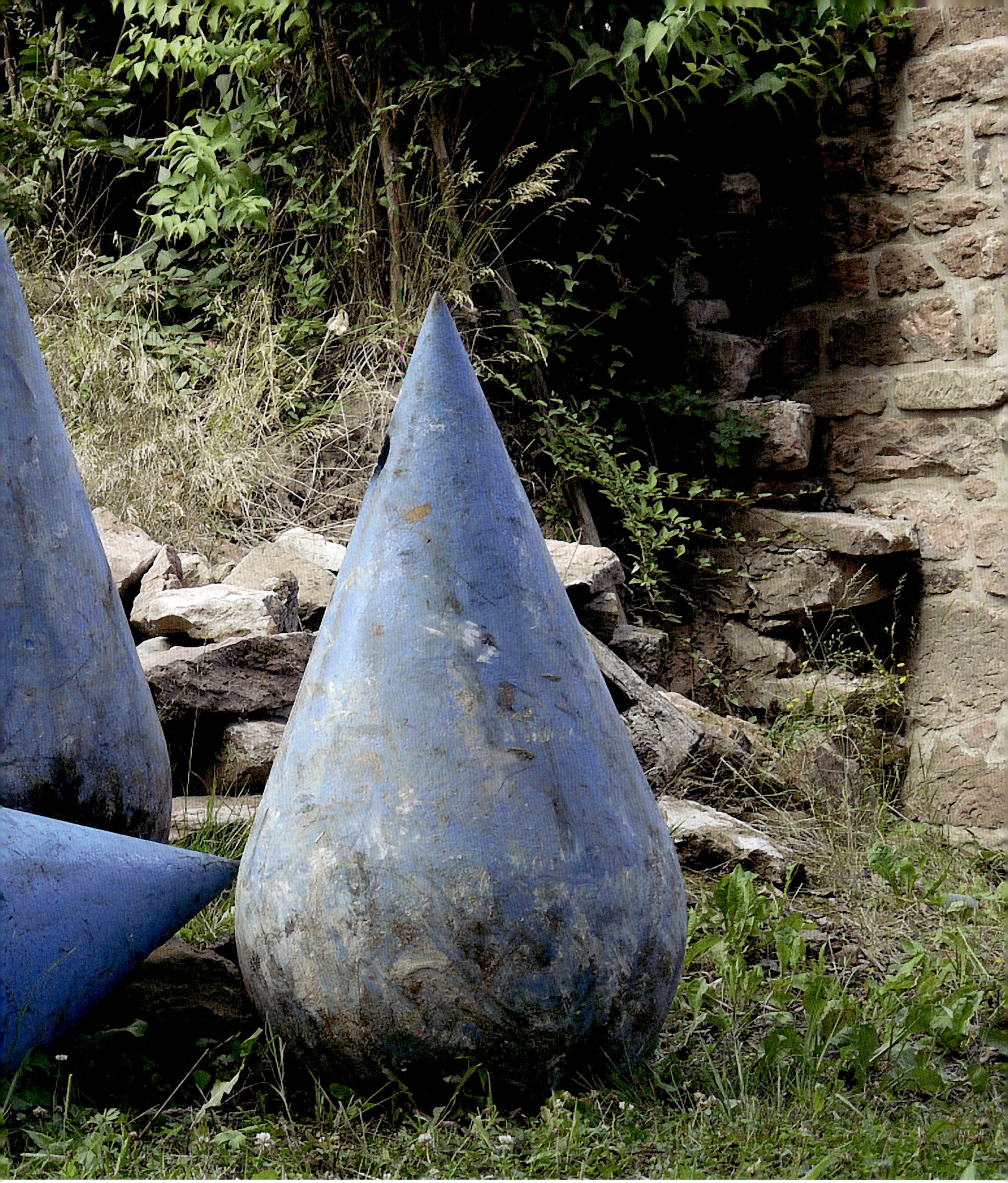

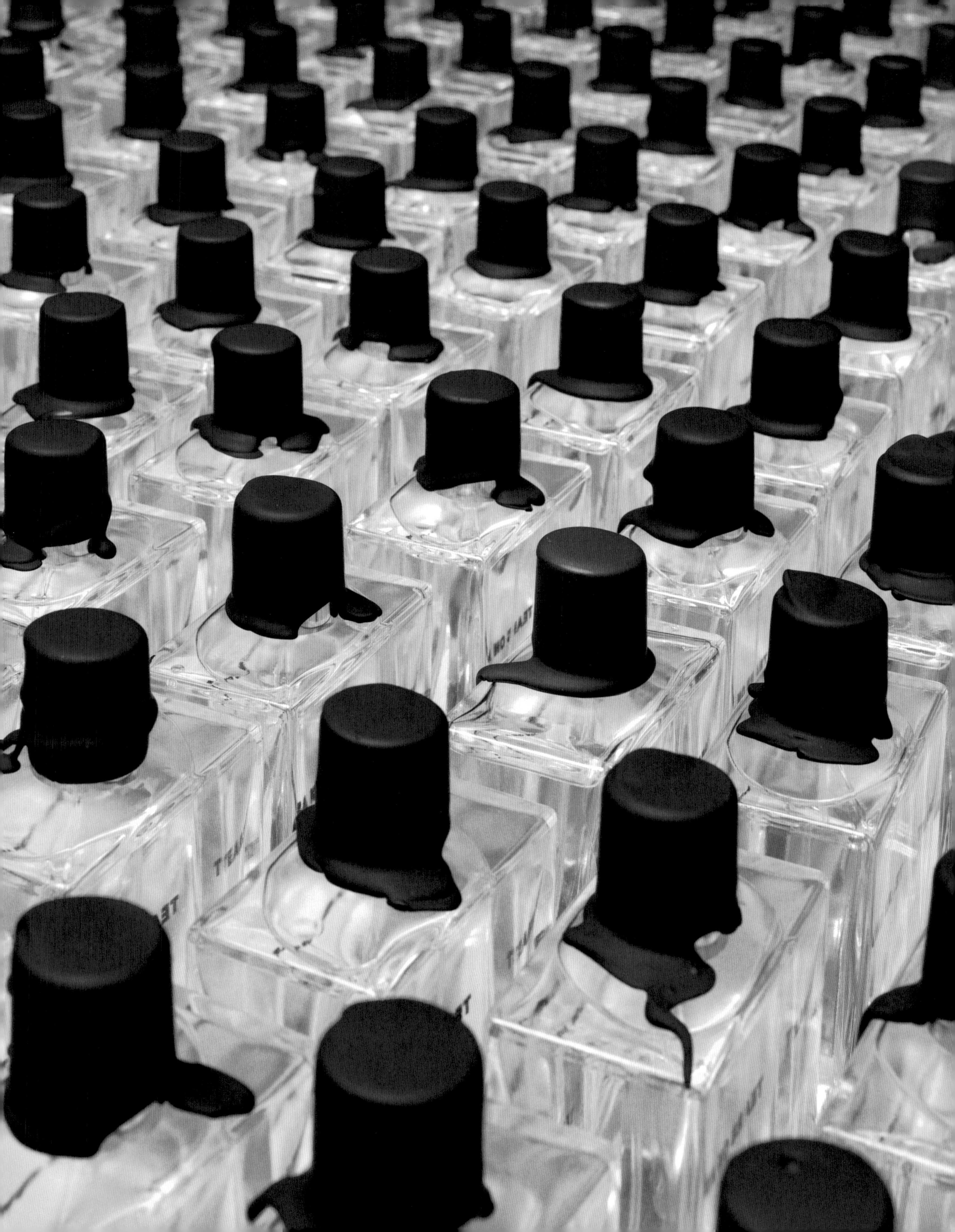

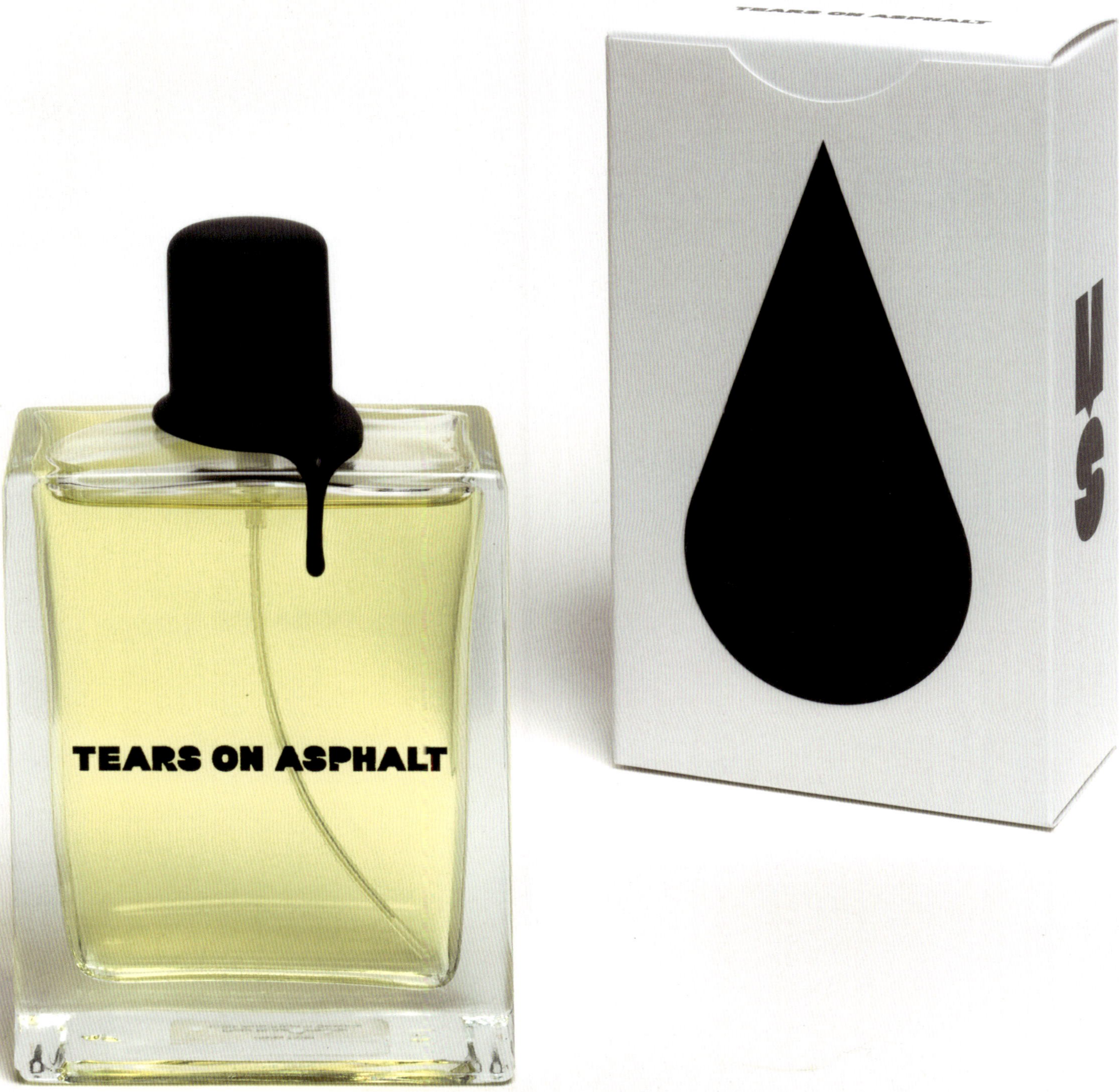

Tears On Asphalt, 2022
Perfume / Parfum

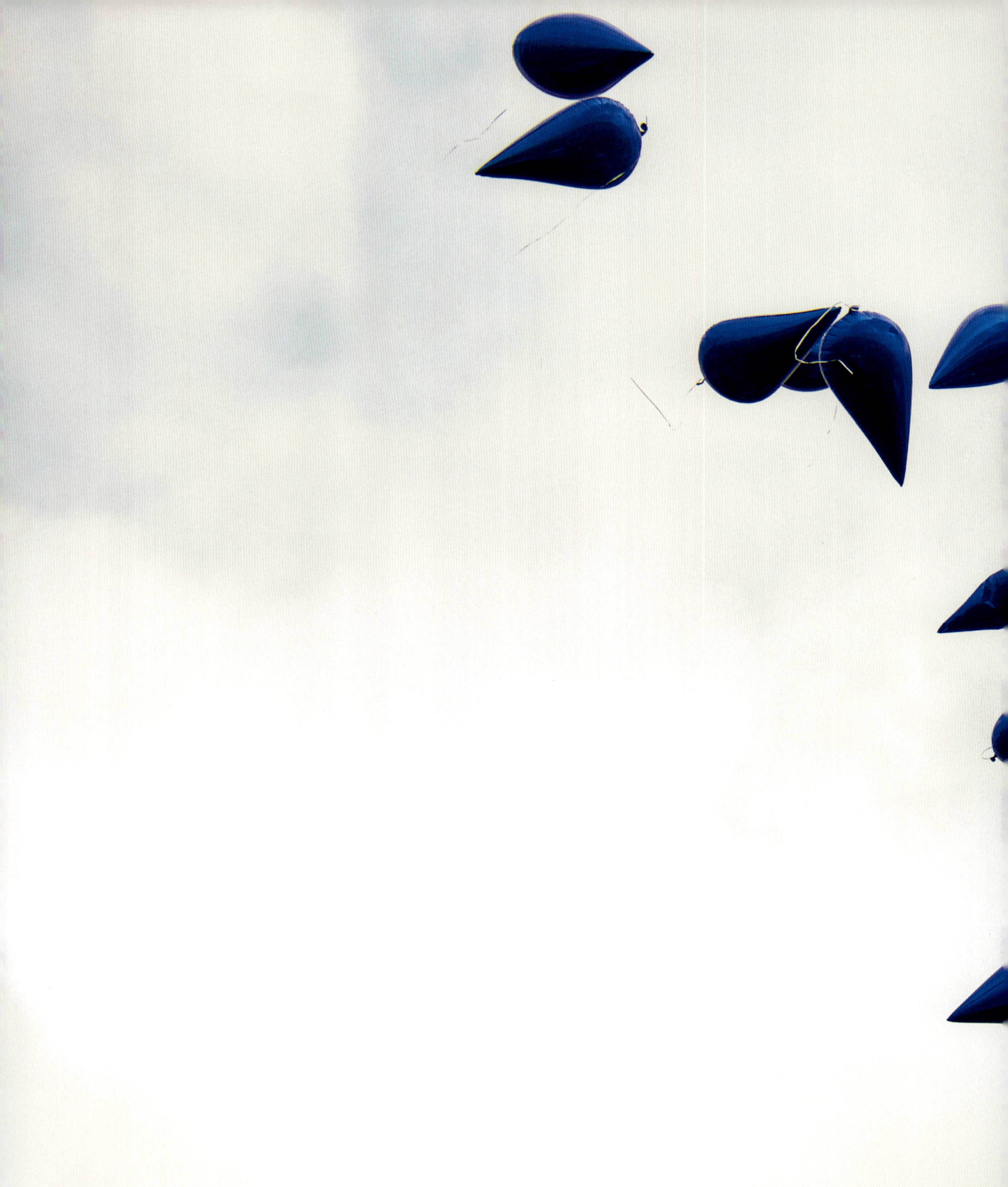

Tear Balloons, 2018

Balloons / Ballons

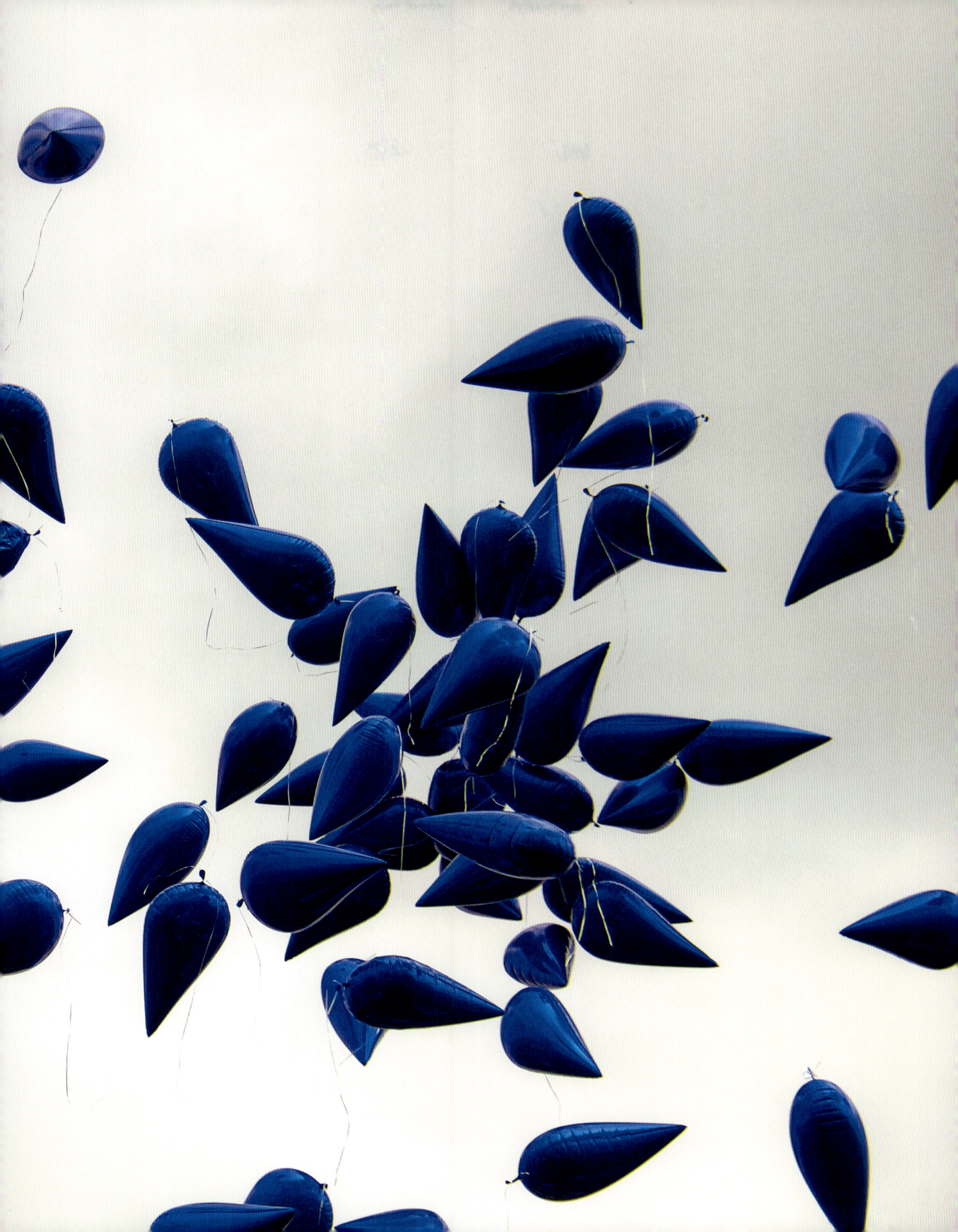

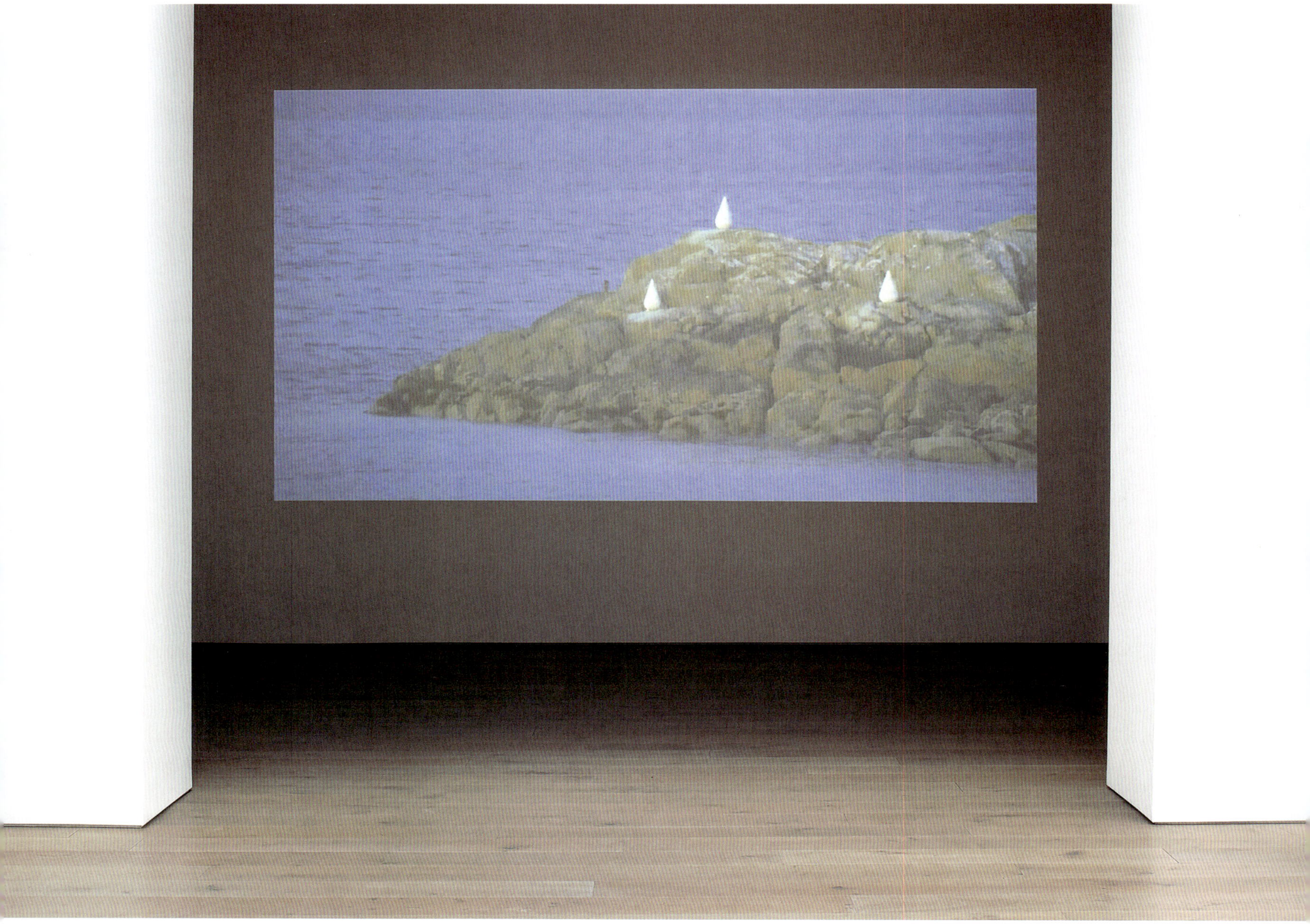

Salt, 2019

Video livestream

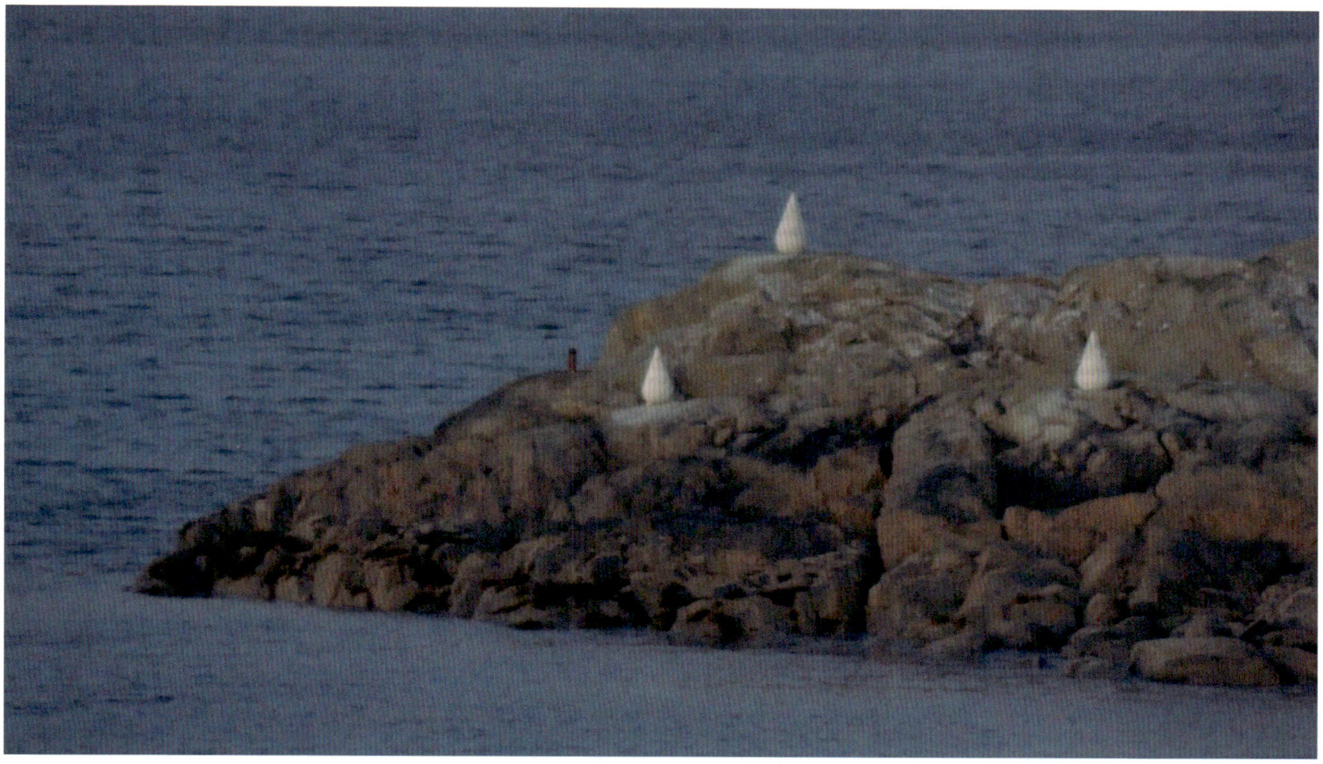

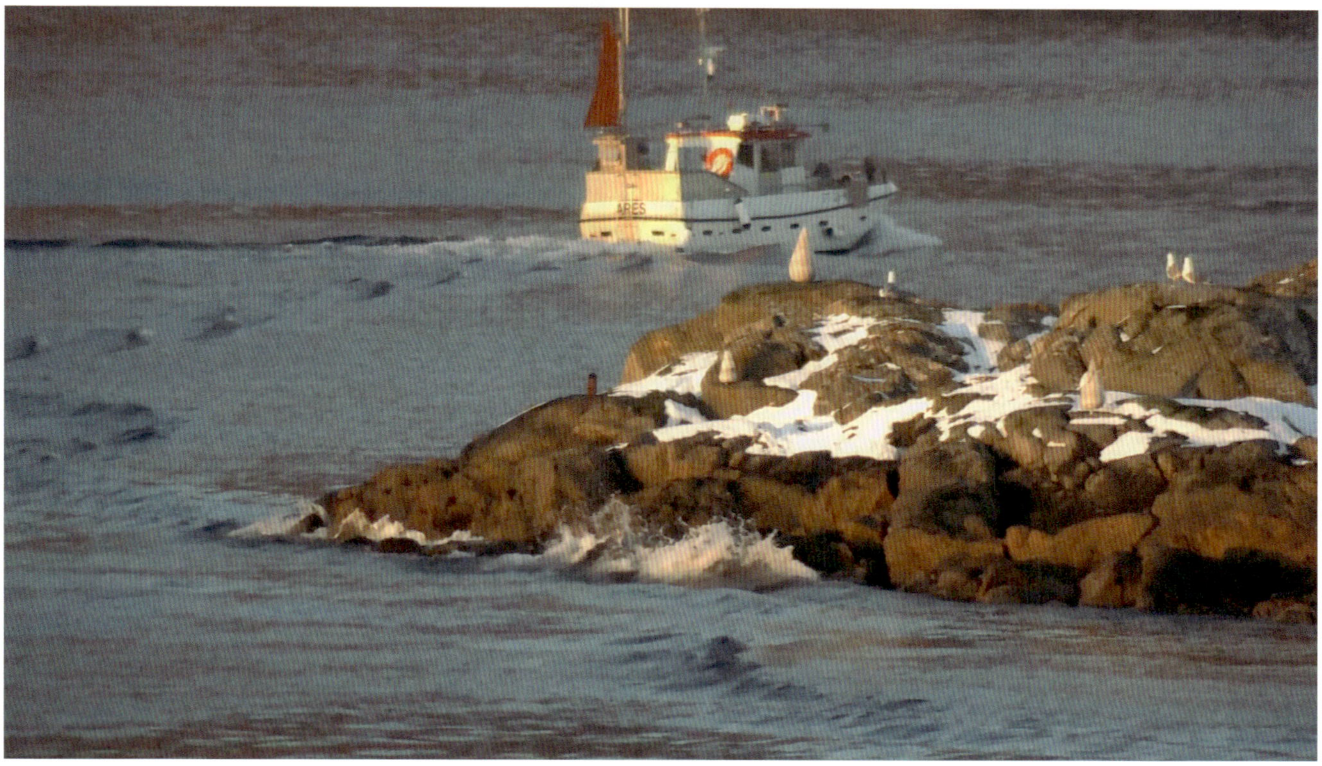
ARES

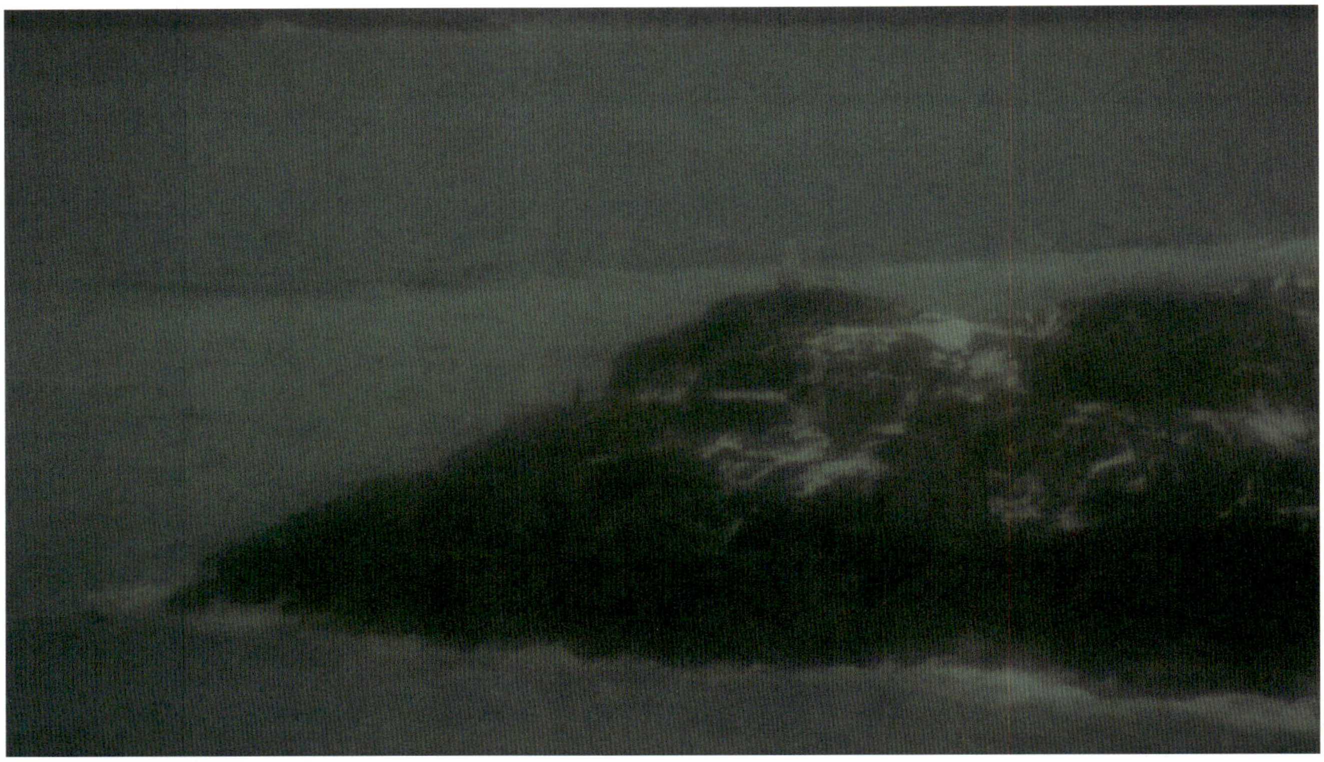

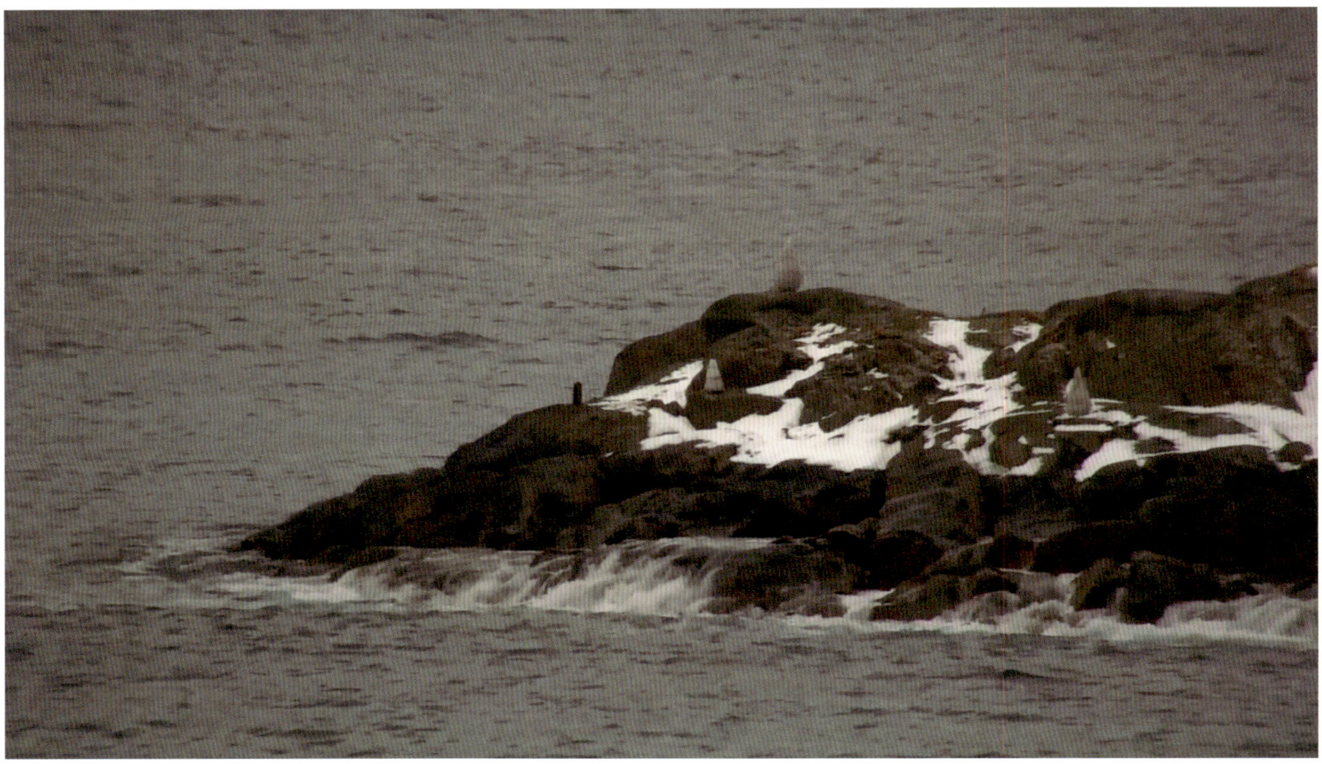

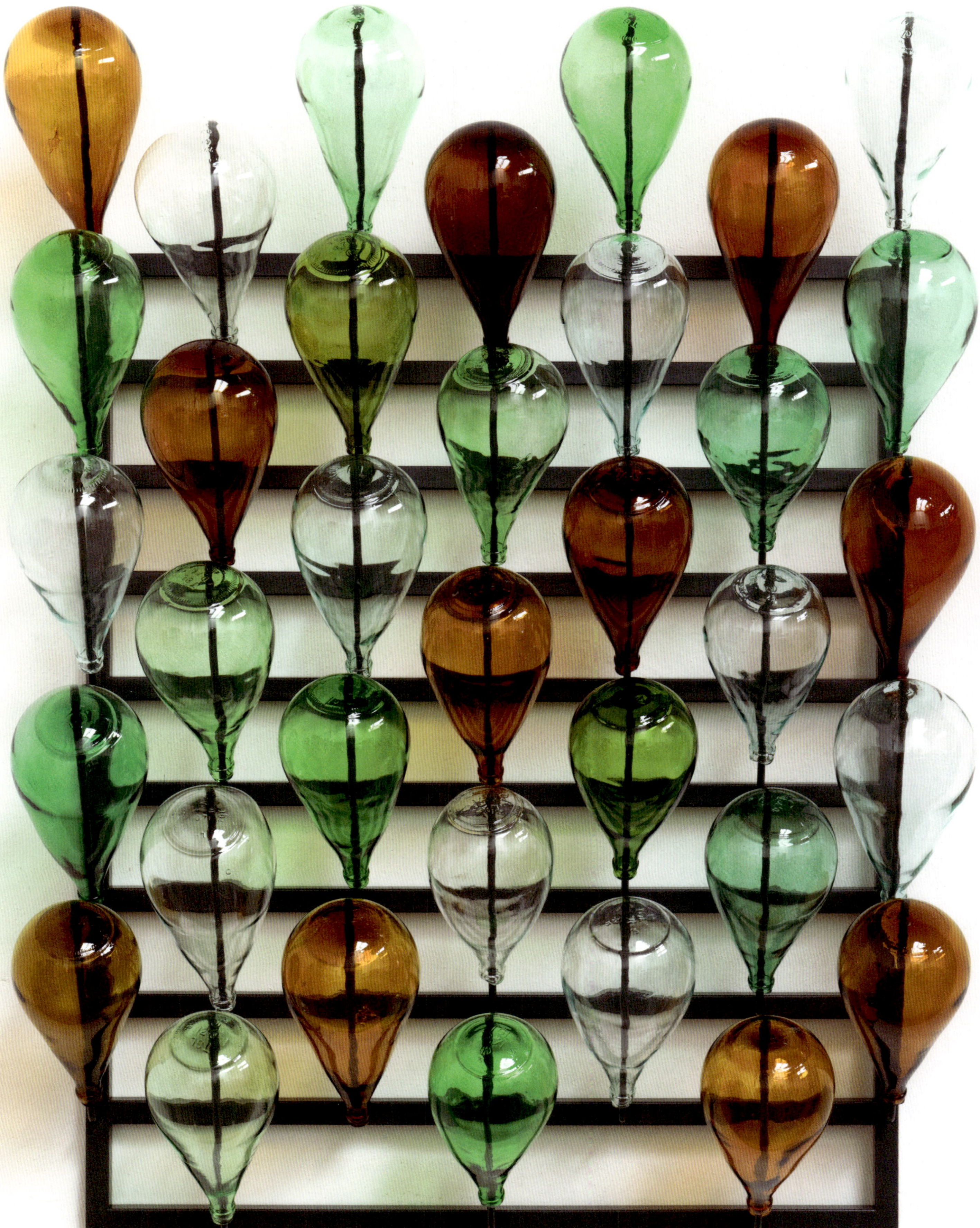

Tränentrockner Köln, 2019

Steel, glass / Stahl, Glas, 130 × 97 × 28 cm

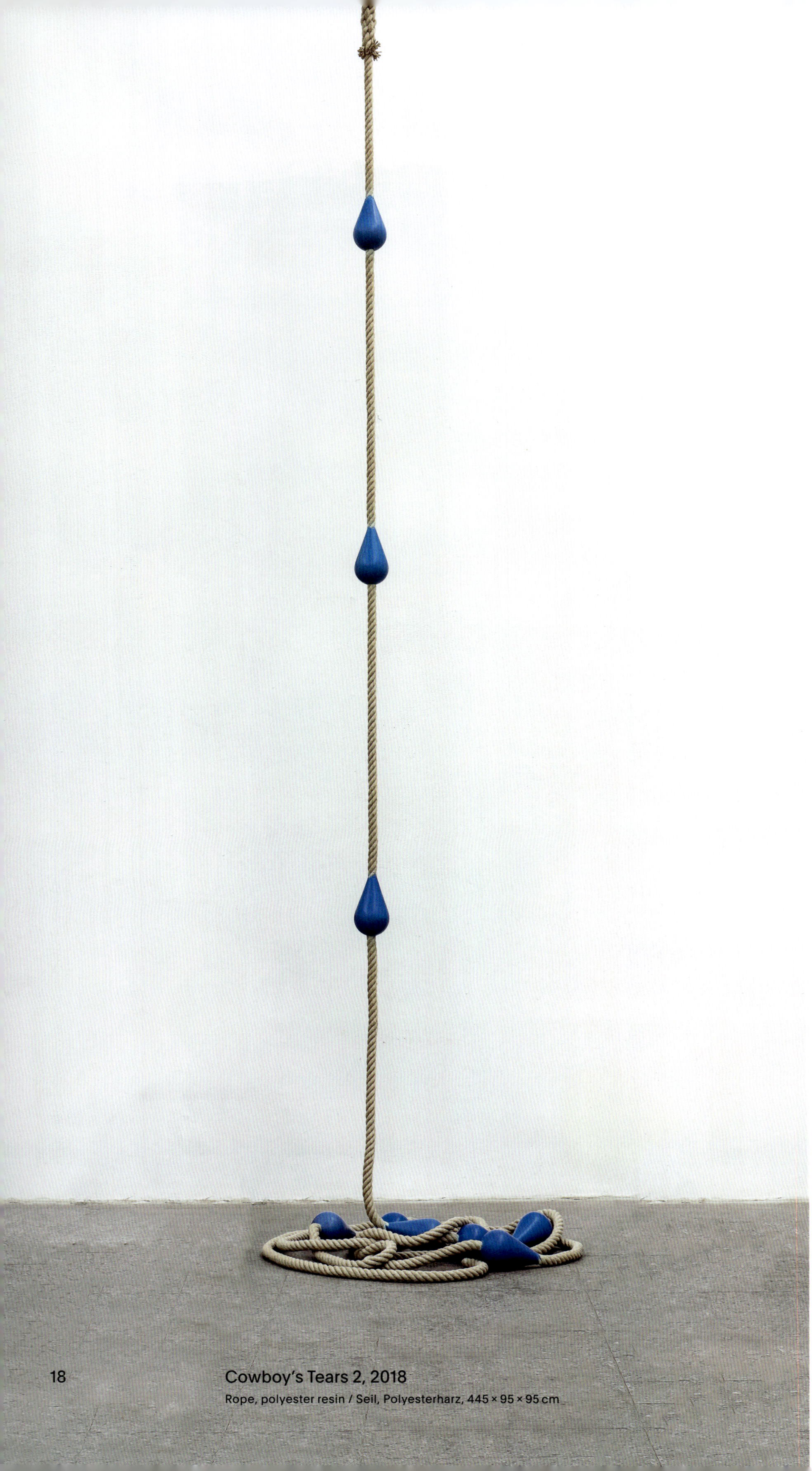

Cowboy's Tears 2, 2018

Rope, polyester resin / Seil, Polyesterharz, 445 × 95 × 95 cm

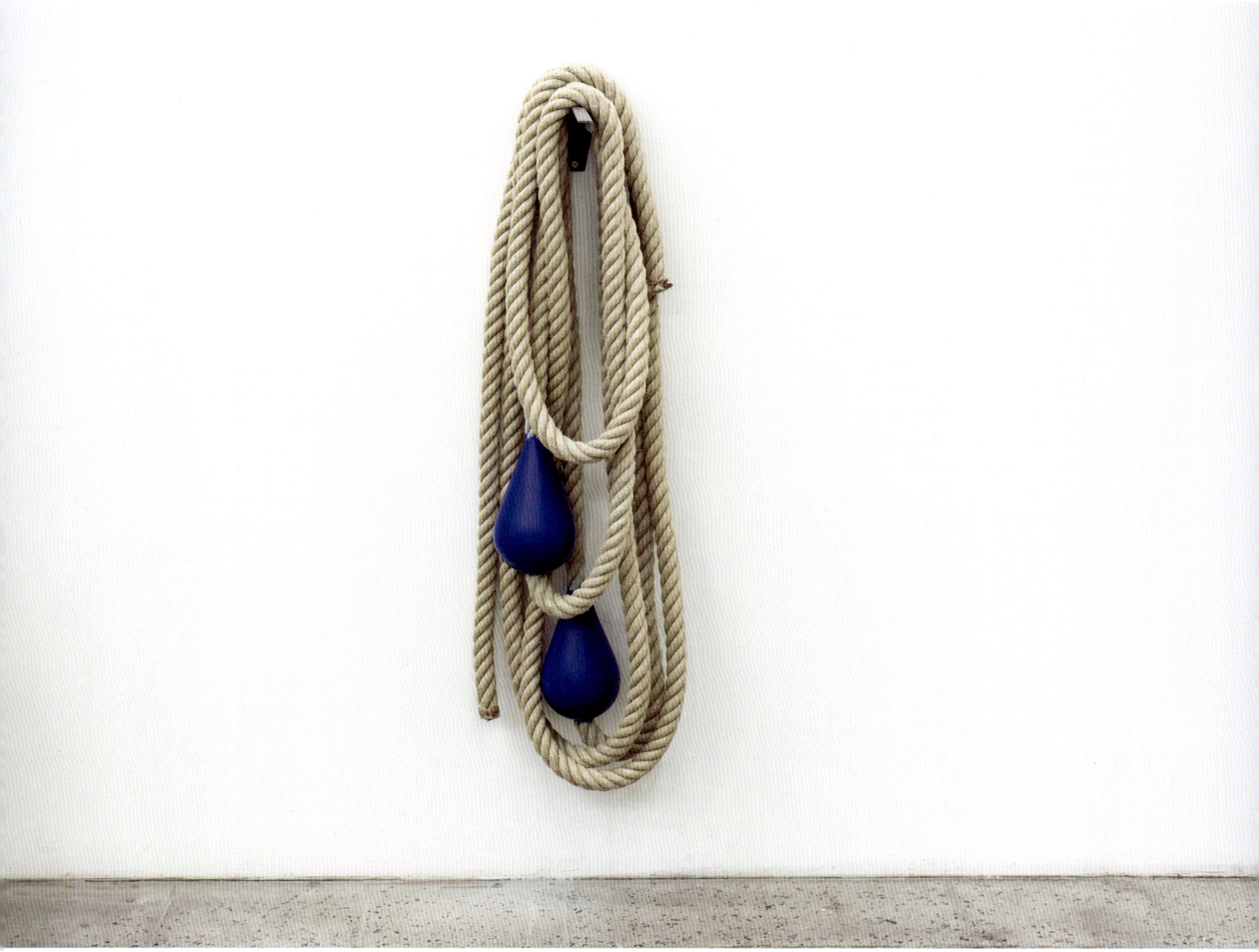

Cowboy's Tears 1, 2018

Rope, polyester resin, steel / Seil, Polyesterharz, Stahl, 107 × 30 × 30 cm

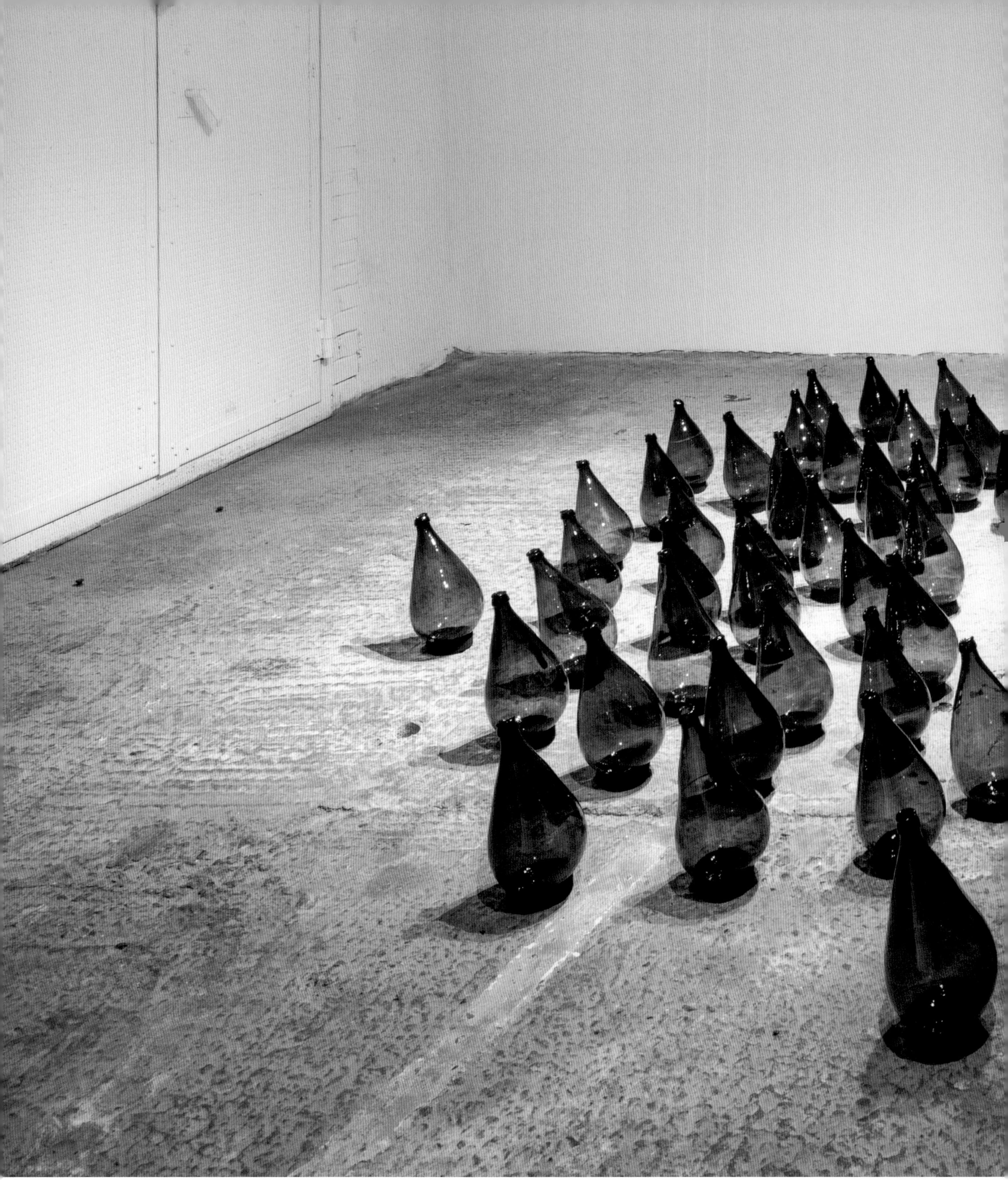

20

Regen, 2018

Glass, rubber / Glas, Gummi, Dimensions variable / Maße variabel,
Installation view / Installationsansicht *Tear Show*, König London

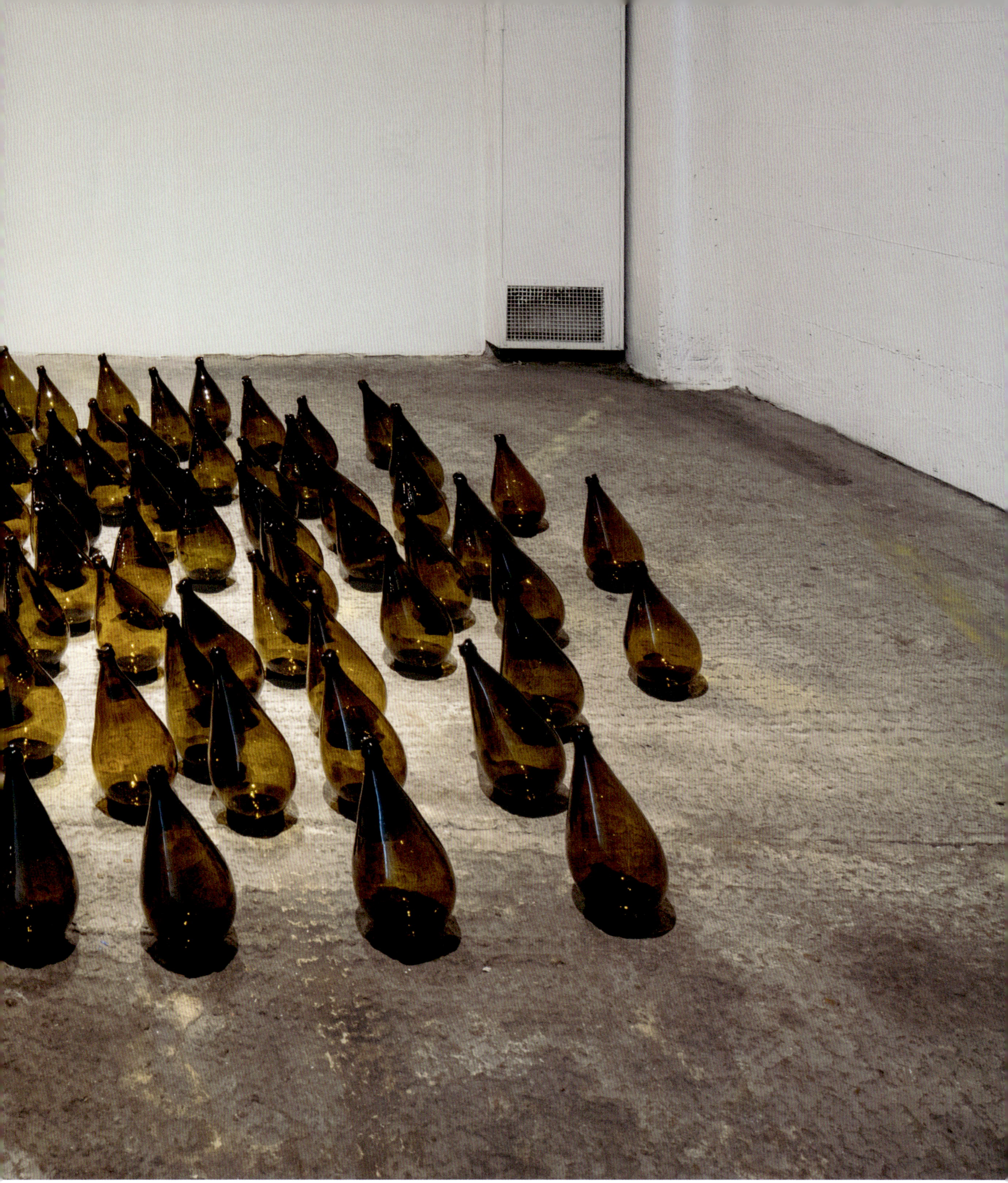

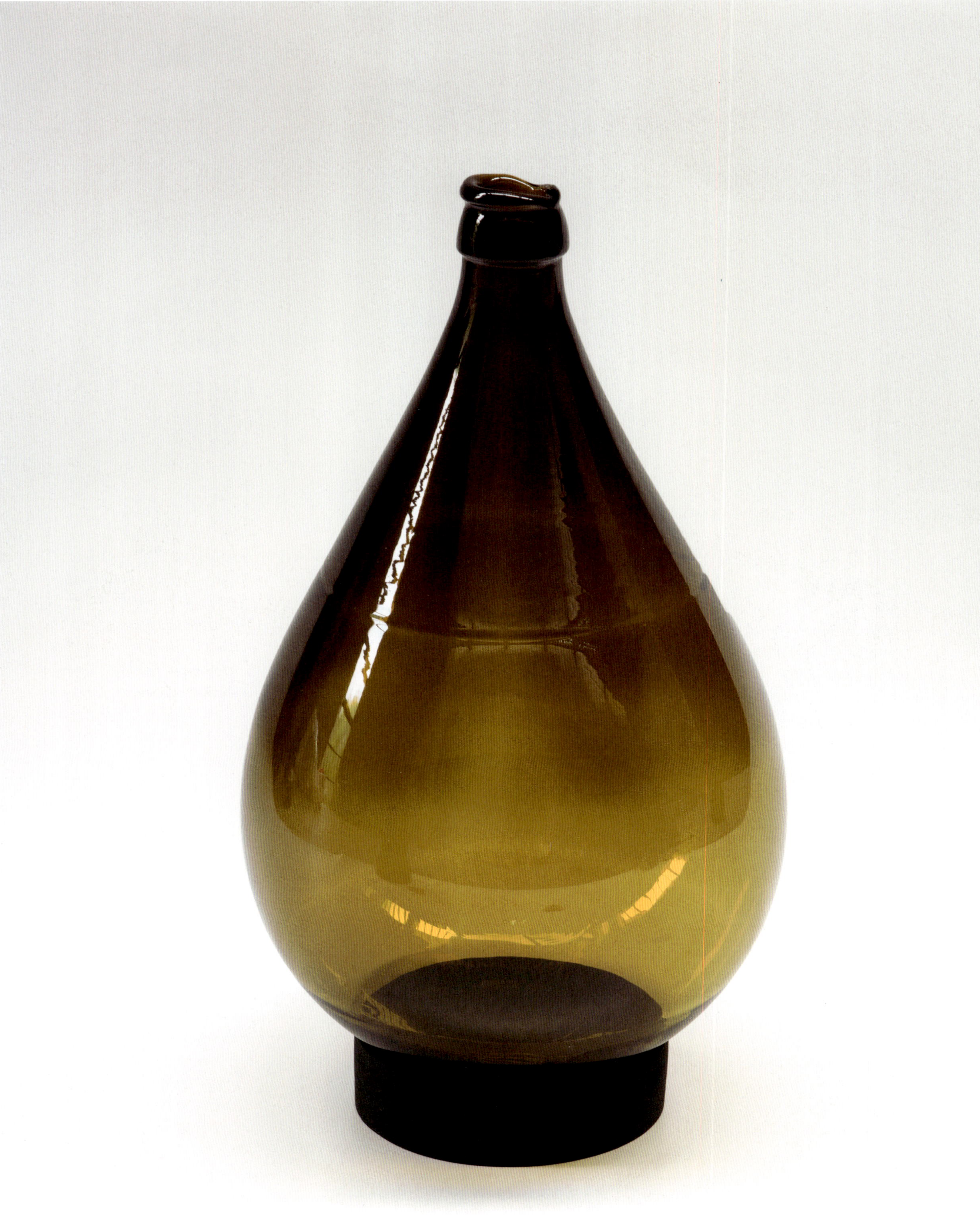

Tear Bottle, 2018

Glass, rubber / Glas, Gummi, 26,5 × 13 × 13 cm

TTV, 2018

Bronze, 220 × 37 × 36 cm

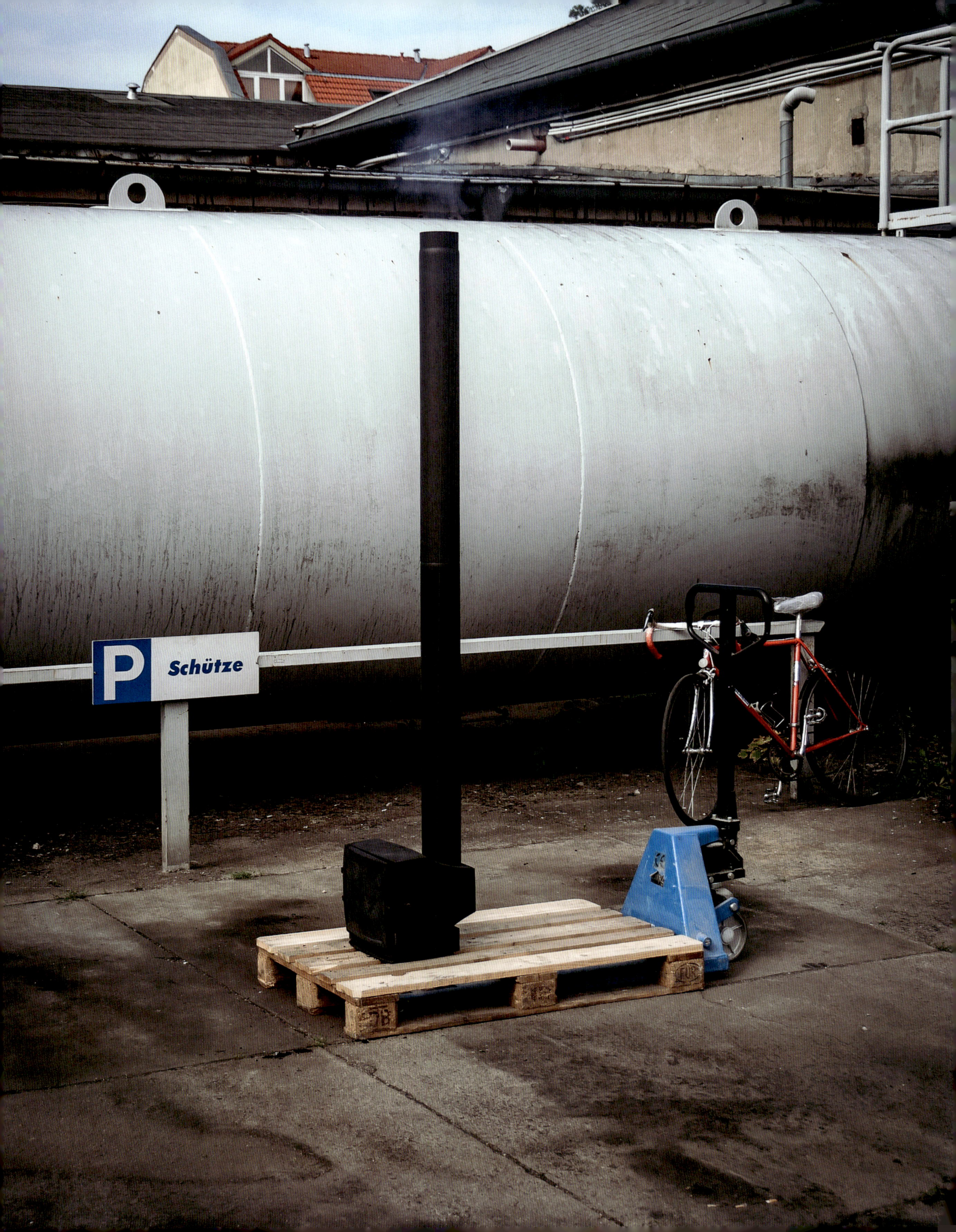
P
Schütze

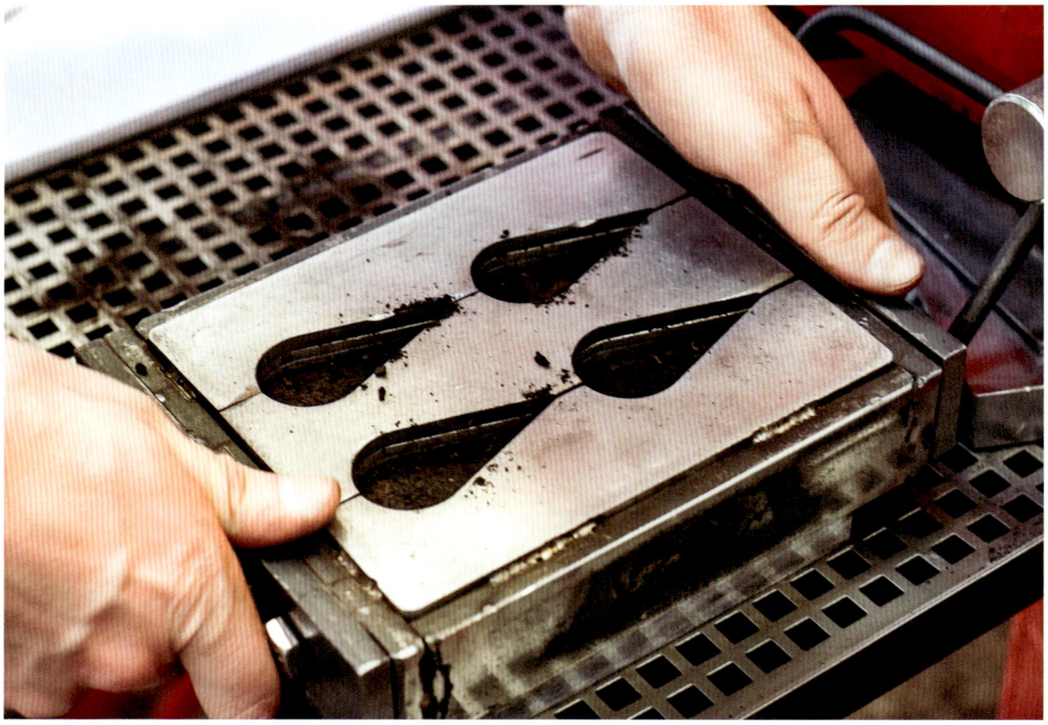

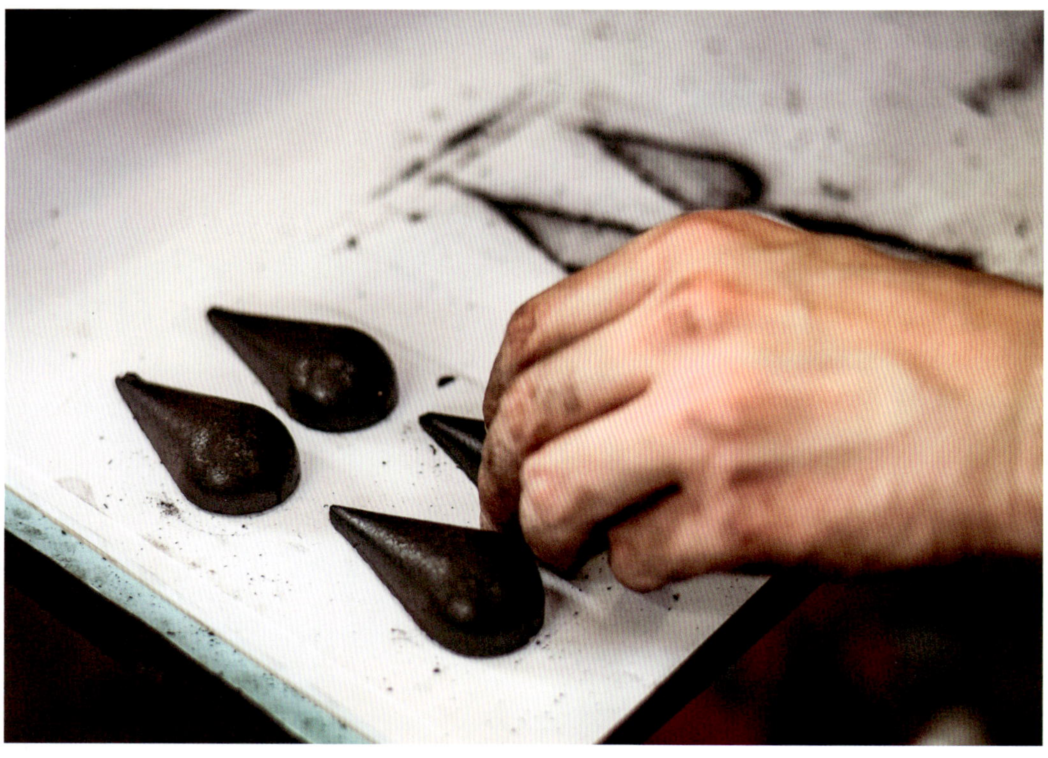

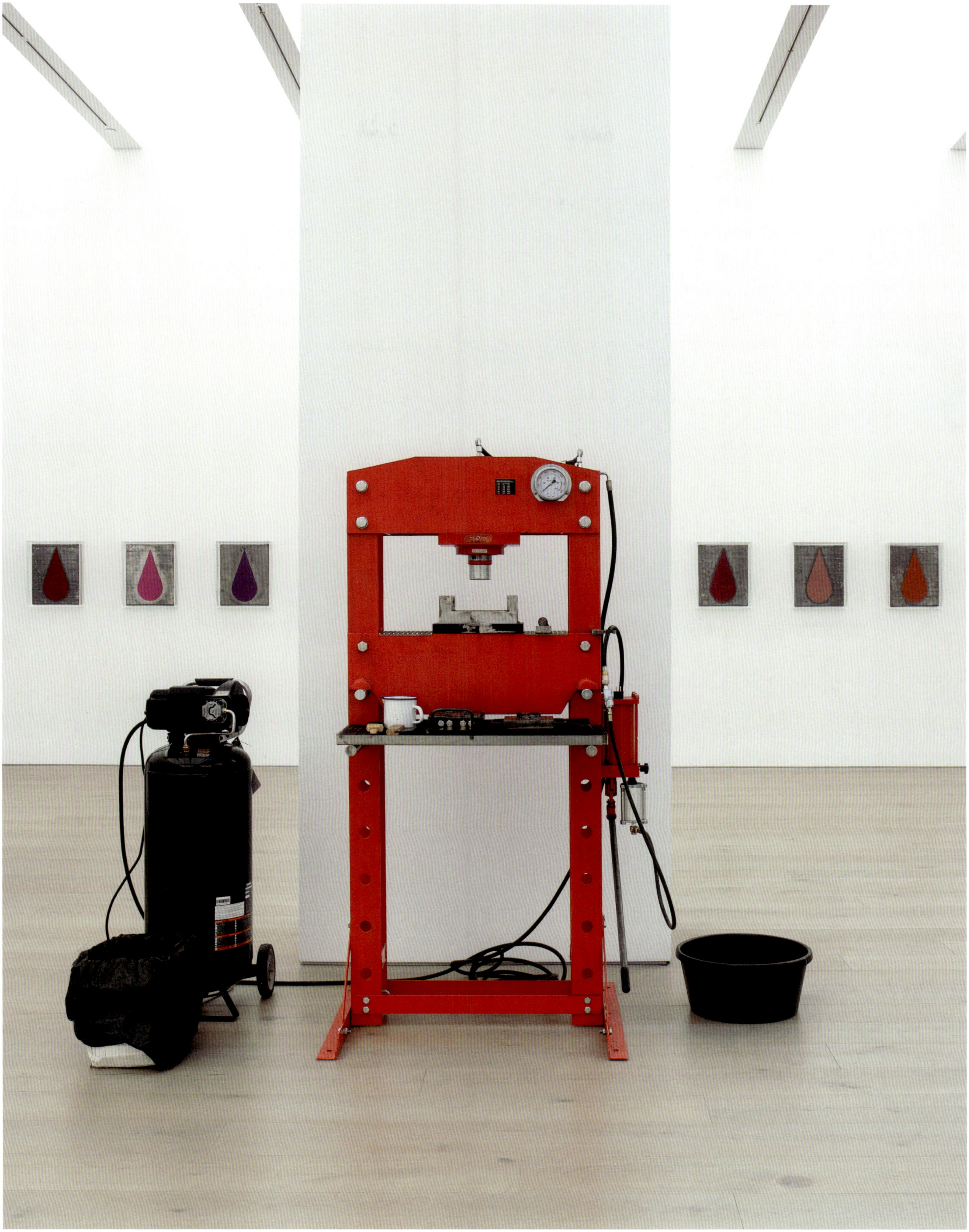

Tränenpresse, 2018

Coal, hydraulic press / Kohle, Hydraulikpresse, 186 × 90 × 85 cm

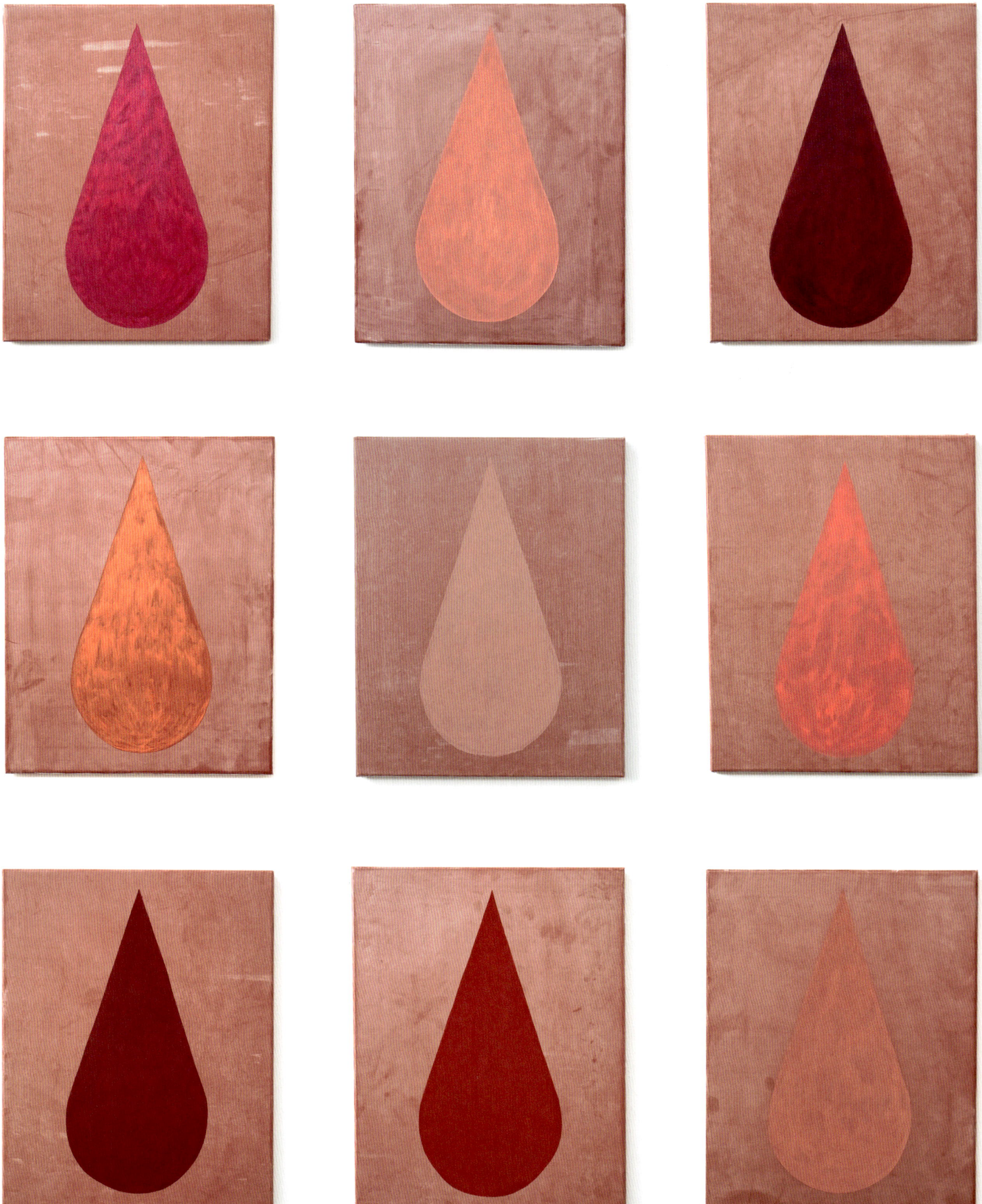

Tears, 2018

Silicone, lipstick / Silikon, Lippenstift, 50 × 40 cm

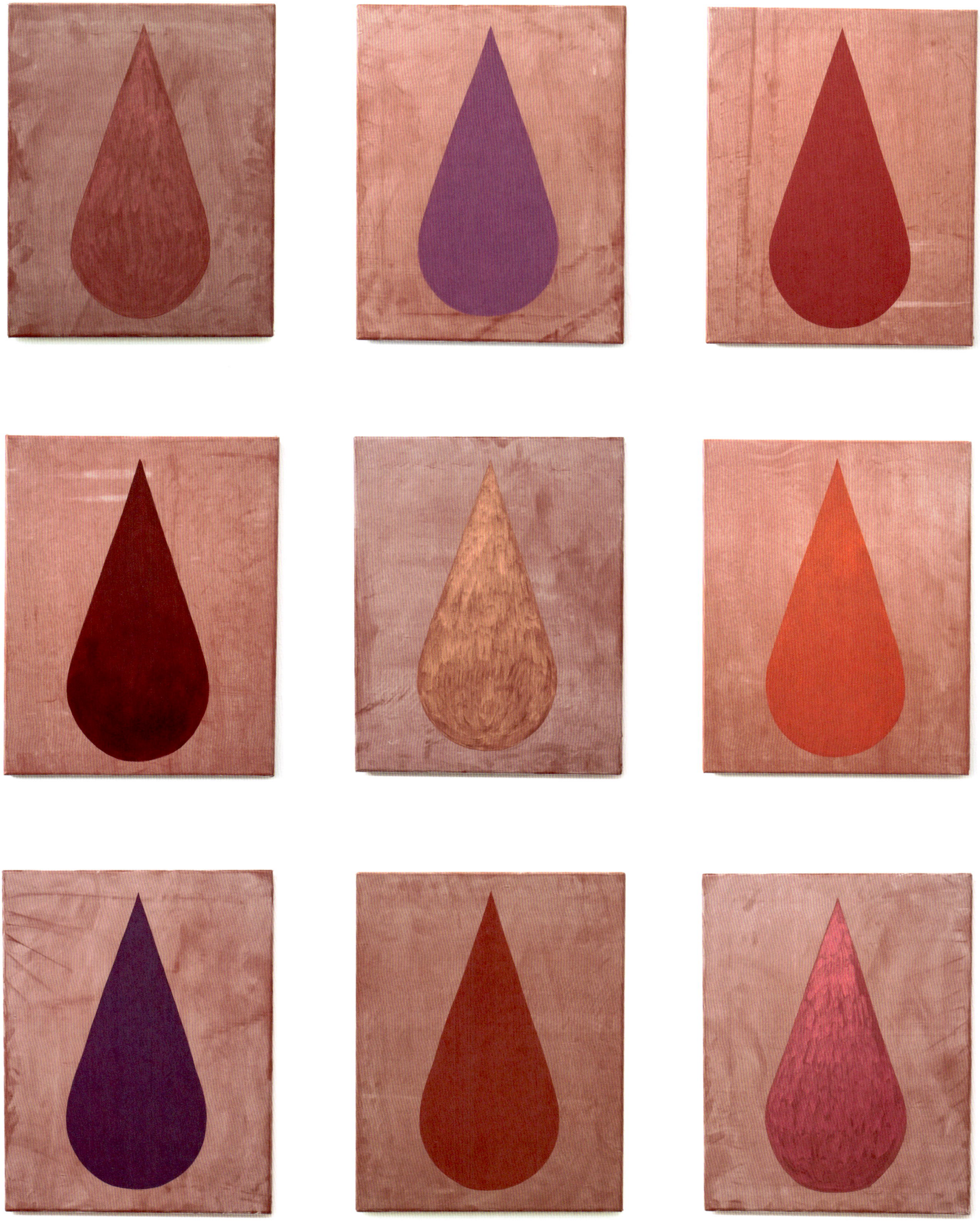

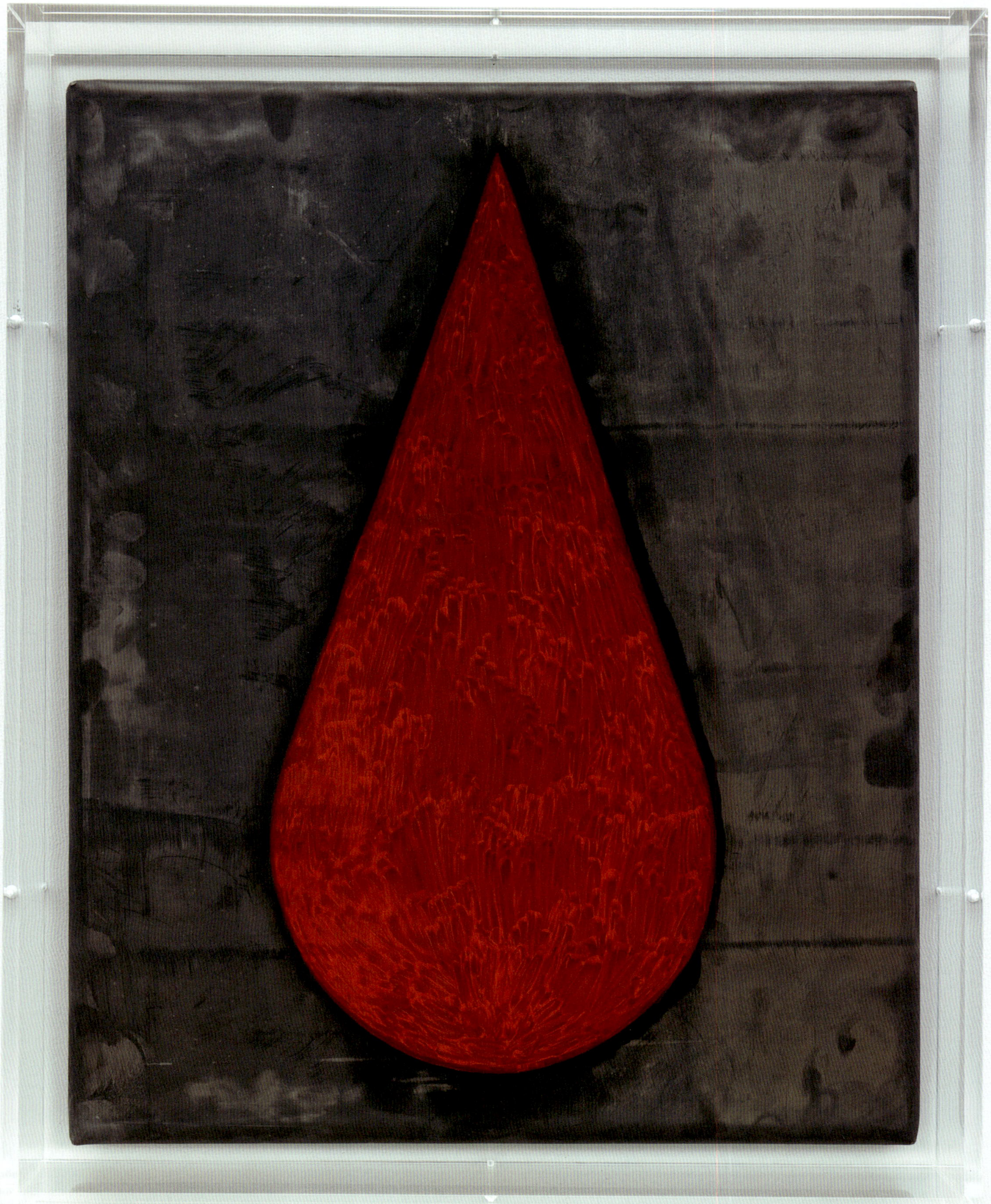

Heavy Tear 05 MAC EROS, 2018

Lead, lipstick / Blei, Lippenstift, 53 × 43 × 8 cm (framed / gerahmt)

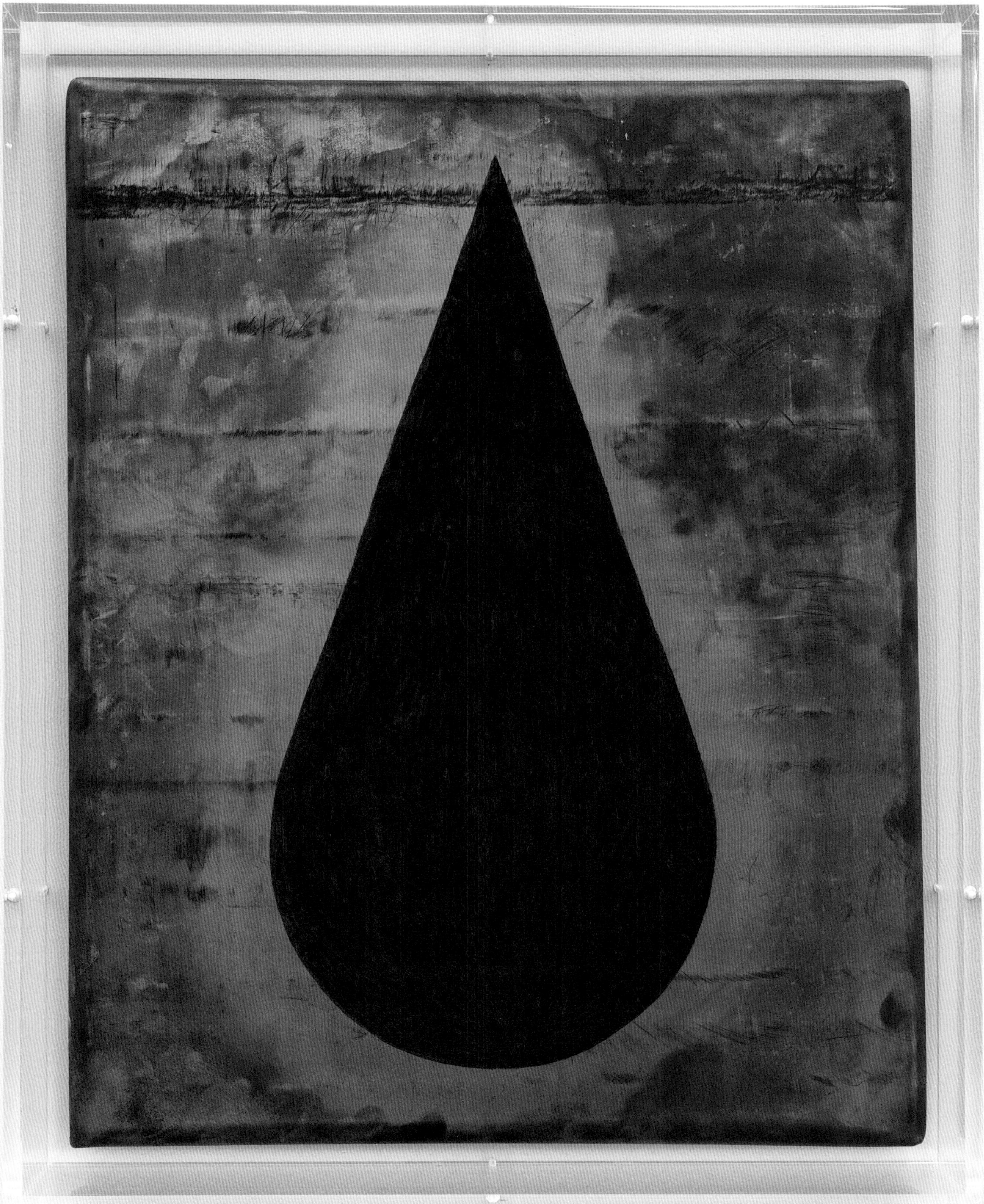

Heavy Tear 39 MAC FLAT OUT FABULOUS, 2018

Lead, lipstick / Blei, Lippenstift, 53 × 43 × 8 cm (framed / gerahmt)

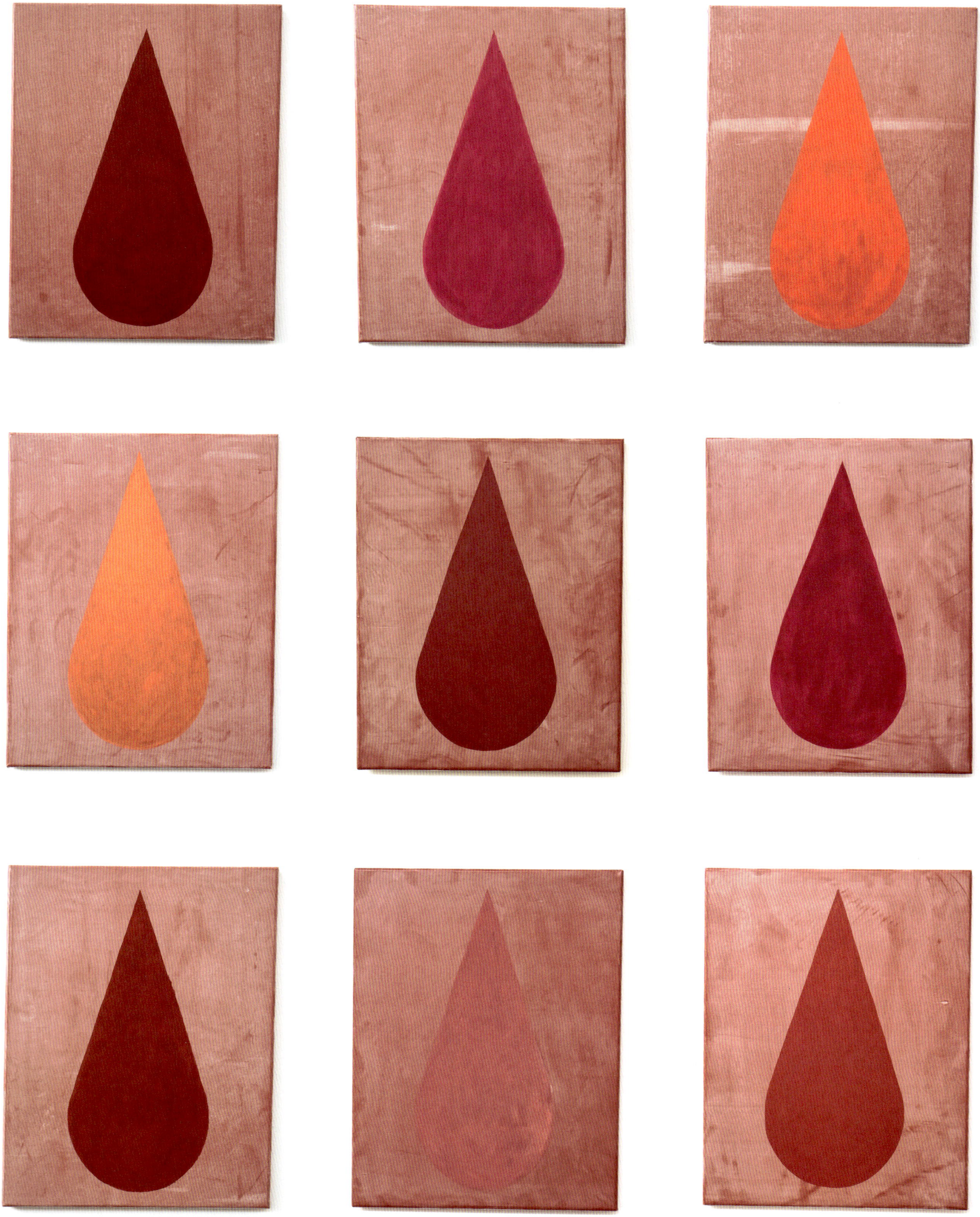

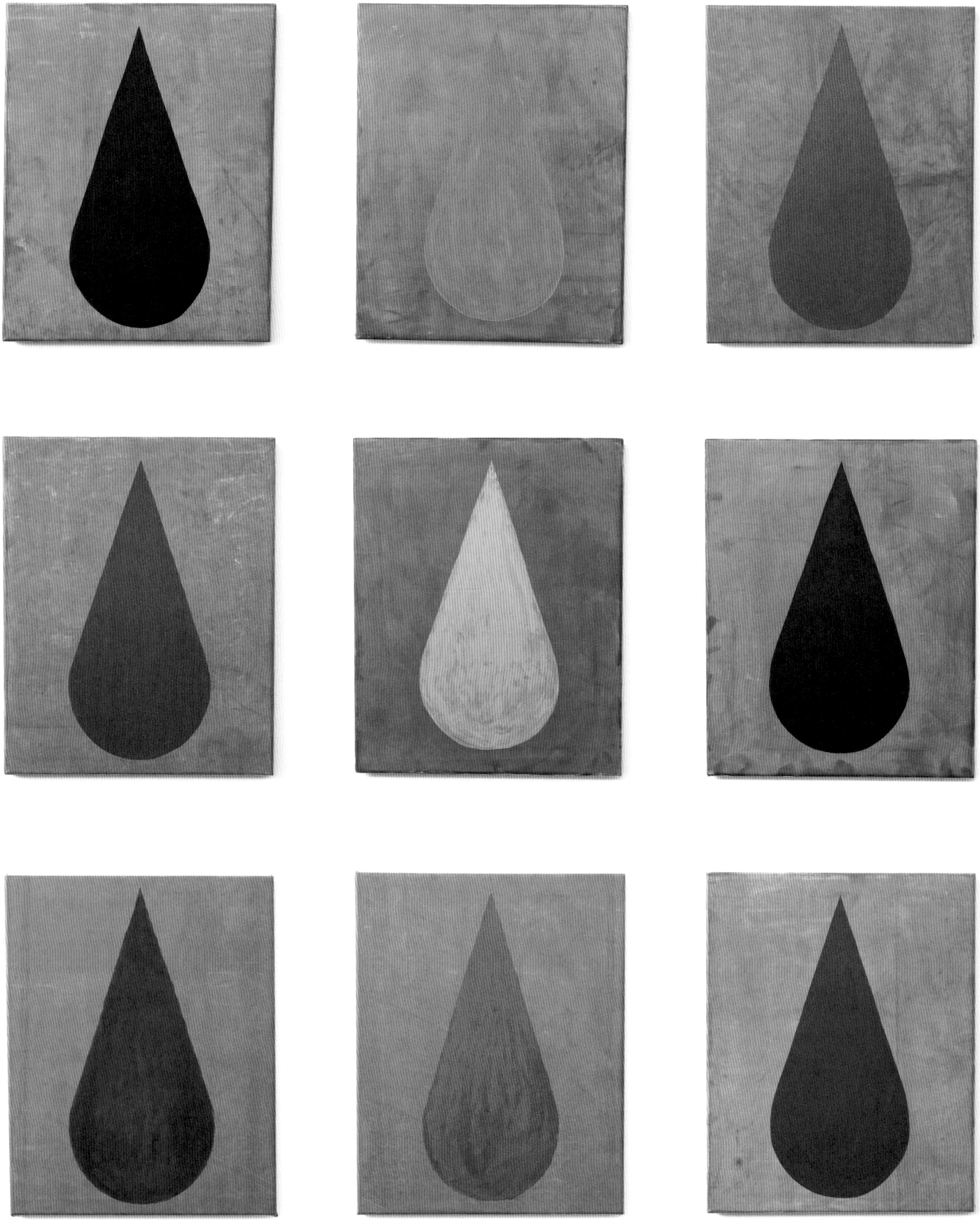

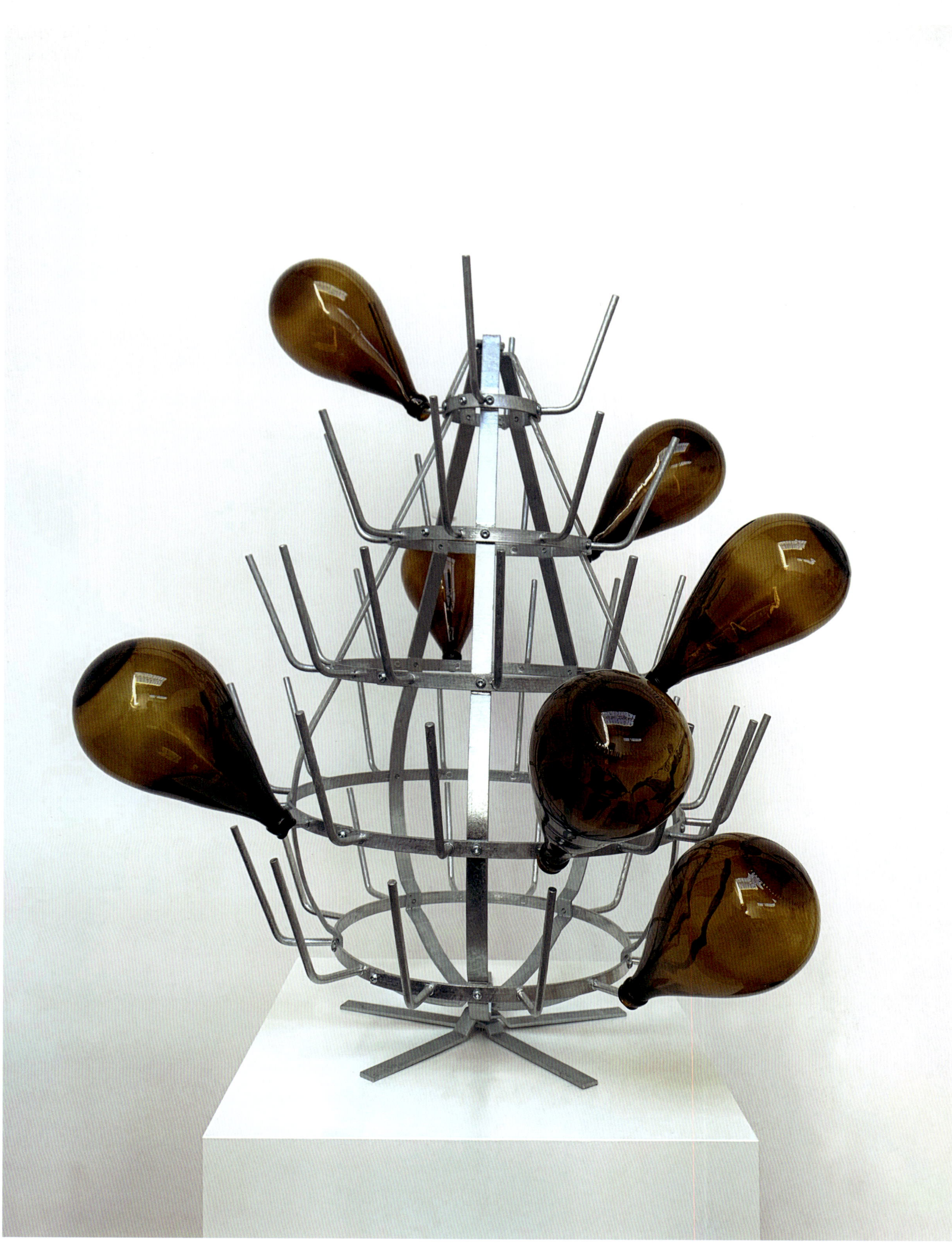

Tränentrockner Tempelhof, 2019

Steel, glass / Stahl, Glas, 80 × 80 × 80 cm

As Tears Go By New York, 2019

Eggs, ceramic, cardboard / Eier, Keramik, Karton, 10 × 16 × 22 cm

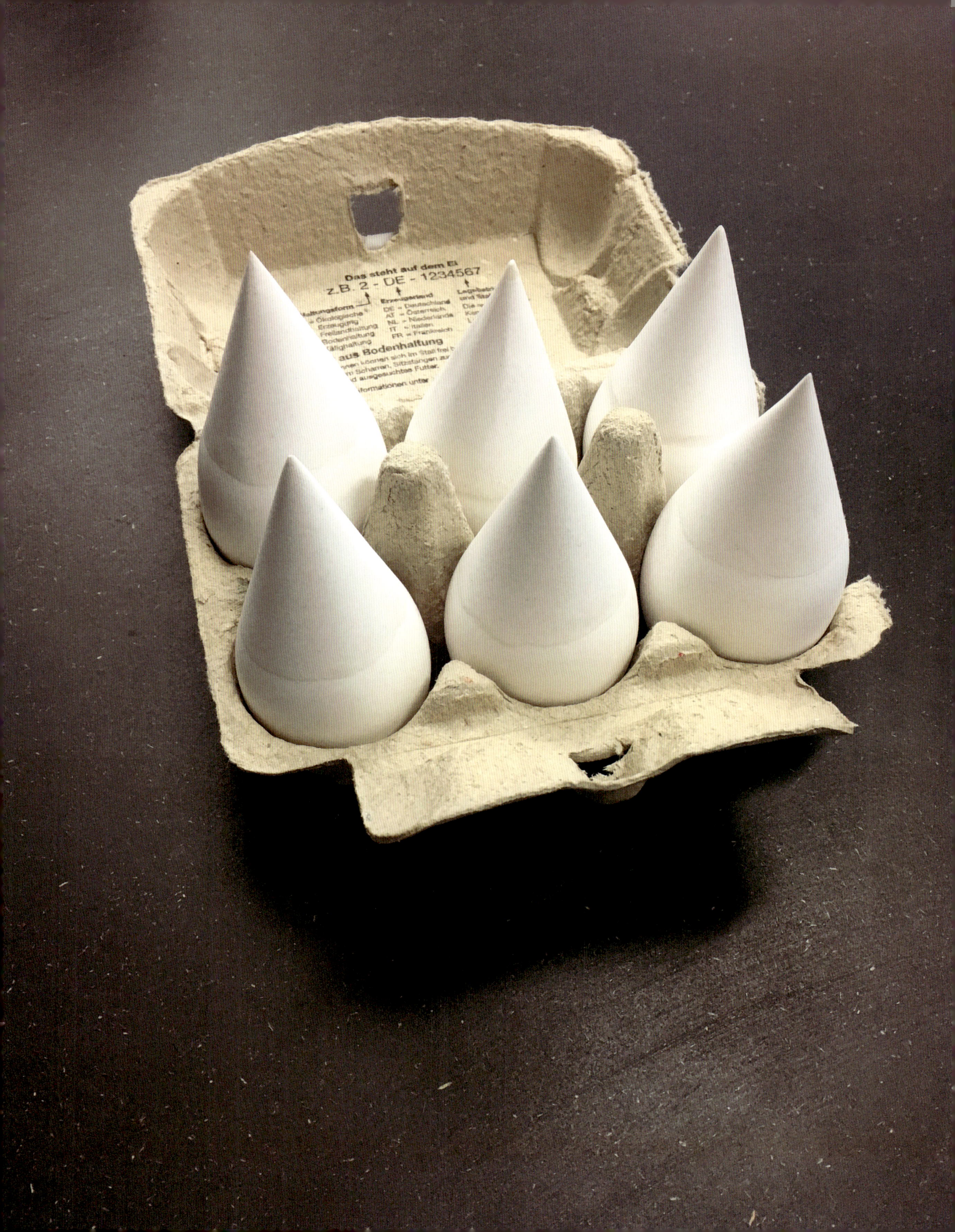
Das steht auf dem Ei
z.B. 2 - DE - 1234567
aus Bodenhaltung

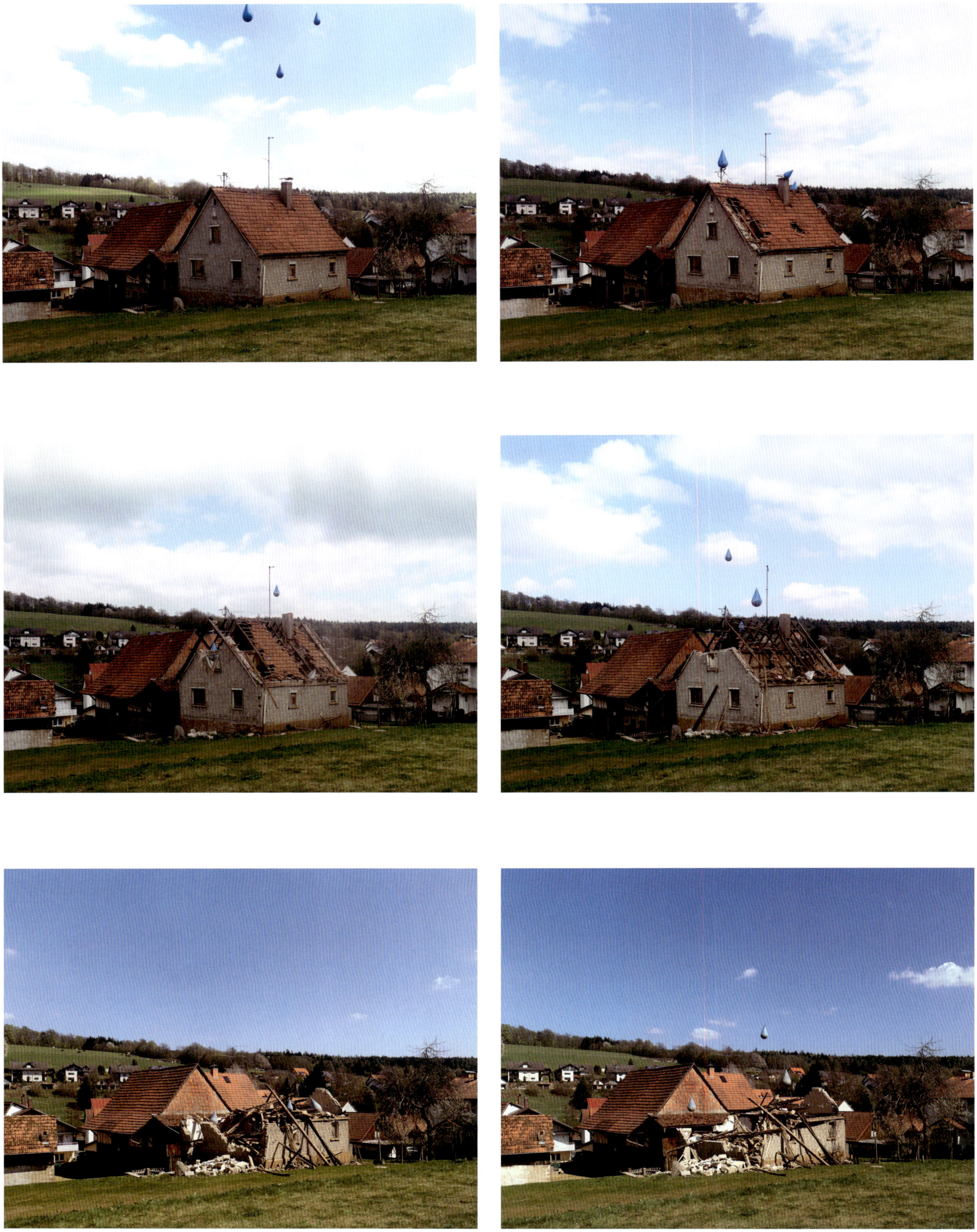

Tränen, 2015

Video, 8 min 33 sec

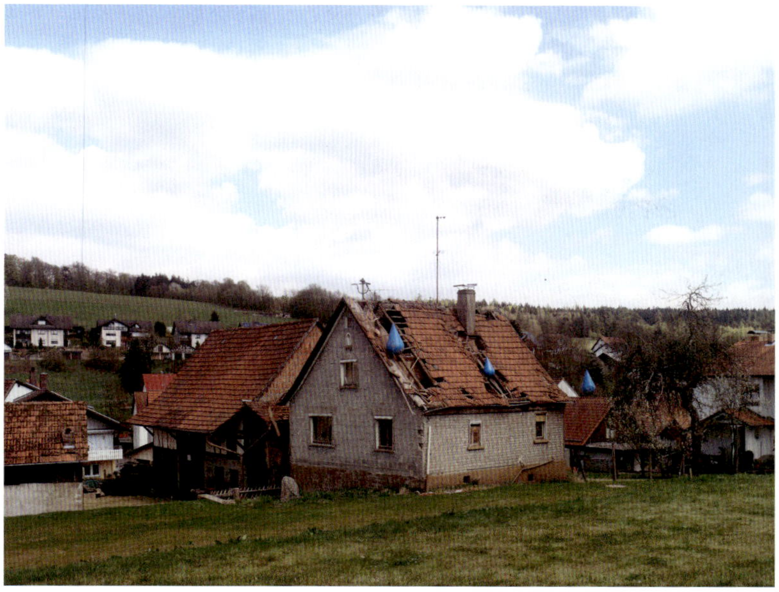
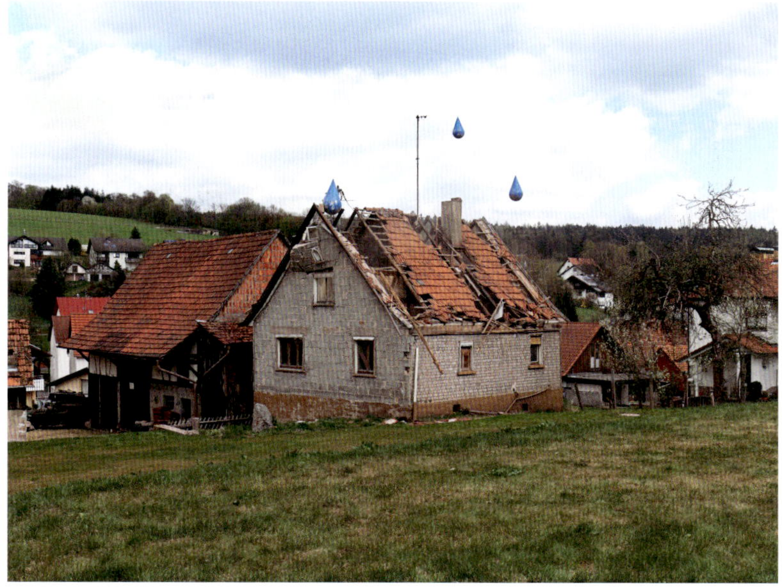
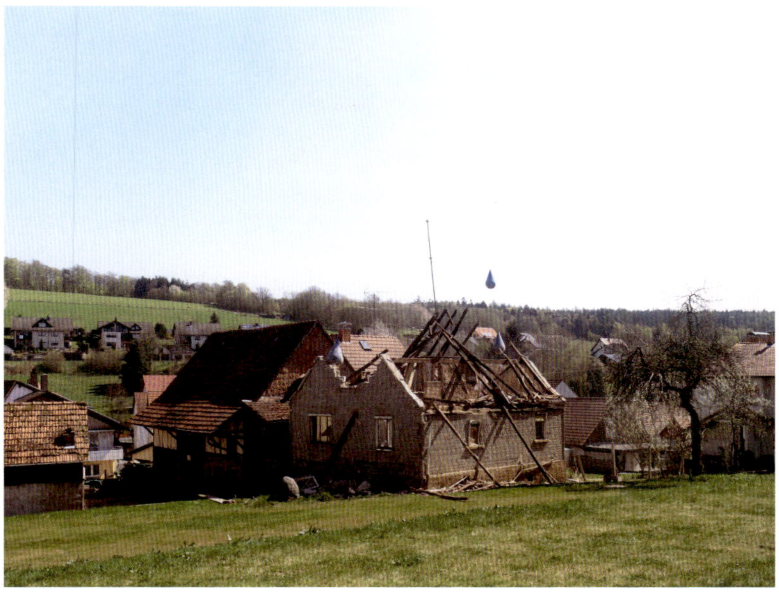
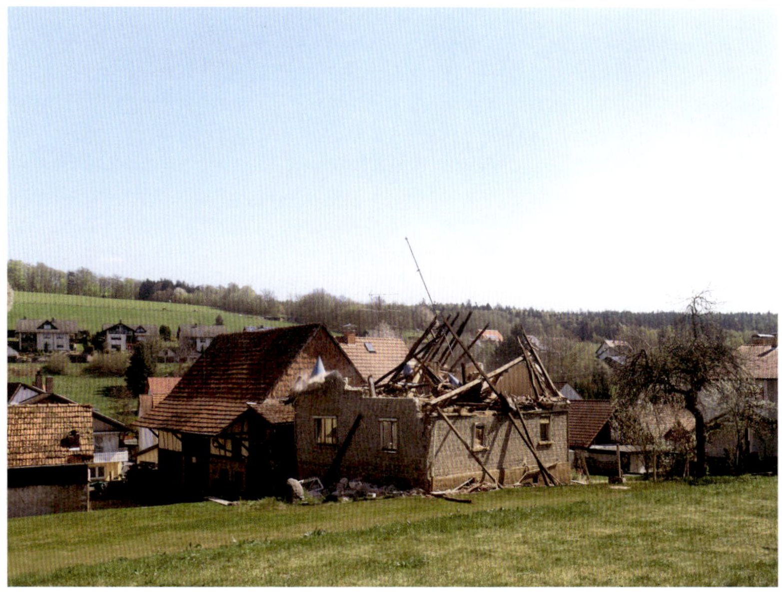
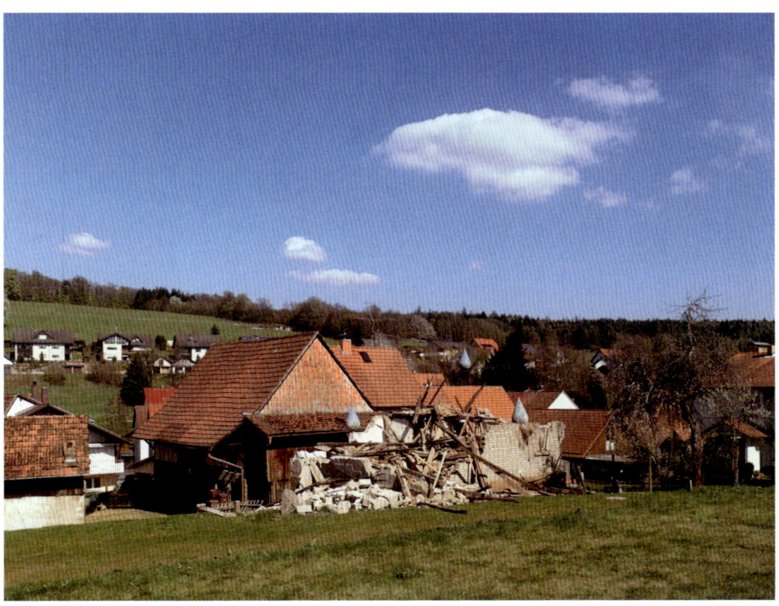
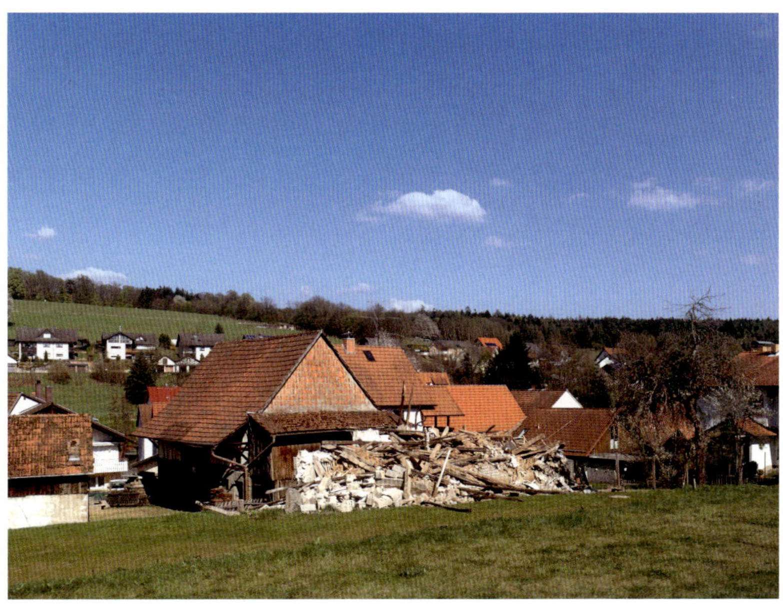

A conversation between
MICHAEL SAILSTORFER
and
JOHANNA and
FRIEDRICH GRÄFLING,
moderated by
DIANDRA DONECKER,
April 3, 2022

DD I'm very pleased to talk with you about the work *Tränen* (Tears) ↗34/35 by Michael Sailstorfer. Also because, for a week now, I've constantly had the print of this work in front of me. The first questions are actually rather obvious: When and how did you meet? What was the mutual fascination to then realize this project? And how did it come about that a couple from Frankfurt am Main and an artist from Berlin end up meeting in the Spessart?
FG It's pretty simple from our side, because Michael Sailstorfer's works were floating around in our heads and, at some point, they were also hanging on our walls. So we knew Michael through his work. He didn't know us at that point, of course, and then we somehow got to know each other personally, probably at a dinner. It intensified when Johanna wrote her master's thesis on "Mythos Berlin" and interviewed Michael on this topic. That was in 2011. We then met time and again and also made studio visits. We perhaps already talked about initial projects, but *Tränen* was in fact our first big project together.
MS I think we met in Berlin, and you told me about the house you own in Wiesen in the Spessart. At that time, you asked me directly whether I could realize a work of art with it.
JG Exactly! But maybe something has to be said about the house: Friedrich, together with his father, translocated a historic half-timbered house. The house was thus dismantled in one place, transported to Wiesen, and rebuilt there 1:1. The vaulted cellar under the *Tränen* house has the same dimensions as the half-timbered house. So, this house from the 1950s had to make way sooner or later. We thought that instead of simply tearing it down, it would, of course, be more exciting to get Michael involved.
FG I wasn't aware that it would happen on such a scale. I thought that Michael would perhaps remove a window, and then a sculpture would emerge from that; or a bit of wallpaper would be scraped off, and that would be used to make a collage or something similar. I didn't realize at the time that the demolition itself would become the artwork.
DD You then traveled there together. How many times did you actually look at the house, the place? And how did this idea come about to destroy the house in this fairy-tale way through "tears"? How exactly did that develop? Dialogically, or was it immediately clear to you, Michael, what direction it might take?
MS I think it really took a while. I first had a photo of the house that Johanna and Friedrich had sent me. And then quite some time went by. I think I walked around for a year with the house in my head, and the work actually developed relatively naturally, out of my particular circumstances. There was a feeling that needed to come out. I made a collage depicting the house and three tears falling on it. At that point, I hadn't seen the house yet. Then we met, and I presented the collage. From that point on, we pushed the project forward; and finally, I traveled to Wiesen with paper models of the tears to see how big they had to be.
DD I immediately have two questions: What does "a feeling that needed to come out" mean—if this question is not too personal? And what did the house you drew look like versus what it then actually looked like? I think it's interesting that you didn't know the place yet, but you already developed an idea of it.
MS It was a feeling of sadness that needed to come out. I always look, of course, at what's important or big enough for me at a particular moment that makes me want to realize it in a work. The collage looked relatively similar to the house because Johanna and Friedrich had given me the photo of it, and I worked with that. The only difference was that I had colored the house white in the draft design because I thought it would then be more neutral or more of an archetype of a house. In the end, though, we didn't do that. We actually left everything as it was.
FG That's right, initially we were talking about a white façade.
MS We had considered painting the house white to make it appear more minimal, but then I decided against it.
DD So you could say the tear is something that is very personally connected to you, an emotion and a form that came out of you. At the same time, however, I see a brutality in the work, because the tear is actually a wrecking ball.
MS Sadness can, of course, also be destructive and break something. I found that interesting, and that's what I associated with the house, which stands for a home, whether small or large.
DD When I first started thinking about it, different ideas came to me. First, I thought the collapse of this house is not only a story of the building, but also of the place. Is it also about a social transformation? And is the house a metaphor for societal change or even demise? In some way as a symbol …
MS Definitely. I had already used the "house" motif in earlier works. For example, in *3 Ster mit Ausblick* (3 Cubic Meters of Wood with a View) ↗219–222, where a house is burned in its own fireplace. I think a house always has a strong symbolic power and stands for living space or for a protected space.
DD How was it for you, Friedrich and Johanna, when you saw the collage? Was it immediately clear to you that it would be like this?
FG As I said, we didn't expect this result. We thought it would be much less elaborate. But we both had no doubt at any moment that it wouldn't work, not even in terms of the concept or content of the work. It was then just a very long process to actually realize it from a technical standpoint.
MS I found it truly exceptional that you supported and enabled the project unconditionally from the very beginning; because, of course, it was indeed a daring proposal. And that's why our collaboration was exceptional for me as well. It had never happened to me before that a collector couple approached me with the option to realize such a work. That's something very special.
DD Do you also want to say something about the technical details, or is that not so interesting for you?
MS By all means. They're a very important factor for the work. First, we determined the size and weight of the teardrops so that it would work both visually and technically. We realized three sizes: 88 cm, 108 cm, and 120 cm. The heaviest tear weighed two and a half tons. Friedrich and Johanna then organized a crane company that placed three truck-mounted cranes around the house. The tears were hanging from the cranes, and I had a walkie-talkie and was connected to the crane operators with it and directed how they should drop the tears onto the house. We had a camera crew and a photography team documenting everything over two days of shooting. During the shoot, the lighting conditions played an important role. Then, in post-production, the crane cables and all the shadows were erased frame by frame. The result became more surreal; sometimes you think it could be an animation.
DD What was this shot with? I read something about a Hasselblad camera and a drone.

MS The documentation was recorded by the photographers Achim and Tino Kukulies from Düsseldorf. I've done many projects with them. For the photos, they used a Hasselblad camera with a digital back, and the videos were made with a Canon 5D camera. There were microphones around the house to record the sound. We also had a GoPro video camera in the house so we could try out different options when editing. We didn't use that footage later, though.
JG The drone was from the crane company, who also recorded the action for themselves.
FG It took half a year to even find a crane company for the project. It was really very complicated, because everyone refused to do something like that.
MS The company had to have three identical cranes that could drop the tears at virtually the same speed.
JG They couldn't estimate the weight of the tears or the force of the impact. It was then also tricky to pull the sculptures back out of the building. So there were many unpredictable factors.
MS It was an experiment from the very beginning. There was no way to test it. We didn't know how much resistance the house would offer. In the beginning, I was afraid that it might be completely flat after only half an hour. But then the old timber frame inside held out for a very long time. As a result, the whole process took two days.
DD The idea, which is somewhere between poetry and beauty—although, at the same time, it's also about destruction—is very interesting. And then the time it takes to demolish the house, because it resists somehow. I also had to think of dance, of choreography, of music, although there's no music in the video at all. The relationship between the destruction and the way to get there: There's something brutal about this, but also something tender. In your work, there's often a tipping moment between these two poles, which can be seen as antithetical but is, at the same time, cohesive.
JG It's funny that you mention the choreography. We had that feeling when Michael was coordinating the cranes using the walkie-talkies. That was really a choreography. How the tears were then dropped onto the house—because you always had to look where something was falling down now, and which tear made sense next. I think Michael always had in mind how it should look later in the video. That was already a performance!
MS Yes, it was very intense. It was two days of hard work.
DD Michael, you once said, "I want to make changeable sculptures in a place that I like and that also function at the same time." Is the house also a sculpture? Has this place or this building thus become a sculpture?
MS Yes, the building becomes a sculpture. I think the whole project was sculpture. With the citizens of Wiesen coming and sitting there and watching the spectacle. That was somehow sculpture, too. The house was a changeable sculpture in every stage of demolition.
FG You can even compare it to other works, for example *Pulheim gräbt* (Pulheim Digs) ↗288–295. There is still such an aura in that place. These two days, the action and Michael as a person, that resonates a lot and is, in itself, a totality.
DD How was that received by the people standing around?
JG At first, there was a lot of skepticism, because there was no understanding for the project. No one could imagine that a work of art was being produced here, and why three cranes were needed to tear down this small house. This quickly turned into curiosity; and at some point, the mayor actually had beer garden benches brought over. People sat there and watched it all happen. It was nice to see how that developed.
MS Friedrich, because you talked about aura, would you say that the work is still present in people's minds or that they still talk about it today? Has it imprinted itself in their minds, so to speak?
FG Definitely. There are still anecdotes about it. We were recently approached by someone who had flipped through an art magazine in which *Tränen* was illustrated. He then told others in the village about it; this fills us with pride. And there are similar incidents that are repeatedly brought to our attention.
JG You even received a letter from the mayor of the neighboring village.
MS The neighboring village wanted to have a similar project because the press echo in Wiesen was so great.
FG Of course, the subsequent exhibition at the Kunstverein Wiesen also contributed to this. There, your work was presented almost a little retrospectively, with the *Tränen* work as an anchor point. This allowed the citizens and the region to see and understand the action in the context of your work as a whole.
DD The way one deals with terms and their classification is also interesting. Some who saw it would regard it as part of the environment, others would call it a performance. What is sculpture, and what role does photography play in it?
MS *Tränen* is, on the one hand, a performance, which has a temporality, but was always intended for me both as a video work and as a photographic work. I had an image in my mind of tears falling like a continuous rain on this house until it's completely demolished.
DD Tears also play a role conceptually in another work, the *Tränentrockner* (Tear Dryer) ↗17, 32.
MS That's right. All the other tear works are actually a consequence of the work that was created in Wiesen. That was the starting point, and after that came many others, like *Heavy Tears* ↗26, 31 and the *Tränentrockner*, all the way to *Tears on Asphalt* ↗10, 11, a perfume I'm working on right now with Geza Schön. The fragrance is about sadness dissolving into something beautiful. This will then be the final tear work.
DD So, from this project on, the tear had become a part of your work every now and then?
MS Yes, but since this project, the tear is in a state of dissolution.

Gespräch zwischen
MICHAEL SAILSTORFER
und
JOHANNA und
FRIEDRICH GRÄFLING,
moderiert von
DIANDRA DONECKER
am 3. April 2022

DD Ich freue mich sehr, mit euch über die Arbeit *Tränen* ↗34/35 von Michael Sailstorfer zu sprechen. Auch weil ich seit einer Woche immer den Print dieser Arbeit sehe und die erste Frage liegt da eigentlich auf der Hand: Wann und wie seid ihr euch begegnet? Was ist die gegenseitige Faszination gewesen, um dann dieses Projekt zu verwirklichen, und wie kommen ein Paar aus Frankfurt und ein Berliner Künstler in den Spessart?
FG Das ist von unserer Seite ziemlich einfach, weil die Arbeiten von Michael Sailstorfer in unseren Köpfen herumschwirrten und irgendwann auch an unseren Wänden hingen. Dadurch kannten wir Michael über sein Werk. Er kannte uns zu dem Zeitpunkt natürlich noch nicht und dann haben wir uns, wahrscheinlich bei einem Abendessen, kennengelernt. Intensiviert hat es sich, als Johanna ihre Masterarbeit über den „Mythos Berlin" schrieb und dazu Michael interviewte. Das war 2011. So haben wir uns dann immer wieder getroffen und auch Studiobesuche gemacht. Vielleicht haben wir dabei schon über erste Projekte gesprochen, die *Tränen* waren aber tatsächlich unser erstes, gemeinsames, großes Projekt.
MS Ich glaube, wir haben uns in Berlin getroffen und ihr habt mir von dem Haus erzählt, das ihr in Wiesen im Spessart besitzt. Ihr habt mich damals direkt gefragt, ob ich damit ein Kunstwerk realisieren könnte.
JG Genau! Aber vielleicht muss man noch etwas zu dem Haus sagen: Friedrich hat zusammen mit seinem Vater ein historisches Fachwerkhaus transloziert. Das Haus wurde also an einem Ort abgebaut, nach Wiesen transportiert und dort wieder 1:1 aufgebaut. Der Gewölbekeller unter dem *Tränen*-Haus hat die gleichen Maße wie das Fachwerkhaus. Daher musste dieses Haus aus den fünfziger Jahren früher oder später weichen. Wir haben uns gedacht, anstatt es einfach abzureißen, wäre es natürlich spannender, da den Michael einzubinden.
FG Mir war nicht bewusst, dass es in so einem Umfang passieren würde. Ich dachte, Michael baut vielleicht ein Fenster aus und daraus entsteht dann eine Skulptur oder es wird ein bisschen Tapete abgekratzt und das gibt eine Collage oder so etwas Ähnliches. Dass der Abriss das Kunstwerk wird, war mir zu diesem Zeitpunkt nicht bewusst.
DD Ihr seid dann also zusammen dorthin gereist. Wie oft habt ihr euch das Haus, den Ort tatsächlich angeguckt? Und wie kam diese Idee zustande, das Haus auf diese märchenhafte Weise durch „Tränen" zu zerstören? Also wie genau hat sich das entwickelt? Dialogisch oder war dir, Michael, gleich klar, in welche Richtung das gehen könnte?
MS Ich glaube, das hat wirklich eine Weile gedauert. Ich hatte zunächst ein Foto von dem Haus, das Johanna und Friedrich mir geschickt hatten. Und dann ist eine ganze Zeit vergangen. Ich denke, ich bin ein Jahr mit dem Haus im Kopf herumgelaufen und die Arbeit hat sich eigentlich relativ natürlich, aus meinen Lebensumständen, entwickelt. Da war ein Gefühl, das raus musste. Ich habe eine Collage gemacht, die das Haus und drei Tränen zeigt, die auf dieses Haus fallen. Zu dem Zeitpunkt hatte ich das Haus noch nicht real gesehen. Dann haben wir uns getroffen und ich habe die Collage präsentiert. Von da an haben wir das Projekt vorangetrieben und schließlich bin ich mit Papiermodellen der Tränen nach Wiesen gefahren, um zu gucken, wie groß die sein müssen.
DD Da habe ich sofort zwei Fragen: Was heißt, „ein Gefühl musste raus zu der Zeit", wenn die Frage nicht zu persönlich ist? Und wie sah das Haus, das du gezeichnet hast, im Vergleich zum wirklichen Haus aus? Ich finde interessant, dass du den Ort noch nicht kanntest, aber schon eine Vorstellung davon entwickelt hattest.
MS Es war ein Gefühl der Traurigkeit, das raus musste. Ich schaue natürlich immer, was für mich momentan wichtig oder groß genug ist, dass ich es in einer Arbeit realisieren will. Die Collage sah relativ ähnlich wie das Haus aus, weil Johanna und Friedrich mir ein Foto davon gegeben hatten und ich damit gearbeitet habe. Der einzige Unterschied war, dass ich das Haus im Entwurf weiß eingefärbt hatte, weil ich dachte, dass es dann neutraler oder mehr ein Archetyp von einem Haus ist. Am Ende haben wir das aber nicht gemacht. Wir haben eigentlich alles so gelassen.
FG Stimmt, zunächst war eine weiße Fassade im Gespräch.
MS Wir hatten überlegt, ob wir das Haus weiß streichen, damit es minimaler erscheint, aber dann habe ich mich dagegen entschieden.
DD Man könnte also sagen, die Träne ist etwas, was ganz persönlich mit dir verbunden ist, eine Emotion und eine Form, die aus dir heraus entstanden ist. Gleichzeitig sehe ich aber auch eine Brutalität in der Arbeit, da die Träne ja eigentlich eine Abrissbirne ist.
MS Traurigkeit kann natürlich auch zerstörerisch sein und etwas kaputt machen. Das fand ich interessant und das habe ich mit dem Haus assoziiert, das für ein Zuhause im Kleinen wie im Großen steht.
DD Als ich mich das erste Mal damit auseinandergesetzt habe, kamen mir verschiedene Ideen. Zunächst dachte ich, der Zerfall dieses Hauses ist nicht nur eine Geschichte des Gebäudes, sondern auch des Ortes. Geht es dabei auch um eine soziale Veränderung und ist das Haus eine Metapher für gesellschaftlichen Wandel oder sogar Untergang? Irgendwie als Symbol …
MS Auf jeden Fall. Ich habe ja in früheren Arbeiten schon das Motiv „Haus" benutzt. Zum Beispiel bei *3 Ster mit Ausblick* ↗219–222, wo ein Haus im eigenen Kamin verheizt wird. Ich glaube, ein Haus hat immer eine starke Symbolkraft und steht für Lebensraum oder für einen geschützten Raum.
DD Wie war das für euch, Friedrich und Johanna, als ihr die Collage gesehen habt, war euch da sofort klar, dass es so sein wird?
FG Wie schon gesagt, mit diesem Ergebnis haben wir nicht gerechnet. Wir dachten, es wird wesentlich unaufwändiger. Aber wir haben beide zu keinem Moment bezweifelt, dass das nicht gehen würde, auch nicht, was das Konzeptuelle oder Inhaltliche der Arbeit betrifft. Es war dann lediglich ein sehr langer Prozess, es technisch umzusetzen.
MS Ich fand es wirklich einzigartig, dass ihr das Projekt von Anfang an vorbehaltlos unterstützt und ermöglicht habt, weil es natürlich schon ein waghalsiger Vorschlag war. Und deshalb war unsere Zusammenarbeit für mich auch einzigartig. Es ist mir noch nie passiert, dass ein Sammlerpaar die Option an mich herangetragen hat, so eine Arbeit zu realisieren. Das ist etwas ganz Besonderes.
DD Wollt ihr zu den technischen Details auch etwas sagen oder ist das für euch nicht so interessant?
MS Doch, die sind ja ein ganz wichtiger Faktor für die Arbeit. Zunächst haben wir die Größe und das Gewicht der Tränen-Tropfen bestimmt, damit es optisch und technisch funktioniert. Wir haben drei Größen realisiert: 88 cm, 108 cm und 120 cm. Die schwerste Träne wog zweieinhalb Tonnen. Friedrich und Johanna haben dann eine Kranfirma organisiert, die drei Autokräne um das Haus herum platziert hat. An den Kränen hingen die Tränen und ich hatte ein Walkie-Talkie

und war darüber mit den Kranführern verbunden und habe dirigiert, wie sie die Tränen auf das Haus fallen lassen sollten. Wir hatten ein Kamera- und ein Fotografenteam, die alles an zwei Drehtagen dokumentiert haben. Beim Dreh spielten die Lichtverhältnisse eine wichtige Rolle. In der Postproduktion wurden dann die Kranseile und alle Schatten Bild für Bild retuschiert. Das Ergebnis wurde dadurch surrealer, manchmal denkt man, es könnte auch eine Animation sein.
DD Mit was wurde das aufgenommen? Ich habe etwas von einer Hasselblad-Kamera und einer Drohne gelesen.
MS Die Dokumentation wurde von den Fotografen Achim und Tino Kukulies aus Düsseldorf aufgezeichnet, mit den beiden habe ich schon viele Projekte realisiert. Für die Fotos haben sie eine Hasselblad-Kamera mit digitalem Rückteil verwendet, die Videos wurden mit einer Canon- 5D-Kamera gemacht. Um das Haus verteilt, standen Mikrofone, um den Ton aufzunehmen. Wir hatten auch eine GoPro-Videokamera im Haus, um beim Schnitt verschiedene Möglichkeiten ausprobieren zu können. Das Material haben wir später aber nicht benutzt.
JG Die Drohne war von der Kranfirma, die die Aktion auch für sich aufgezeichnet hat.
FG Es hat ein halbes Jahr gedauert, überhaupt eine Kranfirma dafür zu finden. Das war wirklich sehr kompliziert, weil sich alle geweigert haben, sowas zu machen.
MS Die Firma musste über drei identische Kräne verfügen, die quasi in gleicher Geschwindigkeit die Tränen herunterlassen können.
JG Sie konnten das Gewicht der Tränen nicht einschätzen und auch nicht die Wucht des Einschlags. Es war dann auch heikel, die Skulpturen wieder aus dem Gebäude zu ziehen. Es gab also viele unvorhersehbare Faktoren.
MS Es war von Anfang an ein Experiment. Man konnte das ja nicht testen. Wir wussten nicht, wie viel Widerstand das Haus leisten würde. Anfangs habe ich befürchtet, dass es vielleicht schon nach einer halben Stunde platt sein würde. Dann hat das alte Fachwerk im Inneren aber doch sehr lange standgehalten. Dadurch hat der ganze Prozess zwei Tage gedauert.
DD Die Idee, die irgendwo zwischen Poesie und Schönheit liegt, obwohl es gleichzeitig um Zerstörung geht, ist sehr interessant. Und dann die Zeit, die es braucht, um das Haus kleinzubekommen, weil es sich irgendwie wehrt. Ich musste auch an Tanz denken, an Choreografie, an Musik, obwohl im Video gar keine Musik zu hören ist. Die Beziehung zwischen der Zerstörung und dem Weg dahin, das hat etwas Brutales, aber auch etwas Zärtliches. In deinen Arbeiten gibt es oft einen Kippmoment zwischen diesen beiden Polen, die man als konträr, aber gleichzeitig auch als zusammenhängend empfinden kann.
JG Es ist lustig, dass du die Choreografie erwähnst. Dieses Gefühl hatten wir auch, als Michael die Kräne mit Hilfe der Walkie-Talkies koordiniert hat. Das war wirklich eine Choreografie. Wie die Tränen dann auf das Haus herabgelassen wurden, weil man ja immer schauen musste, wo jetzt etwas zusammenfällt und welche Träne als nächste Sinn macht. Ich denke, Michael hatte auch immer im Kopf, wie es später im Video aussehen soll. Das war schon eine Performance!
MS Ja, das war sehr intensiv. Es waren zwei Tage schwere Arbeit.
DD Michael, du hast einmal gesagt: „Ich möchte an einem Ort, der mir gefällt, veränderliche Skulpturen machen, die gleichzeitig auch funktionieren." Ist das Haus auch eine Skulptur? Also ist dieser Ort oder dieses Gebäude zu einer Skulptur geworden?
MS Ja, das Gebäude wird eine Skulptur. Ich glaube, das ganze Projekt war Skulptur. Mit den Bürgern von Wiesen, die kamen und dasaßen und sich das Spektakel angesehen haben. Das war irgendwie auch Skulptur. Das Haus war in jedem Stadium des Verfalls eine veränderliche Skulptur.
FG Man kann es sogar mit anderen Arbeiten vergleichen, beispielsweise mit *Pulheim gräbt* ↗288–295. An diesem Ort gibt es immer noch so eine Aura. Diese zwei Tage, die Aktion und Michael als Person, das schwingt schon sehr mit und ist in sich eine Gesamtheit.
DD Wie wurde das von den Leuten aufgenommen, die da drum herum standen?
JG Da war zuerst einmal große Skepsis, weil es kein Verständnis für das Vorhaben gab. Niemand konnte sich vorstellen, dass hier ein Kunstwerk produziert wird, und warum man drei Kräne braucht, um dieses kleine Haus einzureißen. Daraus wurde schnell Neugier und irgendwann wurden dann wirklich vom Bürgermeister Bierbänke aufgestellt. Die Leute saßen da und haben alles mitverfolgt. Es war schön, zu sehen wie sich das entwickelt hat.
MS Friedrich, weil du von Aura gesprochen hast, würdest du sagen, dass die Arbeit noch in den Köpfen der Leute präsent ist oder dass sie heute noch darüber reden? Hat sich das irgendwie eingeprägt?
FG Definitiv. Dazu gibt es immer noch Anekdoten. Vor Kurzem wurden wir von jemandem angesprochen, der in einem Kunstmagazin geblättert hatte, in dem die *Tränen* abgebildet waren. Er hat das danach im Dorf weitererzählt, sowas erfüllt uns mit Stolz. Ähnliche Begebenheiten, die uns zugetragen werden, gibt es immer wieder.
JG Du hast doch sogar einen Brief vom Bürgermeister aus dem Nachbardorf erhalten.
MS Der Nachbarort wollte ein ähnliches Projekt haben, weil das Presse-Echo in Wiesen so groß war.
FG Natürlich hat auch die anschließende Ausstellung im Kunstverein Wiesen dazu beigetragen. Dort wurde dein Werk fast schon ein wenig retrospektiv vorgestellt, wobei die *Tränen*-Arbeit einen Ankerpunkt bildete. So konnten die Bürger und die Region die Aktion im Kontext deines Œuvres sehen und verstehen.
DD Der Umgang mit den Begriffen und ihrer Zuordnung ist auch interessant. Wahrscheinlich speichern das manche, die es gesehen haben, als Environment ab, andere würden es als Performance bezeichnen. Was ist Skulptur und welche Rolle spielt die Fotografie dabei?
MS *Tränen* ist einerseits eine Performance, die eine Zeitlichkeit hat, war aber für mich immer als Video- und als Fotoarbeit gedacht. Ich hatte ein Bild von Tränen im Kopf, die wie ein kontinuierlicher Regen auf dieses Haus fallen, bis es komplett zerstört ist.
DD Tränen spielen begrifflich auch in einer anderen Arbeit eine Rolle, dem *Tränentrockner* ↗17, 32.
MS Stimmt. Alle weiteren Tränen-Arbeiten sind eigentlich eine Konsequenz aus der Arbeit, die in Wiesen entstanden ist. Das was der Startpunkt, danach kamen viele andere, wie die *Heavy Tears* ↗26, 31 und der *Tränentrockner* bis hin zu *Tears on Asphalt* ↗10, 11, ein Parfum, an dem ich gerade mit Geza Schön arbeite. Bei dem Duft geht es darum, dass sich die Traurigkeit in etwas Schönem auflöst. Das ist die dann letzte Tränen-Arbeit.
DD Seit diesem Projekt ist die Träne also immer mal wieder ein Teil deiner Arbeiten?
MS Ja, aber seit diesem Projekt befindet sich die Träne in Auflösung.

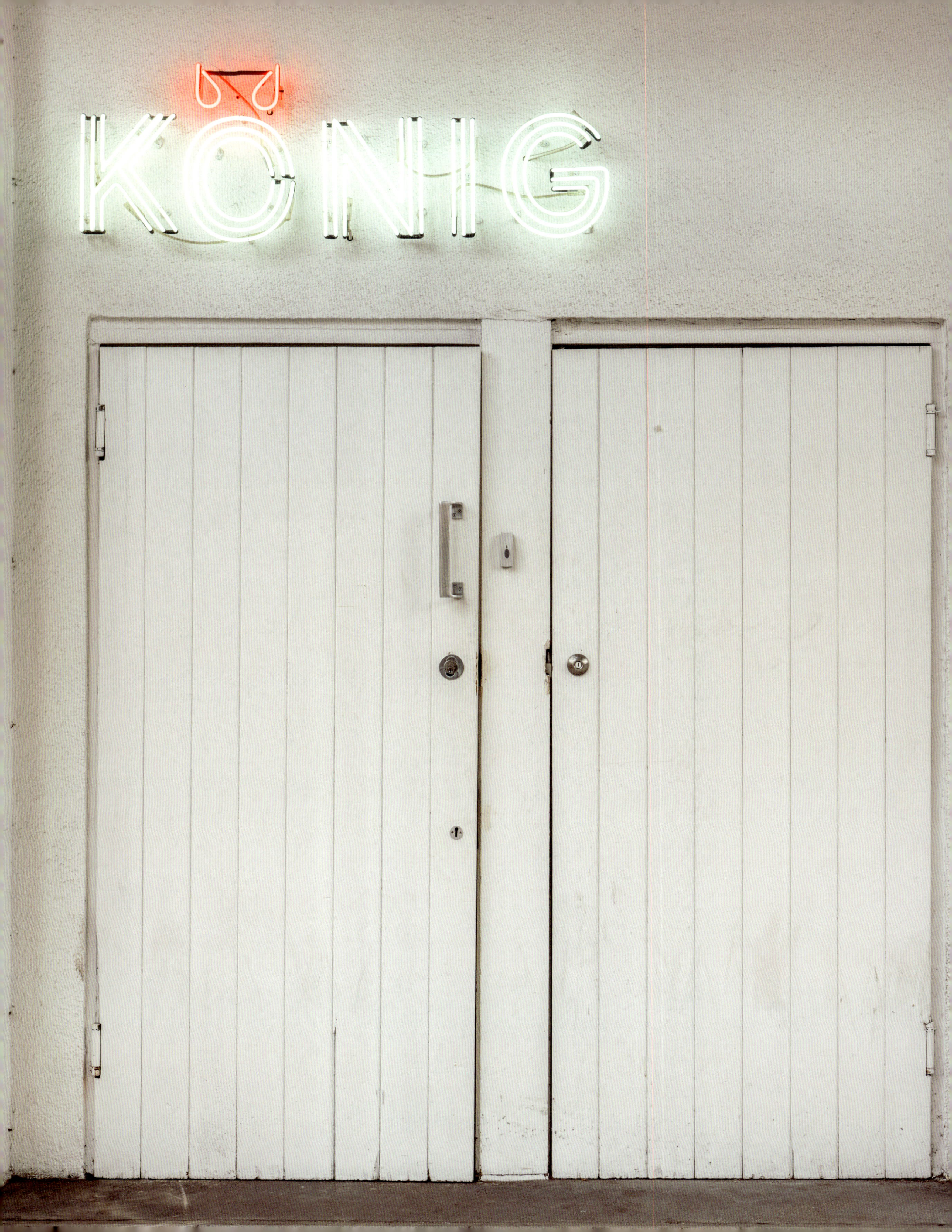
KÖNIG

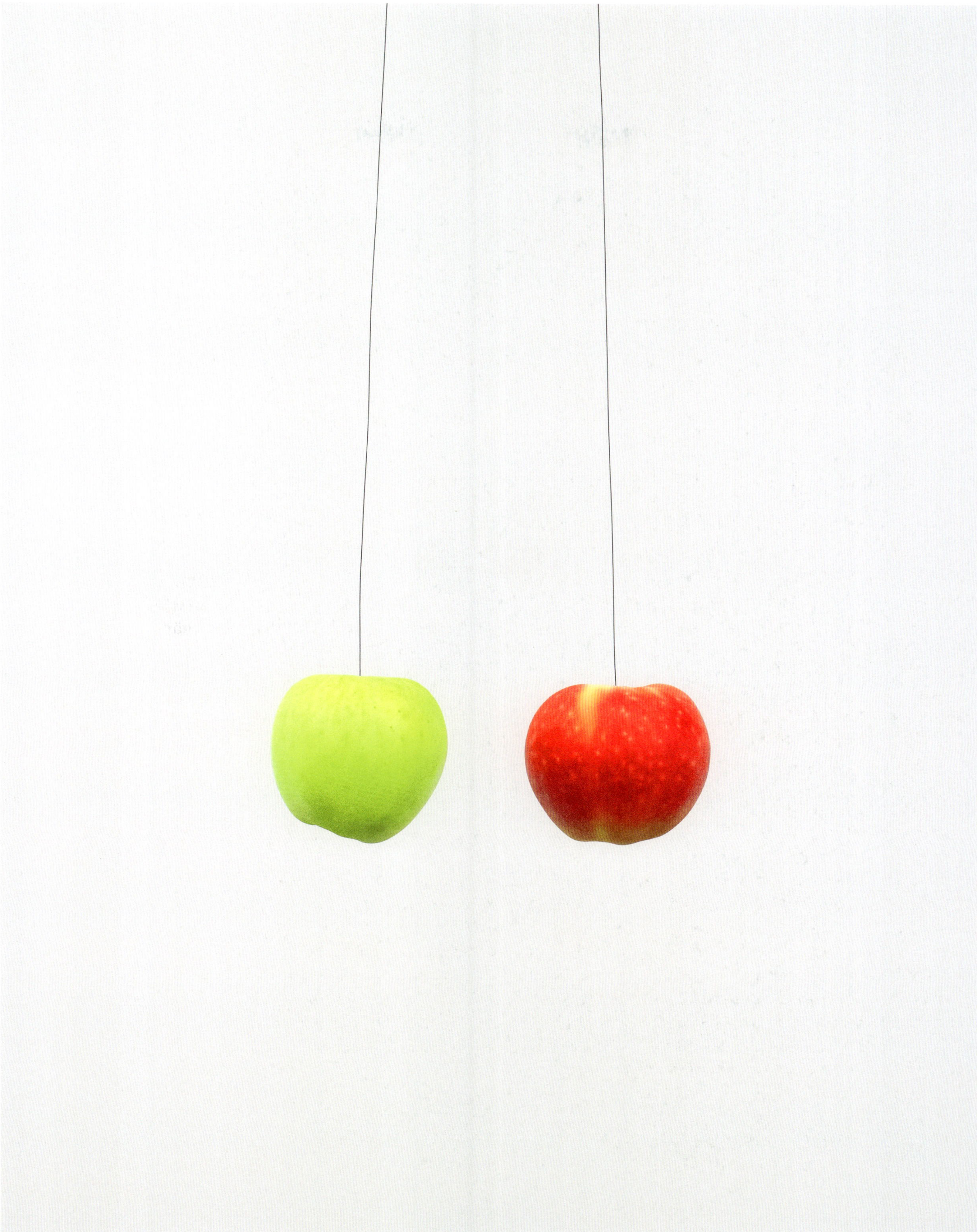

Two Tears, 2018

Neon tubes / Neonröhren, 39 × 125 cm, Installation view / Installationsansicht *Tear Show*, König London

Zwei Äpfel (--), 2018

Polystyrene, paint, electricity / Polystyrol, Farbe, Elektrizität, 170 × 50 × 20 cm

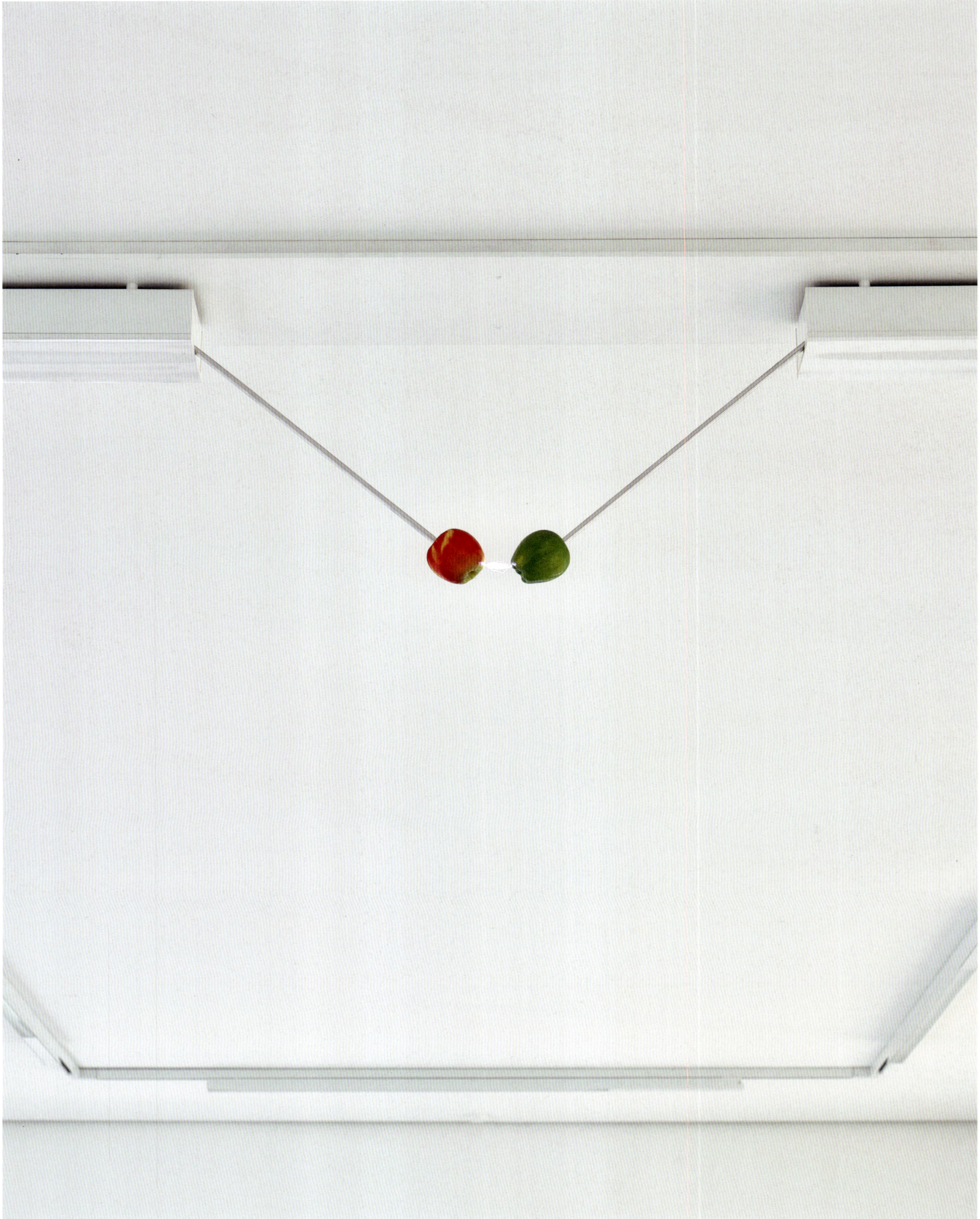

Zwei Äpfel (+-), 2017

Aluminum, paint, electricity / Aluminium, Farbe, Elektrizität, 47 × 241 × 28 cm

Kreuzknoten RG, 2020

Neon tubes / Neonröhren, 7 × 29 × 6 cm

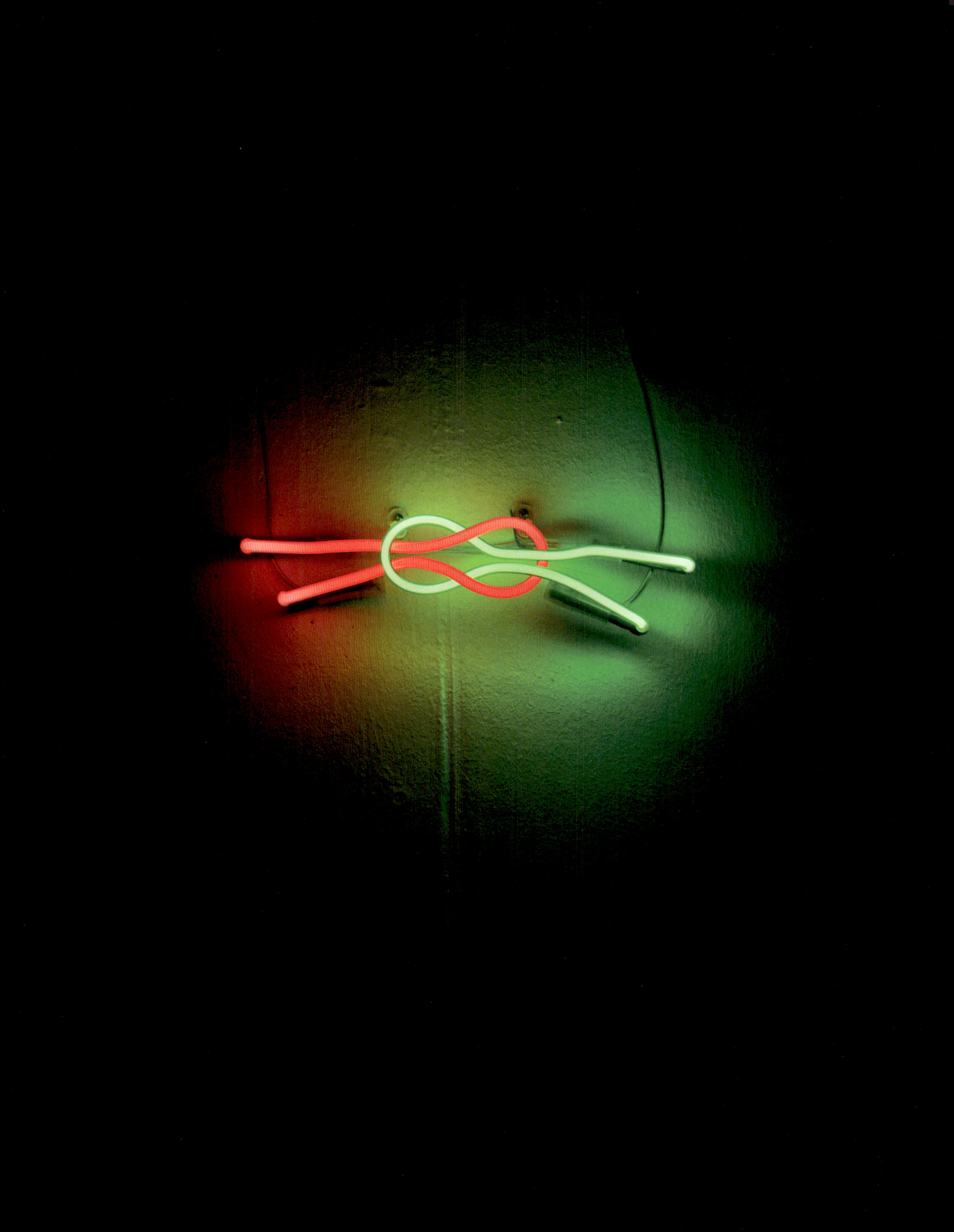

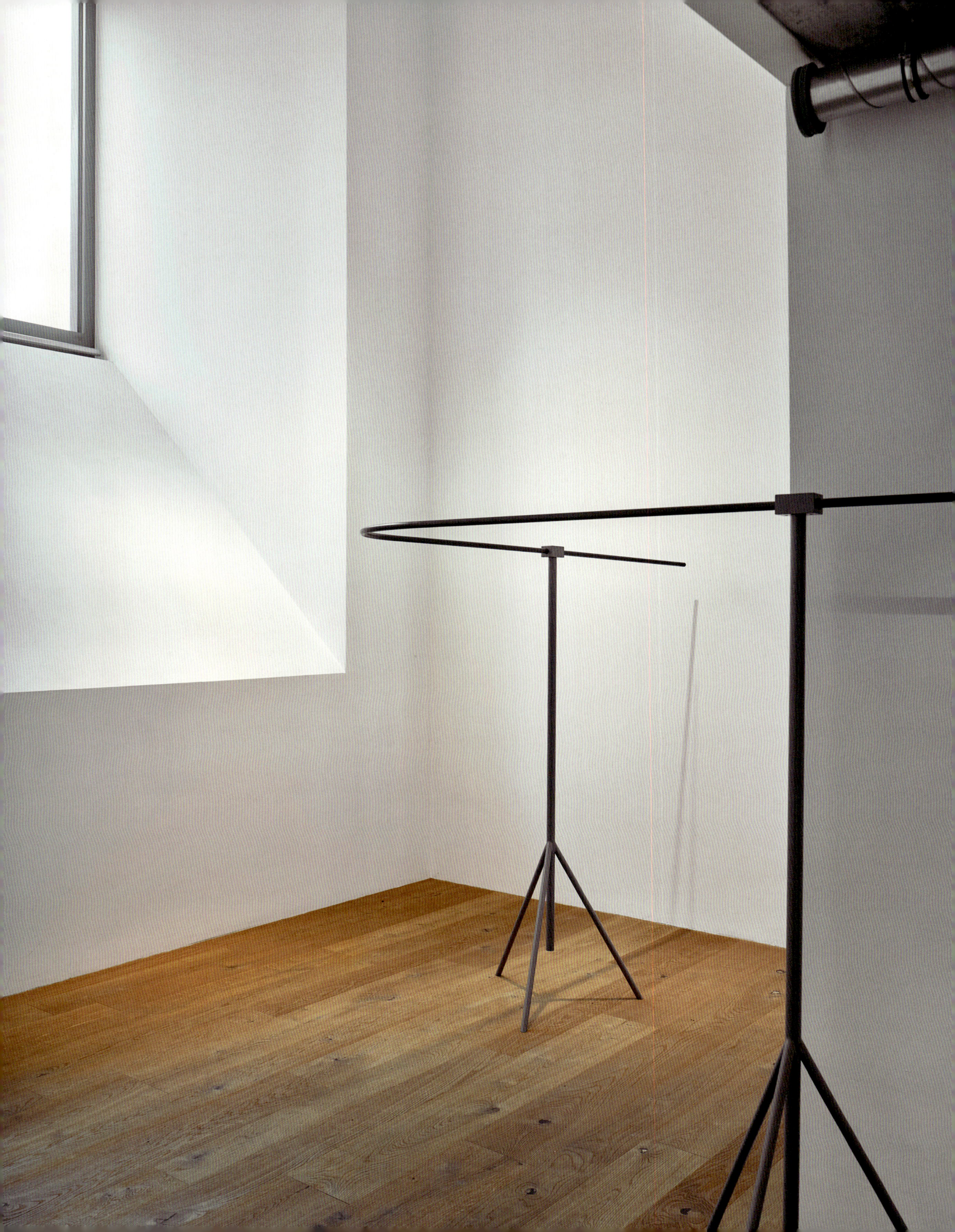

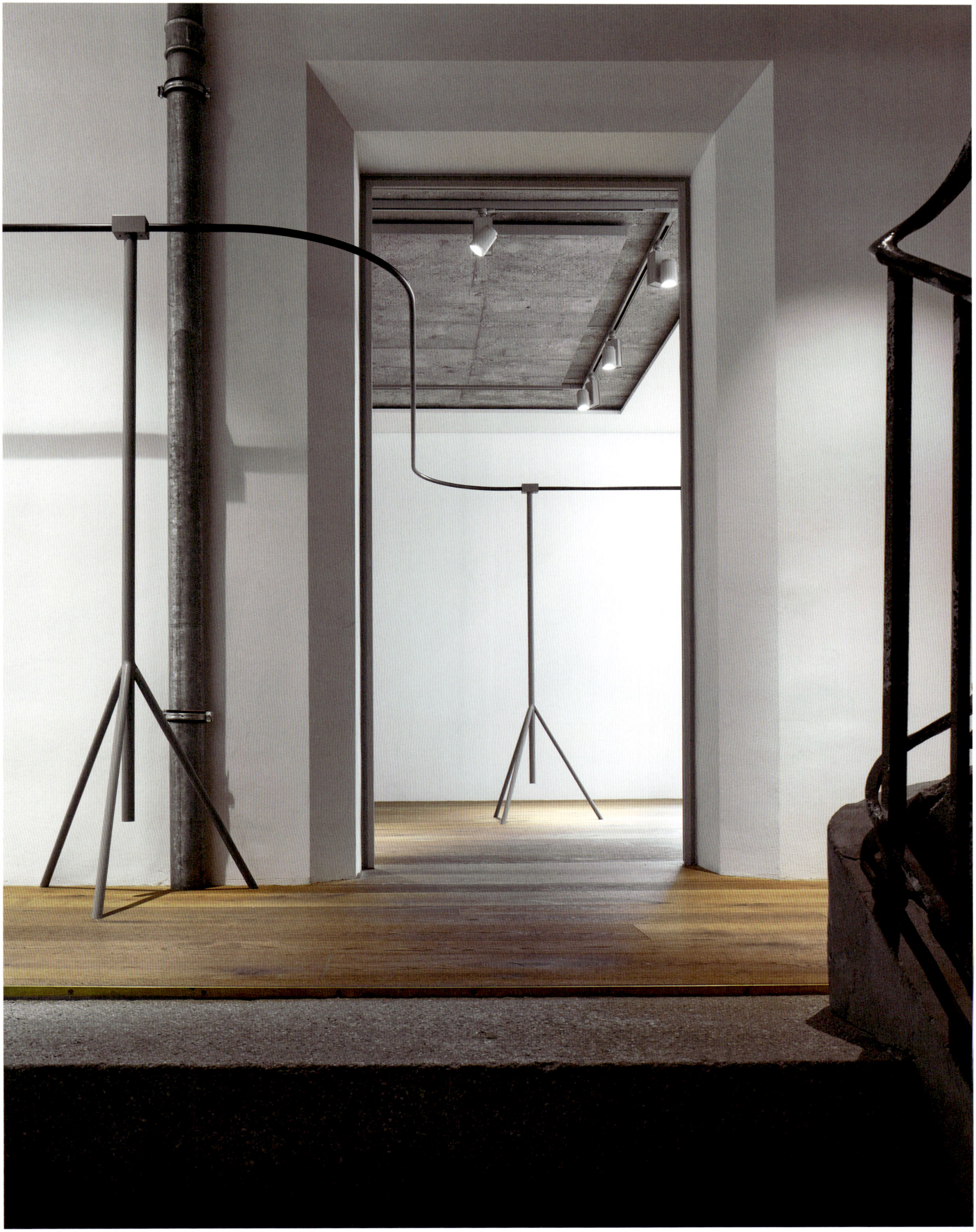

Augenhöhe, 2019

Air gun, steel / Luftgewehr, Stahl, Dimensions variable / Maße variabel, Installation view / Installationsansicht, BNKR, Munich / München

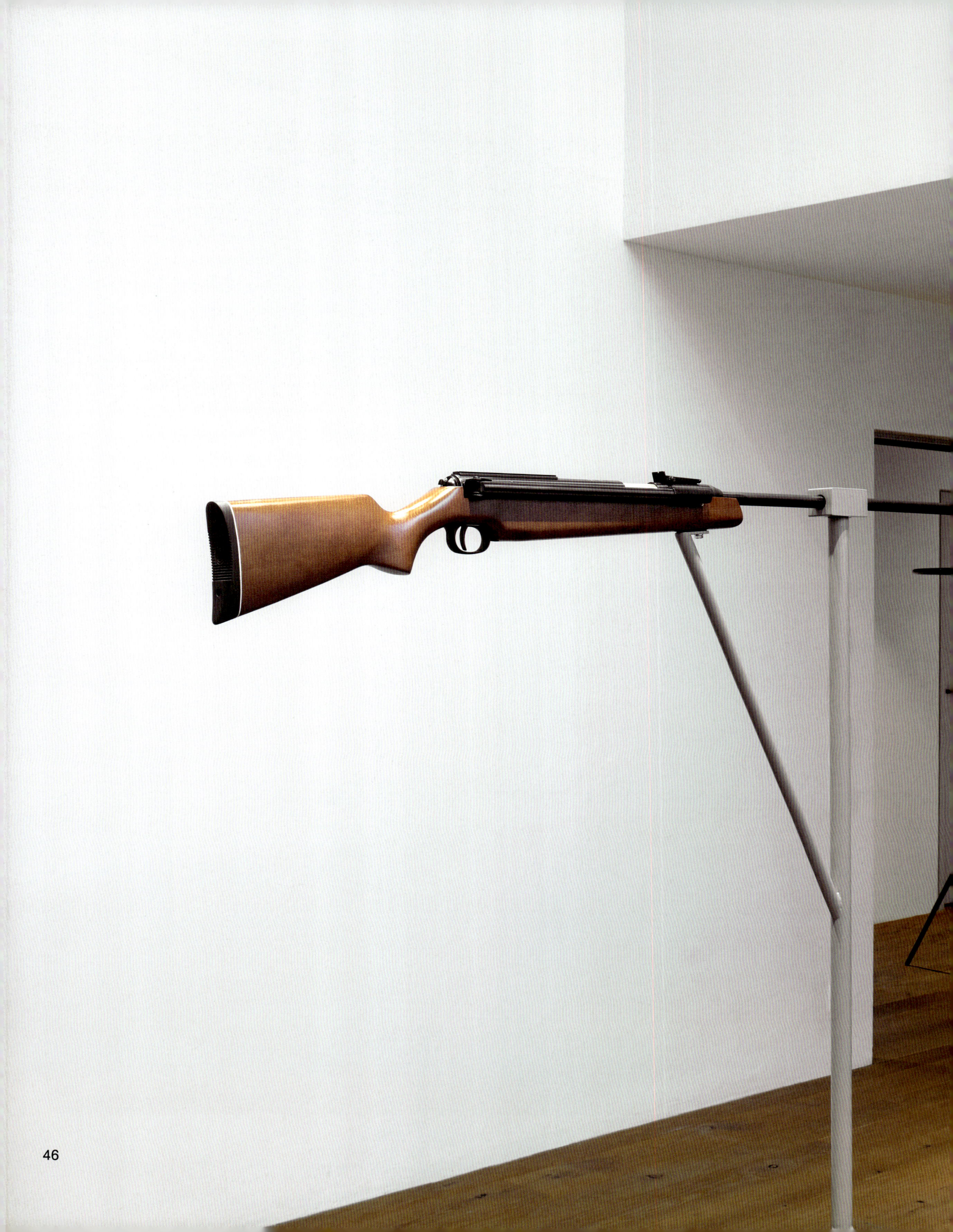

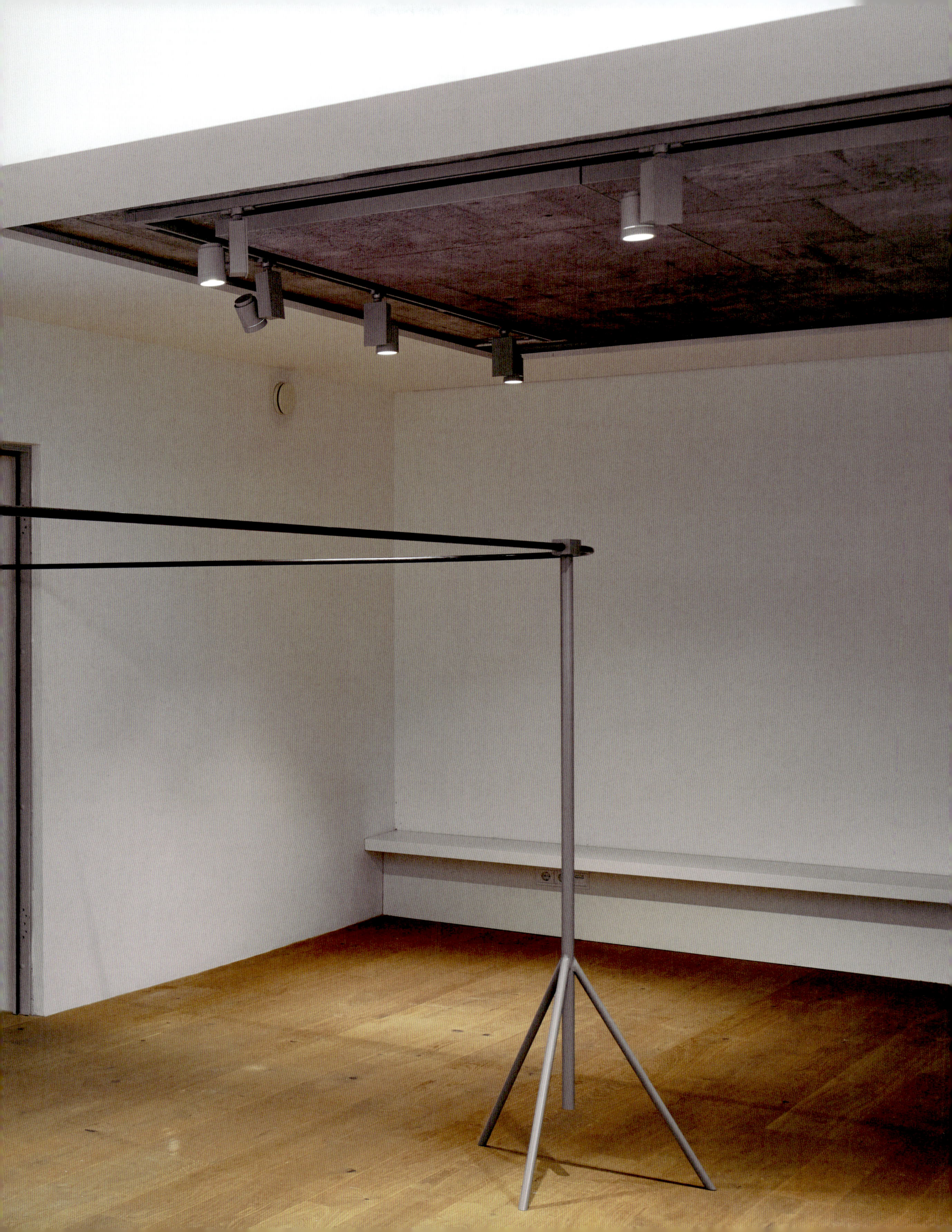

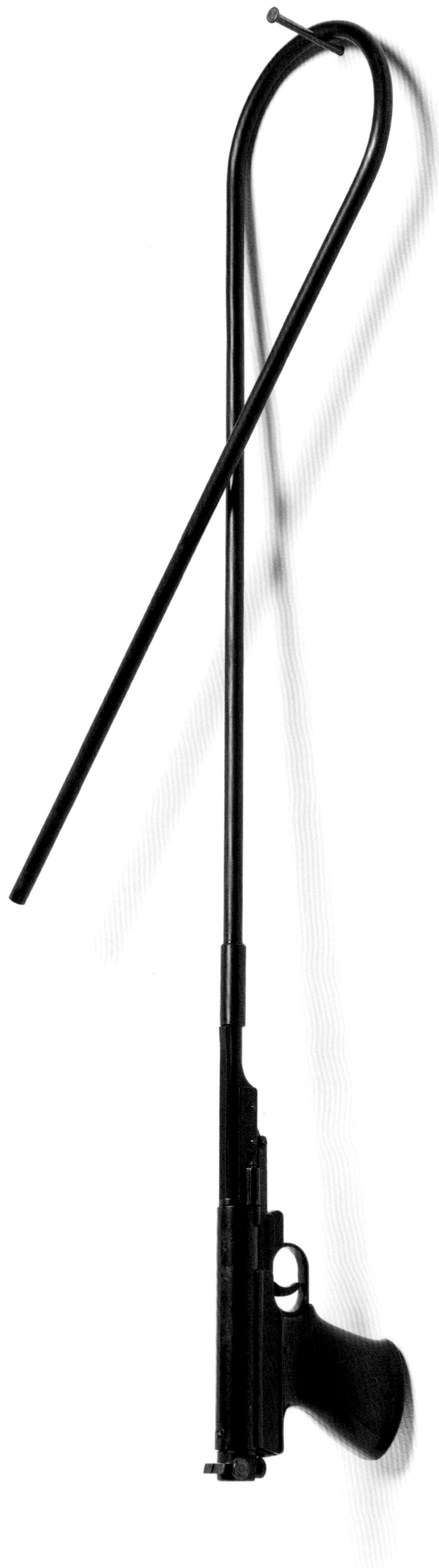

Gun 1, 2020

Air gun, steel / Luftpistole, Stahl, 92 × 32 × 15 cm

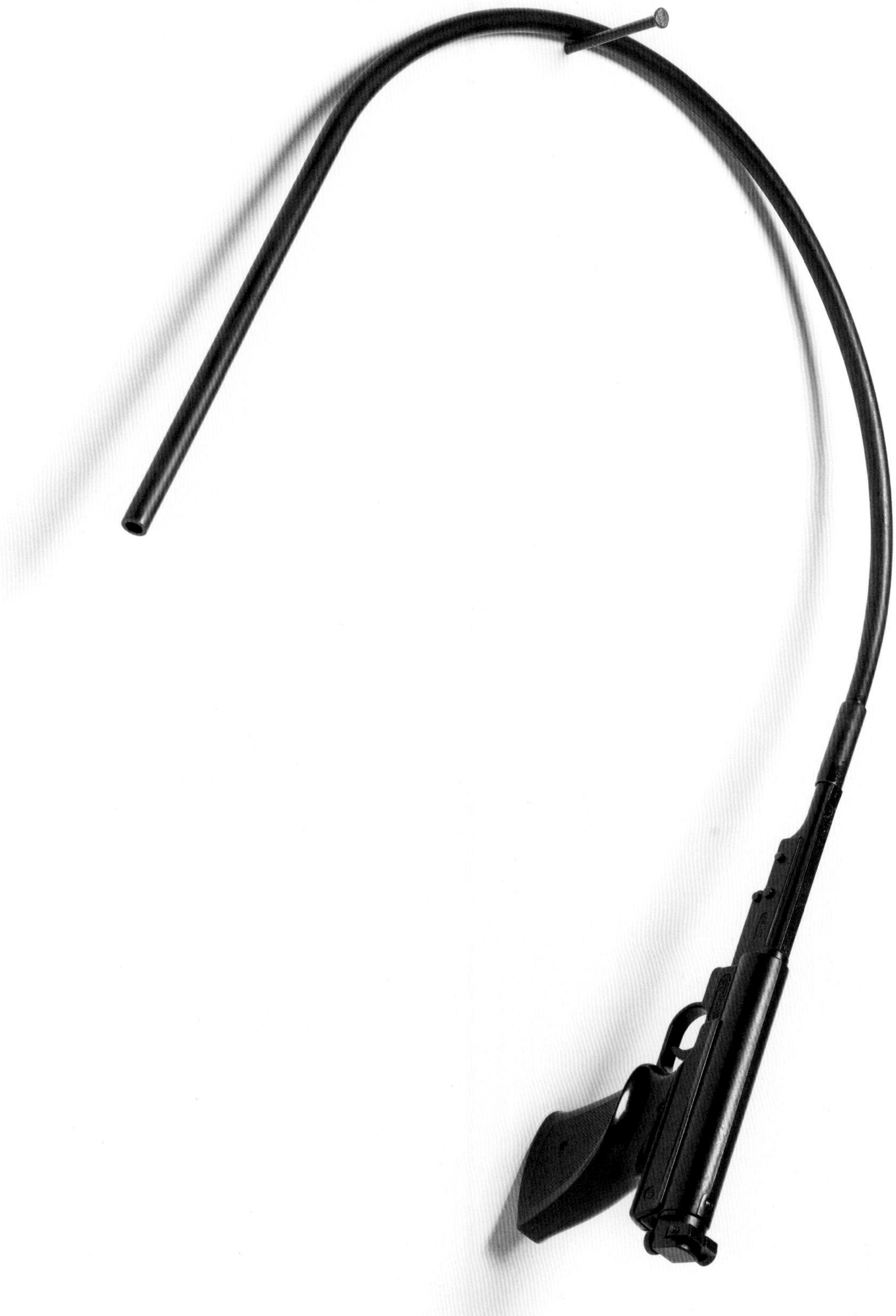

Gun 2, 2020

Air gun, steel / Luftpistole, Stahl, 57 × 45 × 15 cm

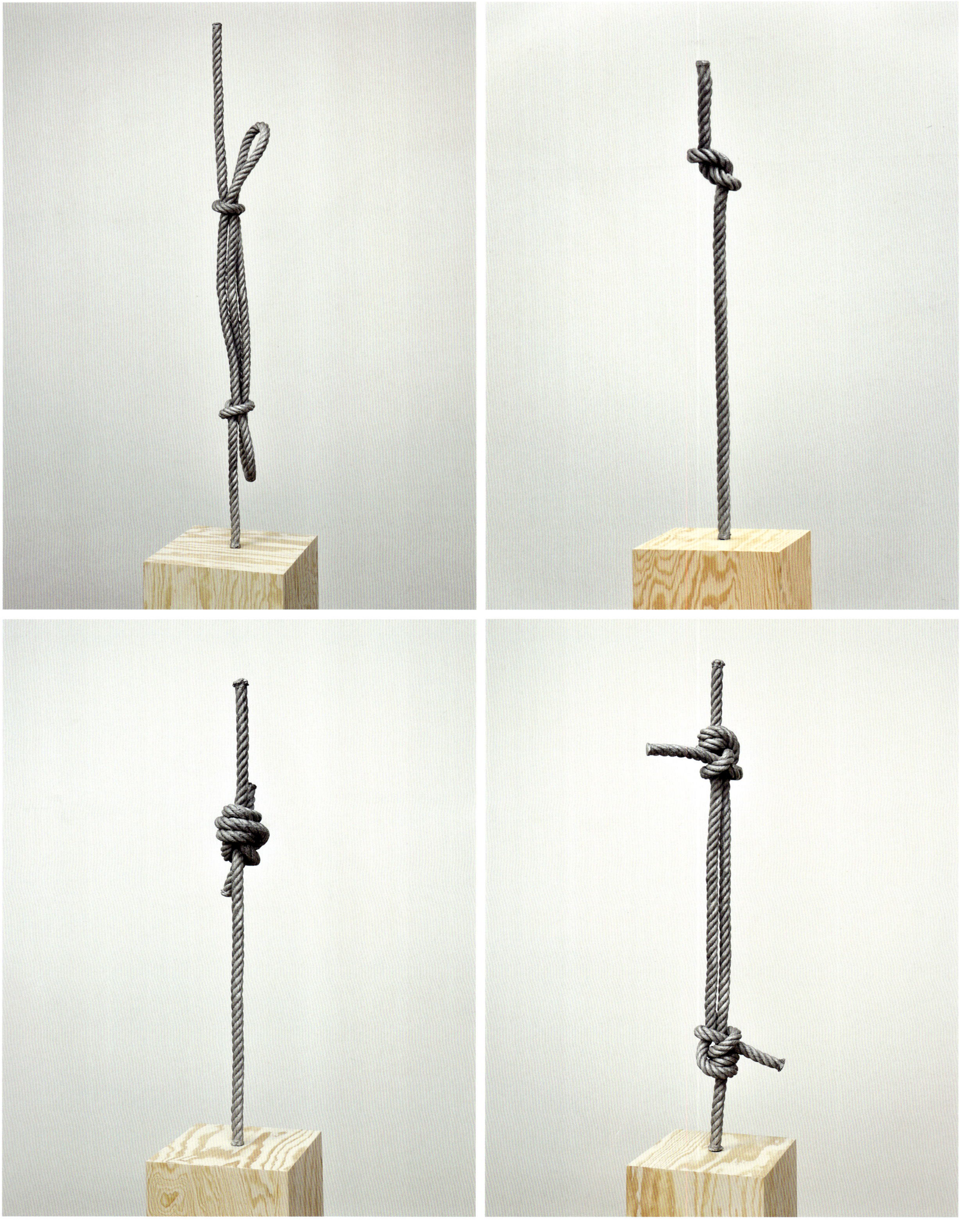

Knoten, 2010

Aluminum / Aluminium

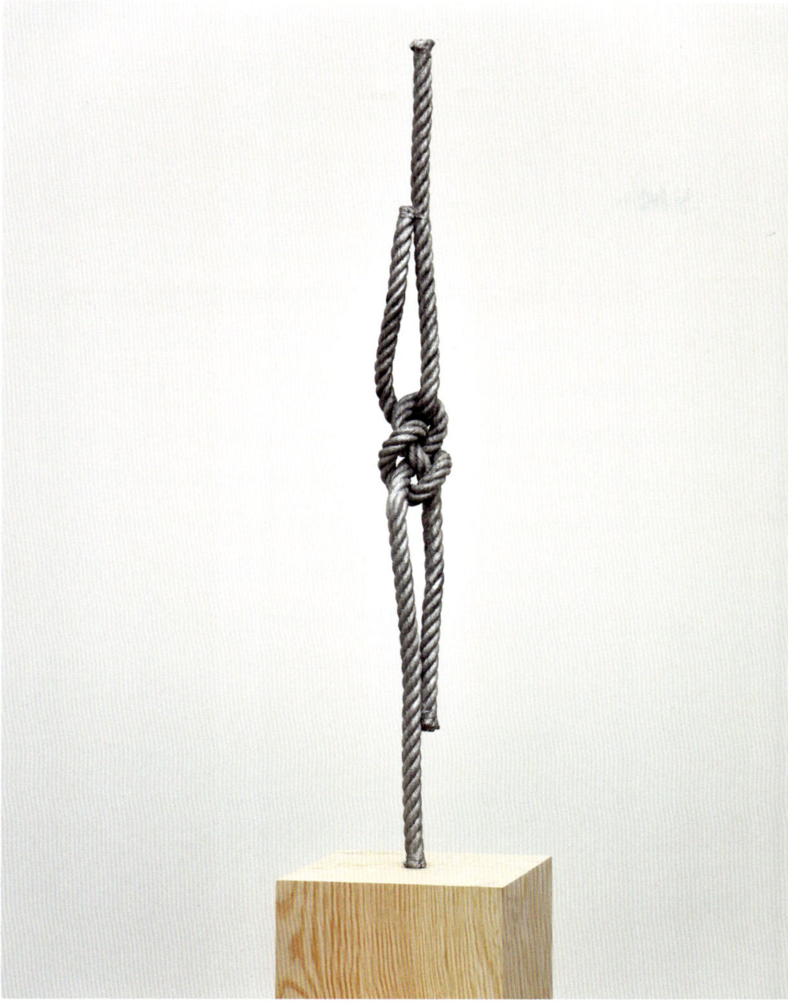
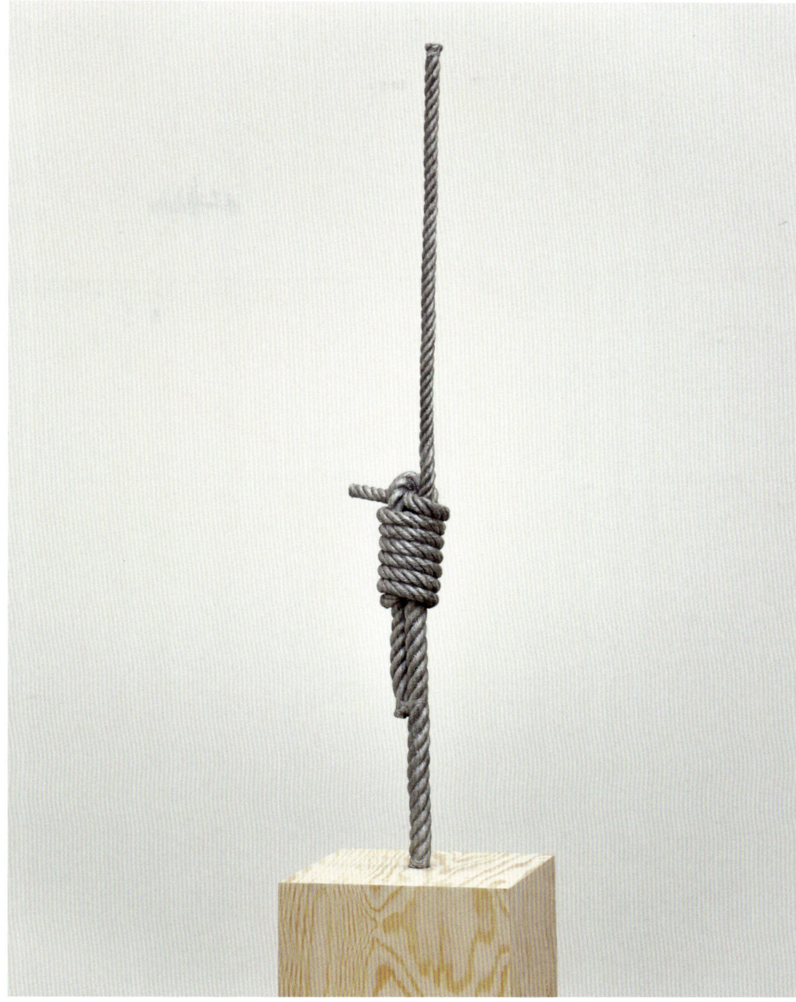
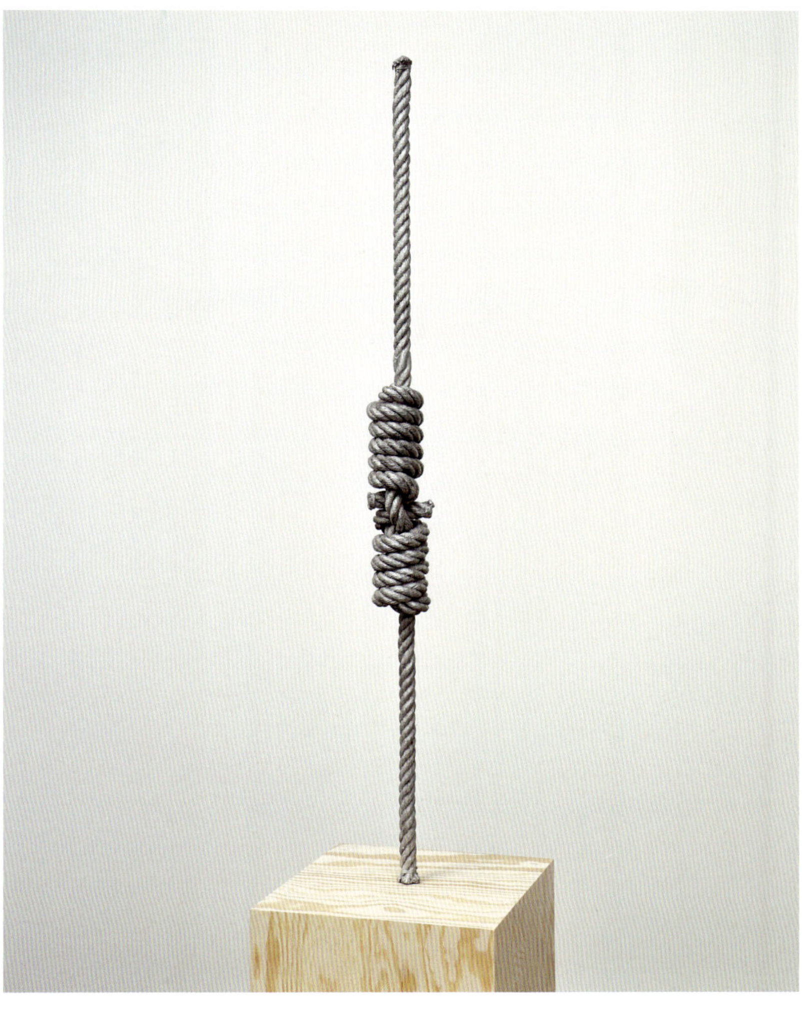
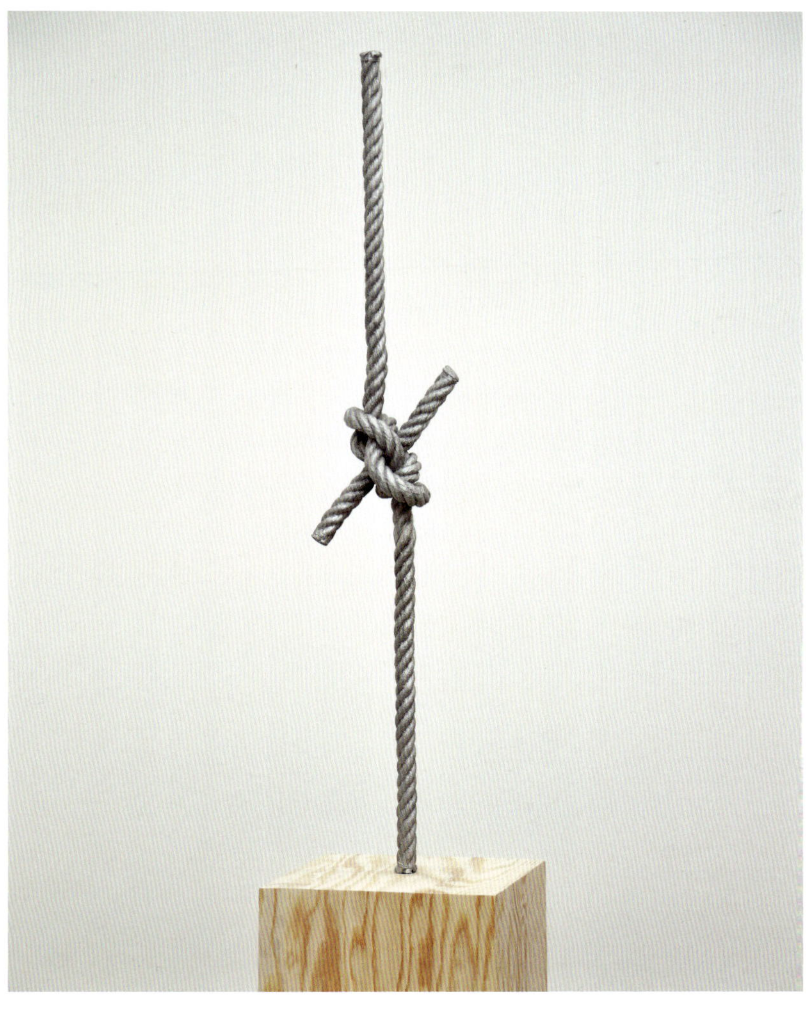

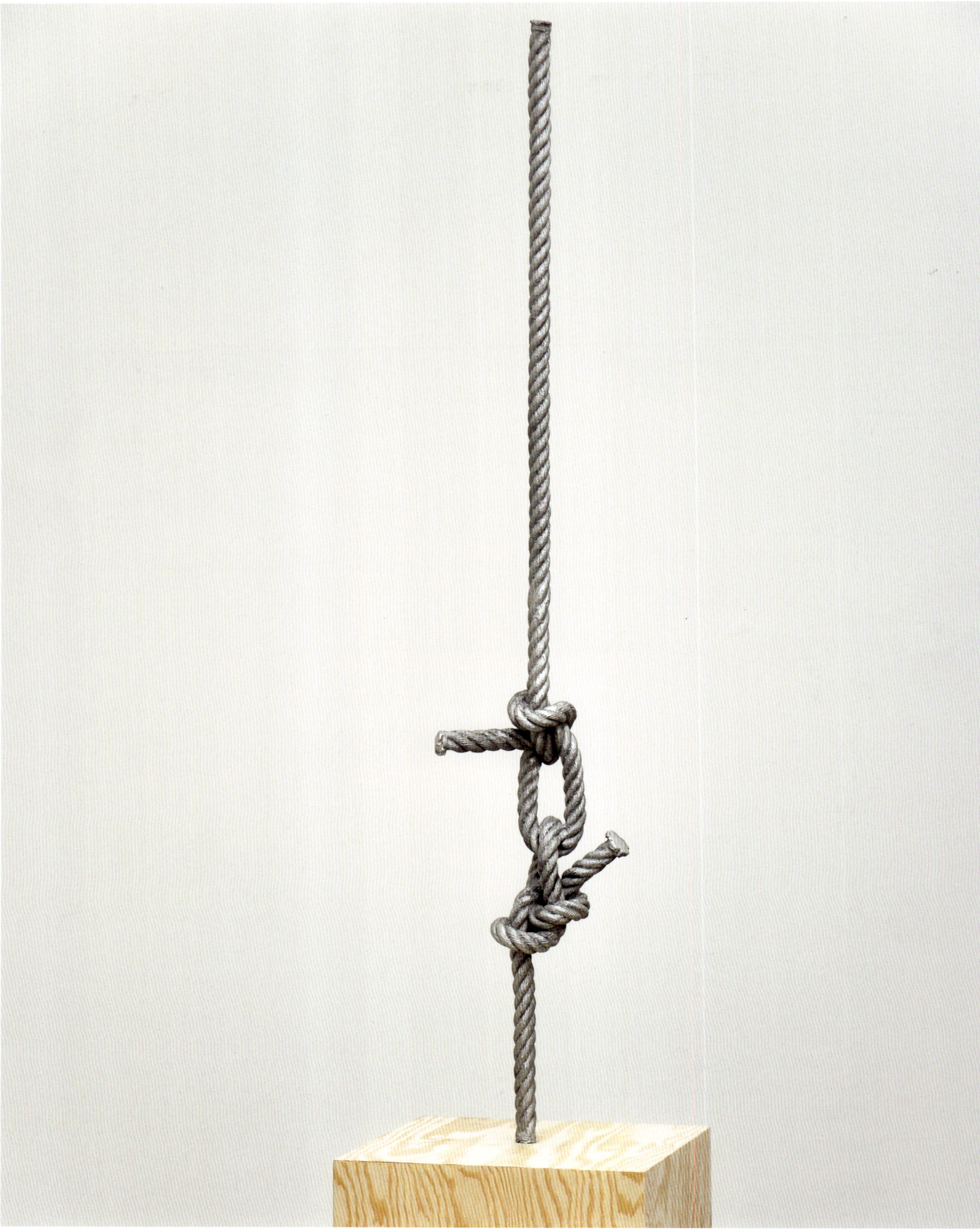

Knoten 20, 2010

Aluminum / Aluminium, 114 × 23 × 23 cm

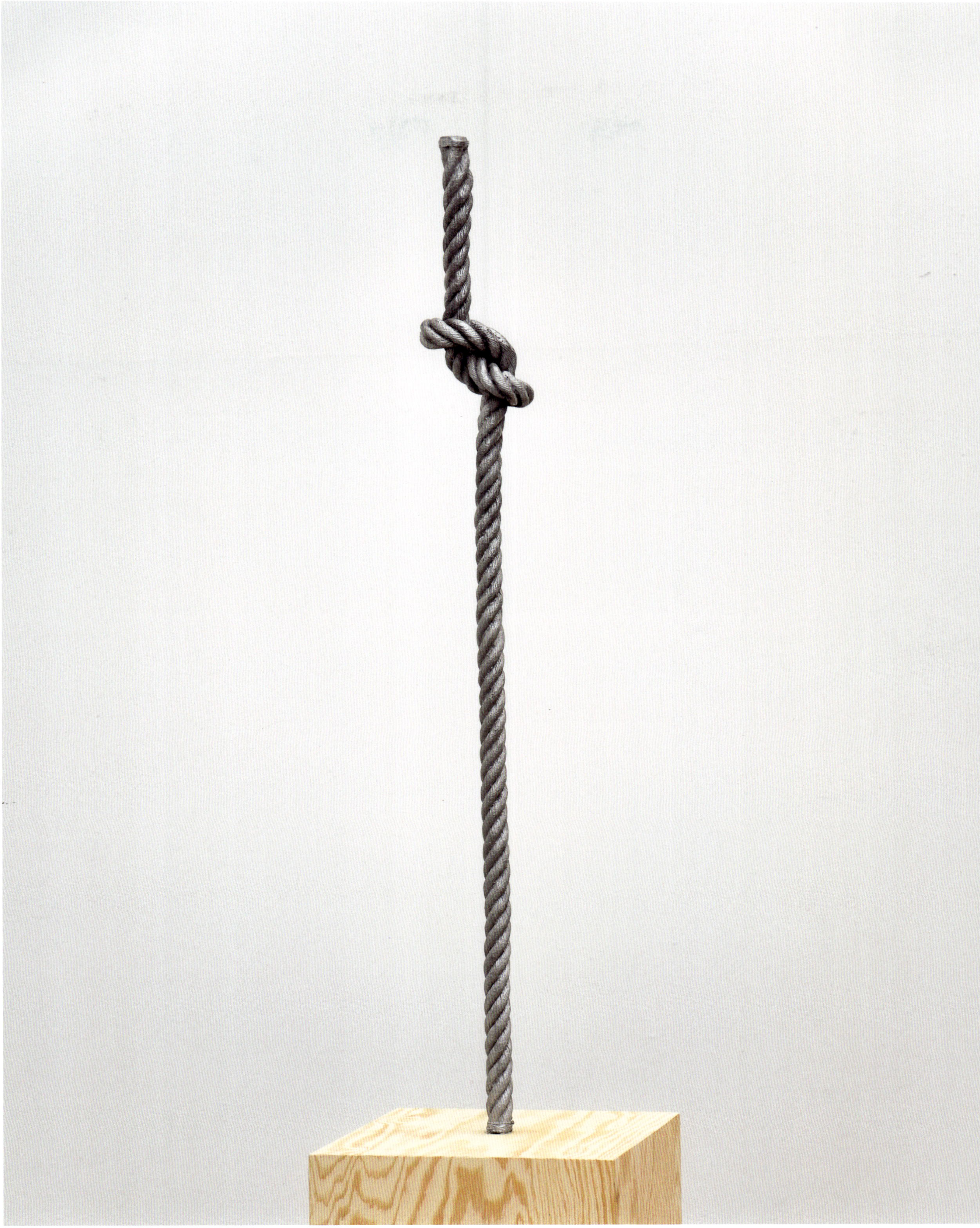

Knoten 25, 2010

Aluminum / Aluminium, 104 × 14 × 14 cm

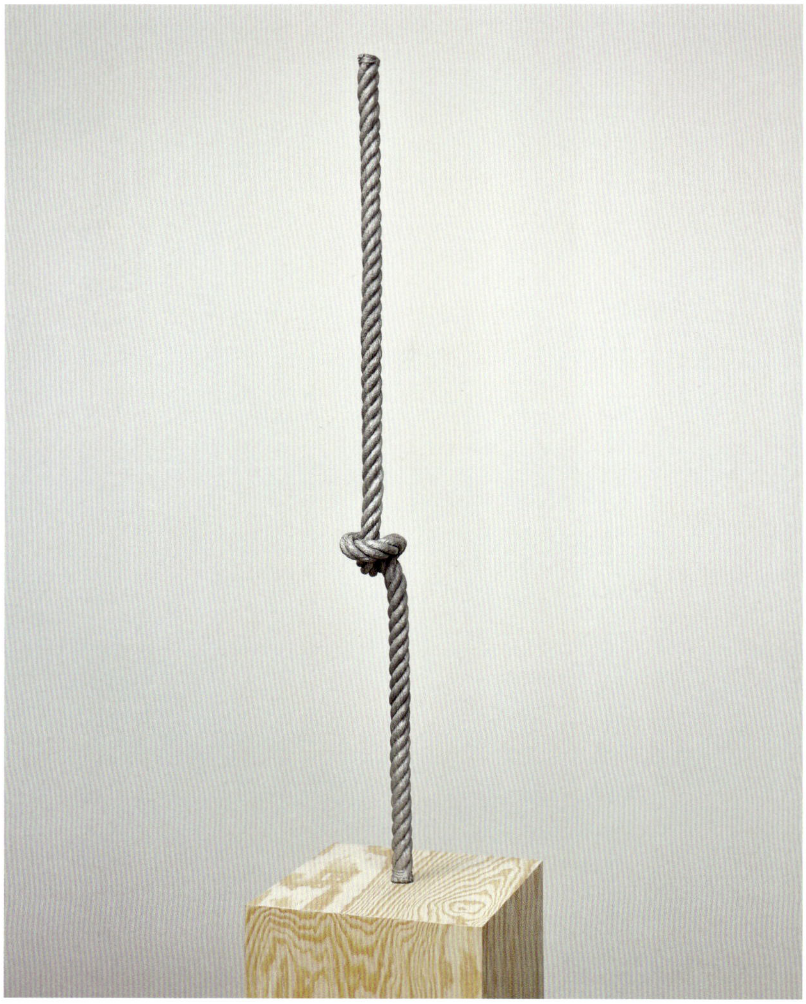
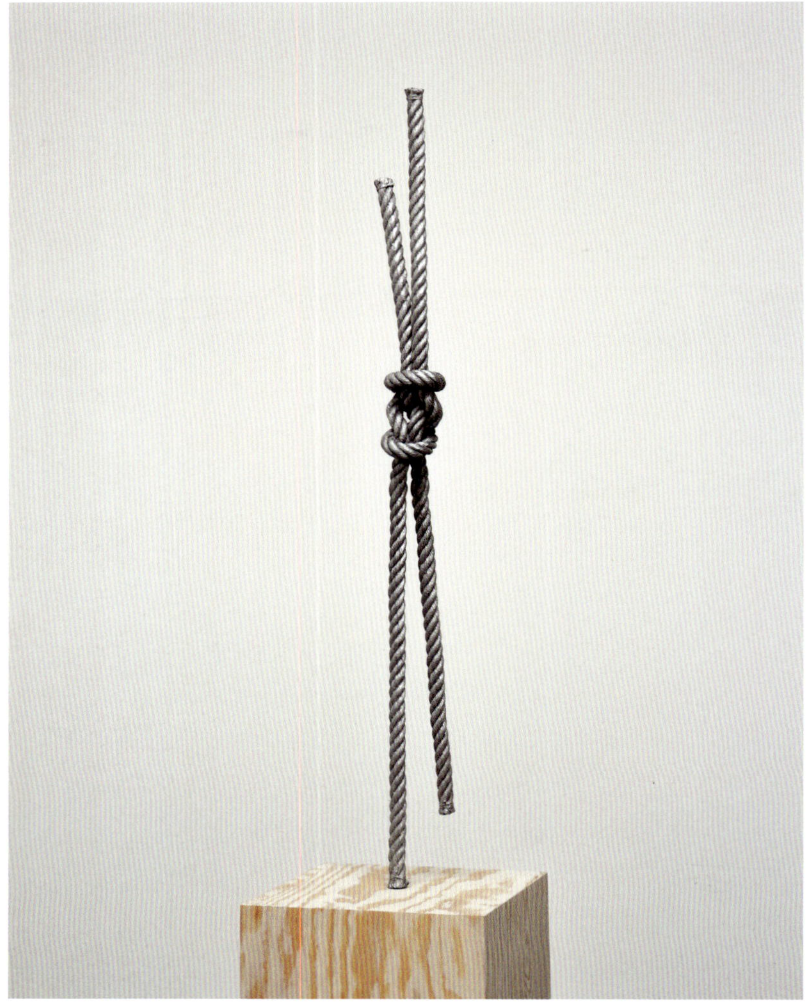
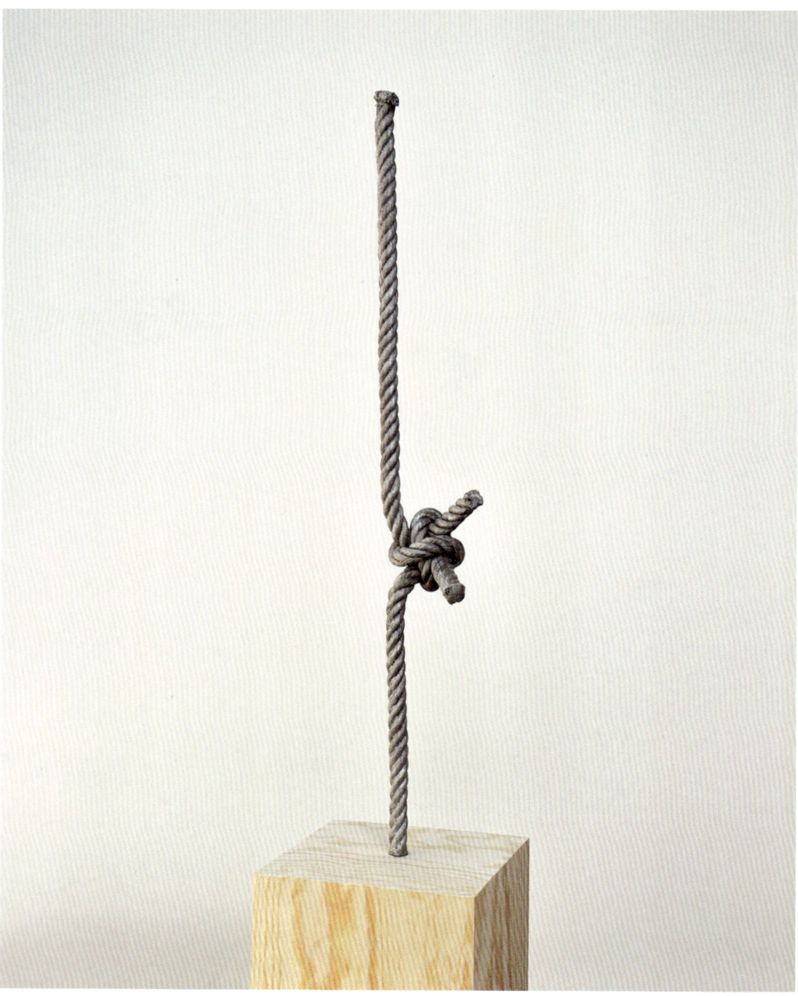
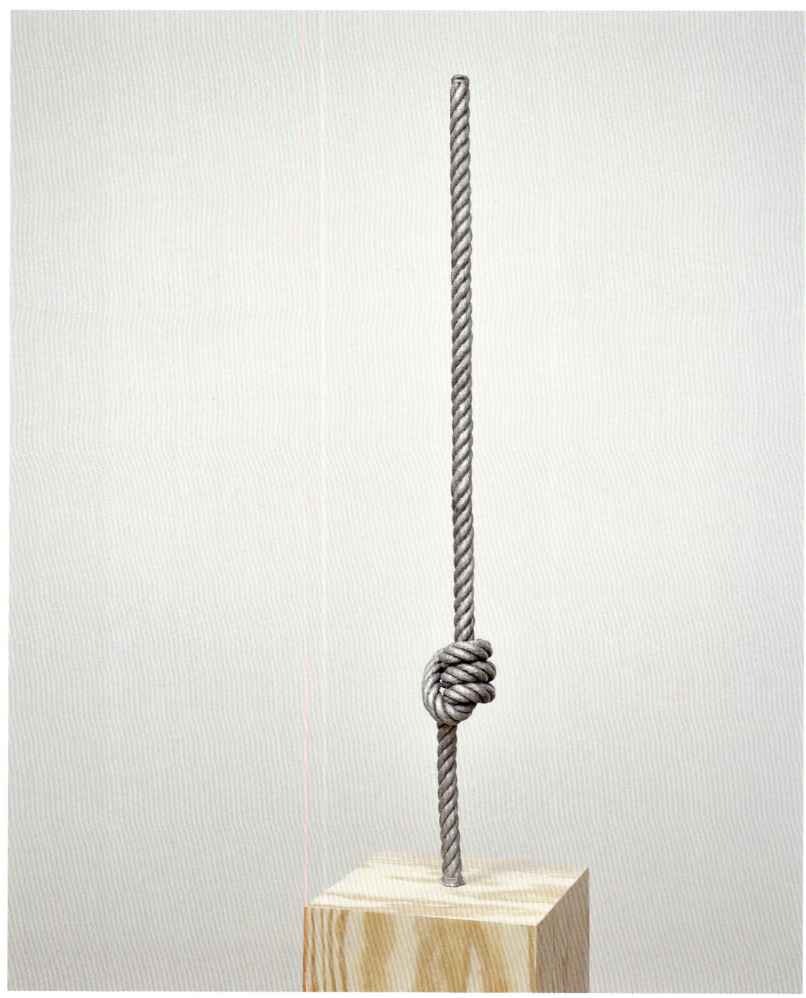

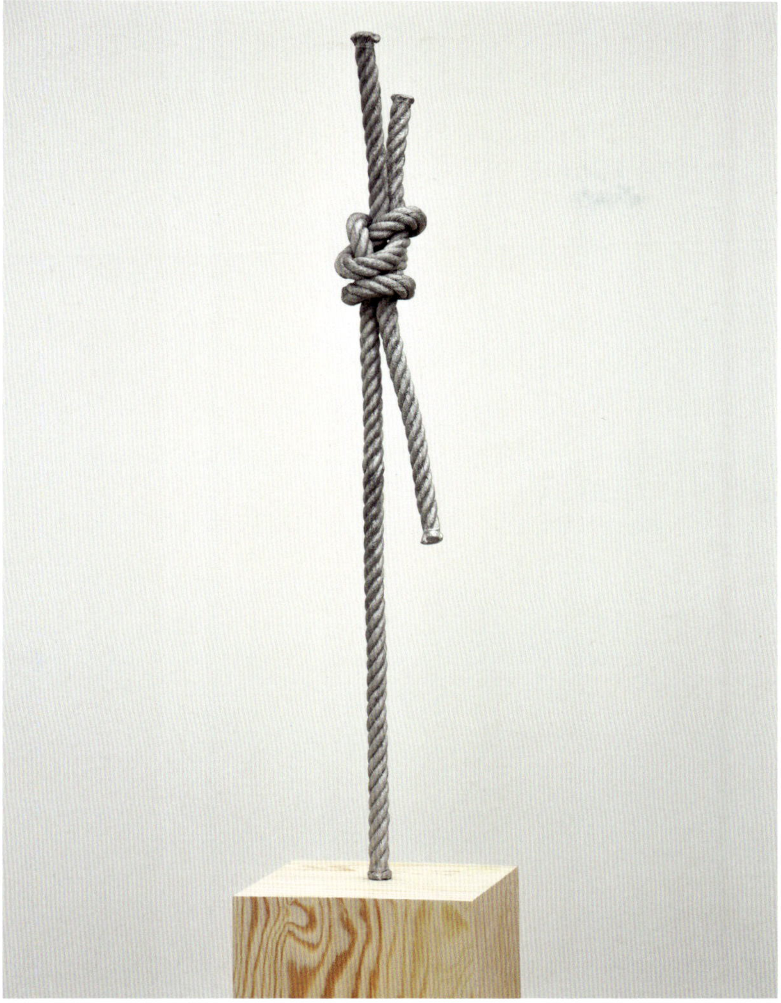
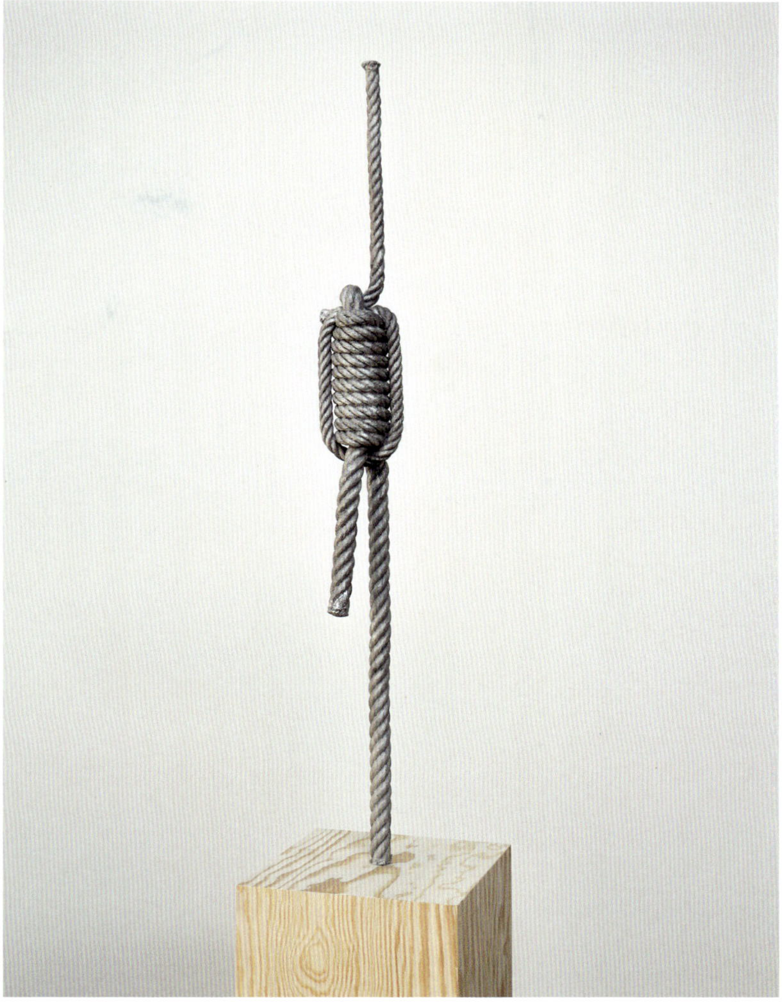
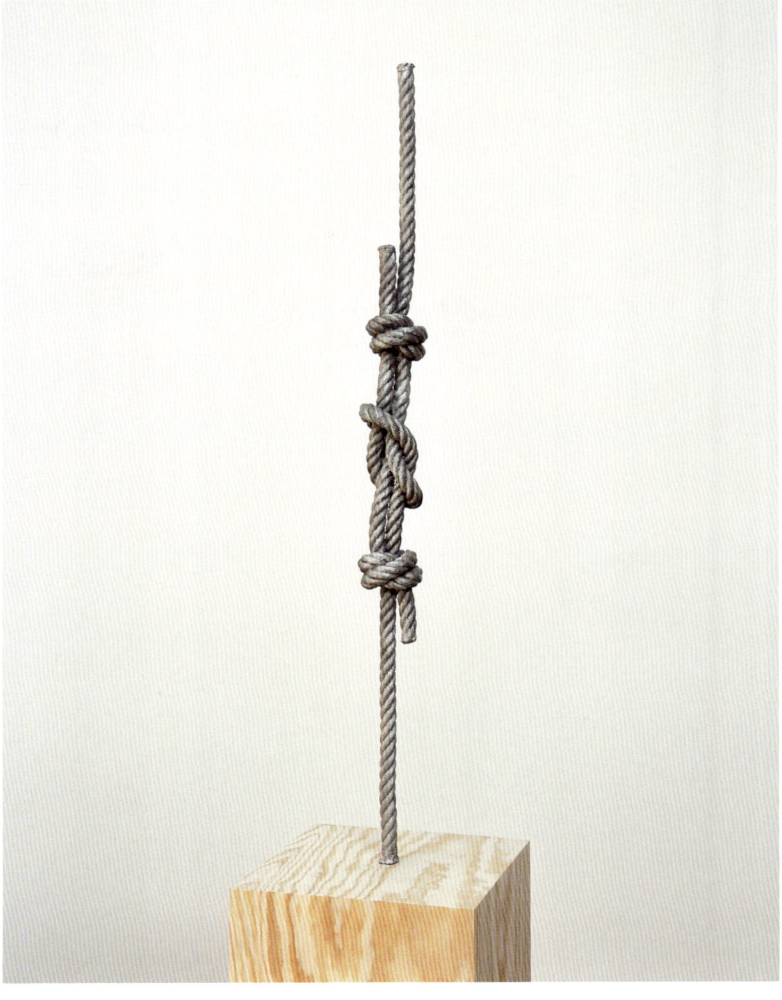
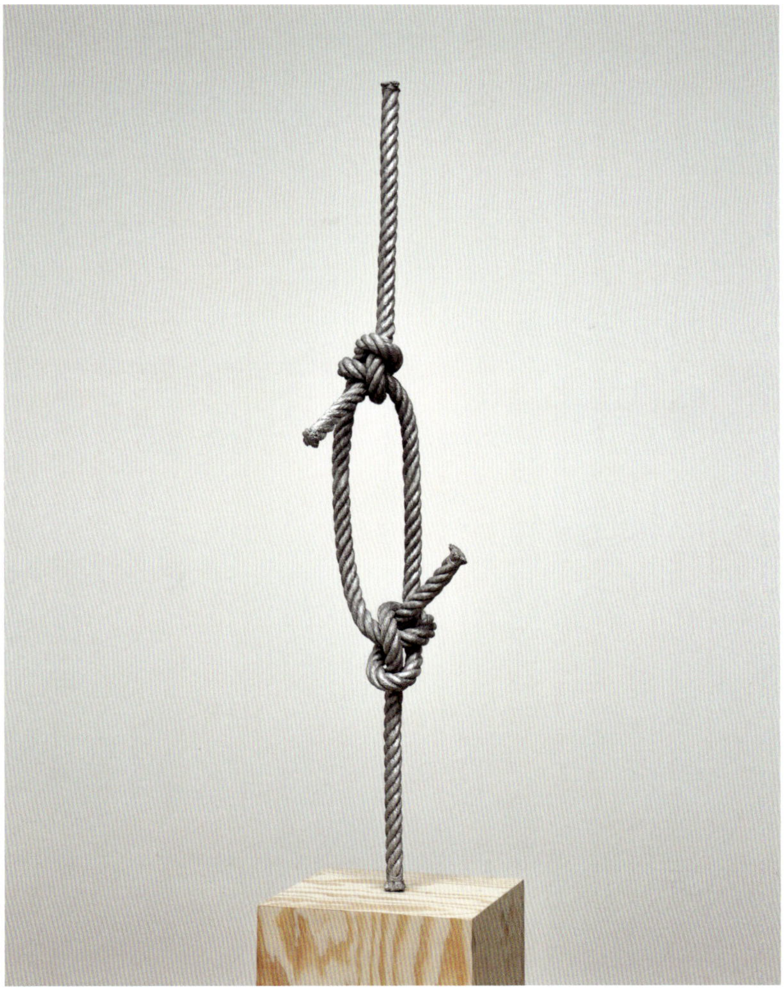

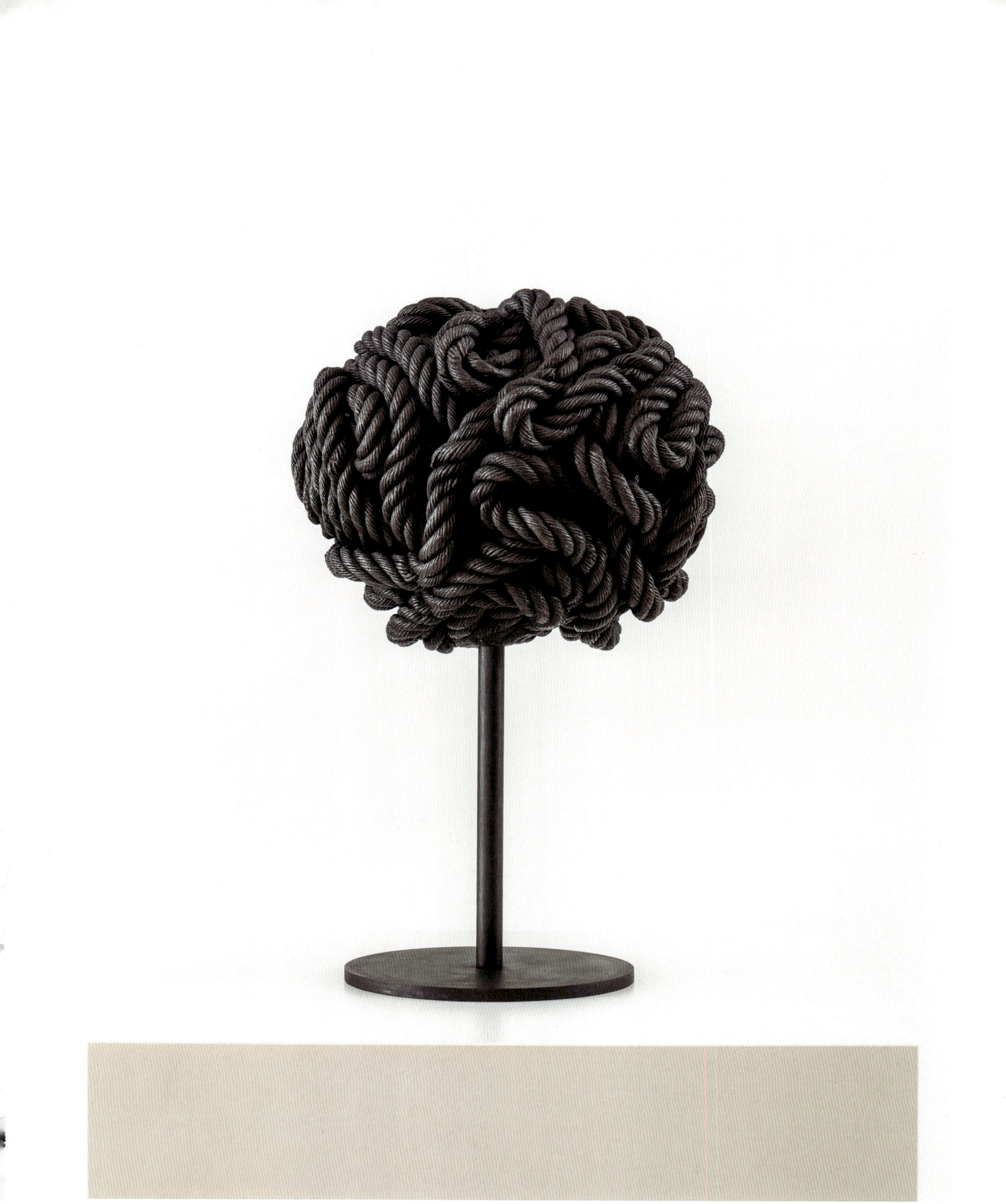

Brain U, 2020
Bronze, 52 × 24 × 32 cm

Brain T, 2020
Bronze, 59 × 31 × 35 cm

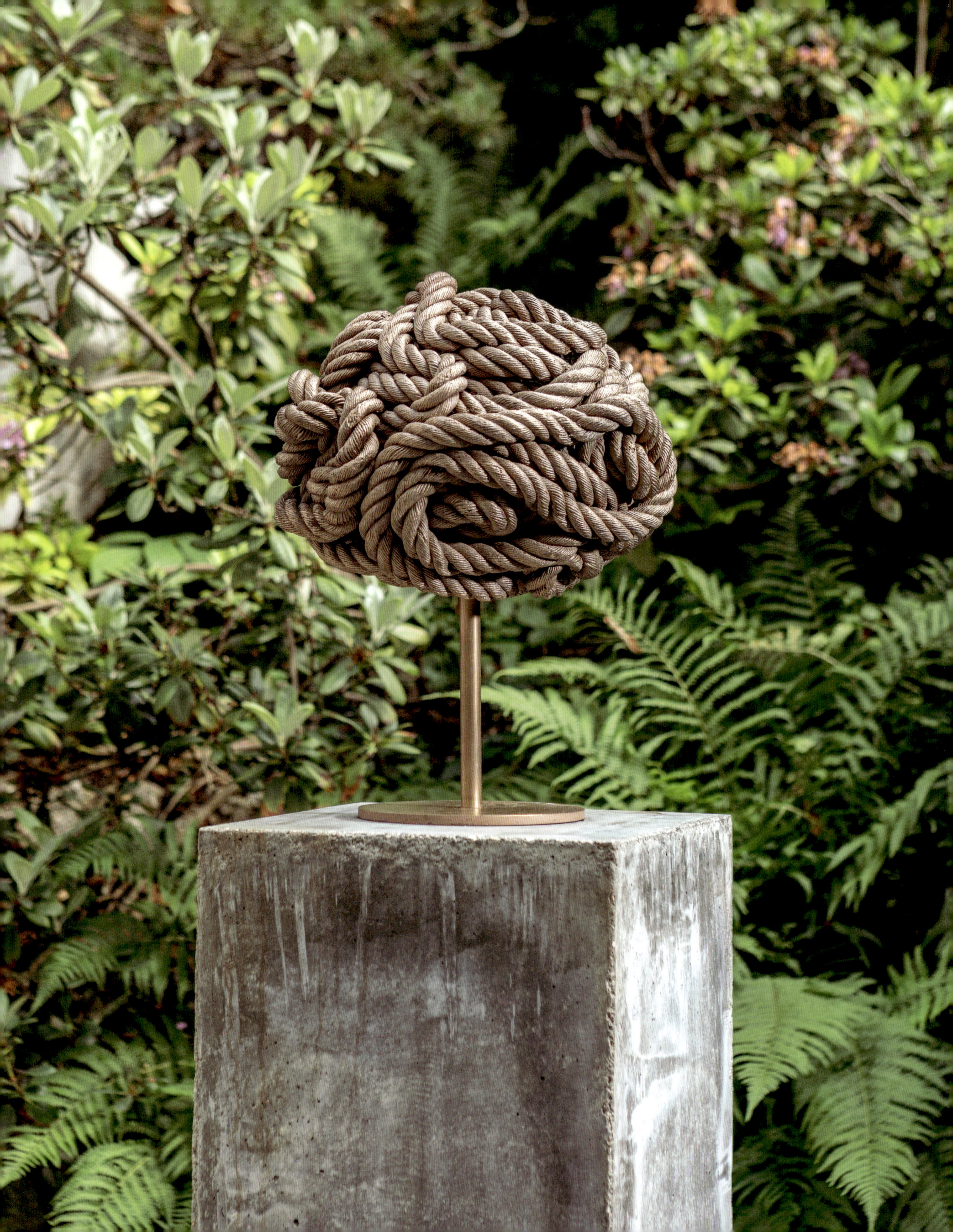

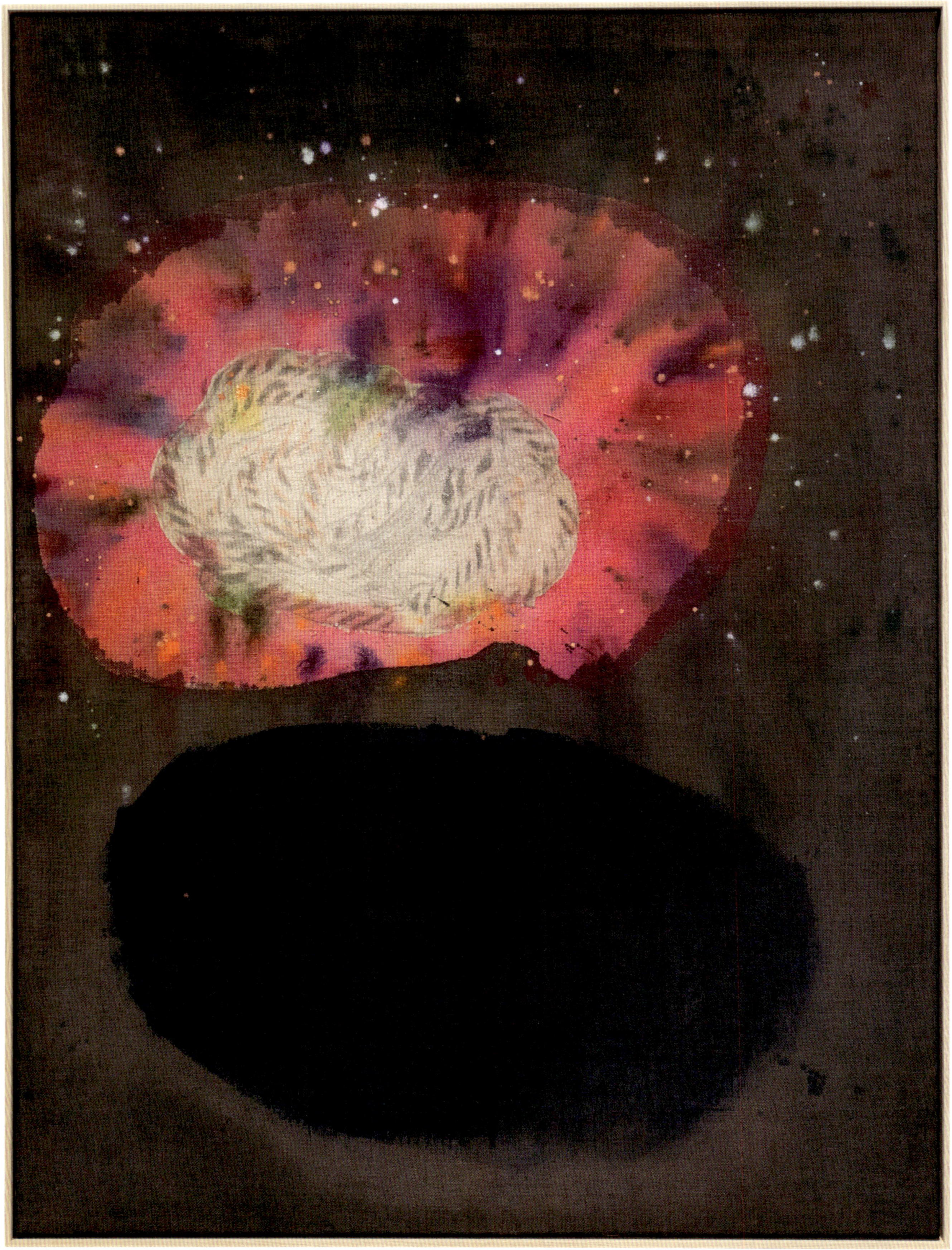

Brain 1, 2020

Pencil, salt and ink on jute / Bleistift, Salz und Tusche auf Jute, 153 × 118 cm (framed / gerahmt)

Brain B2, 2020

Bronze, 74 × 53 × 40 cm

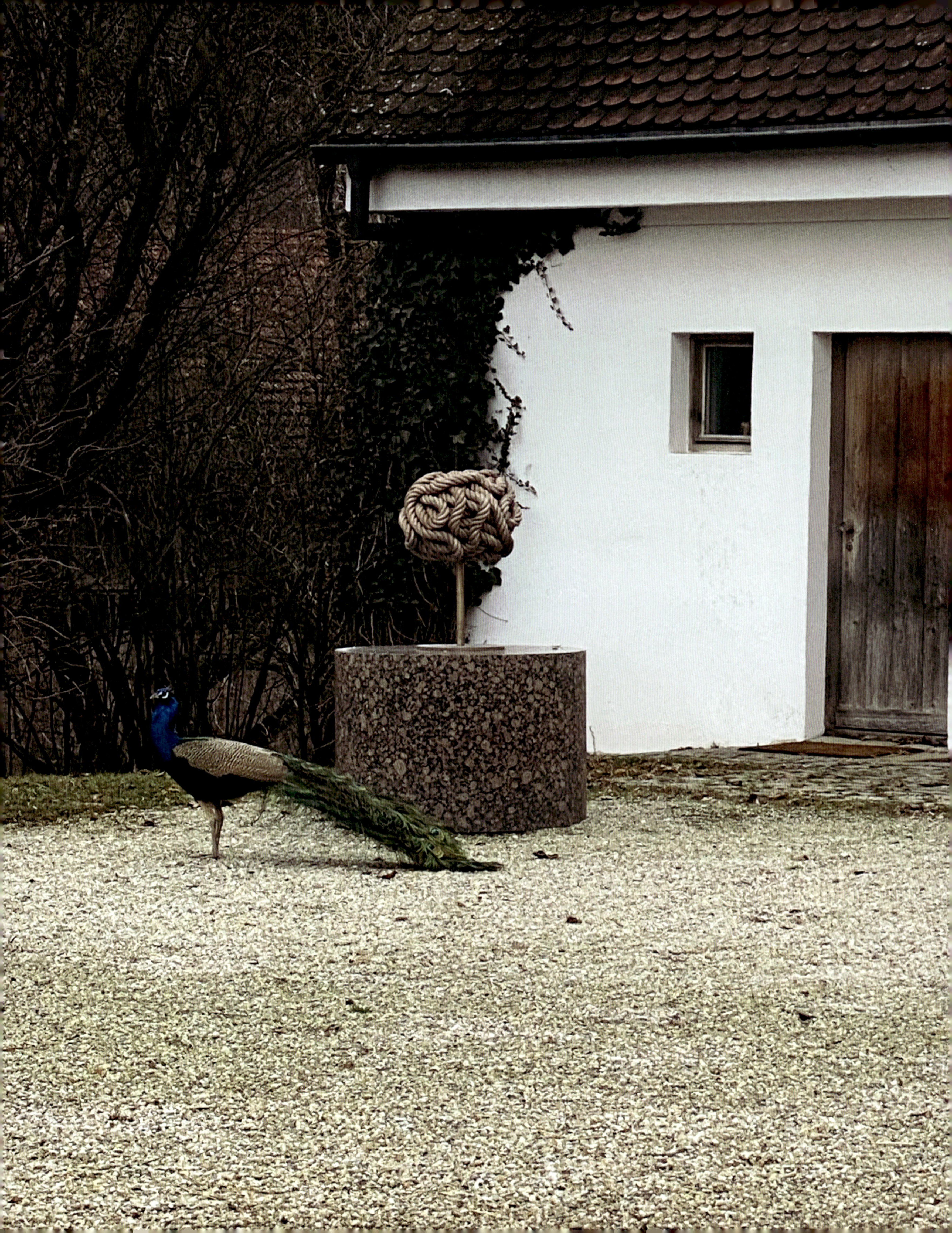

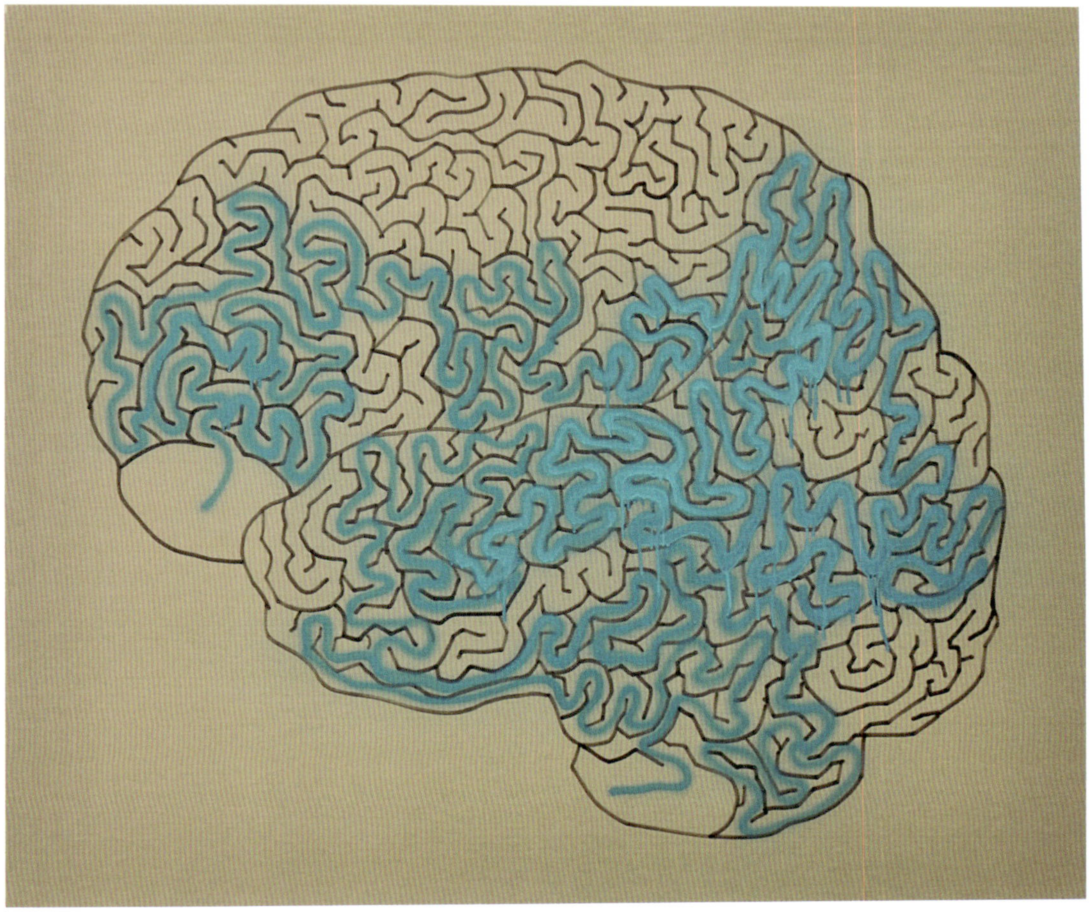

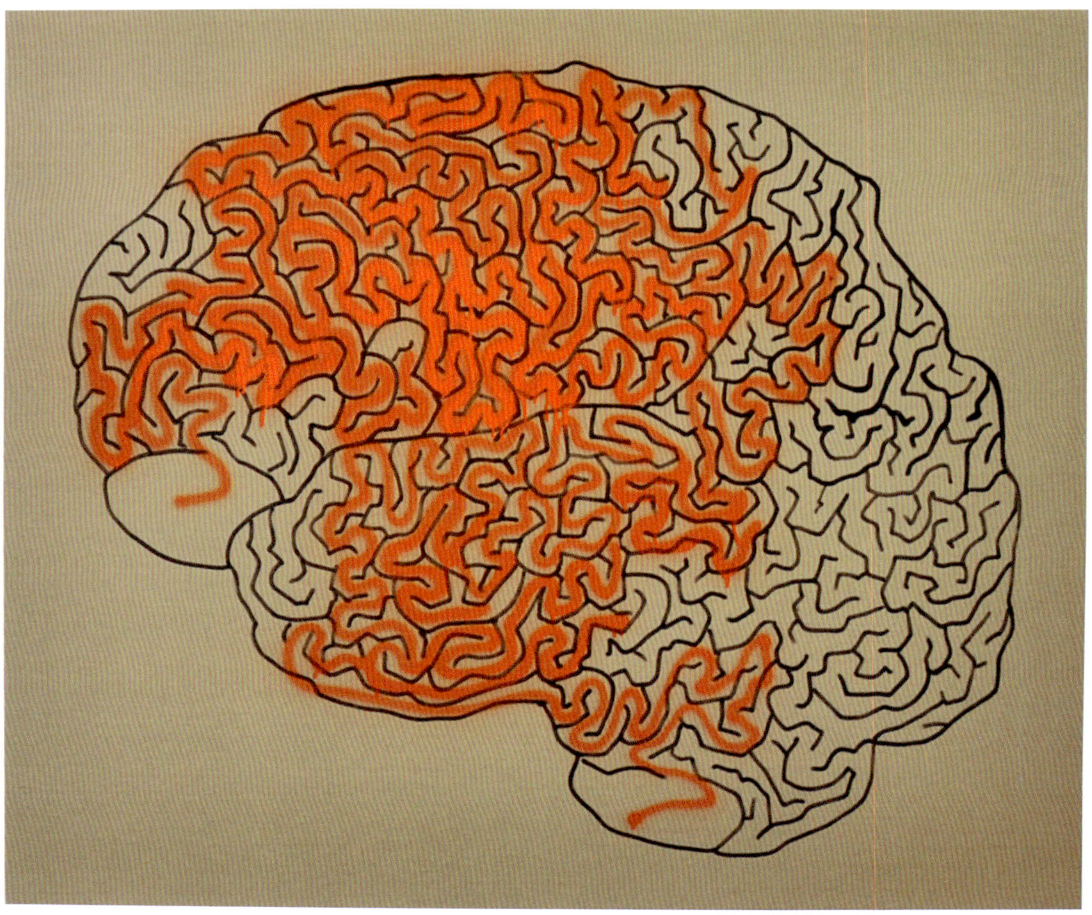

Maze 28, 2012

Maze 34, 2012

Ink and spray paint on linen / Tusche und Sprühfarbe auf Leinen, 190 × 230 cm

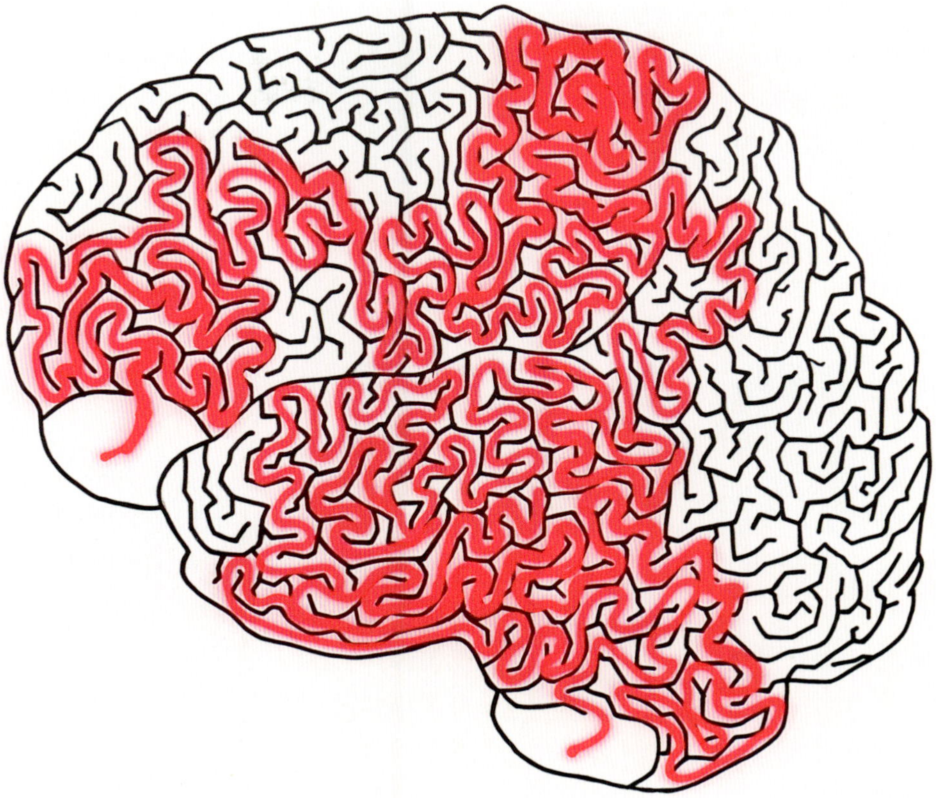

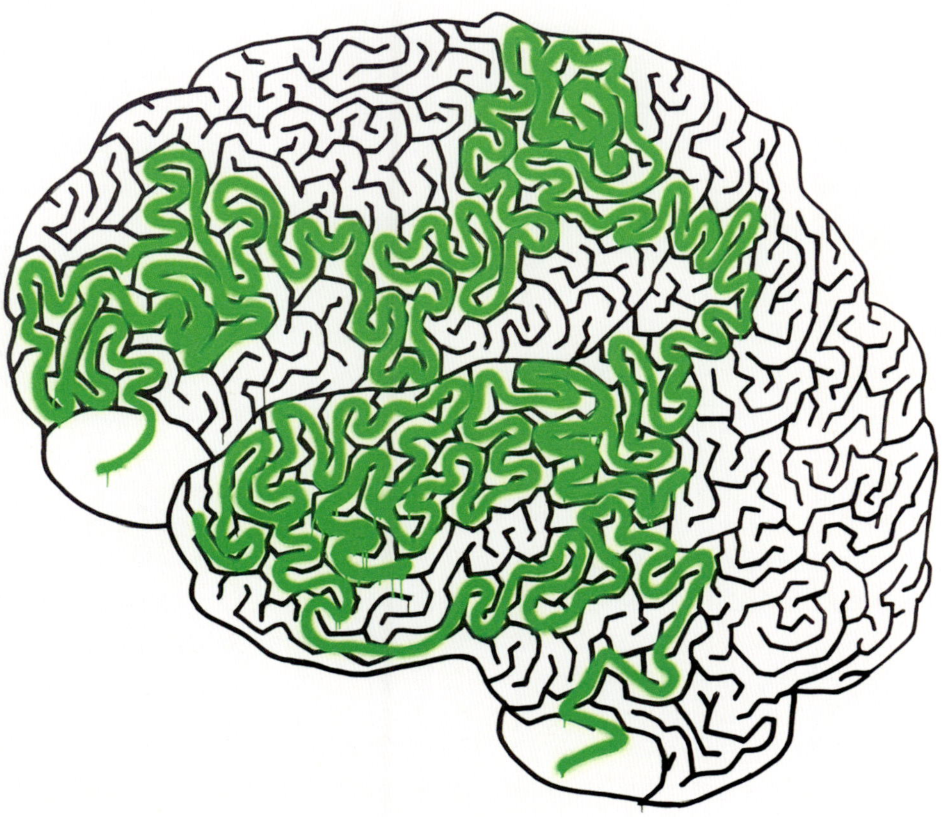

Maze 29, 2012

Maze 30, 2012

Ink and spray paint on canvas / Tusche und Sprühfarbe auf Leinwand, 190 × 230 cm

Johanna Adam

THE BRAIN SERIES

"If the human brain were so simple that we could understand it, we would be so simple that we couldn't."

EMERSON PUGH, 1977

„Wenn das menschliche Gehirn so einfach wäre, dass wir es verstehen könnten, dann wären wir so einfach, dass wir es nicht verstehen würden."

EMERSON PUGH, 1977

DIE *BRAIN*-SERIEN ↗56–59

The sobering insight of the American scientist Emerson Pugh reads like a paradox. The human brain is one of those areas of research that have so far constantly raised—and, as the quote suggests, will continue to constantly raise—new questions as our knowledge grows. This uncertainty offers room for speculative considerations. When the first EEG was recorded roughly one hundred years ago, expectations could hardly have been greater. Soon, it was thought, it would be possible to write in "electric brain writing"; the possibilities of mindreading and telepathy seemed within reach. Today, despite more advanced technical imaging techniques and the resulting insights, hopes and expectations are much more subdued. And yet pessimism would be misplaced at this point. In fact, it is even due to the considerably improved understanding of how the brain works that, today, neuroscientists are far less emphatic: "If brain research has shown one thing in the last thirty years, it is that it is in principle possible to learn something about a person's mindset by taking a look at his or her brain processes," explains Prof. John-Dylan Haynes of the Bernstein Center for Computational Neuroscience at the Charité, Berlin. The hope that the "language of the brain" will soon be deciphered is, however, not reflected in this prognosis. As our knowledge grows, so does our awareness of the

Die ernüchternde Erkenntnis des amerikanischen Wissenschaftlers Emerson Pugh liest sich wie ein Paradoxon. Das menschliche Gehirn gehört zu jenen Forschungsbereichen, die bislang – und, wie das Zitat nahelegt, auch in Zukunft – mit wachsenden Erkenntnissen stets neue Fragen aufwerfen. Die Ungewissheit bietet Raum für spekulative Überlegungen. Als vor etwa hundert Jahren das erste EEG aufgezeichnet wurde, konnten die Erwartungen kaum größer sein. Bald werde man in „Gehirnschrift" schreiben können; die Möglichkeiten des Gedankenlesens und der Telepathie schienen zum Greifen nah. Heute nehmen sich die Hoffnungen und Erwartungen trotz weiterentwickelter technischer Verfahren der Bildgebung und der daraus resultierenden Einsichten deutlich verhaltener aus. Und dennoch wäre Pessimismus an dieser Stelle verfehlt. Tatsächlich liegt es sogar am erheblich verbesserten Verständnis der Funktionsweise des Gehirns, dass Neurowissenschaftler heute weit weniger emphatisch formulieren: „Wenn die Hirnforschung in den letzten dreißig Jahren eines gezeigt hat, dann dass es prinzipiell möglich ist, etwas über die Gedankenwelt einer Person zu erfahren, indem man einen Blick auf ihre Hirnprozesse wirft", konstatierte Prof. John-Dylan Haynes vom Bernstein Center for Computational Neuroscience an der Charité, Berlin. Die Hoffnung, man könne sehr bald die „Sprache des Gehirns" entschlüsseln, spiegelt

limitations of our knowledge. In this context, the following observation is crucial: Our brains function in a highly individual way—each brain speaks its own language. And: It changes, learns and unlearns, throughout our lives. The fact that our identity is formed in a complex way from our biography, from our experiences and observations, but also from our genetic dispositions, is impressively demonstrated by this continuous changeability of our brain. This organ, in which we locate the seat of our mind, is linked to our personality more than any other part of our body. But how do we find images for everything that makes us who we are and what is going on inside us? How can these—according to Emerson Pugh ultimately incomprehensible—processes be at least roughly understood? With our language, we formulate metaphors that bear witness to how we imagine the processes in the brain. These images depend on the time and culture in which we live. Plato described that our memories are imprinted like impressions on the wax tablets that were common in his time. Goethe compared the thought process to the shuttle of a loom, whizzing back and forth to create a web of thought made up of many interwoven threads. Today, we like to use the image of our brain as a super-computer or network. Nevertheless, it is true that no technical system can ever come close to the complexity of our brain.

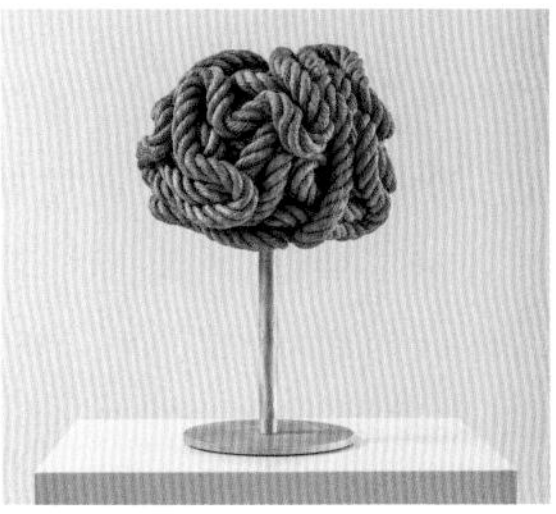

Brain I2, 2021

With his *Brain* series ↗56–59, Michael Sailstorfer finds new ways of thinking about the brain not only through the form itself. As is often the case with his works, it is the multi-layered interplay of content and materiality that opens up a wide space for thought. In this context, the sculptural work *Brain I2* (2021) provides a particularly vivid example. The slightly more than head-sized ball of strong rope, as it is used in seafaring, immediately allows the association of a brain and its convolutions. If the ball were unwound, the rope would have a length of roughly thirty-five meters. Our cortex would also take up an astonishingly large area if unfolded and would not come close to finding room under the skullcap. The folding has the advantage that regions that would be far apart on a surface are brought closer together, allowing them to exchange information more quickly. The rope Sailstorfer chose consists of a large number of individual threads that are twisted together. These, in turn, are spun from countless fibers, resulting in a highly complex, very strong structure. From this image, numerous ideas can be spun

sich in dieser Prognose allerdings nicht wider. Mit wachsenden Erkenntnissen nimmt auch das Wissen um die begrenzten Erkenntnismöglichkeiten zu. In diesem Zusammenhang ist die folgende Feststellung ausschlaggebend: Unsere Gehirne funktionieren auf hochindividuelle Weise – jedes Gehirn spricht seine eigene Sprache. Und: Es verändert sich, lernt und verlernt, ein Leben lang.

Dass sich unsere Identität auf komplexe Weise aus unserer Biografie, unseren Erfahrungen und Erlebnissen, aber auch aus unseren genetischen Dispositionen formt, lässt sich an dieser fortwährenden Veränderlichkeit unseres Gehirns eindrucksvoll ablesen. Jenes Organ, in dem wir den Sitz unseres Geistes verorten, ist mehr als jeder andere Teil unseres Körpers mit unserer Persönlichkeit verknüpft. Wie aber finden wir Bilder für all das, was uns ausmacht und was in uns vorgeht? Wie sind diese – nach Emerson Pugh letztlich unbegreiflichen – Prozesse zumindest annäherungsweise nachzuvollziehen? Mit unserer Sprache bilden wir Metaphern, die davon zeugen, wie wir uns die Vorgänge im Gehirn vorstellen. Diese Bilder sind abhängig von der Zeit und der Kultur, in der wir leben. Platon beschrieb, dass sich unsere Erinnerungen einprägen wie Abdrücke auf den Wachstäfelchen, die zu seiner Zeit gebräuchlich waren. Goethe verglich den Denkprozess mit dem Schiffchen eines Webstuhls, das hin- und hersaust und ein Gedankengewebe erzeugt, das aus vielen ineinander verwobenen Fäden besteht. Heute bemühen wir gerne das Bild von unserem Gehirn als Supercomputer oder Netzwerk. Dennoch gilt: Kein technisches System kann je an die Komplexität unseres Gehirns heranreichen.

In seinen *Brain*-Serien ↗56–59 findet Michael Sailstorfer nicht nur über die Form zu einem neuen Nachdenken über das Gehirn. Wie häufig in seinen Arbeiten ist es das vielschichtige Zusammenspiel von Inhalt und Materialität, das einen weiten Denkraum eröffnet. In diesem Kontext liefert die skulpturale Arbeit *Brain I2*, 2021, ein besonders anschauliches Beispiel. Das etwas mehr als kopfgroße Knäuel aus starkem Tau, wie es in der Seefahrt verwendet wird, lässt unmittelbar die Assoziation an ein Gehirn und seine Windungen zu. Würde man das Knäuel auseinanderwickeln, hätte das Seil eine Länge von etwa 35 Metern. Auch unser Cortex würde auseinandergefaltet eine erstaunlich große Fläche einnehmen und nicht annähernd Platz unter der Schädeldecke finden. Die Faltung hat den Vorteil, dass Regionen, die auf einer Oberfläche weit auseinanderliegen würden, dichter zusammengebracht werden und so schneller Informationen austauschen können. Das Tau, das Sailstorfer ausgewählt hat, besteht aus einer großen Anzahl von Fäden, die miteinander verdreht sind. Diese wiederum werden aus unzähligen Fasern gesponnen und ergeben eine hochkomplexe, sehr feste Struktur. Von diesem Bild aus lassen sich viele Ideen weiterspinnen: die Analogie zu den Hirnsträngen und Nervenbahnen bis

further: the analogy to brain strands and nerve tracts to the often difficult-to-reconstruct twists and turns of our thoughts that the intertwined rope recreates.
This notion also seems to be taken up by the labyrinths which Sailstorfer thematized in his *Mazes* (2011–2014) ↗60/61, 99–105, 193–199. For this series, he appropriated labyrinths from magazines as templates and transferred these onto large-format canvases using a screen-printing process. The task of finding the way out of the labyrinth by drawing a line through the twists and turns to the sole exit was carried out by Sailstorfer freehand with spray paint. Inevitably, the trail of paint occasionally goes off the track laid out by the screen-printed lines of the labyrinth. When an idea crosses our mind, we like to imagine how the thought literally moves through our brain. As in a labyrinth, it wanders through the twists and turns, at times getting lost or running into a dead end—and every now and then, it seems to get off track and leave the predefined paths. Here, we are reminded of those moments when a thought breaks off or we ourselves are "thrown off course," but also of situations in which thinking "off the beaten track" helps us to gain new insights.

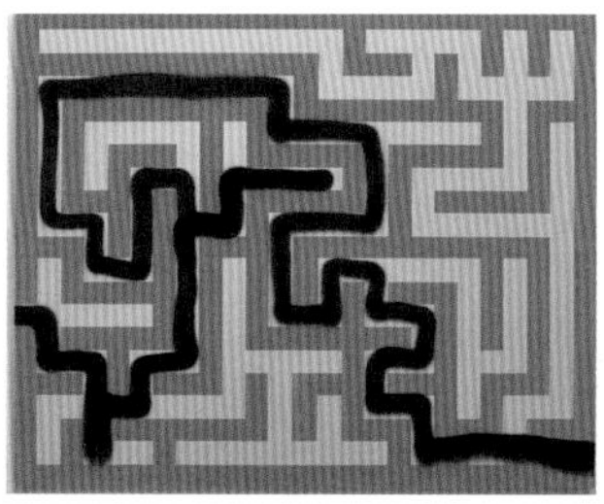

Maze, 2011

Inspirations, ideas, and flashes of genius are difficult to force. They emerge as if by themselves. Today, however, the neurobiological processes involved in many things that seem to happen "only in the mind" can already be made visible. Nevertheless, recognizing the physical operations that take place in our brain during a thought process usually seems insufficient when it comes to describing the complexity of our trains of thought. Michael Sailstorfer's *Atomic Brains* series (2020) ↗65 provides an apt image for the sensation that surges through us when a great idea forms inside us. A new, as yet untested idea is like the result of nuclear fusion, releasing enormous energies—and yet it appears threatening. It is these free-associative images that Sailstorfer expresses with his works and that generate vast fields of thought. At the interface between figurative and abstract sculpture, he deliberately allows interstices to emerge that are only filled with concrete thoughts through the mental process that is triggered. As if thinking were also a material, it becomes an integral part of a work that yields its own sense of meaning above all in the eye—or brain—of the respective beholder.

hin zu den oft schwer zu rekonstruierenden Irrungen und Wirrungen unserer Gedanken, die das verschlungene Seil nachempfindet.
Diese Vorstellung scheinen auch die Labyrinthe aufzugreifen, die Sailstorfer in seinen *Mazes* ↗60/61, 99–105, 193–199 aus den Jahren 2011 bis 2014 thematisiert. Für diese Serie hat er Rätsellabyrinthe aus Zeitschriften als Vorlage genommen und sie im Siebdruckverfahren auf eine großformatige Leinwand übertragen. Die Aufgabe, den Weg aus dem Labyrinth zu finden, indem man eine Linie durch die Windungen bis zum einzigen Ausgang zeichnet, hat Sailstorfer wiederum freihändig mit einer Farbspraydose ausgeführt. Unvermeidlich, dass die Farbspur manchmal über die Bahn hinaustritt, die die vorgedruckten Linien festlegen. Wenn uns etwas durch den Kopf geht, stellen wir uns gerne vor, wie der Gedanke sich wortwörtlich durch unser Gehirn bewegt. Wie in einem Labyrinth durchstreift er die Windungen, verirrt sich mitunter oder läuft in eine Sackgasse – und scheint hin und wieder auch aus der Bahn zu geraten und vorgezeichnete Wege zu verlassen. Hier lässt sich an jene Momente denken, in denen ein Gedanke abreißt oder wir selbst „aus der Spur" geraten, aber auch an Situationen, in denen uns das Denken abseits der festgelegten Bahnen zu neuen Erkenntnissen verhilft.
Inspirationen, Ideen und Geistesblitze lassen sich nur schwerlich forcieren. Sie entstehen wie von selbst. Dabei können die neurobiologischen Vorgänge bei vielem, was scheinbar „nur im Geiste" geschieht, heute bereits sichtbar gemacht werden. Die physischen Abläufe zu erkennen, die während eines Denkprozesses in unserem Gehirn ablaufen, scheint uns jedoch meist nicht auszureichen, wenn es darum geht, die Komplexität unserer Gedankengänge zu beschreiben. Michael Sailstorfers Serie der *Atomic Brains*, 2020 ↗65, liefert ein treffendes Bild für das Gefühl, das uns durchströmt, wenn sich ein großer Gedanke in unserem Inneren formt. Eine neue, noch unerprobte Idee ist wie das Ergebnis einer Kernfusion, die enorme Energien freisetzt – und doch bedrohlich erscheint. Es sind diese frei zu assoziierenden Bilder, die Sailstorfer in seinen Arbeiten zum Ausdruck bringt und die weite Denkfelder erzeugen. An der Schnittstelle zwischen figürlicher und abstrakter Bildhauerei lässt er bewusst Zwischenräume entstehen, die sich erst durch den angestoßenen Denkprozess mit konkreten Gedanken füllen. Als sei auch das Denken ein Material, wird es zum integralen Bestandteil eines Werkes, das vor allem im Auge – oder im Gehirn – des jeweiligen Betrachters einen eigenen Sinn ergibt.

Atomic Brain 1, 2020
Ceramic, concrete, paint / Keramik, Beton, Farbe, 158 × 35 × 35 cm

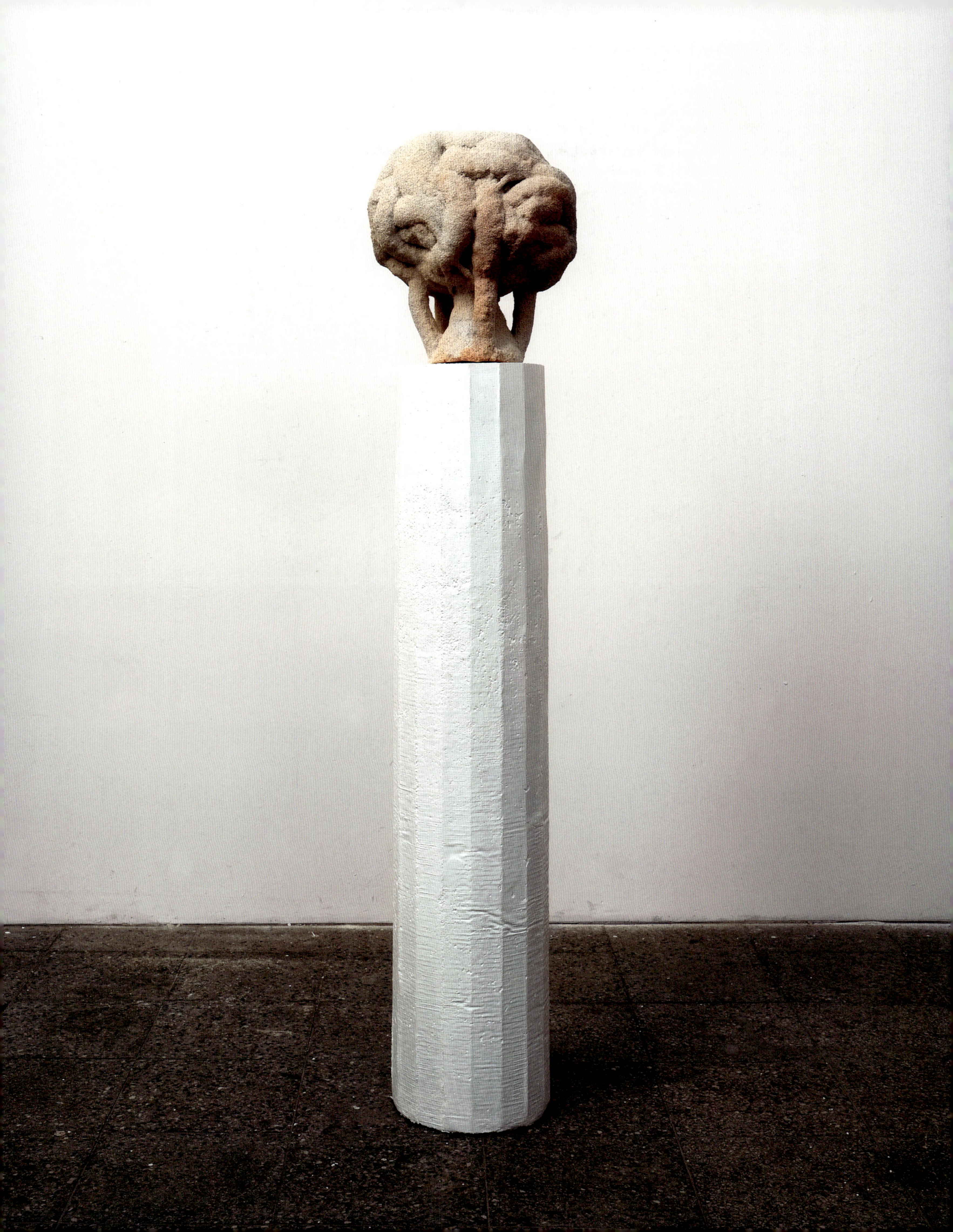

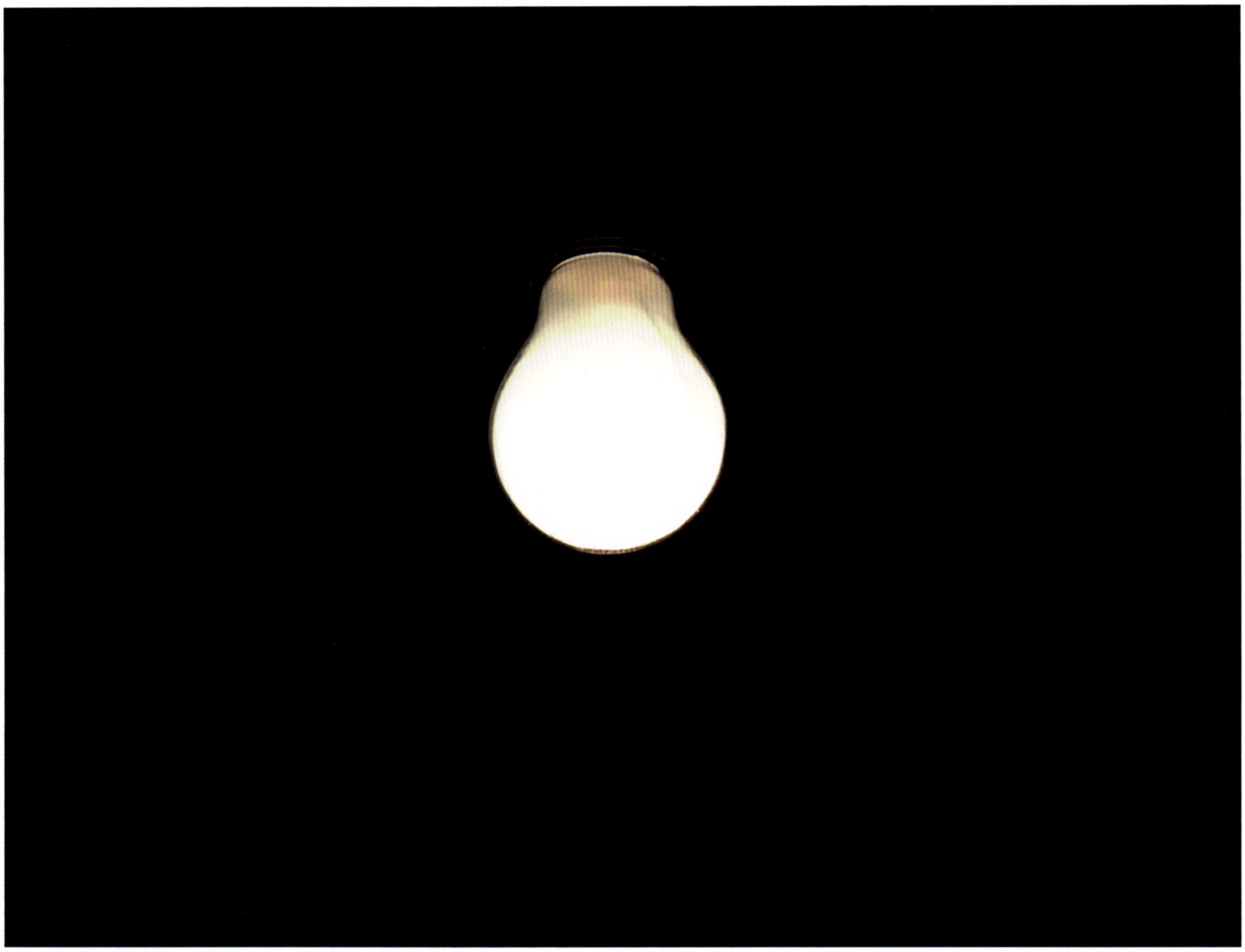

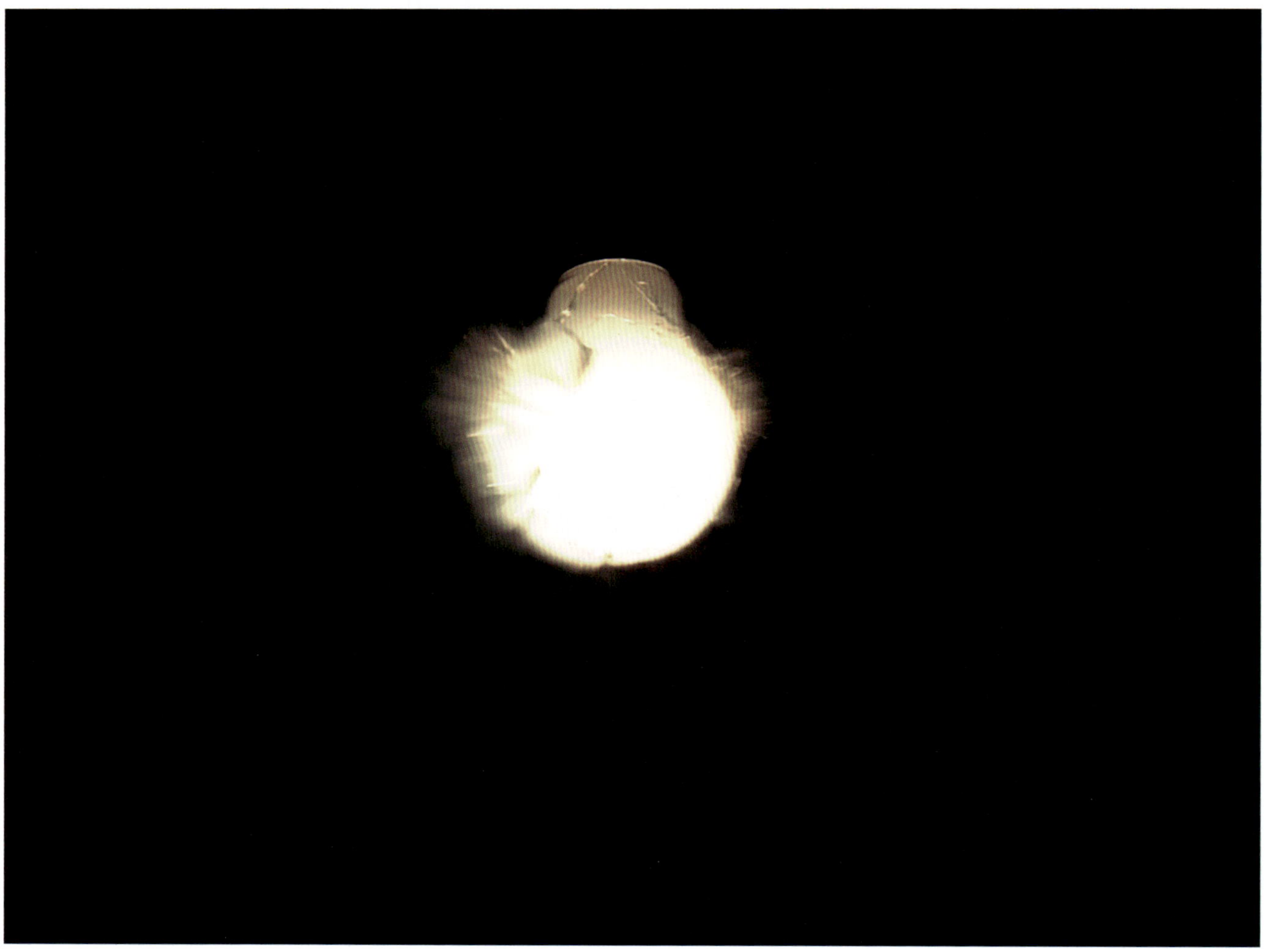

Bulb, 2010

16 mm film, loop, 1 min 59 sec

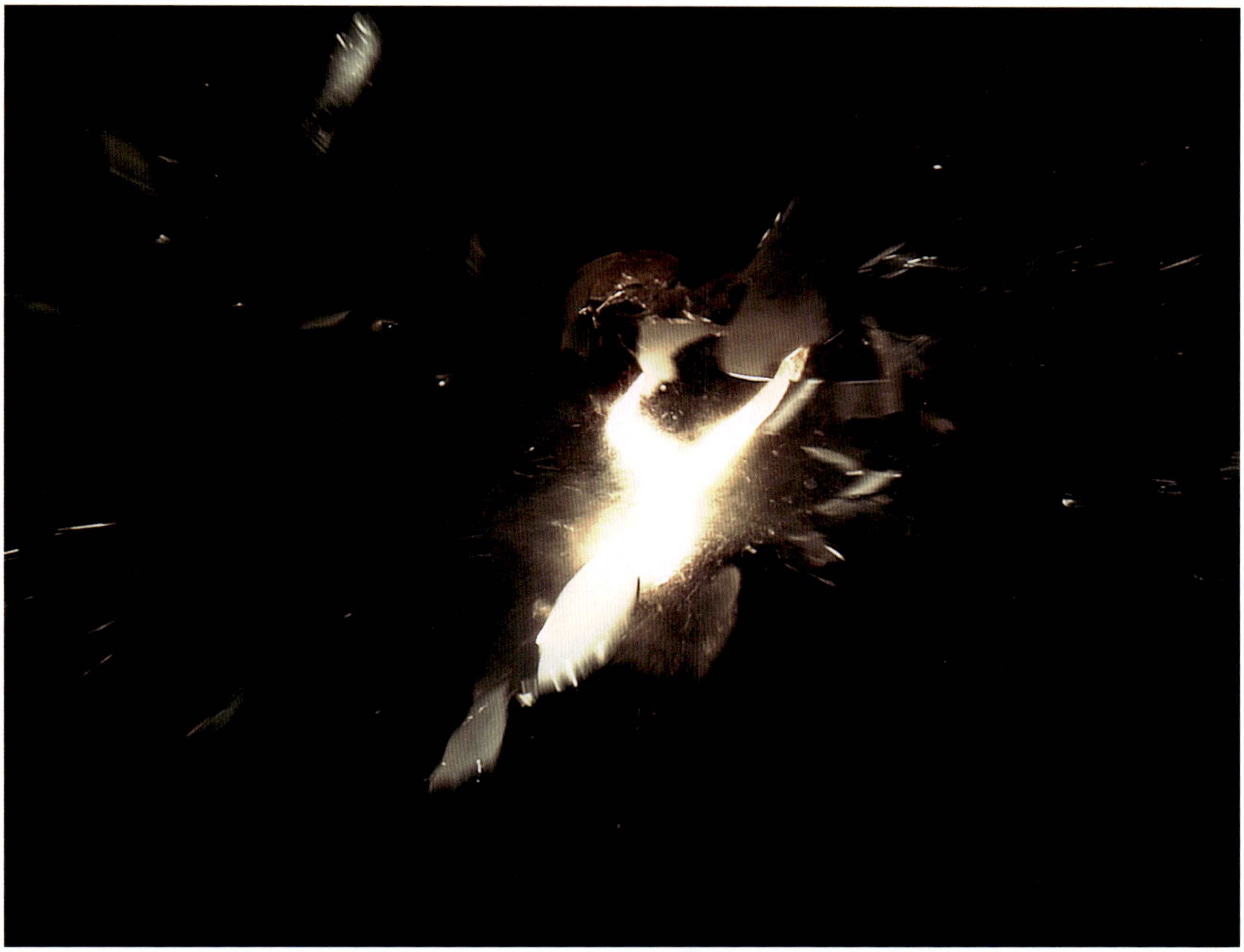

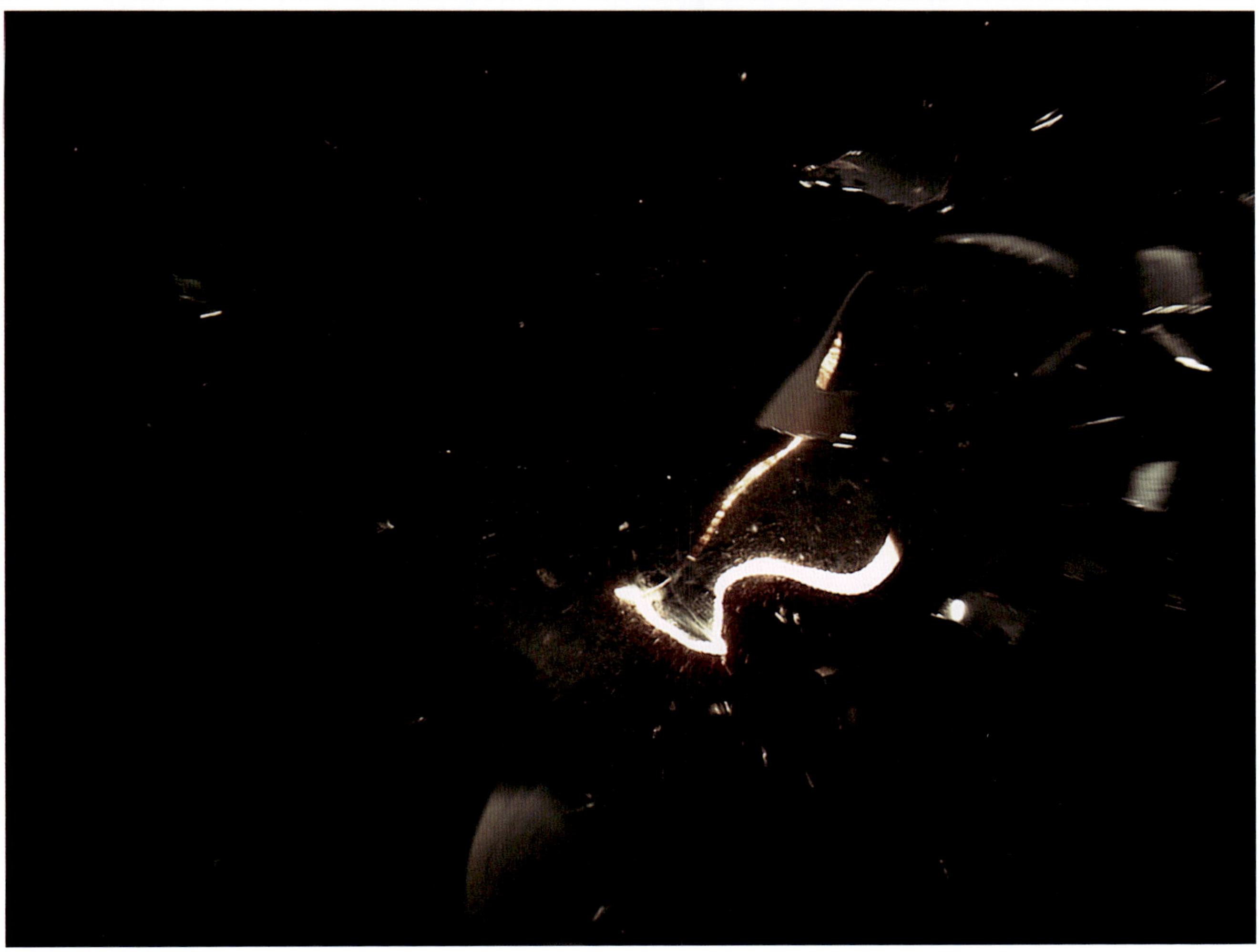

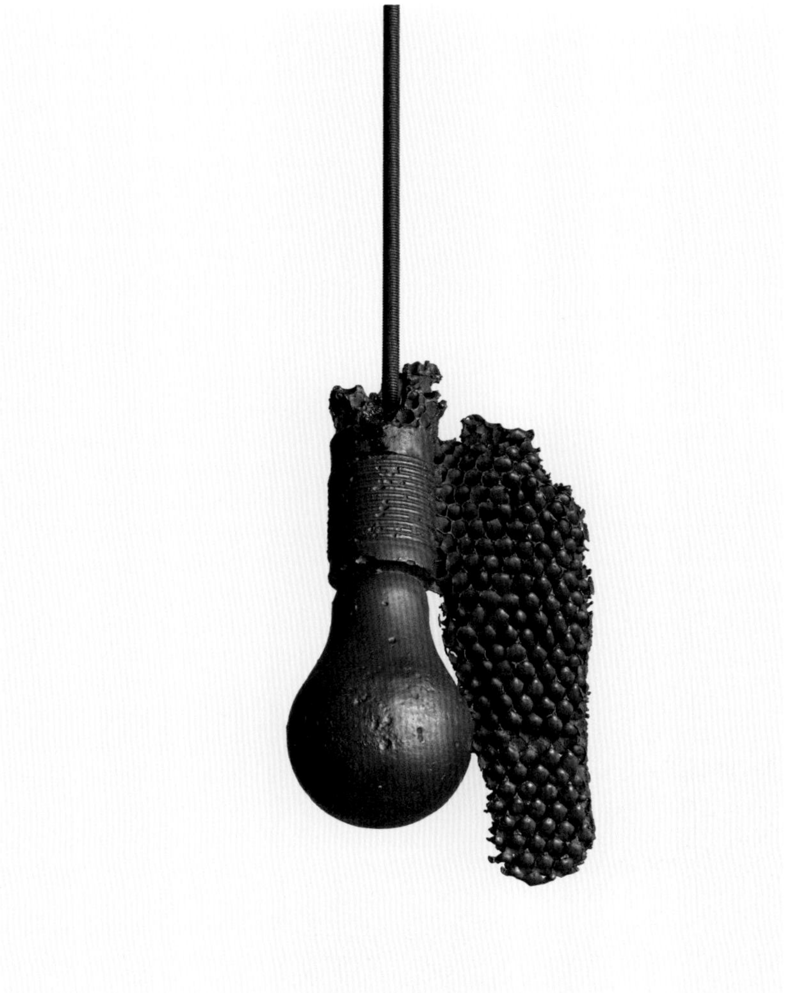
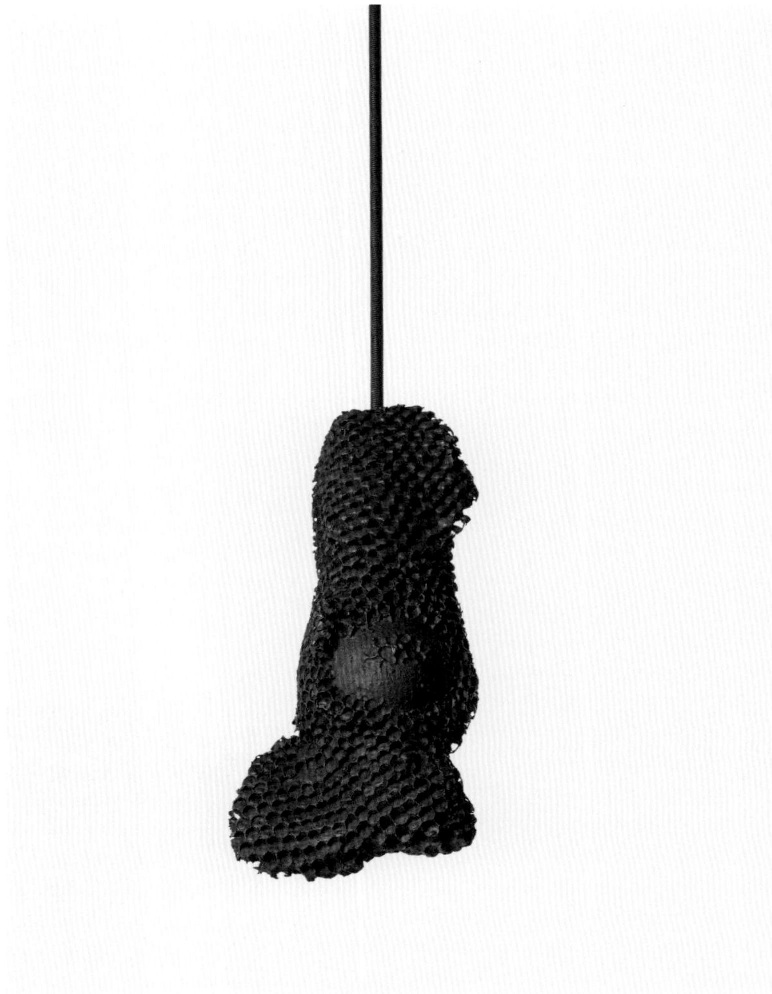
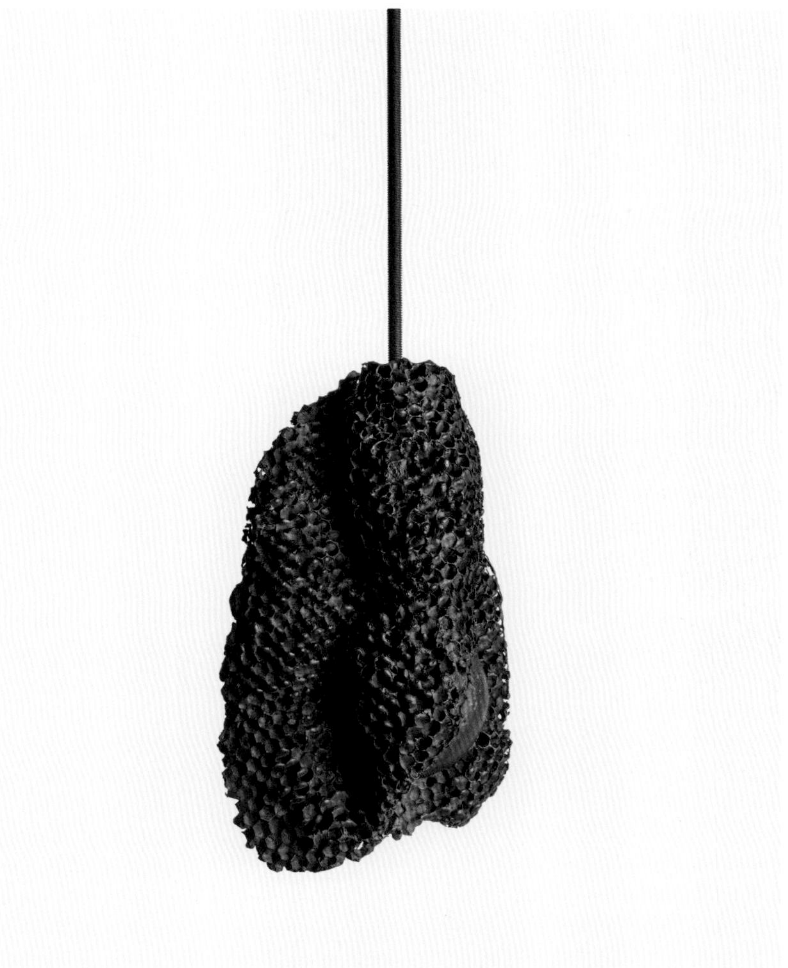
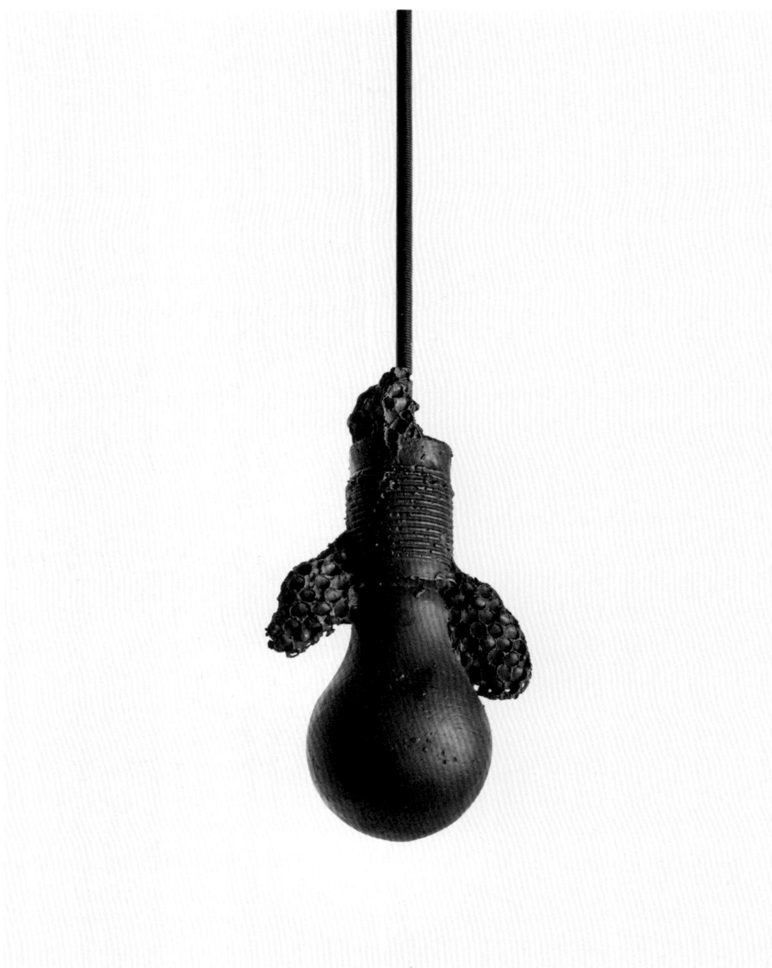

Batterie 5
Batterie 13

Batterie 11
Batterie 2

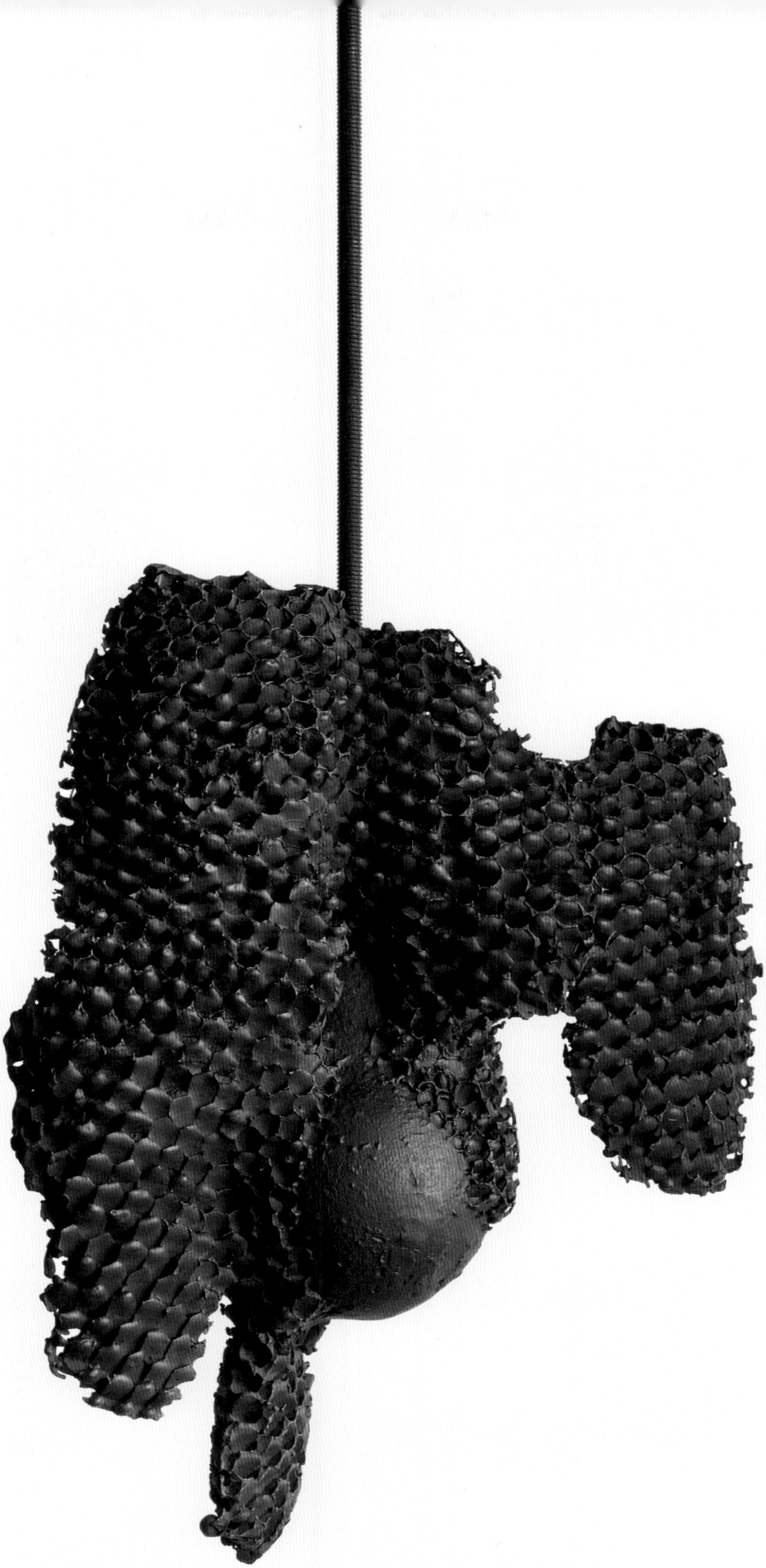

Batterie 9, 2019
Bronze, 19 × 16,5 × 7,5 cm

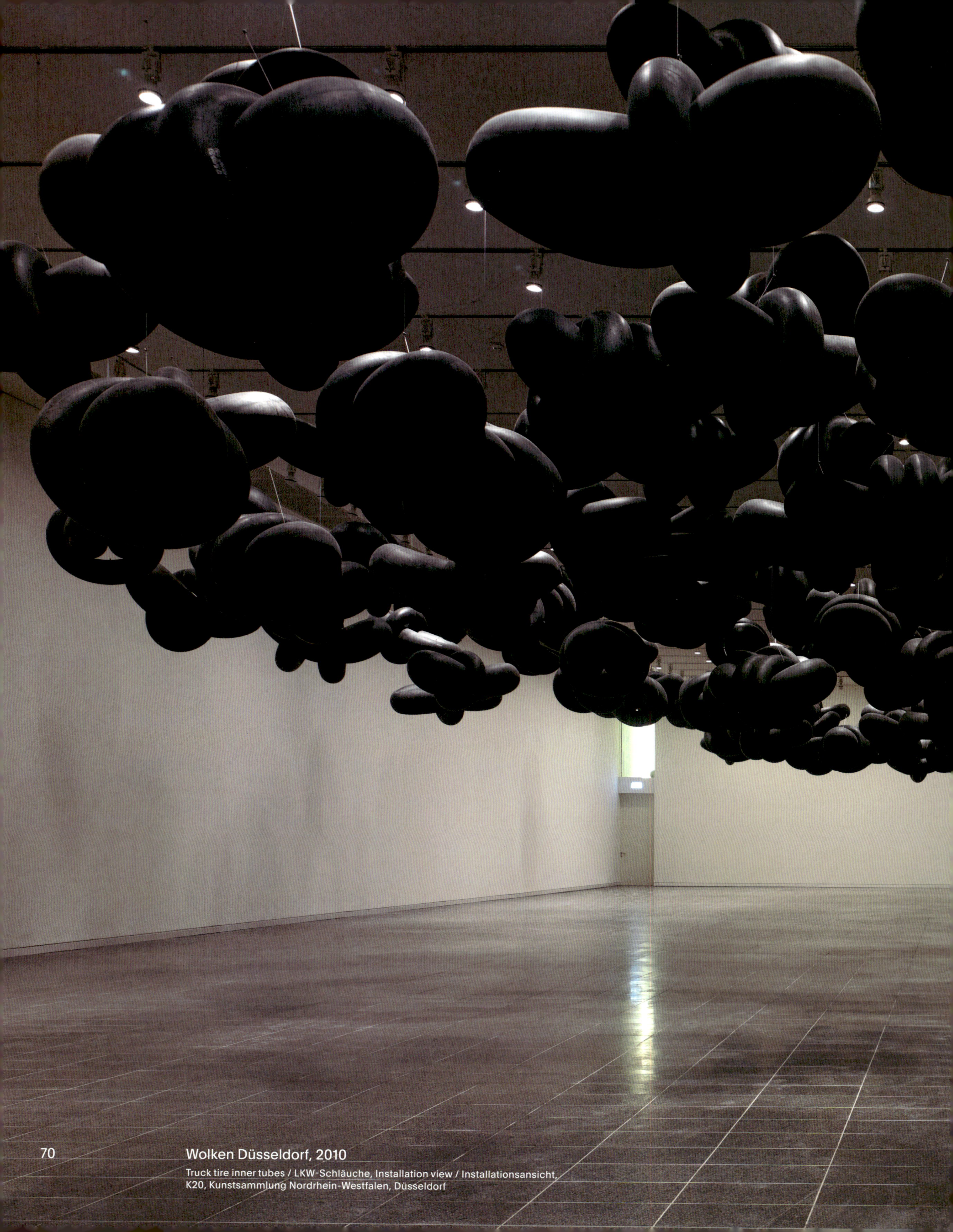

Wolken Düsseldorf, 2010

Truck tire inner tubes / LKW-Schläuche, Installation view / Installationsansicht, K20, Kunstsammlung Nordrhein-Westfalen, Düsseldorf

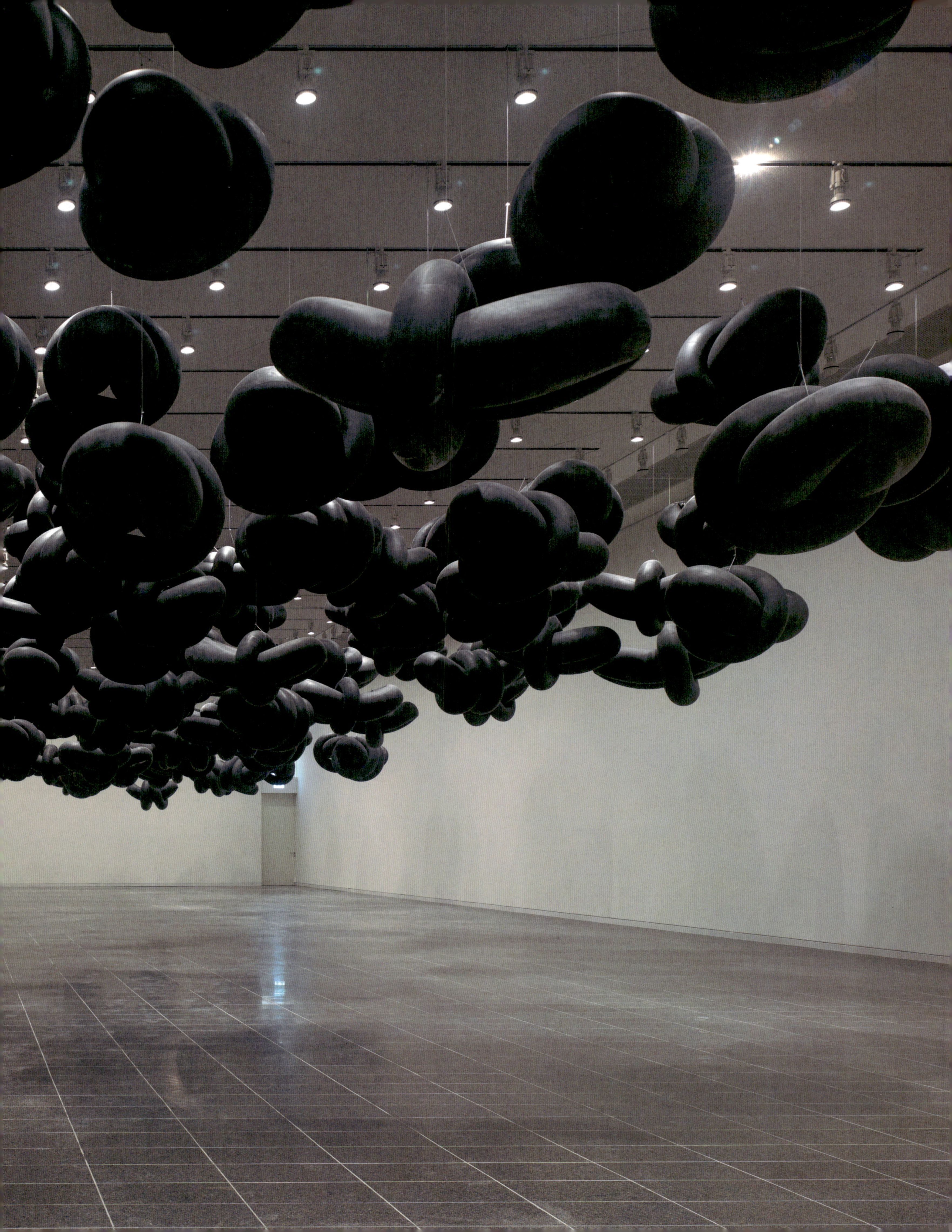

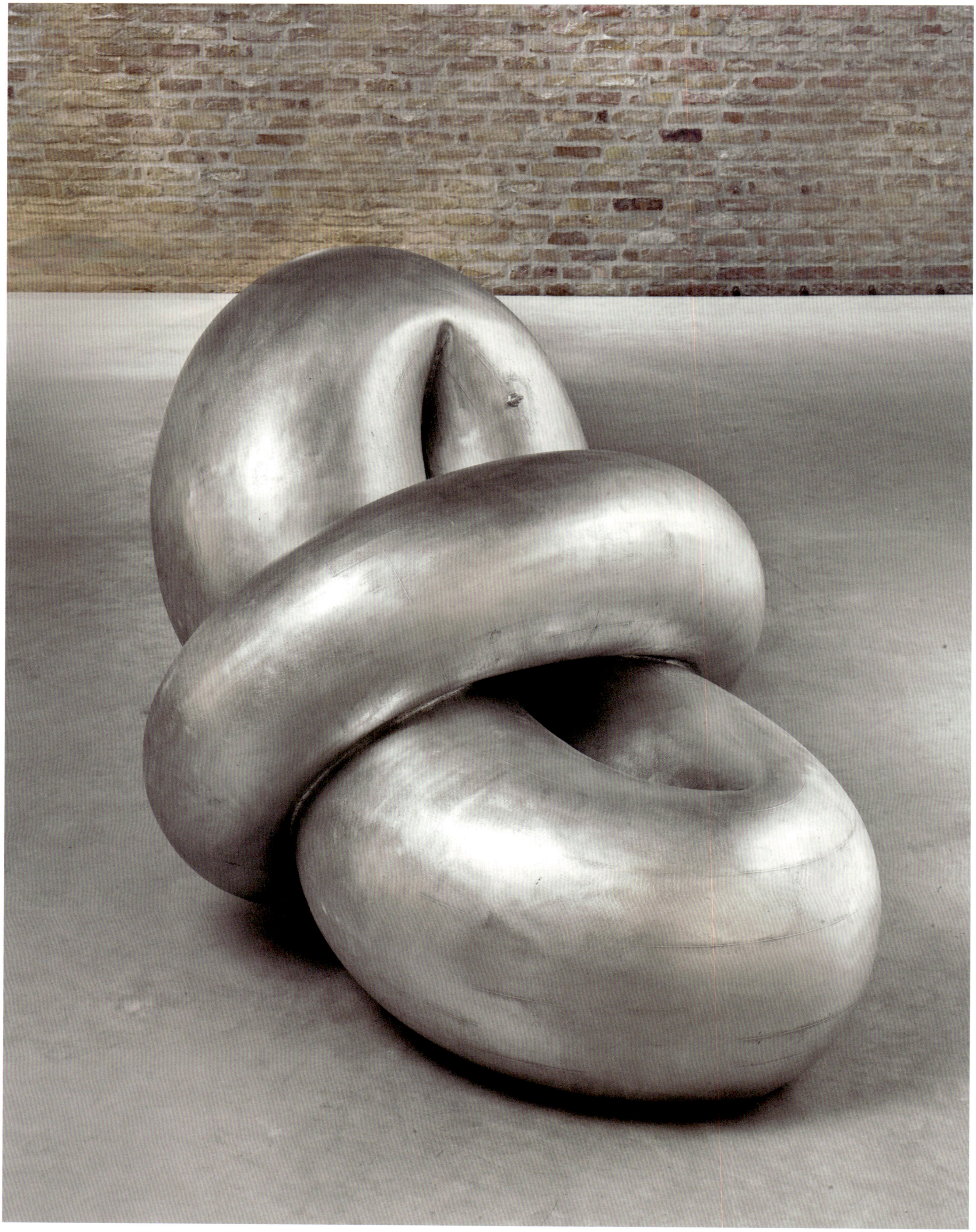

Silver Cloud, 2017

Aluminum / Aluminium, 190 × 130 × 95 cm

Tornado, 2011

Truck tire inner tubes, steel, concrete / LKW-Schläuche, Stahl, Beton, 10 × 5 × 5 m, Doris C. Freedman Plaza, Central Park, New York

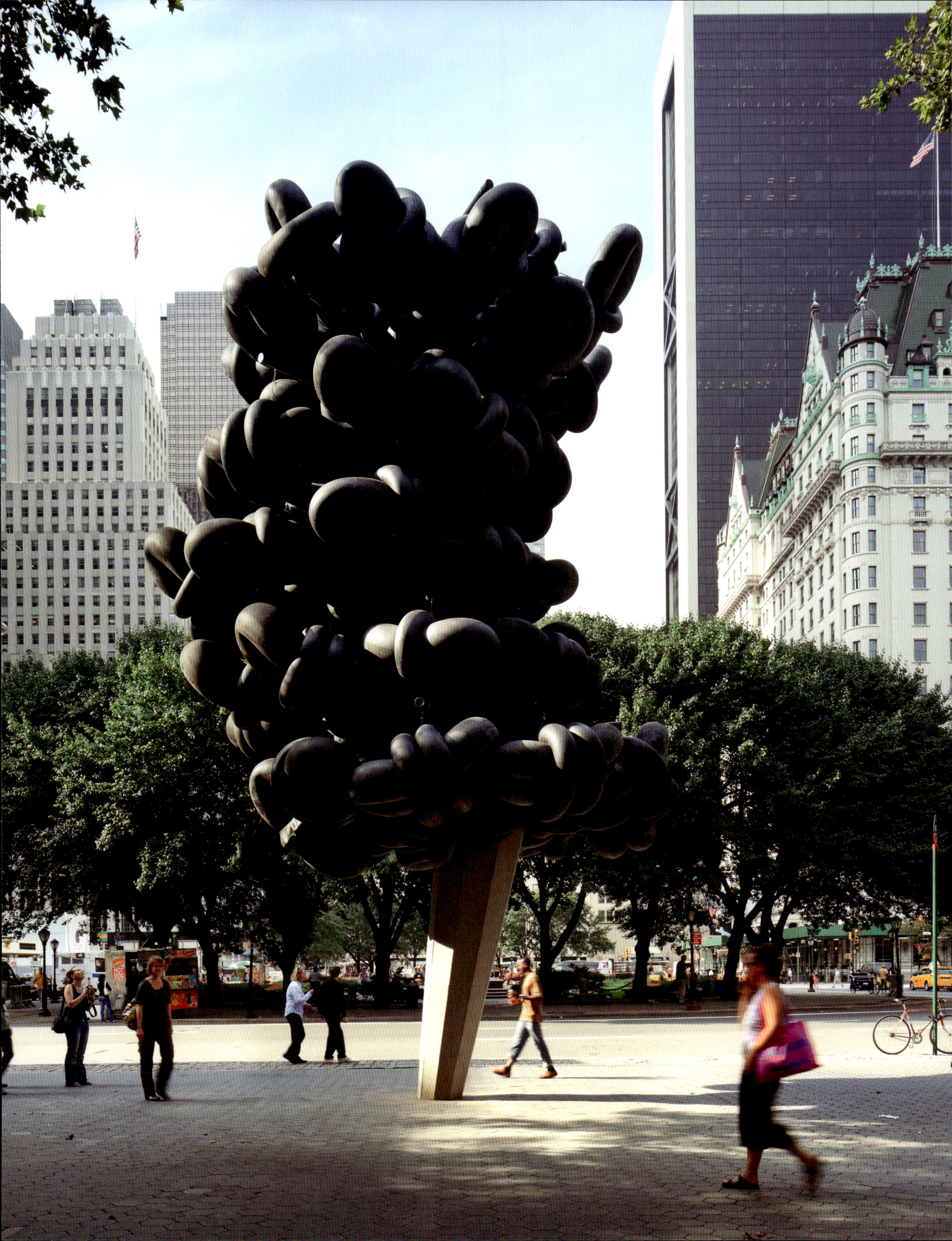
HOT DOG

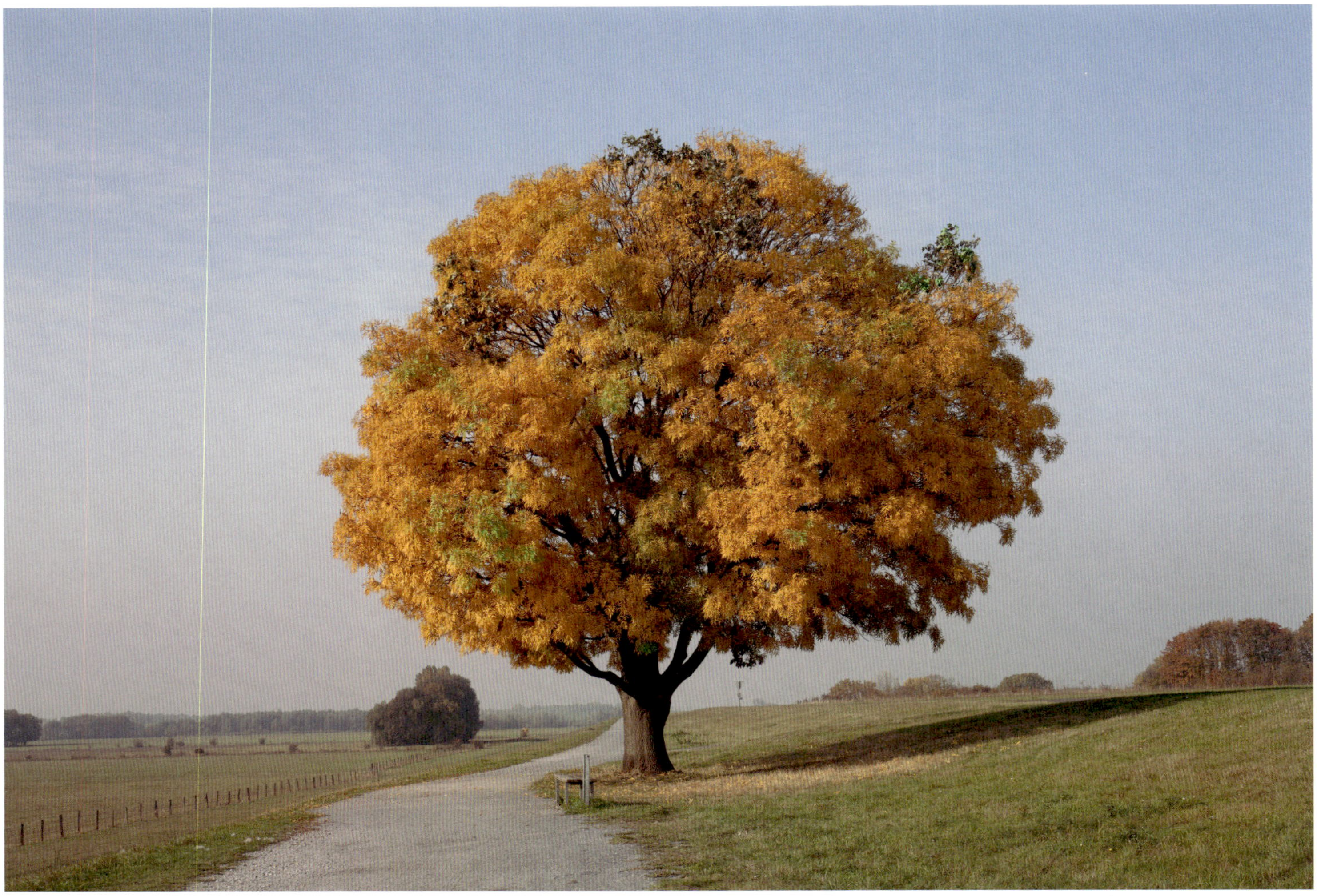

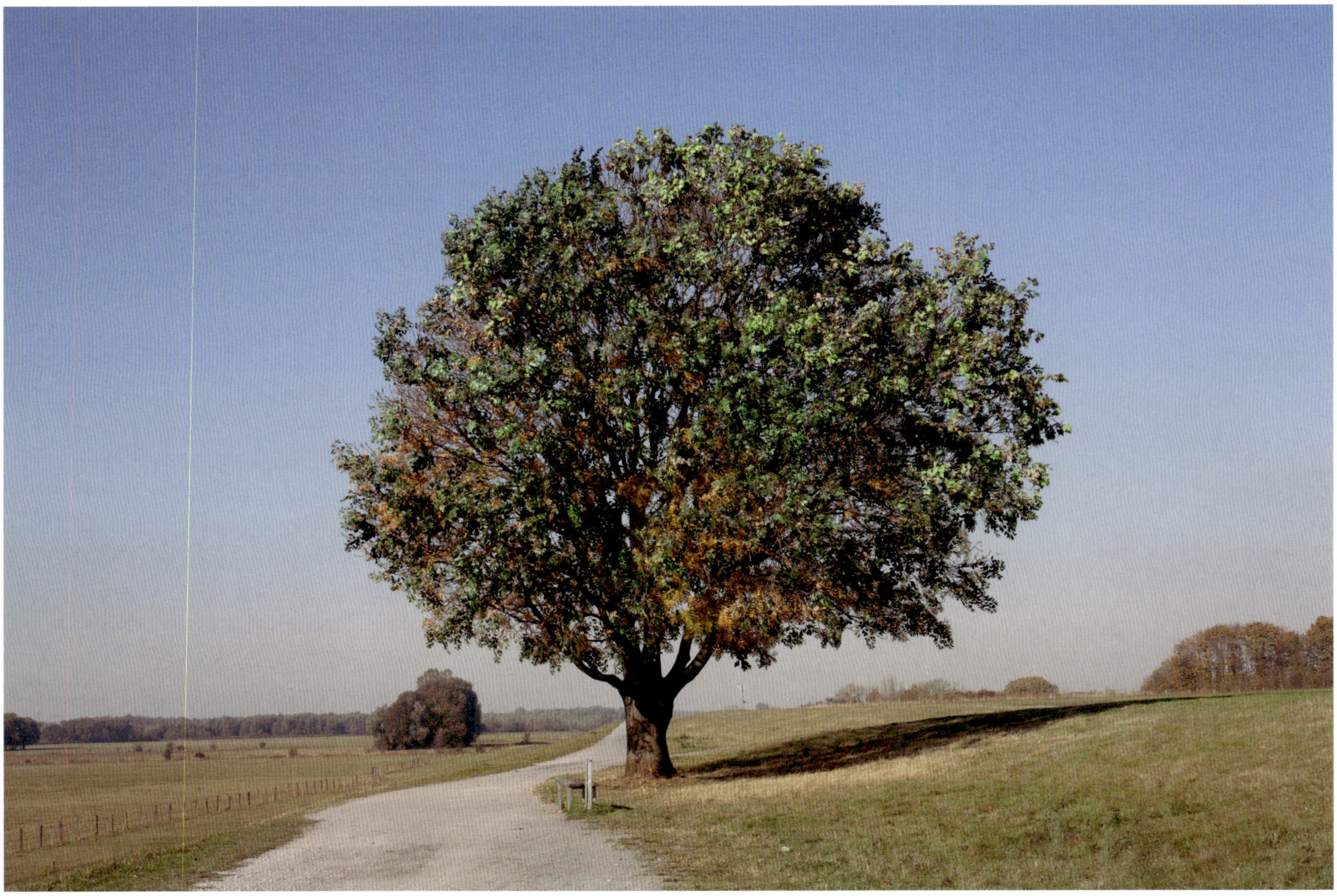

Antiherbst, 2012 / 2013

Video, 12 min 13 sec

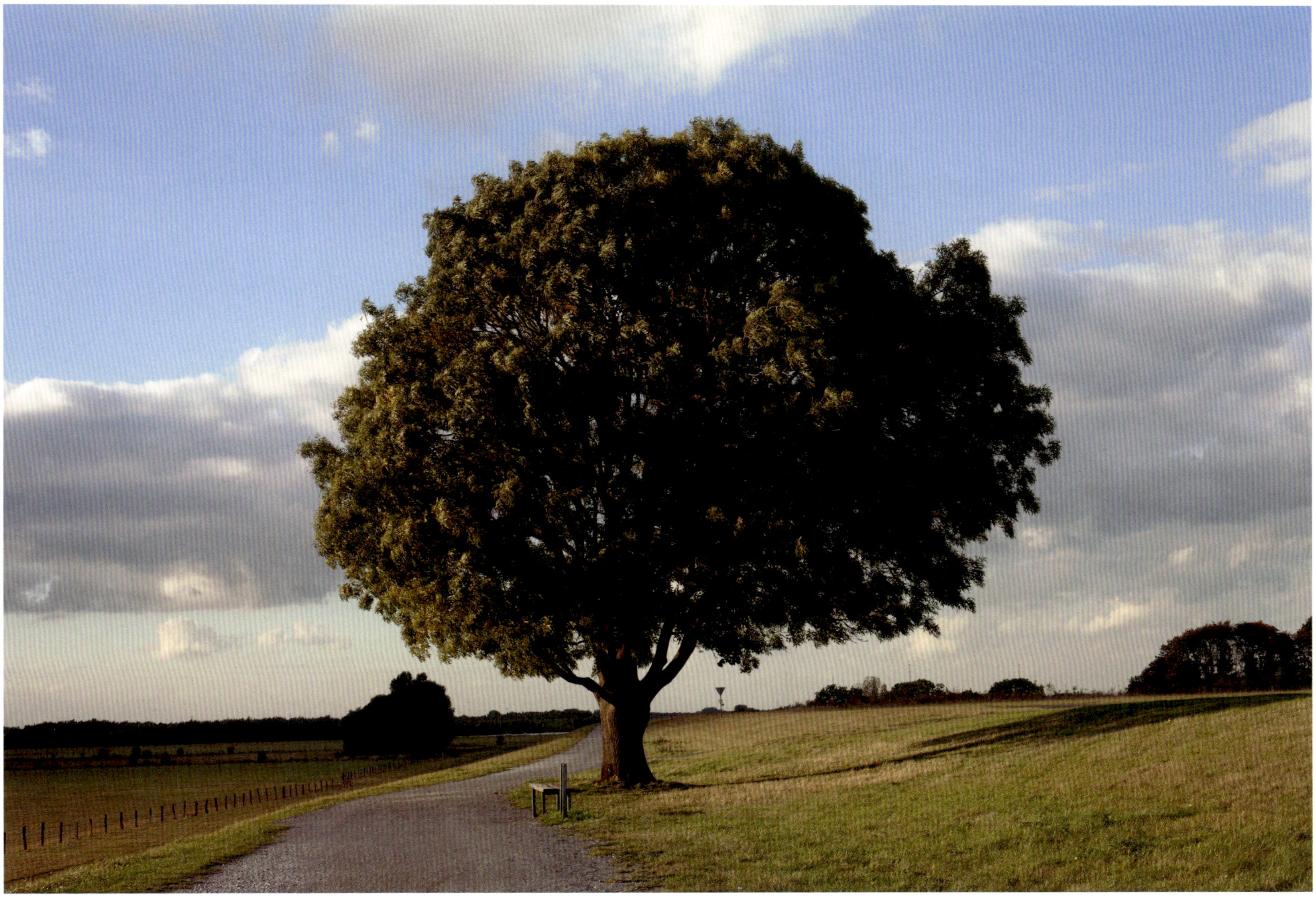

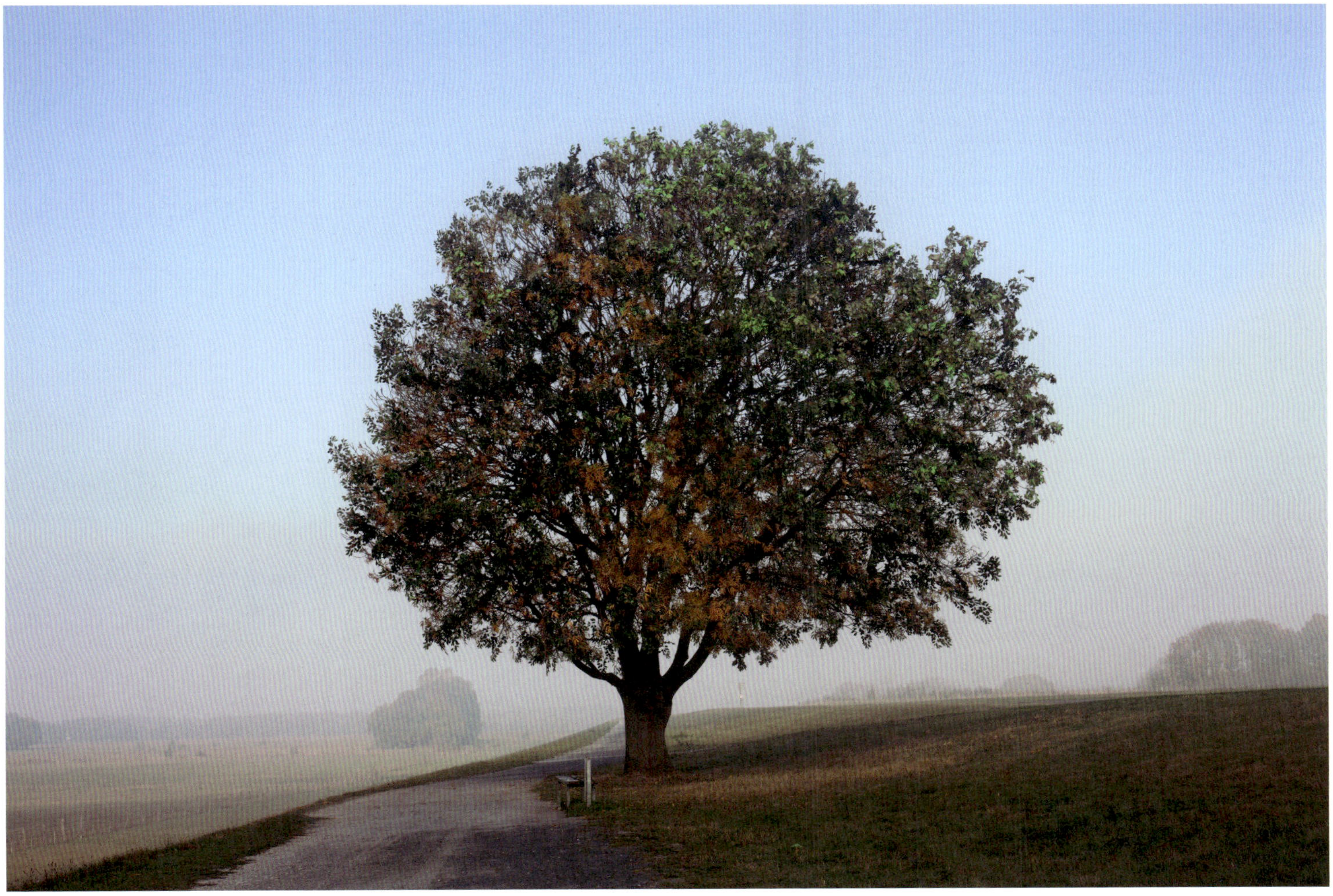

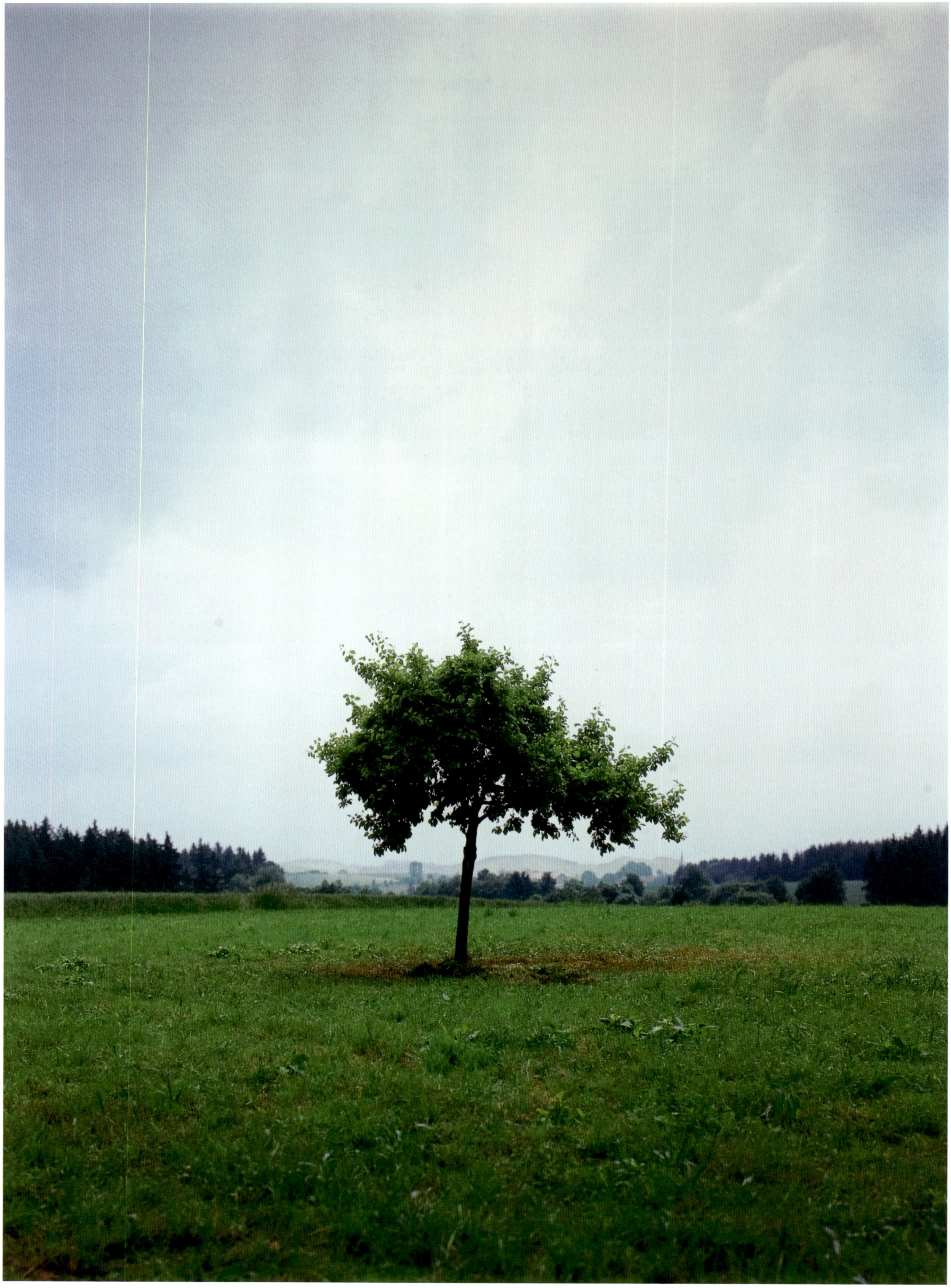

Raketenbaum 1, 2008

C-print, 210 × 160 cm (framed / gerahmt)

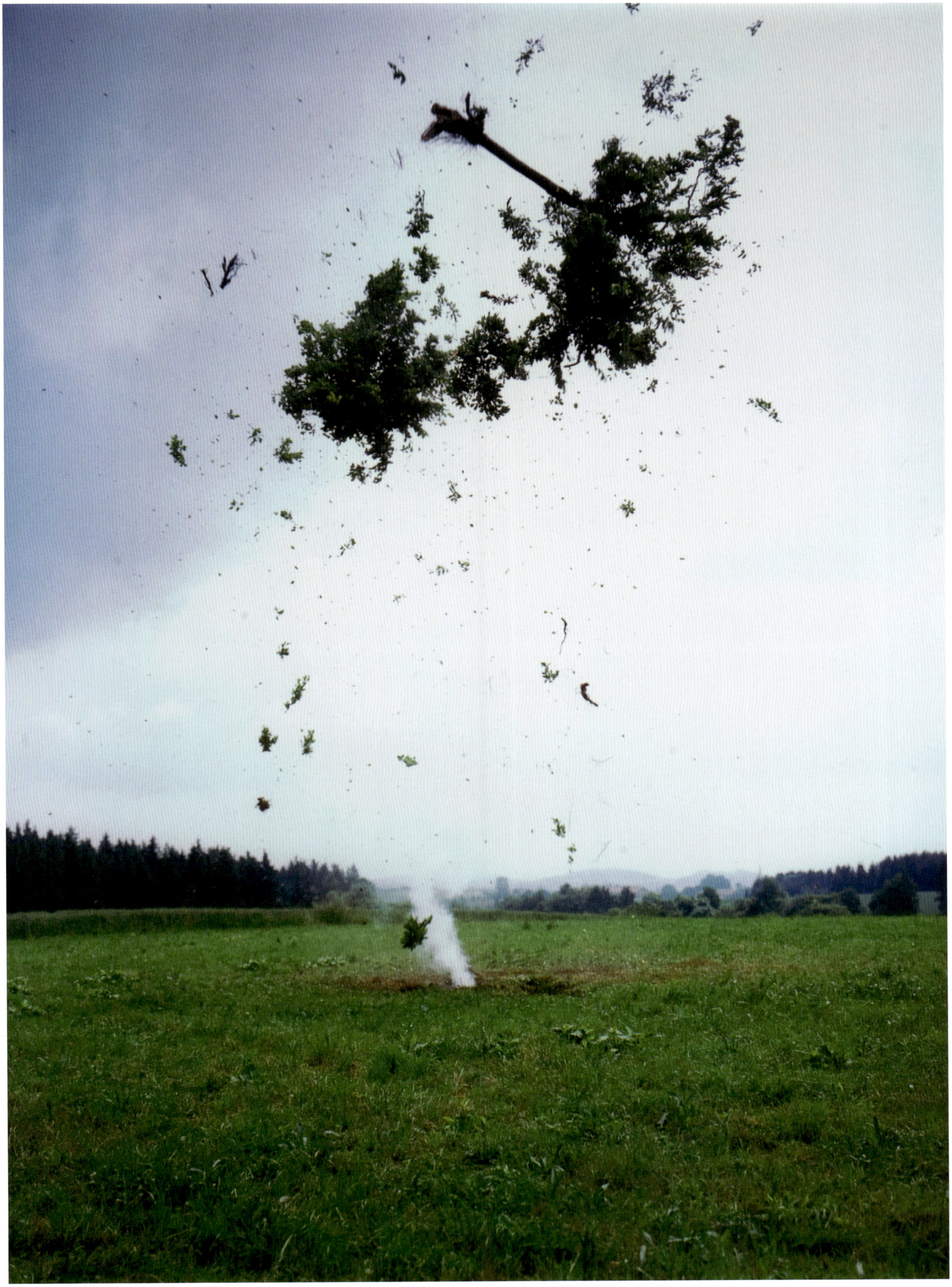

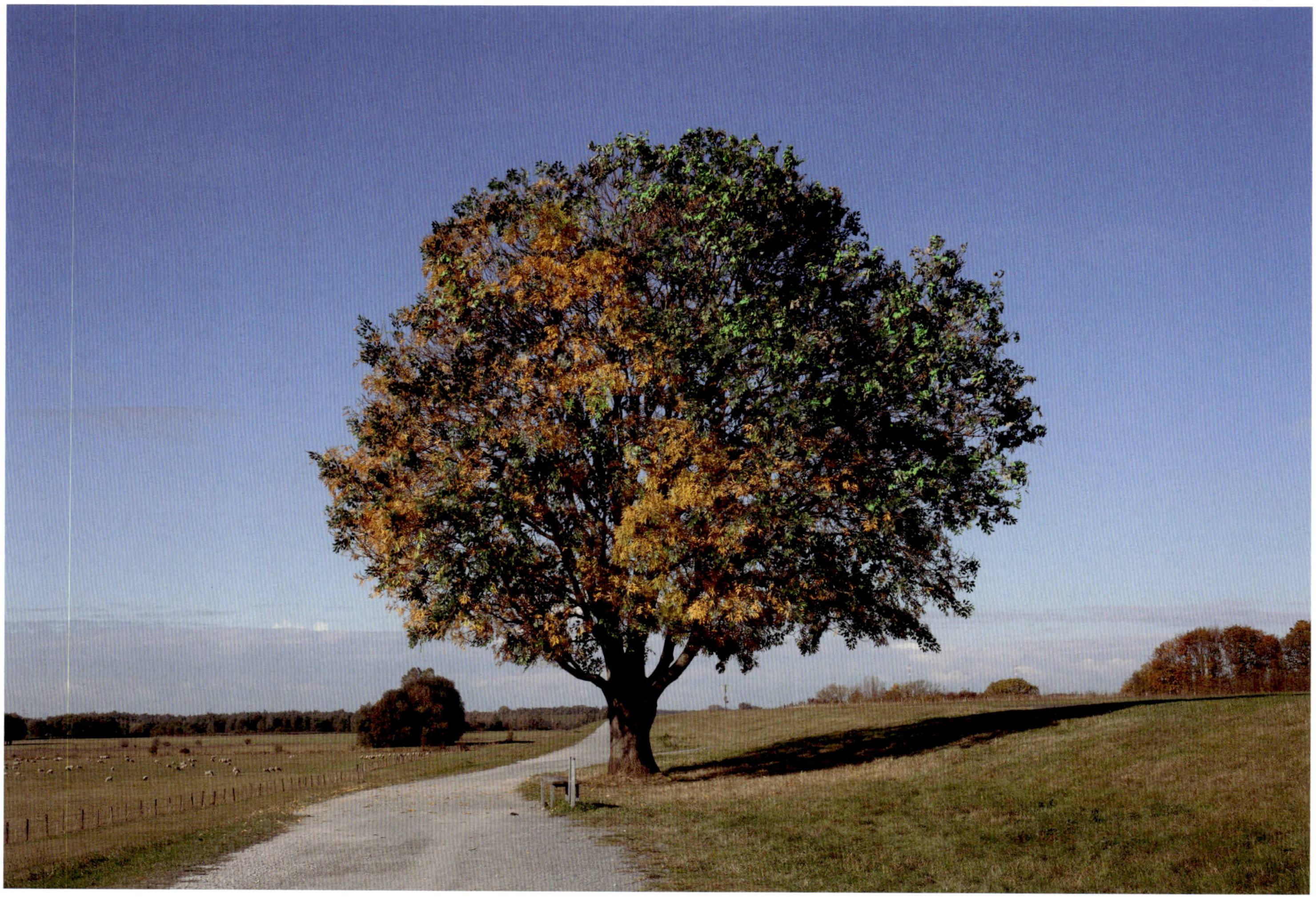

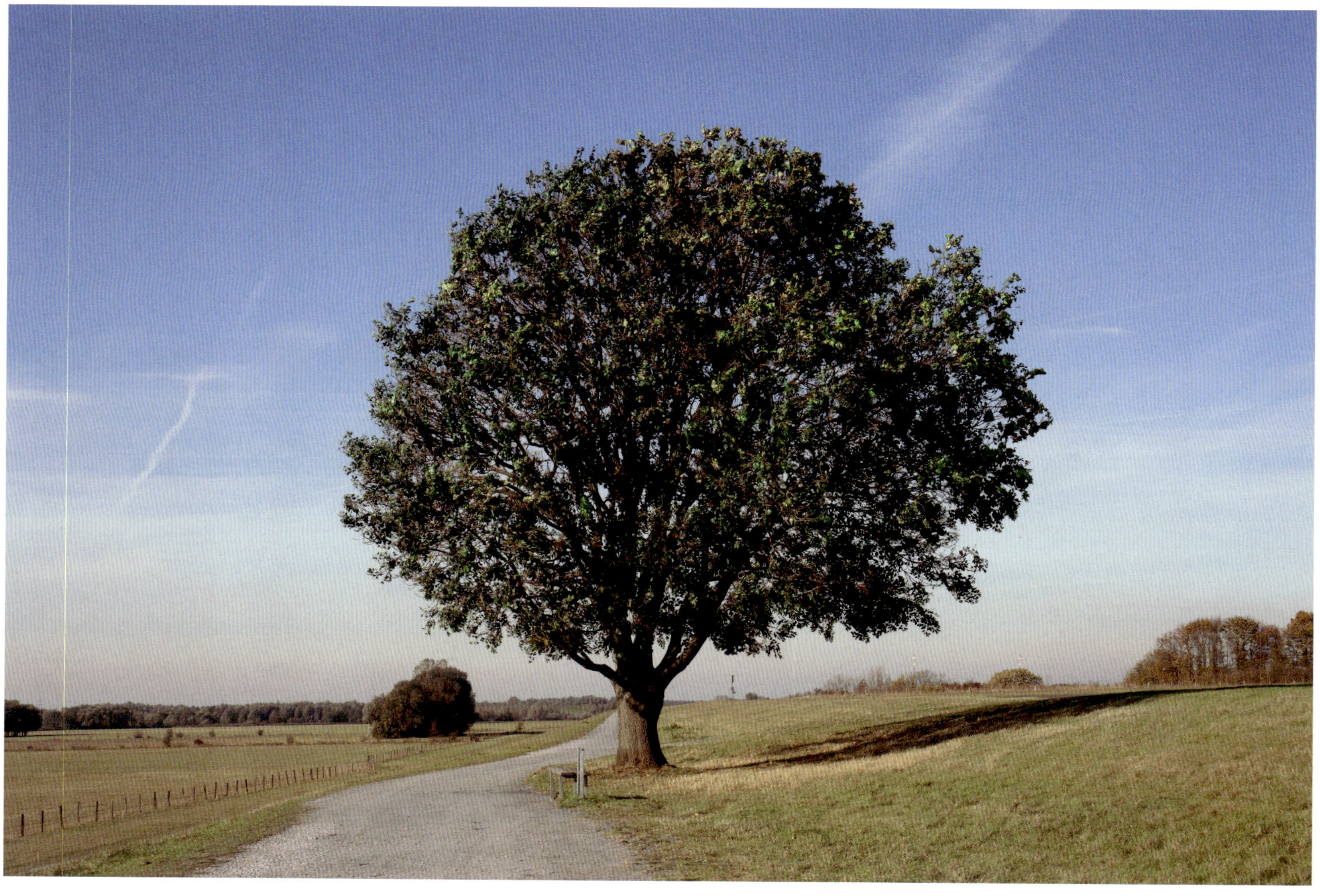

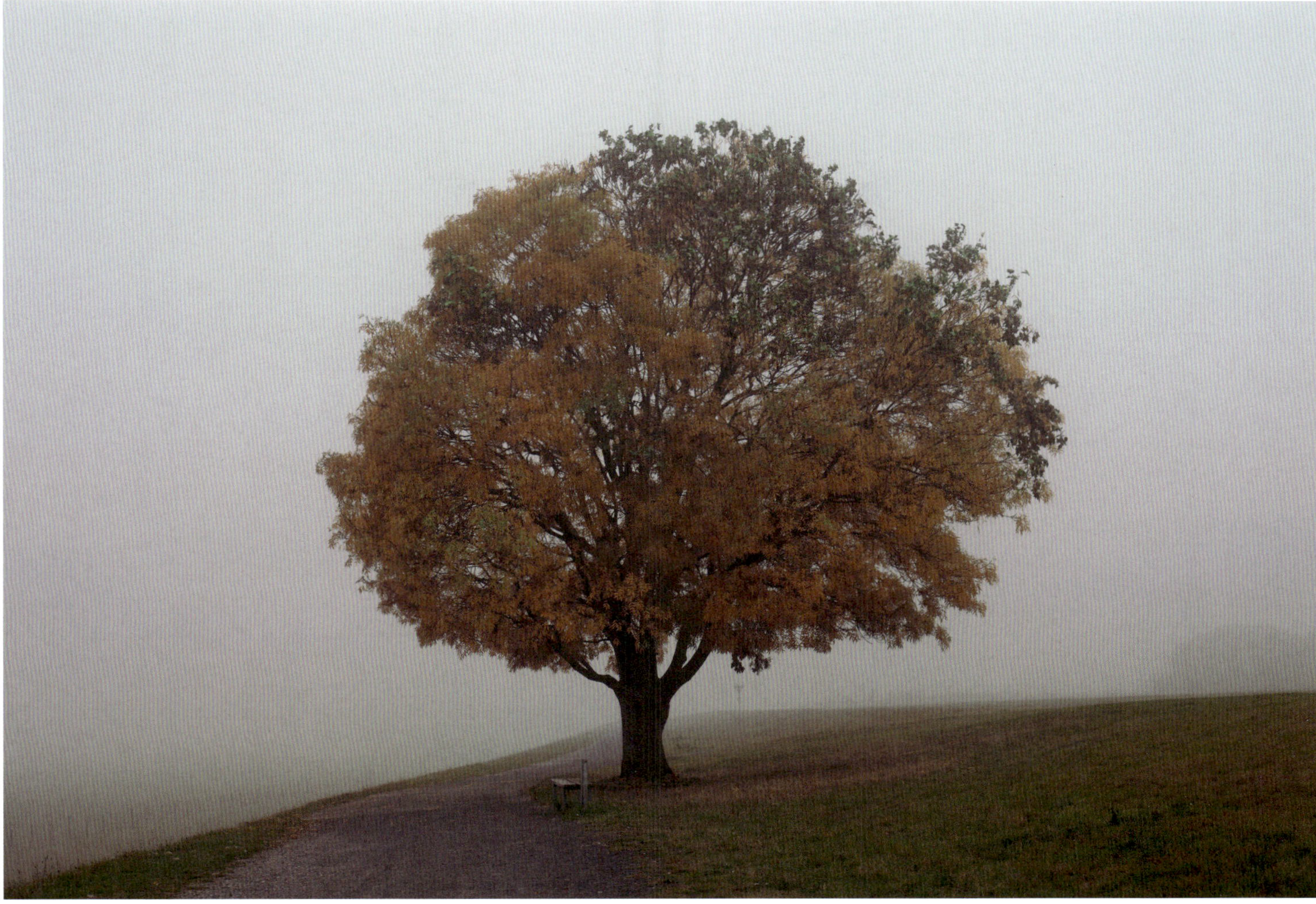

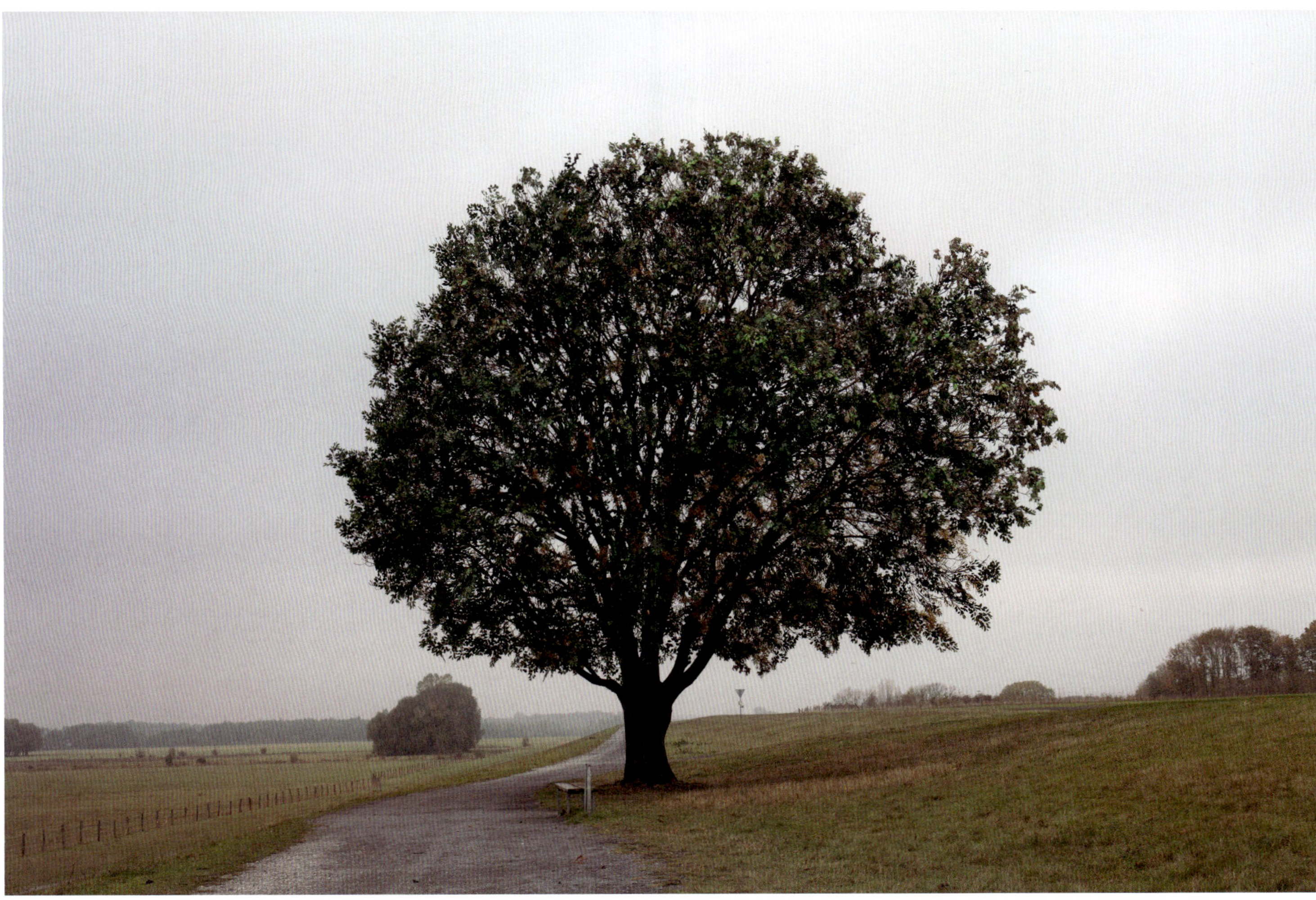

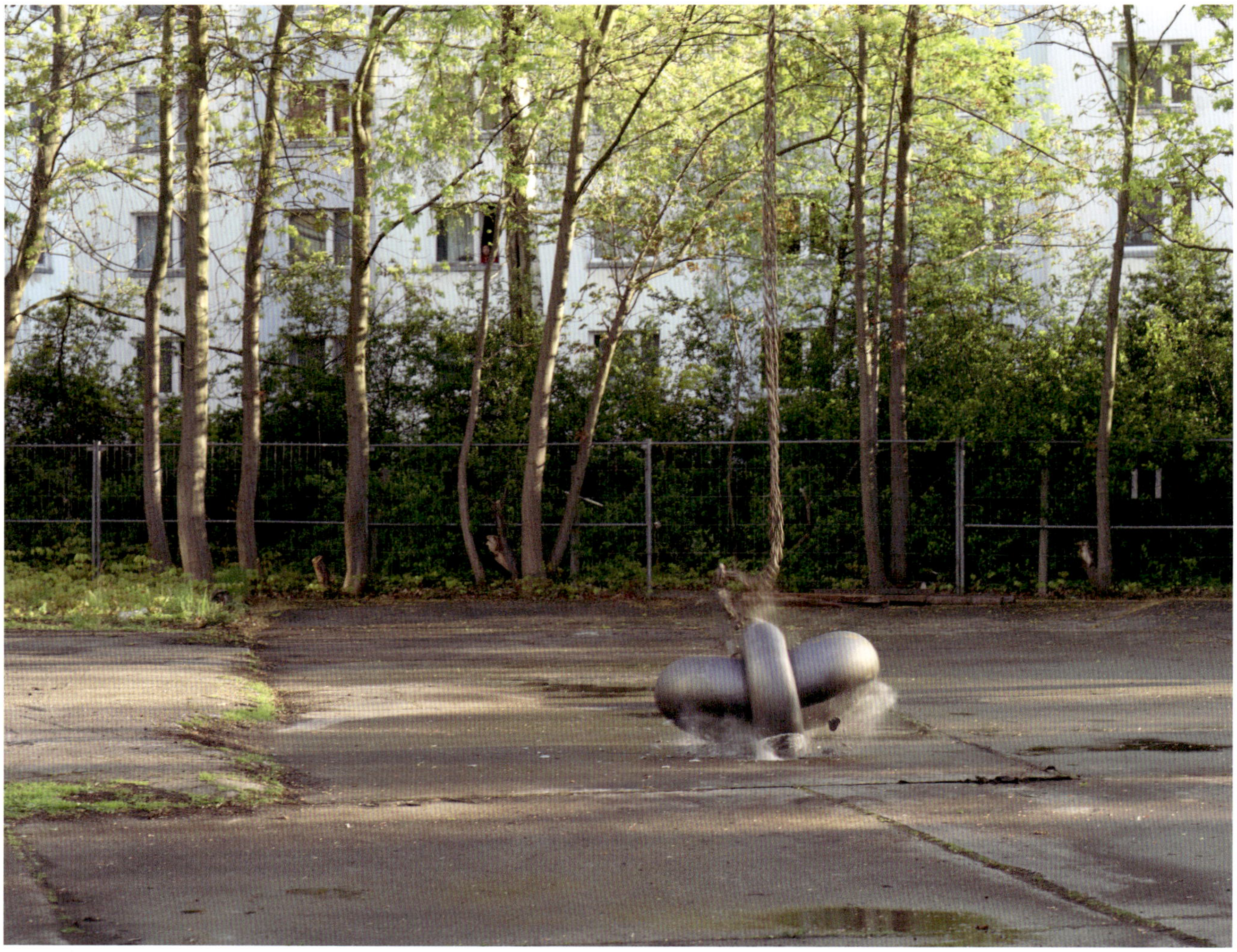

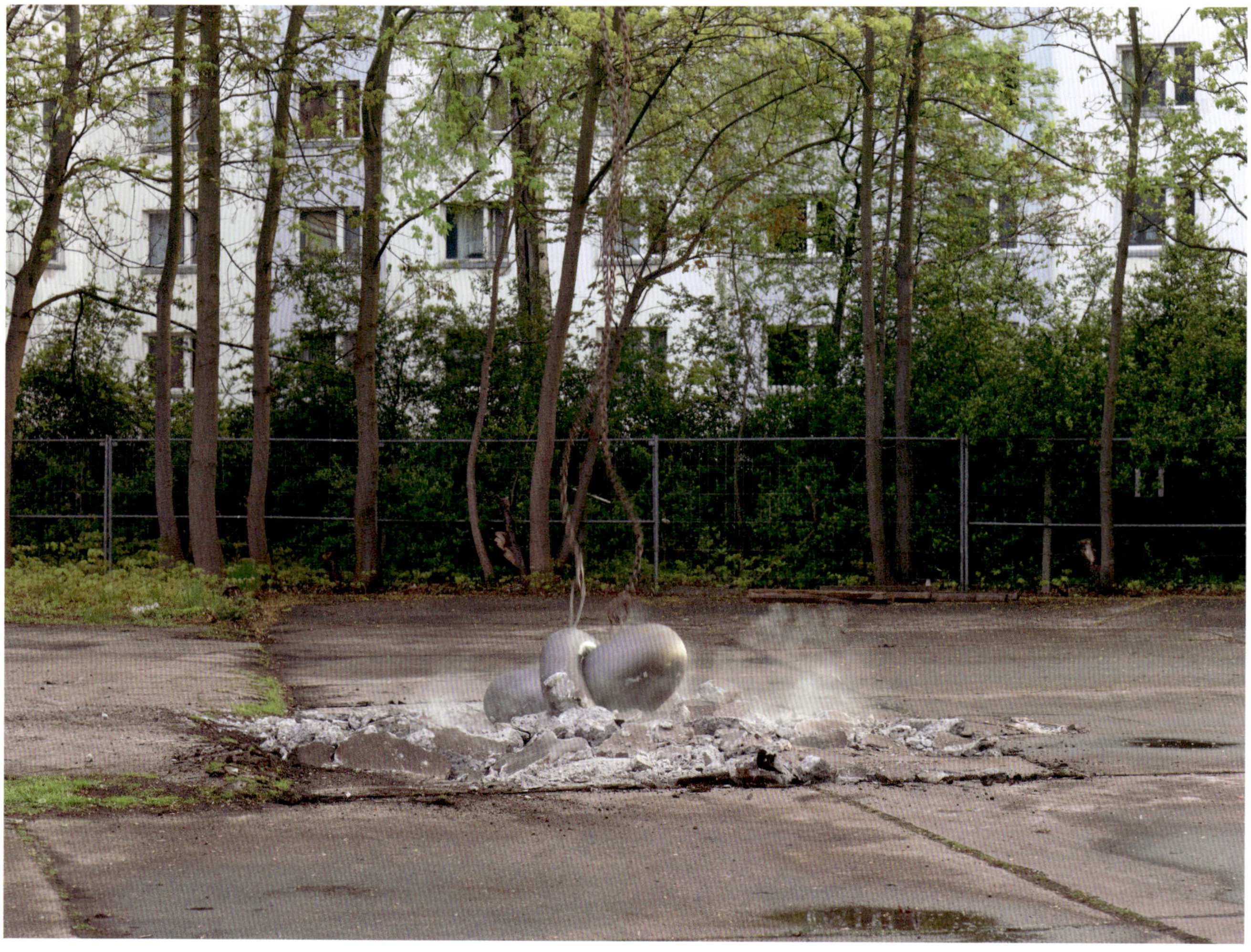

Berlin Depression, 2016

Video, 1 min

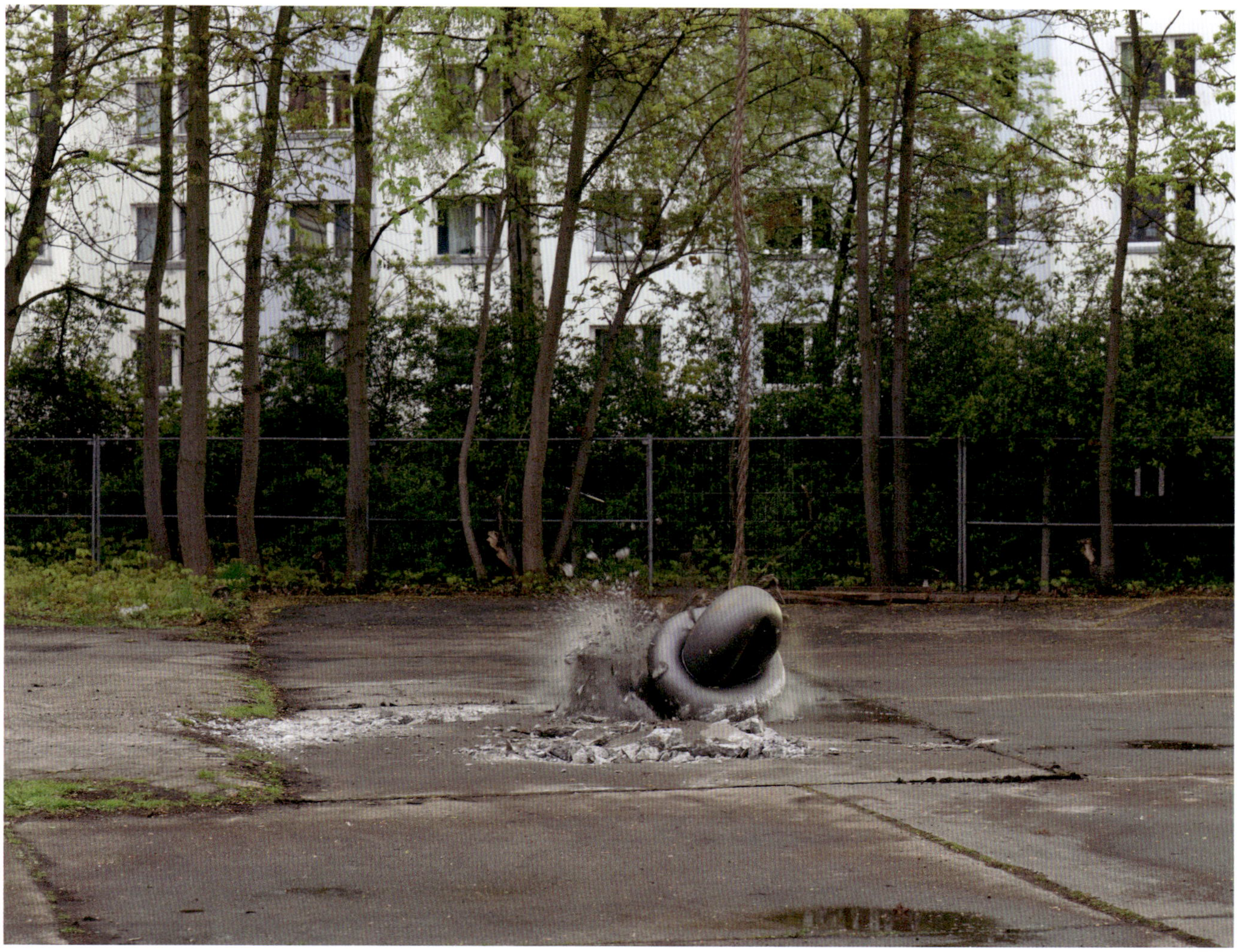

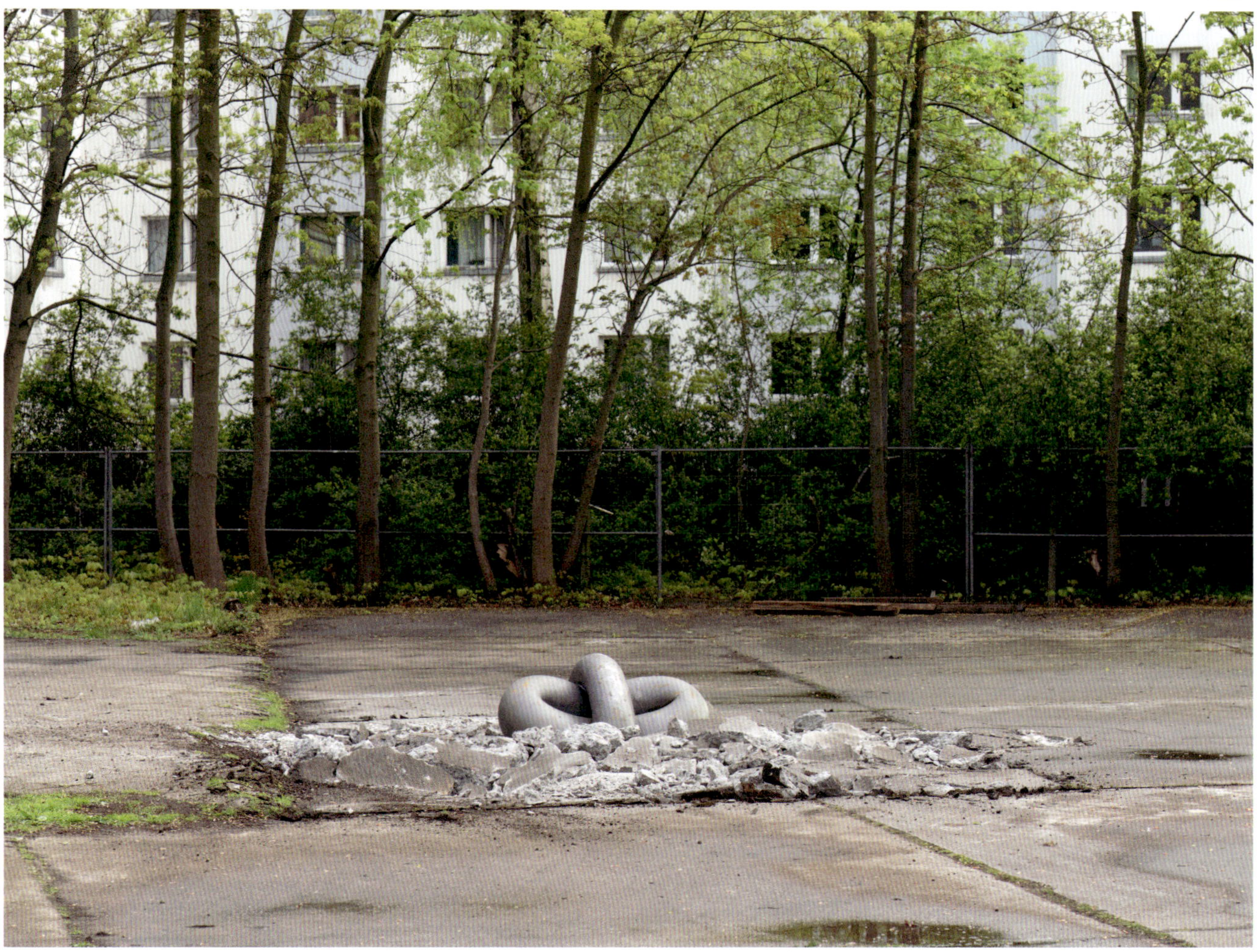

Magdalena Mai

CLOUD ATLAS

Michael Sailstorfer's Cloud Sculptures and the Materialization of the Ephemeral

At all times, in all countries where the sky is not always clear and blue, clouds must have seduced people's imagination with their changing and often whimsical, bizarre forms. People must have always divined in them the imaginary or real beings which occupy their mind. Everyone can find in them what they like; the contour of these vapors is so light, so vague … a breeze transforms them, a breath destroys them.

MARCEL PROUST, DIE WOLKEN (THE CLOUDS)[1]

The meteorological phenomenon of clouds was not only for Marcel Proust a source of fascination and projection. The volatile celestial figures have always inspired people's imagination. From fleecy clouds to translucent veils, from pink clouds to gloomy clouds—based on the natural laws of the ephemeral, the thermal, constantly newly forming structures provide material for dreaming and meditating on intangibility, boundlessness, and ultimately also on the transience of earthly existence.[2]

From a scientific point of view, clouds are so-called hydrometeors, consisting of tiny water and/or ice particles—condensed water vapor, among which tiny, suspended particles such as exhaust gases, dust, and smoke particles can mix. It is in the nature of clouds to hover in the sky. They only come into contact with the ground in the form of fog, haze, or dew.[3] Clouds accumulate and disperse, they rise, sink, pass by. The "flying fog" affects the heating and cooling of the planet by blocking or reflecting sunlight—and produces precipitation. In short, clouds affect the atmosphere.[4]

From both a meteorological and poetic perspective, clouds are genuinely ephemeral, constantly in transformation—a cloud is intangible, volatile matter. This is not the case with Michael Sailstorfer's cloud sculptures,

„Zu allen Zeiten, in allen Ländern, wo der Himmel nicht immer nur klar und blau ist, müssen die Wolken mit ihren wechselnden und oft skurril-bizarren Formen die Einbildungskraft des Menschen verführt haben. Immer muß der Mensch die imaginären oder realen Wesen in ihnen erraten haben, die seinen Geist beschäftigen. Ein jeder kann darin finden, was ihm gefällt; der Umriß dieser Dämpfe ist so leicht, so unbestimmt … eine Brise verwandelt sie, ein Hauch zerstört sie."[1]

MARCEL PROUST, DIE WOLKEN

WOLKENATLAS

Michael Sailstorfers Wolkenskulpturen und die Materialisierung des Flüchtigen

Das meteorologische Phänomen Wolke ist nicht allein für Marcel Proust Faszinosum und Projektionsfläche zugleich. Die volatilen Himmelsfiguren beflügeln die Imagination der Menschen seit jeher. Von der Schäfchenwolke über durchscheinende Schleier, von rosaroten Wolken bis hin zum düsteren Gewölk – auf den Gesetzmäßigkeiten des Flüchtigen basierend, liefern die thermischen, sich ständig neu formierenden Gebilde Stoff zum Träumen und Meditieren über das Nichtfassbare, Grenzenlose und schließlich auch über die Vergänglichkeit irdischen Daseins.[2]

Naturwissenschaftlich gesehen sind Wolken sogenannte Hydrometeore, die aus winzigen Wasser- und/oder Eisteilchen bestehen – kondensierter Wasserdampf also, unter den sich winzige Schwebeteilchen wie Abgase, Staub- und Rauchpartikel mischen können. Es liegt in der Natur der Wolken, in der Luft zu schweben. Nur in Form von Nebel, Dunst oder Tau kommen sie mit dem Boden in Kontakt.[3] Wolken häufen und zerstreuen sich, sie steigen, sinken, ziehen vorüber. Die „fliegenden Nebel" wirken auf Erwärmung und Abkühlung des Planeten ein, indem sie Sonnenlicht abblocken oder reflektieren, und sie erzeugen Niederschlag. Kurzum: Wolken beeinflussen die Atmosphäre.[4]

Sowohl aus meteorologischer als auch aus poetischer Perspektive sind Wolken genuin ephemer, befinden sich

which consist of solid, natural or artificial materials that are given a constantly recurring form defined by the sculptor. The artist develops the formal language of his *Clouds* ↗70–72 from inflated truck tire inner tubes, which he brings together in pairs as well as in threes and presents in various formations: Often, dozens of these hang from the ceiling on cables; later variants made of iron or bronze stand alone as individual objects, lying heavily on the floor with a silvery or polished black finish.

MOTHER CLOUDS – THE BERLIN SKY IN SÃO PAULO Michael Sailstorfer's sculptural interest in clouds was aroused in 2010 in the course of preparations for the exhibition for *Knoten wie Wolken / Nós Como Nuvens* at Galeria Fortes Vilaça in São Paulo. In the exhibition space, the artist arranged eight sculptural works from his *Knoten* (Knots, 2010) ↗50–55 series. Sailstorfer's sailor's knots, tied in rope and cast in aluminum, rise vertically, like lightning rods, into the air from the wooden base, seeming to defy gravity.

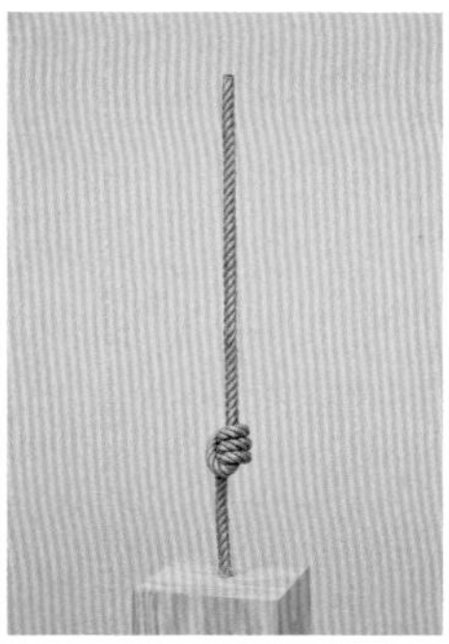

Knoten, 2010

In between, the filmic work *Lohma* (2008) ↗276/277 was projected onto a wall. A windowless sheet metal hall in a wintry landscape can be seen, deforming in slow motion due to a detonation triggered inside: Wobbling, the sheet metal skin yields to the shock wave and inflates, finally returning to its original form. Playing back this sequence as a loop creates the image of a pulsating, almost breathing object.[5] What remains hidden from view, however, is the discharge of the accumulating forces, the bursting of the hall. The broadly drawn roar of the explosion, reminiscent of powerful gusts of wind or the sound of breathing, accompanies the visible deformation of the otherwise stable building structure, which loses its form and creates flowing waves.

To present this video work as a 16mm projection, the light naturally entering the gallery space had to be shielded without darkening it too much. Sailstorfer developed an artistic solution and integrated the Berlin "export product cloud"[6] in the form of an expansive installation: At various heights, the aforementioned clouds made of truck tire inner tubes, which pick up on the shape of the knot sculptures, were hung in a dense formation from the gallery ceiling. They appeared grayish black, like heavy thunderclouds that gathered above the heads of the viewers. The

konstant in Transformation – eine Wolke ist ungreifbare, flüchtige Materie. Nicht so bei Michael Sailstorfer: Seine Wolkenskulpturen bestehen aus festen, natürlichen oder künstlichen Materialien, die in eine vom Bildhauer definierte, sich immer wiederholende Form gebracht werden. Die Formensprache seiner *Clouds* ↗70–72 entwickelt der Künstler aus aufgepumpten LKW-Schläuchen, die er sowohl paarweise als auch zu dritt ineinandersteckt und in verschiedenen Formationen präsentiert: Oft hängen sie zu Dutzenden an Seilen von der Decke, später treten Varianten aus Eisen oder Bronze als Einzelobjekte in Erscheinung, die silbrig oder schwarz poliert schwer auf dem Boden liegen.

MUTTERWOLKEN – BERLINER HIMMEL IN SÃO PAULO Michael Sailstorfers bildhauerisches Interesse an den Wolken wird 2010 im Zuge der Ausstellungsvorbereitungen für *Knoten wie Wolken / Nós Como Nuvens* in der Galeria Fortes Vilaça in São Paulo geweckt. Im Ausstellungsraum arrangiert der Künstler acht skulpturale Arbeiten der Serie *Knoten*, 2010 ↗50–55. In Taue geschlagene, von Sailstorfer in Aluminium übersetzte Seemannsknoten ragen senkrecht wie Blitzableiter vom hölzernen Sockel aus in die Luft und scheinen dabei der Schwerkraft zu trotzen.

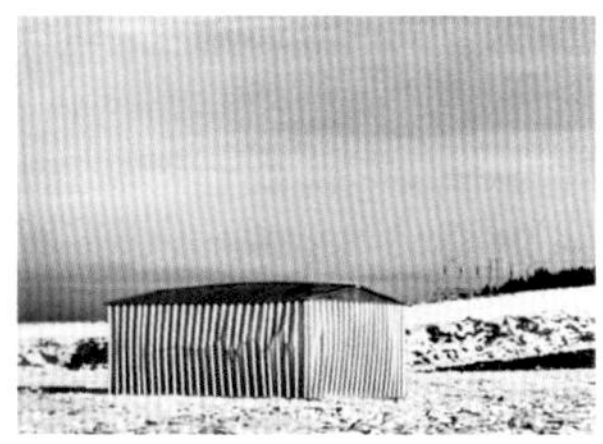

Lohma, 2008

Dazwischen wird die filmische Arbeit *Lohma*, 2008 ↗276/277, auf eine Wand projiziert. Zu sehen ist eine fensterlose Blechhalle in winterlicher Landschaft, die sich aufgrund einer im Inneren ausgelösten Detonation in Zeitlupe verformt: Wabernd gibt die Blechhaut der Druckwelle nach und bläht sich auf, um schließlich wieder in ihre Ausgangsform zurückzufinden. Durch das Abspielen dieser Sequenz als Loop entsteht das Bild eines pulsierenden, geradezu atmenden Objekts.[5] Dem Blick verwehrt, bleibt indes die Entladung der sich anstauenden Kräfte, das Bersten der Halle. Das breitgezogene Dröhnen der Explosion, das wie kräftige Sturmböen oder Atemgeräusche klingt, begleitet die sichtbare Deformation der festen Bausubstanz, die aus der Form gerät und fließende Wellen schlägt.

Um diese Videoarbeit auf 16 mm zu zeigen, soll das natürlich in den Galerieraum einfallende Licht abgeschirmt werden, ohne diesen zu stark abzudunkeln. Sailstorfer entwickelt eine künstlerische Lösung und integriert hierfür das Berliner „Exportgut Wolke"[6] in Form eines raumgreifenden Kunstwerks: Auf unterschiedlichen Höhen werden die eingangs beschriebenen, die Form der Knotenskulpturen aufnehmenden Wolken aus LKW-Schläuchen in dichter Formation von der Galeriedecke in den Raum hineingehängt.

arrangement and volume of the *Clouds* led to the desired effect of clouding over the light and at the same time far beyond this—as an atmospheric change of the space and the artworks gathered in it that influences perception.

The specific staging of the disparate, yet interrelated works mentally revives Marcel Duchamp's *Twelve Hundred Coal Bags Suspended from the Ceiling over a Stove,* an expansive installation developed for the *Exposition Internationale du Surréalisme* in Paris in 1938.[7] Above the exhibits arranged in the main room, Duchamp fixed 1,200 coal sacks stuffed with newspaper, from which fine coal dust trickled down. A sinister, Surrealistic cosmos had been created, in which the selective perception of the individual works receded in favor of the overall staging.[8]

Michael Sailstorfer's cloud formation in the gallery space evokes a comparable impression. It unfolds the effect of a metaphorical bracket around the assembled works, between which an interplay of physical forces unfolds: Charging, tension, and discharging form a closed circuit.

The contradictions of material and form inherent in the works create a sense of tense friction—the sheet metal flows in waves, the ropes solidify into unbreakable knots, the image of the fluid cloud is captured in a clearly delineated form. The solid appears fluid, the malleable solid, the ephemeral materialized.

THE OBSERVATION OF CLOUDS

The motif of the cloud opens a wide range of associations. Dark clouds promise rain, potentially accompanied by violent thunderstorms. Symbolically, they stand for melancholy, looming disaster, or conflict. Due to their nature of mutable essence and ultimate intangibility, clouds refer to metaphysical and psychic dimensions of human existence—the soul, the (day)dream, (life) time, emotions.

Michael Sailstorfer seems to bring the phenomenon of transient celestial bodies back down to earth: Due to their clearly defined form, his *Clouds* profoundly contradict the ephemeral appearance of actual clouds. And: they do not hover, they hang. They do not consist of air, but rather carry it within themselves as a form-giving element. A humorous gesture that is also reflected formally and aesthetically in the stylized realization of the motif.

Sailstorfer's *Clouds* create alternative systems of reference via the industrial material and the blackness inherent in it: They point to urban phenomena such as traffic, exhaust fumes, and smog, and introduce themes such as environmental pollution and the consumption of resources. Sailstorfer thus shifts the metaphorically charged, often romanticized image of the cloud without completely dissolving it. The cloud oscillates between poetry and the banality of everyday life.

Gräulich schwarz wirken sie wie schwere Gewitterwolken, die sich über den Köpfen der Betrachter*innen zusammengebraut haben. Die Anordnung und das Volumen der *Clouds* führen zum gewünschten Effekt der Eintrübung des Lichtes und zugleich weit darüber hinaus – als eine die Wahrnehmung prägende, atmosphärische Veränderung des Raumes und der darin versammelten Kunstwerke.

Die spezifische Inszenierung der unterschiedlichen, dennoch aufeinander bezogenen Werke lässt gedanklich Marcel Duchamps *Twelve Hundred Coal Bags Suspended from the Ceiling over a Stove* aufleben, eine raumgreifende Installation, die er 1938 für die *Exposition Internationale du Surréalisme* in Paris entwickelt hatte.[7] Über den im Hauptraum arrangierten Exponaten fixierte Duchamp 1200 mit Zeitungspapier ausstaffierte Kohlesäcke, aus denen feiner Kohlestaub herabrieselte. Ein finsterer, surrealistischer Kosmos war entstanden, in dem die selektive Wahrnehmung der einzelnen Werke zugunsten der Gesamtinszenierung zurücktrat.[8]

Einen vergleichbaren Effekt evoziert Michael Sailstorfers Wolkenformation im Galerieraum. Sie entfaltet die Wirkung einer metaphorischen Klammer um die versammelten Arbeiten, zwischen denen sich ein Wechselspiel physikalischer Kräfte entspinnt: Aufladung, Spannung und Entladung bilden einen geschlossenen Kreislauf. Durch die den Werken inhärenten Widersprüchlichkeiten von Material und Form entsteht spannungsvolle Reibung – das Blech fließt in Wellen, die Taue erstarren zu unlösbaren Knoten, das Bild der fluiden Wolke wird in eine klar umrissene Form gebannt. Festes erscheint fließend, Formbares fest, Flüchtiges wird materialisiert.

WOLKENBEOBACHTUNG

Das Motiv der Wolke eröffnet einen breiten Assoziationsraum. Dunkle Wolken verheißen Regen, unter Umständen begleitet von heftigem Gewitter. Sinnbildlich stehen sie für Melancholie, aufziehendes Unheil oder Streit. Ihrer Natur des wandelbaren Wesens und ultimativer Nicht-Greifbarkeit nach verweisen Wolken auf metaphysische und psychische Dimensionen des Menschlichen – die Seele, den (Tag-)Traum, die (Lebens-)Zeit, Emotionen.

Michael Sailstorfer scheint das Phänomen der flüchtigen Himmelskörper auf den Boden der Tatsachen zu holen: Aufgrund ihrer klar definierten Form stehen seine *Clouds* in profundem Widerspruch zur ephemeren Erscheinung Wolke. Und: Sie schweben nicht, sie hängen. Sie bestehen nicht aus Luft, sie tragen sie aber als formgebendes Element in sich. Eine humorvolle Geste, die sich auch formal-ästhetisch in der stilisierten Umsetzung des Motivs widerspiegelt.

Über den industriellen Werkstoff und die im Material angelegte Schwärze stellen Sailstorfers *Clouds* dabei alternative Bezugssysteme her: Sie deuten auf urbane Phänomene wie Verkehr, Abgase, Smog, setzen Themen wie

CLOUD COURSE

After the gloomy Berlin sky had invaded sunny São Paulo, variants of the cloud sculptures were shown in very different exhibition situations, each reacting to and interacting with the space surrounding it.

In 2010, for example, Michael Sailstorfer realized *Wolken Düsseldorf* ↗70/71, a powerful installation, in the more than one-thousand-square-meter-large Klee Hall of K20 – Kunstsammlung Nordrhein-Westfalen in Düsseldorf, where nearly three hundred cloud nodes moved into the otherwise empty space. The impressive size of the work put the viewer in relation to the spectacle of nature that had become sculpture, which, relocated to the interior, was domesticated, as it were, under an artificial starry sky of five hundred spotlights.

Similar to Philippe Parreno's floating *Speech Bubbles* (since 1997), the clouds hanging above viewers' heads prove to be carriers of meaning without a clearly legible message. Like placeholders for statements and thoughts, they ask to be filled. However, what is written in Sailstorfer's clouds remains open.

In 2011, the artist brought a cloud sculpture from the museum interior to the urban exterior, namely to the Doris C. Freedman Plaza in Central Park in New York. For *Tornado* (2011) ↗73, he wound dozens of his clouds, made of nearly 200 knotted rubber hoses, around a vertical, funnel-shaped rotating axis made of concrete and steel. The dark knots hung down in bulging tangles from the steel branches and at the same time rose up roughly ten meters in the air. The natural force of the storm with its at times immeasurable destructive potential, the image of which the artist used here, appeared tamed as a construct of its basic element: rotating air. Through its placement between the park and Midtown Manhattan, the most important business district in the United States, the sculpture reflected the dynamics of its surroundings: It mirrored the busy streets of New York—including smog, exhaust fumes, and asphalt—as well as the inner-city green space of Central Park, into whose groups of trees *Tornado* surprisingly blended in. The movement of the cloud knots in the wind poetically combined gentleness and strength, lightness and weight.[9]

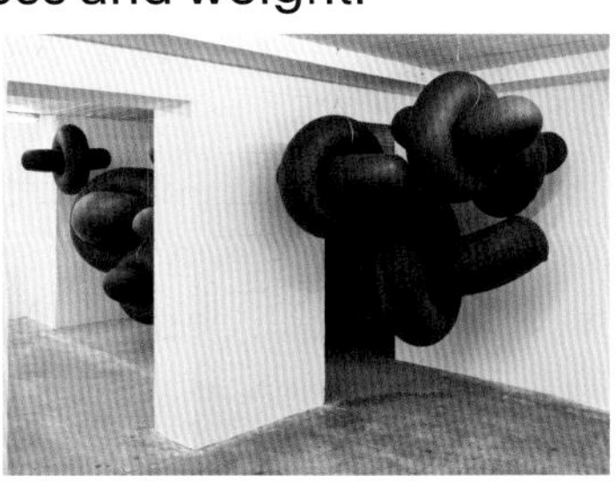

Himmel Berlin, 2012

Himmel Berlin (Sky Berlin, 2012), a dense cluster of clouds spilling out from all sides of the small space reserved for it in the former bunker of the Boros Collection, seemed to inhibit any movement. The clouds completely occupied

Umweltverschmutzung und Verbrauch von Ressourcen ins Bild. Damit verschiebt Sailstorfer das metaphorisch aufgeladene, oftmals romantisch-verklärte Bild der Wolke, ohne es vollständig aufzulösen. Die Wolke oszilliert zwischen Poesie und der Banalität des Alltäglichen.

WOLKENZUG

Nach dem Einzug des düsteren Berliner Himmels ins sonnige São Paulo werden Varianten der Wolkenskulpturen in ganz unterschiedlichen Ausstellungssituationen gezeigt, jeweils auf den sie umgebenden Raum reagierend und mit ihm interagierend.

So realisiert Michael Sailstorfer mit *Wolken Düsseldorf*, 2010 ↗70/71, eine wirkmächtige Installation, in der über eintausend Quadratmeter großen Klee Halle des K20 in Düsseldorf, wo annähernd dreihundert Wolkenknoten in den ansonsten leeren Raum ziehen. Die beeindruckende Größe der Arbeit setzt die Betrachter*innen in Relation zum Skulptur gewordenen Naturschauspiel, das, ins Innere verlagert, unter einem künstlichen Sternenhimmel aus fünfhundert Strahlern gewissermaßen domestiziert wird.

Ähnlich wie Philippe Parrenos schwebende Sprechblasen (*Speech Bubbles*, 1997 fortlaufend) erweisen sich die über den Köpfen hängenden Wolken dabei als Bedeutungsträger ohne eindeutig lesbare Botschaft. Wie Platzhalter für Äußerungen und Gedanken laden sie dazu ein, befüllt zu werden. Was in Sailstorfers Wolken geschrieben steht, bleibt offen.

Vom musealen Innenraum bringt der Künstler 2011 eine Wolkenskulptur in den urbanen Außenraum, auf der Doris C. Freedman Plaza im Central Park in New York. In *Tornado*, 2011 ↗73, windet er Dutzende seiner Wolken aus annähernd 200 verknoteten Gummischläuchen um eine senkrechte, trichterförmige Drehachse aus Beton und Stahl. Von den auslaufenden Stahlästen hängen die dunklen Knoten in wulstigen Knäueln herab und türmen sich zugleich rund zehn Meter in die Höhe. Die Naturgewalt des Wirbelsturms mit seinem teils unermesslichen Zerstörungspotenzial, dessen Bild sich der Künstler hierbei bedient, erscheint gebändigt als Konstrukt seines Grundelements: rotierende Luft. Durch ihre Platzierung zwischen Park und Midtown Manhattan, dem wichtigsten Geschäftsviertel der USA, reflektiert die Skulptur die Dynamik der Umgebung: Sie spiegelt die vielbefahrenen Straßen New Yorks – samt Smog, Abgasen und Asphalt – ebenso wie die innerstädtische Grünfläche des Central Parks, in dessen Baumgruppen sich *Tornado* überraschend einfügt. Durch die Bewegung der Wolkenknoten im Wind verbinden sich auf poetische Weise Sanftheit und Stärke, Leichtigkeit und Schwere.[9]

Als jegliche Bewegung hemmend erscheint *Himmel Berlin*, 2012, in der ein dichtes Wolkencluster von allen Seiten aus dem Kabinett im ehemaligen Bunker der Boros Collection herausquillt. Die Wolken besetzen den Raum vollständig,

the space, making it inaccessible. The impenetrable wall of clouds between the thick concrete walls of the bunker opened up a connection that is both humorous and paradoxical: The aesthetic form of the cloud sculpture thus proved to be a condensation *and* inversion of the functions and properties of the bunker. The sculpture potentiated the effect of the spatial confinement by taking complete possession of the limited niche, warding off any intrusion and defending its space both boldly and belligerently.

AND CLOUDS DO INDEED FALL FROM THE SKY!

In 2016, Sailstorfer used the traditional sculptural material steel for the first time for one of his *Clouds*, which this time appeared as a single object. In addition to the materiality, the coloration also changed—the black clouds condensed into a high-gloss silver cloud, which, as a powerful element, penetrated the surroundings like lightning: Amid great thunderous noise, Michael Sailstorfer realized the performative installation *Silver Cloud (Berlin Depression)* ↗80/81 on the grounds of his studio in Berlin-Weißensee. With the help of a crawler crane, the artist let the silver cloud slam onto the asphalt from various heights. Over and over again, it hit the ground with full force, shattering the asphalt until it was reduced to rubble and gravel. Deep furrows in the ground were left behind. A video recorded the event and the force of the impact of the two-ton sculpture in trembling images. Although the analogy of the titles creates a mental connection to Andy Warhol's *Silver Clouds* (1966), it quickly becomes clear that this can at most be an ironic and humorous quotation. For while Warhol's helium-filled, silver cushions whirl around the space as if they had a life of their own,[10] Sailstorfer's *Silver Cloud (Berlin Depression)* inverts the playful lightness into destructive heaviness.
What is more, this sensational art action opened up concrete references to Michael Heizer's work *Bern Depression* (1969). As part of the iconic exhibition *When Attitudes Become Form,* Heizer maltreated the forecourt of the Kunsthalle Bern with a wrecking ball, thus making the "experience of the artistic process"[11] central to the exhibition visible in the shattered ground, also after the fact.
With *Silver Cloud (Berlin Depression)* Sailstorfer created a kind of remake of Heizer's spectacular action and, to these ends, set the cloud in enormously powerful motion. Transformed into a new materiality, the body once filled with air became a sculpture weighing tons with destructive potential and thus appeared in a new intensity. The hailing cloud (described meteorologically as a "falling hydrometeor"[12]) flashes in the silver surface of the steel sculpture. Destructiveness and incalculability become just as apparent as the creative force of the steel cloud,

machen ihn unbetretbar. Mit der undurchdringlichen Wolkenwand zwischen den dicken Mauern des Bunkers eröffnet sich eine gleichsam humorvolle wie paradoxe Verbindung: So erweist sich die ästhetische Form der Wolkenskulptur als Verdichtung *und* Verkehrung von Funktionen und Eigenschaften des Bunkers. Die Skulptur potenziert die Wirkung der räumlichen Enge, indem sie die begrenzte Nische ganz und gar in Besitz nimmt, jegliches Eindringen abwehrt und ihren Raum ebenso kühn wie angriffslustig verteidigt.

UND WOLKEN FALLEN DOCH VOM HIMMEL! 2016 verwendet Sailstorfer erstmals den traditionellen bildhauerischen Werkstoff Stahl für eine seiner *Clouds*, die diesmal als einzelnes Objekt in Erscheinung tritt. Neben der Materialität verändert sich auch die Farbigkeit – die schwarzen Wolken kondensieren zu einer silbernen Hochglanzwolke, die als kraftvolles Element wie ein Blitz in die Umgebung eindringt: Unter großem Krach realisiert Michael Sailstorfer die performative Installation *Silver Cloud (Berlin Depression)* ↗80/81 auf dem Studiogelände in Berlin-Weißensee. Mittels Seilbagger lässt der Künstler die silberne Wolke aus verschiedenen Höhen auf den Asphalt knallen. Wieder und wieder schlägt sie ungebremst auf dem Boden auf und zertrümmert den Untergrund, bis dieser in Schutt und Schotter gelegt ist. Zurück bleiben tiefe Furchen im Fundament. Ein Video zeichnet das Ereignis und die Wucht des Aufpralls der zwei Tonnen schweren Skulptur in bebenden Bildern auf.
Wenngleich durch die Analogie der Titel eine gedankliche Linie zu Andy Warhols *Silver Clouds*, 1966, entsteht, wird schnell klar, dass es sich höchstens um ein ironisch-humorvolles Zitat handeln kann. Denn während Warhols heliumgefüllte, silberne Kissen luftig-leicht im Raum umherschwirren, als führten sie ein Eigenleben,[10] verkehrt Michael Sailstorfer mit *Silver Cloud (Berlin Depression)* die spielerische Leichtigkeit zu zerstörerischer Schwere.
Die aufsehenerregende Kunstaktion eröffnet indes konkrete Bezüge zu Michael Heizers Arbeit *Bern Depression* von 1969. Im Rahmen der ikonischen Ausstellung *When Attitudes Become Form* malträtierte Heizer mit einer Abrissbirne den Vorplatz der Kunsthalle Bern und machte damit das in der Ausstellung zentrale „Erlebnis des künstlerischen Vorgangs"[11] auch nachträglich im zerschmetterten Boden sichtbar.
Mit *Silver Cloud (Berlin Depression)* schafft Sailstorfer eine Art Remake der spektakulären Aktion Heizers und setzt dafür die Wolke in enorm kraftvolle Bewegung. In eine neue Materialität überführt, wird der einst mit Luft gefüllte Körper in eine tonnenschwere Skulptur mit zerstörerischem Potenzial transformiert und erscheint dadurch in neuer Intensität. Die hagelnde Wolke (meteorologisch als „fallender Hydrometeor"[12] bezeichnet) blitzt im Silber

which inscribes itself into the surroundings in a brutal manner. The force of the impact manifests a discharge of physical forces that is capable of changing, deforming or, if you will, modeling the environment.
Michael Sailstorfer had already addressed this productive side of destruction in 2015 with the video work *Tränen* (Tears) ↗34/35. Here, a house in a rural idyllic landscape crumbles loudly under blue tears, which turn out to be wrecking balls weighing tons that repeatedly strike the building. With the motif of the tear, the artist painted a melancholic picture, placing the progressive transformation from residential building to a pile of rubble in an almost poetic context that counteracts the brutality of the irreversible process.
The systematic work of destruction presented here, which undergoes a positive reevaluation as a sculptural strategy and artistic concept, also locates *Silver Cloud (Berlin Depression)* in the cycle of productive destruction. The destructive tears have metaphorically condensed into a cloud—a coherent further development of the idea. As a genuinely ephemeral phenomenon, the cloud does not dissolve *itself,* but rather the asphalt.
The paradox between the fleeting phenomenon of the cloud and the form of the silver cloud fixed in the material is amplified in the bronze and steel versions, which—like *Very Heavy Cloud* (2021)—ultimately lie isolated, heavy as tons, and motionless on the gallery floor. The phenomenon taken to absurdity: The cloud is grounded.

READING CLOUD IMAGES

The sky: the ceiling of the gallery. The clouds: made of parts of vehicles. They hang in space or fall to the ground, defying the evanescence inherent in their essence. With his cloud works, Michael Sailstorfer gives the mutable, the intangible a solid form and opens up a broad, associative space in which the motif of the cloud oscillates between natural phenomenon, poetic metaphor, and the everyday.
The translation of the dazzling motif into the form-giving base material of knotted truck tire inner tubes creates a fascinating contrast that transfers the image of the cloud into new contexts with a serene gaze and humorous tranquility, without thwarting the poetic moment—the work titles anchor the cloud motif quite explicitly.
Following the trail of Michael Sailstorfer's clouds, one can observe the continuous development of the basic idea. Starting from one and the same object, the cloud knot, changing constellations, material variation, and embedding in various contexts lead to different, ambivalent readings, each of which establishes a relationship to the spatial situation: The *Clouds* do not reflect the light, but rather their surroundings, and likewise have an effect on them.

der Stahlplastik auf. Zerstörungswille und Unkalkulierbarkeit werden ebenso gewahr wie die Gestaltungskraft der Stahlwolke, die sich auf brachiale Weise in die Umgebung einschreibt. In der Wucht des Aufschlags manifestiert sich eine Entladung physikalischer Kräfte, die es vermag, die Umgebung zu verändern, zu deformieren oder, wenn man so will, zu modellieren.
Die produktive Seite des Zerstörens thematisierte Michael Sailstorfer bereits 2015 in der Videoarbeit *Tränen* ↗34/35. Ein Haus in ländlicher Idylle zerbröckelt dort lautstark unter blauen Tränen, die sich als tonnenschwere Abrissbirnen entpuppen und wiederholt auf das Gebäude einschlagen. Im Motiv der Träne zeichnet der Künstler ein melancholisches Bild und setzt die fortschreitende Transformation vom Wohnhaus zum Trümmerhaufen in einen nahezu poetischen Kontext, der die Brutalität des unwiderruflichen Vorgangs konterkariert.
Die hier vor Augen geführte, systematische Zerstörungsarbeit, die als bildhauerische Strategie und künstlerisches Konzept eine positive Umwertung erfährt, verortet auch *Silver Cloud (Berlin Depression)* im Kreislauf produktiver Destruktion. Die zerstörerischen Tränen haben sich bildhaft zur Wolke verdichtet – eine kohärente Weiterentwicklung der Idee. Dabei löst die Wolke als genuin ephemere Erscheinung nicht *sich* auf, sondern den Teer.
Das Paradox zwischen flüchtiger Wolkenerscheinung und im Material fixierter Form der Silberwolke potenziert sich in den Ausführungen in Bronze und Stahl, die – wie *Very Heavy Cloud*, 2021 – schließlich vereinzelt, tonnenschwer und bewegungslos auf dem Galerieboden liegen. Das Phänomen ad absurdum geführt: Die Wolke ist geerdet.

WOLKENBILDER LESEN

Der Himmel: die Galeriedecke. Die Wolken: aus Fahrzeugteilen. Sie hängen im Raum oder fallen zu Boden, der Verflüchtigung trotzend, die ihrem Wesen anhaftet. Mit seinen Wolkenarbeiten gibt Michael Sailstorfer dem Wandelbaren, Nicht-Greifbaren eine feste Form und öffnet einen breit gefächerten, assoziativen Raum, in dem das Motiv der Wolke zwischen Naturphänomen, poetischer Metapher und Alltäglichem changiert.
Durch die Übersetzung des schillernden Motivs in den formgebenden Basiswerkstoff verknoteter LKW-Schläuche entsteht ein spannungsreicher Kontrast, der das Bild der Wolke mit abgeklärtem Blick und in humorvoller Unaufgeregtheit in neue Kontexte überführt, ohne das poetische Moment zu tilgen – die Werktitel verankern das Wolkenmotiv ganz explizit.
Folgt man dem Zug von Michael Sailstorfers Wolken, so lässt sich die kontinuierliche Weiterentwicklung der Grundidee beobachten. Ausgehend von ein und demselben Objekt, dem Wolkenknoten, führen sich wandelnde Konstellationen, materielle Variation und die Einbettung

In the early stage of this series of works, the basic properties of the meteorological phenomenon were particularly prominent in the sculptures. The basic element of air conditions the outer form, the placement ("hanging in the air"), and the resulting change of atmosphere in space. With place and time, density and formation also change. In the form of a tornado, Sailstorfer suggests a movement from the earth into the air that promises destructive power. The development of the motif ultimately led to the dissolution of the cloud formation and culminated in a sculpture weighing tons: The cloud falls, precipitation occurs. The *Cloud* itself now appears as a form-giving element, acting with all its might on its surroundings. In the end, it appears as a single object at rest on the Earth, which completely negates the properties of the natural phenomenon.

The original idea of the cloud is visibly condensed: The sculptural process leads from multiplicity to singularity, from air to earth, and from lightness to weight. Sailstorfer's *Clouds* are inscribed with a poetic story of transformation.

in unterschiedliche Kontexte zu verschiedenen, ambivalenten Lesarten, die jeweils einen Bezug zur räumlichen Situation herstellen: Die *Clouds* reflektieren nicht das Licht, sondern ihre Umgebung und wirken ebenso auf sie zurück. Zu Beginn der Werkserie treten besonders die grundlegenden Eigenschaften des meteorologischen Phänomens in den Skulpturen hervor. Das Basiselement Luft bedingt die äußere Form, die Platzierung („in der Luft hängend") und die daraus resultierende Veränderung der Atmosphäre im Raum. Mit Ort und Zeit wandeln sich auch Dichte und Formierung. In Gestalt des Wirbelsturms deutet Sailstorfer eine Bewegung von der Erde in die Luft an, die zerstörerische Kraft verheißt. Die Entwicklung des Motivs führt schließlich zur Auflösung der Wolkenformation und kulminiert in einer tonnenschweren Plastik: Die Wolke stürzt, es kommt zum Niederschlag. Die *Cloud* erscheint nun selbst als formgebendes Element, das mit aller Kraft auf die Umgebung einwirkt. Am Ende tritt sie als ruhendes Einzelobjekt auf der Erde in Erscheinung, das die Eigenschaften des Naturphänomens gänzlich negiert.

Die ursprüngliche Idee der Wolke wird zusehends verdichtet: Der bildhauerische Prozess führt von der Vielheit zur Vereinzelung, von der Luft auf die Erde und von der Leichtigkeit zur Schwere. Sailstorfers *Clouds* ist eine poetische Geschichte der Transformation eingeschrieben.

1 Marcel Proust: "Die Wolken," in: idem, *Essays, Chroniken und andere Schriften,* Frankfurt Edition, ed, Luzius Keller, Works I / Volume 3 (Frankfurt am Main: Suhrkamp, 2003), pp. 26–29, here p. 26 [translated].

2 Cf. John Ruskin, in: Klaus Reichert, *Wolkendienst. Figuren des Flüchtigen,* 2nd edition (Frankfurt am Main: S. Fischer Verlag, 2016), p. 9.

3 See: Deutscher Wetterdienst (ed.), *Internationaler Wolkenatlas,* part 1/2, 2nd edition (Offenbach am Main: Deutscher Wetterdienst, 1990), p. 3.

4 See: Christian Meier, "Wasser mit nebulöser Wirkung," in: Max Planck Forschung, *Fokus Wolken. Schwebende Wasserspeicher als Klimafaktor,* no. 1/2010, 2010, pp. 16–23, here p. 17.

5 Michael Sailstorfer in conversation with the author on December 17, 2021.

6 Ibid. [translated].

7 Cf. Dieter Daniels, *Duchamp und die anderen. Der Modellfall einer künstlerischen Wirkungsgeschichte in der Moderne* (Cologne: DuMont Buchverlag, 1992), pp. 131–132.

8 Cf. Niels Werber and Ruhr-Universität Bochum (eds.), *Ringvorlesung Avantgarden der Kunst und Literatur: Surrealismus, Kunstkörper, Fotografie,* December 1, 1999, https://homepage.ruhr-uni-bochum.de/niels.werber/Avantgarden/Sykora.htm [last accessed on August 18, 2022].

9 See: Public Art Fund, *Michael Sailstorfer: Tornado. About the Exhibition,* https://www.publicartfund.org/exhibitions/view/tornado/ [last accessed on August 21,2022].

10 See: Thomas Morgan Evans, *3D Warhol. Andy Warhol and Sculpture* (London and New York: I.B. Tauris, 2017), pp. 60f.

11 Harald Szeemann, *Zur Ausstellung,* https://kunsthalle-bern.ch/images/max/ausstellung_8.jpg [last accessed on August 21, 2022] [translated].

12 Deutscher Wetterdienst 1990 (see note 3), p. 59 [translated].

1 Marcel Proust, „Die Wolken", in: ders., *Essays, Chroniken und andere Schriften*, Frankfurter Ausgabe, hrsg. von Luzius Keller, Werke I/ Band 3, Frankfurt am Main: Suhrkamp 2003, S. 26–29, hier S. 26.

2 Vgl. John Ruskin, zit. nach Klaus Reichert, *Wolkendienst. Figuren des Flüchtigen*, Frankfurt am Main: S. Fischer Verlag 2016, S. 9.

3 Vgl. Deutscher Wetterdienst (Hg.), *Internationaler Wolkenatlas*, Teil 1/2, Offenbach am Main: Selbstverlag des Deutschen Wetterdienstes 1990, S. 3.

4 Christian Meier, „Wasser mit nebulöser Wirkung", in: Max Planck Forschung, *Fokus Wolken. Schwebende Wasserspeicher als Klimafaktor*, Heft 1/2010, Berlin 2010, S. 16–23, hier S. 17.

5 Michael Sailstorfer im Gespräch am 17.12.2021, nach Aufzeichnungen der Autorin.

6 Vgl. ebd.

7 Vgl. Dieter Daniels, *Duchamp und die anderen. Der Modellfall einer künstlerischen Wirkungsgeschichte in der Moderne*, Köln: DuMont Buchverlag 1992, S. 131–132.

8 Vgl. Niels Werber und Ruhr-Universität Bochum (Hg.), *Ringvorlesung Avantgarden der Kunst und Literatur: Surrealismus, Kunstkörper, Fotografie*, 1. Dezember 1999, unter: https://homepage.ruhr-uni-bochum.de/niels.werber/Avantgarden/Sykora.htm (abgerufen am 10.1.2022).

9 Vgl. Public Art Fund, *Michael Sailstorfer: Tornado. About the Exhibition*, unter: https://www.publicartfund.org/exhibitions/view/tornado/ (abgerufen am 12.1.2022).

10 Vgl. Thomas Morgan Evans, *3D Warhol. Andy Warhol and Sculpture*, London/New York: I.B. Tauris 2017, S. 60–61.

11 Harald Szeemann, *Zur Ausstellung*, unter: https://kunsthalle-bern.ch/images/max/ausstellung_8.jpg (abgerufen am 21.1.2022).

12 Deutscher Wetterdienst (siehe Anm. 3), S. 59.

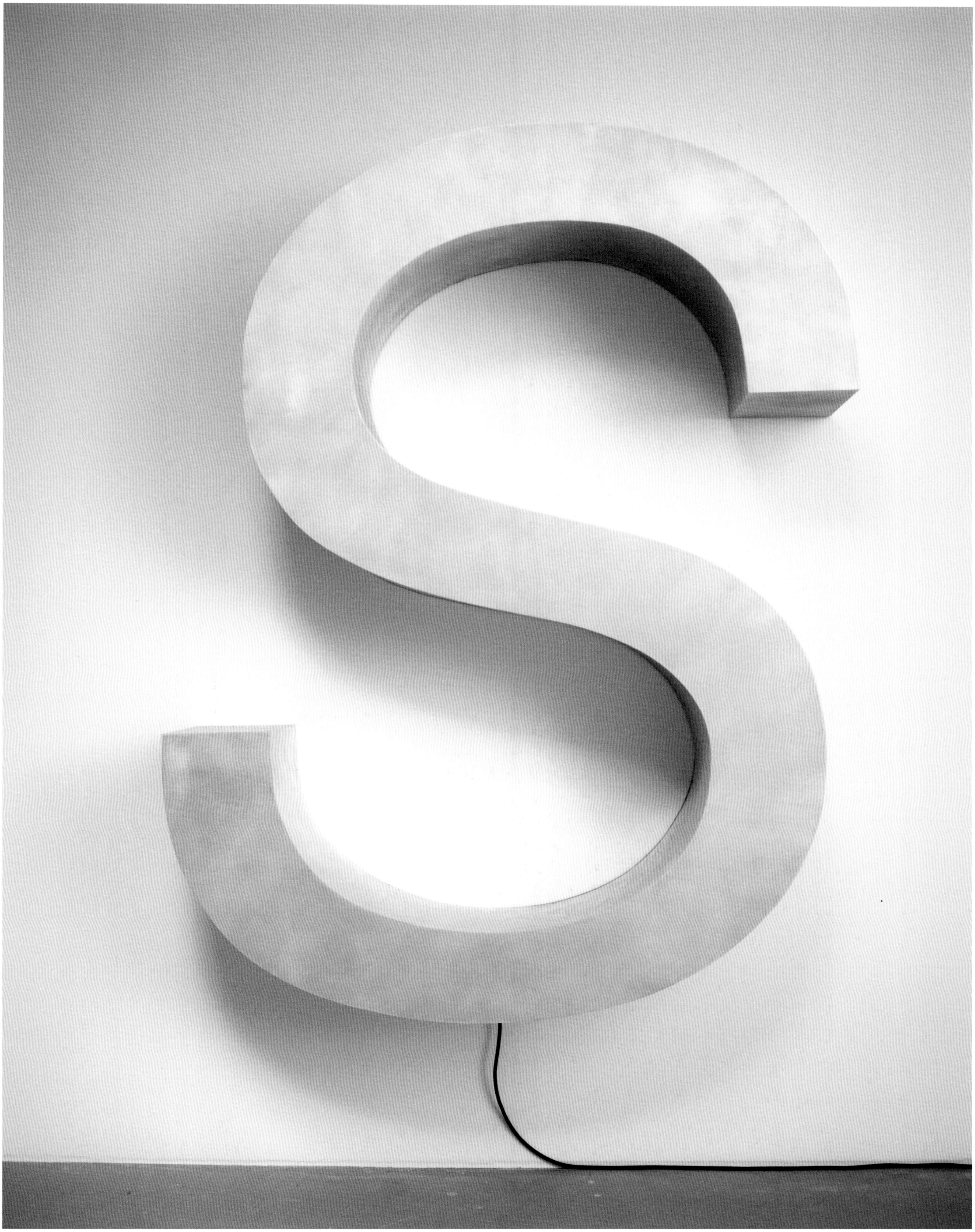

Musikalisches „S“, 2008

Aluminum, loudspeaker, mp3 player / Aluminium, Lautsprecher, MP3-Player, 200 × 165 × 30 cm

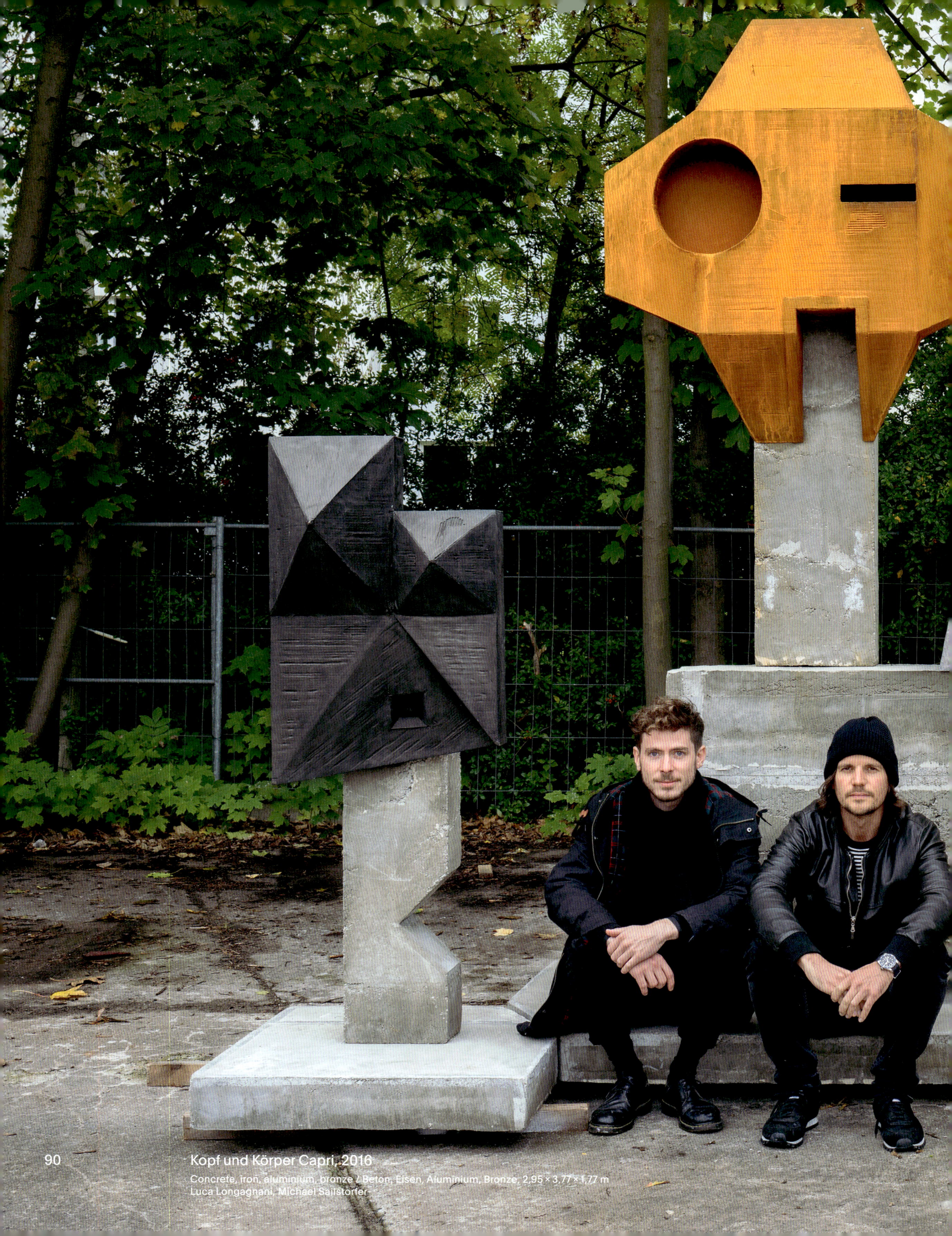

Kopf und Körper Capri, 2016

Concrete, iron, aluminium, bronze / Beton, Eisen, Aluminium, Bronze, 2,95 × 3,77 × 1,77 m
Luca Longagnani, Michael Sailstorfer

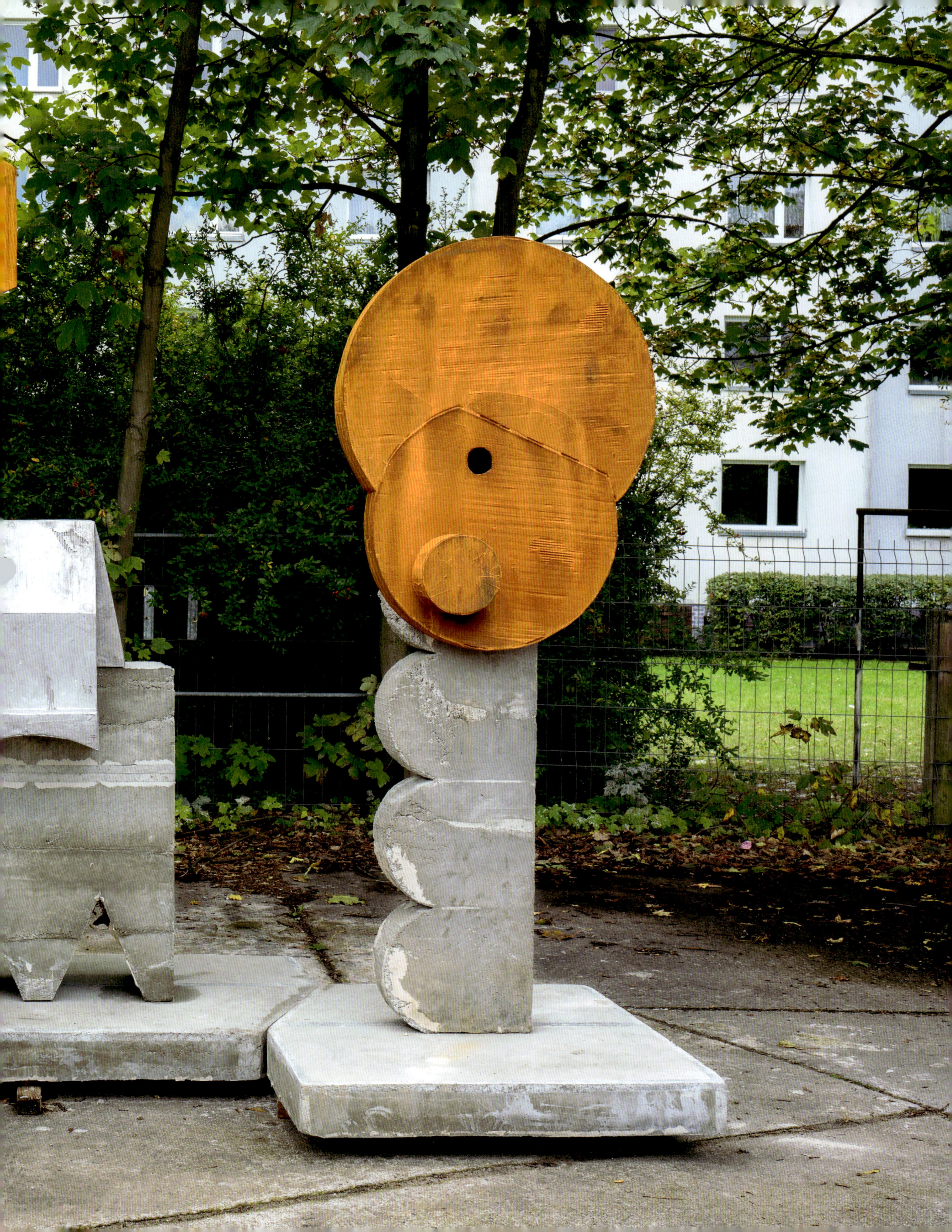

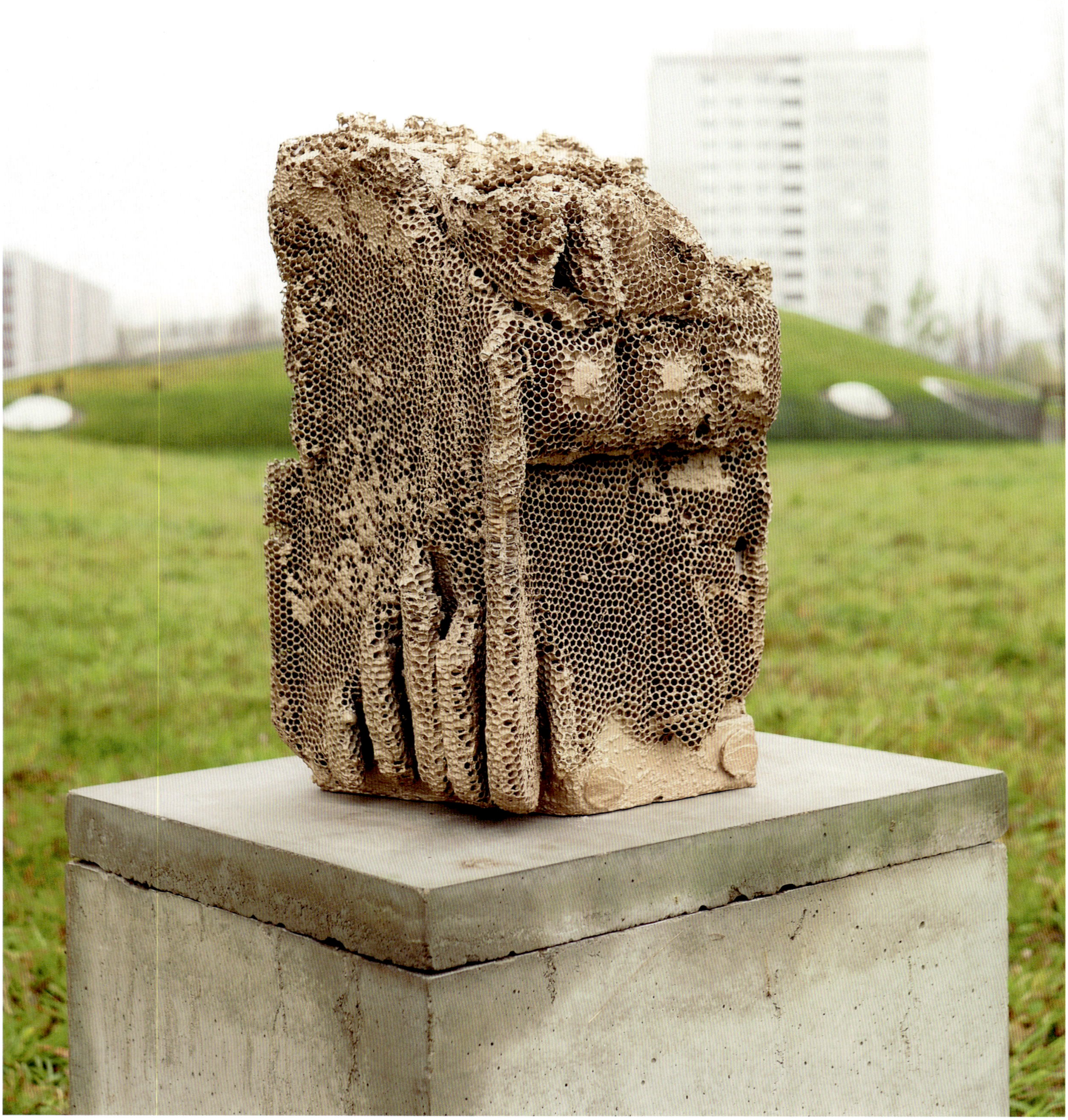

Kopf und Körper Marzahn 02, 2017

Bronze, concrete / Bronze, Beton, 113 × 55 × 44 cm

Kopf und Körper Marzahn 03, 2017

Bronze, concrete / Bronze, Beton, 112 × 55 × 44 cm

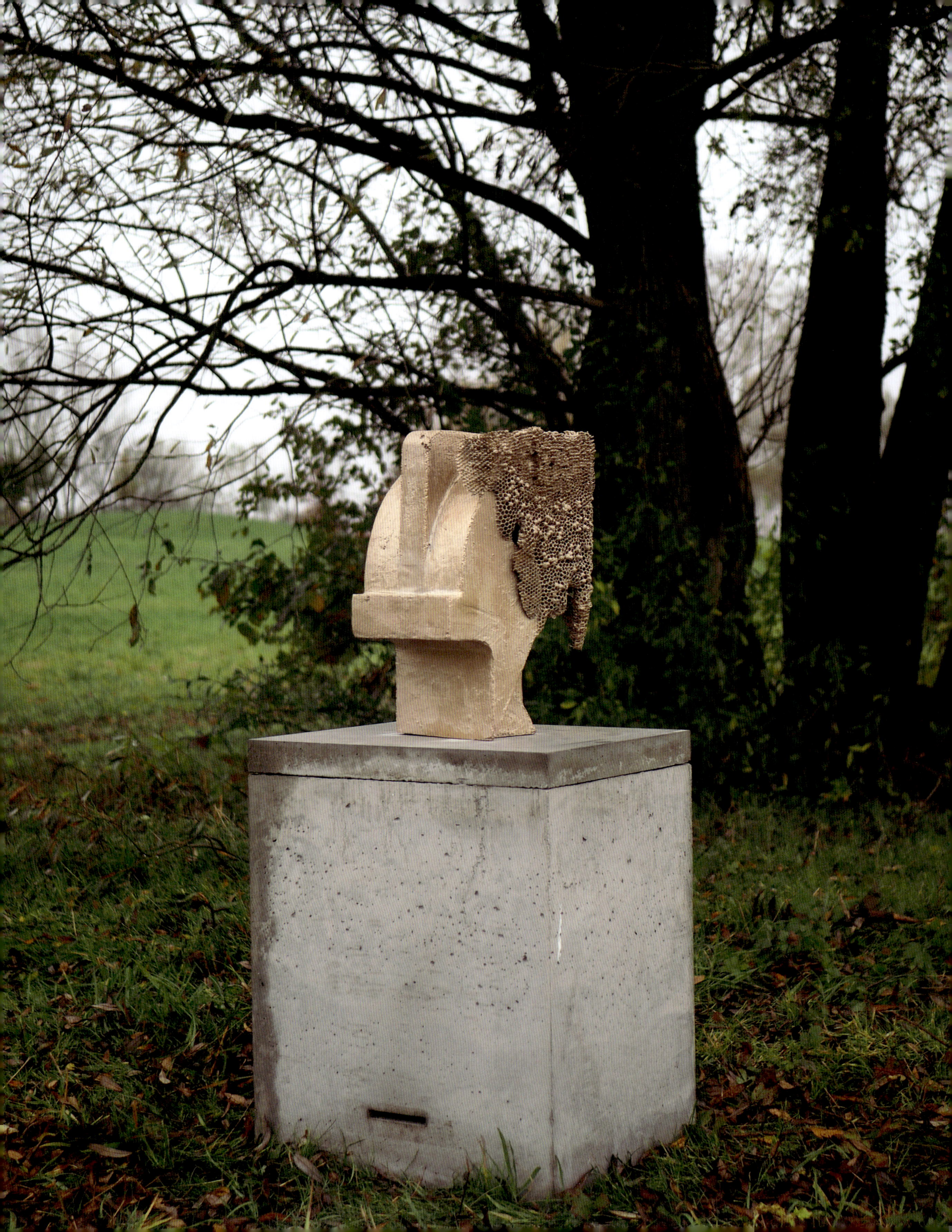

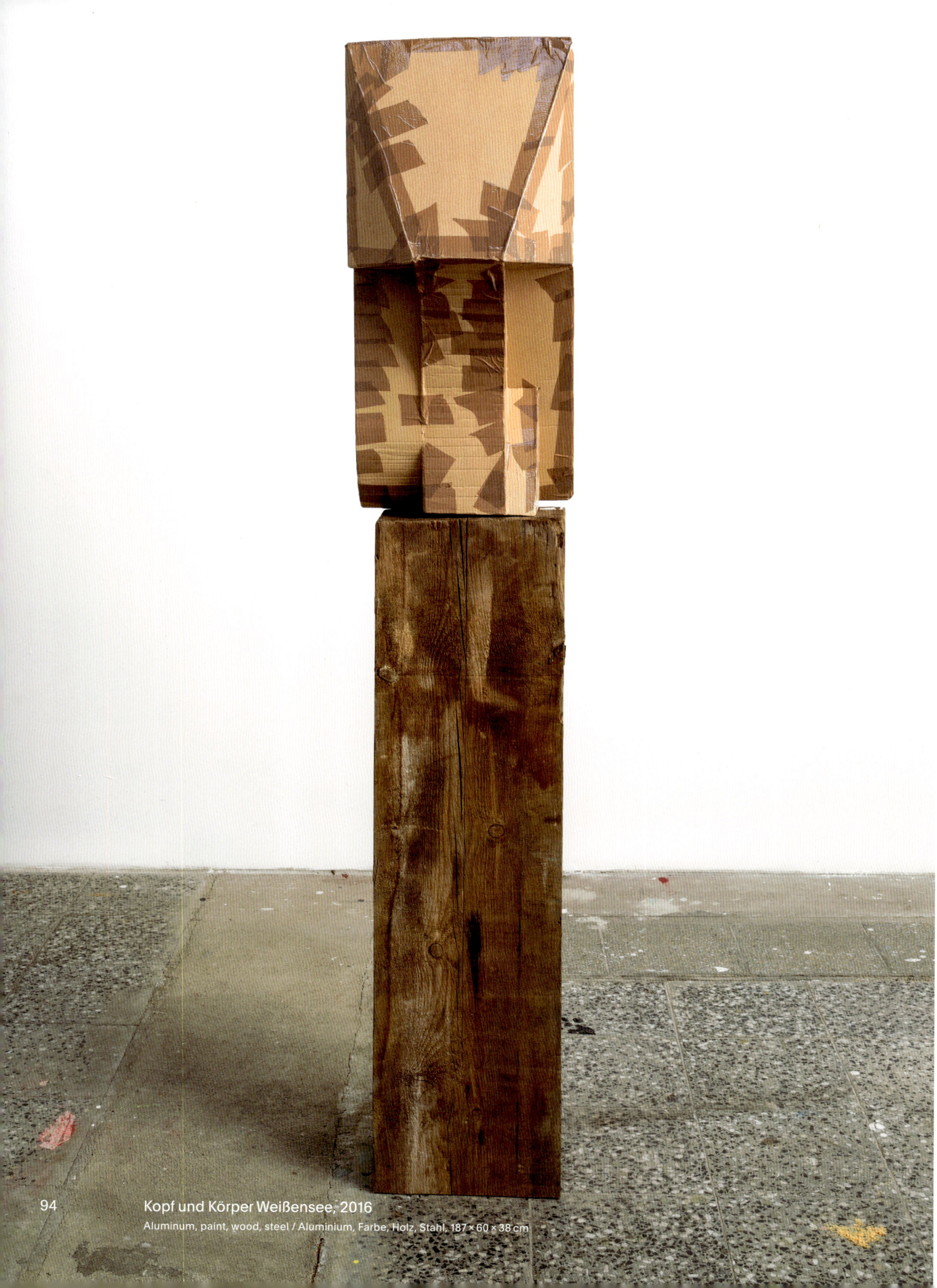

Kopf und Körper Weißensee, 2016

Aluminum, paint, wood, steel / Aluminium, Farbe, Holz, Stahl, 187 × 60 × 38 cm

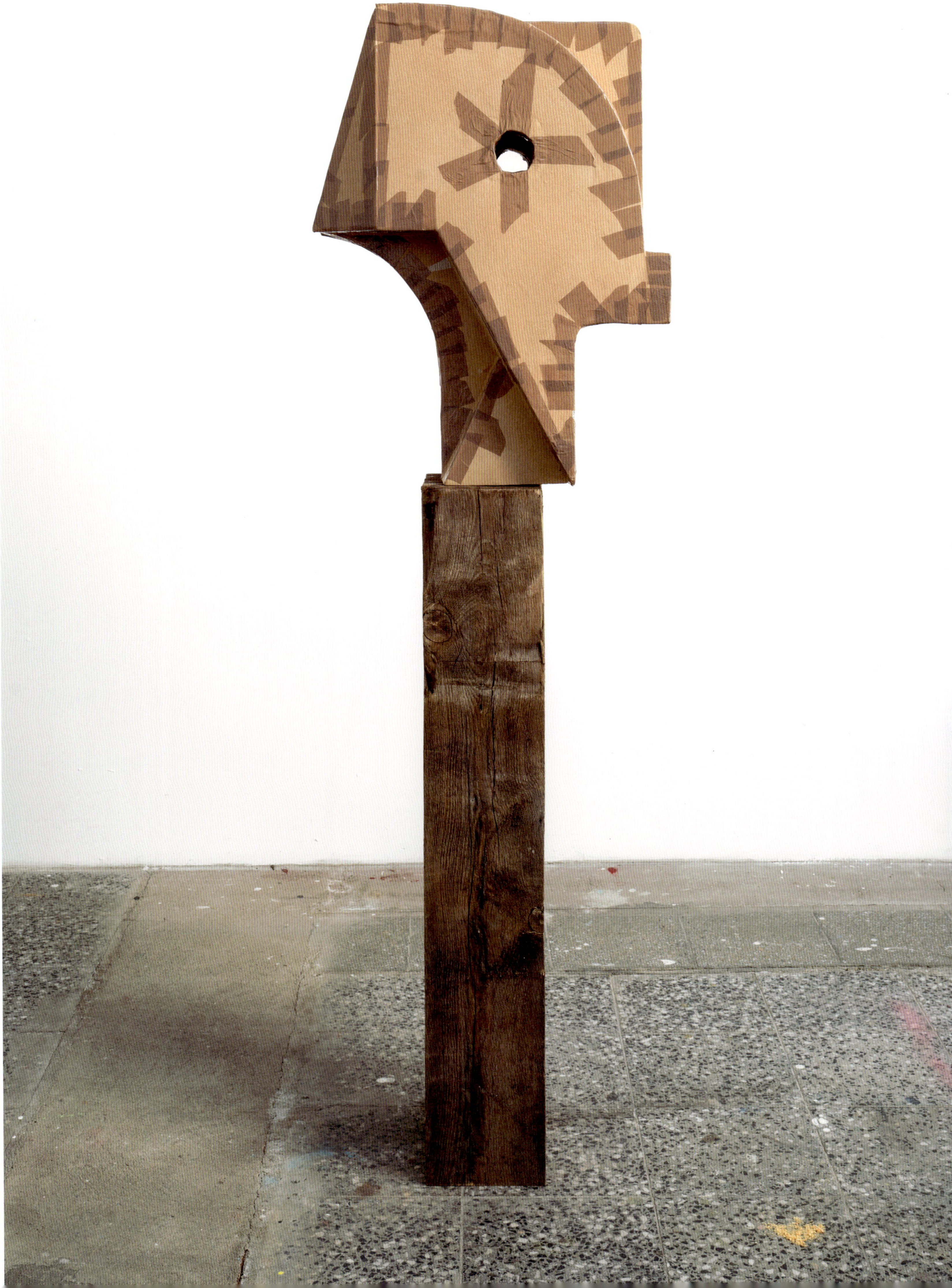

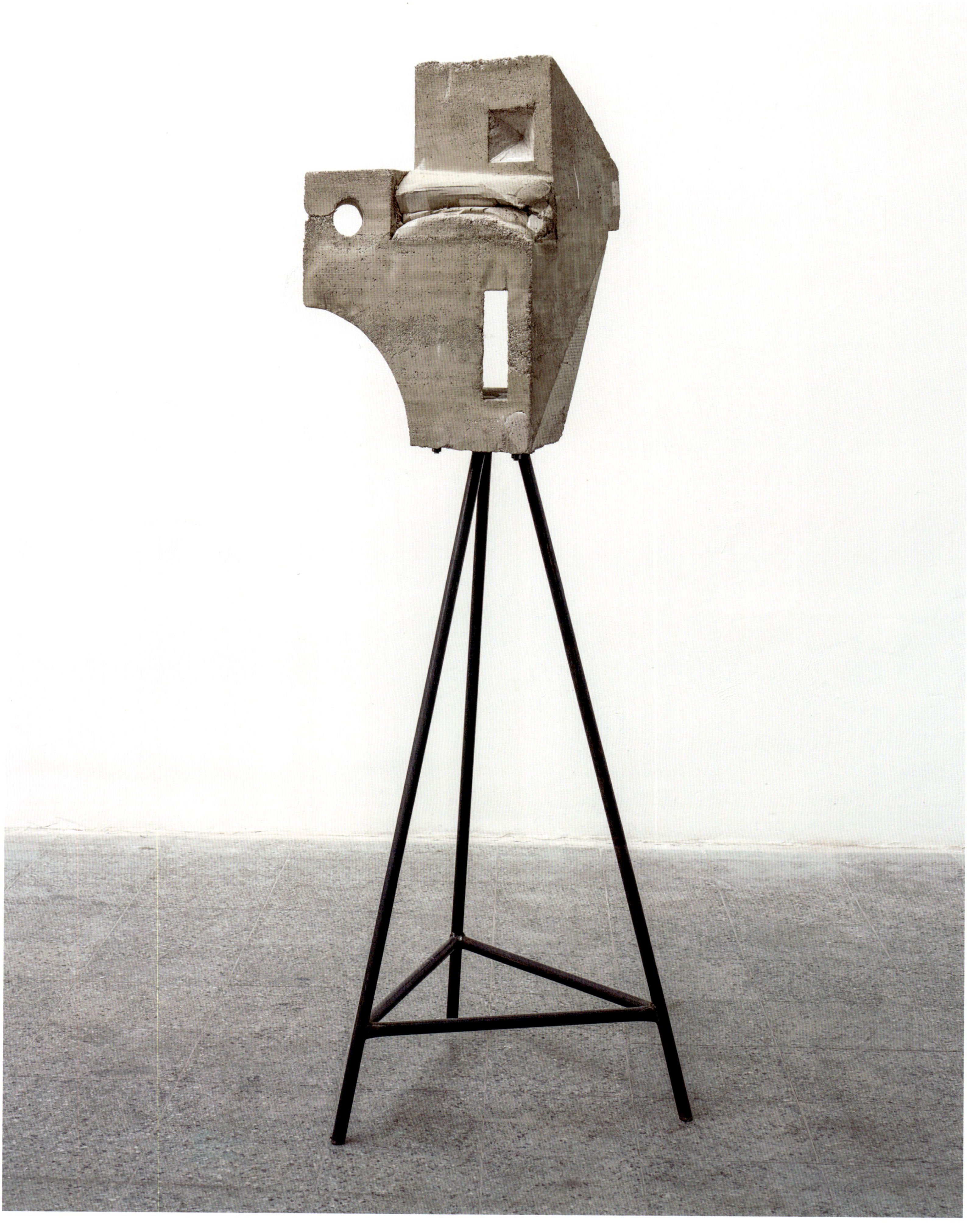

Kopf und Körper Braunschweig I, 2015

Concrete, steel / Beton, Stahl, 208 × 74 × 65 cm

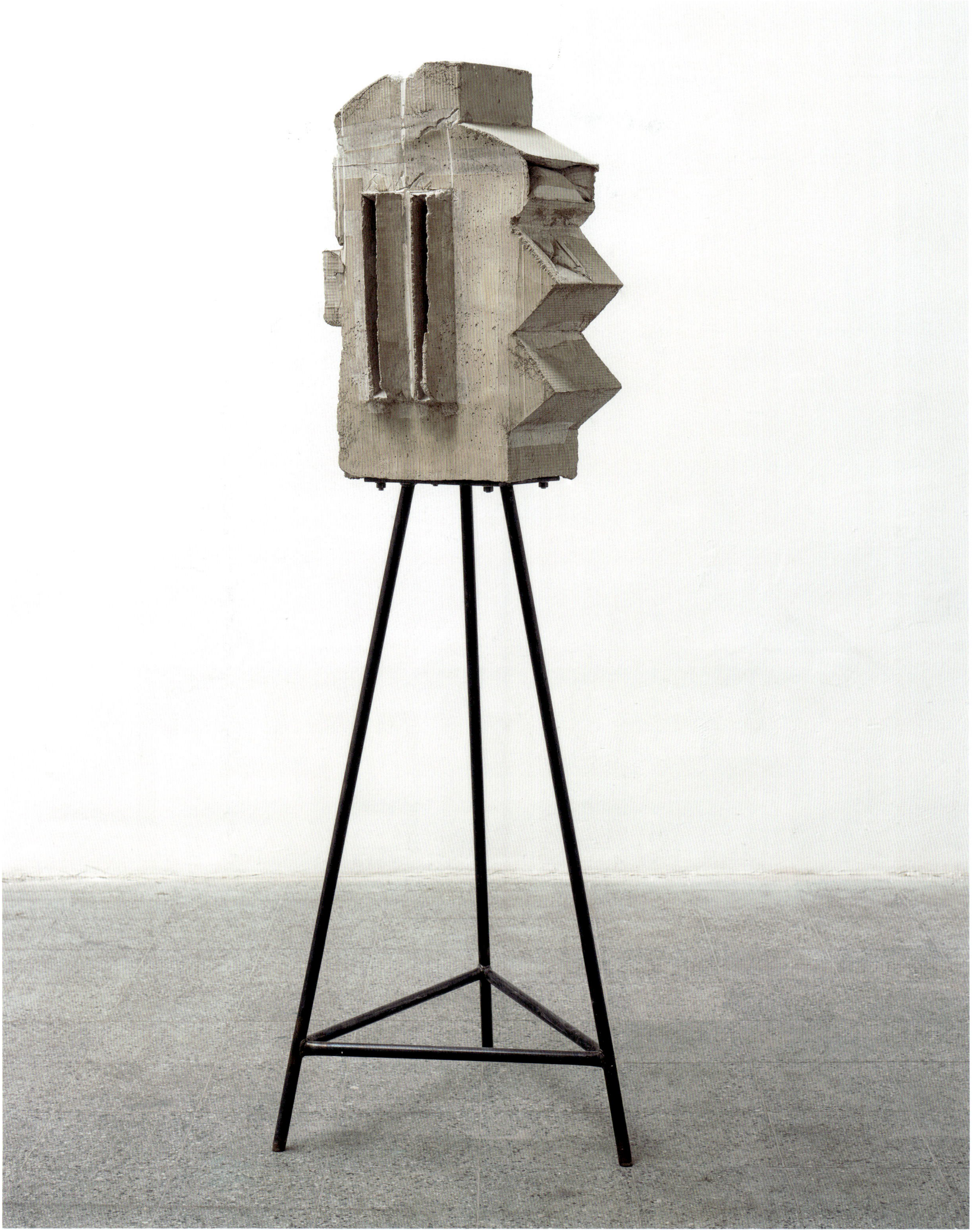

Kopf und Körper Braunschweig II, 2015

Concrete, steel / Beton, Stahl, 212 × 74 × 65 cm

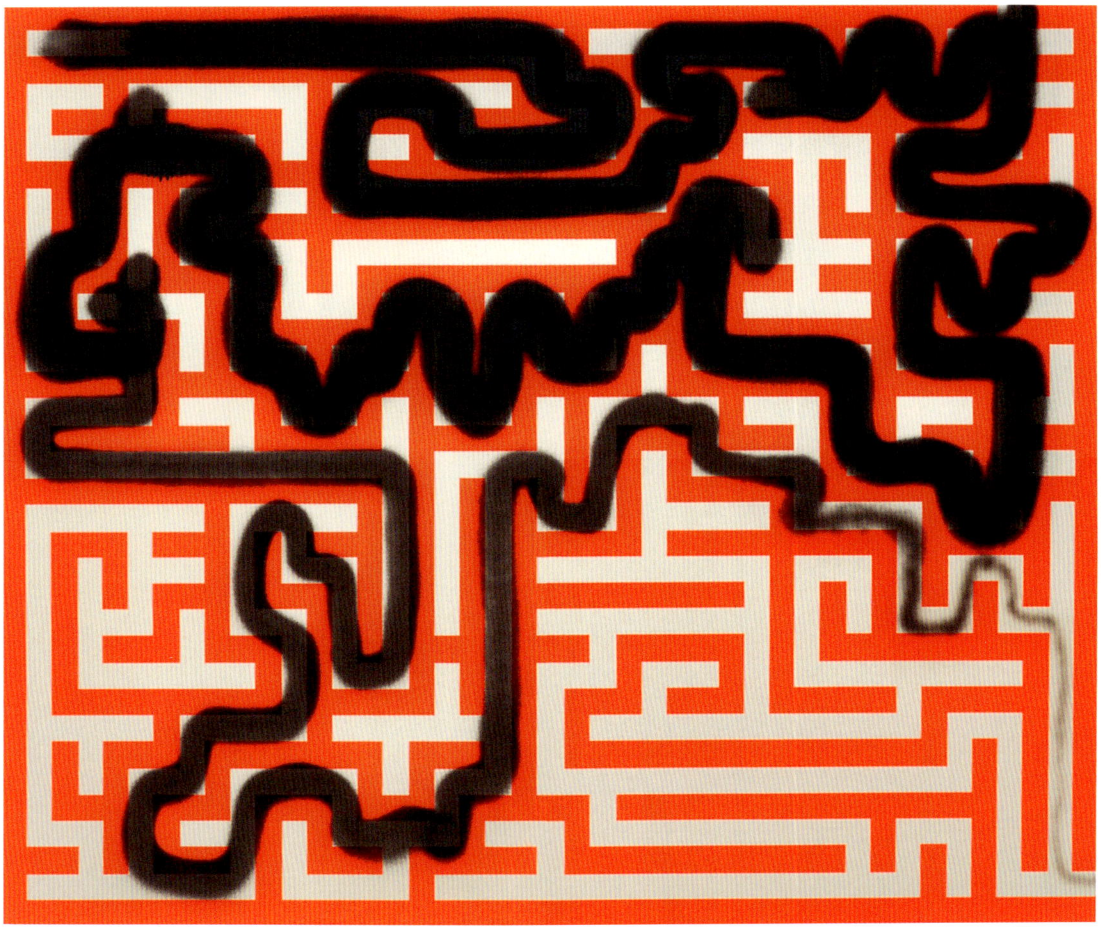

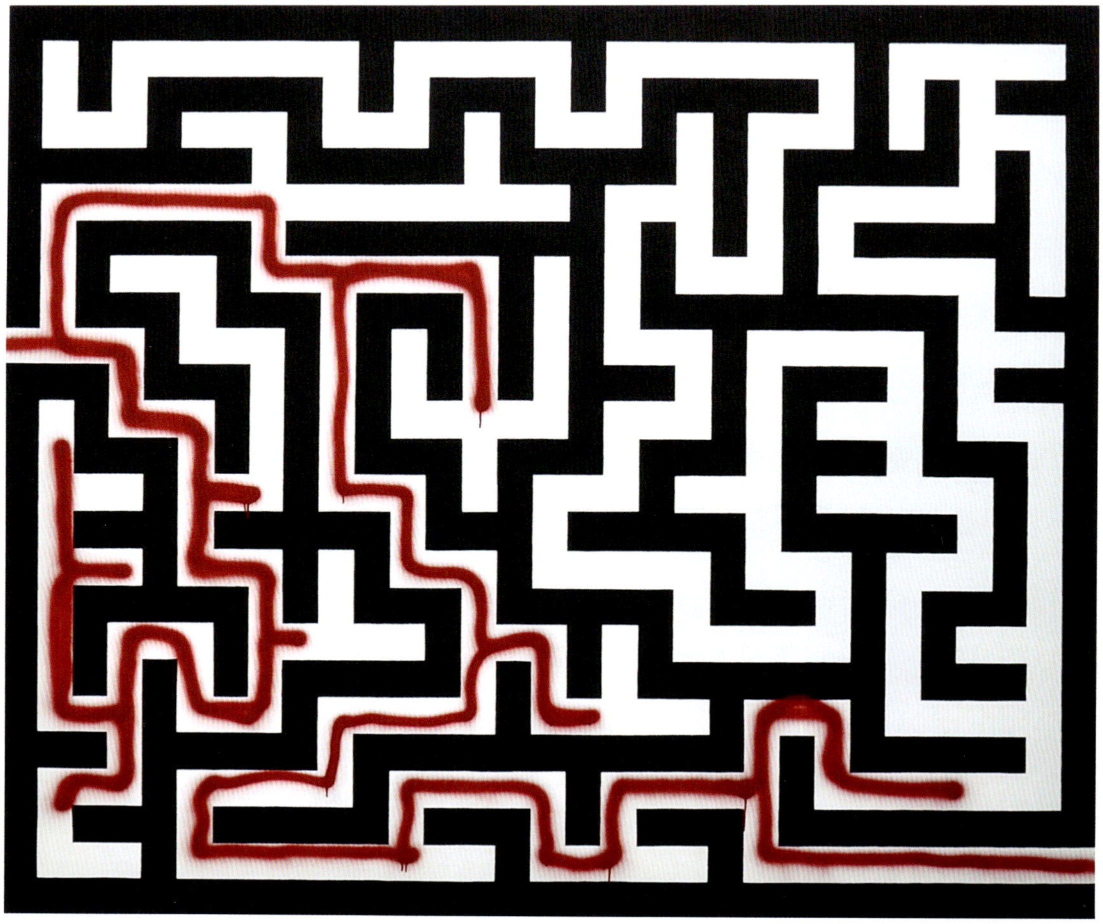

Mazes, 2011/2012

Screen print and spray paint on canvas / Siebdruck und Sprühfarbe auf Leinwand, 190 × 230 cm

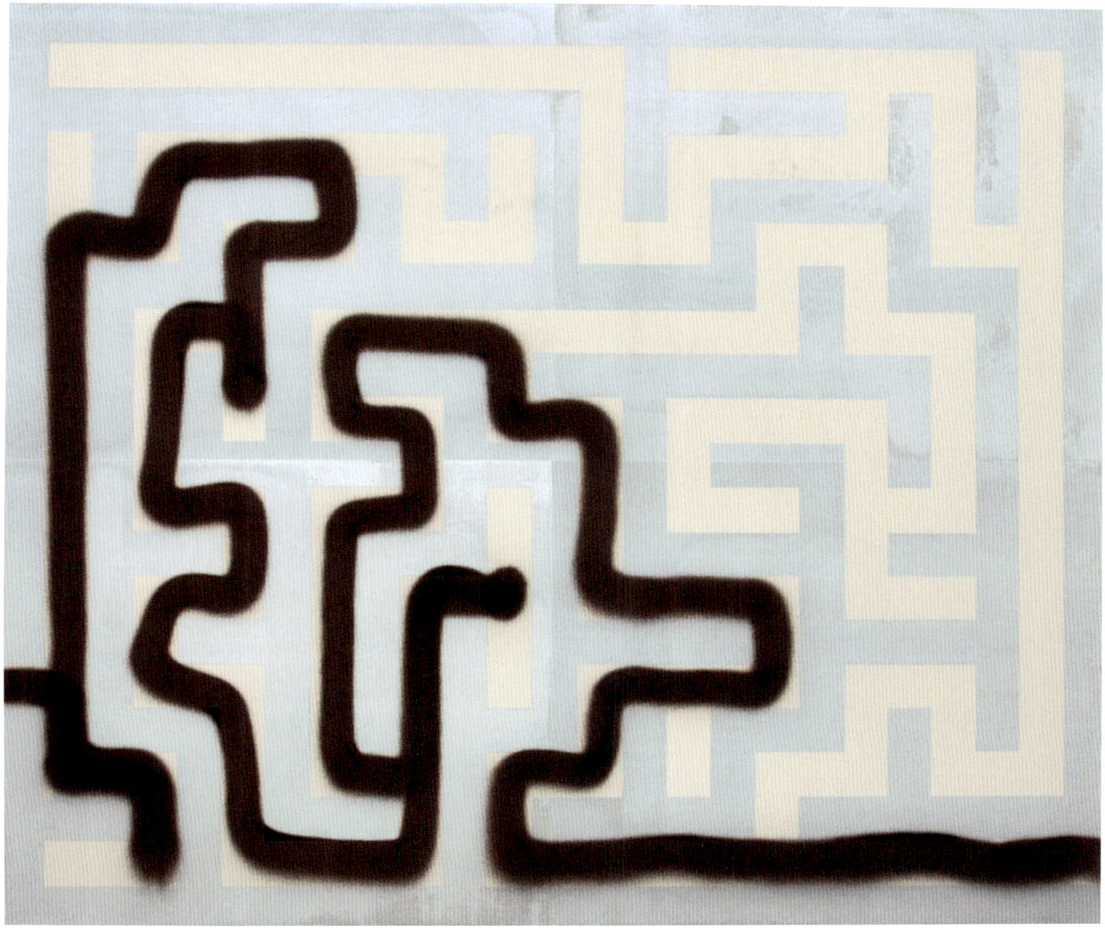

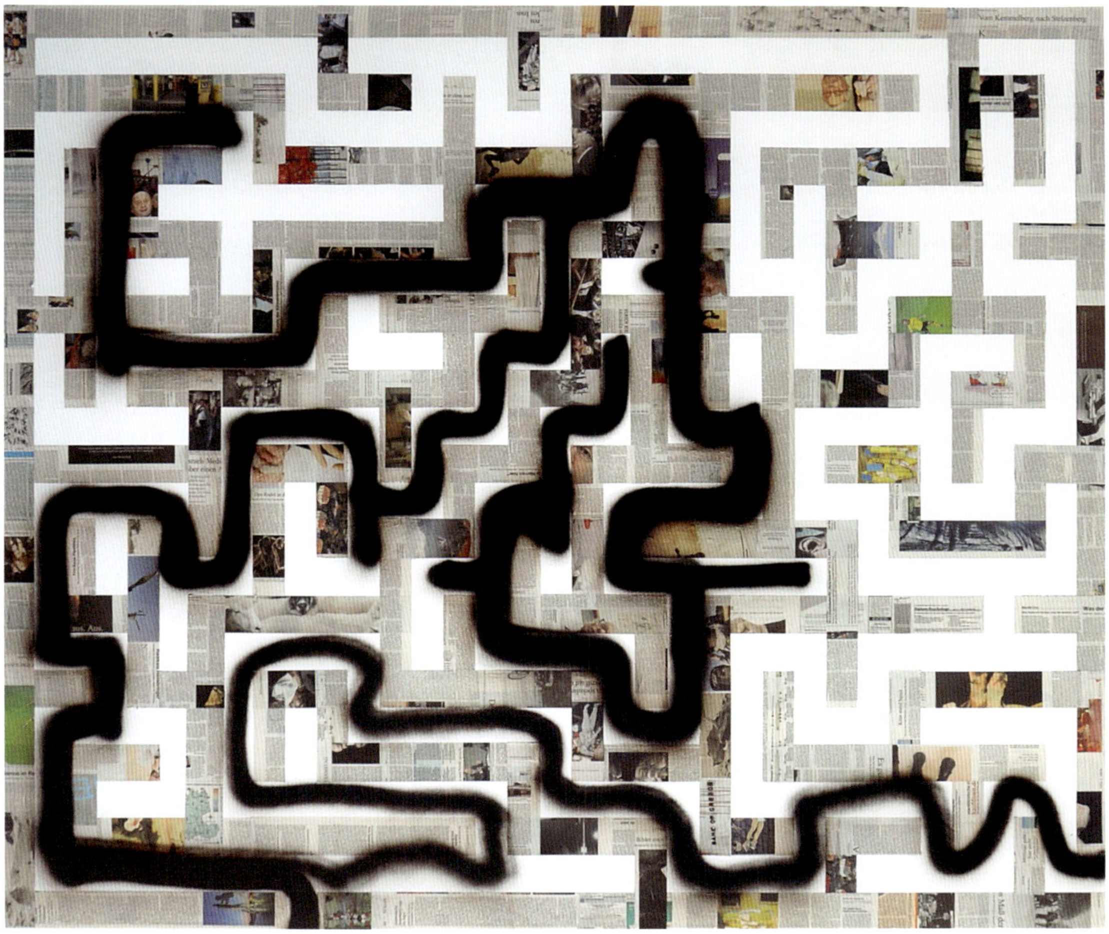

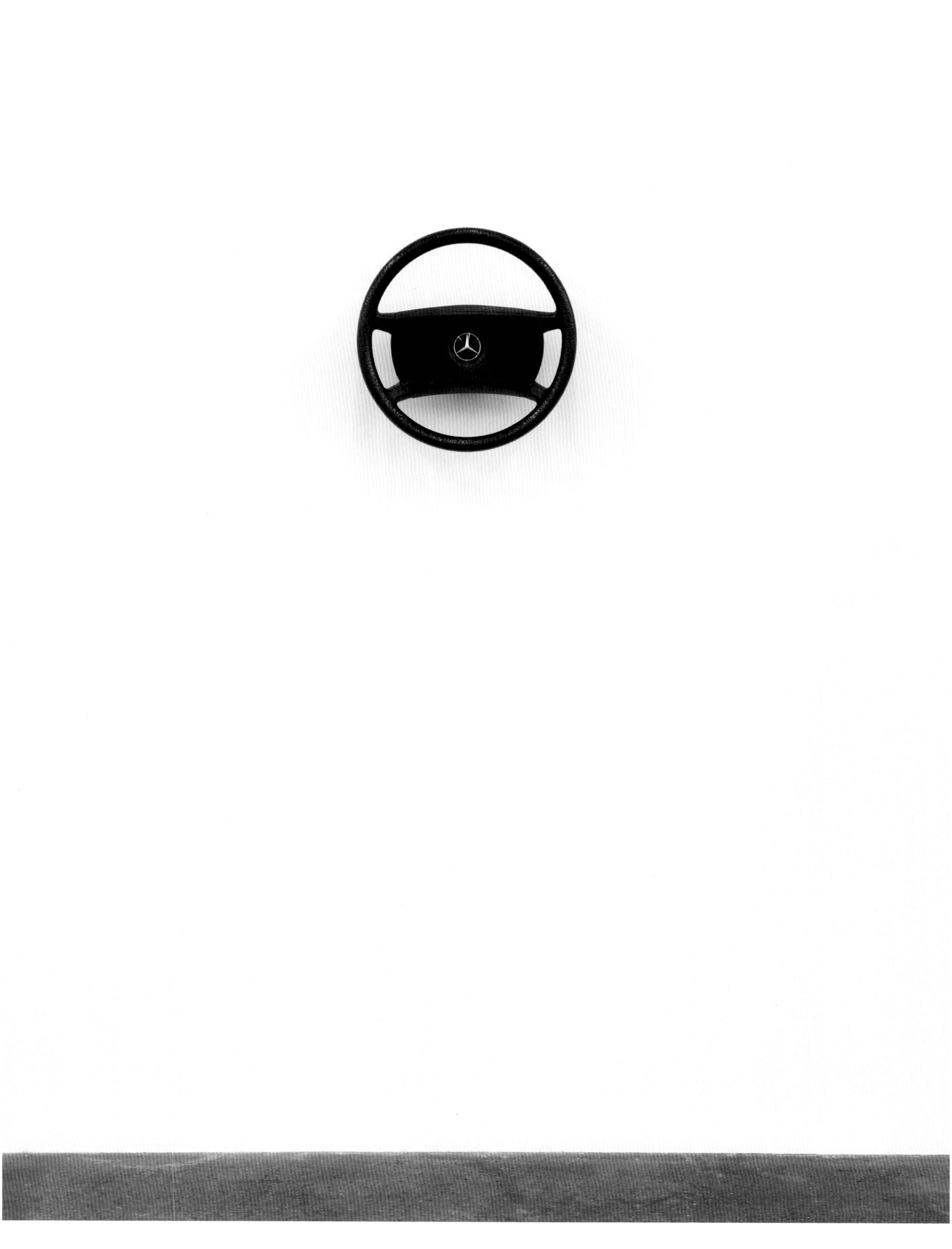

Lenker 3, 2012

Steering wheel, electric motor / Lenkrad, Elektromotor, 40 × 40 × 16,5 cm

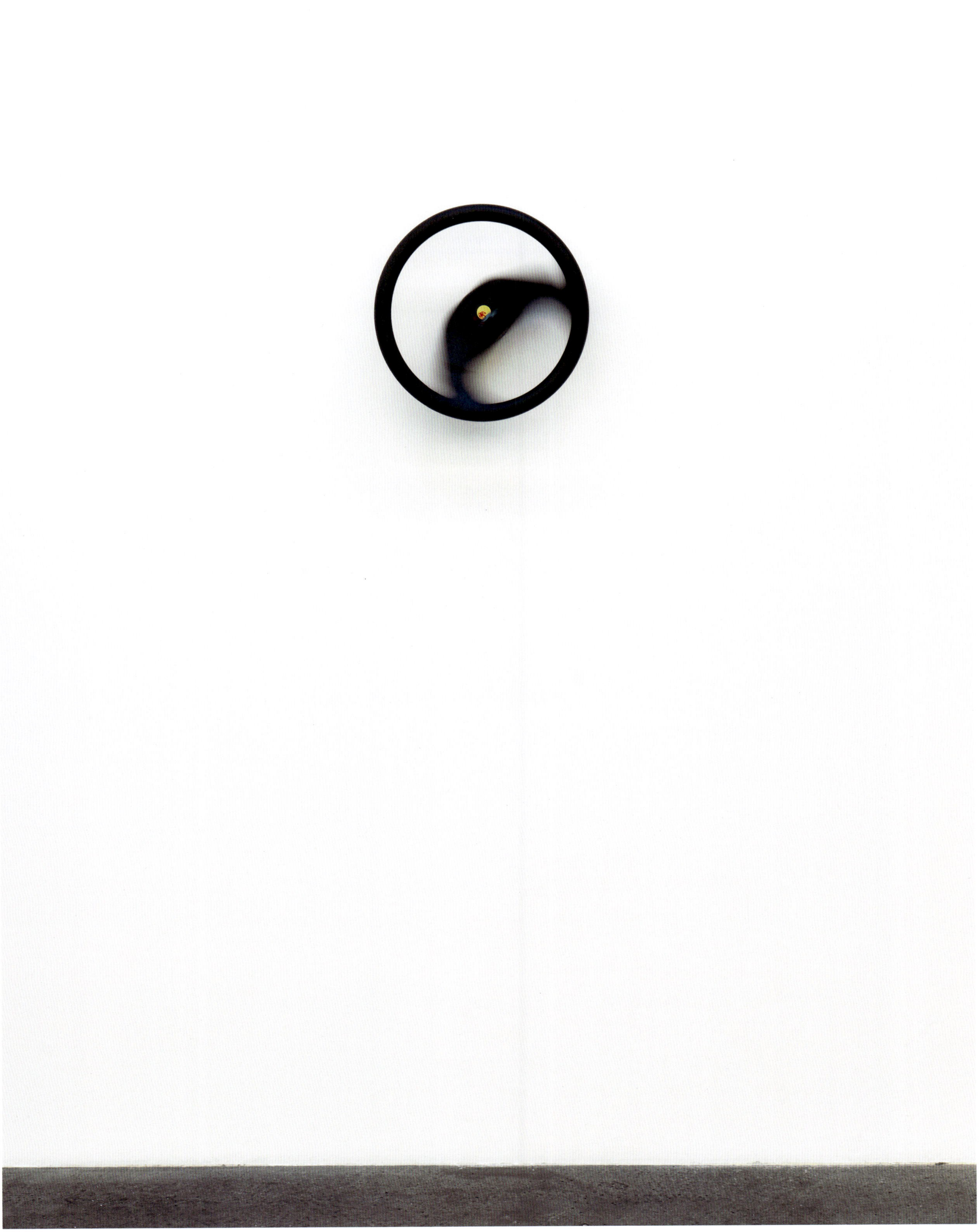

Lenker 1, 2012

Steering wheel, electric motor / Lenkrad, Elektromotor, 36 × 36 × 15 cm

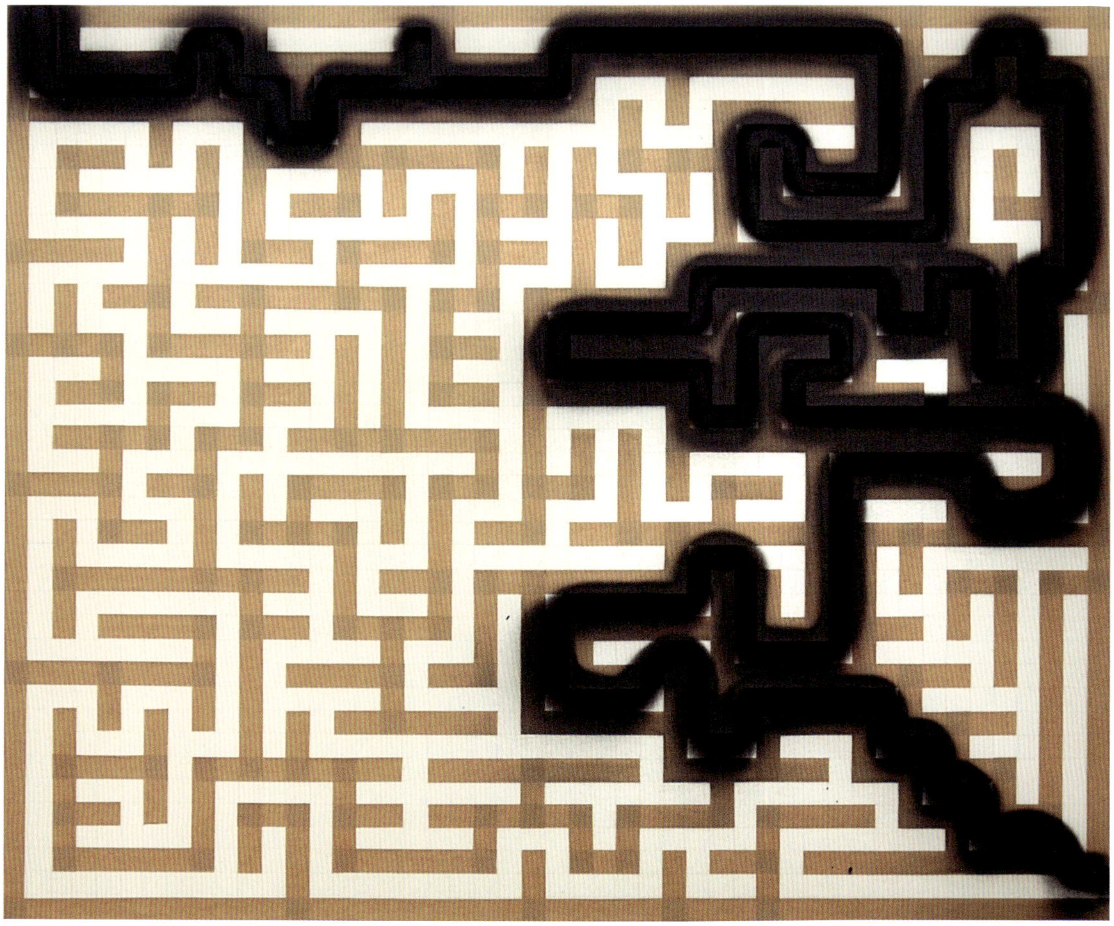

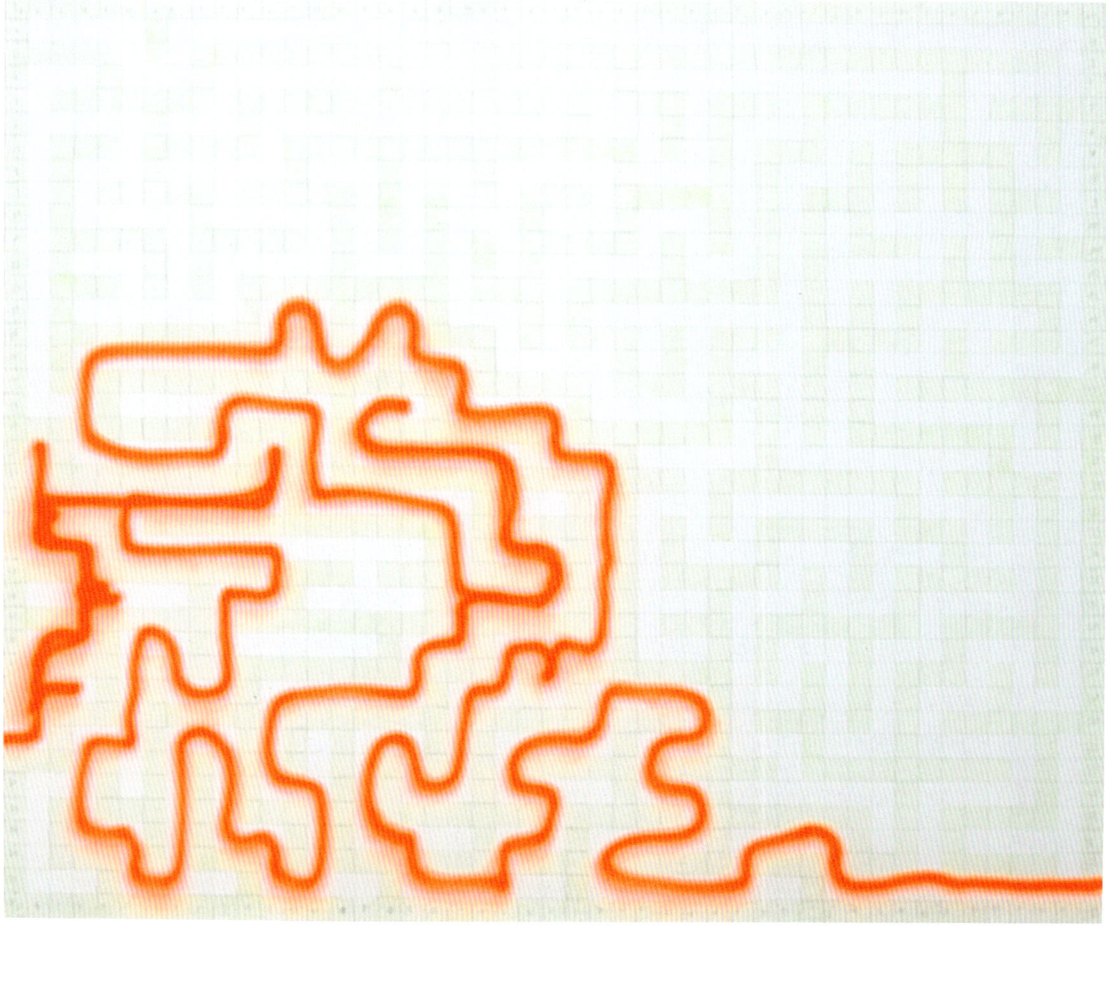

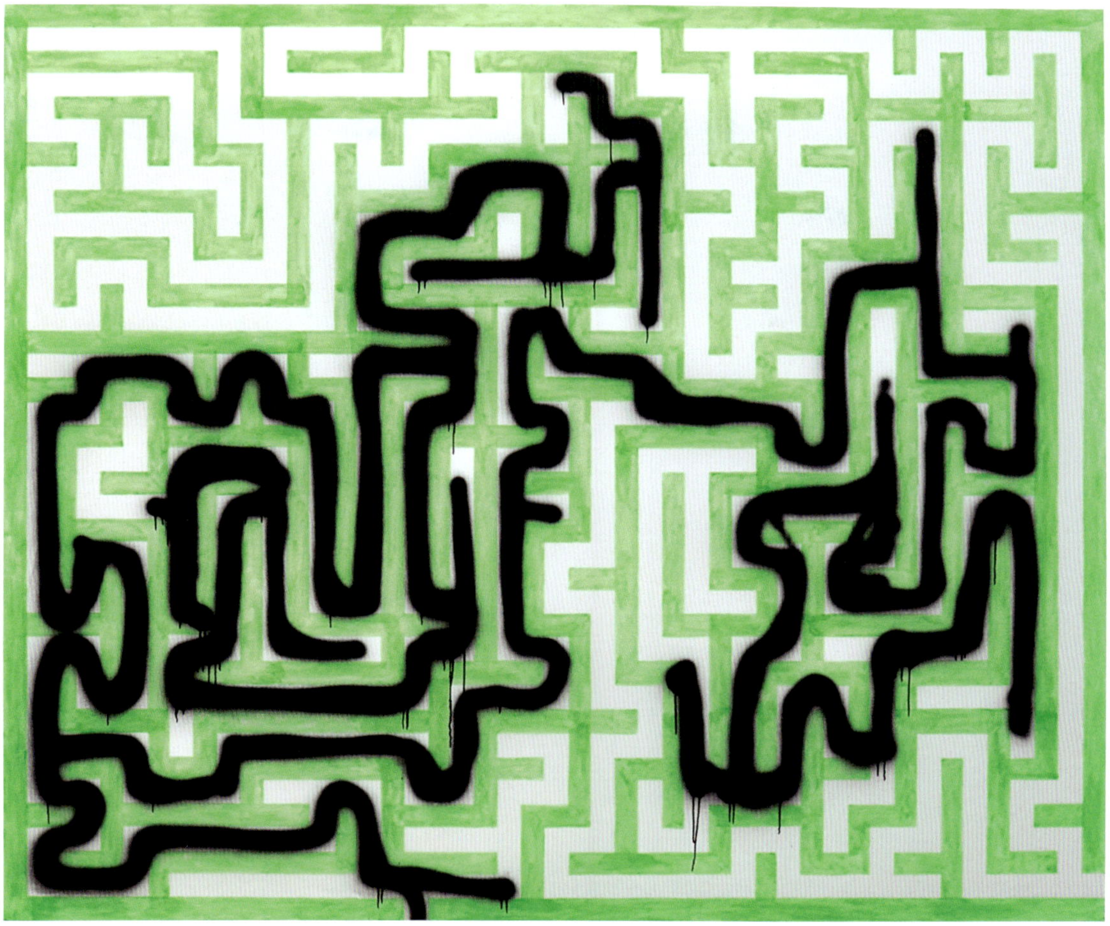

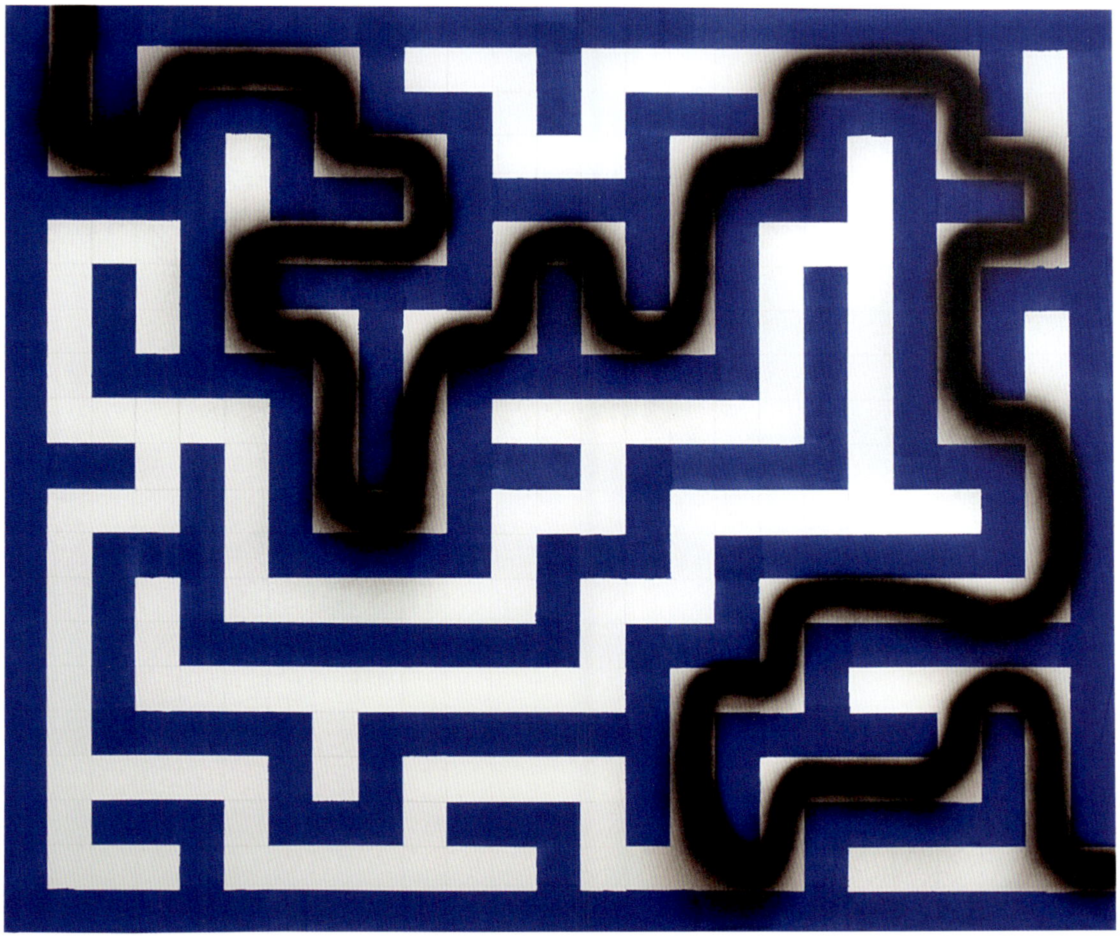

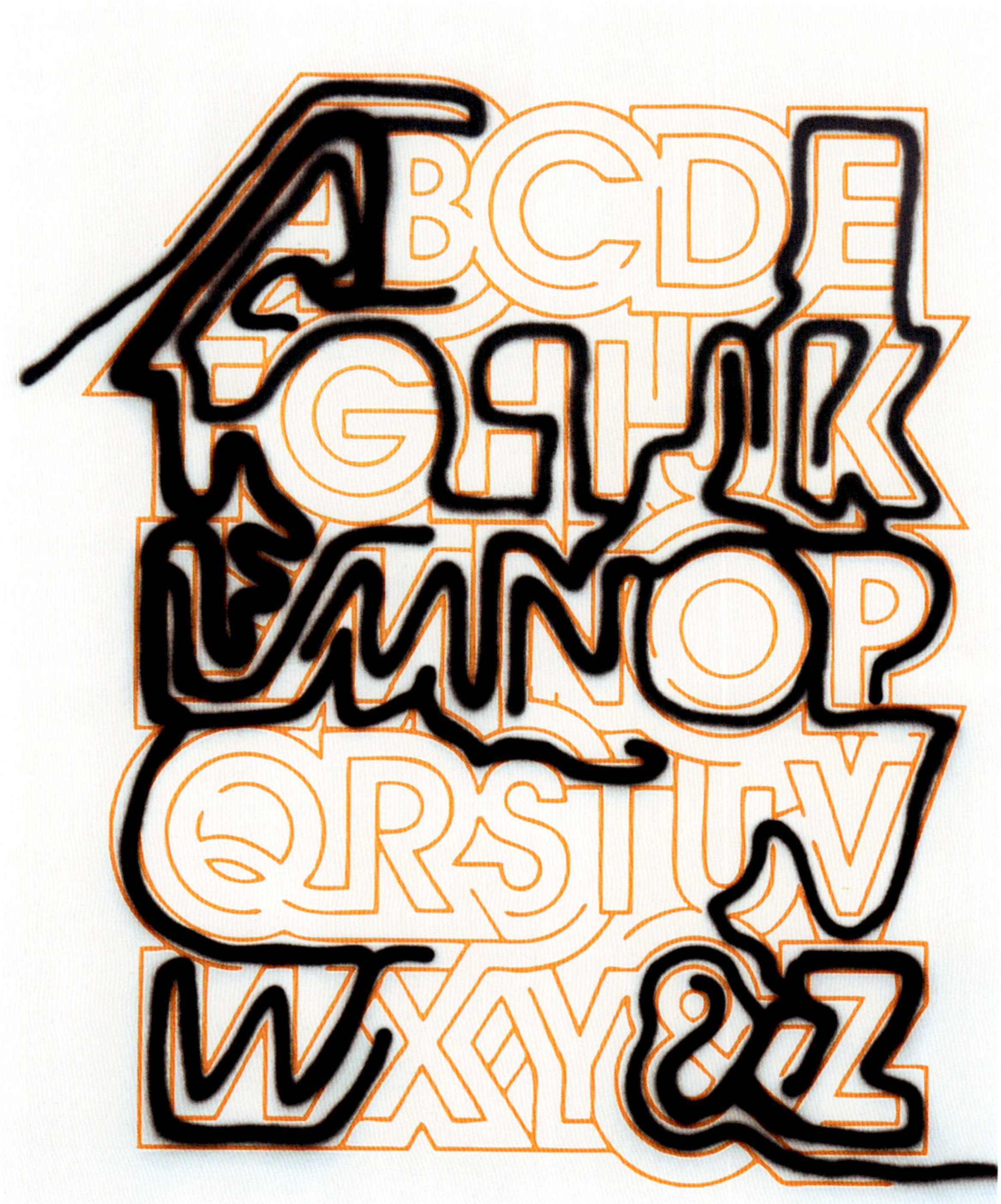

Maze 46, 2012

Screen print and spray paint on canvas / Siebdruck und Sprühfarbe auf Leinwand, 230 × 190 cm

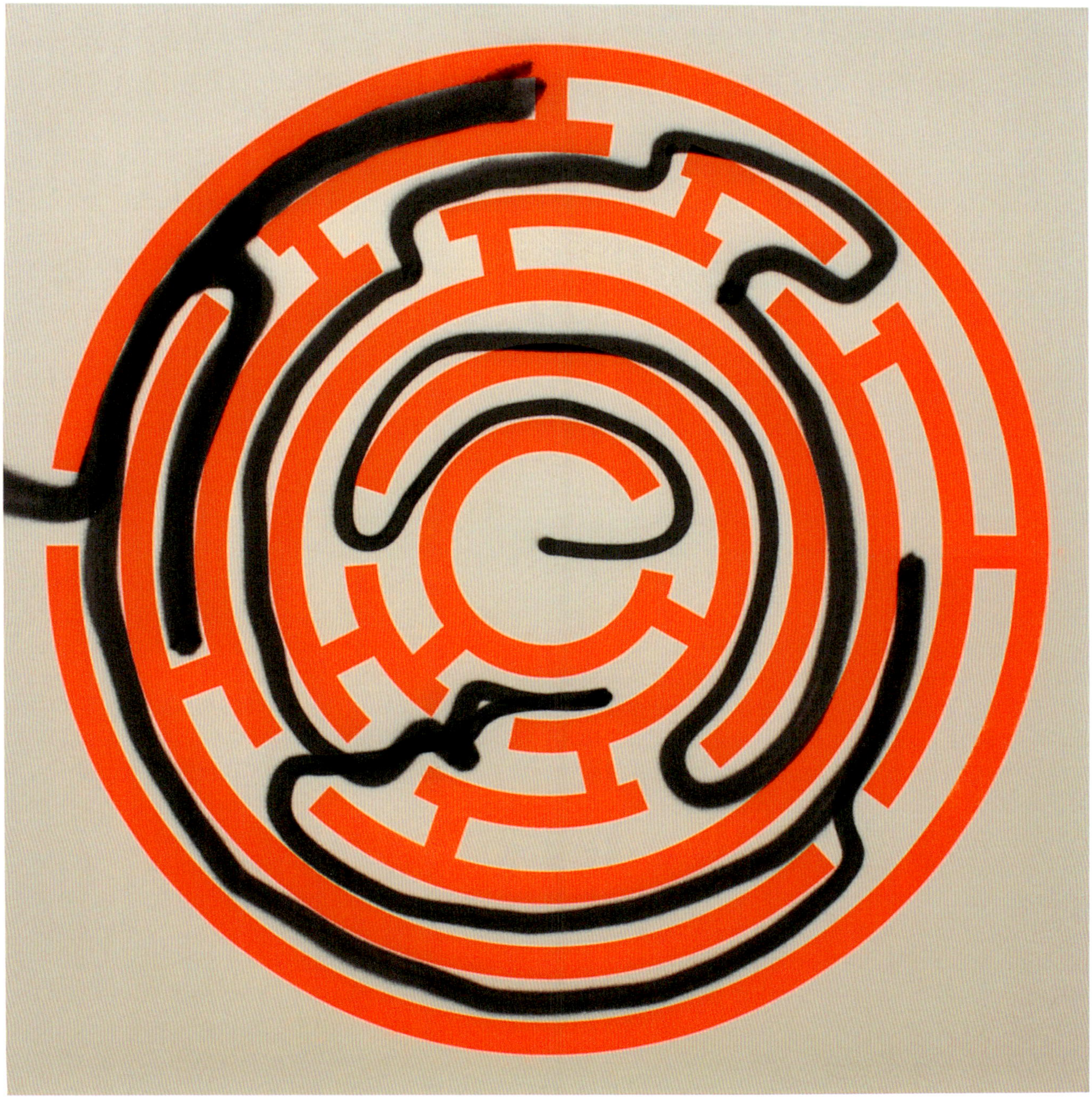

Maze 18, 2011

Screen print and spray paint on canvas / Siebdruck und Sprühfarbe auf Leinwand, 190 × 190 cm

Maria Bremer

MATERIAL IN RELATION

"All the material becomes expressive. It is the affect that is metallic, crystalline, stony."[1]

„Die gesamte Materie wird expressiv: Der Affekt ist metallisch, kristallin, steinern."[1]

Sculptures 2000–2022

For over twenty years now, Michael Sailstorfer has been sounding out elementary questions of sculpture in the ambivalent mode of playful seriousness. In doing so, he deals in particular with the contexts of use and properties of the sculptural material and extends his works into space and time. In terms of art history, his works refer to Marcel Duchamp's concept of the ready-made, to Dadaist purposeless mental games, and to practices of land art, kinetics, and (post-)minimalism. The conceptualism employed speaks an immediate language and engages the viewer without "thoroughly trained intellectuality, background knowledge, or instruction manuals."[2] Likewise, the artist avoids "the mystical level" and relies instead on "subtle exaggeration."[3] The appeal of his works is based on an unexpected handling of generally familiar objects and phenomena from the fields of nature and technology: the forest, the sea, the moon, houses, found objects, vehicles, lamps, car tires.[4] Things that already exist become the source material for sculptural objects that are either processual or leave their production process visible in the result: "The process of producing [...] is the most important part [...], even more important than the finished object. Therefore, in the end, every step must be clearly visible in the work. It must be clear where the material comes from, just as all traces of the sculpture's production must be visible."[5] Sailstorfer also regularly creates experimental arrangements that set unforeseen sequences of creative effects in motion. A geometric

MATERIAL IN BEZIEHUNG
Skulpturen 2000–2022

Seit über zwanzig Jahren lotet Michael Sailstorfer im ambivalenten Modus spielerischer Ernsthaftigkeit elementare Fragen der Skulptur aus. Dabei setzt er sich insbesondere mit den Nutzungszusammenhängen und Eigenschaften des bildhauerischen Materials auseinander und dehnt seine Werke in Raum und Zeit aus. Kunsthistorisch beziehen sich seine Arbeiten auf Duchamps Readymade-Konzept, auf dadaistische zweckfreie Gedankenspiele sowie auf Praktiken der Land-Art, Kinetik und des (Post-)Minimalismus. Der in Anschlag gebrachte Konzeptualismus spricht eine unmittelbare Sprache und bindet die Betrachter*in ohne „durchtrainierte Intellektualität, Hintergrundwissen oder Gebrauchsanweisungen"[2] ein. Ebenso umgeht der Künstler „die mystische Ebene" und setzt vielmehr auf „hintersinnige Übertreibung"[3]. Der Reiz seiner Werke beruht auf einem unerwarteten Umgang mit allgemein vertrauten Gegenständen und Phänomenen aus den Bereichen der Natur und der Technik: dem Wald, dem Meer, dem Mond, Häusern, Fundstücken, Fahrzeugen, Leuchten, Autoreifen.[4] Vorhandenes wird zum Ausgangsmaterial für skulpturale Objekte, die entweder prozessual angelegt sind oder ihren Produktionsprozess im Ergebnis sichtbar belassen: „Der Prozess der Herstellung (...) ist der wichtigste Teil (...), sogar noch wichtiger als das fertige Objekt. Deshalb muss letztlich jeder Schritt in dem Werk klar zu erkennen sein. Es muss klar sein, wo das Material herkommt, genauso wie alle Spuren der Herstellung der Skulptur."[5] Darüber hinaus schafft Sailstorfer regelmäßig Versuchsanordnungen, die

clearing in the forest [*Waldputz* (Cleaning the Forest), 2000 ↗298/299]; a car tire rubbing against the wall of a gallery [*Zeit ist keine Autobahn* (Time Is No Freeway) ↗243–246]; endlessly producing popcorn machines built from concrete mixers that fill the exhibition space with popcorn [*1:43–47* ↗224, 225, 227]; a wooden cabin that is dismantled piece by piece and burned in its own woodstove [*3 Ster mit Ausblick* (3 Cubic Meters of Wood with a View), 2002 ↗219–222]. In such "reformatting of objects and materials,"[6] the works become sites of semantic destabilization: Common meanings and practices of use shift.

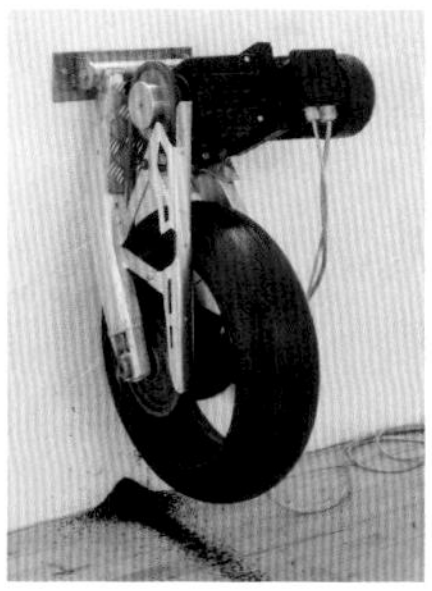

Zeit ist keine Autobahn Straubing, 2008

Thus far, Sailstorfer's works have mostly been discussed as an examination of the boundaries between nature and culture, interior and exterior. Or aspects of transience and slapstick have been highlighted.[7] New works by the artist continue to contribute to this thematic range. At the same time, however, they expand it to include a search movement that more obviously revolves around the relational potential of sculpture. On the one hand, affective resonances, material transformations, and processes of "vivification" are now more in focus, while, on the other hand, language games, symbolic or metaphorical charges, move into the background. In other words, the material itself, including its manifold relationships, is examined artistically. This shift connects Sailstorfer's work with the trend of New Materialisms. In the course of the last decades, an appreciation of the intrinsic logic of matter and artifacts has encompassed various fields of knowledge, adding a material counterpart to the long-standing general interest in discursive processes, cultural practices, or social constructions.[8] Against this background, Sailstorfer's preoccupation with visual connections, as well as with material relations and cycles, gains contemporary conciseness.

STRUCTURES OF THE GAZE

For the work *Kopf und Körper 1* and *2* [Head and Body, 2014], two large, oxidized boiler parts were erected frontally and mounted on shiny iron frames. Round openings gape on the curved circular surfaces of the boiler parts. With custom-made panes of glass, their position evokes eyes and mouths. Through the erection and partial glazing, the dilapidated relics of an industrial laundry take on anthropomorphic features. Correspondingly, the frames supporting the oversized "heads" suggest stylized

unvorhergesehene Abläufe mit gestalterischen Effekten in Gang bringen. Eine geometrische Lichtung im Wald (*Waldputz*, 2000 ↗298/299). Ein Autoreifen, der sich an der Galeriewand abreibt (*Zeit ist keine Autobahn* ↗243–246). Endlos produzierende, aus Betonmischern gebaute Popcornmaschinen, die den Ausstellungsraum mit Popcorn füllen (*1:43–47* ↗224, 225, 227). Eine Holzhütte, die Stück für Stück abgebaut und in ihrem eigenen Holzofen verbrannt wird (*3 Ster mit Ausblick*, 2002 ↗219–222). Bei diesen „Umformatierungen von Objekten und Materialien"[6] werden die Werke zu Schauplätzen semantischer Destabilisierung: Es verschieben sich gängige Bedeutungen und Nutzungspraktiken. Bisher wurden Sailstorfers Arbeiten zumeist als Auseinandersetzung mit den Grenzen zwischen Natur und Kultur, innen und außen besprochen. Oder es wurden Aspekte der Vergänglichkeit und des Slapsticks hervorgehoben.[7] Neue Werke des Künstlers tragen zwar weiterhin zu dieser thematischen Bandbreite bei. Sie erweitern sie jedoch zugleich um eine Suchbewegung, die offensichtlicher um das relationale Potenzial der Skulptur kreist. Affektive Resonanzen, Materialtransformationen und Prozesse der „Verlebendigung" stehen nun stärker im Fokus. Sprachspiele, symbolische oder metaphorische Aufladungen rücken hingegen in den Hintergrund. Anders gewendet wird das Material selbst einschließlich seiner vielfältigen Beziehungen künstlerisch untersucht. Diese Verschiebung verbindet Sailstorfers Arbeiten mit der Tendenz der Neuen Materialismen. Im Laufe der letzten Jahrzehnte hat eine Aufwertung der Eigenlogik der Materie und Artefakte verschiedene Wissensbereiche erfasst und das langjährige allgemeine Interesse für diskursive Prozesse, kulturelle Praktiken oder soziale Konstruktionen um einen materiellen Gegenpol ergänzt.[8] Sailstorfers Beschäftigung mit Blickbeziehungen, Materialverhältnissen und -kreisläufen gewinnt vor diesem Hintergrund an zeitgenössischer Prägnanz.

BLICKGEFÜGE

Für die Arbeit *Kopf und Körper 1* und *2*, 2014, wurden zwei imposante oxidierte Kesselteile frontal aufgerichtet und auf glänzende Eisengestelle montiert. Auf den gewölbten kreisförmigen Flächen der Kesselteile klaffen runde Öffnungen auf. Passgenau verglast, evozieren sie durch ihre Position Augen und Münder. Durch die Aufrichtung und die teilweise Verglasung nehmen die verwahrlosten Relikte einer Großwäscherei anthropomorphe Züge an. Entsprechend lassen die Gestelle, die die überdimensionierten „Köpfe" stützen, an stilisierte Körper oder Füße denken. Als Masken oder als Alien-Darstellungen ziehen sie die Betrachter*innen in ihren Bann.[9] Diese Einschreibung quasi subjekthafter Eigenschaften in skulpturale Objekte erprobt Sailstorfer seitdem auf kleinerem Maßstab weiter. Die daraus entstandene Werkreihe richtet eine unmittelbare Ansprache an die Betrachter*in. Insgesamt

bodies or feet. As masks or as representations of aliens, they captivate the viewer.[9] Sailstorfer has since continued to test this inscription of quasi-subjective qualities into sculptural objects on a smaller scale. The resulting series of works addresses the viewer directly. In general, it suggests masks or façades. Instead of incorporating already existing objects, the sculptures are formed, cast, or designed from various materials: ceramic, concrete, aluminum, bronze. Despite obvious material differences, they appear relatively uniform when hung on the wall or installed in a space. By hanging them or placing them on a pedestal, usually at eye level, the effect of a presence is achieved that speaks directly to the viewer. Markings, perforations, and openings on the sculptural surfaces suggest eyes and mouths that are pressed shut or locked in profile or frontal view. They trigger a disparate dynamic of an exchange of glances.

The ability of this group of works to have such an appeal to the viewer lies first of all in its reference. Masks serve to enter into interaction. Because they are meant to be experienced like faces, we react directly to their optical specifications. They signal something, but at the same time withdraw what lies behind them from perception. Masks have been used in various contexts since prehistory. As artifacts that conceal the face, they are essential in social practices of disguise, protection, and ritual. The transformative act of putting on a mask is accompanied by cultural and social concerns that also play a role in the proliferation of the mask motif in the visual arts. Beyond the design aspect, the artistic use of the mask can stand in for the politically occupied themes of cultural appropriation, gender transformation, or protest.[10]

Rather than explicitly laying claim to a symbolic or political reflection, the reference to the mask motif in Sailstorfer's oeuvre pursues an objective that instead locates itself on the concrete level of mediality and materiality. The series of works immediately signalizes its constructedness. It invites the viewer to retrace the material processes underlying the various objects. Drawn in by the anthropomorphic or zoomorphic features, one discovers at second glance that the bronze and aluminum sculptures "store" the ephemeral materiality of the cardboard models from which they were cast. Those places where the cardboard has been dented, torn, or glued together inscribe themselves in the cast along with the corrugated structure and the traces of adhesive tape. With this surface design, not only is the production method made transparent; at the same time, as an artifact, the object is tied back to the sense of touch, and the priority of the visual aspect is interrupted.

In addition, the processing is occasionally continued in refining finishes of gold leaf, or a *trompe l'oeil* painting layer deceptively reproduces the initial cardboard

lässt sie Masken oder Fassaden assoziieren. Anstatt bereits vorhandene Objekte einzubinden, sind die Skulpturen aus unterschiedlichen Materialien geformt, gegossen oder gestaltet: Keramik, Beton, Aluminium, Bronze. Trotz offensichtlicher materieller Unterschiede treten sie, an die Wand gehängt oder raumgreifend installiert, formal relativ einheitlich in Erscheinung. Durch ihre Hängung oder Aufsockelung, meist auf Augenhöhe, wird der Effekt einer Präsenz erzielt, die die Betrachter*innen unmittelbar anspricht. Markierungen, Durchbrüche und Öffnungen auf den skulpturalen Oberflächen lassen an zugepresste oder aufgesperrte Augen und Münder in Profil- oder Frontalansicht denken. Sie lösen eine ungleiche Dynamik des Blickaustauschs aus.

Das Affizierungsvermögen dieser Werkgruppe liegt zunächst in ihrer Referenz begründet. Masken dienen dazu, in Interaktion zu treten. Weil sie wie Gesichter erlebt werden sollen, reagieren wir unmittelbar auf ihre optischen Vorgaben. Sie signalisieren etwas, entziehen das Dahinterliegende jedoch zugleich der Wahrnehmung. Seit der Urgeschichte kommen Masken in verschiedenen Kontexten zum Einsatz. Als Artefakte, die das Gesicht verdecken, sind sie in sozialen Praktiken der Verkleidung, des Schutzes und des Rituals unerlässlich. Mit dem transformativen Akt des Maskenaufsetzens gehen kulturelle und gesellschaftliche Anliegen einher, die auch bei der Verbreitung des Maskenmotivs in der bildenden Kunst eine Rolle spielen. Über den gestalterischen Aspekt hinaus kann die künstlerische Verwendung der Maske für die politisch besetzten Themen der kulturellen Aneignung, der Geschlechtsverwandlung oder des Protests einstehen.[10]

Anstatt ausdrücklich eine symbolische oder politische Reflexion zu beanspruchen, verfolgt die Referenz auf das Maskenmotiv in Sailstorfers Werk eine Zielsetzung, die sich vielmehr auf der konkreten Ebene der Medialität und Materialität verortet. Unmittelbar signalisiert die Werkreihe ihre Gestaltetheit. Sie lädt zum Nachvollzug der materiellen Prozesse ein, die den verschiedenen Objekten zugrunde liegen. Von den anthropomorphen oder zoomorphen Merkmalen angesprochen entdeckt man auf einen zweiten Blick, dass die Plastiken aus Bronze und Aluminium die ephemere Materialität der Pappmodelle, von denen sie abgegossen wurden, „speichern". Diejenigen Stellen, an denen die Pappe eingedrückt, aufgerissen oder zusammengeklebt wurde, schreiben sich zusammen mit der Wellenstruktur und den Klebstreifenbahnen in den Abguss ein. Mit dieser Oberflächengestaltung ist nicht nur die Produktionsweise transparent gemacht, zugleich wird das Objekt als Artefakt an den Tastsinn rückgebunden und die Priorität des Visuellen durchbrochen.

Zudem setzt sich die Verarbeitung teils in veredelnden Beschichtungen aus Blattgold fort oder eine Trompe-l'Œil-Malschicht reproduziert täuschend echt das Ausgangsmodell aus Pappe, in bestimmten Fällen sogar einschließlich

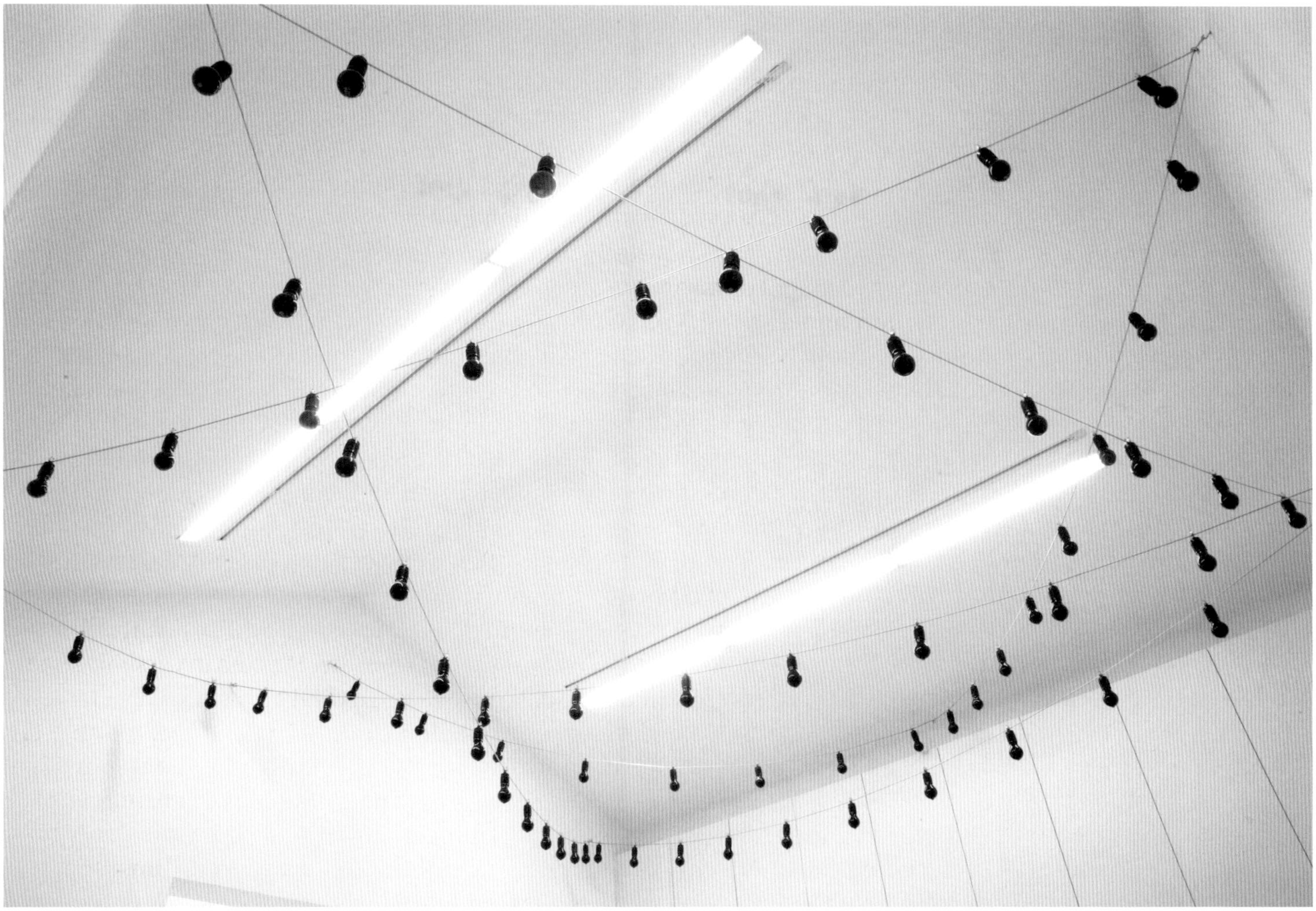

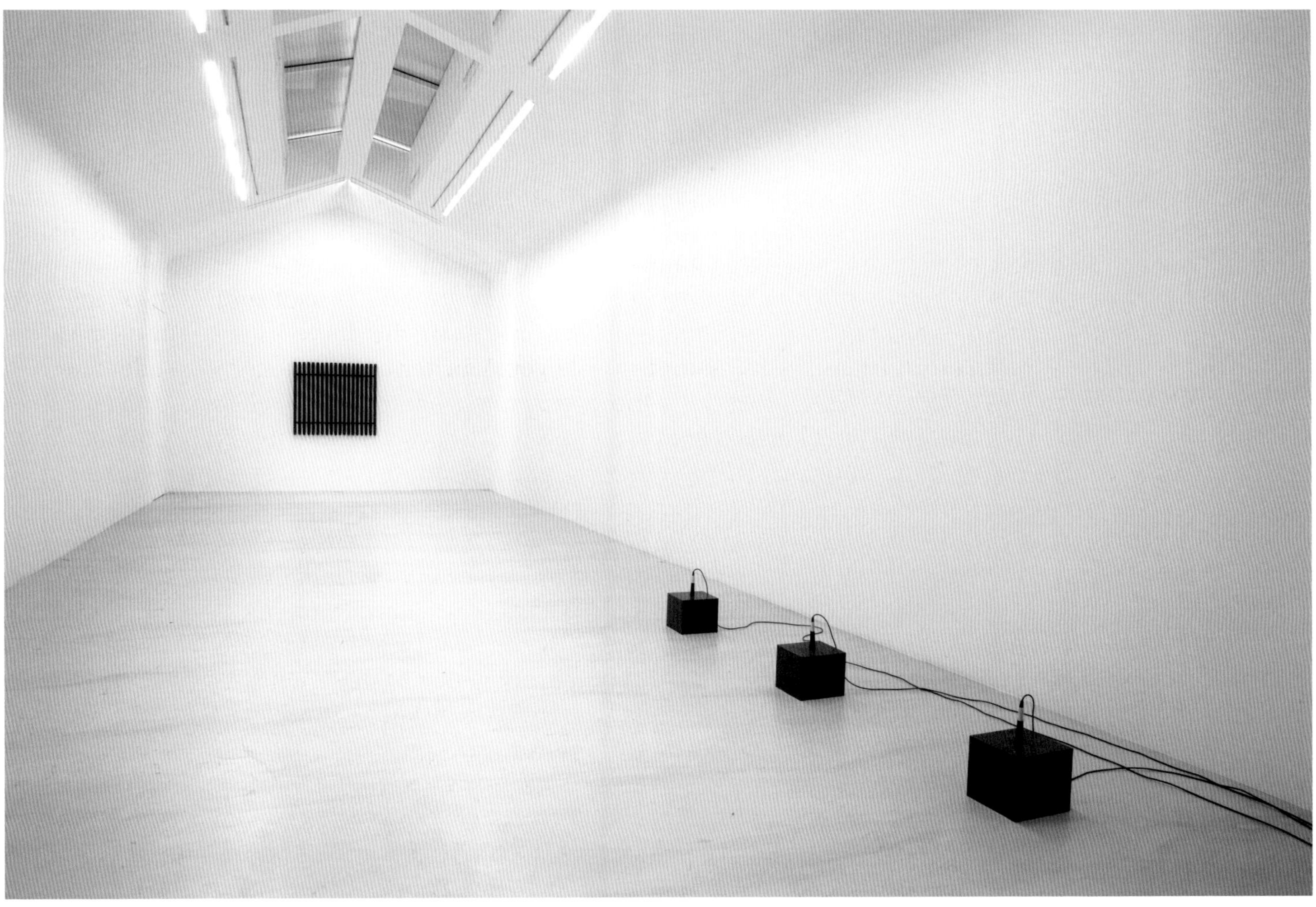

Installation view / Installationsansicht *No light*, 2009, Perrotin, Paris

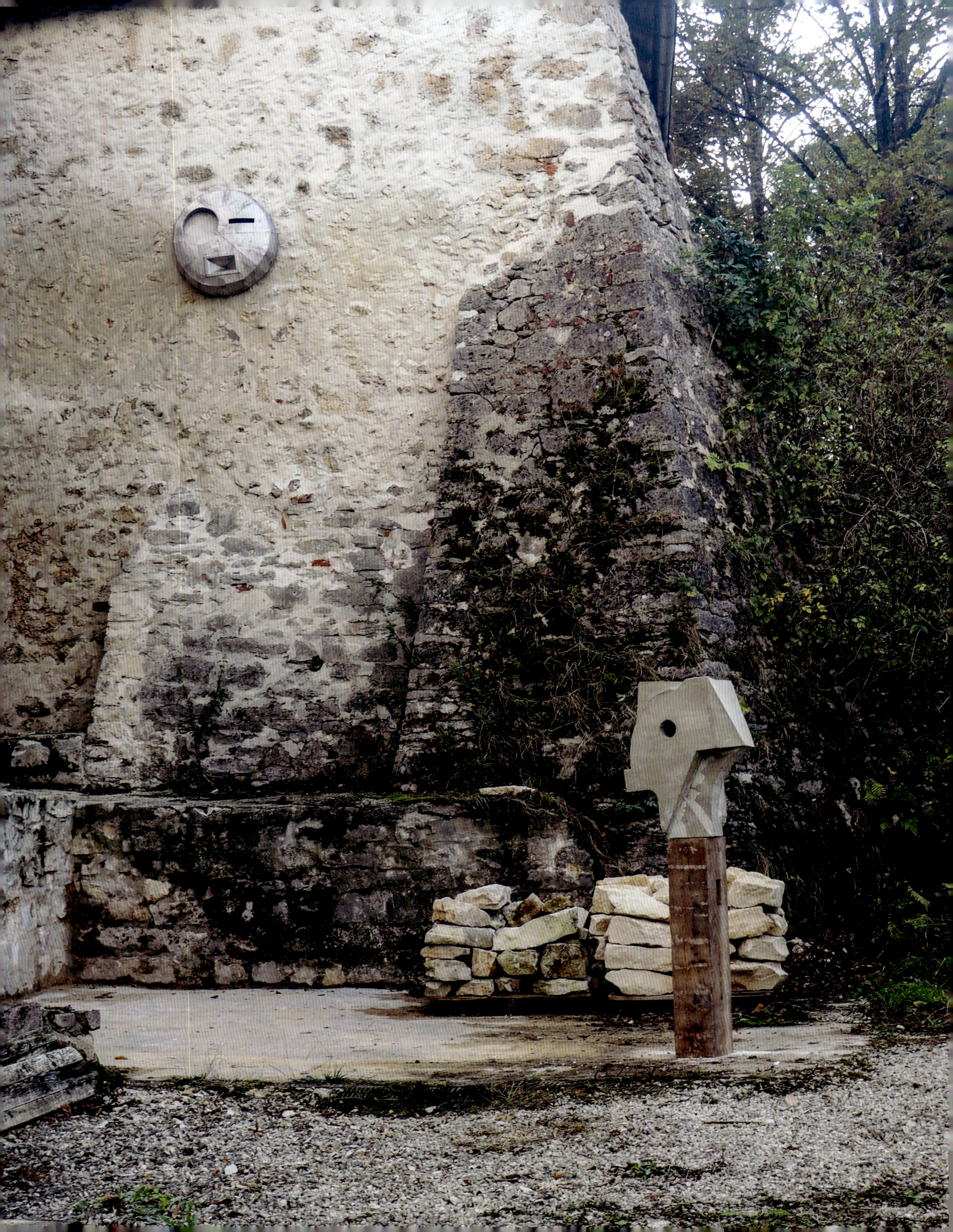

model, in certain cases even including colorful shipping labels and barcodes [*M. 80*, 2021]. In contrast, the ceramic masks and sculptures, which were first formed by hand and then fired, have uneven or speckled glazes that gleam in different colors and textures. The material layering processes thus become a sculptural theme. The manner of use of the subject depicted—as transformative masquerade or disguise—is taken up by incorporating it into the production process.

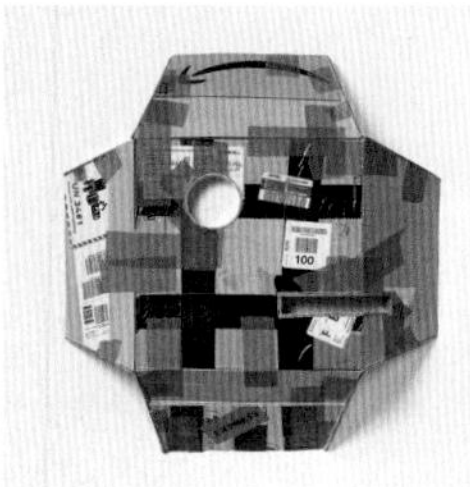

M. 80, 2021

In contrast to the objects reminiscent of masks, the concrete castings reinforced with iron fittings from the *Kopf und Körper Braunschweig* series are left raw and crumbly. The formal design here is multidimensional and thus more complex. The material used shifts the subject away from a sculptural study of a head to an architectural ruin. In buildings, as with masks, organic correspondences between body and architecture can often be discerned. Not only because architecture finds its beginnings in animal skins, that is to say, in hides or protective covers—which further solidified in relation to the vulnerability of human life. Anthropomorphic associations are also composed into the ground plan of buildings, or they serve to structure façades.[11] Modes of action and reaction are thus predetermined via a certain physiognomy of the buildings. Sailstorfer's concrete studies tie in with these archaic and essential connotations of architecture.

In contrast, the three-dimensional ceramic sculptures, which are staged on lower pedestals like architectural models, convey conceptions of isolation. The black and white *Altenheim für Kosmonauten* [Retirement Home for Cosmonauts ↗166 and its counterpart, the *Altenheim für Astronauten* [Retirement Home for Astronauts] ↗165, both from 2017, are reminiscent of space suit helmets and at the same time also of makeshift shelters. These and other similar sculptures, which vaguely reference building typologies such as palaces or factories, are closed. The surface design is forbidding, the view into the interior blocked.

Because the scale of this series of works remains manageable throughout, one gains the overall impression of an experimental design. As if the transfer of human or animal characteristics to artifacts is being tested in a model-like manner through an idiosyncratic vocabulary of forms. We immediately imagine expressions, moods, or even a lack of expression in the motionless objects.

bunter Versandaufkleber und Barcodes (*M. 80*, 2021). Die erst handgeformten und anschließend gebrannten Keramikmasken und -skulpturen weisen hingegen Glasuren auf. Ungleichmäßig verlaufen oder gesprenkelt leuchten sie in verschiedenen Farben und Texturen. Damit werden die materiellen Schichtungsprozesse zum skulpturalen Thema. Die Verwendungsweise des dargestellten Sujets – als transformierende Verkleidung oder Tarnung – wird aufgegriffen, indem sie in den Produktionsprozess miteinfließt.

Im Gegensatz zu den Objekten, die an Masken erinnern, sind die mit Eisenarmaturen verstärkten Betongüsse *Kopf und Körper Braunschweig I* und *II* hingegen roh und bröckelig belassen. Die formale Ausgestaltung ist hier mehrdimensional und damit komplexer. Das verwendete Material rückt das Sujet weg von einer skulpturalen Kopfstudie hin zu einer architektonischen Ruine. Wie bei Masken lassen sich auch bei Bauwerken oftmals organische Übereinstimmungen zwischen Körper und Architektur ausmachen. Nicht nur, weil die Architektur ihre Anfänge in Tierfellen, also in Häuten oder Schutzhüllen – die sich in Relation zur Ausgesetztheit des Menschen weiter verfestigten – findet. Zudem werden anthropomorphe Assoziationen in den Grundriss von Bauwerken hineinkomponiert, oder sie dienen der Gliederung von Fassaden.[11] Über eine bestimmte Physiognomie der Bauwerke werden also Wirkungs- und Reaktionsweisen vorgegeben. An diese archaischen und wesenhaften Konnotationen der Architektur knüpfen Sailstorfers Betonstudien an.

Die dreidimensionalen Keramikskulpturen, die auf tiefer liegenden Sockeln wie Architekturmodelle inszeniert werden, transportieren hingegen Vorstellungen der Abschottung. Das *Altenheim für Kosmonauten*, 2017 ↗166, und sein Gegenpart, das *Altenheim für Astronauten*, 2017 ↗165, erinnern in dunkel und hell an Helme von Raumanzügen und zugleich auch an behelfsmäßige Unterkünfte. Diese und weitere ähnliche Skulpturen, die vage auf Gebäudetypologien wie Paläste oder Fabriken referieren, sind geschlossen gehandhabt. Die Oberflächengestaltung ist abweisend, der Einblick in den Innenraum versperrt.

Weil der Maßstab dieser Werkreihe durchgehend überschaubar bleibt, gewinnt man insgesamt den Eindruck eines gestalterischen Versuchsaufbaus. Als werde die Übertragung menschlicher oder tierischer Merkmale auf Artefakte modellhaft durch ein eigenwilliges Formvokabular erprobt. In einem Augenblinzeln meinen wir bei den unbewegten Objekten Expressionen, Stimmungen oder Ausdrucksleere zu erfassen. Die Skulpturen scheinen unseren Blick zu erwidern oder sich diesem zu verweigern. Unwillkürlich assoziieren wir damit Spuren zurückgezogenen Lebens. Erzielt wird dieser Effekt jedoch gerade nicht, indem die Künstlichkeit der Objekte unterschlagen wird. Im Gegenteil: Materialbeschaffenheit und -verwandlung werden zum

Installation view / Installationsansicht *Freundschaft*, 2015, Galerie Zink, Waldkirchen

The sculptures seem to return our gaze or to refuse it. Involuntarily, we associate them with traces of a withdrawn life. However, this effect is not achieved by concealing the artificiality of the objects. On the contrary, the characteristics and transformation of the material used become a design principle. Thus, when viewing the artifacts, we experience the animistic address, as it were, as all the more paradoxical. In addition to a presence *for* a subject, the works themselves unfold a quasi-subjective presence.

MATERIAL RELATIONSHIPS

The provocative question as to how powerful the material, with which artistic work is done, is to be understood continues in further works. Interesting in this context is the *Heavy Eyes* series ↗168–179, 182–185, which transfers the medium of sculpture to the surface and performs material interactions in the pictorial format, so to speak. Commercially available sheets of lead are attached to stretcher frames and form the substrate for further design processes. Eye shadows in various combinations and hues are applied to the leaden surface. The texture of the surface—grooves, scratches, traces of wear, discoloration, or imprints of stickers—provides design guidelines for overpainting. The aleatory aspect of this extraction of figures or compositions makes one think of abstract forms that are created when lead is poured over a flame and used for divination. Since ancient times, the heavy metal has been used in the manufacture of weapons, water pipes, and vessels. While its effects are harmful to health, lead is also used to protect against dangers such as aggressive acids or radioactive rays. To this day, it is used for lucky charms as well as for protection against X-rays. As a white pigment (white lead), it was also added to makeup until the eighteenth century, despite its side effects on health.[12]

In Sailstorfer's series of works, figure and substrate appear both toxic and seductive. The disproportionately applied eyeshadow shimmers strikingly synthetically on the leaden pictorial ground. The *Heavy Eyes* thus also evoke themes of danger, protection, and camouflage. However, the eyelids alluded to in the title are abstracted to the rectangular image format and, as it were, closed under the pressure of leaden fatigue. With the exception of the overpainting, the artist refrains from any further figurative design measures. Sailstorfer's abstractions thus clearly focus on the properties of the combination of the materials used. Indeed, although they are fixed with a transparent varnish, lead and eyeshadow remain in a process of interaction. While the eyeshadow adheres to the surface, shiny traces of grease settle on the substrate. The lead also flows downward internally: Its molecules are unstable and exposed to the force of gravity. Because they obviously emphasize their own materiality,

Gestaltungsprinzip. So erleben wir bei der Betrachtung der Artefakte die gleichsam animistische Ansprache als umso paradoxer. Neben einer Präsenz *für* ein Subjekt entfalten die Werke selbst eine quasi subjekthafte Präsenz.

MATERIALVERHÄLTNISSE

Die provokative Frage danach, wie wirkmächtig die Materie zu verstehen ist, mit der künstlerisch gearbeitet wird, setzt sich in weiteren Arbeiten fort. Interessant ist in diesem Zusammenhang die *Heavy Eyes*-Reihe ↗168–179, 182–185, die das Medium Skulptur auf die Fläche überträgt und materielle Interaktionen gleichsam im Bildformat aufführt. Handelsübliche Bleiblätter werden auf Keilrahmen aufgespannt und bilden den Untergrund für weitere Gestaltungsverfahren. Lidschatten in verschiedenen Zusammensetzungen und Farbtönen werden auf den bleiernen Grund aufgetragen. Die Textur des Grundes – Rillen, Kratzer, Abnutzungsspuren, Verfärbungen oder Abdrücke von Aufklebern – bietet Gestaltungsvorgaben für die Übermalung. Der aleatorische Aspekt dieser Figuren- bzw. Kompositionsgewinnung lässt an abstrakte Glücksfiguren denken, die beim Bleigießen über der Flamme entstehen und zur Weissagung dienen. Seit der Antike wird das Schwermetall bei der Herstellung von Waffen, Wasserrohren oder Gefäßen verwendet. Seine Effekte sind gesundheitsschädlich, dennoch vermag Blei wiederum vor Gefahren wie aggressiven Säuren oder radioaktiven Strahlen zu schützen. Auch heute findet es für glücksbringende Amulette bis hin zur Röntgen-Schutzkleidung Verwendung. Als Weißpigment (Bleiweiß) wurde es zudem trotz gesundheitlicher Nebeneffekte noch bis ins 18. Jahrhundert der Schminke beigefügt.[12]
In Sailstorfers Werkreihe erscheinen Figur und Grund gleichermaßen giftig und verführerisch. Der überproportioniert aufgetragene Lidschatten schimmert auf den bleiernen Bildgründen auffallend synthetisch. Auch die *Heavy Eyes* evozieren damit Themen der Gefahr, des Schutzes und der Tarnung. Jedoch sind die im Titel angedeuteten Augenlider zum rechteckigen Bildformat abstrahiert und gewissermaßen unter dem Druck bleierner Müdigkeit geschlossen. Bis auf die Übermalung wird von figurativen Gestaltungsmaßnahmen abgesehen. Sailstorfers Abstraktionen legen den Fokus also eindeutig auf die Eigenschaften der eingesetzten Materialkombination. Obwohl sie mit einem durchsichtigen Lack fixiert werden, befinden sich Blei und Lidschatten nämlich weiterhin im Prozess. Während die Farbe an der Oberfläche haftet, setzen sich glänzende Fettspuren auf dem Untergrund ab. Auch das Blei fließt im Inneren abwärts: Seine Moleküle sind instabil und der Anziehungskraft ausgesetzt. Weil sie augenscheinlich ihre Stofflichkeit betonen, unterscheiden sich diese Bilder von vorangehenden künstlerischen Einsätzen des Bleis, etwa zur Veranschaulichung zeitlicher Transformation (bei Richard Serra), alchemistischer Prozesse (bei Anselm

these images differ from previous artistic uses of lead, such as to illustrate temporal transformation (Richard Serra), alchemical processes (Anselm Kiefer), or methods of remembrance (Joseph Beuys).[13] Instead, Sailstorfer's works are more in line with the lead paintings of Günther Förg, which likewise mobilize the material in terms of its organic effect but counteract the original patinations with linear geometric figurations.[14]

Under the title *Heavy Tears* ↗26, 31, a further group of works insists on the affective appeal of make-up. In all the paintings of the series, a large-scale, stylized drop shape stands out from the lead ground. The title of the work reveals it to be a tear. The bright red, pink, or orange tones of the various tear figures, together with their impasto consistency, indicate the use of lipstick. The materiality of the make-up usually achieves its effect in dynamics of desire. Here, lipstick is used to claim a correspondingly sensual reception experience. Through the expropriation of the haptically protruding teardrop figure, the image intervenes in the space of contemplation.

In other work contexts as well, the tear—stylized as a figure of fluidity, of flowing, dissolving, disintegrating, of permeability and material transformation—plays a central role. Because it transcends bodily boundaries from the inside to the outside, the tear symbolizes the medial and formal breakthroughs on which the artistic works are based in each case.[15] Notable in this regard are the *Tränentrockner* (Tear Dryer) ↗17, 32 created between 2019 and 2022. Reminiscent of Duchamp's emblematic readymade prototype, Sailstorfer resorts to bottle drying racks in various wall and free-standing formats. Opaque glass sculptures in the form of teardrops are placed over the steel pins. The green or brown tones of the sculptures refer to their previous life as beer bottles. The artist had the recycled glass blown within a closed material cycle and hand-formed into a teardrop shape that would be unsuitable as a bottle. The focus is thus on the transformation of form to which the amorphous solid glass is subjected. The ability of the glass to melt and thereby further change its respective shape defines a virtual field of action, which the drops take up iconically. In contrast to the lead paintings, it is not the ongoing process itself that is presented, yet the result attests to the reservoir of possibilities of glass as a material. The individually crafted glass teardrops contrast with the found and unprocessed bottle drying rack.

With other works, the sculpture is produced through a border-crossing, collaborative endeavor. The *Batterie* bouquet from 2019 ↗68/69 consists of suspended, dark bronze castings in the shape and size of light bulbs. The idiosyncratic materiality and surface result from a surprising interconnection of different approaches and their participants. Wax casts of light bulbs were further

Kiefer) oder Erinnerungsverfahren (bei Joseph Beuys).[13] Vielmehr verhält sich Sailstorfer hier zu Günther Förgs Bleibildern, die das Material ebenfalls im Hinblick auf seine organische Wirkung mobilisieren, den ursprünglichen Patinierungen jedoch mit gradlinig geometrischen Figurationen entgegenwirken.[14]

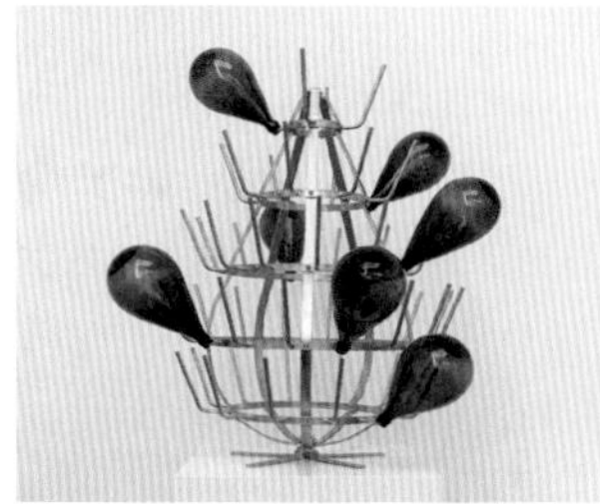

Tränentrockner Tempelhof, 2019

Eine weitere Werkgruppe insistiert unter dem Titel *Heavy Tears* ↗26, 31 auf den affektiven Appell des Make-ups. Vom Bleigrund hebt sich in allen Bildern eine großformatige stilisierte Tropfenform ab. Der Werktitel enttarnt sie als Träne. Die leuchtend roten, pinken bis orangen Töne der verschiedenen Tränenfiguren indizieren zusammen mit ihrer pastosen Konsistenz den Einsatz von Lippenstift. Die Stofflichkeit des Make-ups erzielt gewöhnlich bei Dynamiken des Begehrens ihren Effekt. Hier wird mit dem Lippenstift eine entsprechend sinnliche Rezeptionserfahrung beansprucht. Durch die Entäußerung der haptisch hervortretenden Tränenfigur greift das Bild in den Raum der Betrachtung ein.

Auch in anderen Werkzusammenhängen spielt die Träne – zur Figur der Flüssigkeit, des Fließenden, Zerfließenden, Zergehenden, der Durchlässigkeit und Materialtransformation stilisiert – eine zentrale Rolle. Weil sie Körpergrenzen von innen nach außen überschreitet, versinnbildlicht die Träne die medialen und formalen Durchbrüche, auf denen die künstlerischen Arbeiten jeweils gründen.[15] Bemerkenswert sind in dieser Hinsicht die zwischen 2019 und 2022 entstandenen *Tränentrockner* ↗17, 32. In Erinnerung an Duchamps emblematischen Readymade-Prototyp greift Sailstorfer auf Flaschentrockner in verschiedenen Wand- und Raumformaten zurück. Den Stahlarmen werden blickdurchlässige Glasskulpturen in Tränenform übergestülpt. Die Grün- oder Brauntöne der Skulpturen verweisen auf ihren vorangehenden Lebensabschnitt als Bierflaschen. Der Künstler hat das Altglas innerhalb eines geschlossenen Stoffkreislaufs neu blasen und von Hand in eine Tränenform, die als Flasche untauglich wäre, bringen lassen. Somit liegt die Aufmerksamkeit auf dem Formwandel, dem der amorphe Feststoff Glas unterworfen wird. Das Vermögen des Glases, zu schmelzen und dadurch seine jeweilige Formbestimmung weiter zu verändern, definiert ein virtuelles Handlungsfeld, das die Tropfen ikonisch aufgreifen. Anders als zuvor bei den Bleibildern ist nicht der laufende Prozess selbst präsentiert, dennoch belegt das Ergebnis den Möglichkeitsvorrat des Materials Glas. Die einzel gefertigten Glastränen stehen in Spannung zu dem vorgefundenen und unbearbeitet präsentierten Flaschentrockner.

processed by honeybees in custom-made hives until the industrial appearance of the casts was overgrown by island-shaped honeycombs. The wax sculptures were then cast in bronze and sandblasted. They thus continuously oscillate between technical and animal production.

CYCLES

In addition to those works that make affective appeals to the viewer or present material interactions, Sailstorfer designs more complex sculptural constellations. In these, a "lively" exchange occurs in real time. It is less about the single sculpture, but rather about a relational structure that encompasses a plurality of agents and objects. In art historical terms, this expanded concept of sculpture is based on system-oriented approaches of the 1960s and '70s. One is reminded, for example, of Hans Haacke's *Franziskanische Serie*, (Franciscan Series, 1965–1972), which placed plants and animals in relation to one another in so-called "real-temporal systems."[16] The move away from the individual object at that time was motivated by the popularization of cybernetics, or the theory of dynamic systems. This approach presupposed an analogy of machine and organism, and examined the ways in which matter, energy, and information bring different elements into a system and control its behavior. With the contemporary turn of sculpture to the "situation"—with Pierre Huyghe, for example—this conceptual tradition gains relevance. The materiality of the artistic work is extended to the environment. Processes are set in motion. The performed relational structures expand in time. In the work of Sailstorfer, however, instead of condensing into scientifically closed systems, such processual and relational experimental set-ups claim a relative openness. Both the possibilities of development and the reality content of the arranged cycle remain in abeyance, as it were. The event generally stands "in a special relation to the fictive."[17] Contingency, loss of control, and dynamics of destruction take the place of scientific goal-orientation. As productive tactics, these aspects produce "a high degree of attention and images."[18] With regard to Sailstorfer's approach, Kristin Schrader has noted that "everything [...] is an event and thus nothing special. Unless the ratio of means is good."[19] In Sailstorfer's artistic "event economies,"[20] this relationship is up for discussion each time anew.

In some cases, individual works are taken up and embedded in intersubjective structures. The artist thus placed tear sculptures several times in a natural environment. The drops are first sculpturally extracted from rock salt. Because of their gray-white iridescent grains, they appear to be made of marble or granite. The sedimentary rock is, however, a fossil, formed over thousands of years from concentrated seawater. Thus, when the salt crystals

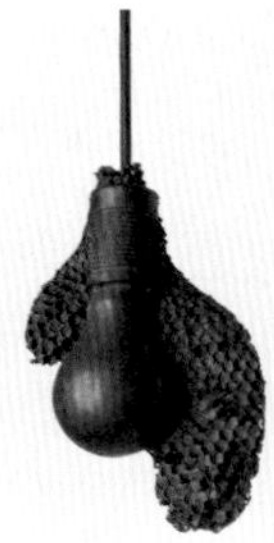

Batterie 10, 2019

Bei weiteren Werken wird die Skulptur durch ein gemeinsames Unterfangen, das Artengrenzen überbrückt, produziert. Der *Batterie*-Strauß, 2019 ↗68/69, besteht aus schwebend inszenierten dunklen Bronzegüssen in Form und Größe von Glühbirnen. Die eigenwillige Materialität und Oberfläche resultiert aus einer überraschenden Vernetzung verschiedener Vorgehensweisen und ihrer Beteiligten. Wachsabgüsse von Glühbirnen wurden in maßgerecht gefertigten Bienenkästen durch Honigbienen weiterbearbeitet, bis das industrielle Erscheinungsbild der Güsse von inselförmigen Waben überwuchert war. Anschließend wurden die Wachsskulpturen in Bronze gegossen und sandgestrahlt. So oszillieren sie unablässig zwischen technischer und tierischer Fertigung.

KREISLÄUFE

Neben denjenigen Werken, die affektive Appelle an die Betrachter*innen richten oder materielle Interaktionen präsentieren, entwirft Sailstorfer komplexere skulpturale Anordnungen. Darin ereignet sich ein „lebendiger" Austausch in Realzeit. Es geht hier weniger um die singuläre Skulptur, sondern vielmehr um ein Beziehungsgefüge, das eine Mehrzahl an Agent*innen und Objekten umfasst. Kunsthistorisch fußt dieses erweiterte Konzept des Skulpturalen auf systemorientierten Vorgehensweisen der 1960er und 1970er Jahre. Man denke etwa an Hans Haackes *Franziskanische Serie*, 1965–1972, die Pflanzen und Tiere in sogenannten „real-zeitlichen Systemen" zueinander in Relation setzt.[16] Die damalige Abwendung vom Einzelobjekt war durch die Popularisierung der Kybernetik, also der Theorie dynamischer Systeme, begründet. Dieser Ansatz setzte eine Analogie von Maschine und Organismus voraus und untersuchte die Art und Weise, wie Materie, Energie und Informationen verschiedene Elemente in ein System bringen und dessen Verhalten steuern. Durch die heutige Hinwendung der Skulptur zur „Situation" – etwa bei Pierre Huyghe – gewinnt diese konzeptuelle Tradition an Relevanz. Die Materialität der künstlerischen Arbeit wird auf die Umgebung erweitert. Abläufe werden in Gang gesetzt. Die aufgeführten Beziehungsgefüge dehnen sich zeitlich aus. Anstatt sich zu wissenschaftlich geschlossenen Systemen zu verdichten, beanspruchen solche prozessualen und relationalen Versuchsanordnungen bei Sailstorfer jedoch eine relative Offenheit. Sowohl die Entwicklungsmöglichkeiten als auch der Realitätsgehalt des arrangierten

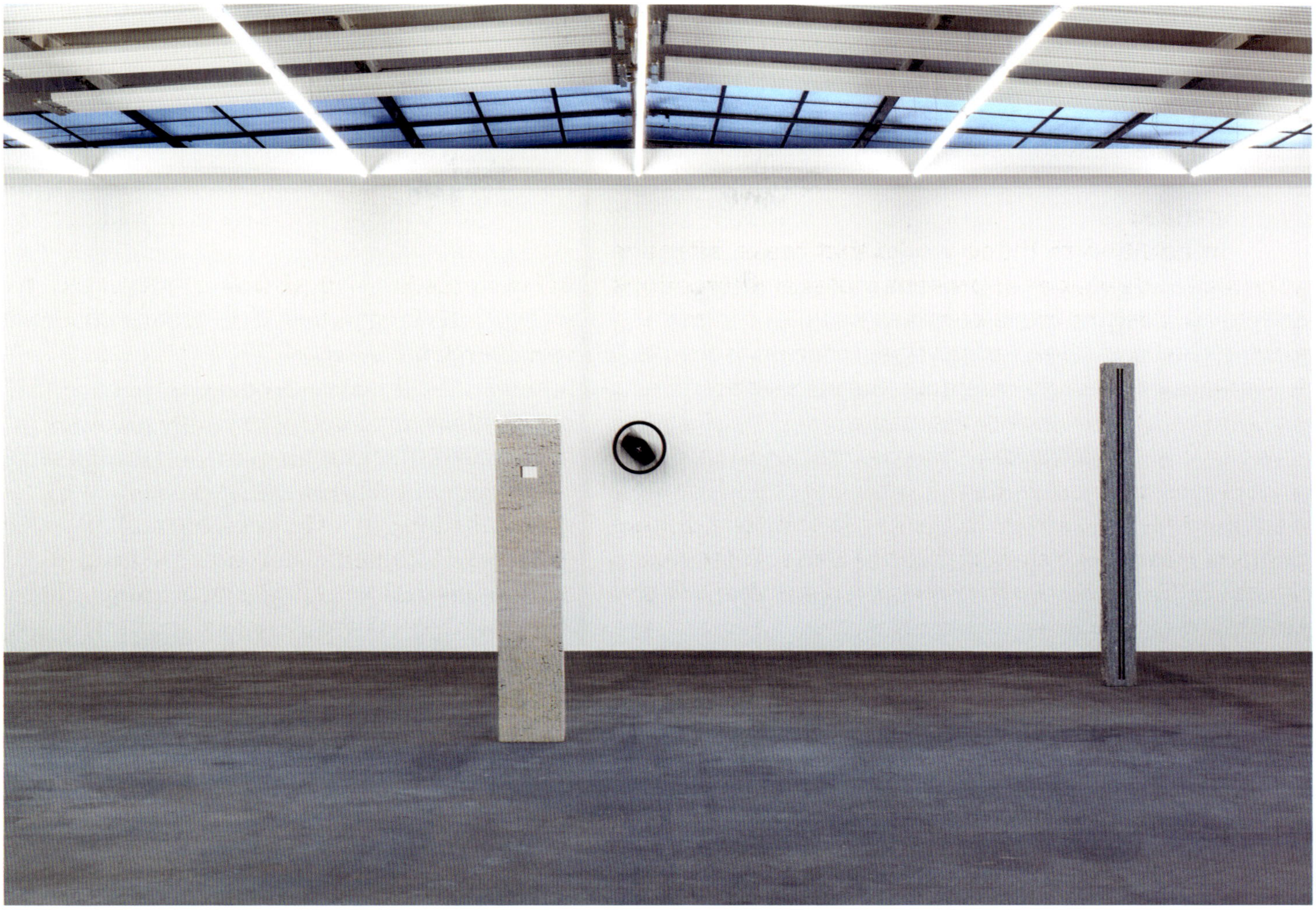

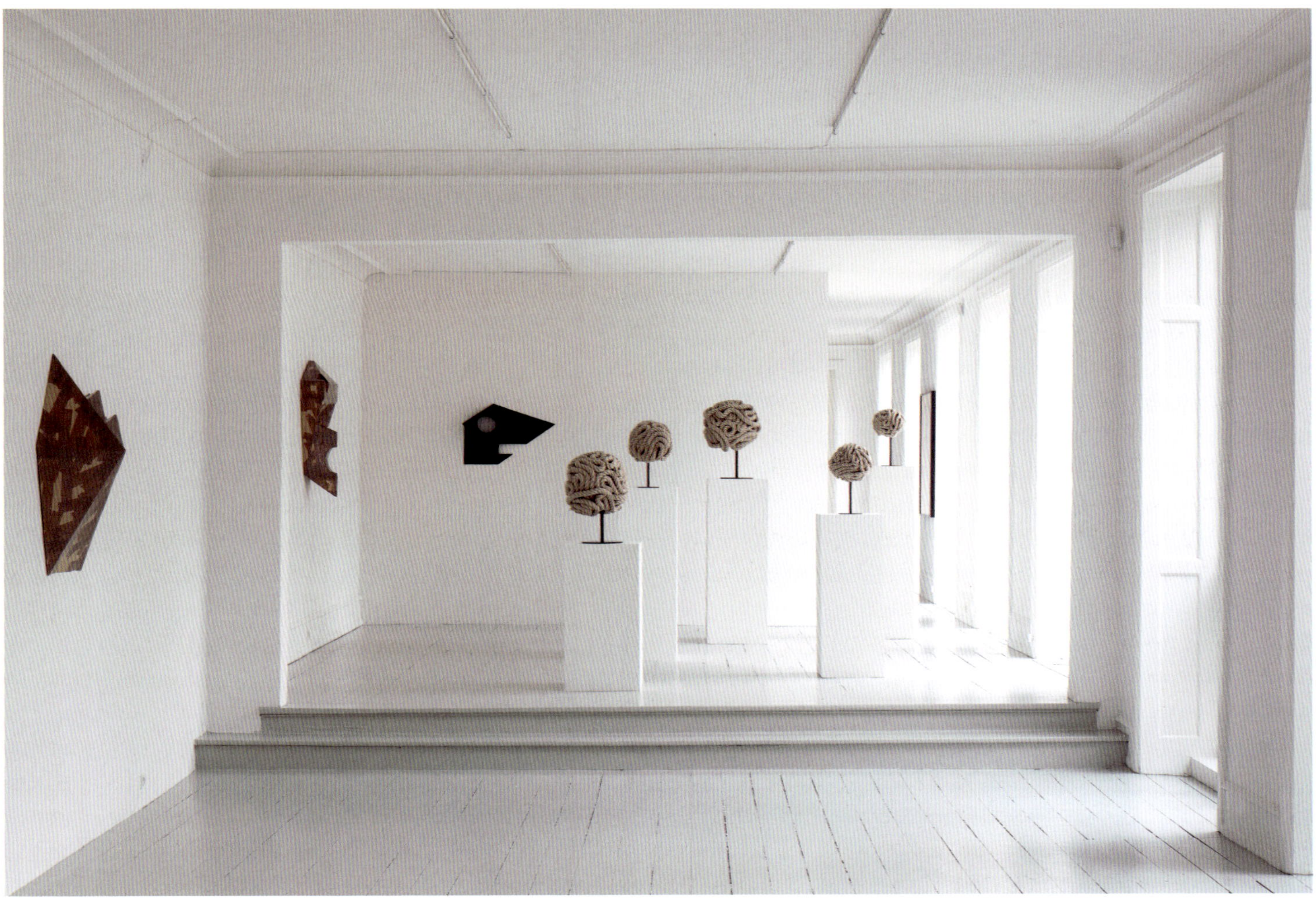

Installation view / Installationsansicht *Josef Sailstorfer & Michael Sailstorfer*, 2012, König Galerie, Berlin
Installation view / Installationsansicht *Brainspotting,* 2018, Alvskarl, Copenhagen / Kopenhagen

are exposed to water molecules, they begin to deliquesce again. The artistic design—the droplet—summarizes the origin and future scenario of the material used. For the work *Salt* from 2018, the sculptures stand in an animal enclosure with goats and are exposed to their behavior. In this constellation, the tear form appears distinctly culturally coded. From the perspective of the animals, its iconic meaning is obviously irrelevant: Rather, the sculptures become salt supplies and thus the building blocks of species-appropriate ruminant feeding. In another execution of the work *Salt* from 2019 ↗14/15, the artist positioned three teardrop sculptures made of rock salt on a cliff in Lofoten. Exposed to the weather and waves, the sculptures completely dissolved over the course of a few weeks. In this way, the fossil seawater was transformed once again into liquid sea. In both cases, the re-location allows the sculptures to be revealed as artistic interventions in a natural material. Over the course of the sculptural situation, the design measures are undone by indifferent natural forces.

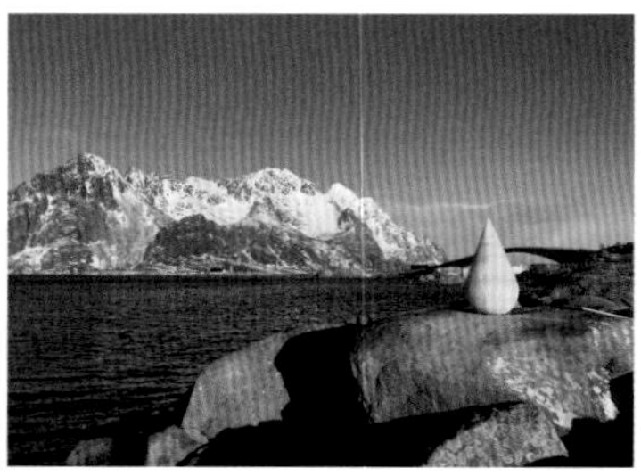

Salt, 2019

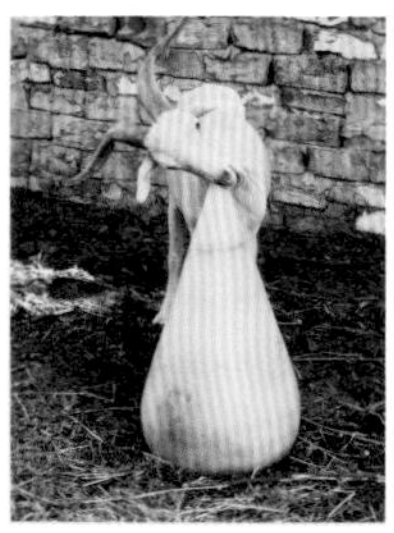

Tearcracker, 2018

The eating away of the rock salt by the goats took place outdoors and eventually resulted in a photographic work [*Tearcracker*, 2018 ↗7]. The processes of melting, sublimation, and evaporation in Lofoten could be followed via video transmission in the exhibition space at Galerie Perrotin in New York. Within the frameworks of the *Tear-Show*, this work served as a set piece of a more complex exhibition structure from March to April 2019 that connected various materials and formats through a consistent repetition of the tear form.[21] While the Lofoten video captured evaporation processes, another video work in this context, *Tears* (2015) ↗34/35 illustrated a peculiar precipitation. Blue-painted raindrops cast from iron fall relentlessly on a nondescript country house, turning it into rubble. Because the cranes and steel cables that originally controlled the oversized "rain" were retouched away in the post-production process, the trigger of the process is hidden; nevertheless, its effects—demolition by iron weights—remain visible. In an ostensibly deserted location, the iron sculptures thus virtually sculpt the house. In this video work, the "vitality" and efficacy of matter appears obviously staged. It is real, however, in that the weights relate destructively to the wood and masonry. While their form suggests lightness and fluidity, the iron castings prove to be heavy and solid. The discrepancy

Kreislaufs sind gewissermaßen in der Schwebe belassen. Das Ereignis steht zumeist „in einem besonderen Verhältnis zum Fiktiven".[17] Anstelle wissenschaftlicher Zielgerichtetheit treten Kontingenz, Kontrollverlust und Zerstörungsdynamiken. Als produktive Taktiken bringen diese Aspekte „hohe Aufmerksamkeit und Bilder"[18] hervor. In Bezug auf Sailstorfers Vorgehen hat Kristin Schrader angemerkt, dass „alles (...) Ereignis (ist) und damit nichts Besonderes. Außer das Verhältnis der Mittel ist gut."[19] Dieses Verhältnis steht bei Sailstorfers künstlerischen „Ereignisökonomien"[20] jedes Mal neu zur Disposition.

Teils werden Einzelwerke aufgegriffen und in intersubjektive Gefüge eingelassen. So hat der Künstler Tränenskulpturen mehrfach in eine natürliche Umgebung platziert. Die Tropfen werden zuerst bildhauerisch aus Salzgestein gewonnen. Wegen ihrer grau-weiß schillernden Maserungen lassen sie an Marmor oder Granit denken. Jedoch ist das Sedimentgestein ein Fossil: Über Jahrtausende hinweg ist es aus konzentriertem Meerwasser entstanden. Wenn die Salzkristalle Wassermolekülen ausgesetzt werden, beginnen sie also erneut zu zerfließen. Die künstlerische Formgebung – der Tropfen – fasst das Ursprungs- und Zukunftsszenario des verwendeten Materials zusammen. Für die Arbeit *Salt*, 2018, stehen die Skulpturen in einem Tiergehege mit Ziegen und sind deren Verhalten ausgesetzt. In dieser Konstellation erscheint die Tränenform deutlich kulturell codiert. Aus einer Tierperspektive ist ihre ikonische Bedeutung offensichtlich irrelevant: Vielmehr werden die Skulpturen zum Salzvorrat und damit zu Bausteinen einer artgerechten Wiederkäuerfütterung. In einer weiteren Ausführung der Arbeit *Salt*, 2019 ↗14/15, positionierte der Künstler drei Tränenskulpturen aus Steinsalz auf einer Felsklippe auf den Lofoten. Der Witterung und den Wellen ausgesetzt, lösten sich die Skulpturen im Laufe weniger Wochen vollständig auf. Auf diese Weise verwandelte sich das fossile Meerwasser erneut in liquides Meer. In beiden Fällen ermöglicht es die Neuverortung, die Skulpturen als künstlerische Eingriffe in ein Naturmaterial zu entlarven. Im Verlauf der skulpturalen Situation werden die gestalterischen Maßnahmen durch indifferente natürliche Kräfte wieder aufgehoben.

Die Einverleibung des Salzgesteins durch die Ziegen fand im Außenbereich statt und mündete schließlich in eine fotografische Arbeit (*Tearcracker*, 2018 ↗7). Die auf die Lofoten ausgelagerten Prozesse des Schmelzens, Sublimierens und Verdunstens konnten per Videoübertragung im Ausstellungsraum der Galerie Perrotin in New York mitverfolgt werden. Im Rahmen der *Tear-Show* diente diese Arbeit von März bis April 2019 als Versatzstück eines komplexeren Ausstellungsgefüges, das verschiedene Materialien und Formate durch eine konsequente Wiederholung der Tränenform verband.[21] Während das Lofoten-Video Verdunstungsprozesse einfing, veranschaulichte eine

between appearance and substance gives the materiality an enigmatic indecision. It is suggested that material relations precede aesthetic and semantic encodings and can occur independently of these.

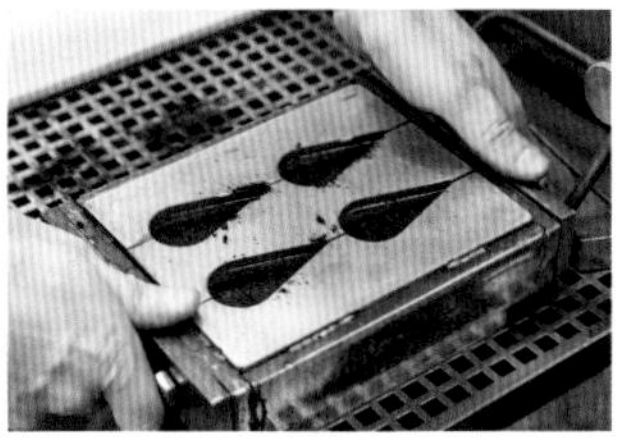

Tränenpresse, 2018

Two other works in the *Tear-Show* pick up on the divergence between form and behavior while at the same time suggesting a further material cycle. *Tränenpresse* [Tear Press, 2018] ↗24/25 consists of a functioning hydraulic press; under high pressure, it is used to press and stamp out small materials into solid units. With a template specially made for the task, this machine can be used to press coal briquettes into a teardrop shape—a process that took place within the context of the exhibition. The new shape of the briquettes refers to liquid and thus not only contradicts their solid state, but also the potentially pending incineration process. The material nature is predisposed to burning. One possibility for this is offered by the work *TTV* (2018) ↗23: a bronze casting consisting of a sculptural assemblage of a television and a stove. Here, the punched-out drops can be further heated and burned. The inherent logic of material relations expressed in the context of the *Tear-Show* is thus not necessarily congruent with cultural attributions of meaning.

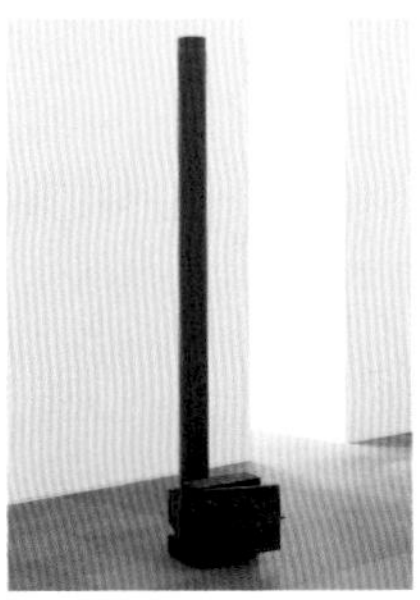

TTV, 2018

Sailstorfer's examination of aggregate states and ecological cycles, however, is not content with valorizing the material's reservoir of possibilities and relativizing humankind as a creative instance that provides meaning. On the occasion of the solo exhibition *Hitzefrei* at König Galerie in Berlin in the winter of 2017, the artist relied on synesthetic addressing and thus involved the viewers in the bonds and relationships staged. The centerpiece of the exhibition was a large-scale installation of six brand-new car frames [*Brenner* (Combustor), 2017 ↗257–261]. These were arranged as if in a double production line and occupied the entire upper floor of the former Church of St. Agnes. Before the exhibition, the vehicles' engines were replaced with wood-burning stoves. Throughout the course of the show, the stoves were in operation. The pipes conducted the smoke through the roof of the

weitere Videoarbeit (*Tränen*, 2015 ↗34/35) in diesem Kontext einen eigentümlichen Niederschlag. Blau bemalte, aus Eisen gegossene Regentropfen fallen unerbittlich auf ein unscheinbares Landhaus und verwandeln es in Trümmer. Weil die Kräne und Stahlseile, die ursprünglich den überdimensionierten „Regen" steuerten im Postproduktionsprozess wegretuschiert wurden, ist der Auslöser des Prozesses ausgeblendet, seine Effekte – der Abbruch durch Eisengewichte – bleiben hingegen sichtbar. Auf einem vermeintlich menschenleeren Schauplatz bearbeiten die Eisenskulpturen das Haus also gewissermaßen bildhauerisch. Die „Lebendigkeit" und Wirkmacht der Materie erscheint in dieser Videoarbeit offensichtlich inszeniert. Sie ist jedoch insofern real, als sich die Gewichte zerstörerisch zu dem Holz und Gemäuer verhalten. Während ihre Form Leichtigkeit und Flüssigkeit suggeriert, erweisen sich die Eisengüsse als schwer und fest. Die Diskrepanz zwischen Erscheinung und Substanz verleiht der Materialität eine rätselhafte Unentschiedenheit. Es wird nahegelegt, dass Materialverhältnisse ästhetischen und semantischen Codierungen vorangehen und sich unabhängig davon ereignen können.
Zwei weitere Arbeiten, die in der *Tear-Show* vertreten waren, nehmen die Divergenz zwischen Form und Verhalten auf und suggerieren zugleich einen weiteren Materialkreislauf. Die *Tränenpresse*, 2018 ↗24/25, besteht aus einer funktionsfähigen Hydraulikpresse, unter hohem Druck werden damit Kleinstoffe zu festen Einheiten verpresst und ausgestanzt. Mit einer speziell für die Arbeit angefertigte Schablone lassen sich mit dieser Maschine Kohlebriketts in Tropfenform pressen – ein Vorgang, der im Rahmen der Ausstellung stattfand. Die neue Form der Briketts referiert auf Flüssigkeit und steht damit nicht nur in Widerspruch zu ihrem festen Zustand, sondern auch zum potenziell anstehenden Verbrennungsprozess. Die materielle Beschaffenheit ist für eine Kombustion, prädisponiert. Eine Möglichkeit dazu bietet die Arbeit *TTV*, 2018 ↗23: ein Bronzeguss, der aus einer skulpturalen Assemblage eines Fernsehers und eines Ofens besteht. Darin können die ausgestanzten Tropfen weiter angeheizt und verbrannt werden. Die Eigenlogik der Materialverhältnisse, die im Rahmen der *Tear-Show* zum Ausdruck gebracht wird, ist mit kulturellen Bedeutungszuschreibungen also nicht notwendigerweise deckungsgleich.
Sailstorfers Auseinandersetzung mit Aggregatzuständen und ökologischen Zyklen begnügt sich jedoch nicht damit, das Möglichkeitsreservoir des Materials aufzuwerten und den Menschen als gestalterische und bedeutungsstiftende Instanz zu relativieren. Aus Anlass der Einzelausstellung *Hitzefrei* in der König Galerie in Berlin setzt der Künstler im Winter 2017 auf synästhetische Adressierung und involviert damit die Betrachter*innen in die aufgeführten Bindungen und Beziehungen. Herzstück der Ausstellung ist eine aufwändige Installation aus sechs nagelneuen Fahrzeugrahmen (*Brenner*, 2017 ↗257–261). Diese sind wie in einer

gallery. Painted matte black, the sculptural entities appeared like strange minimalist skeletons: clean yet used, powered yet immobile. Above all, they radiated a dangerous heat. The combustion that took place in the ovens did not simply raise the internal temperature of the Brutalist space, but also connected the metabolic process of art to an external ecology. Because the exceptional situation became physically tangible, the title of the exhibition, which denotes time off from school or work due to exceptionally hot weather, took on a threatening meaning. Without explicitly formulating the question of complicity and ecological responsibility, the installation inevitably evoked familiar associations. Involuntarily, one thinks here of car factories, hyperproduction, and energy consumption. An association with overheated server centers is also not farfetched. Through a physical borderline situation, the material basis of capitalist-neoliberal systems is called into consciousness.

In these more recent works by Michael Sailstorfer, matter thus becomes "expressive"—it takes on quasi-subjective properties, enters into interactions, involves us in its cycles. In the words of Jane Bennett: "The extra attention paid to matter and the power inherent in it [...] will not eradicate the problem of exploitation and oppression [...], but it can sensitize us to the sheer extent of the interconnectedness between bodies that are [...] inextricably intertwined."[22] Beyond commentary or illustration, Sailstorfer's works affirm the environment as a web of reciprocal relationships. These involve natural, human, and animal forces. Their physical concreteness continues in synesthetic fields of action. What is decisive here is that the differently weighted interventions and relations that condition the creation of the work and its course are not nullified. They remain visible in the artistic result. By wanting to be reconstructed, they stand for processes of becoming and interrelating that concern us. As sensual-conceptual syntheses, the works also make an important contribution to the contemporary possibilities of sculpture.

doppelten Fertigungsstraße angeordnet und nehmen das gesamte Obergeschoss der ehemaligen St. Agnes-Kirche ein. Die Motoren der Fahrzeuge wurden zuvor durch Holzöfen ersetzt. Während der Laufzeit der Ausstellung sind sie in Betrieb. Die Rohre leiten den Rauch durch das Dach der Galerie. Mattschwarz lackiert erschienen die skulpturalen Gebilde wie seltsame minimalistische Skelette: sauber und doch gebraucht, angetrieben und doch unbeweglich. Vor allem aber strahlen sie eine gefährliche Hitze aus. Die Verbrennung, die in den Öfen stattfindet, erhöht nicht einfach nur die Innentemperatur des brutalistischen Raumes, sondern verbindet den Stoffwechsel der Kunst mit einer äußeren Ökologie. Weil der Ausnahmezustand physisch erfahrbar wird, erhält der Titel der Ausstellung eine bedrohliche Bedeutung. Ohne die Frage nach Komplizenschaft und ökologischer Verantwortung ausdrücklich zu formulieren, drängt die Installation vertraute Assoziationen auf. Unwillkürlich denkt man hier an Autofabriken, Hyperproduktion und Energieverbrauch. Auch der Gedanke an überhitzte Server-Zentren liegt nicht weit entfernt. Durch eine physisch grenzwertige Situation wird die materielle Grundlage kapitalistisch-neoliberaler Systeme ins Bewusstsein gerufen.

In neueren Arbeiten von Michael Sailstorfer wird die Materie also „expressiv" – sie nimmt quasi subjekthafte Eigenschaften an, geht Interaktionen ein, bezieht uns in ihre Kreisläufe ein. Mit Jane Bennett gesprochen, wird „das Mehr an Aufmerksamkeit, das man der Materie und der Kraft, die ihr innewohnt, zuteilwerden lässt, (...) das Problem der Ausbeutung und Unterdrückung (...) nicht aus der Welt schaffen, aber es kann uns für das schiere Ausmaß der Verbundenheit zwischen Körpern sensibilisieren, die (...) untrennbar miteinander verwoben sind."[22] Jenseits von Kommentar oder Illustration vergewissern sich Sailstorfers Arbeiten der Umwelt als Geflecht wechselseitiger Beziehungen. Sie involvieren natürliche, menschliche und tierische Kräfte. Ihre physische Konkretheit setzt sich in synästhetischen Wirkungsfeldern fort. Entscheidend ist dabei, dass die verschieden gewichteten Eingriffe und Relationen, die Werkentstehung und Ablauf bedingen, nicht zunichte gemacht werden. Sie bleiben im künstlerischen Ergebnis sichtbar. Indem sie nachvollzogen werden wollen, stehen sie für Prozesse des Werdens und des Sich-Zueinander-Verhaltens ein, die uns angehen. Als sinnlich-konzeptuelle Synthesen liefern die Werke zugleich einen wichtigen Beitrag zu den zeitgenössischen Möglichkeiten der Skulptur.

1 Gilles Deleuze and Felix Guattari, *What Is Philosophy?*, trans. Hugh Tomlinson and Graham Burchili (London and New York: Verso 1994), p. 167.

2 Veit Görner, "Vorwort," in: *Michael Sailstorfer*, exh. cat. Kestner Gesellschaft, Hanover et al. (Berlin: Distanz 2010), p. 12 [translated].

3 Ellen Seifermann, "Handlungsbedarf. Über den erweiterten Skulpturbegriff in Michael Sailstorfers Werken," in: exh. cat. Hanover 2010 (see note 2), pp. 128–141, here p. 138 [translated].

4 See: Kito Nedo, "Material-ABC," in: *Michael Sailstorfer. Reibungsverlust am Arbeitsplatz*, exh. cat. Museum Kurhaus Kleve – Ewald Mataré Sammlung et al. (Berlin: Distanz 2015), pp. 125–148.

5 Michael Sailstorfer, in: Neville Wakefield, "Reaktor. Neville Wakefield im Gespräch mit Michael Sailstorfer," in: *Michael Sailstorfer. Reaktor* (New York: Lukas & Sternberg 2008), pp. 93–104, here p. 95 [translated].

6 Seifermann 2010 (see note 3), p. 128 [translated].

7 See, for example: B. Martin Germann, "Sailstorfers Prototypen," in: exh. cat. Hanover et al. 2010 (see note 2), pp. 22–43; Kris Douglas, "Michael Sailstorfers (Material-) Romanze," in exh. cat. Kleve at al. 2015 (see note 4), pp. 41–48.

8 For more on the manifestation of this movement in the arts, see: Susanne Pfeffer (ed.), *Speculations on Anonymous Materials, Nature After Nature, Inhuman*, exh. cat. Museum Fridericianum, Kassel (London: Koenig Books 2018).

9 See: Melanie Bono [in conversation with Michael Sailstorfer], "Kunst muss ja erst mal gar nichts …," in: exh. cat. Kleve et al. 2015 (see note 4), pp. 81–92.

10 See, for example: Madeleine Schuppli, *Maske. In der Kunst der Gegenwart* (Zurich, Scheidegger & Spiess 2019).

11 See, for example: Hasso Hohmann, *Fassaden mit Gesichtern* (Graz: Verl. der Technischen Universität 2014).

12 See: Thomas Macho, "So leicht wie Blei," in Christiane Heibach and Carsten Rohde (eds.), *Ästhetik der Materialität* (Paderborn: Wilhelm Fink Verlag 2015), pp. 199–212.

13 Ibid.

14 See: *Günther Förg. Zwölf Bleibilder 1989*, ed. Uli Knecht et al., exh. cat. Galerie Bärbel Grässlin, Frankfurt am Main (Cologne: Snoeck 2013).

15 See: Geraldine Spiekermann, *Tränen in der modernen Kunst*, PhD diss. Humboldt University of Berlin, 2012.

16 See: Ursula Ströbele, "Real-zeitliches System und skulpturale Situation: Hans Haacke und Pierre Huyghe," in idem and Martina Dobbe (eds.), *Gegenstand: Skulptur* (Paderborn et al.: Wilhelm Fink Verlag 2020), pp. 97–118.

17 Kristin Schrader, "Ereignisökonomien," in: *Michael Sailstorfer*, exh. cat. Kestner Gesellschaft, Hanover et al. (Berlin: Distanz 2010), pp. 62–85, here p. 70 [translated].

18 Ibid. [translated].

19 Ibid., p. 78 [translated].

20 Ibid. [translated].

21 The tear form appeared here in the *Heavy Tear* pictures and in the rock salt sculptures, as part of a *Tränentrockner* work and in the sculptural installation *Cowboy's Tears* (2018).

22 Jane Bennett, quoted in: Kirsty Bell, "Perverse Objekte, Plastiglomerate und pulsierende Materie in der natürlichen Welt," in Pfeffer 2018 (see note 7), pp. 307–313, here p. 312 [translated].

1 Gilles Deleuze, Felix Guattari, *Was ist Philosophie?*, Frankfurt am Main: Suhrkamp 2000, S. 195.

2 Veit Görner, „Vorwort", in: *Michael Sailstorfer*, Ausst.-Kat. Kestner Gesellschaft, Hannover u. a., Berlin: Distanz 2010, S. 12.

3 Ellen Seifermann, „Handlungsbedarf. Über den erweiterten Skulpturbegriff in Michael Sailstorfers Werken", in: *Michael Sailstorfer*, Ausst.-Kat. Kestner Gesellschaft, Hannover u. a., Berlin: Distanz 2010, S. 128–141, hier S. 138.

4 Vgl. Kito Nedo, „Material-ABC", in: *Michael Sailstorfer. Reibungsverlust am Arbeitsplatz*, Ausst.-Kat Museum Kurhaus Kleve – Ewald Mataré Sammlung u. a., Berlin: Distanz 2015, S. 125–148.

5 Michael Sailstorfer in: Neville Wakefield, „Reaktor. Neville Wakefield im Gespräch mit Michael Sailstorfer", in *Michael Sailstorfer. Reaktor*, New York: Lukas & Sternberg 2008, S. 93–104, hier S. 95.

6 Seifermann 2010 (s. Anm. 3), hier S. 128.

7 Vgl. z. B. Martin Germann, „Sailstorfers Prototypen", in: *Michael Sailstorfer*, Ausst.-Kat. Kestner Gesellschaft, Hannover u. a., Berlin: Distanz 2010, S. 22–43; Kris Douglas, „Michael Sailstorfers (Material-)Romanze", in: *Michael Sailstorfer. Reibungsverlust am Arbeitsplatz*, Ausst.-Kat. Museum Kurhaus Kleve – Ewald Mataré Sammlung u. a., Berlin: Distanz 2015, S. 41–48.

8 Zu dem Niederschlag dieser Bewegung in den Künsten siehe Susanne Pfeffer (Hg.), *Speculations on Anonymous Materials, Nature After Nature, Inhuman*, Ausst.-Kat. Museum Fridericianum, Kassel, London: Koenig Books 2018.

9 Vgl. Melanie Bono im Gespräch mit Michael Sailstorfer, „Kunst muss ja erst mal gar nichts …", in: *Michael Sailstorfer. Reibungsverlust am Arbeitsplatz*, Ausst.-Kat. Museum Kurhaus Kleve – Ewald Mataré Sammlung u. a., Berlin: Distanz 2015, S. 81–92.

10 Vgl. dazu etwa Madeleine Schuppli, *Maske. In der Kunst der Gegenwart*, Zürich: Scheidegger & Spiess 2019.

11 Vgl. z. B. Hasso Hohmann, *Fassaden mit Gesichtern*, Graz: Verl. der Technischen Universität 2014.

12 Vgl. Thomas Macho, „So leicht wie Blei", in: Christiane Heibach, Carsten Rohde (Hg.), *Ästhetik der Materialität*, Paderborn: Wilhelm Fink Verlag 2015, S. 199–212.

13 Vgl. ebd.

14 Vgl. Uli Knecht u. a. (Hg.), *Günther Förg. Zwölf Bleibilder 1989*, Ausst.-Kat. Galerie Bärbel Grässlin, Frankfurt am Main, Frankfurt am Main, Köln: Snoeck 2013.

15 Vgl. Geraldine Spiekermann, *Tränen in der modernen Kunst*, Dissertation, Berlin: Humboldt-Univ. 2012.

16 Vgl. Ursula Ströbele, „Real-zeitliches System und skulpturale Situation: Hans Haacke und Pierre Huyghe", in: dies., Martina Dobbe (Hg.), *Gegenstand: Skulptur*, Paderborn u. a.: Wilhelm Fink Verlag 2020, S. 97–118.

17 Kristin Schrader, „Ereignisökonomien", in: *Michael Sailstorfer*, Ausst.-Kat. Kestner Gesellschaft, Hannover u. a., Berlin: Distanz 2010, S. 62–85, hier S. 70.

18 Ebd.

19 Ebd., S. 78.

20 Ebd.

21 Die Träne trat hier in den *Heavy Tear*-Bildern, in den Salzgestein-Skulpturen, im Rahmen einer Tränentrockner-Arbeit und der skulpturalen Installation *Cowboy's Tears*, 2018, auf.

22 Jane Bennett, zit. nach Kirsty Bell, „Perverse Objekte, Plastiglomerate und pulsierende Materie in der natürlichen Welt", in: Pfeffer 2018 (Anm. 8), S. 307–313, hier S. 312.

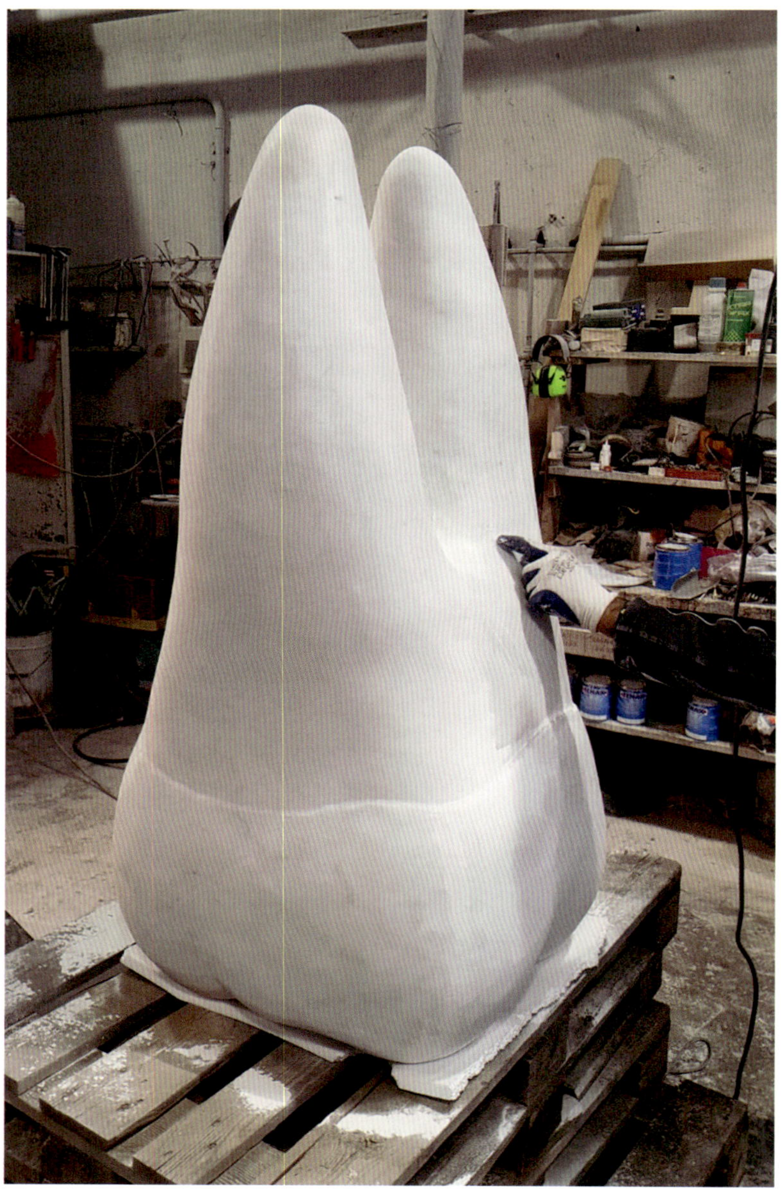

Z 46, 2020

Marble / Marmor, 70 × 70 × 130 cm

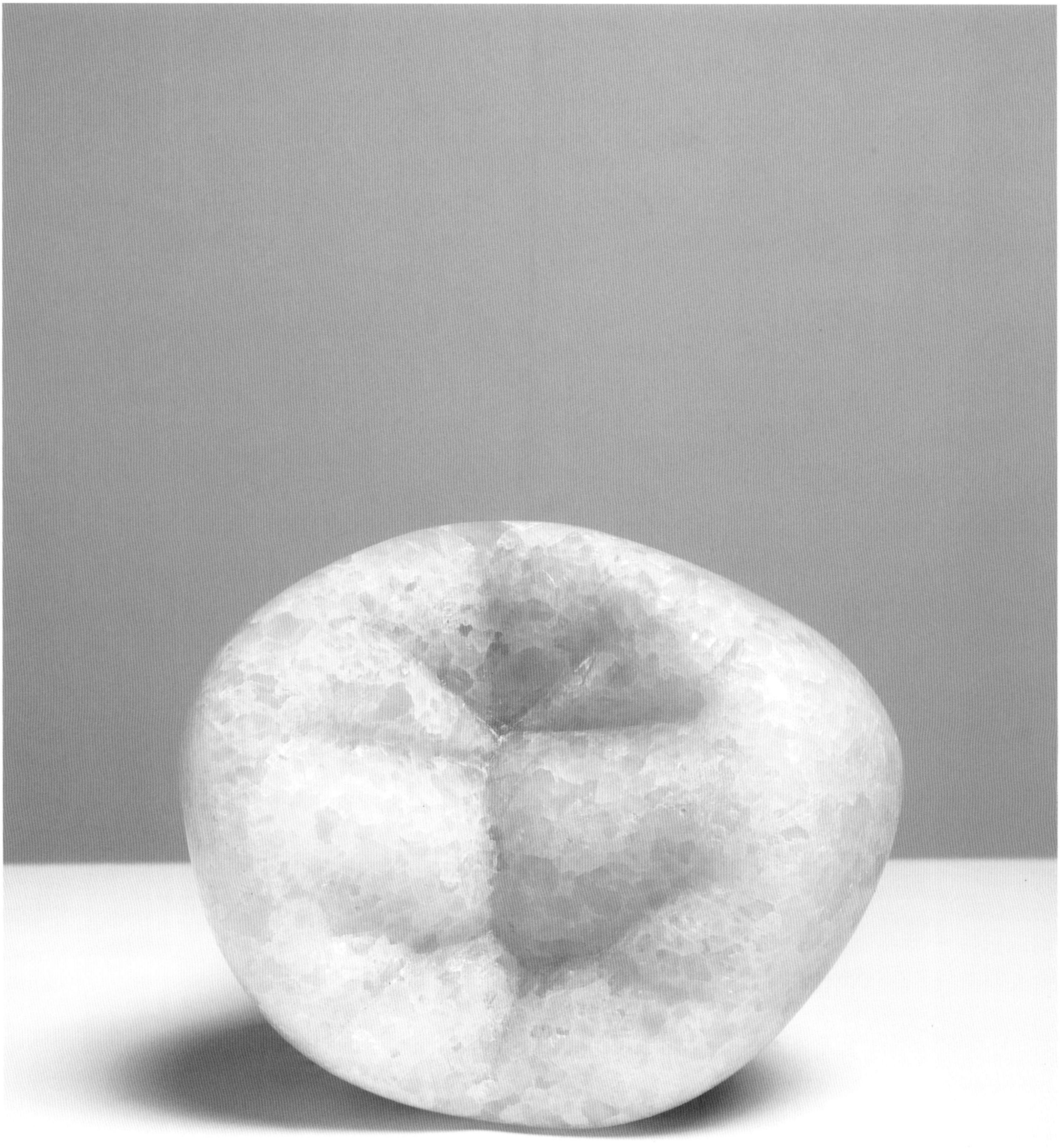

45, 2020

Salt / Salz, 13,5 × 35 × 15,5 cm

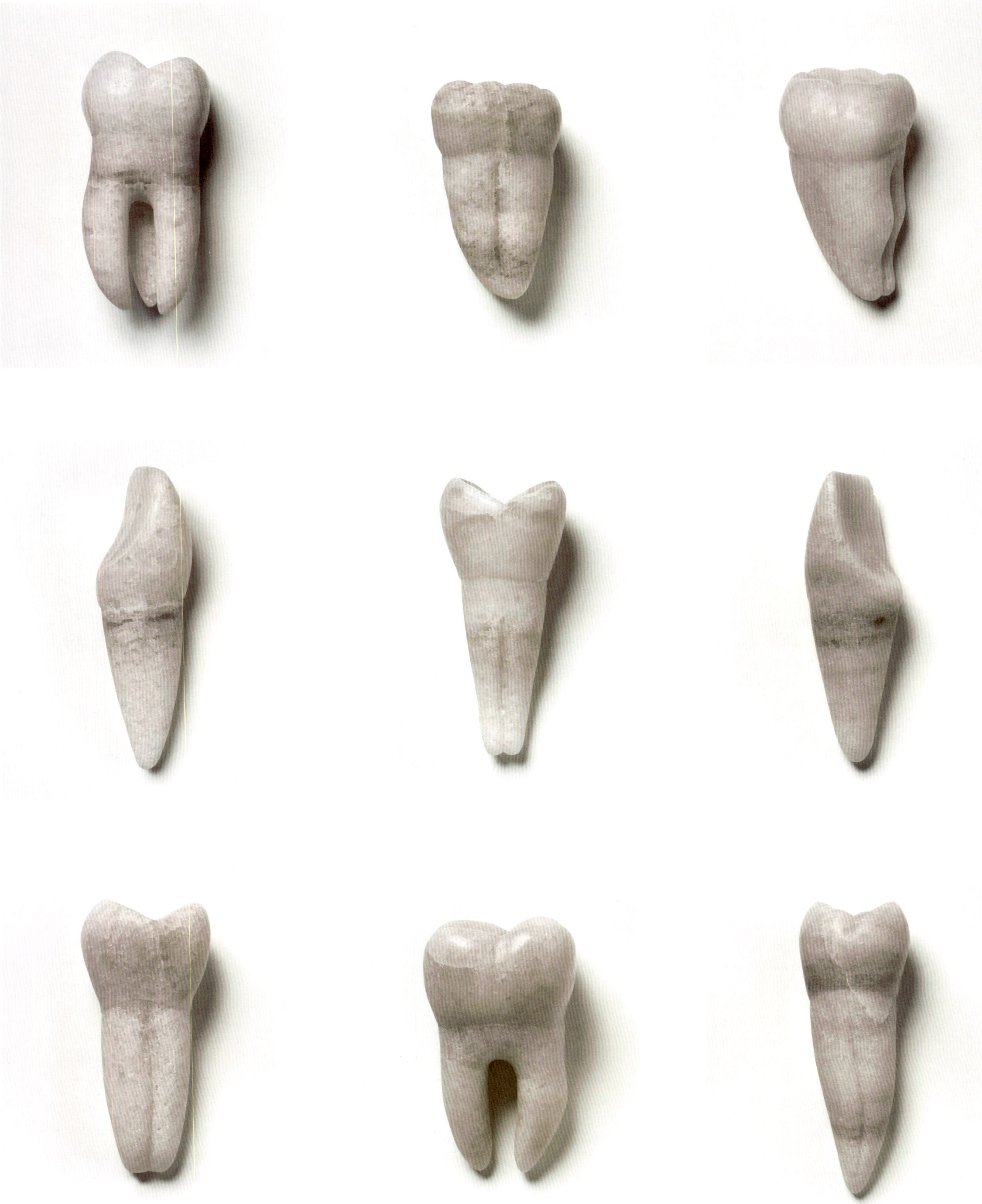

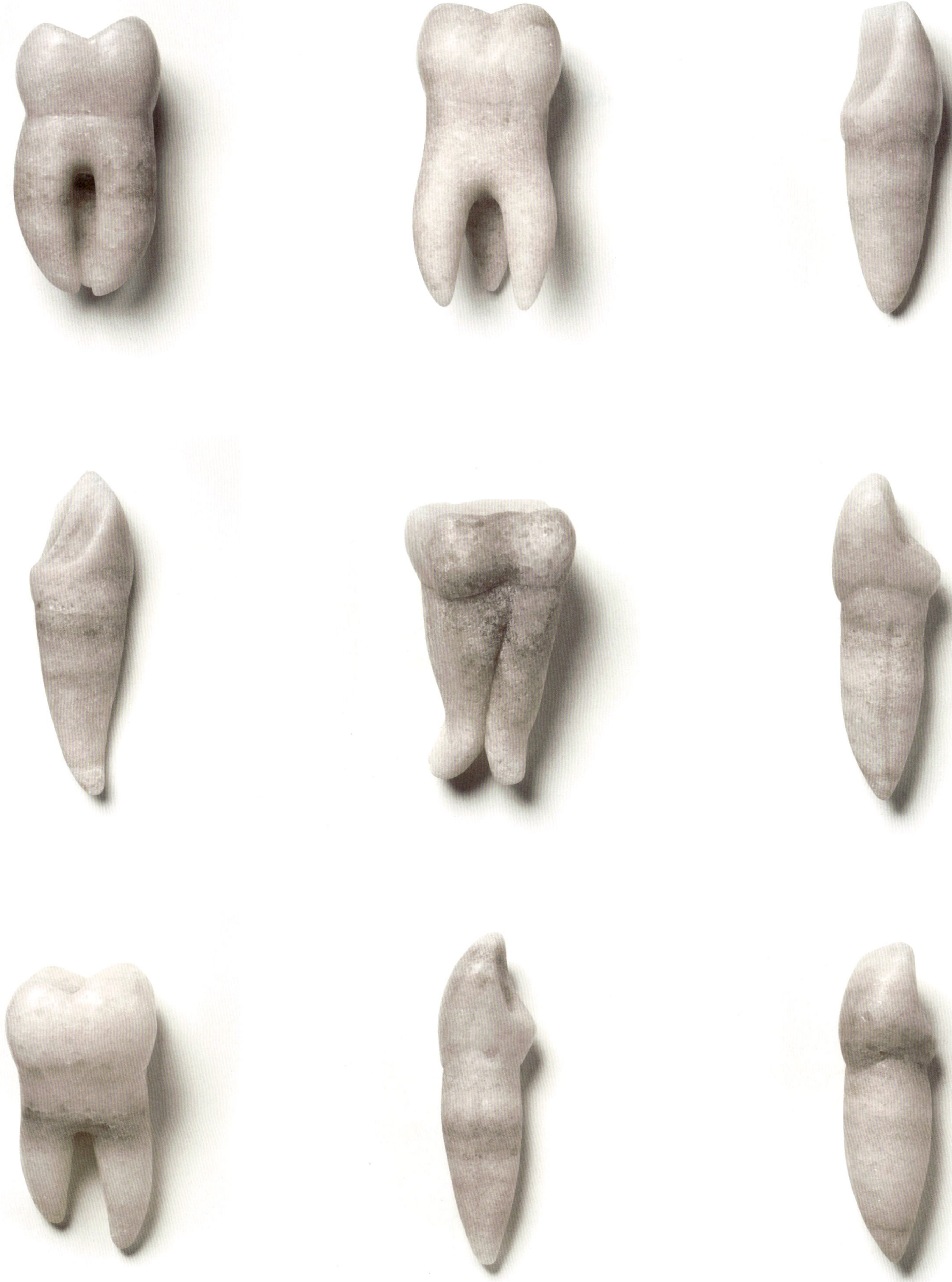

1–32, 2020
Salt / Salz

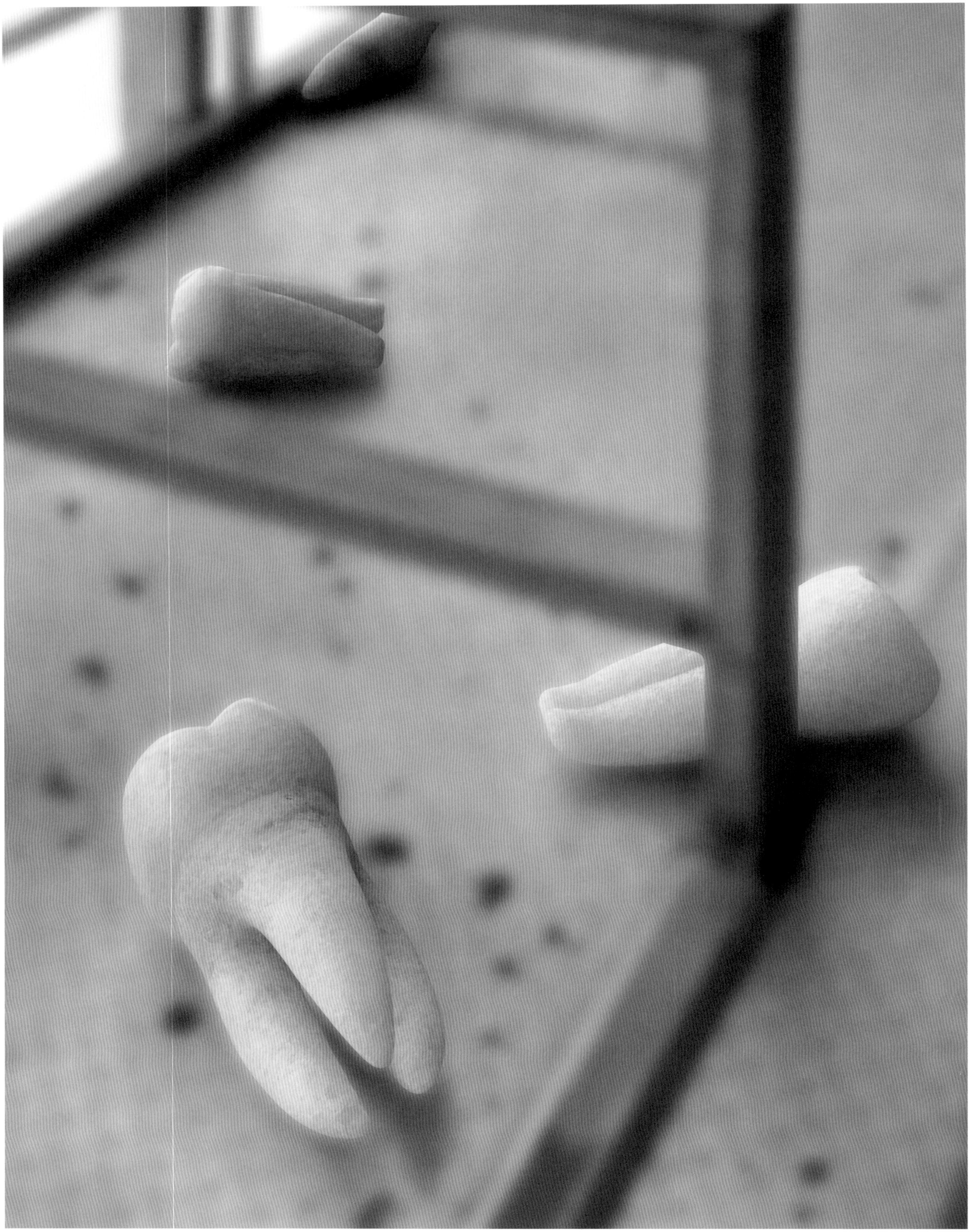

1–32, 2020

Salt / Salz, Installation view / Installationsansicht
Studio Berlin, Berghain, Berlin

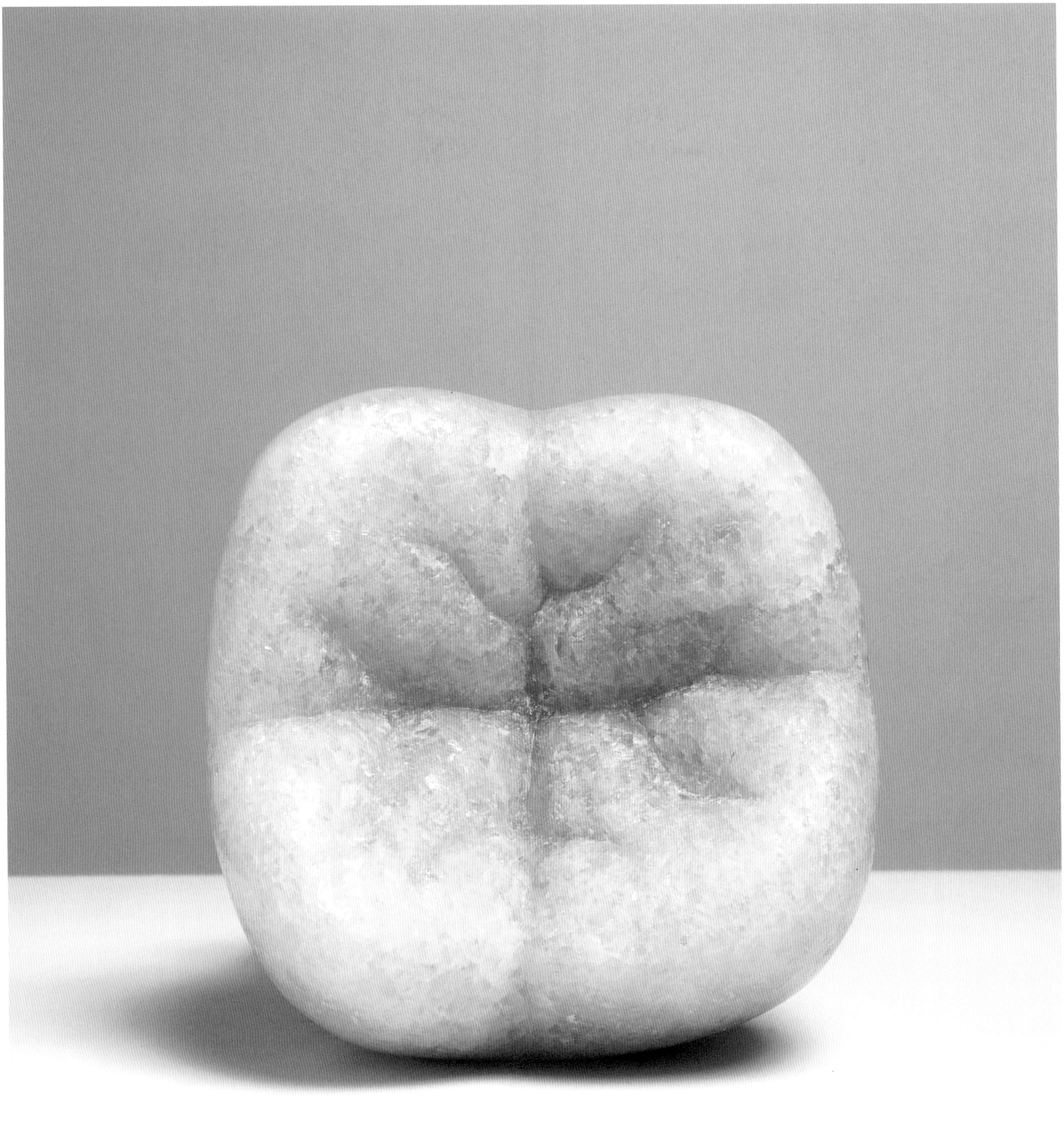

47, 2020
Salt / Salz, 15 × 28 × 16 cm

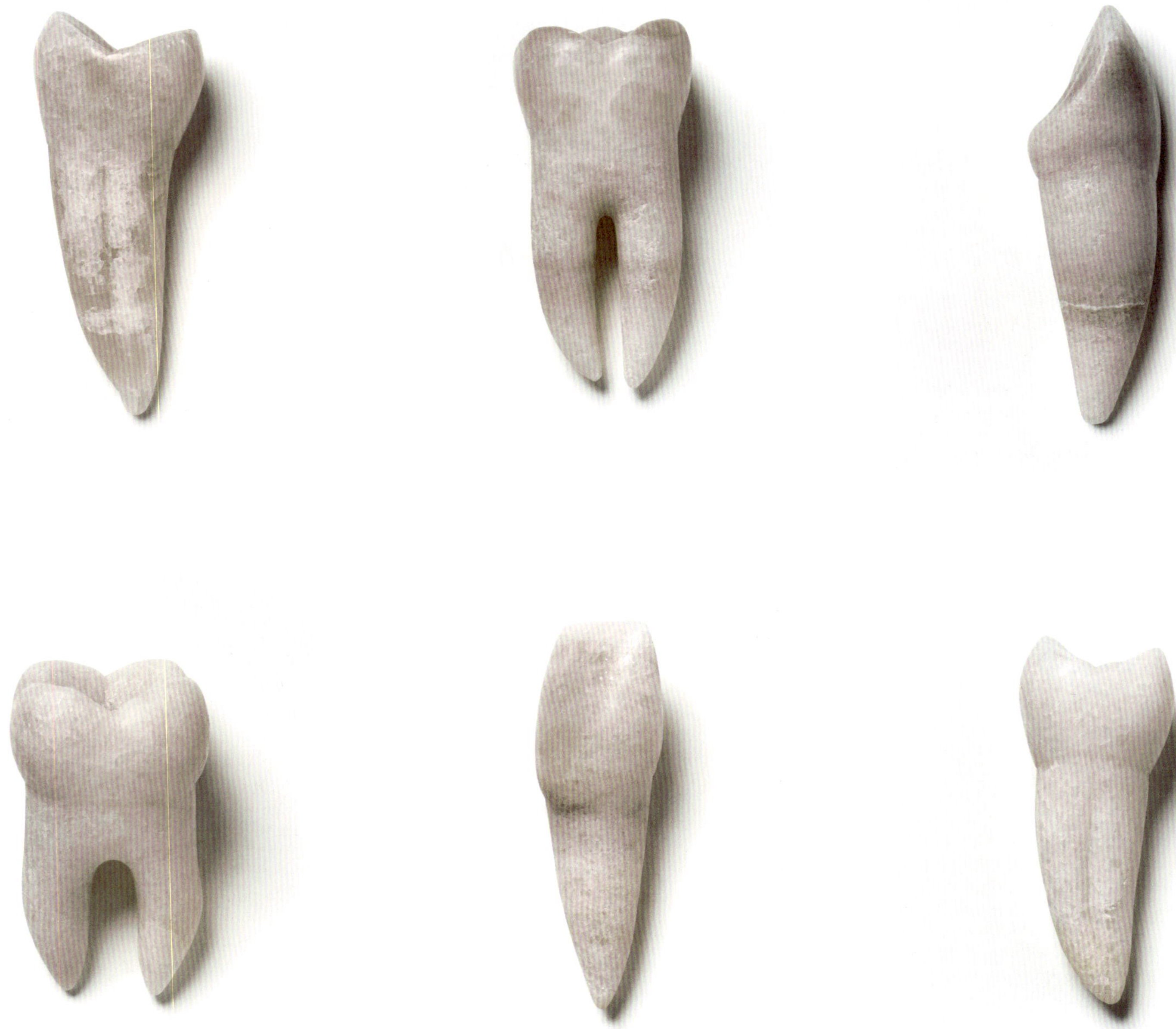

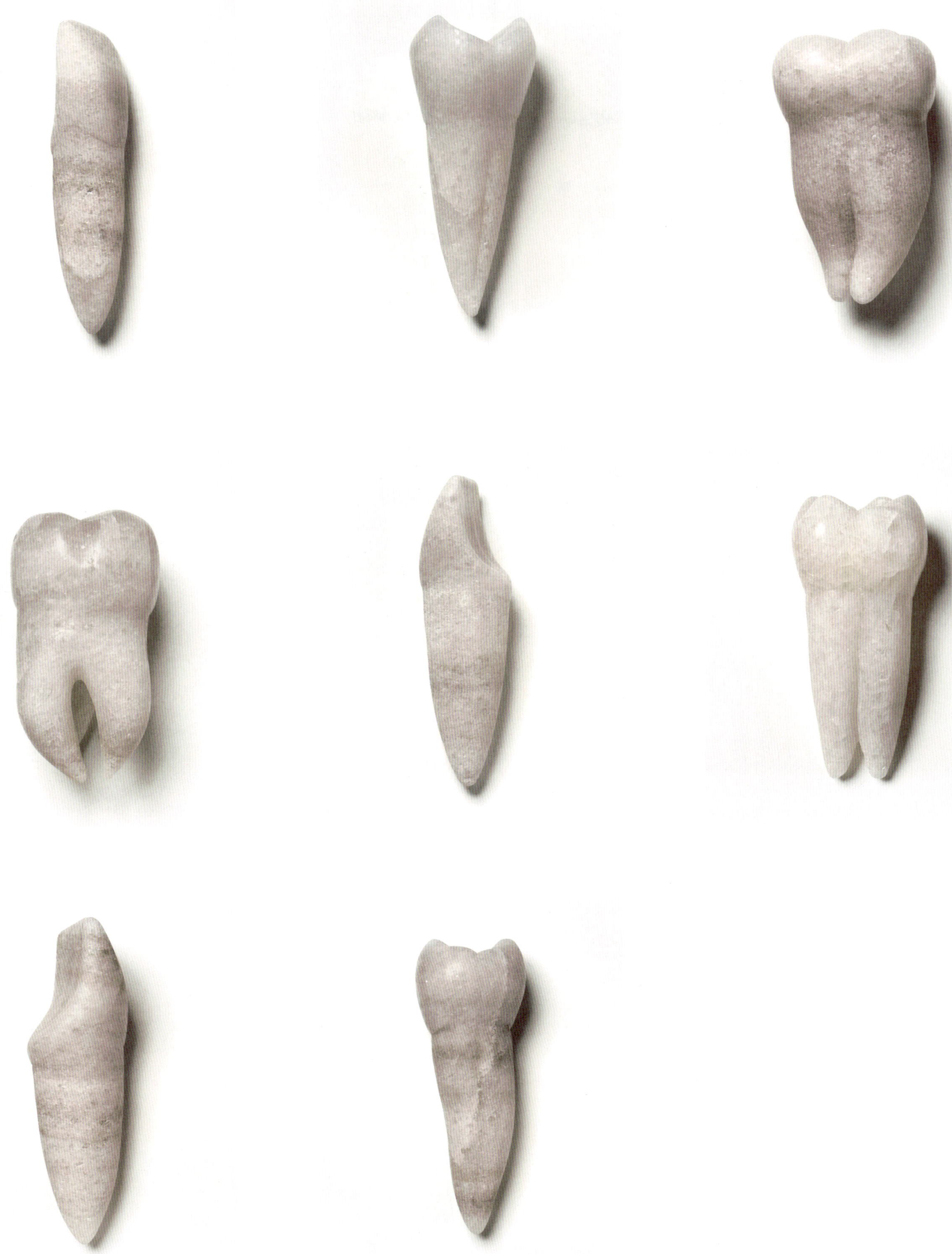

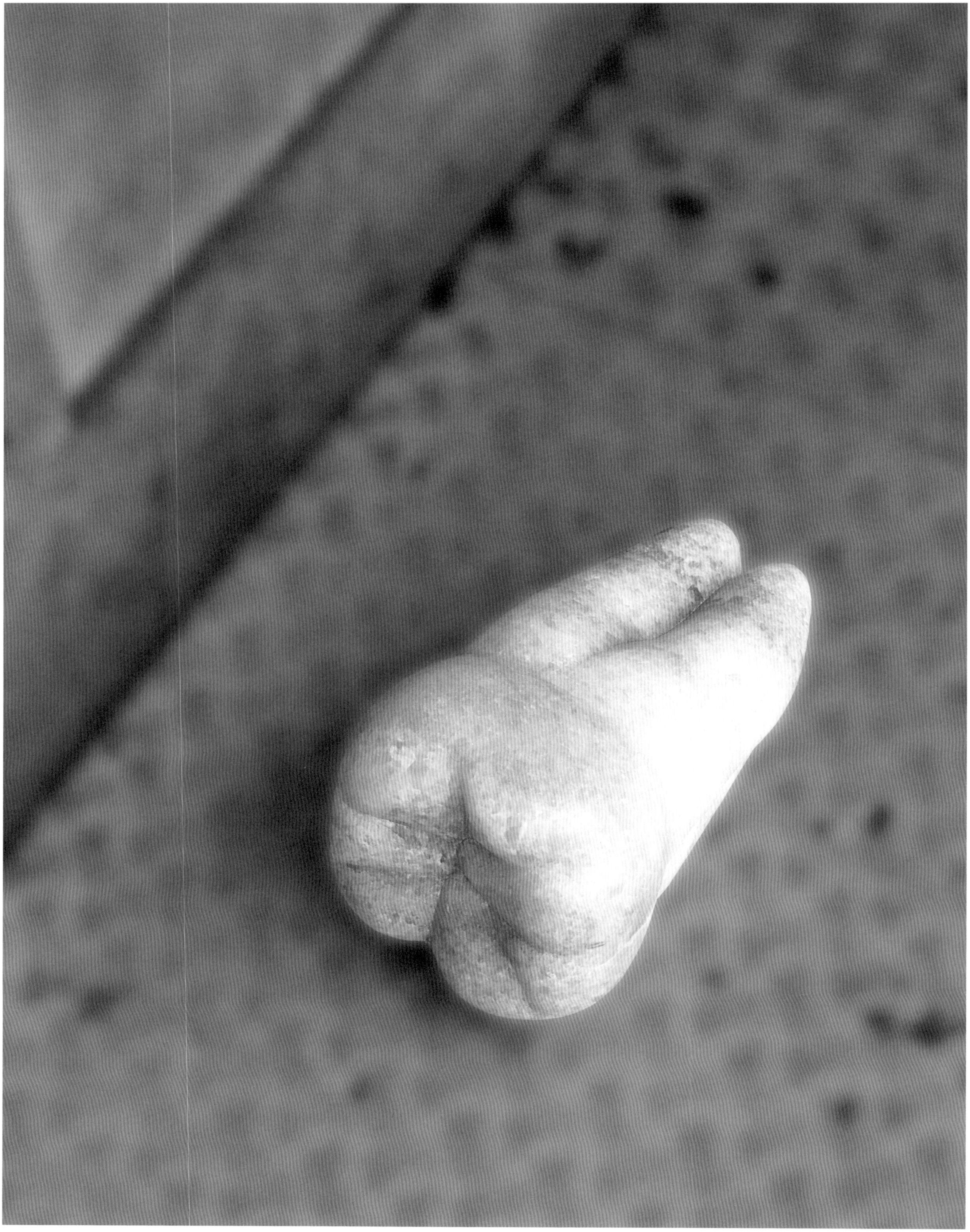

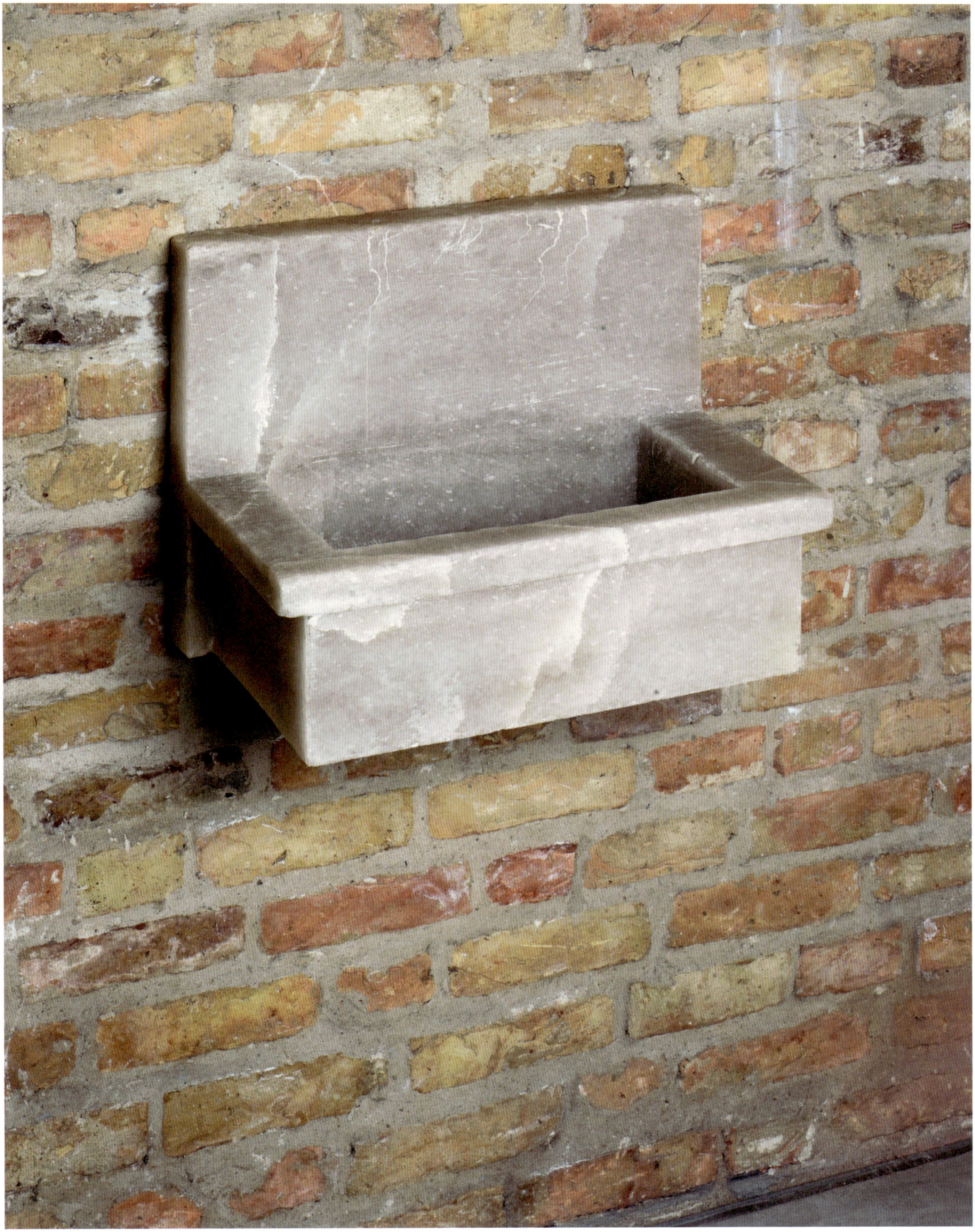

Sink, 2019

Salt, water / Salz, Wasser, 40 × 50 × 36,5 cm

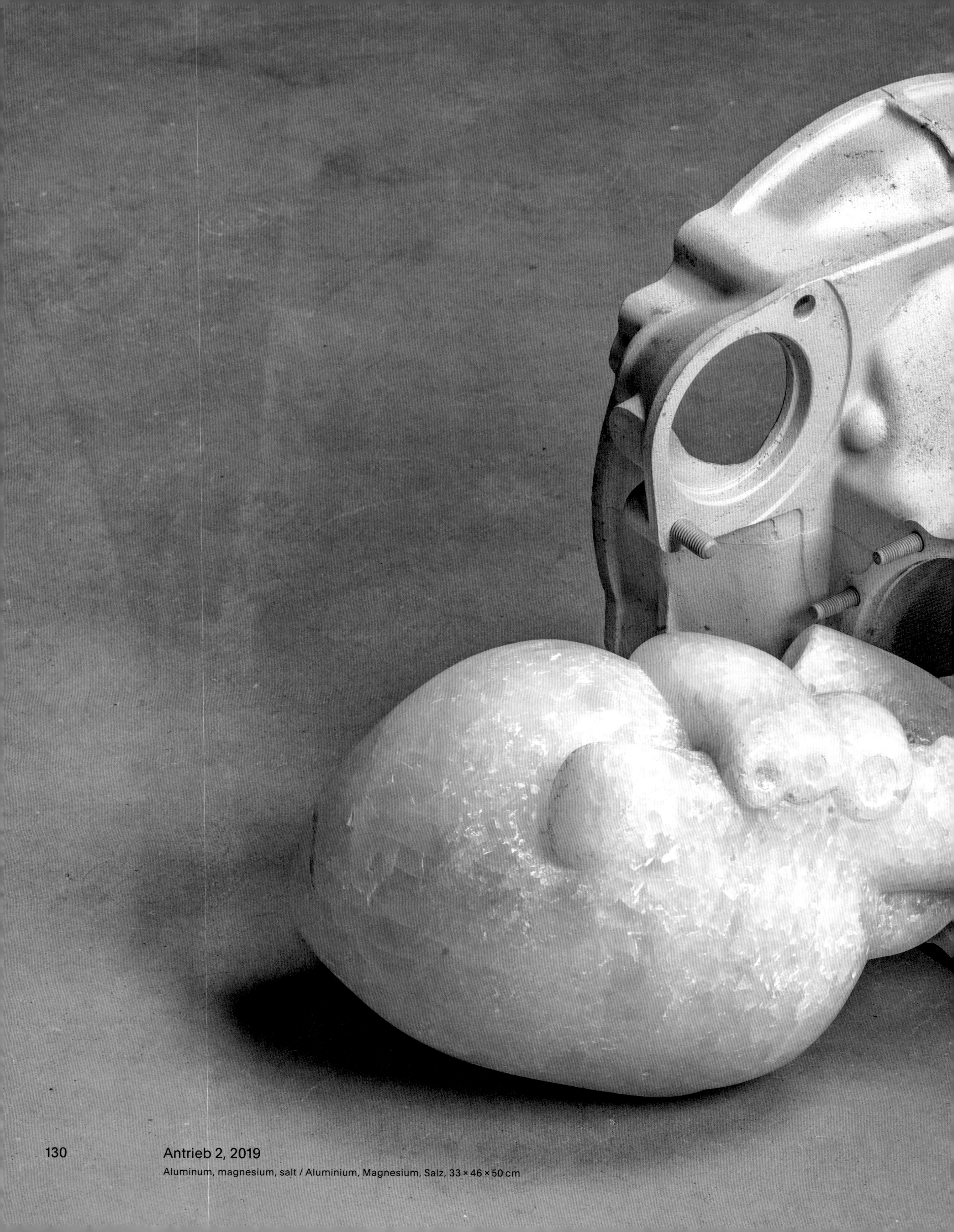

Antrieb 2, 2019

Aluminum, magnesium, salt / Aluminium, Magnesium, Salz, 33 × 46 × 50 cm

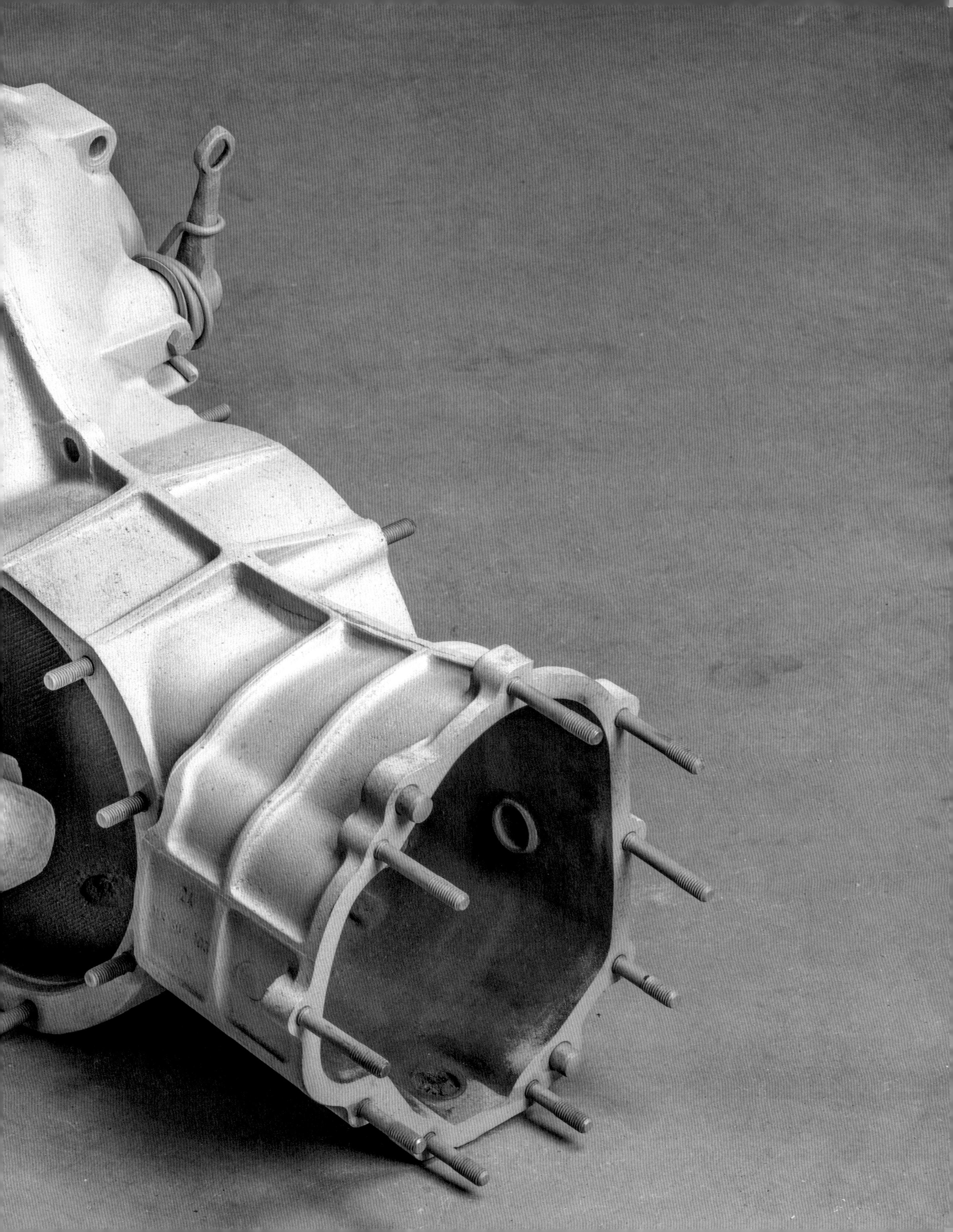

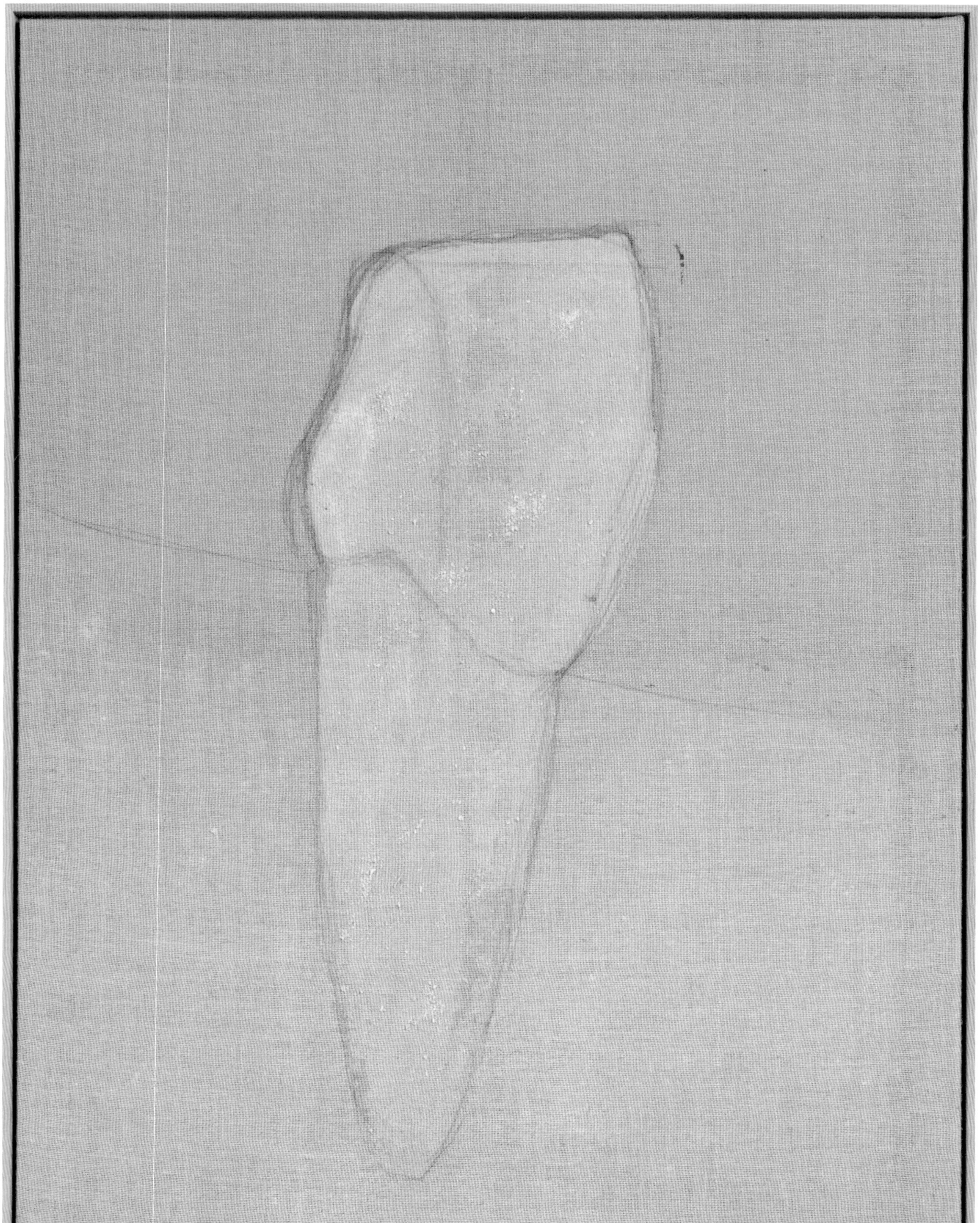

Zahn 5, 2020

Pencil, salt and ink on jute / Bleistift, Salz und Tusche auf Jute, 118 × 93 cm (framed / gerahmt)

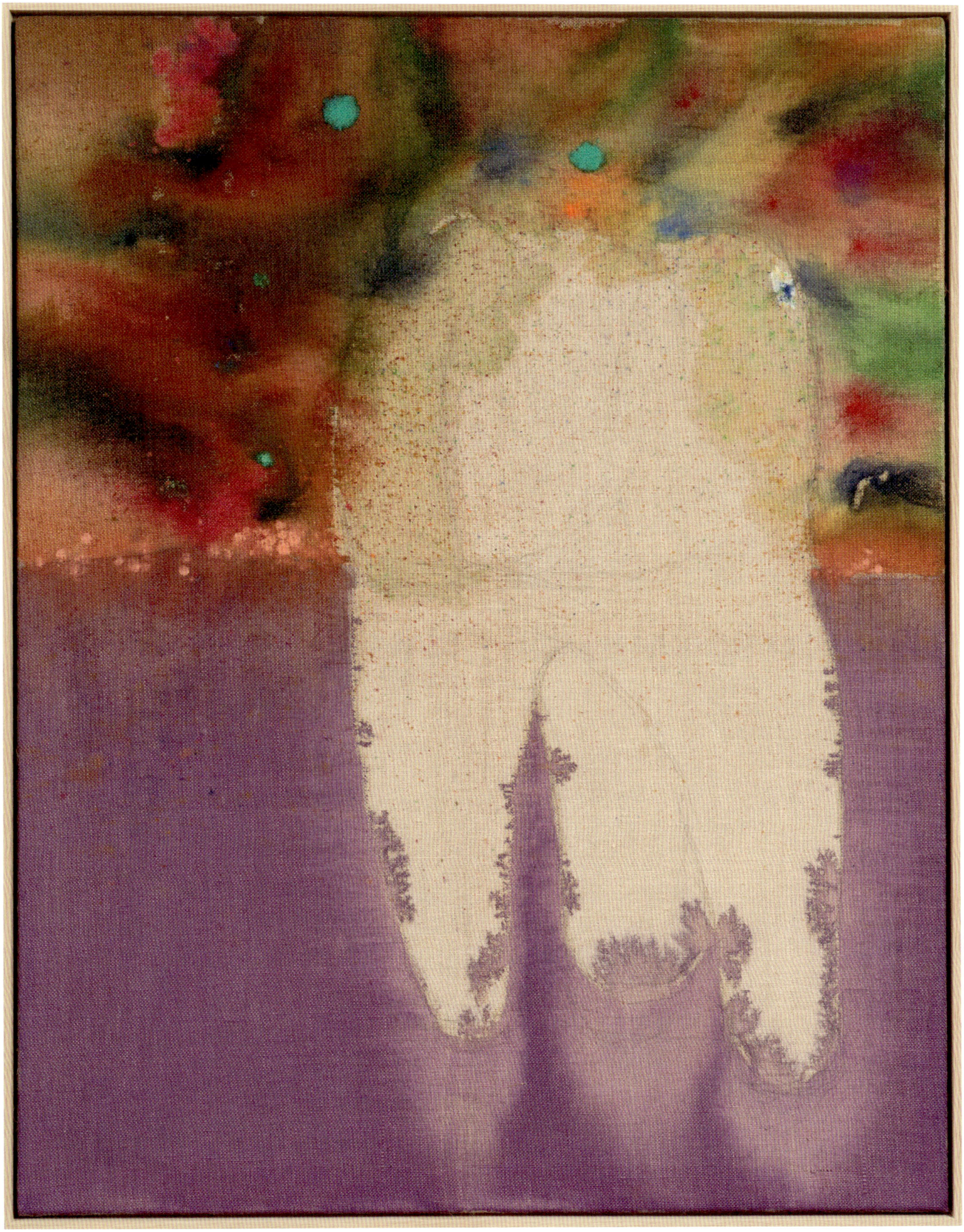

Zahn 2, 2019

Pencil, salt and ink on jute / Bleistift, Salz und Tusche auf Jute, 118 × 93 cm (framed / gerahmt)

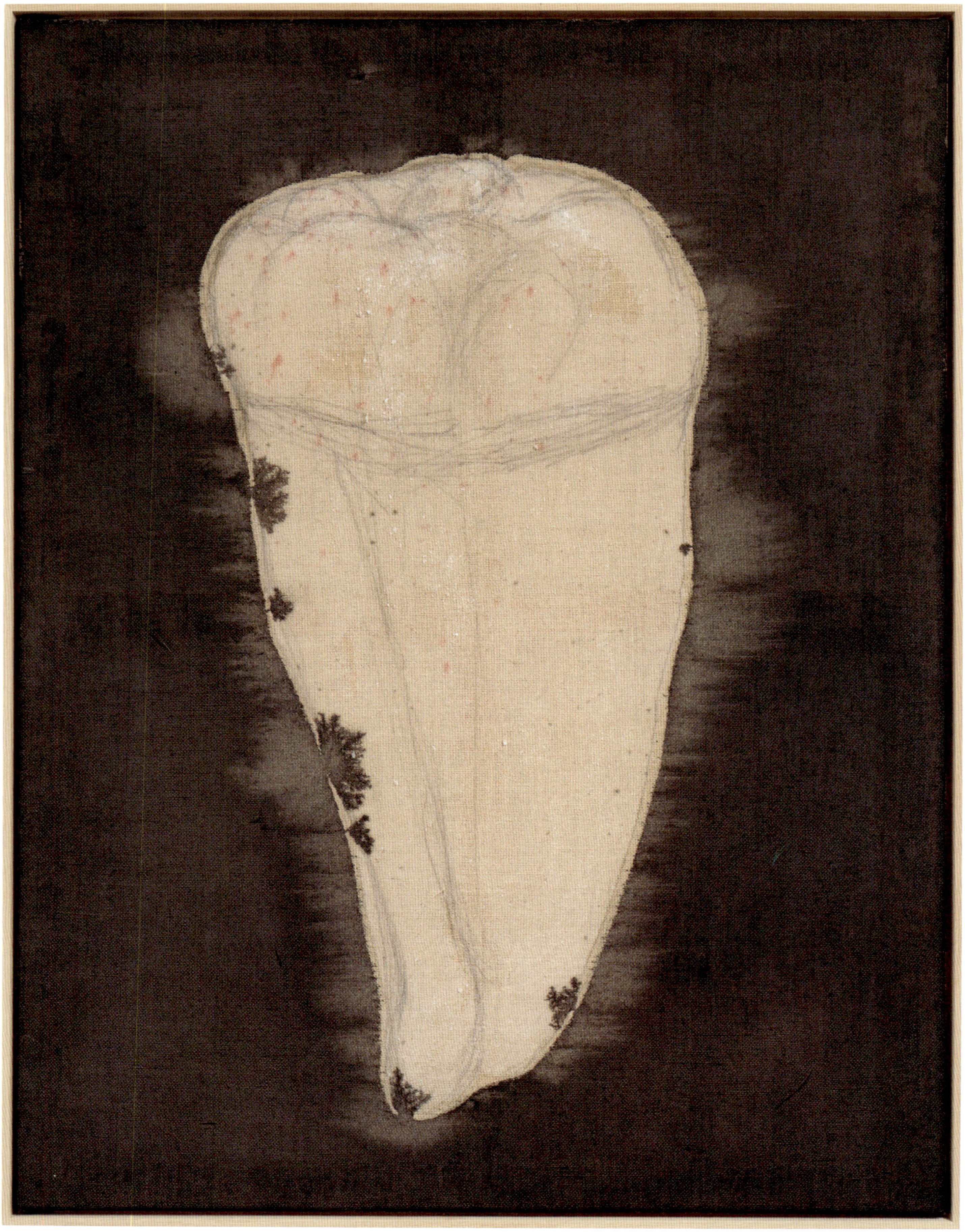

Zahn 3, 2020

Pencil, salt and ink on jute / Bleistift, Salz und Tusche auf Jute,
118 × 93 cm (framed / gerahmt)

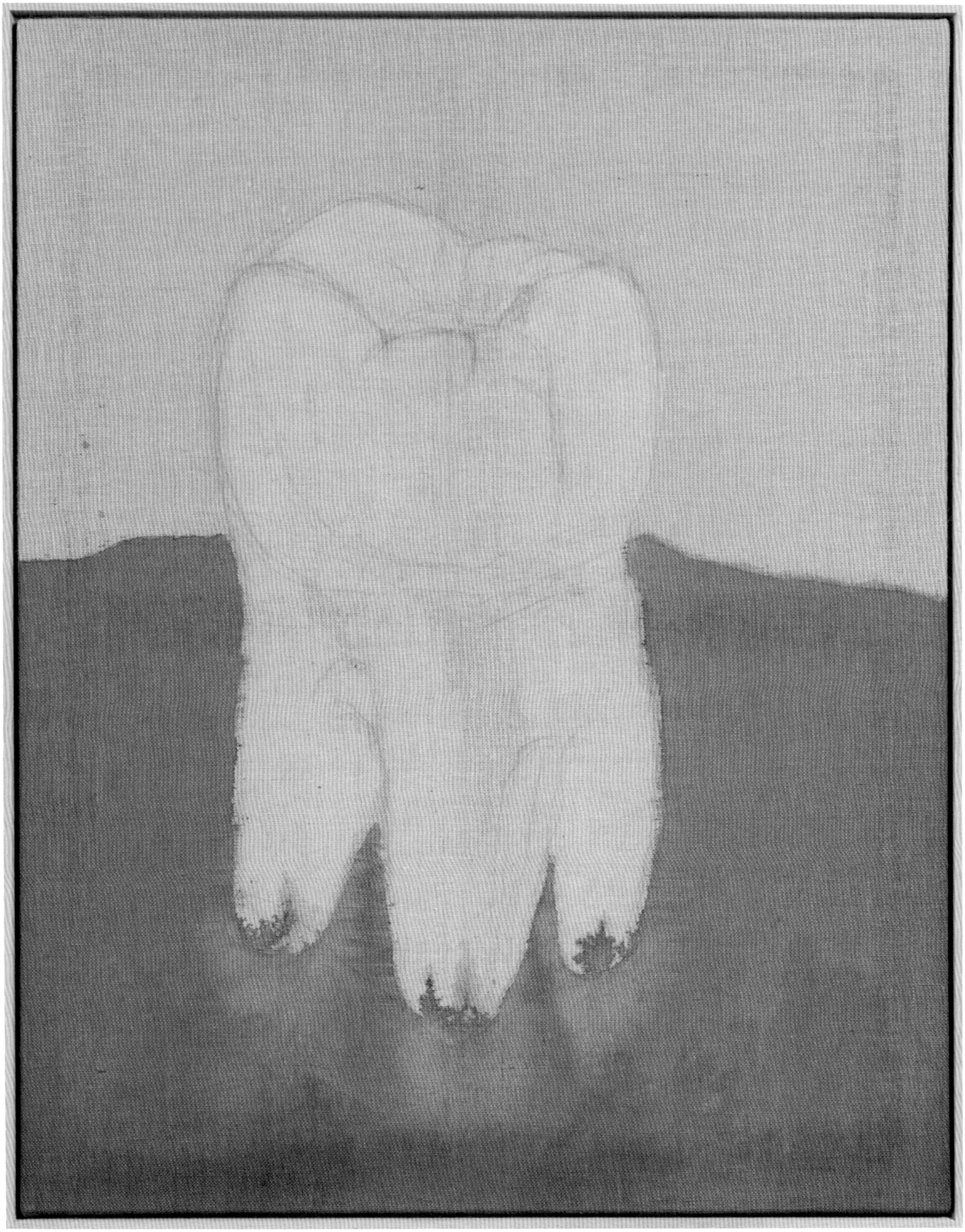

Zahn 1, 2019

Pencil, salt and ink on jute / Bleistift, Salz und Tusche auf Jute, 118 × 93 cm (framed / gerahmt)

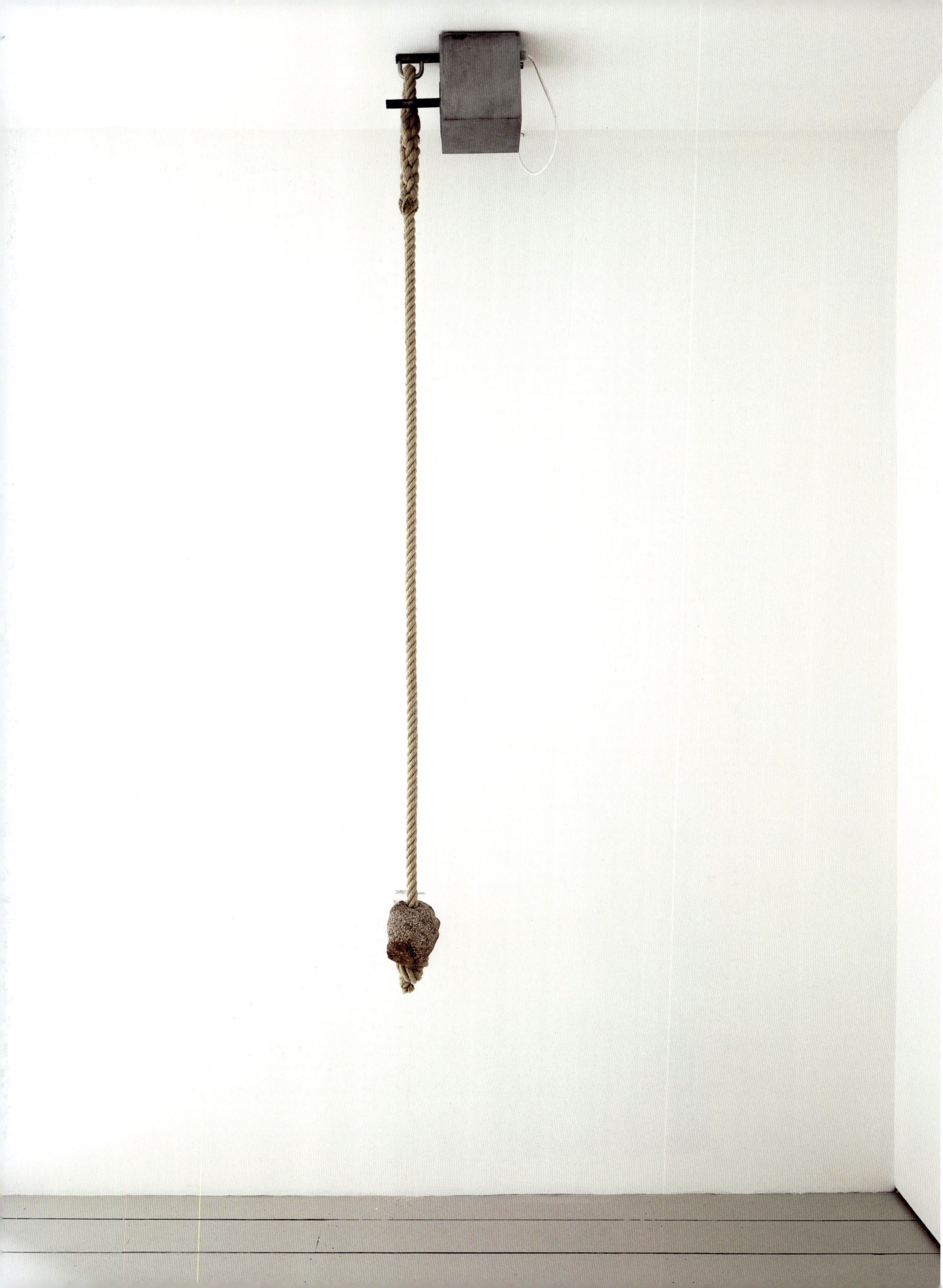

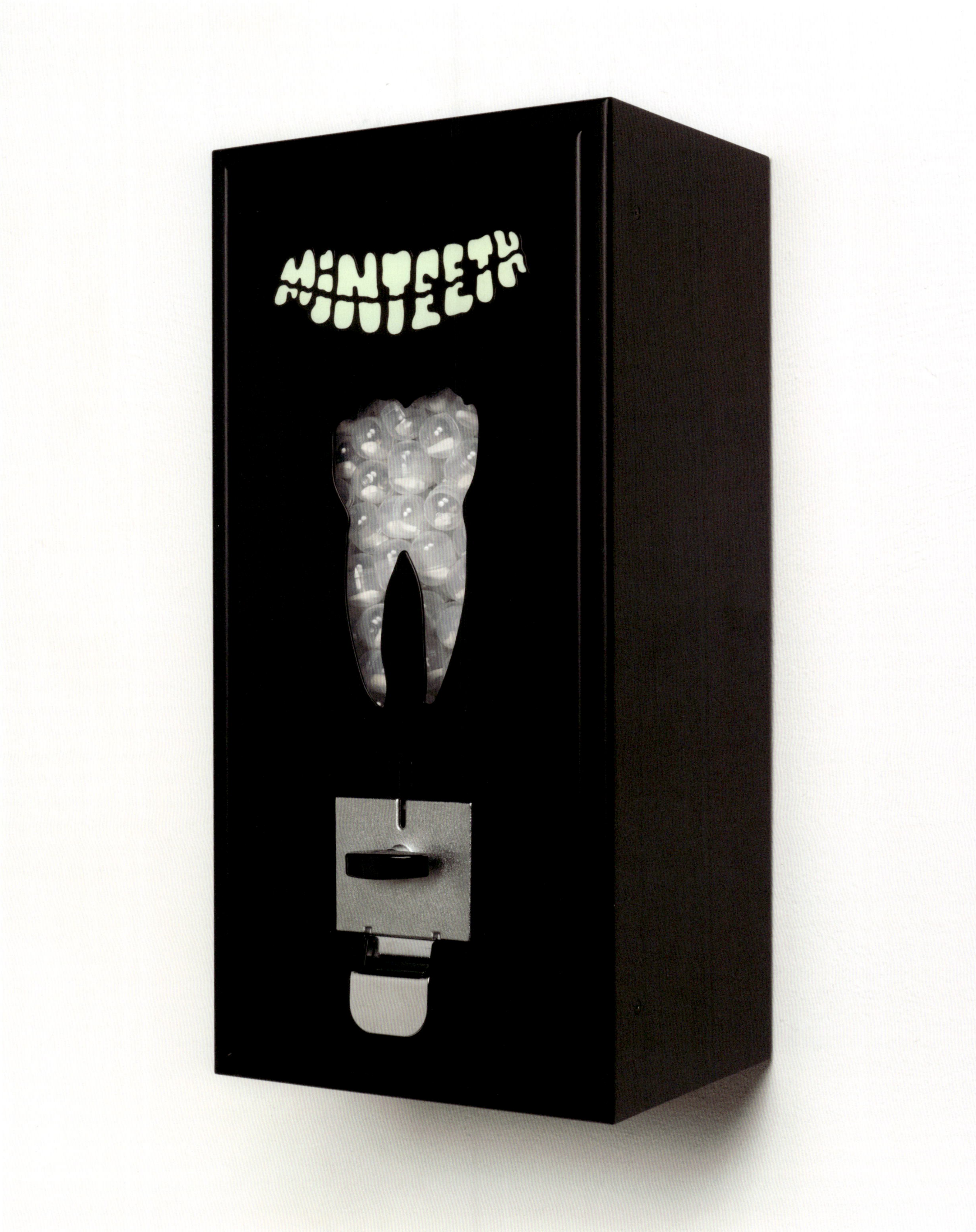

Granite 1, 2018

Granite, rope, motor / Granit, Seil, Motor, Dimensions variable / Maße variabel

Minteeth, 2022

Vendor / Automat, 56,5 × 28 × 21cm

Sigurd Larsen

SALT

SALZ

Strange white objects, shaped like teeth from an oversized human were scattered around the floor and stairs of the Studio Berlin's exhibition in Berghain during lockdown. Michael Sailstorfer's work with salt was immediately inspiring to me. Both because of the beauty of the white translucent surface, but also because of the sinister idea that if you touch or interfere with it, it will disintegrate and be gone.

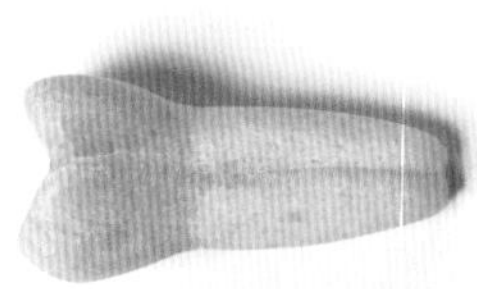

4, 2020

To create objects that are perishable seem to me like a new interpretation of Vanitas symbols. They remind us that life on earth is temporary and should be enjoyed while it lasts. A great match with the exhibition space in Berghain which is famous for its long hedonistic parties, week after week, year after year. But not for all eternity.
The material of the art piece might disintegrate and evaporate if you touch it with your wet hands. It might be absorbed by your body through the skin. At first it appears like fine white marble, but it does not possess the same longevity of statues that last for hundreds of generations. This salt is only here in this shape for a while.
When the teeth sculptures were carved out from a block, salt grains were the only leftover material. With these grains, Michael Sailstorfer made a series of paintings on canvas. One of the paintings has a beautiful curvy shape defined by a slim black line on the raw canvas, made white and textured by salt grains. It can be seen as an elevation of a tooth, or a lower torso with a leg. It could also be a plan drawing of a white building on a rock.
Seeing the painting was love at first sight so I got in touch with Michael. The piece was perfect for a white house we are building on a cliff by the sea on the Greek island Kythnos. The place is defined by a fresh salty breeze from the Aegean Sea, rocky landscapes and vernacular architecture of white chalked walls. In this environment, the salt of the painting might disintegrate leaving the canvas empty. Or it might absorb more salt from the air, and continue its process in a new and exciting chapter.

Merkwürdige weiße Objekte, in Gestalt von Zähnen eines überlebensgroßen menschlichen Wesens, waren auf dem Boden und den Treppen der Ausstellung *Studio Berlin*, die während des Lockdowns im Berghain stattfand, verstreut. Die Arbeit aus Salz von Michael Sailstorfer begeisterte mich sofort. Sowohl wegen der Schönheit ihrer weißen lichtdurchlässigen Oberfläche, als auch wegen der finsteren Idee, dass wenn man sie anfasst oder anderweitig mit ihr in Kontakt kommt, sie sich auflöst und nicht mehr da ist.
Dinge zu erschaffen, die vergänglich sind, erschien mir wie eine neue Interpretation von Vanitas-Symbolen. Sie erinnern uns daran, dass das Leben auf der Erde endlich ist und man es genießen soll, solange es währt. Das passte zu der Ausstellung im Berghain, das berühmt für seine ausschweifenden hedonistischen Partys ist, Woche für Woche, Jahr für Jahr. Aber nicht für alle Ewigkeit.
Das Material des Kunstwerks kann zerfallen und verdunsten, wenn man es mit feuchten Händen berührt. Es kann vom Körper durch die Haut absorbiert werden. Zuerst erscheint es wie feiner weißer Marmor, aber es besitzt nicht die gleiche Langlebigkeit von Statuen, die hunderte von Generationen überdauern. Dieses Salz behält seine Form nur eine Weile.
Als die Zahnskulpturen aus einem Block gemeißelt wurden, blieben nur jede Menge Salzkörner übrig. Mit diesen Körnern machte Michael Sailstorfer eine Serie von Arbeiten auf Leinwand. Eines der Gemälde hat eine wunderbar kurvige Kontur, die von einer dünnen schwarzen Linie auf dem unbearbeiteten, nur durch die Salzkörner weiß texturierten Leinen definiert wird. Es kann als ein Aufriss eines Zahns oder als unterer Torso mit einem Bein gedeutet werden. Es könnte aber auch eine Planzeichnung für ein weißes Gebäude auf einem Felsen sein.
Als ich das Bild sah, war es Liebe auf den ersten Blick, deshalb kontaktierte ich Michael. Die Arbeit war perfekt für das weiße Haus, das wir gerade auf der griechischen Insel Kythnos auf einer Klippe am Meer bauen. Der Ort zeichnet sich durch eine frische salzige Brise von der Ägäis, eine felsige Landschaft und die landestypische Architektur mit weiß gekalkten Mauern aus. In dieser Umgebung könnte sich das Salz auflösen und eine leere Leinwand hinterlassen oder es könnte mehr Salz aus der Luft aufnehmen und seinen Prozess in einem neuen aufregenden Kapitel fortsetzen.

Minteeth, 2022
Mint sweets / Minzbonbons

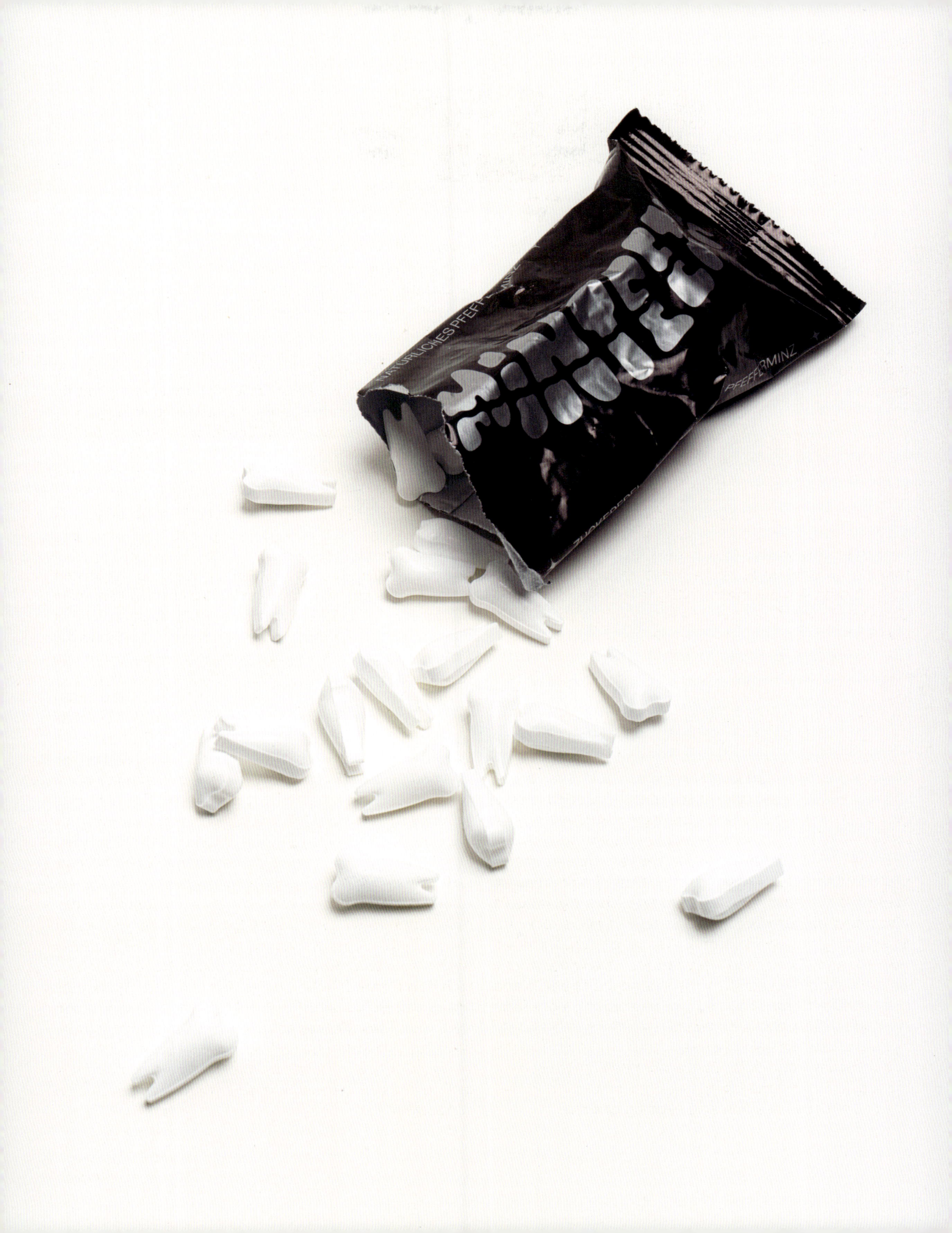
NATÜRLICHES

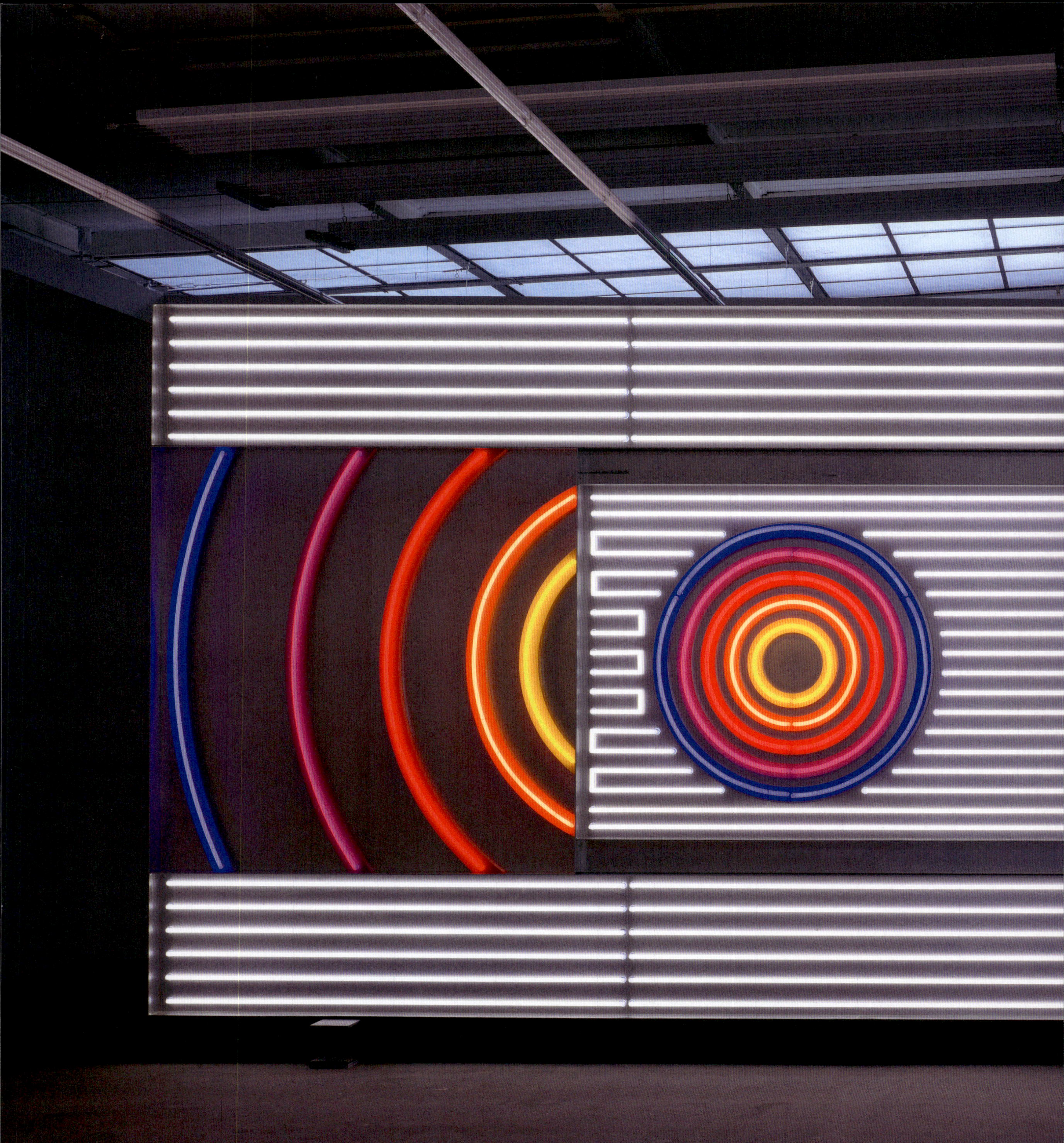

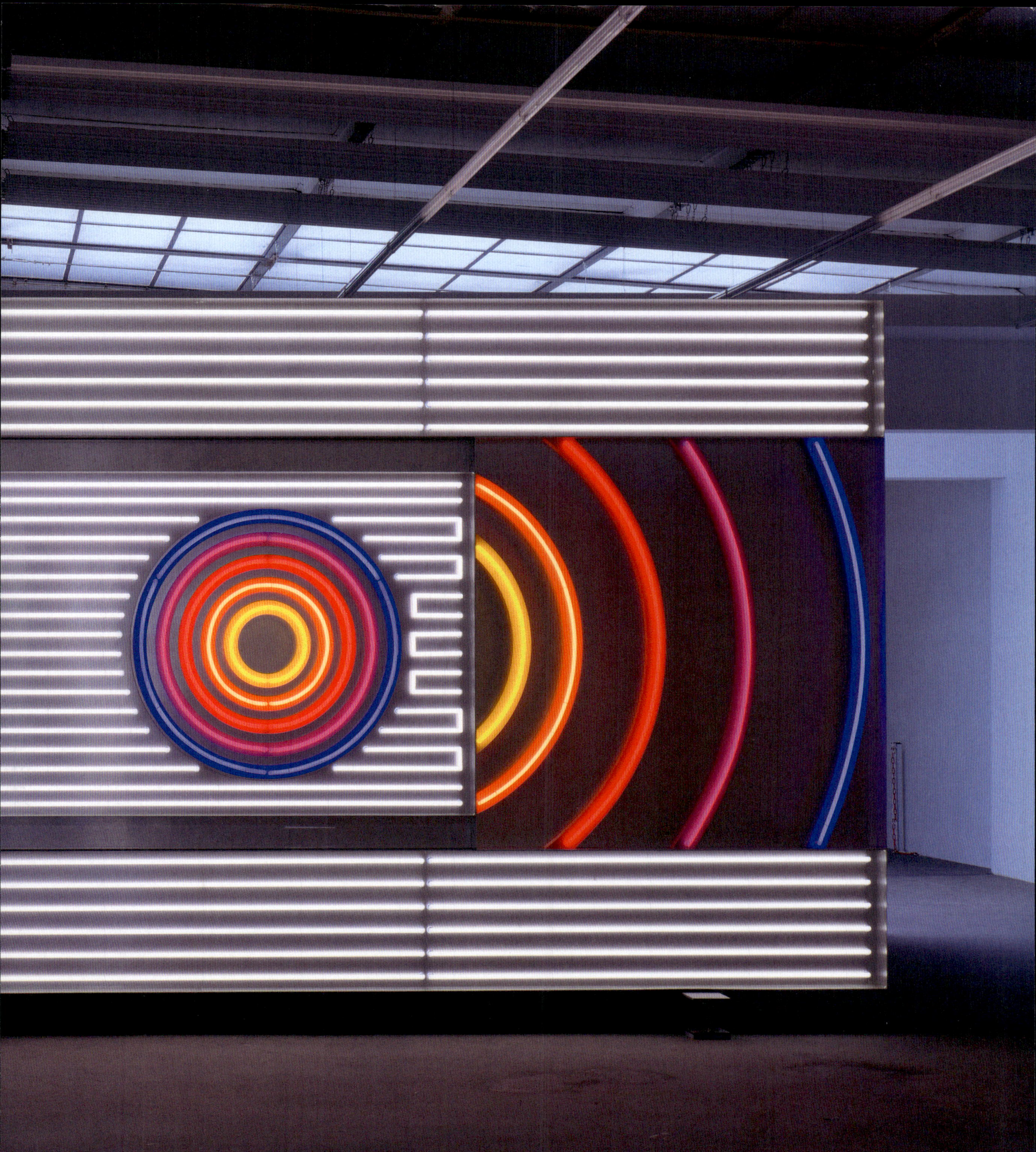

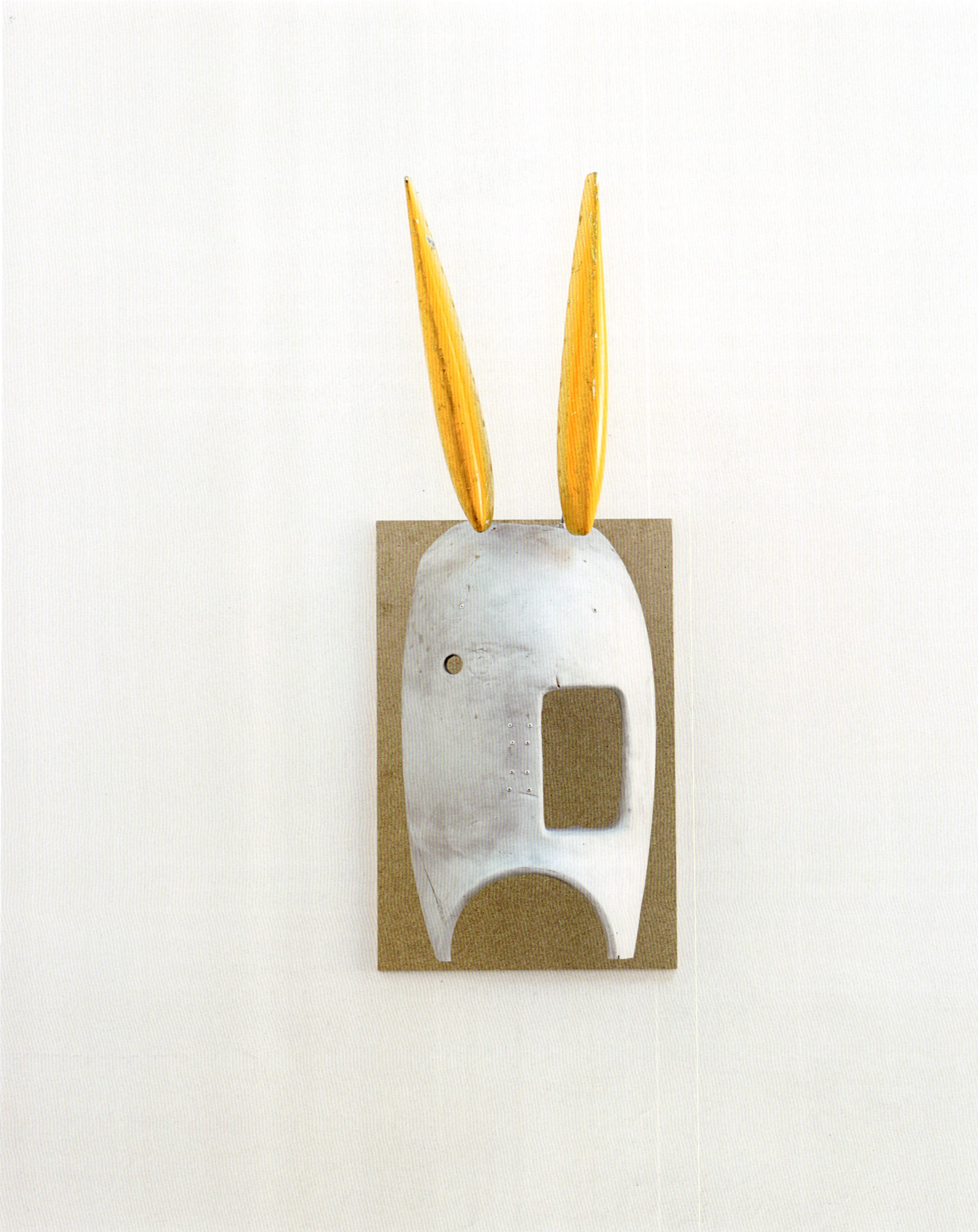

Hase, 2007

Aluminum, wood / Aluminium, Holz, 160 × 60 × 55 cm

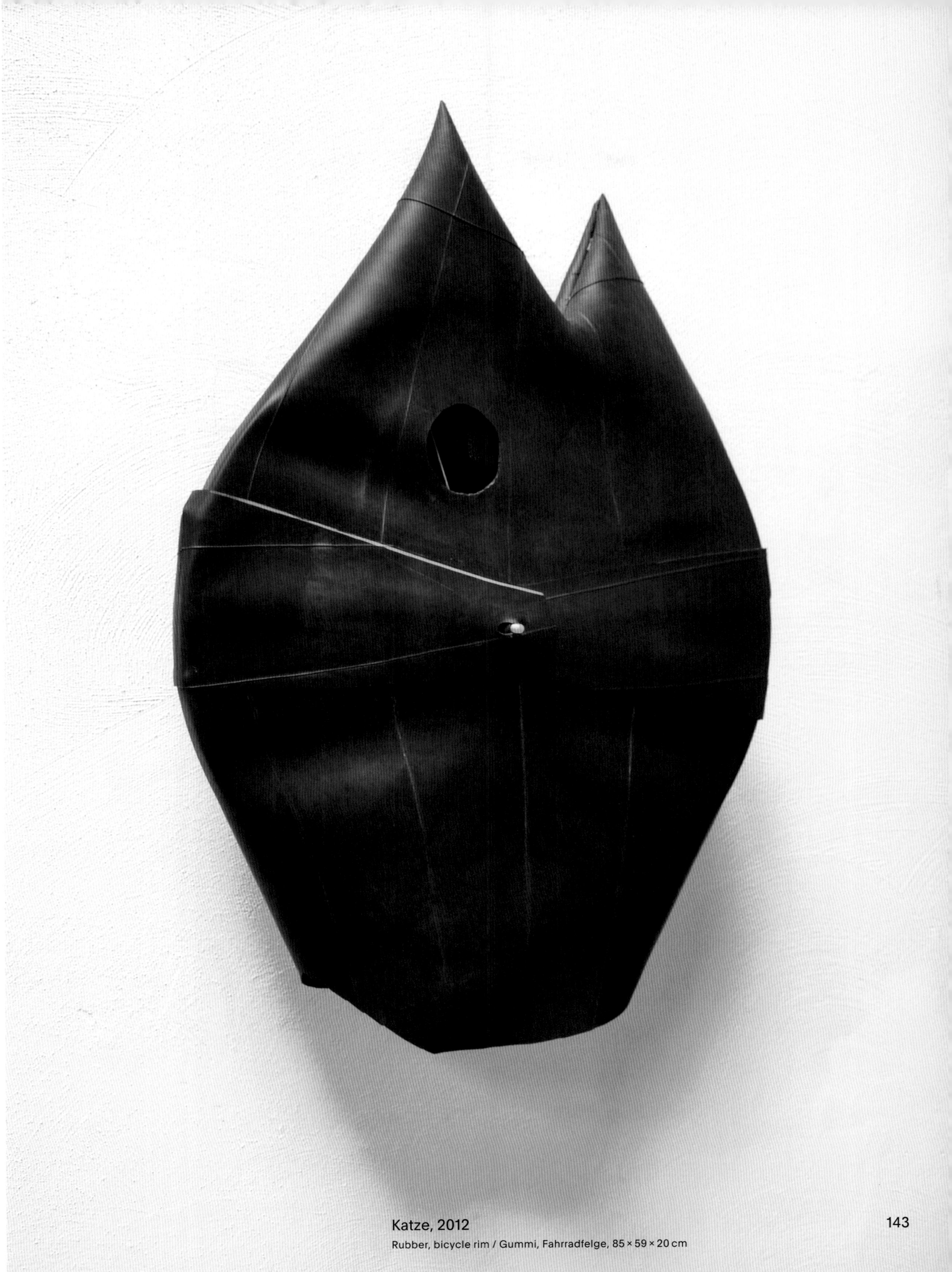

Katze, 2012

Rubber, bicycle rim / Gummi, Fahrradfelge, 85 × 59 × 20 cm

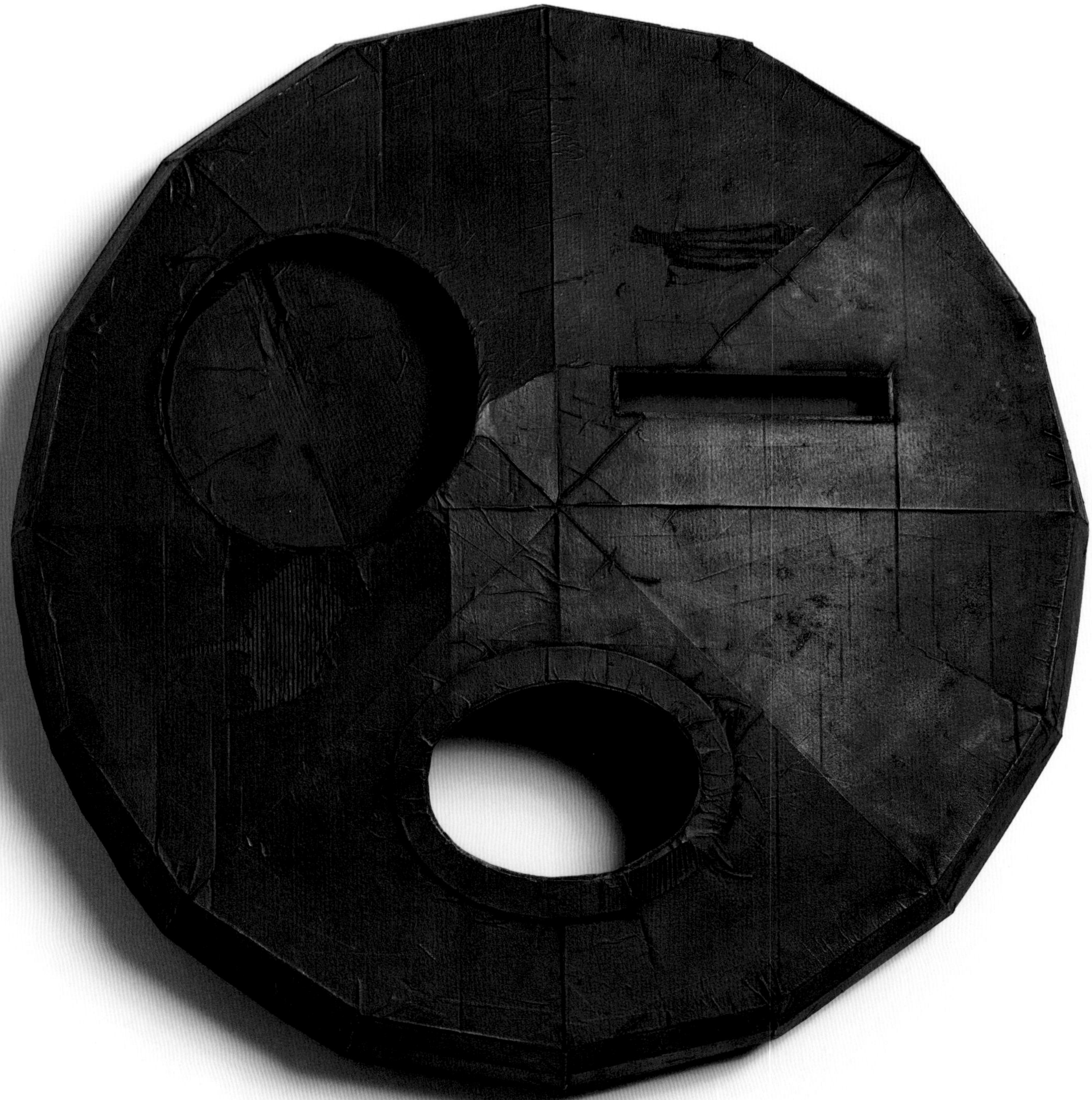

M.84, 2022

Bronze, 86 × 86 × 17 cm

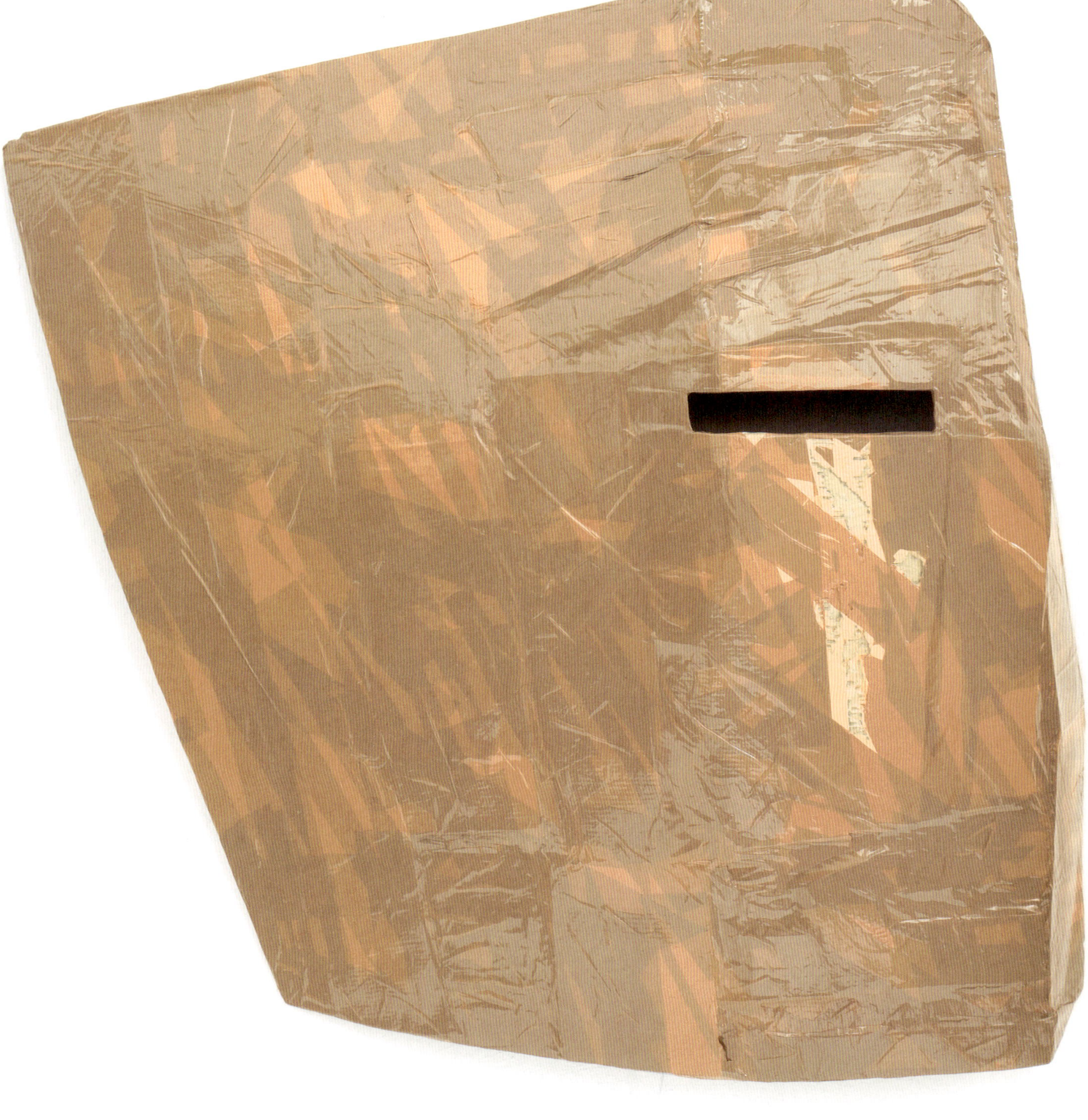

M. 76, 2019

Aluminum, paint / Aluminium, Farbe, 80 × 75 × 24 cm

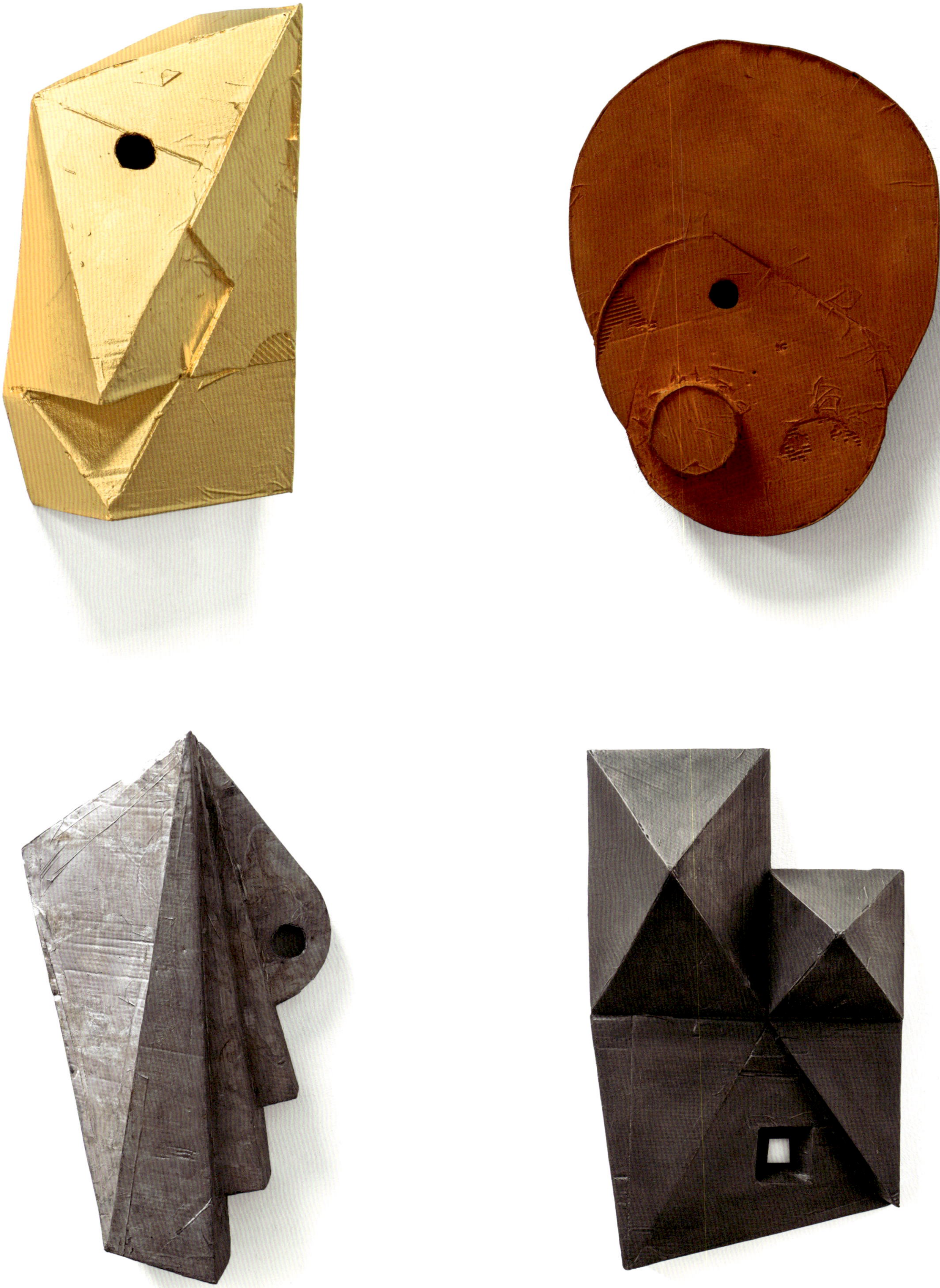

M., 2015–2021

Casts / Güsse, Dimensions variable / Maße variabel

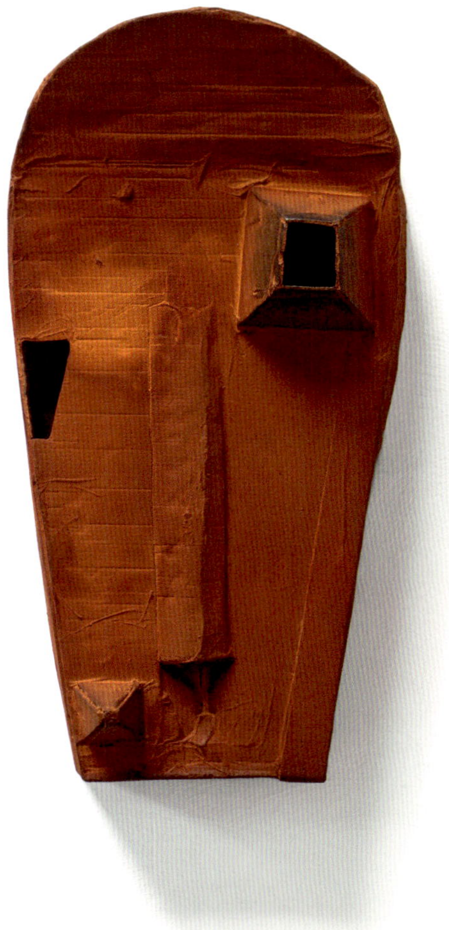

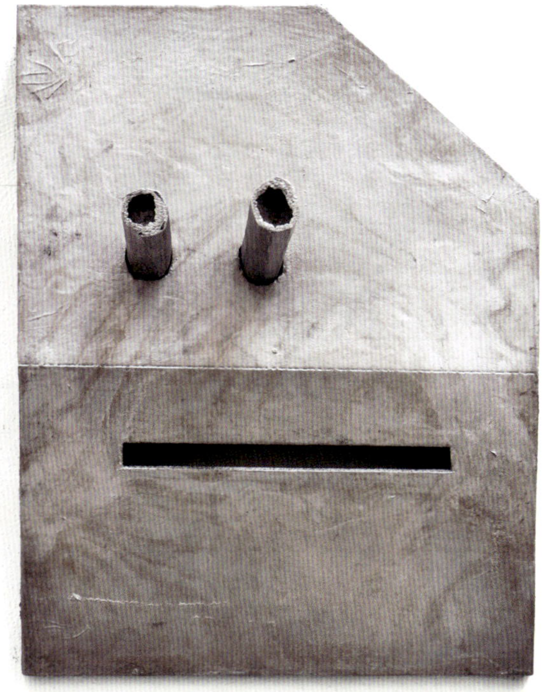

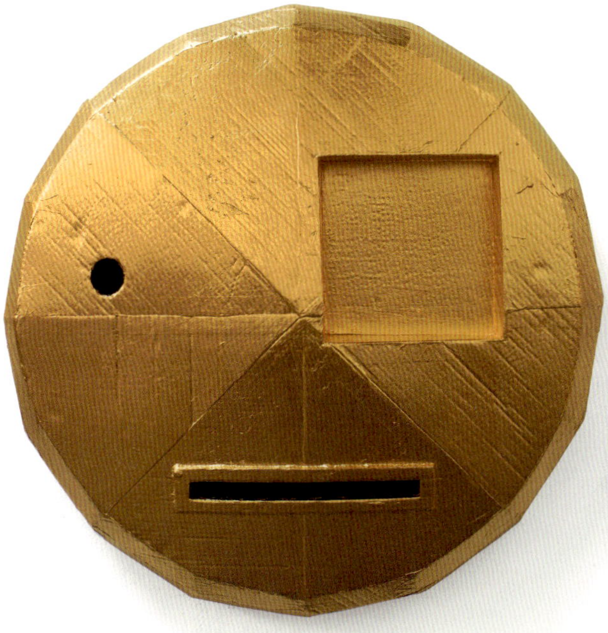

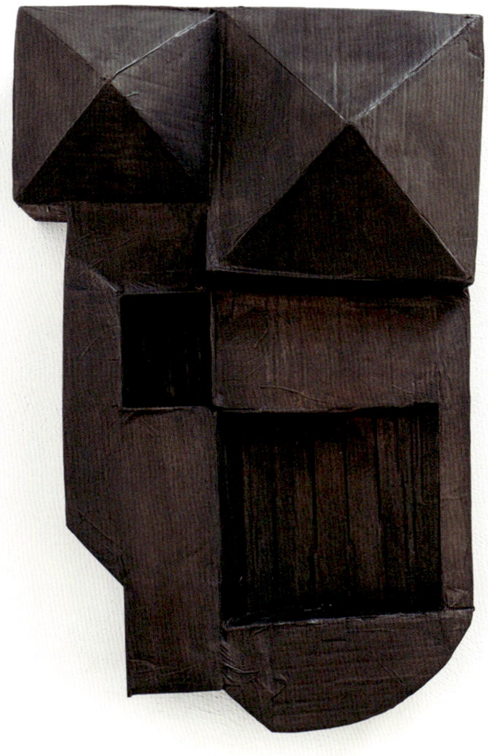

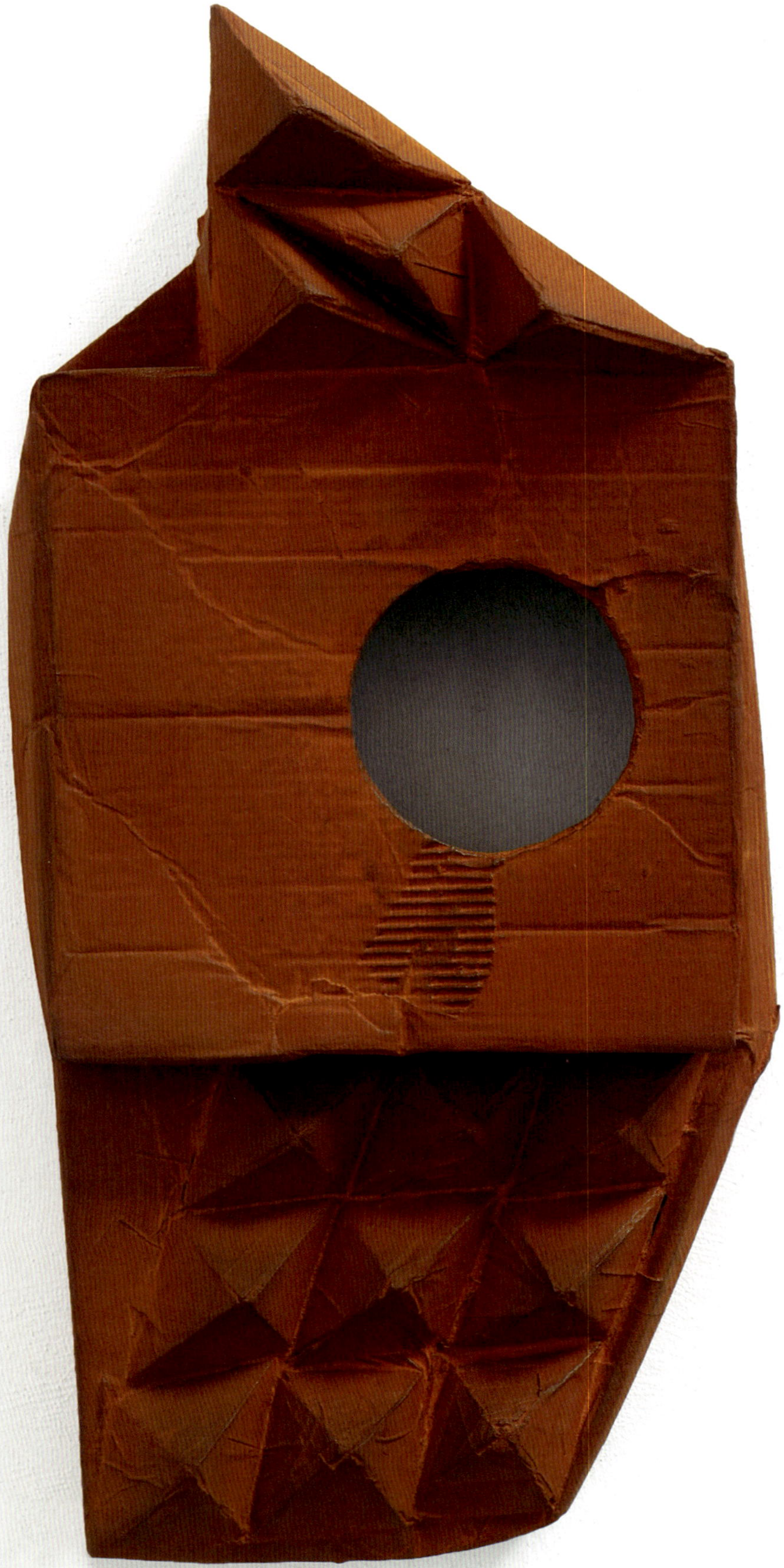

M. 63, 2017

Iron / Eisen, 83 × 43 × 24 cm

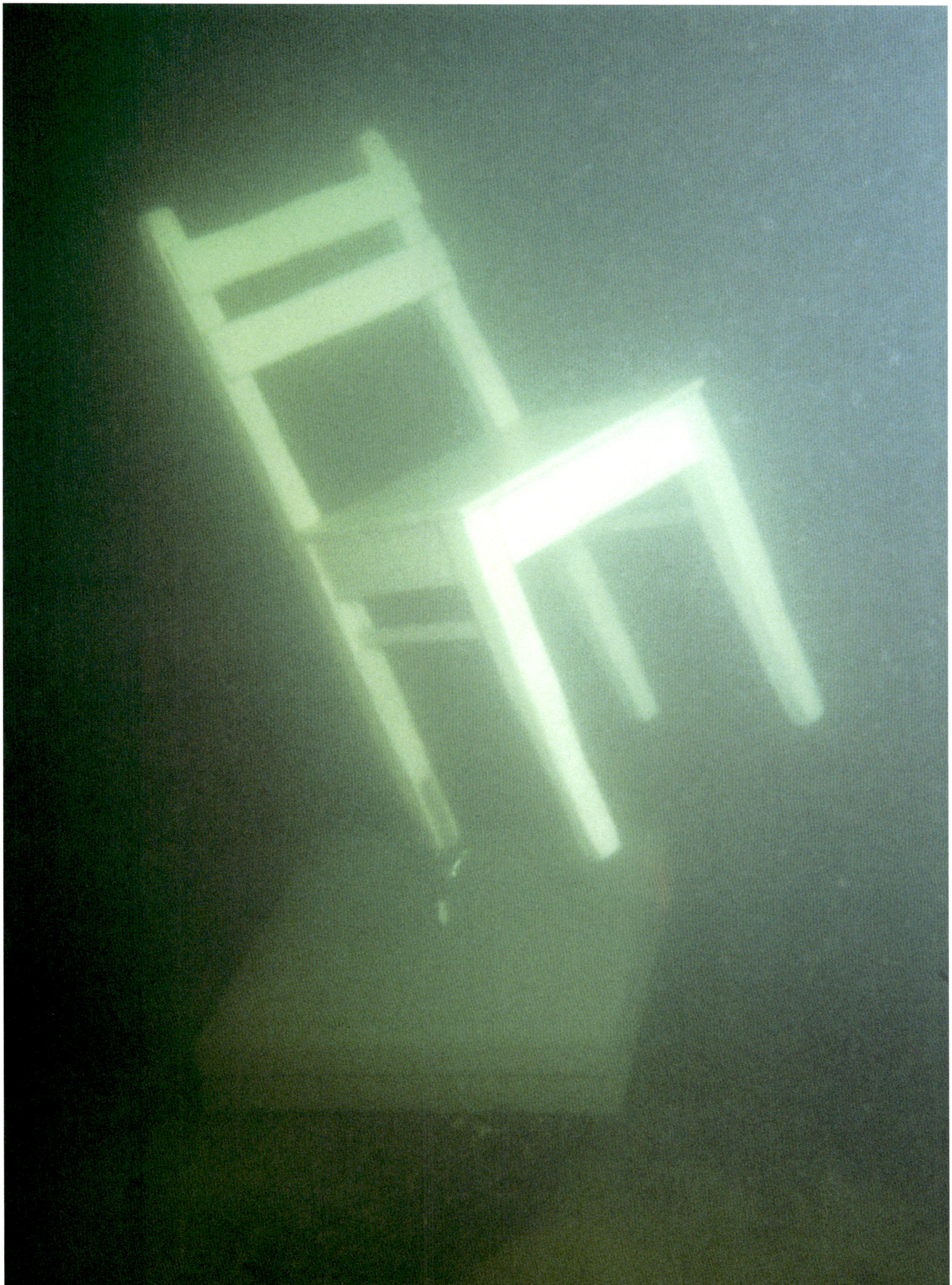

U13, 54° 8' 39,3" N / 12° 7' 59,4" E, 2007

C-print, 75 × 50 cm (framed / gerahmt)

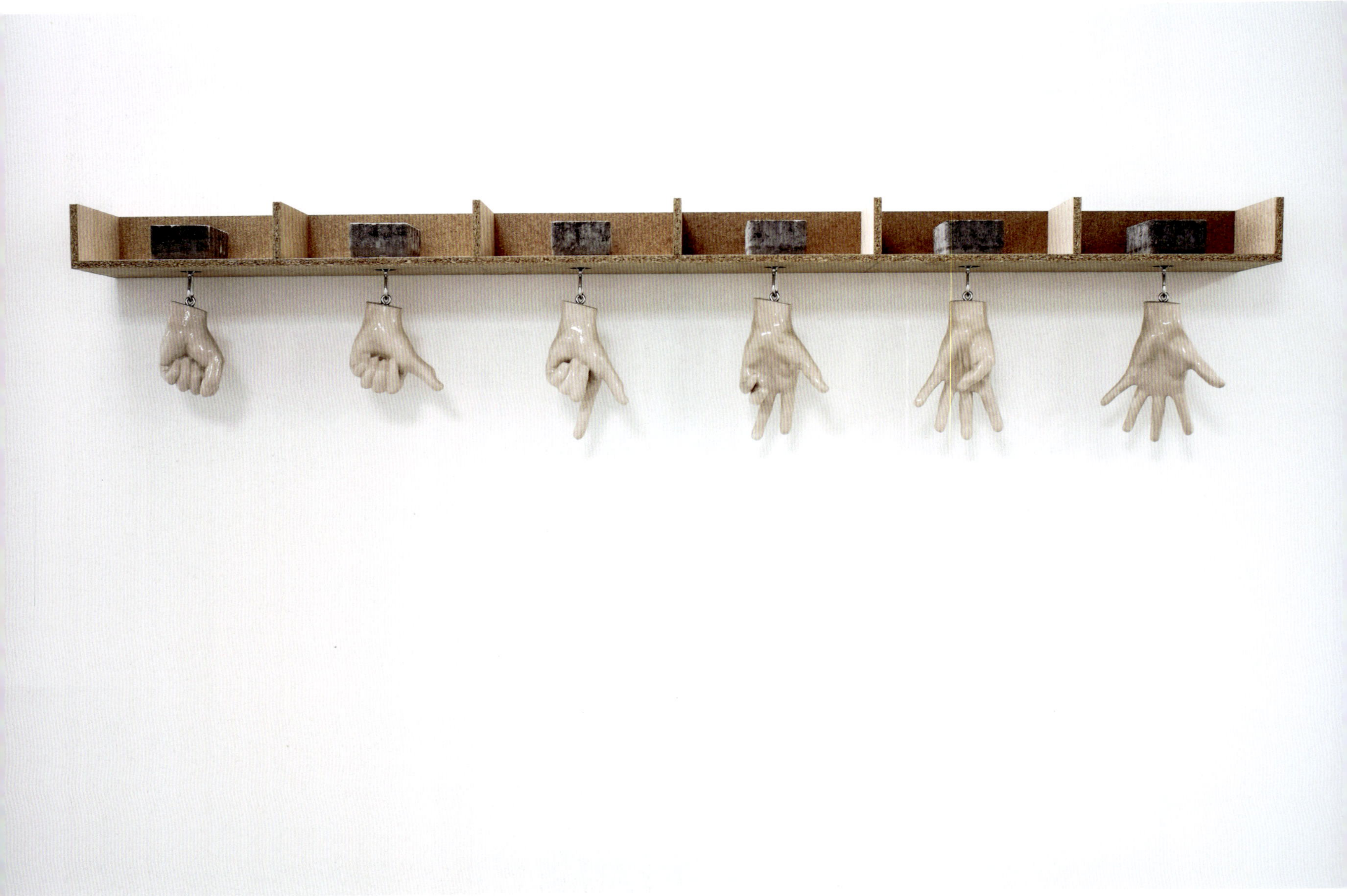

Studie U14, 2008

Concrete, plaster, styrofoam, fiberglass, epoxy resin, wood /
Beton, Gips, Styropor, Glasfaser, Epoxidharz, Holz, 30 × 280 × 60 cm

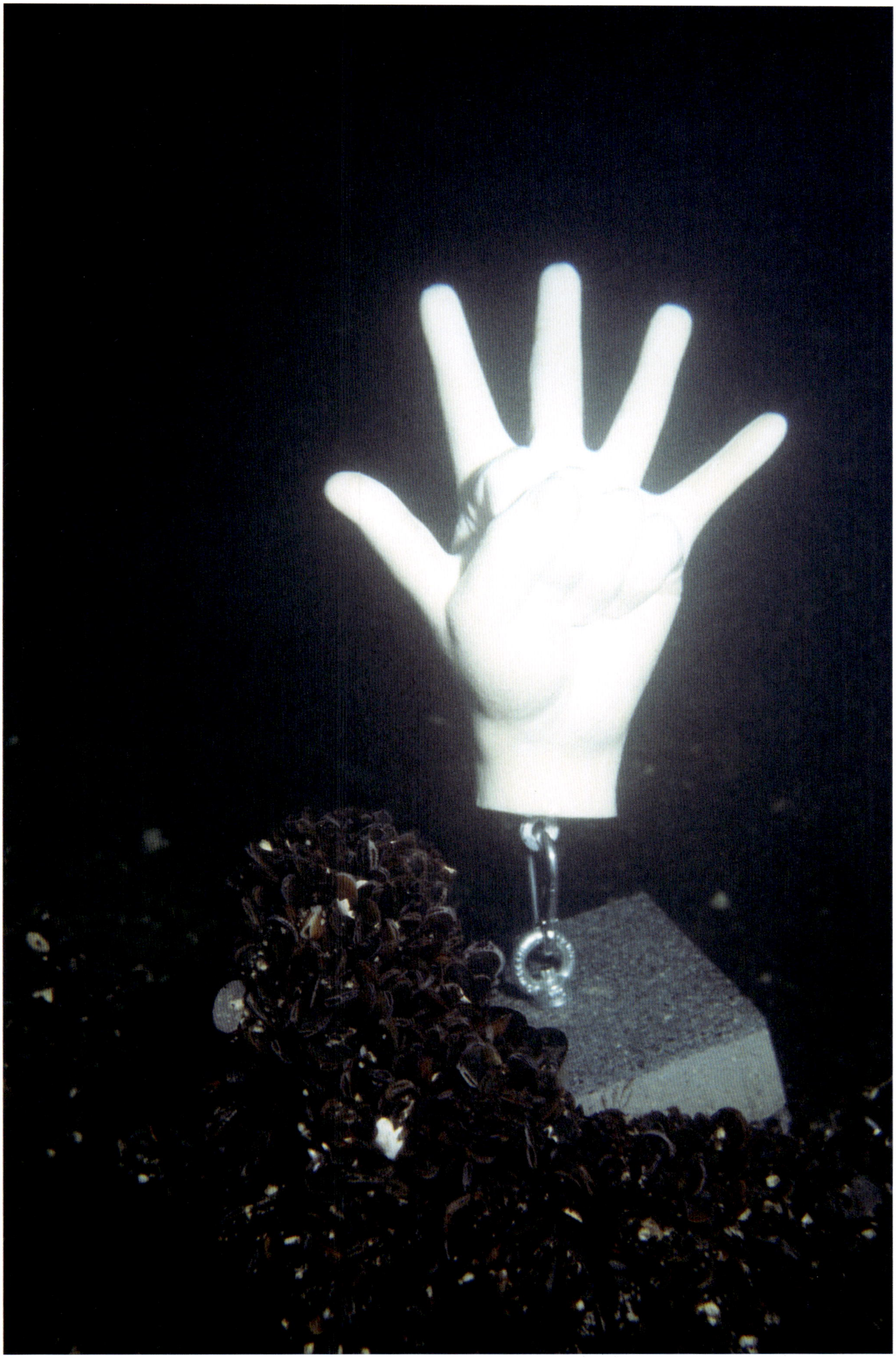

U15, 54° 12' 2,3" N / 12° 08' 8,08" E, 2008

C-print, 75 × 50 cm (framed / gerahmt)

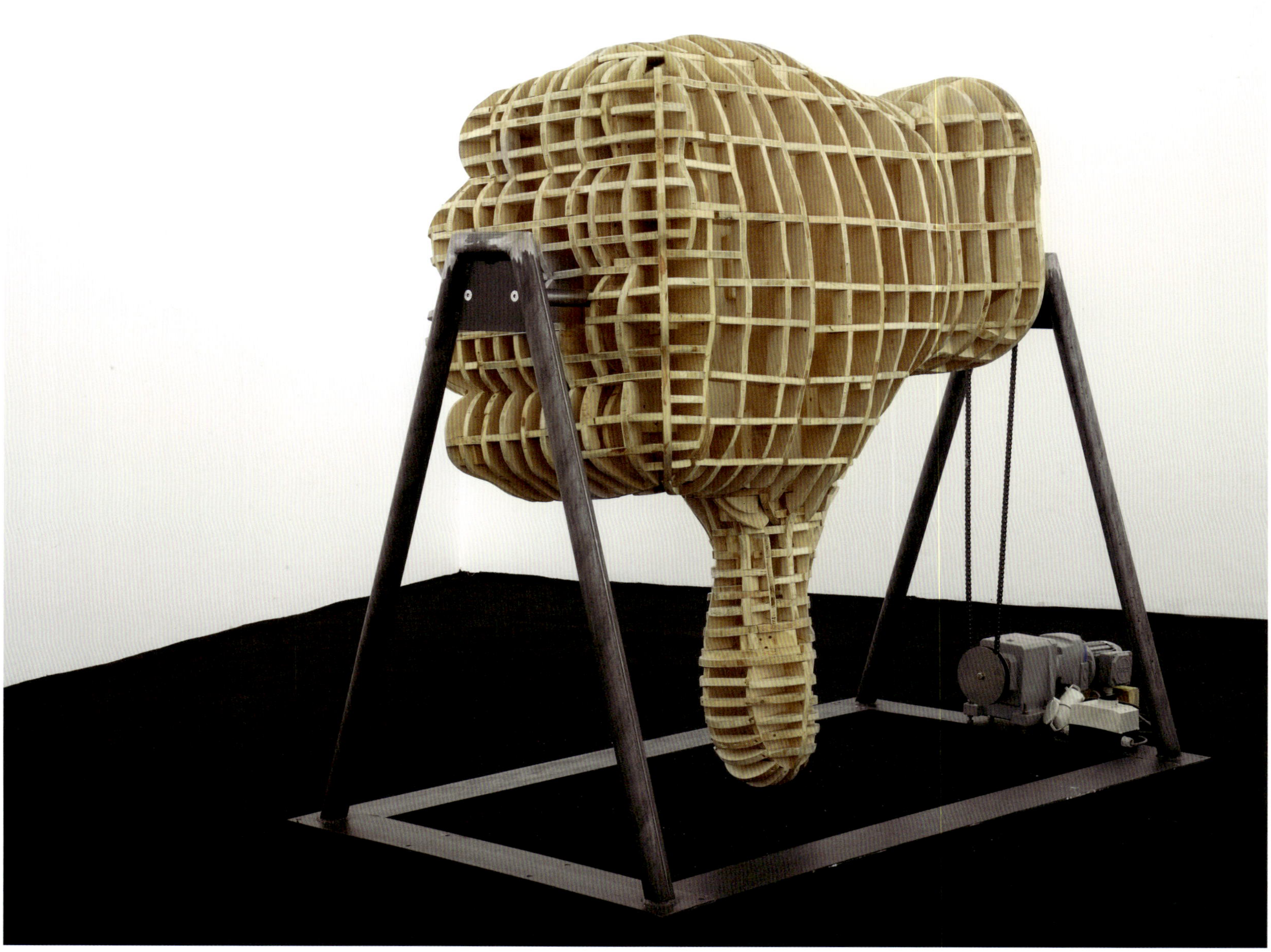

Daumen, 2008

Steel, motor, wood / Stahl, Motor, Holz, 200 × 220 × 110 cm

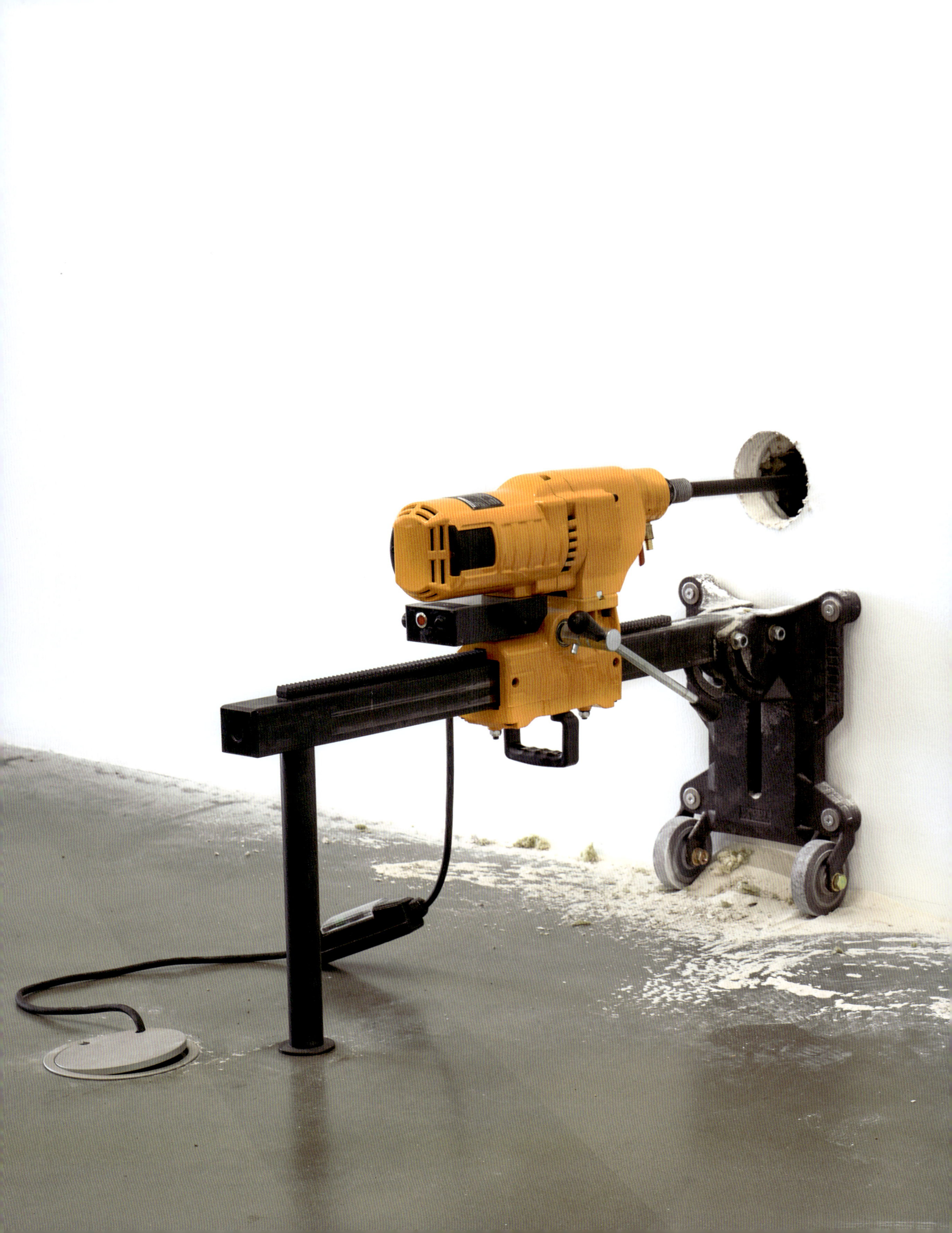

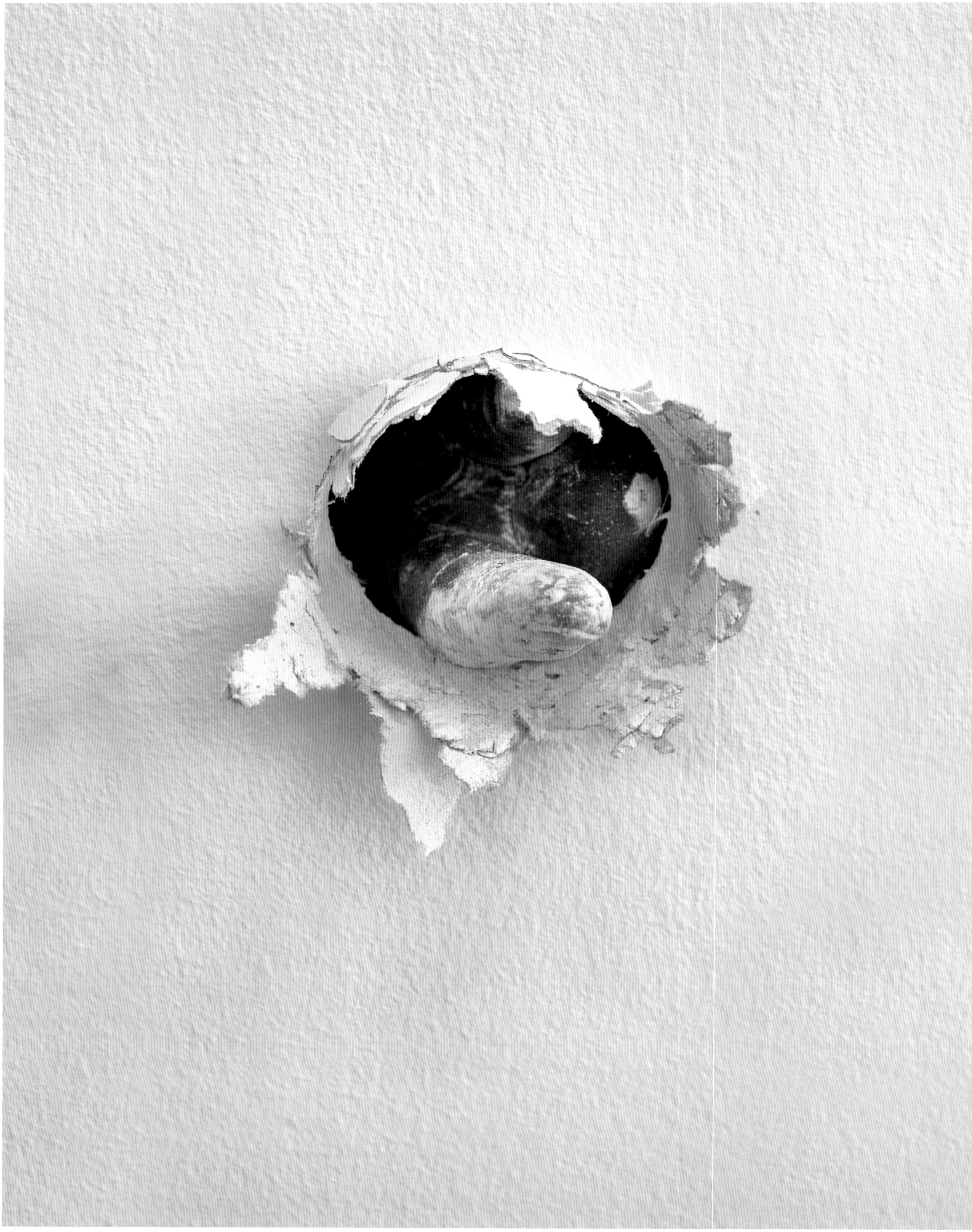

I Want You, 2021

Core drilling machine, steel / Kernbohrmaschine, Stahl, 65 × 45 × 110 cm,
Installation view / Installationsansicht, KINDL – Zentrum für zeitgenössische Kunst, Berlin

Echolot 2, 2022

Bronze, 112,5 × 27 × 9 cm

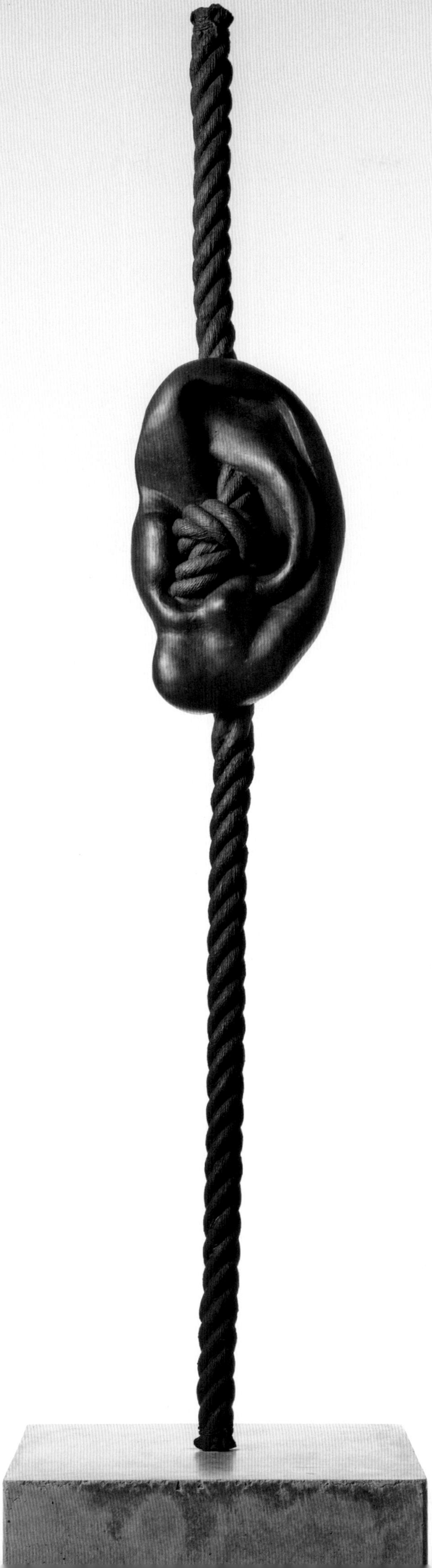

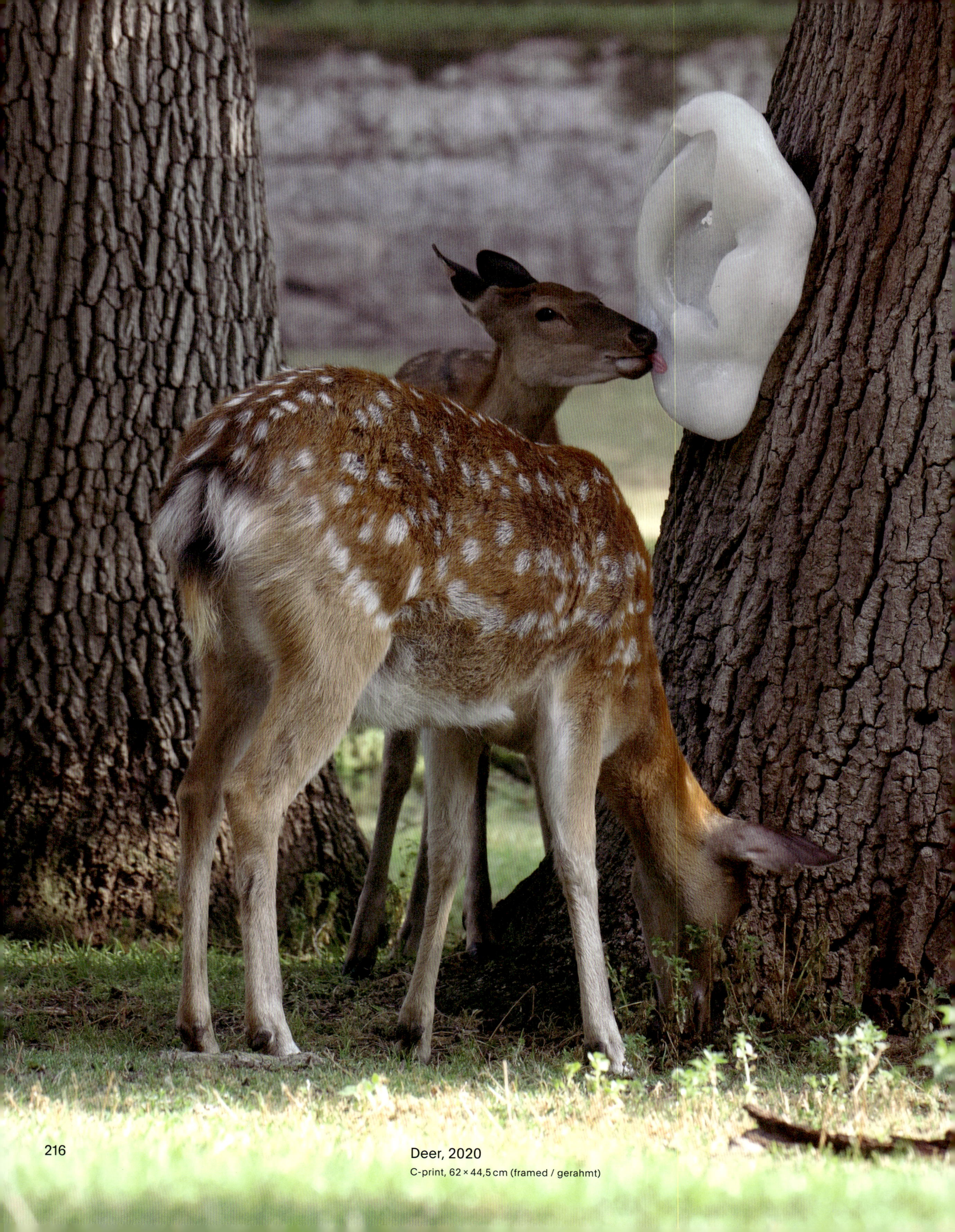

Deer, 2020
C-print, 62 × 44,5 cm (framed / gerahmt)

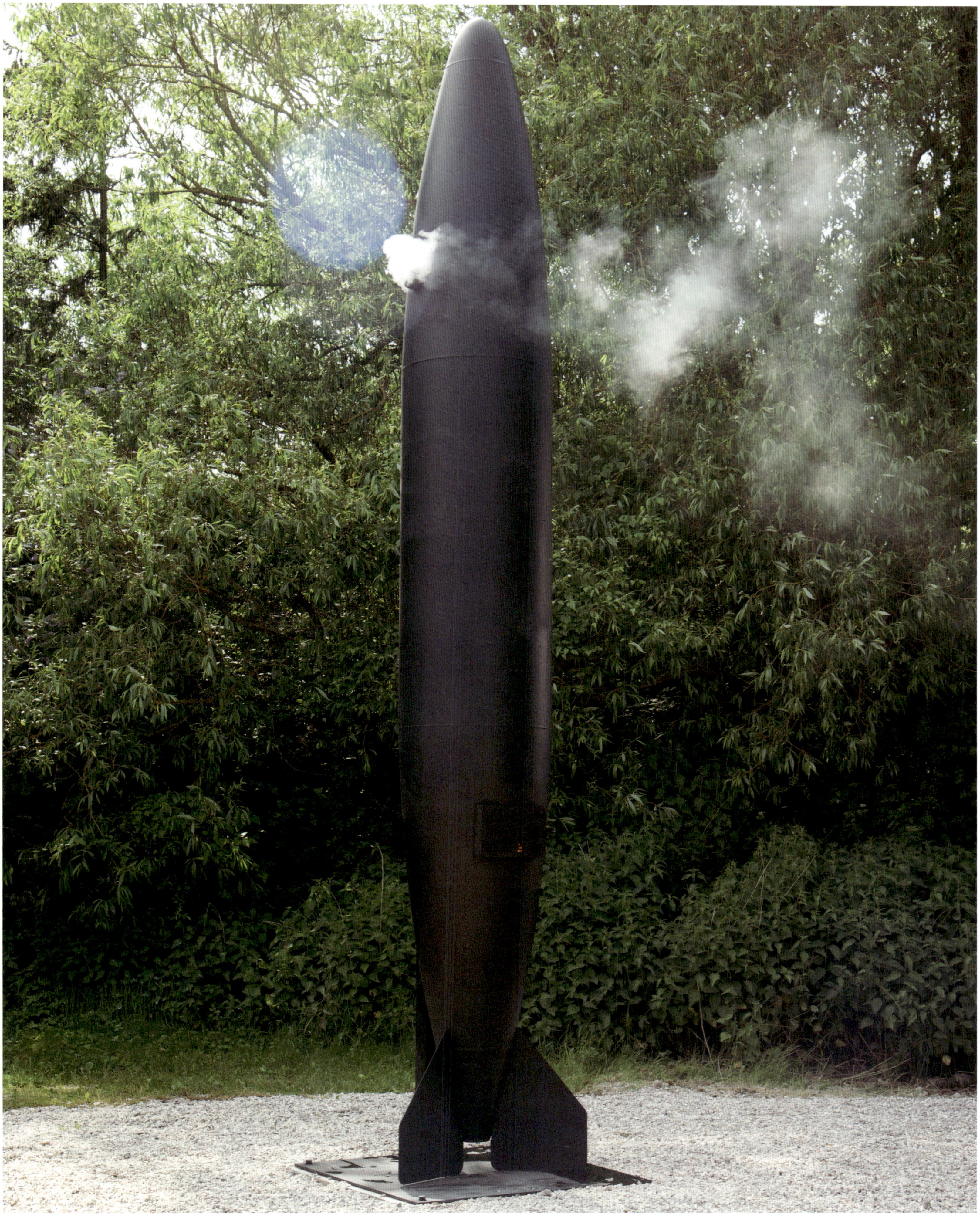

Brenner R02, 2017

Aluminum, steel, paint / Aluminium, Stahl, Farbe, 600 × 80 × 80 cm

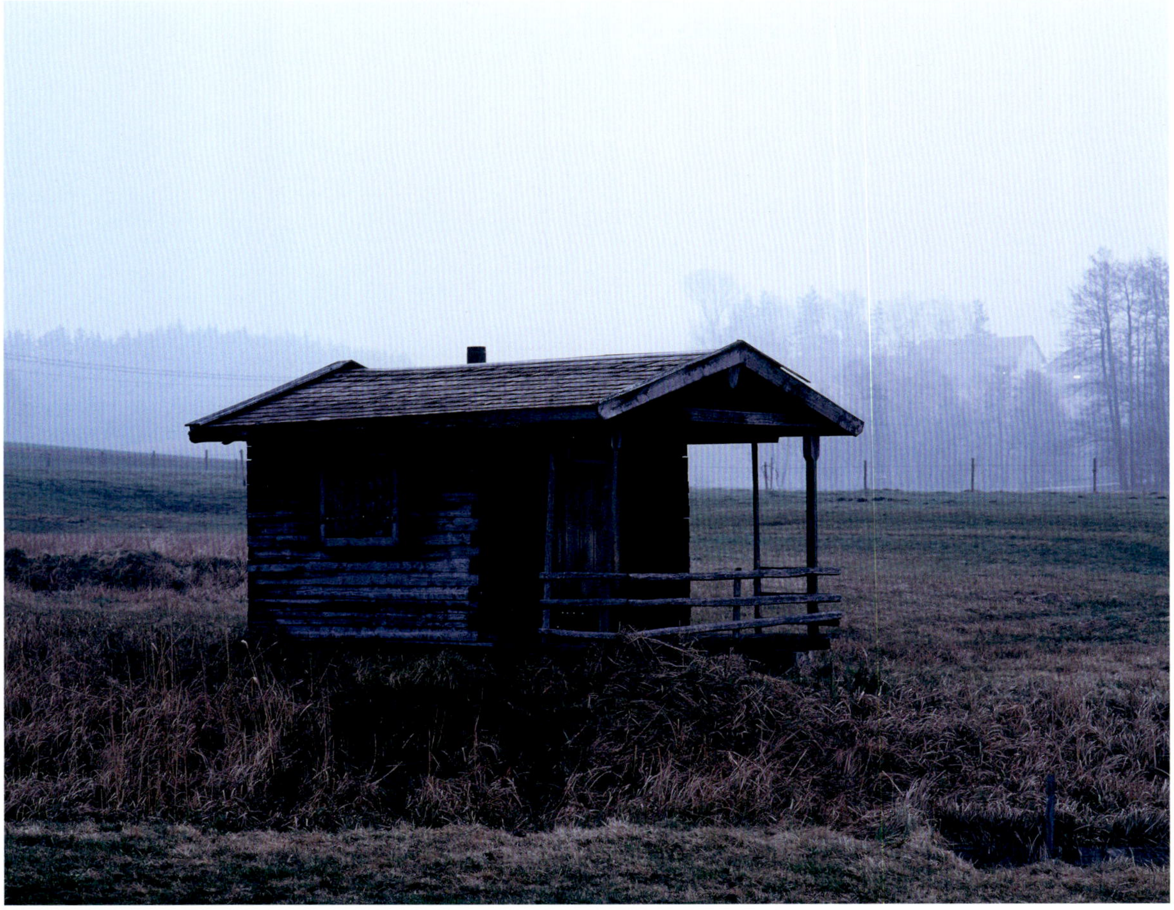

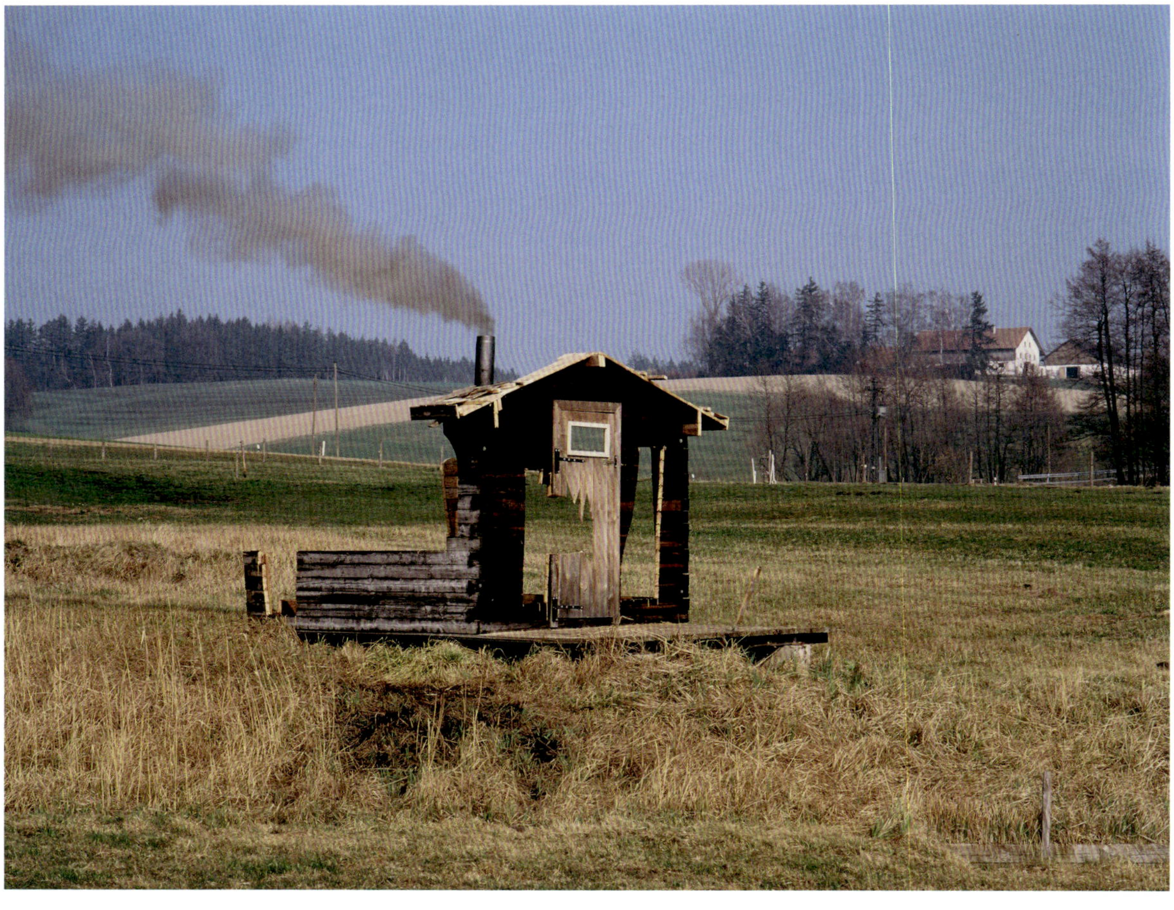

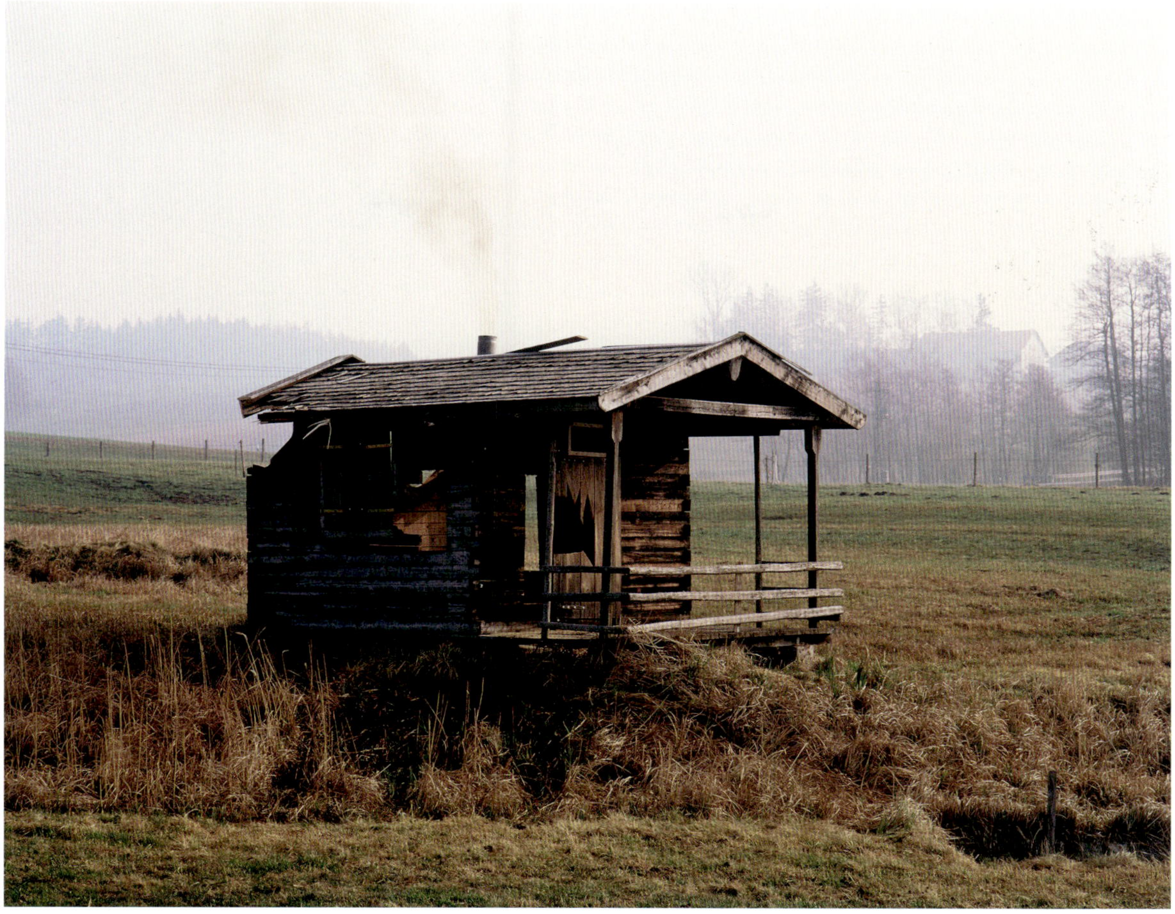

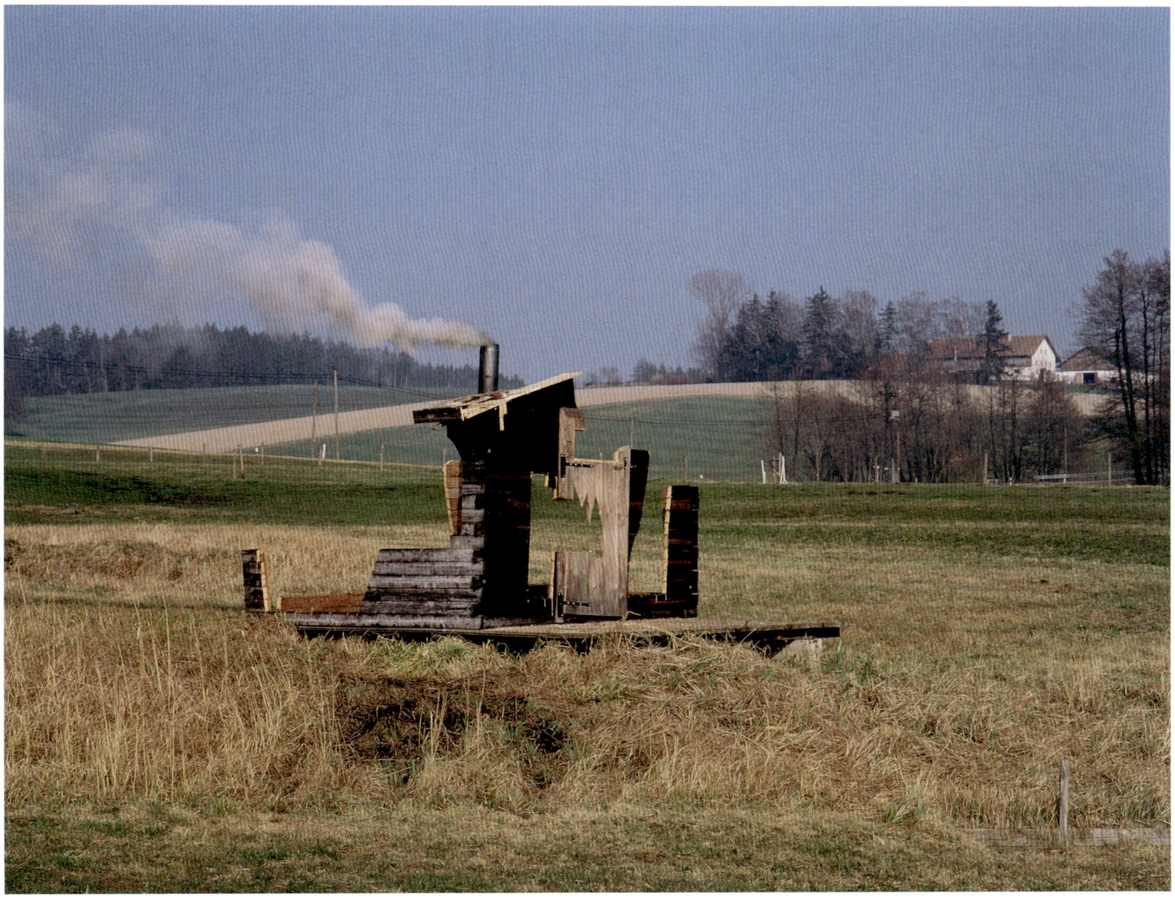

3 Ster mit Ausblick, 2002

Video, 1 min 52 sec, in collaboration with / in Zusammenarbeit mit Jürgen Heinert

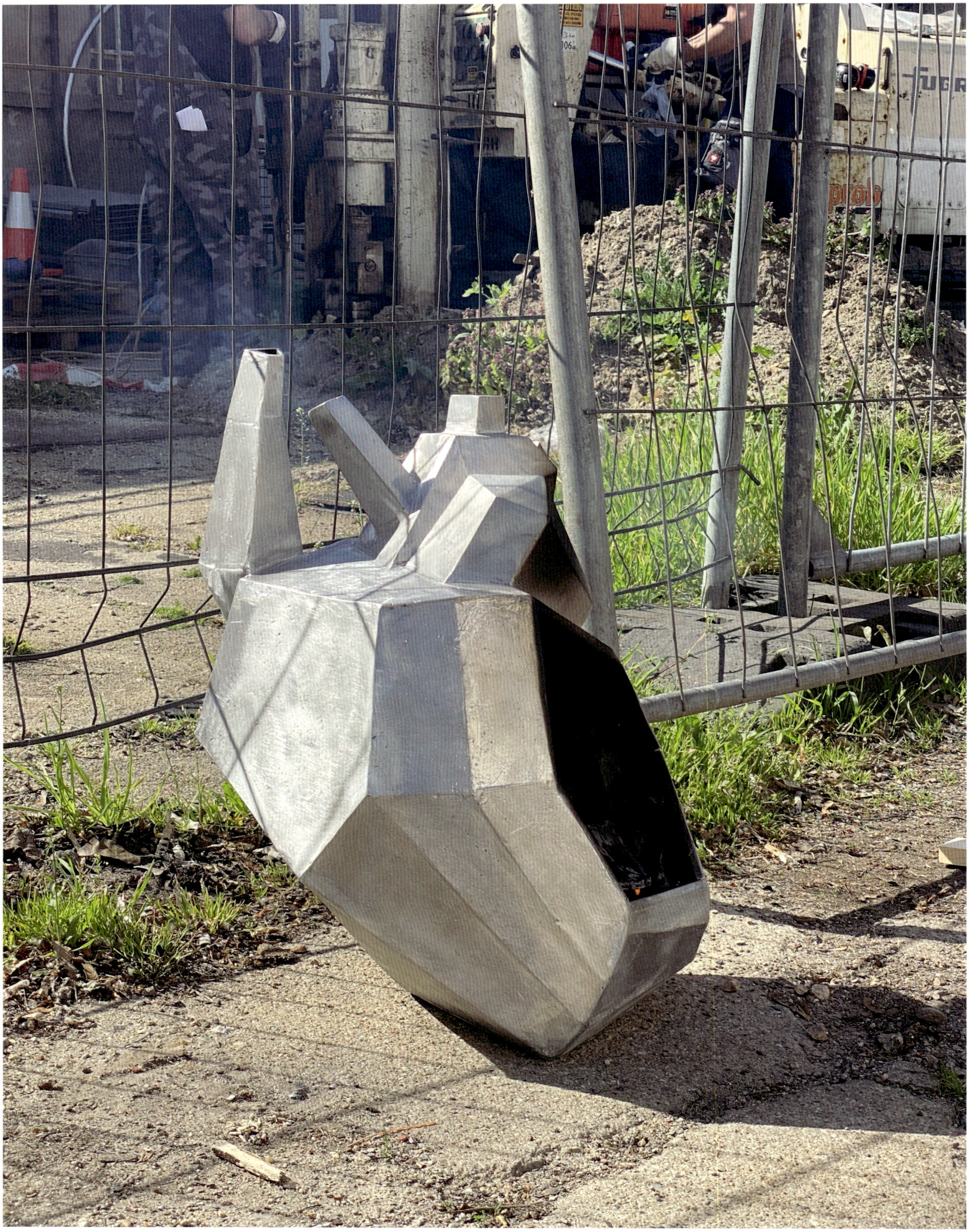

Factory, 2021
Aluminum / Aluminium, 50 × 35 × 25 cm

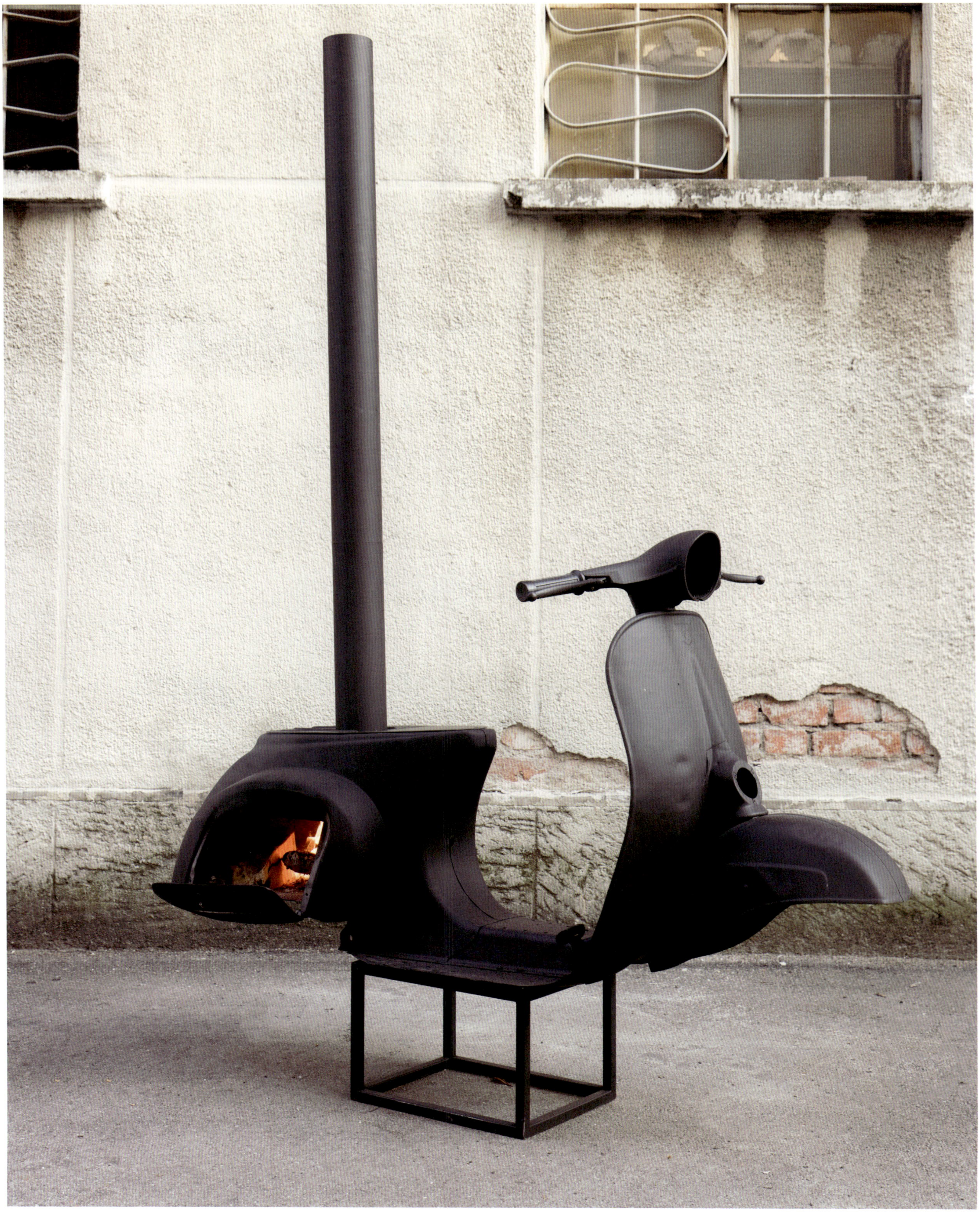

Ofen Mailand, 2017

Steel, paint / Stahl, Farbe, 205 × 168 × 70 cm

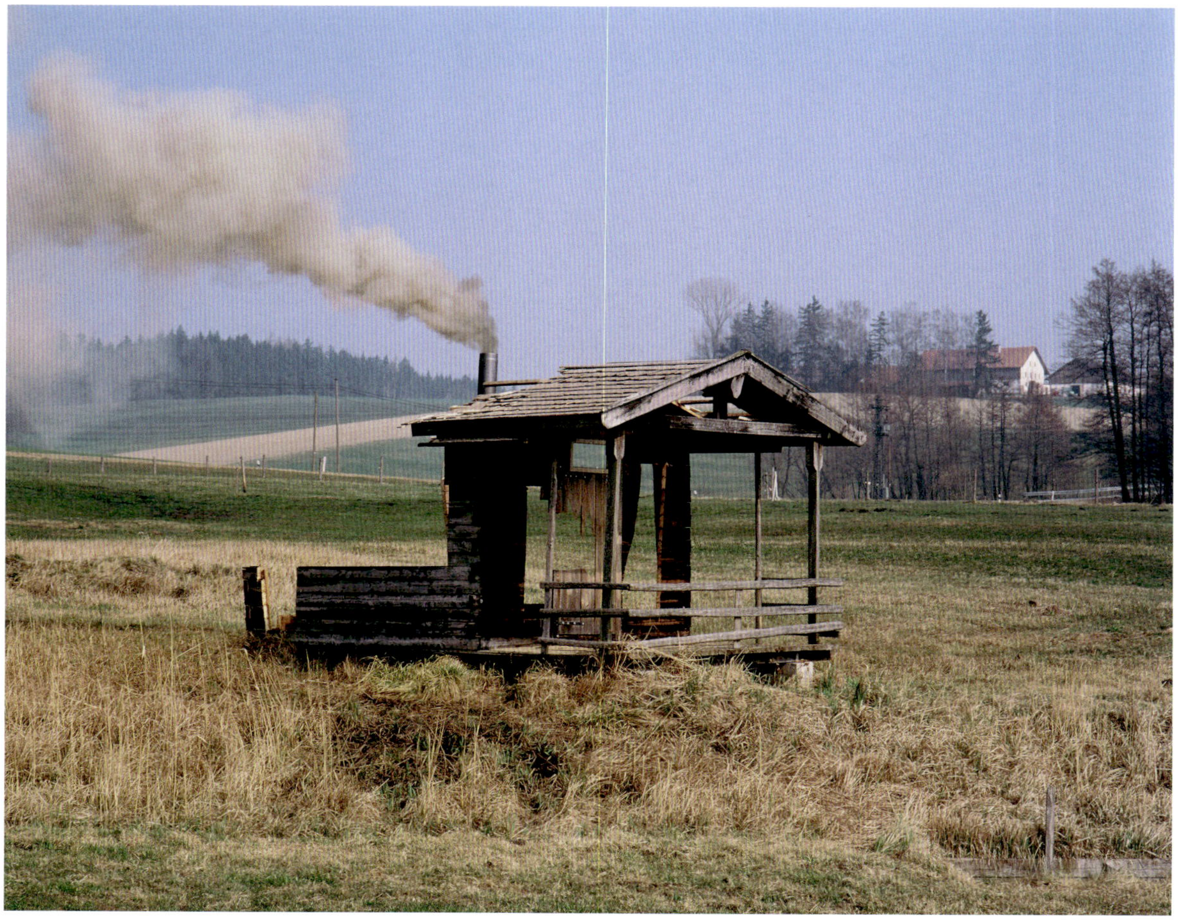

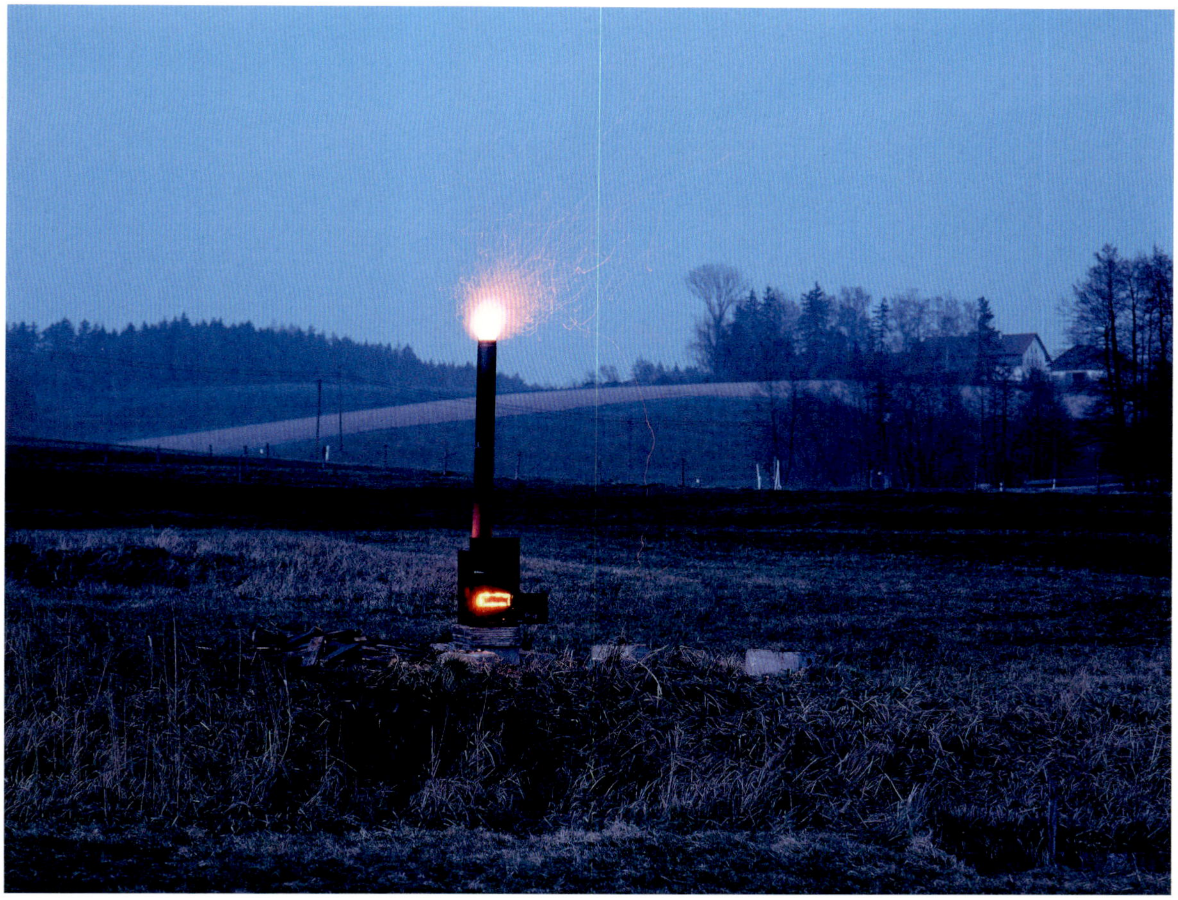

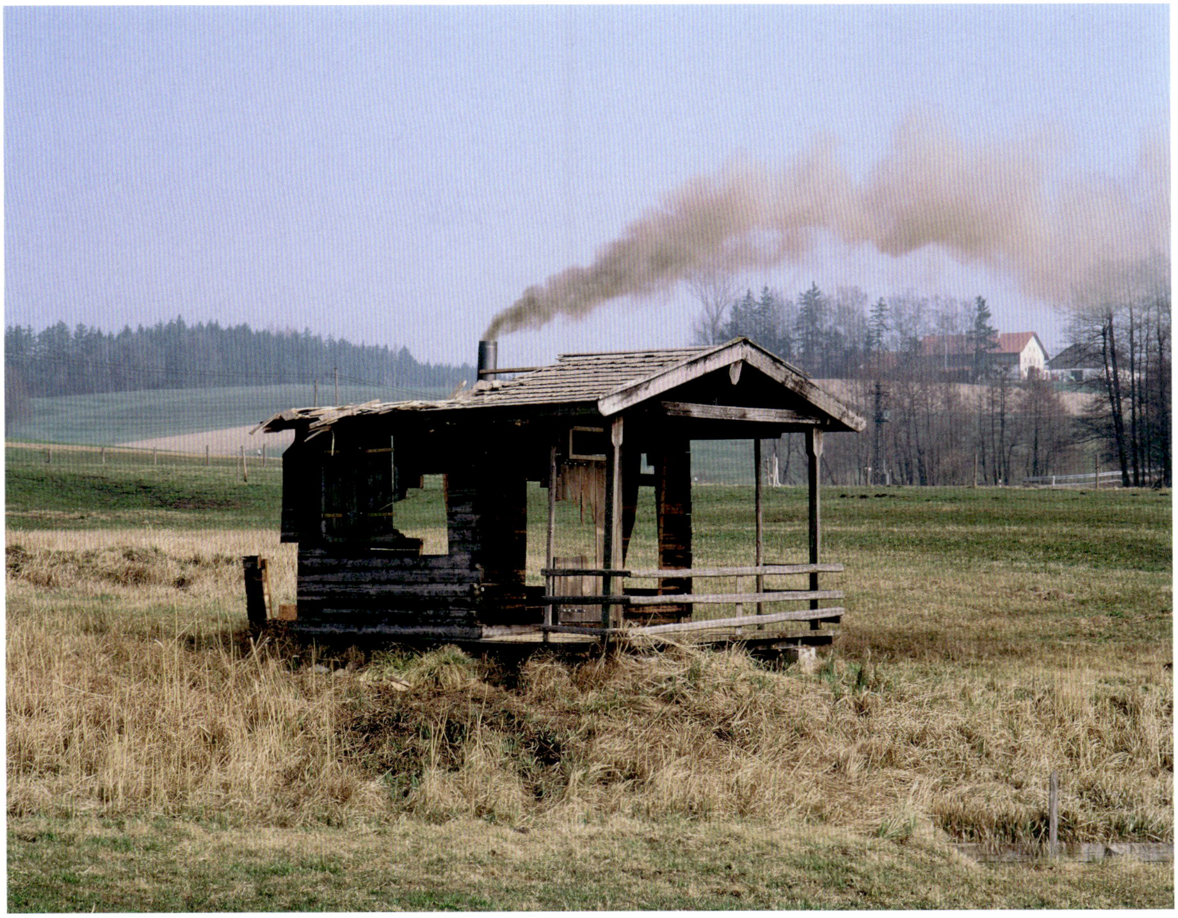

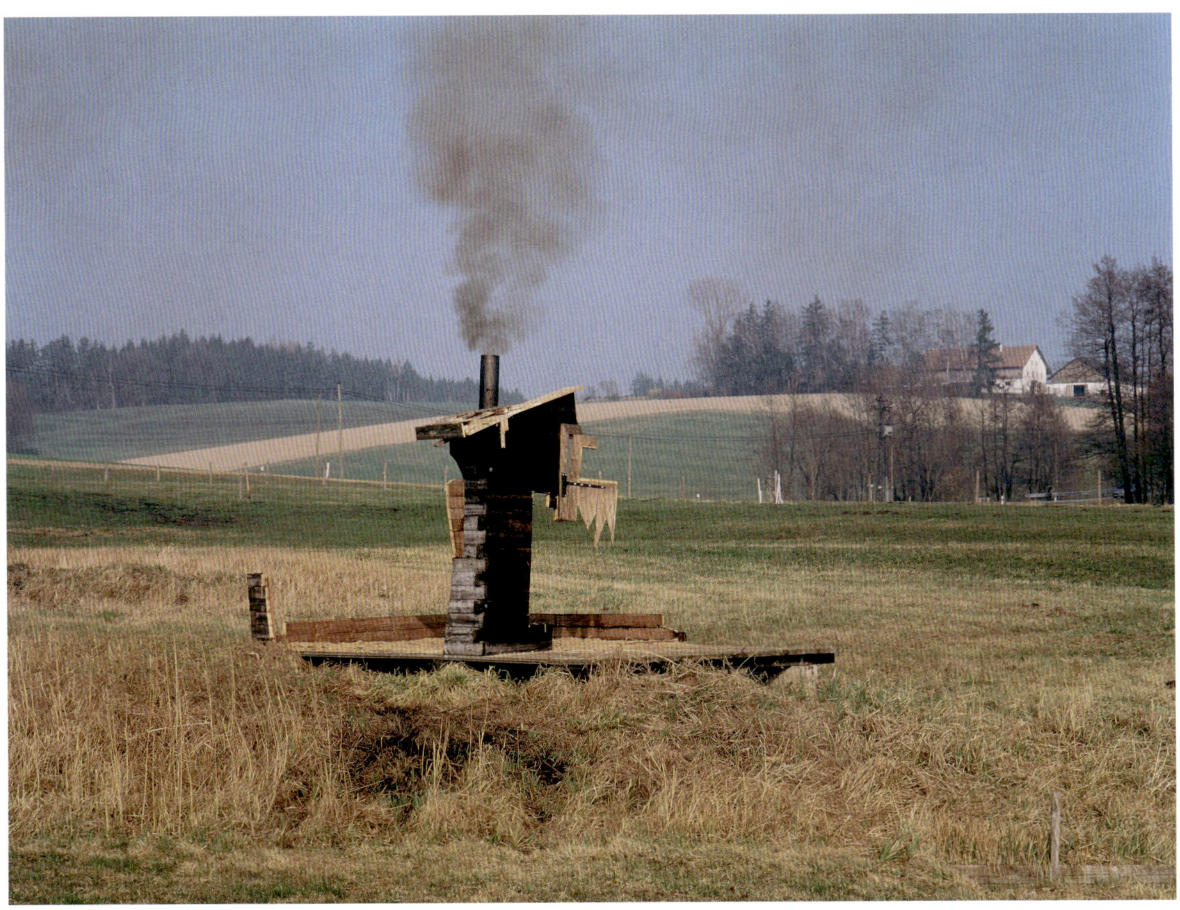

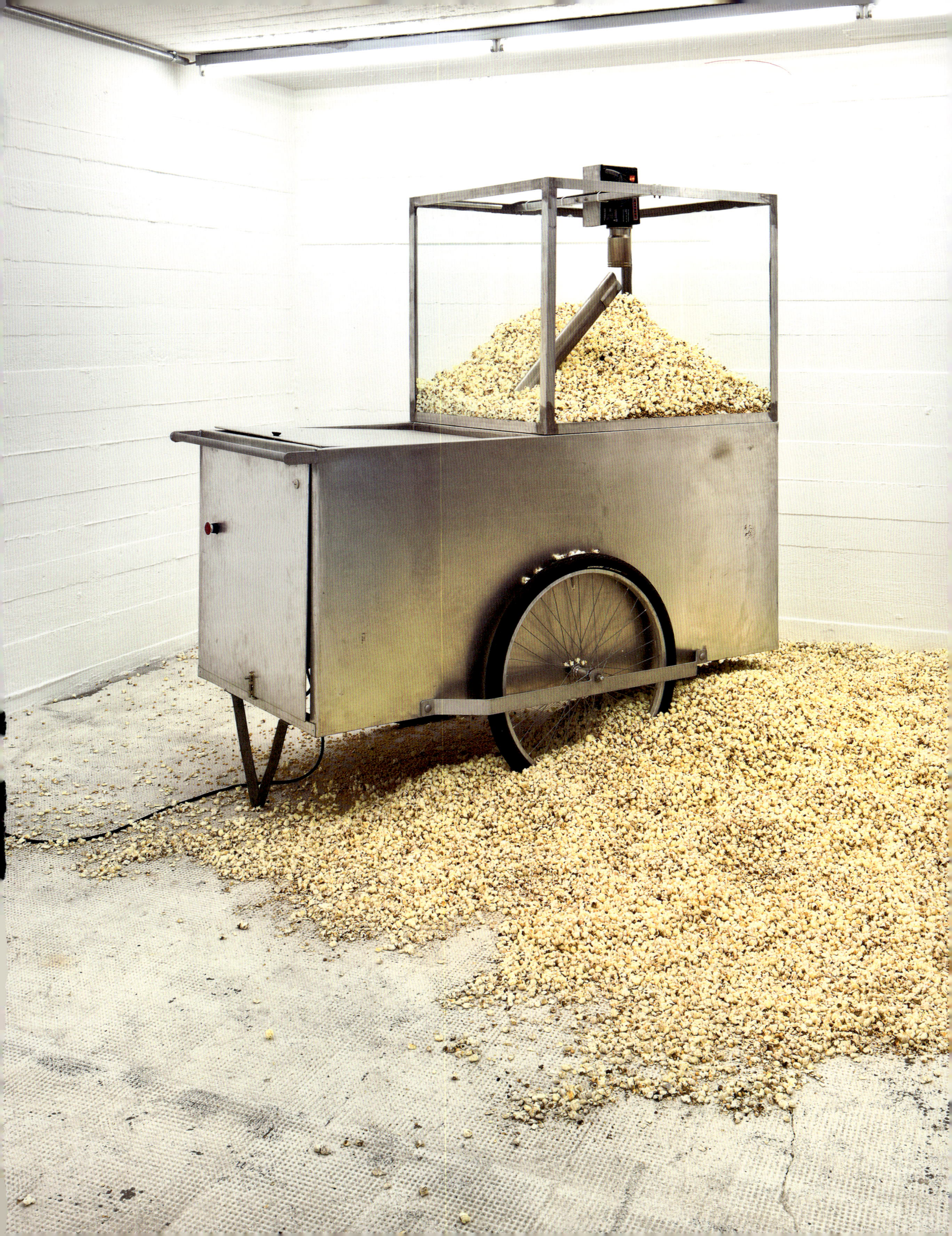

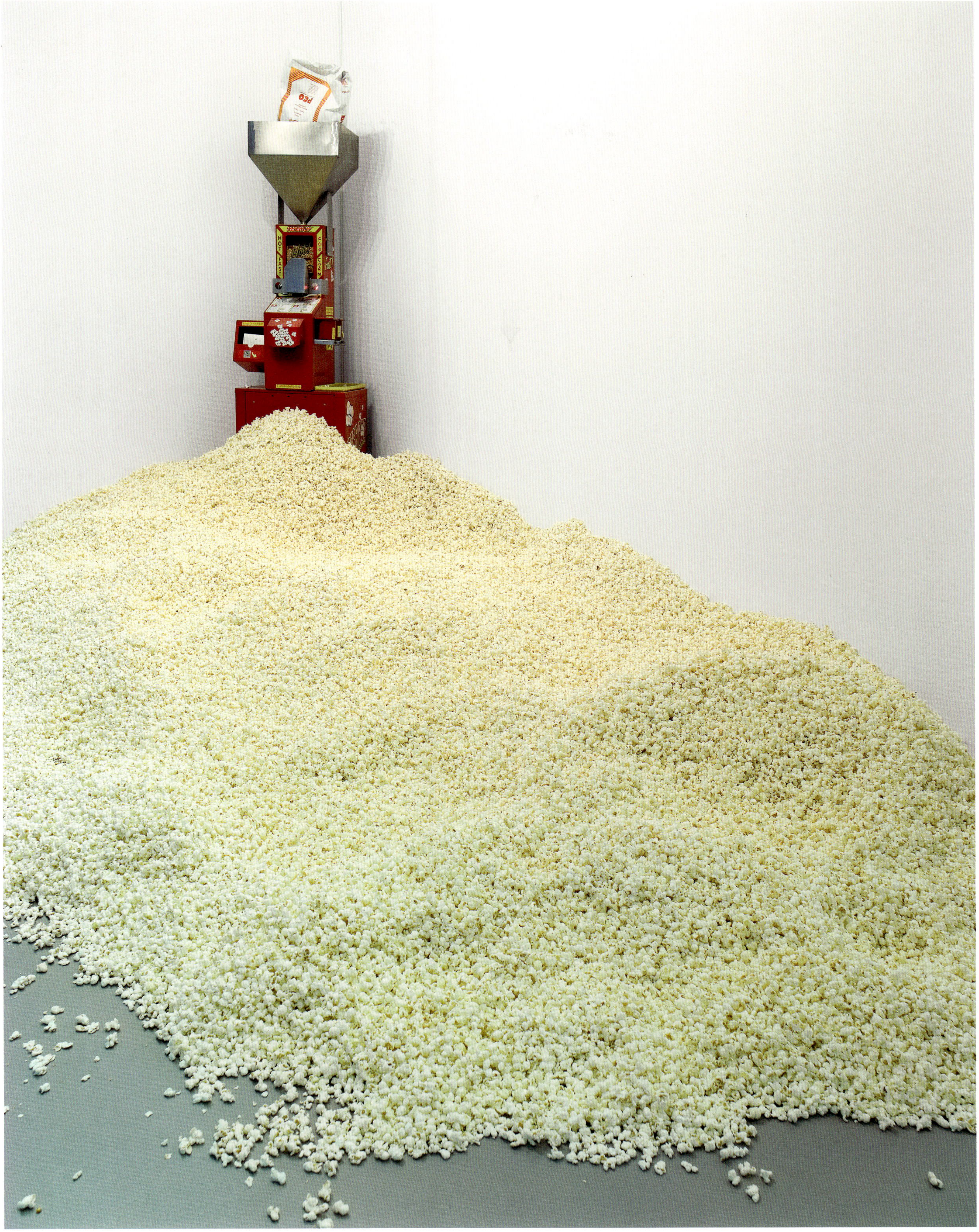

1:43–47, Frankfurt, 2008

Aluminum, steel, rubber, electric motor, hot air gun, popcorn / Aluminium, Stahl, Gummi, Elektromotor, Heißluftpistole, Popcorn, 169 × 97 × 168,5 cm

1:43–47, Nordhorn, 2008

Stainless steel, popcorn machine, popcorn / Edelstahl, Popcornmaschine, Popcorn, 210 × 58 × 50 cm

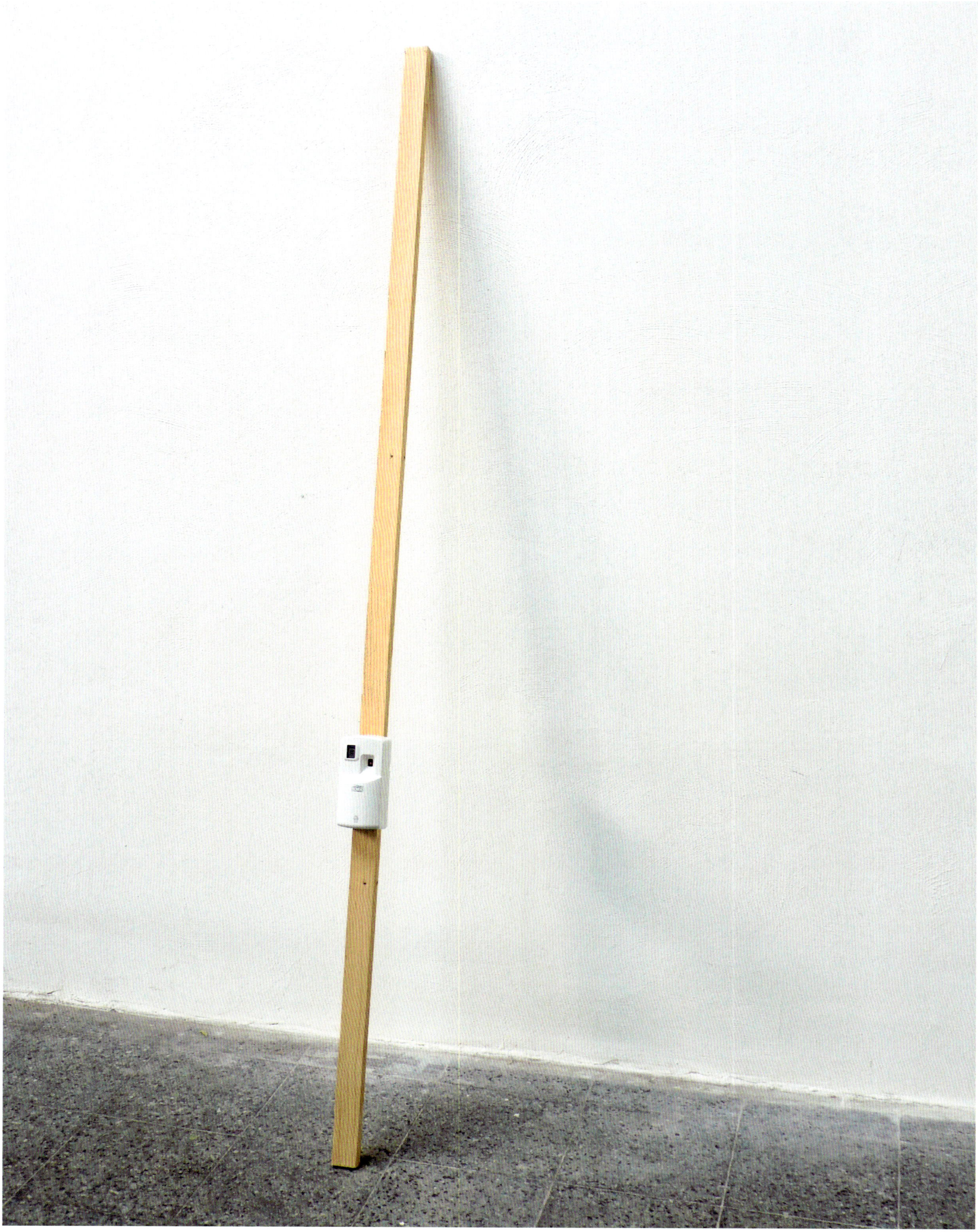

Andy Warhol trägt Parfüm, 2007

Wood, fragrance dispenser / Holz, Duftspender, 210 × 12 × 8 cm

1:43–47, Marl, 2017

Steel, glass, popcorn, hot air gun, motor, controller / Stahl, Glas, Popcorn, Heißluftpistole, Motor, Steuerung, 400 × 85 × 250 cm

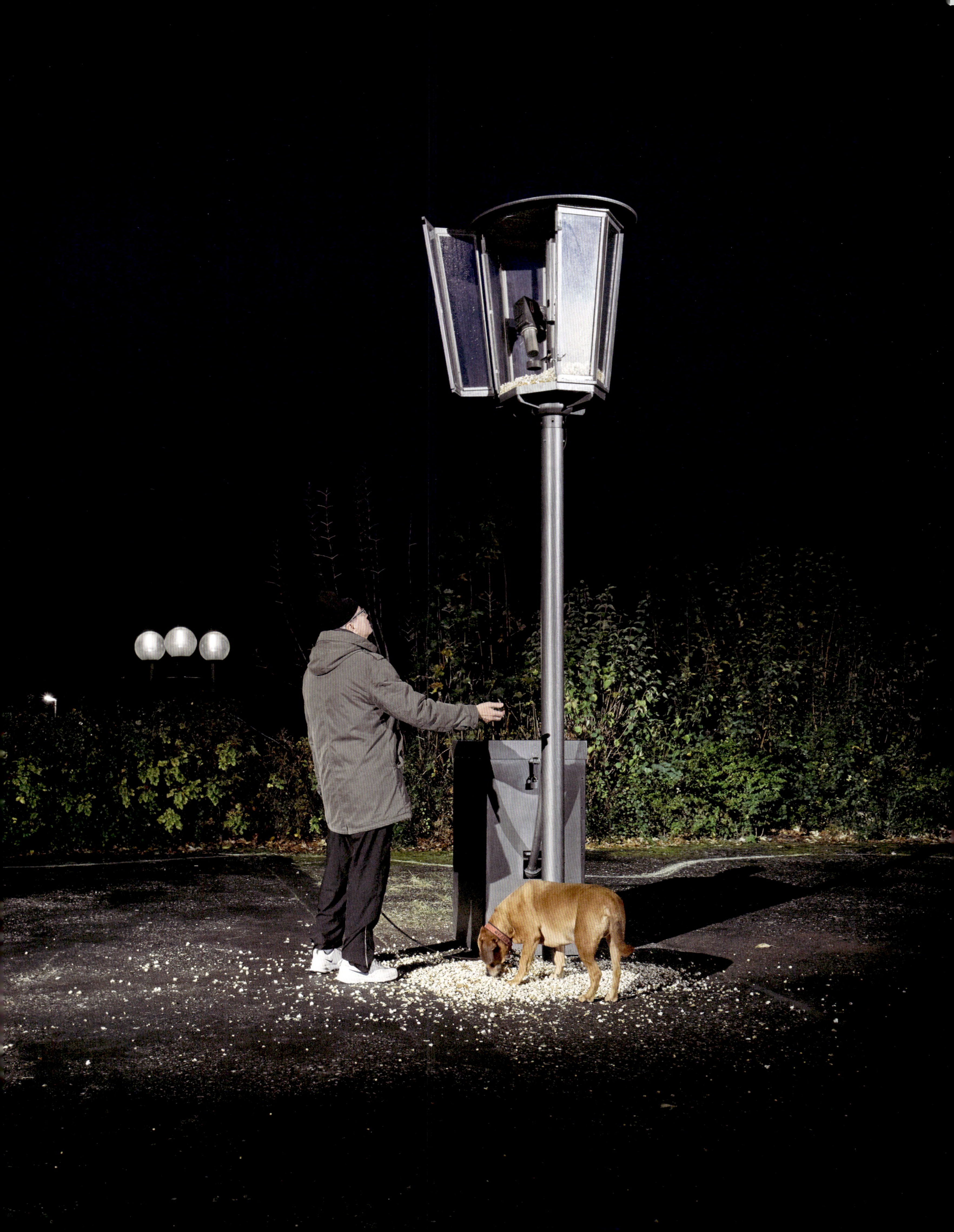

Lukas Feireiss

ATTEMPTS AT LOCALIZATION

A Approaches to Home and Homeland

ORTUNGSVERSUCHE
Annäherungen an Heim und Heimat

Space is the basis of human existence. Extrinsically and intrinsically. Our entire life is located in space. We live, love, laugh, cry, reside, and die in spaces. Space is the storage medium of our historical situatedness and testimony of the cultural structure in which we live. Space is not only the foundation of our very existence, but also a prerequisite for our exploration of the world.

However, when we begin to explore and question the space that surrounds us, to inscribe our experiences into it and leave our individual narratives, our personal traces there, then space transforms into place. Space is to be understood here as a blank slate—an abstract space without essential meaning that has yet to be shaped by personal experience; in contrast, place is to be understood as a space with meaning—a semantic space, as it were, which is created by human experience and whose size is unlimited.

Michael Sailstorfer's early works seem to place precisely such processes of localization at the center of his creativity: the transformation of spaces into places, so to speak, as an artistic approach to the world. With him, this transformation of something that exists into something different takes place essentially through intervention, deconstruction, and reconstruction.

For example, with his very first work, *Waldputz* [Cleaning the Forest, 2000 ↗298/299], he presented a neatly partitioned off rectangular plot of earth in the middle of the forest, which he had cleared of all natural growth. This simple conceptual gesture of material removal creates a clearly

Raum ist die Basis menschlicher Existenz. Umgebend und innewohnend. Unser gesamtes Leben ist im Raum verortet. Wir leben, lieben, lachen, weinen, wohnen und sterben in Räumen. Raum ist Speichermedium unserer historischen Situiertheit und Zeugnis des kulturellen Gefüges, in dem wir leben. Raum ist dabei nicht nur unsere Existenzgrundlage, sondern Grundvoraussetzung für unsere Erkundung der Welt.

Doch wenn wir beginnen, den uns umgebenden Raum zu erkunden und zu hinterfragen, unsere Erfahrungen in diesen einzuschreiben und unsere individuellen Narrative, unsere persönlichen Spuren dort zu hinterlassen, dann verwandelt sich Raum in einen Ort. Raum soll hier als ein unbeschriebenes Blatt verstanden werden – ein abstrakter Raum ohne wesentliche Bedeutung, der noch durch persönliche Erfahrungen geprägt werden muss; der Ort hingegen als Raum mit Bedeutung – ein Bedeutungsraum also, der durch menschliche Erfahrung erschaffen wird und dessen Größe unbegrenzt ist.

Michael Sailstorfers frühe Werke scheinen genau solche Verortungsprozesse ins Zentrum seines Schaffens zu setzen. Die Verwandlung von Räumen in Orte sozusagen als künstlerischer Weltzugang. Diese Transformation des Vorhandenen in etwas Anderes geschieht bei ihm im Wesentlichen durch Intervention, Dekonstruktion und Rekonstruktion.

So zeigt er beispielsweise in seiner allerersten Arbeit *Waldputz*, 2000 ↗298/299, ein sauber abgeteiltes, rechteckiges Stück Erde mitten im Wald, welches er von jeglichem natürlichen

delineated, three-dimensional space in the midst of the uncontrolled growth. At the same time, it creates a concrete place in the abstract space of the forest.

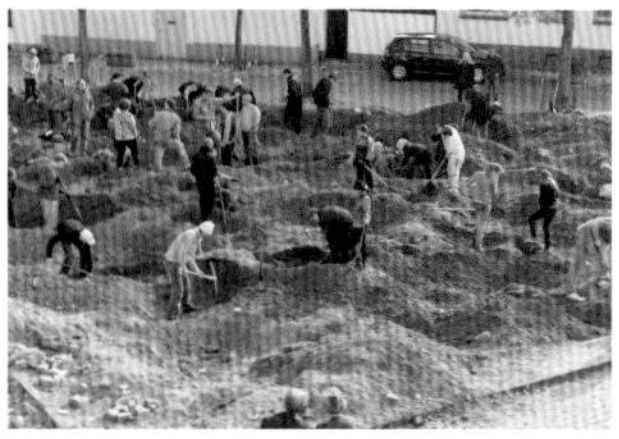

Pulheim gräbt, 2009/2010

With *Pulheim gräbt* [Pulheim Digs, 2009/2010 ↗288–295], he also transformed a fallow space—an inconspicuous grassy area in a small town—into a concrete place of individual as well as collective experience and imagination. After Sailstorfer secretly buried twenty-eight gold bars on the property and later announced this at a press conference, a gold-digging atmosphere arose in the small Rhenish town. What remained after the gold rush died down was a hilly landscape of sculptural appearance, created by many hands working together.

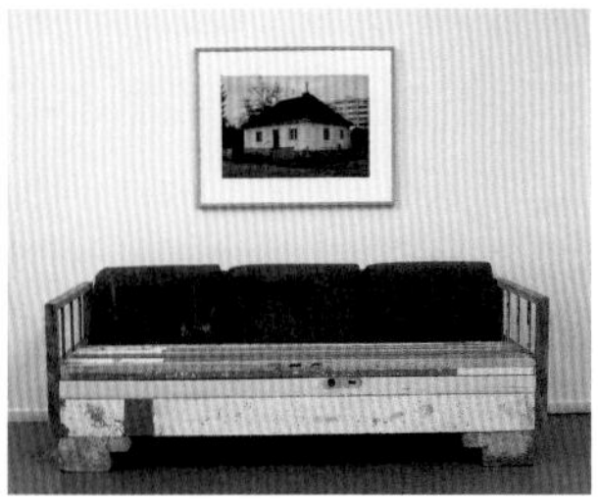

Herterichstraße 119, 2001

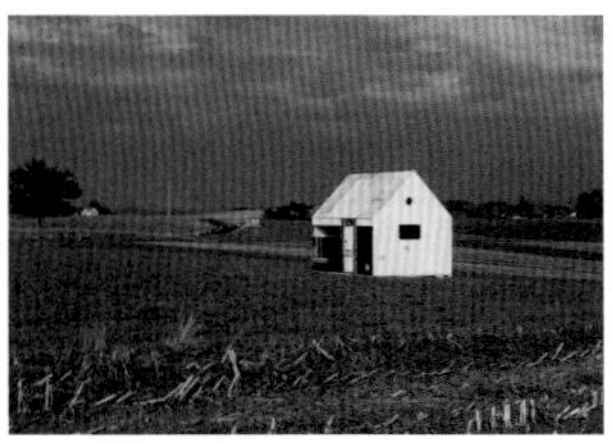

Heimatlied, 2001

With a large series of works, Sailstorfer also playfully questioned different ways of being in a relationship to spaces and places in the immediate vicinity of his parental home. Indeed, questions of home and homeland also seem to be at the center of his artistic exploration—whereby, here, that which is capable of change possesses a mutable permanence and that which seems permanent becomes unstable. Thus, a small hut consumes itself bit by bit in a stove located inside [*3 Ster mit Ausblick* (3 Cubic Meters of Wood with a View), 2002 ↗219–222], four mobile homes are converted into an almost model-like gable-roofed house [*Heimatlied* (Song of Home), 2001 ↗274/275], a demolished house becomes a piece of furniture [*Herterichstraße 119*, 2001 ↗271], and rural bus stops are suddenly transformed into freshly furnished living spaces with bed, toilet, cooking area, table, chair, and shelf [*Wohnen mit Verkehrsanbindung* (Living with Access to Public Transport), 2001 ↗267–270].

At this point—as so often in his artistic practice—Sailstorfer's preoccupation with home and homeland seems to be an expression of his own life: the question regarding

Bewuchs befreit hat. Diese einfache konzeptuelle Geste der Materialentfernung schafft inmitten des Wildwuchses einen klar abgesteckten, dreidimensionalen Raum. Zugleich wird dadurch ein konkreter Ort im abstrakten Waldraum geschaffen.

Auch in *Pulheim gräbt*, 2009/2010 ↗288–295, verwandelt er einen brachliegenden Raum – eine unscheinbare kleinstädtische Grünfläche – in einen konkreten Ort individueller wie kollektiver Erfahrung und Imagination. Nachdem Sailstorfer heimlich achtundzwanzig Goldbarren auf dem Grundstück vergraben und dies später auf einer Pressekonferenz bekannt gegeben hatte, entstand in der rheinischen Kleinstadt eine Goldgräberstimmung. Was nach dem Abebben des Goldrauschs übrig blieb, war eine Hügellandschaft von skulpturaler Anmutung, von vielen Händen gemeinsam geschaffen.

In einer ganzen Reihe von Arbeiten hinterfragt Sailstorfer aber auch spielerisch unterschiedliche Arten des In-Beziehung-Seins zu Räumen und Orten in unmittelbarer Nähe seines Elternhauses. Im Mittelpunkt seiner künstlerischen Auseinandersetzung scheinen dabei tatsächlich auch Fragen nach Heim und Heimat zu stehen, wobei das Veränderliche hier eine wandelbare Dauerhaftigkeit besitzt und das, was permanent scheint, unbeständig wird. So verzehrt sich eine kleine Hütte Stück für Stück in einem darin befindlichen Ofen (*3 Ster mit Ausblick*, 2002 ↗219–222), vier Wohnmobile verwandeln sich in ein fast abziehbildhaftes Satteldachhaus (*Heimatlied*, 2001 ↗274/275), ein Abrisshaus wird zu einem Möbelstück (*Herterichstraße 119*, 2001 ↗271) und ländliche Bushaltestellen verwandeln sich plötzlich in frisch eingerichtete Wohnräume mit Bett, Klo, Kochstelle, Tisch, Stuhl und Regal (*Wohnen mit Verkehrsanbindung*, 2001 ↗267–270).

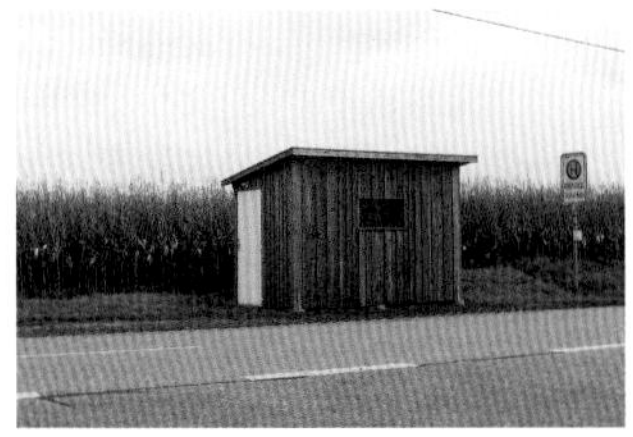

Wohnen mit Verkehrsanbindung, 2001

Diese Beschäftigung mit Heim und Heimat scheint zu diesem Zeitpunkt – wie so oft in seiner Praxis – Ausdruck seines eigenen Lebens zu sein. Die Frage nach dem Mittelpunkt der individuellen Existenz des Menschen, dem Ort der Kindheit, der Geborgenheit und Sicherheit und zugleich die Frage, wo und wie man in Zukunft leben möchte. *Heimatlied* sagt in gewisser Weise, ich will nicht mehr reisen, sondern mich an einem Ort niederlassen, den ich mir ausgesucht habe. Bei *Wohnen mit Verkehrsanbindung* ist das Gegenteil der Fall. Es ist ein Beispiel für Wohnen an einem Ort, von dem man wegfahren will. *3 Ster mit Ausblick* ist laut Sailstorfer ein Modell für ein größeres Haus: „Wenn das ganze Holz verbrannt ist, ist der Blick frei."

Sailstorfers unvoreingenommen künstlerischen Untersuchungen von Heim und Heimat schlagen hier also eine Art Doppelstruktur vor, die sowohl auf eine heimisch-sesshafte

the center of a person's individual existence, the place of childhood, security, and safety; and, at the same time, the question as to where and how one would like to live in the future. In a certain sense, *Heimatlied* says: I don't want to travel anymore; I want to settle down in a place I have chosen. In the case of *Wohnen mit Verkehrsanbindung*, the opposite is true. It is an example of living in a place you want to travel away from. According to Sailstorfer, *3ster mit Ausblick* is a model for a larger house: "When all the wood is burned, the view is clear."

Here, Sailstorfer's unbiased artistic investigations of home and homeland thus suggest a kind of double structure, pointing both to a homey, sedentary side that allows one to form attachments and dwell within oneself, and to a more restless side that leads one to be permanently on the move and not to stop at any adopted attitude or insight.

An ostensible domestication is thereby often countered by transformative acts of destruction. With *Lohma* (2008) ↗276/277, a 16-mm film work, Sailstorfer once again takes up the typology of the house in the form of a corrugated iron building and explodes it in a high-speed looped film. Here, the building first expands for several seconds, only to contract and expand again shortly before the explosion. The building, caught in the loop, becomes a living and breathing thing. In a counterintuitive twist, an inanimate building is thus seemingly brought to life by its imminent destruction. With *Tränen* [Tears, 2015] ↗34/35, Sailstorfer created another filmic work that finds its conclusion in the destruction of a house. The video presents three two-ton, cast-iron, and almost comic-like tears that fall continuously from above onto a single-family house in a rural village setting, slowly but surely reducing it to rubble through their destructive impact.

With *Tränen*, Sailstorfer's explicit preoccupation with the thematic complex of home and homeland also seems to have found a provisional conclusion. They seem like tears of valediction—bidding farewell to each other, to entrenched ideas, perhaps even to an outdated image of family. With a smile in one eye and a tear in the other, space is created here for something new in the erasure of a concrete place. As is so often the case, however, Sailstorfer's multi-layered works naturally allow for various interpretations.

Seite verweist, die es ermöglicht, Bindungen einzugehen und in sich zu wohnen, als auch auf eine eher umtriebige Seite, die dazu führt, permanent unterwegs zu sein und bei keiner eingenommenen Haltung oder Einsicht stehen zu bleiben.

Einer vermeintlichen Domestizierung wird dabei oftmals durch transformative Akte der Zerstörung entgegengewirkt. In *Lohma*, 2008 ↗276/277, einer 16-Millimeter-Filmarbeit, greift Sailstorfer erneut die Typologie des Hauses in Form eines Wellblechgebäudes auf und lässt dieses in einem geloopten Hochgeschwindigkeitsfilm explodieren. Dabei dehnt sich das Gebäude erst mehrere Sekunden lang aus, um sich kurz vor der Explosion wieder zusammenzuziehen und erneut auszudehnen. Das Gebäude wird, im Loop gefangen, zu einem lebenden und atmenden Ding. In einer kontraintuitiven Wendung wird hier also ein unbelebtes Haus durch seine bevorstehende Zerstörung scheinbar zum Leben erweckt. Mit *Tränen*, 2015 ↗34/35, hat Sailstorfer eine weitere filmische Arbeit geschaffen, die ihren Abschluss in der Destruktion eines Hauses findet. Das Video zeigt drei zwei Tonnen schwere, gusseiserne und geradezu comichaft erscheinende Tränen, die kontinuierlich von oben herab auf ein Einfamilienhaus in ländlich-dörflicher Umgebung fallen und dieses durch ihren zerstörerischen Aufschlag langsam, aber sicher in Schutt und Asche legen.

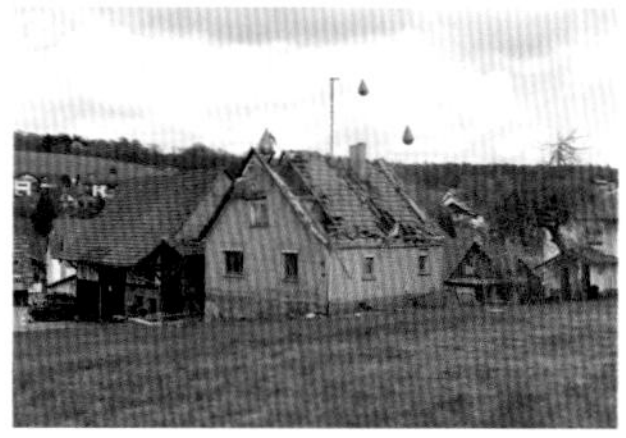

Tränen, 2015

Mit *Tränen* scheint auch Sailstorfers explizite Beschäftigung mit dem Themenkomplex Heim und Heimat einen vorläufigen Abschluss gefunden zu haben. Sie wirken wie Tränen des Abschieds – voneinander, von festgefahrenen Vorstellungen, vielleicht sogar von einem überholten Bild von Familie. Mit einem lachenden und einem weinenden Auge wird hier in der Auslöschung eines konkreten Ortes Raum für Neues geschaffen. Aber wie so oft lassen Sailstorfers vielschichtige Arbeiten natürlich verschiedene Interpretationen zu.

Modell – Reaktor, 2005

Concrete, microphone, loudspeaker / Beton, Mikrofon, Lautsprecher, Dimensions variable / Maße variabel

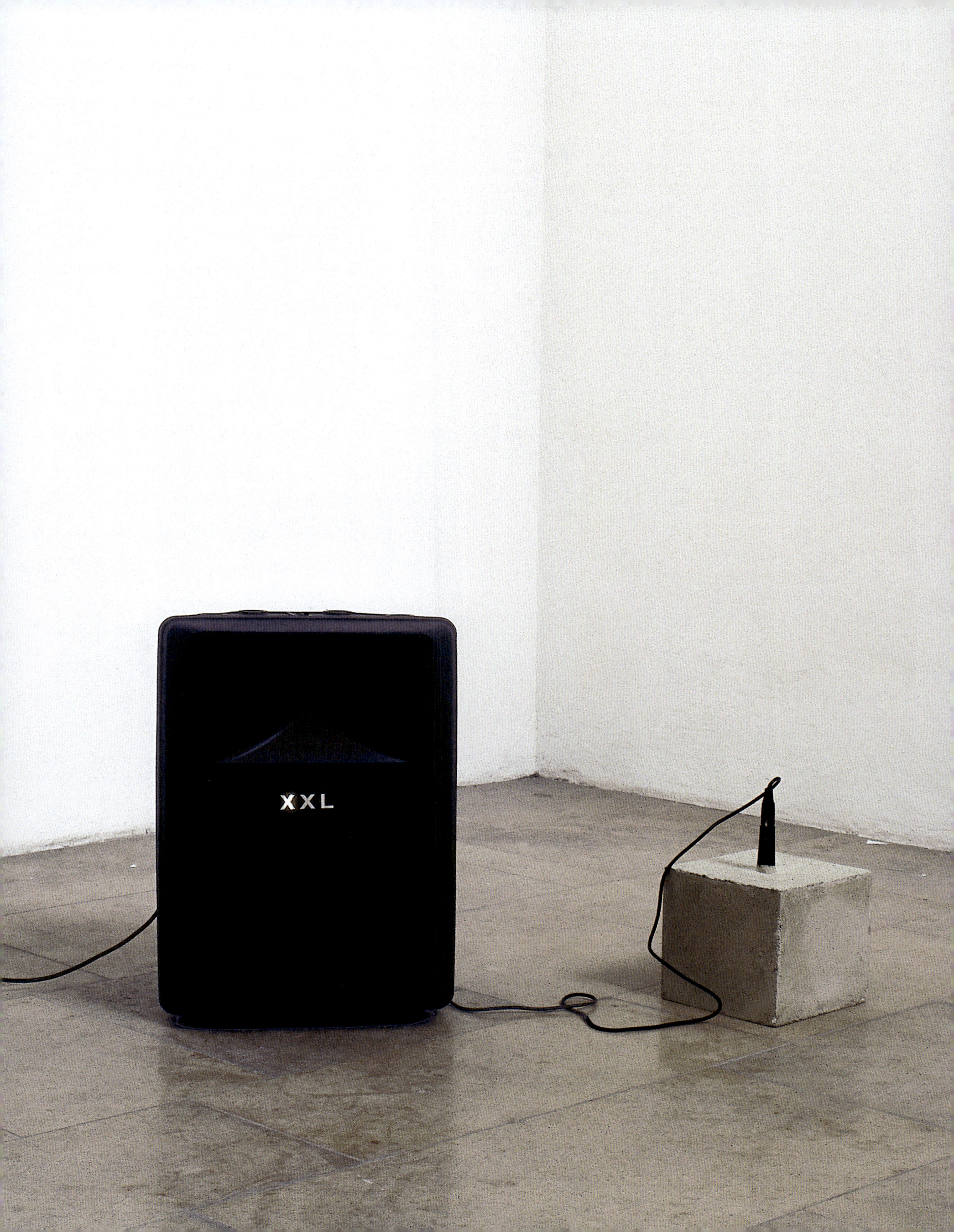
XXL

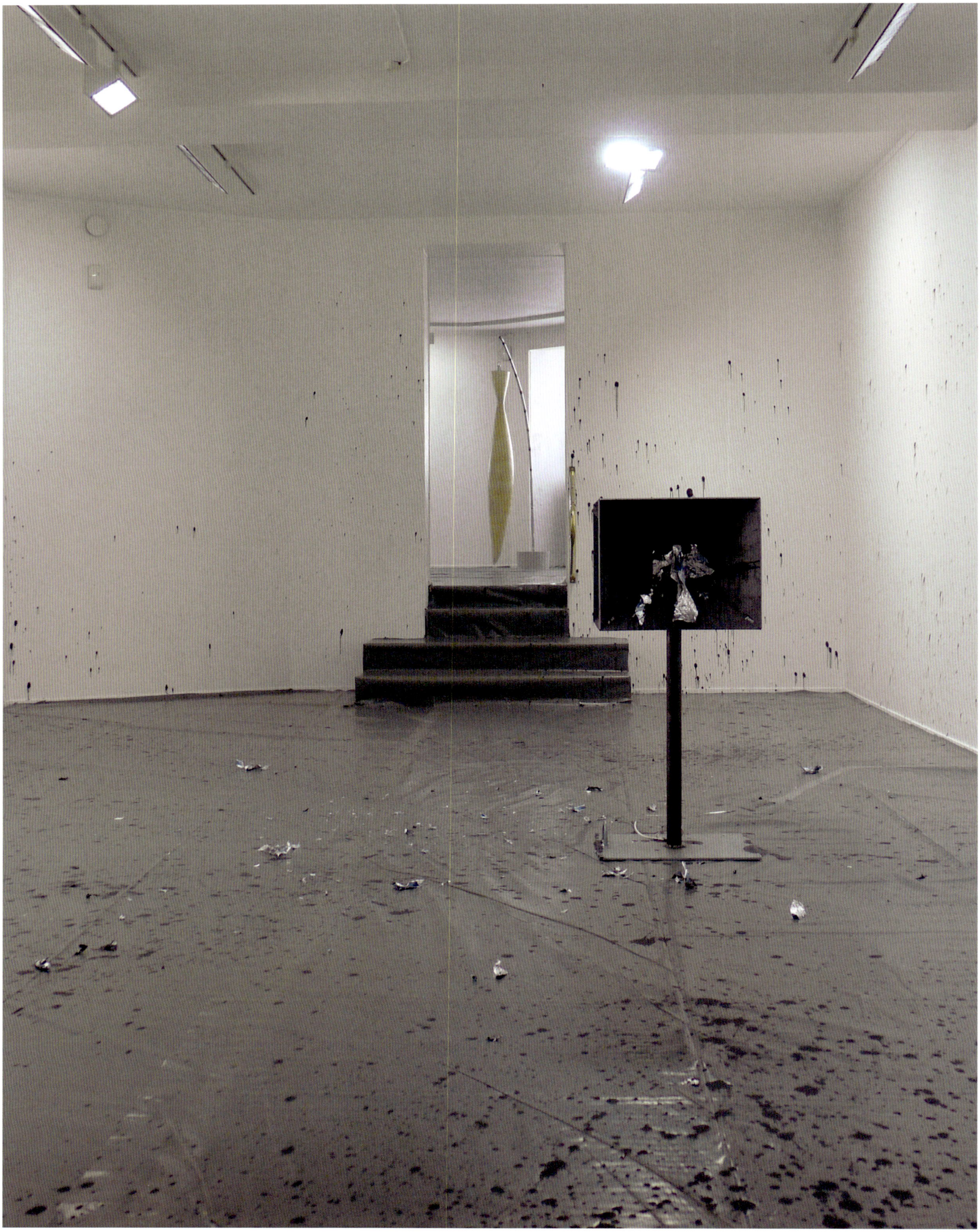

Trichter, 2008

Steel, paint, explosives / Stahl, Farbe, Sprengstoff, Dimensions variable / Maße variabel, Installation view / Installationsansicht *Mollstraße*, Galleri K, Oslo

Reaktor, 2005

Concrete, microphones, mixer, amplifier, loudspeaker / Beton, Mikrofone, Mischpult, Verstärker, Lautsprecher, Dimensions variable / Maße variabel

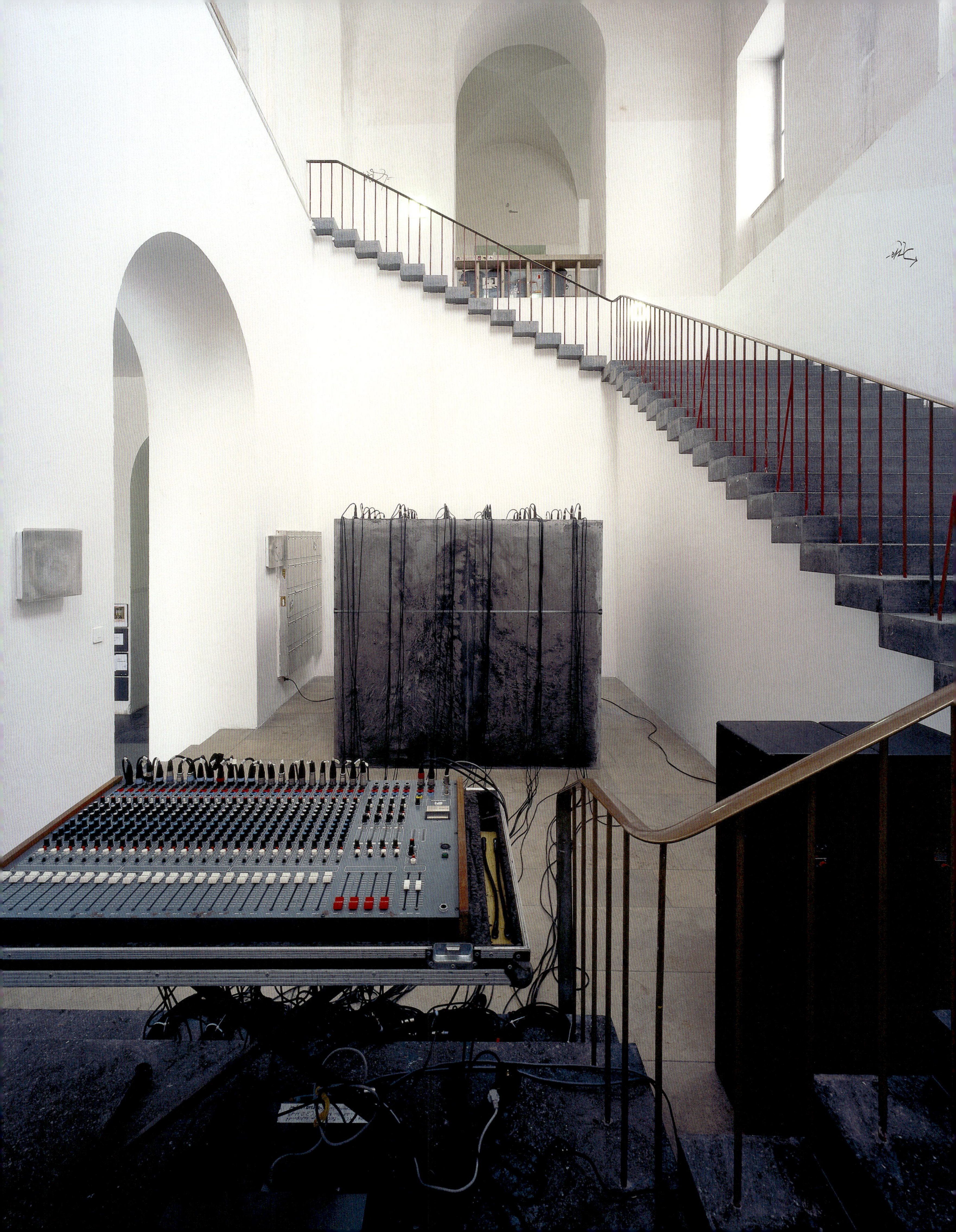

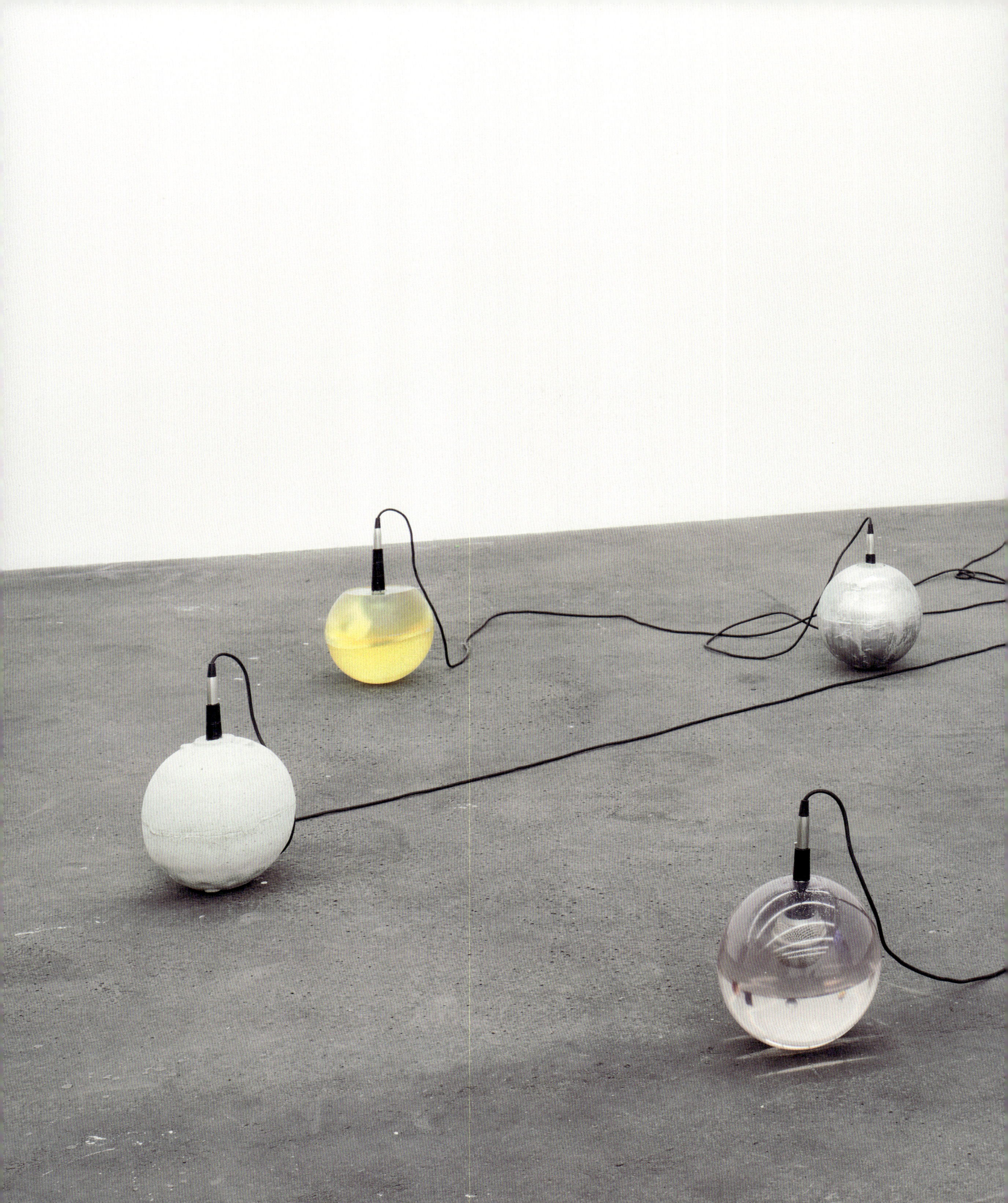

Versuchsreaktor (7k), 2008

Concrete, steel, epoxy resin, polyster resin, polyurethane resin, microphones, mixer, loudspeaker / Beton, Stahl, Epoxidharz, Polyurethanharz, Mikrofone, Mischpult, Lautsprecher, Dimensions variable / Maße variabel

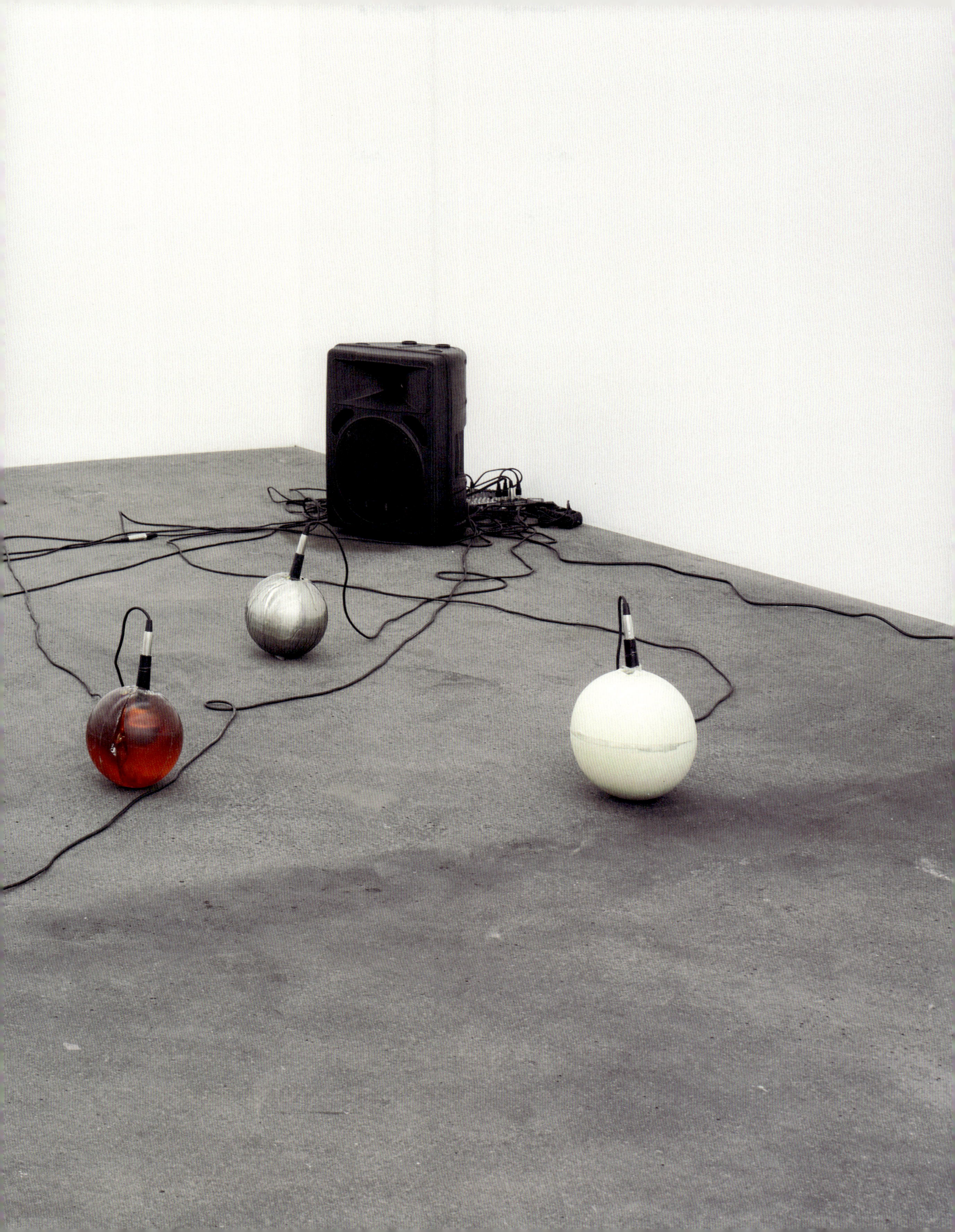

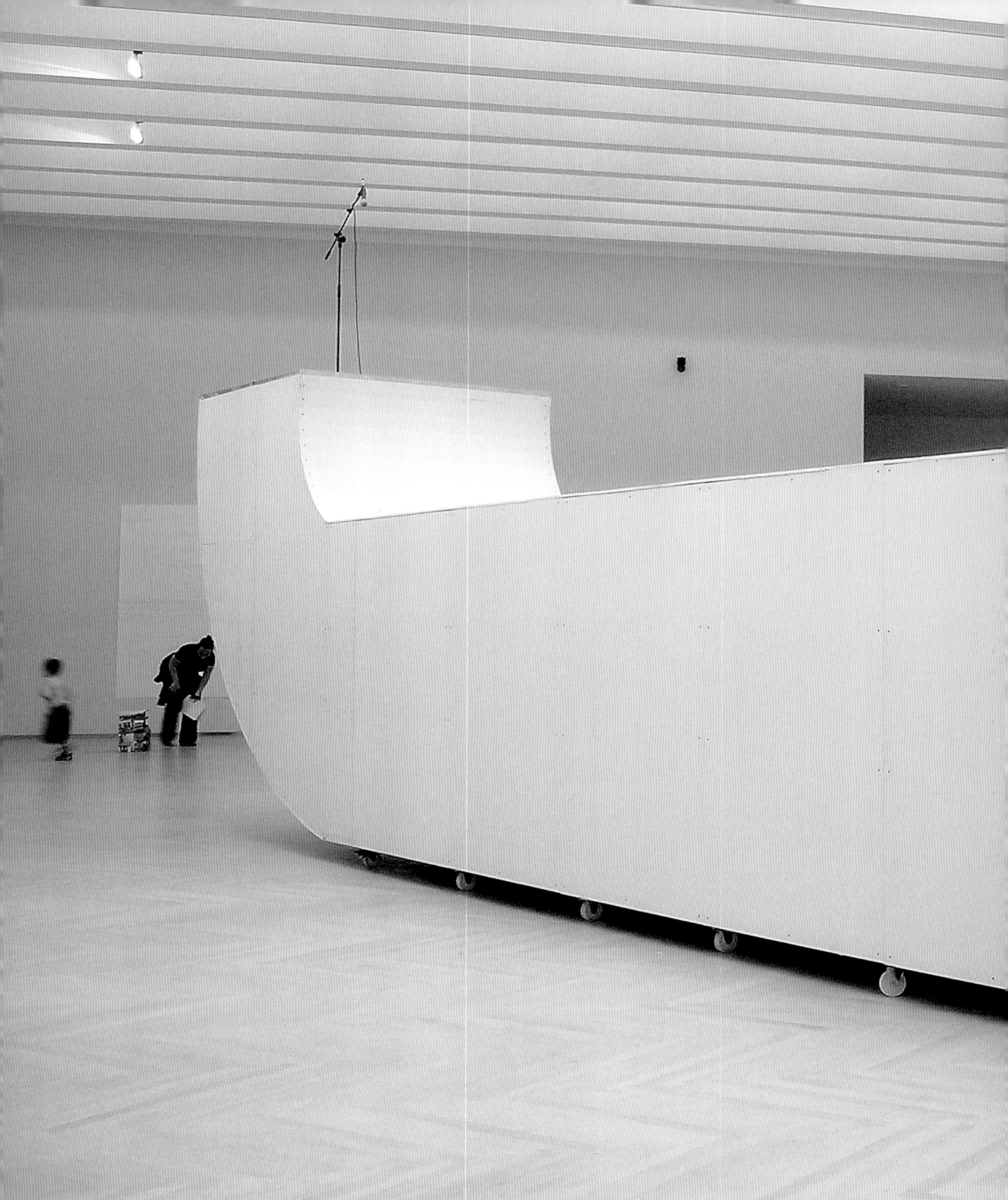

Versuchsaufbau Marilyn, 2004

Fan, steel, plasterboard, wheels, microphone, amplifier, loudspeaker / Ventilator, Stahl, Rigipsplatte, Räder, Mikrofon, Verstärker, Lautsprecher, 460 × 1.100 × 170 cm, Installation view / Installationsansicht *Manifesta 5*, Donostia-San Sebastián

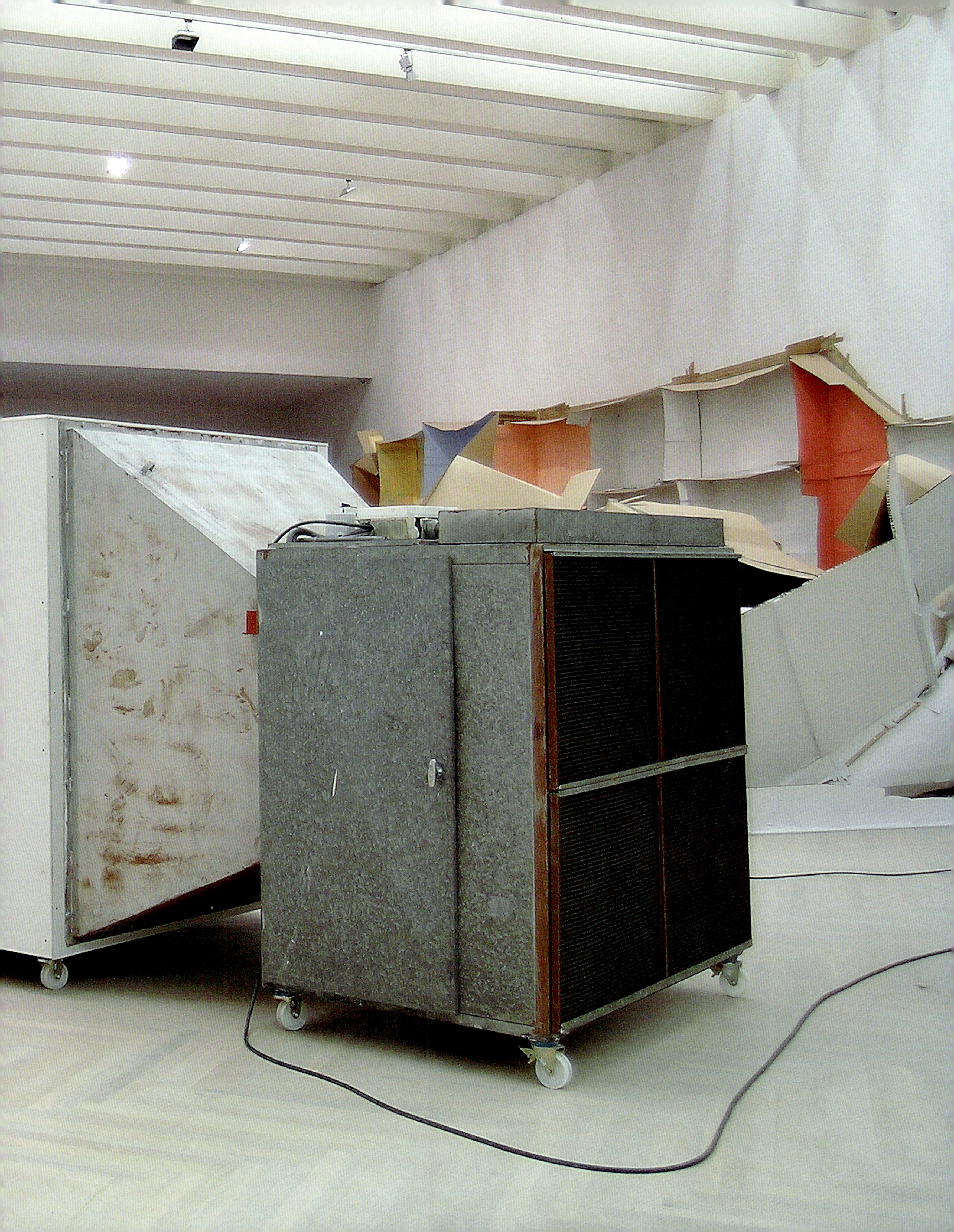

Bethlehem, 2004

Motorbike Simson Duo, current generator, steel, stretch film, neon lamps / Motorrad Simson Duo, Stromgenerator, Stahl, Stretchfolie, Neonlampen, 183 × 193 × 259 cm

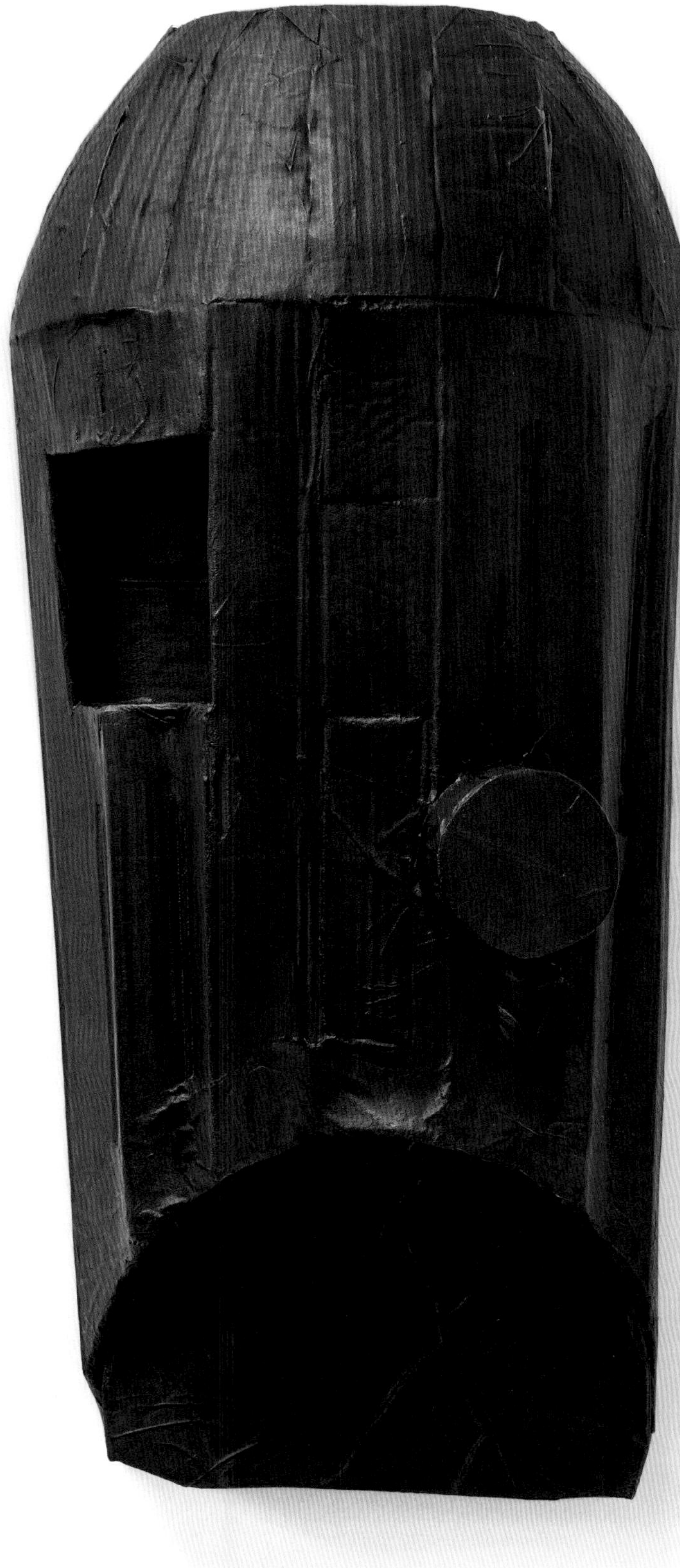

M. 23, 2015

Bronze, 82 × 38 × 21 cm

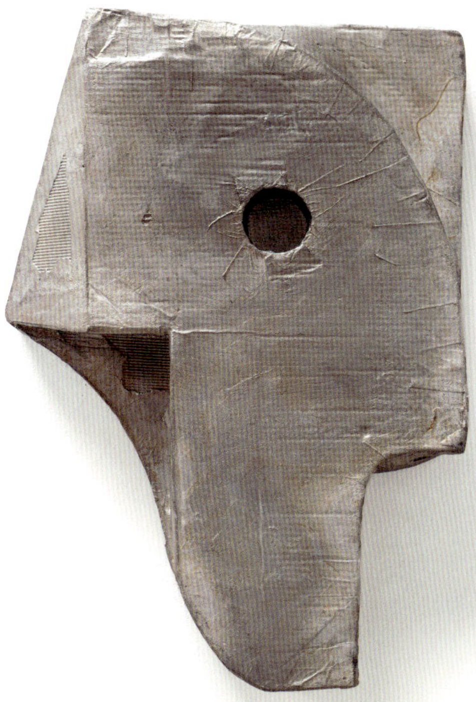

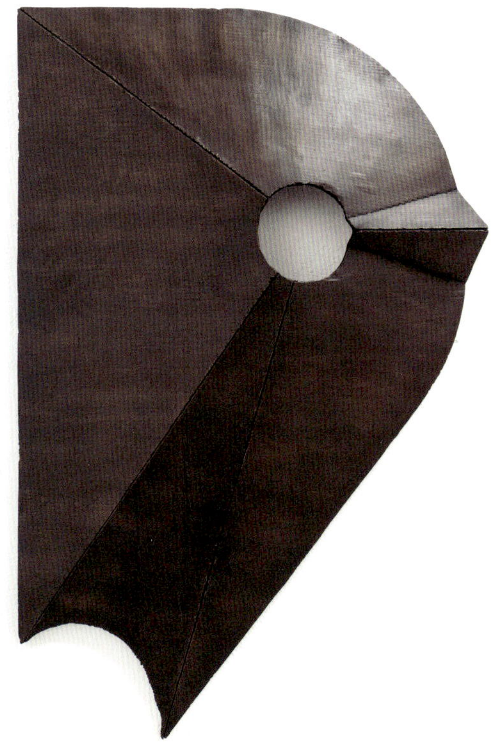

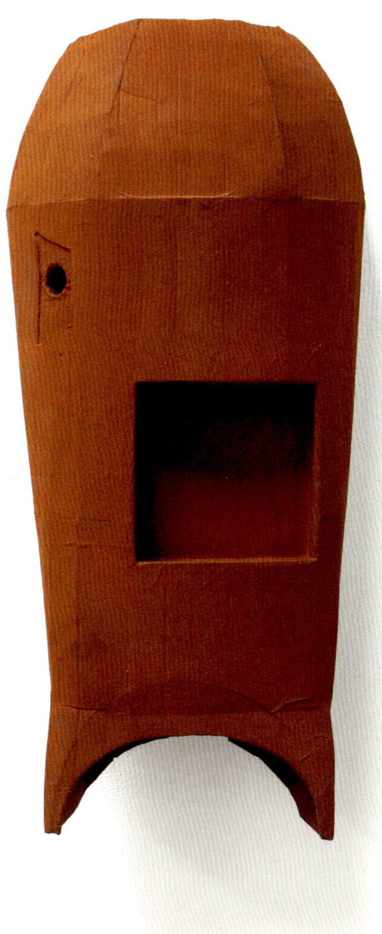

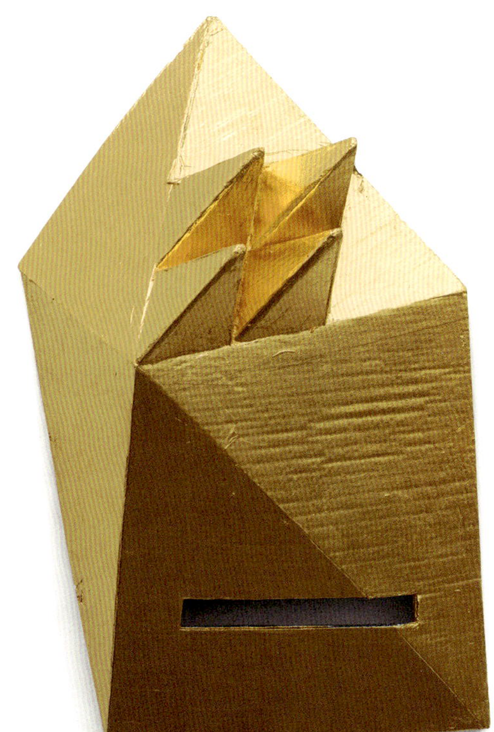

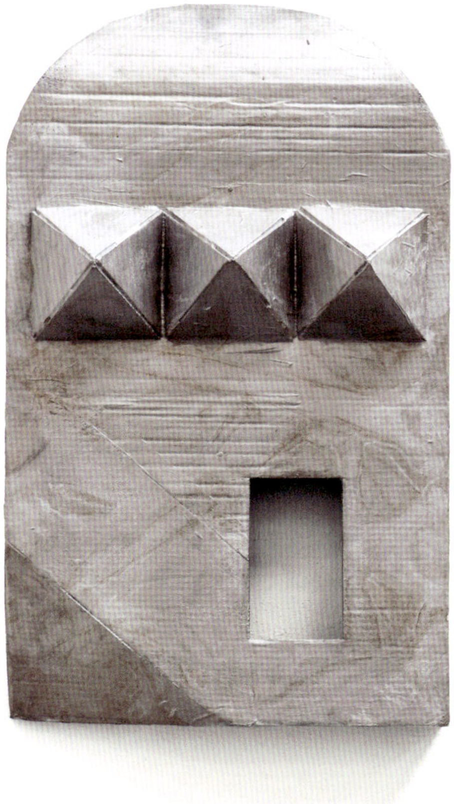

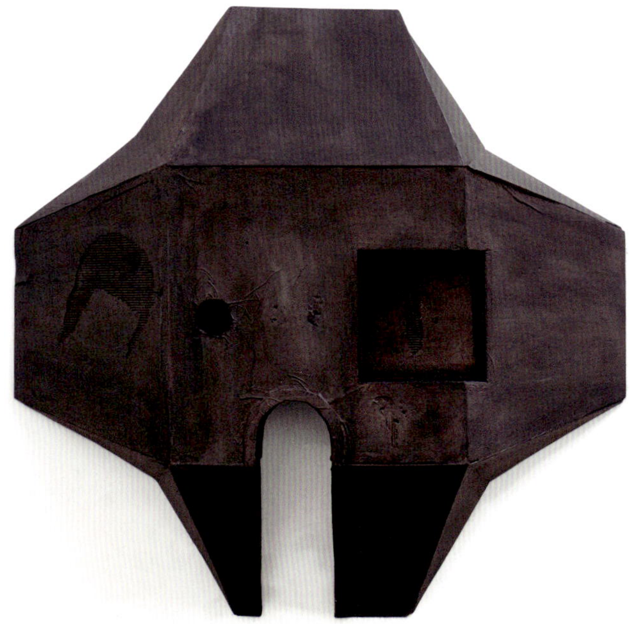

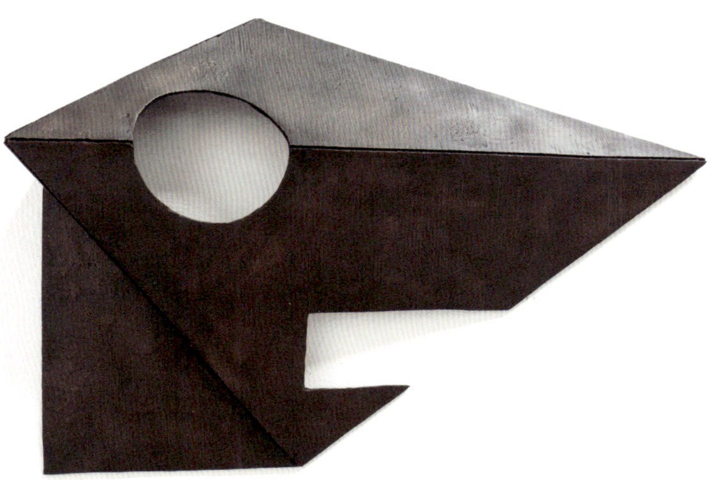

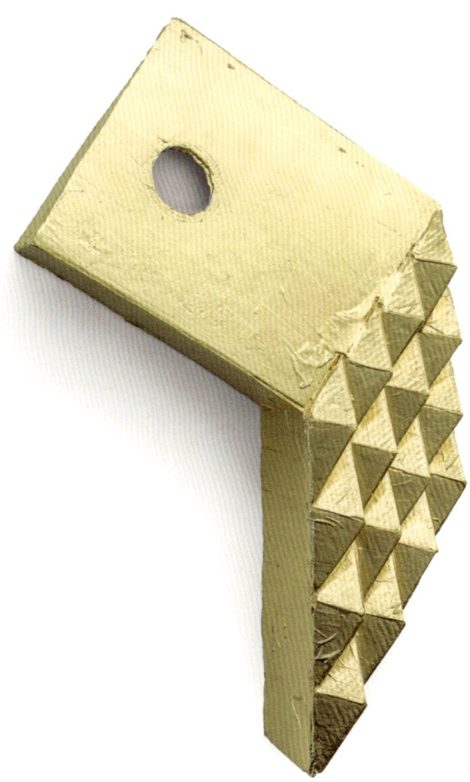

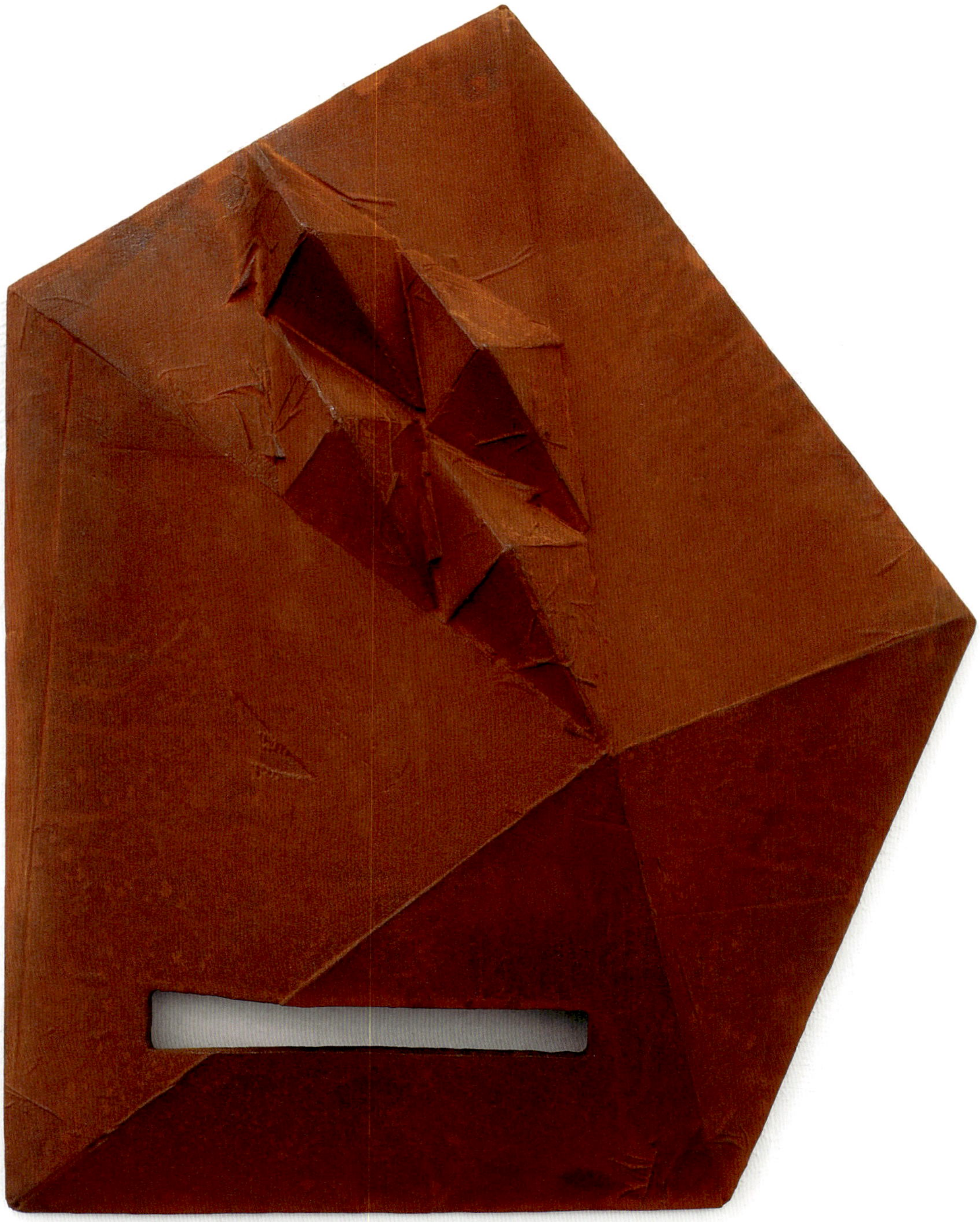

M. 60, 2017
Iron / Eisen, 72 × 57 × 17 cm

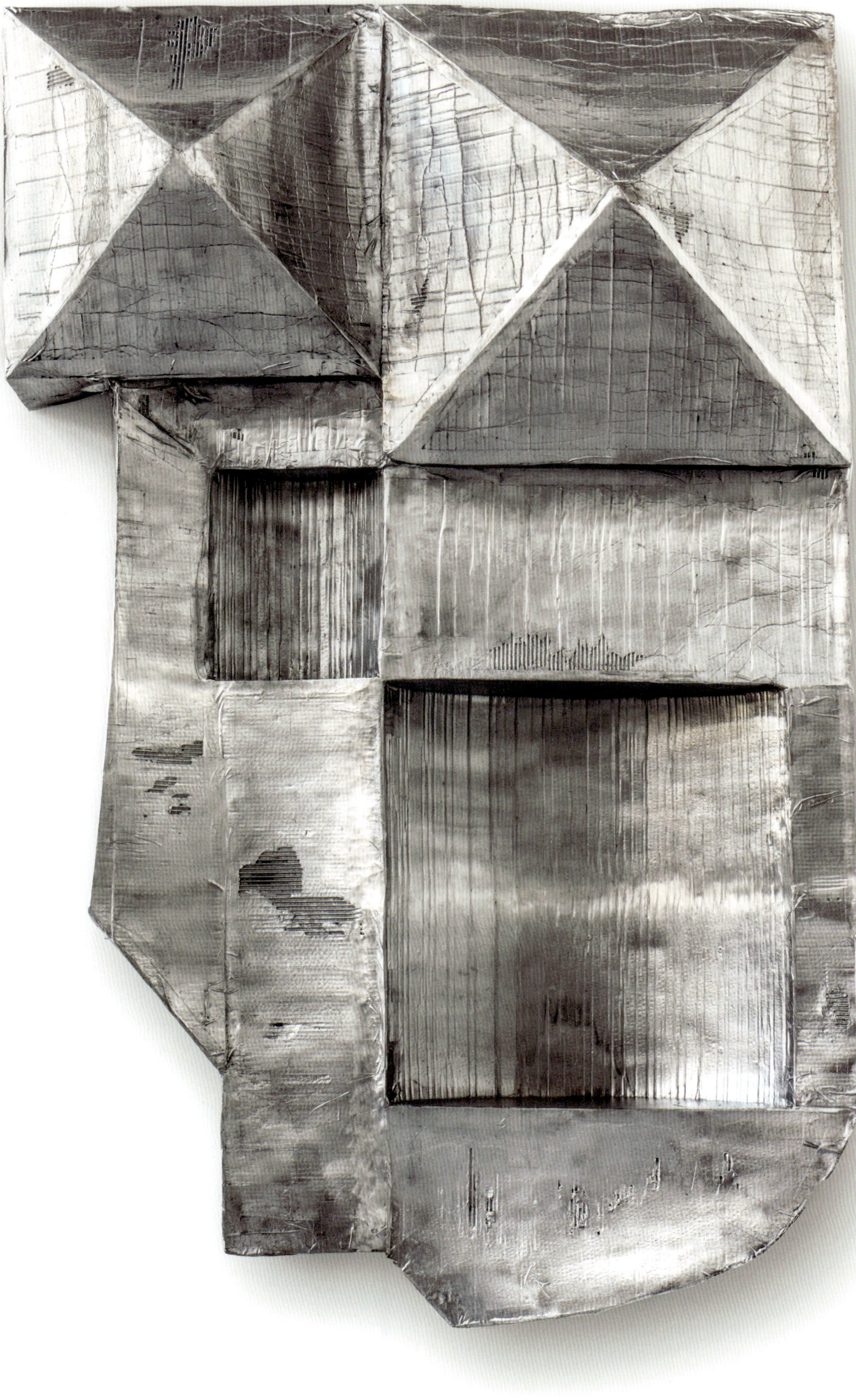

MB1, 2017

Aluminum / Aluminium, 200 × 130 × 55 cm

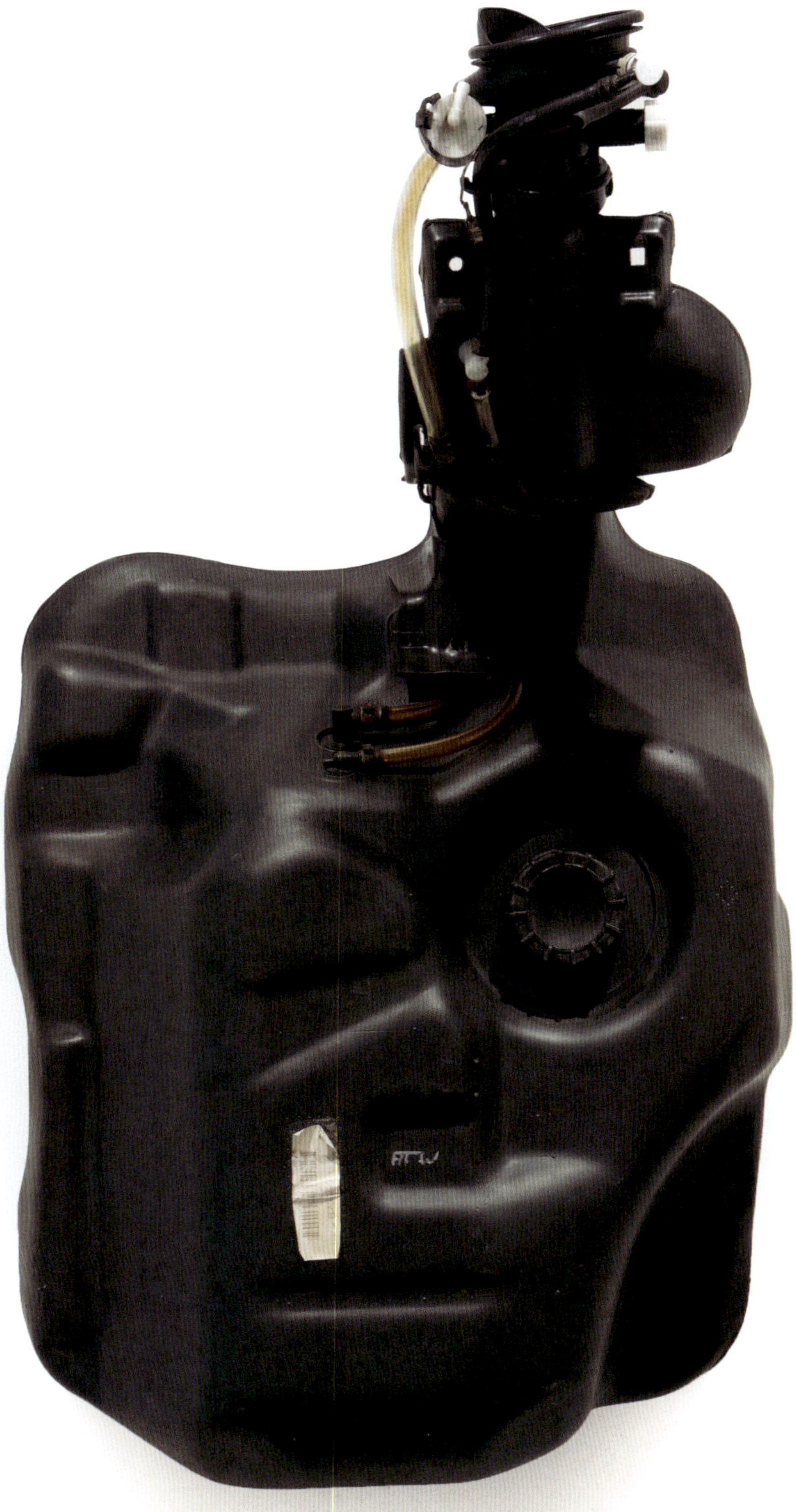

Tank 1, 2020

Fuel tank, loudspeaker / Benzintank, Lautsprecher, 115 × 70 × 75 cm

Kopf und Körper Bad Driburg, 2017

Wood / Holz, 910 × 335 × 313 cm, Installation view / Installationsansicht, Gräflicher Park Bad Driburg

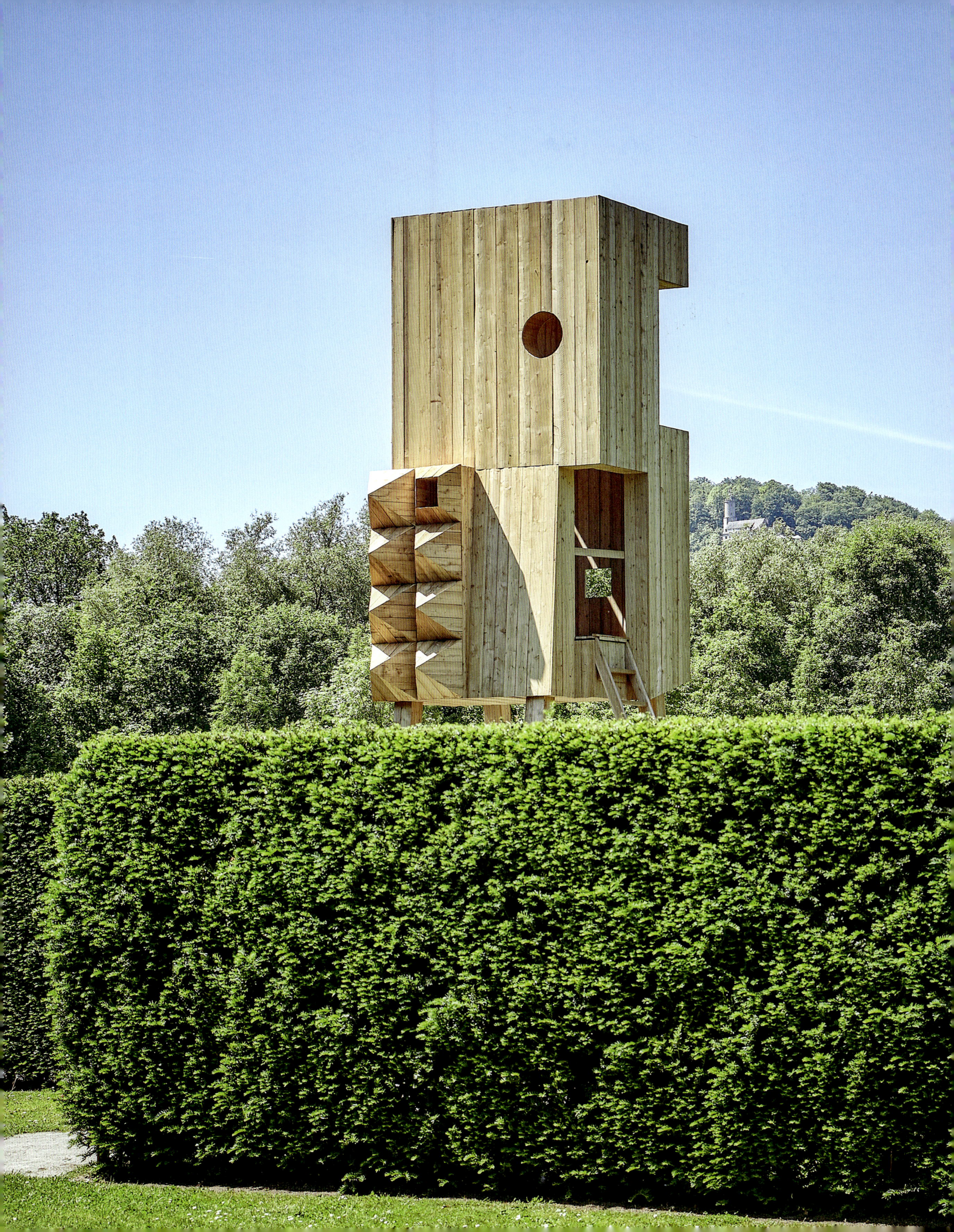

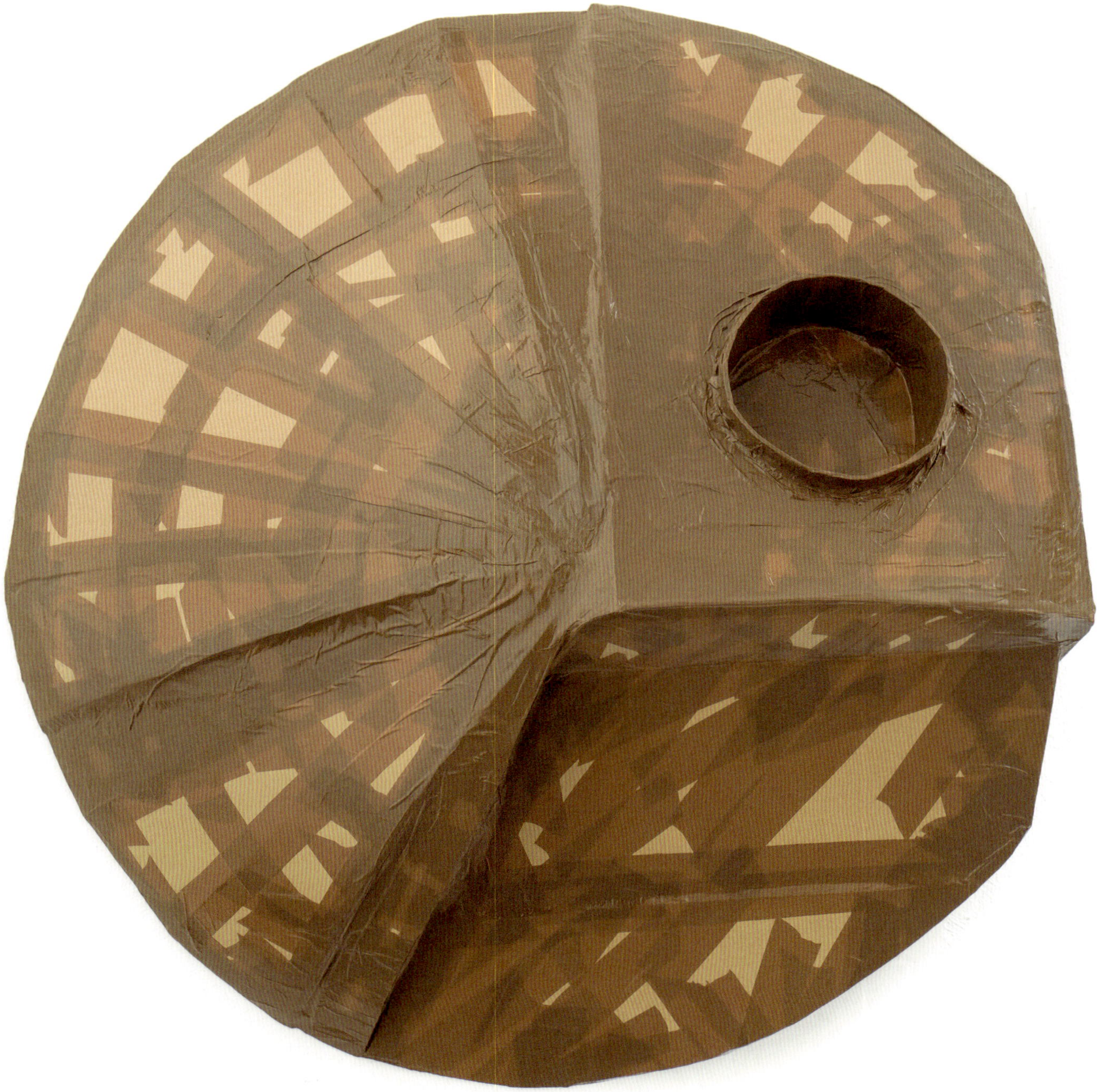

M. 74, 2018

Aluminum, paint / Aluminium, Farbe, 107 × 99,5 × 29 cm

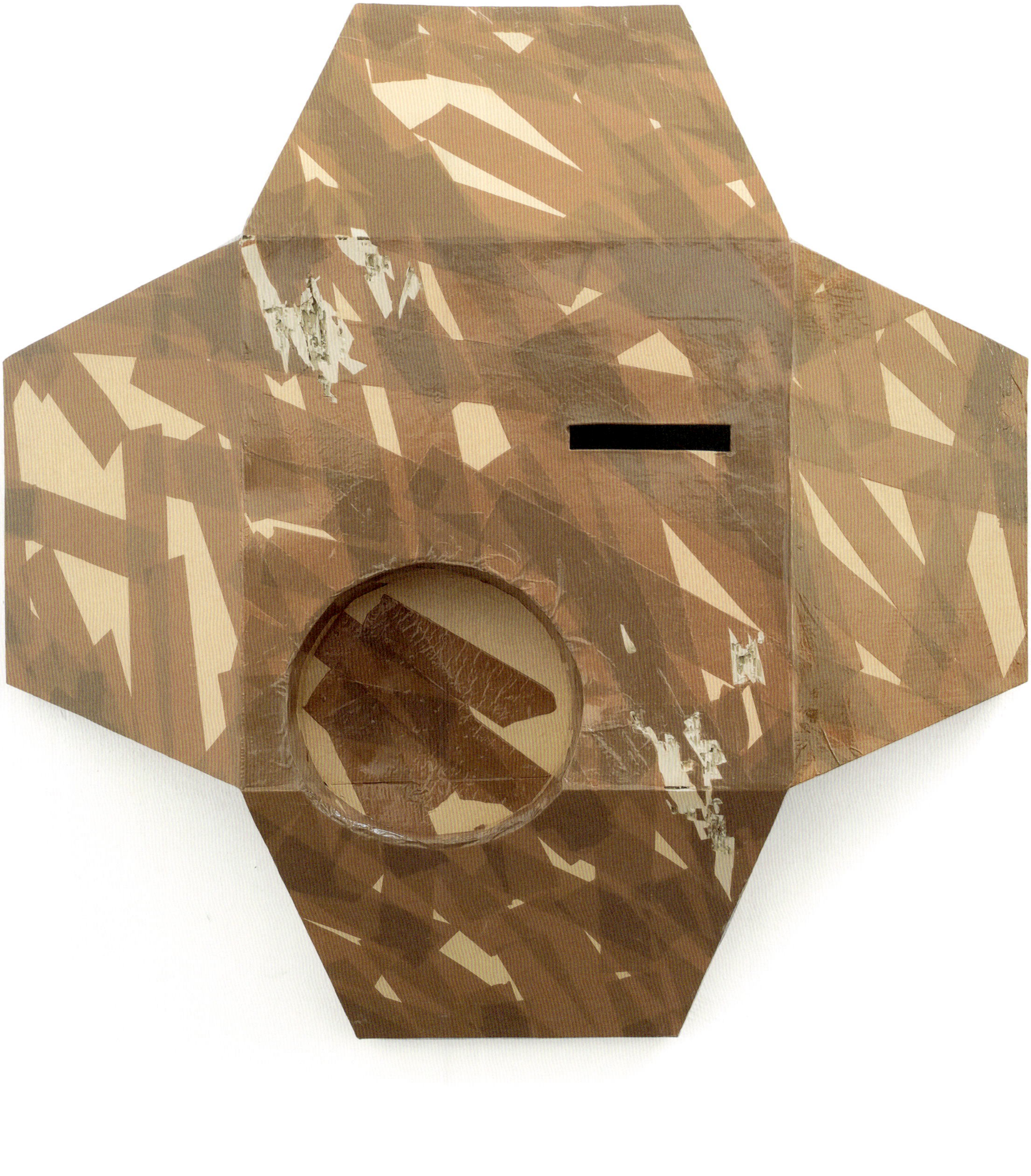

M. 71, 2018

Aluminum, paint / Aluminium, Farbe, 94,5 × 94,5 × 21 cm

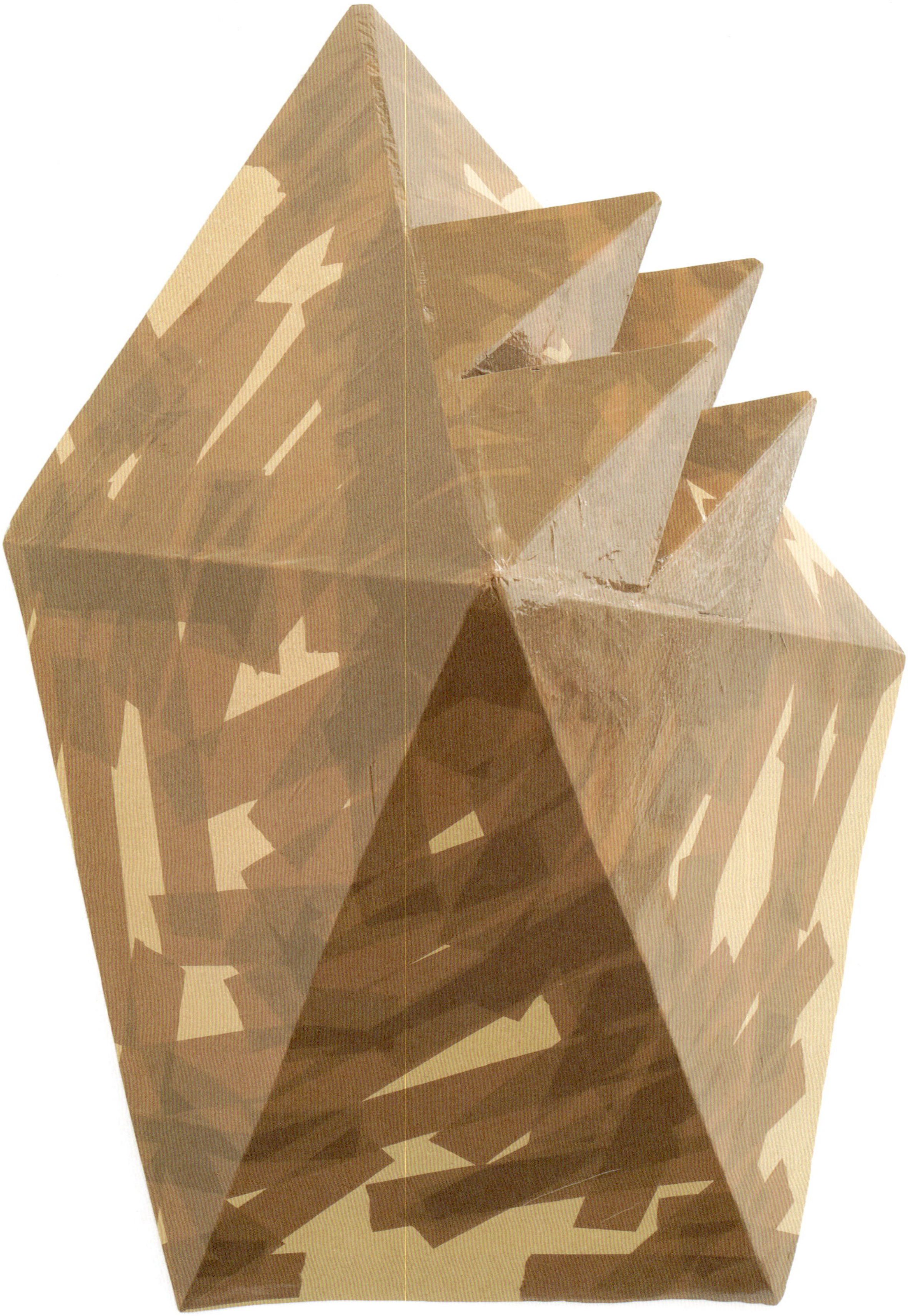

M. 73, 2018

Aluminum, paint / Aluminium, Farbe, 91,5 × 67,5 × 29,5 cm

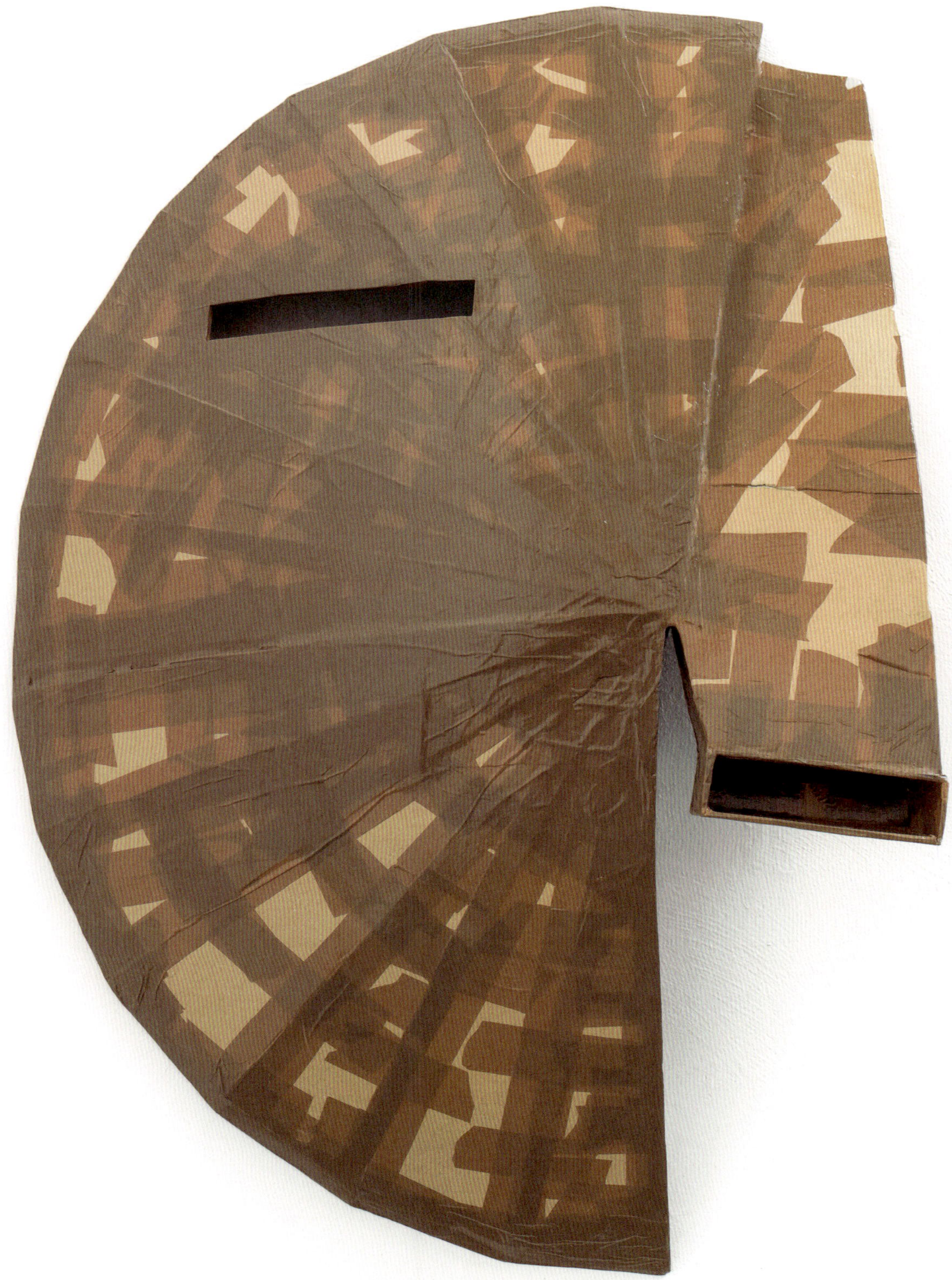

M. 70, 2018

Aluminum, paint / Aluminium, Farbe, 115 × 79,5 × 23,5 cm

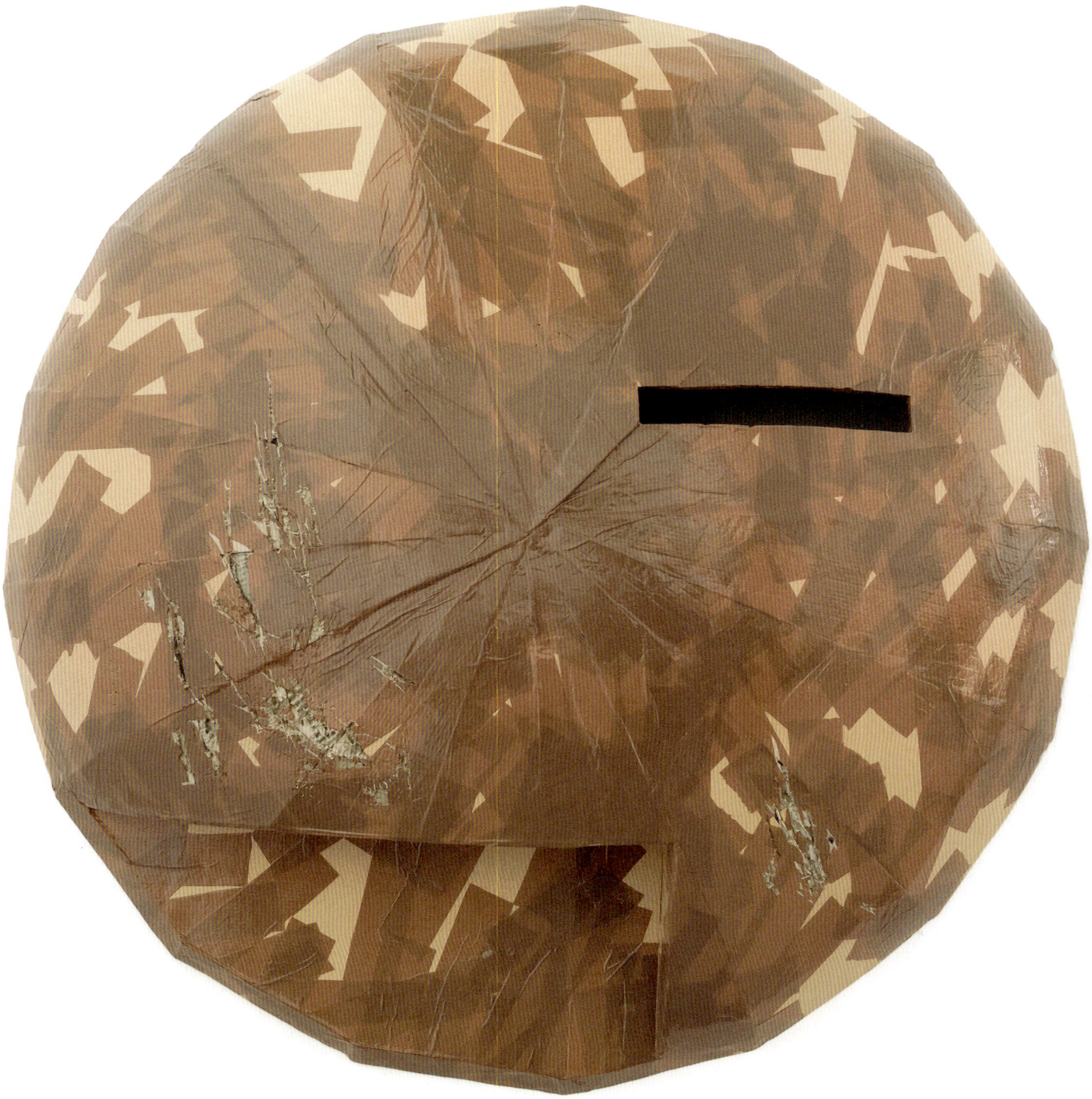

M. 69, 2018
Aluminum, paint / Aluminium, Farbe,
105 × 105 × 18 cm

MB3, 2017
Aluminum, paint / Aluminium, Farbe,
200 × 150 × 30 cm

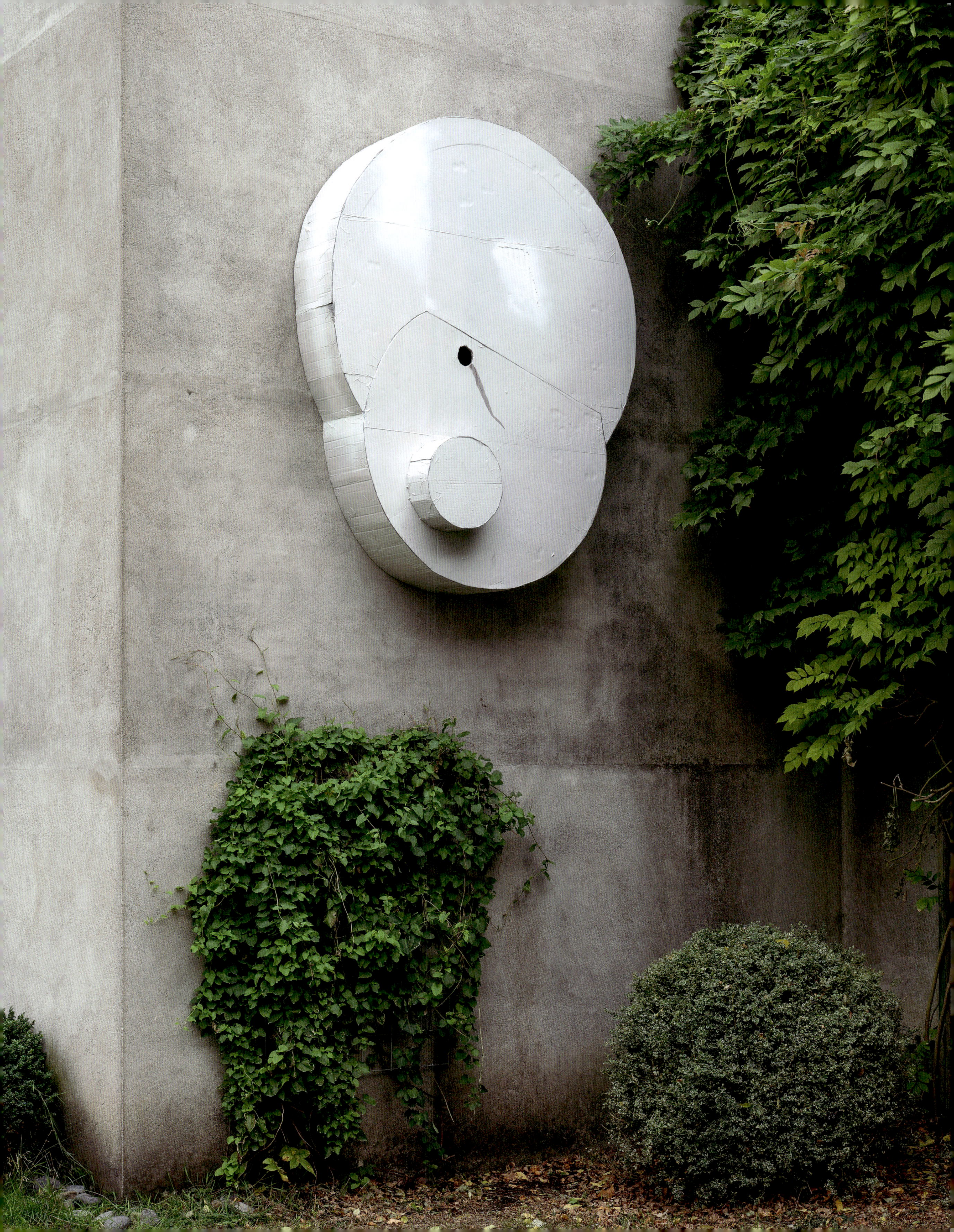

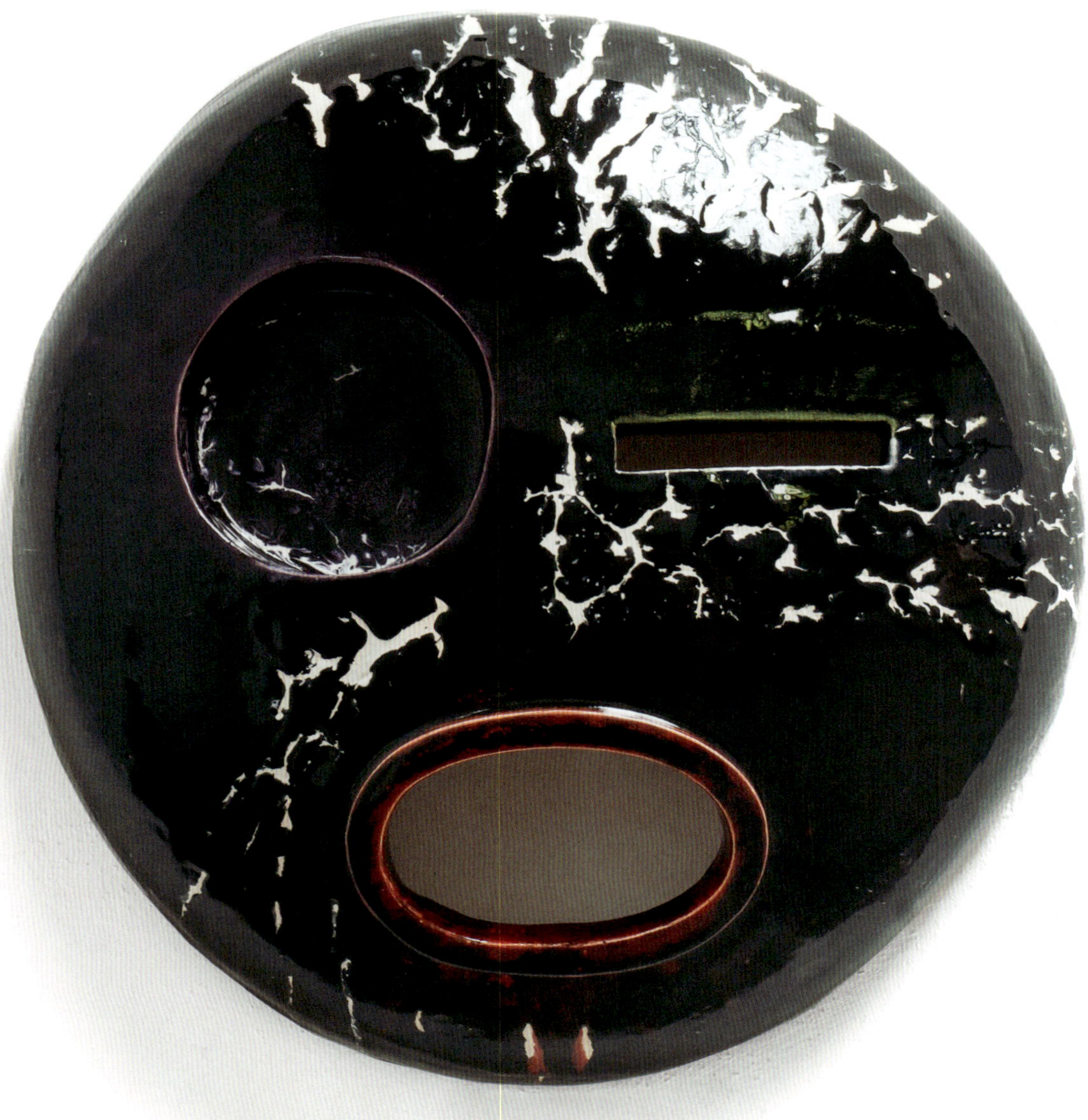

MC28, 2018

Ceramic, glaze / Keramik, Glasur, 52 × 52 × 14 cm

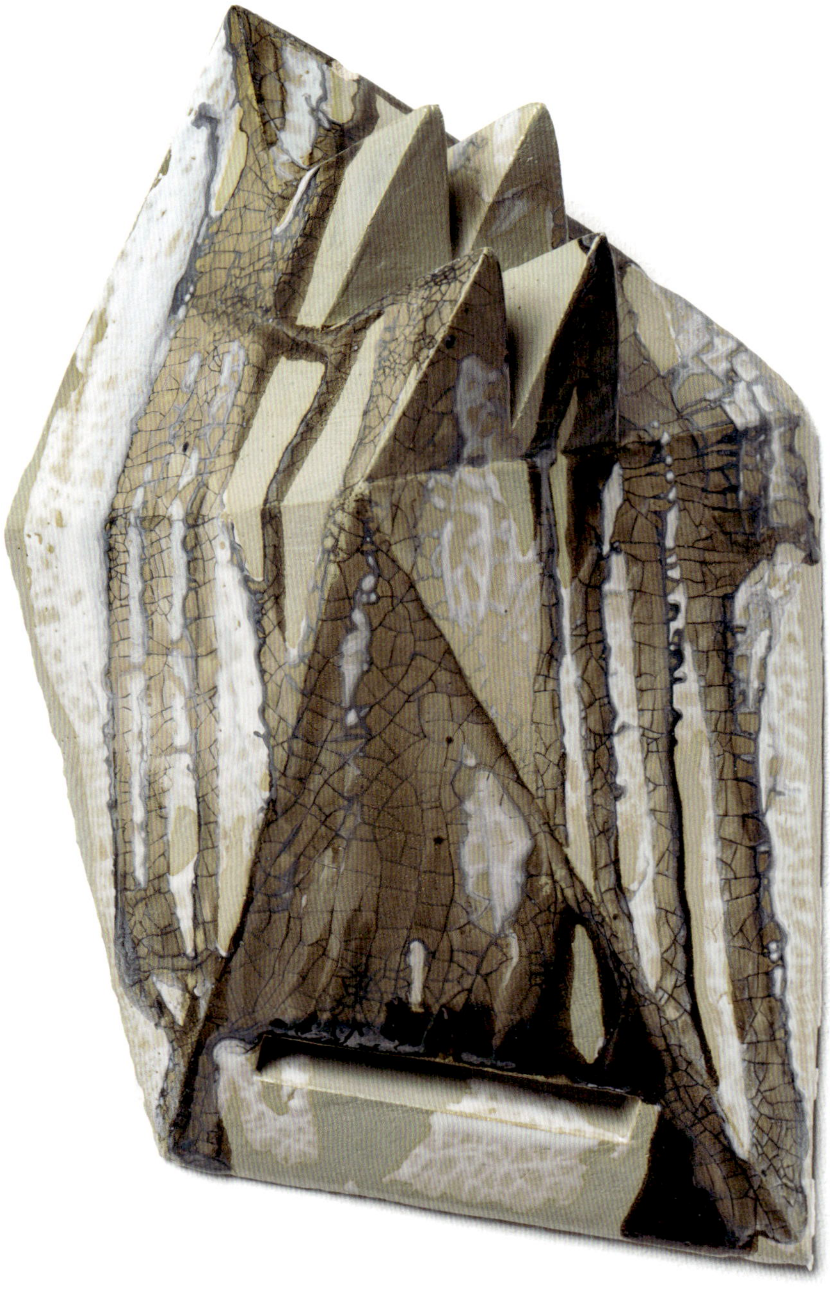

MCS39, 2022

Ceramic, glaze / Keramik, Glasur, 28 × 28 × 6 cm

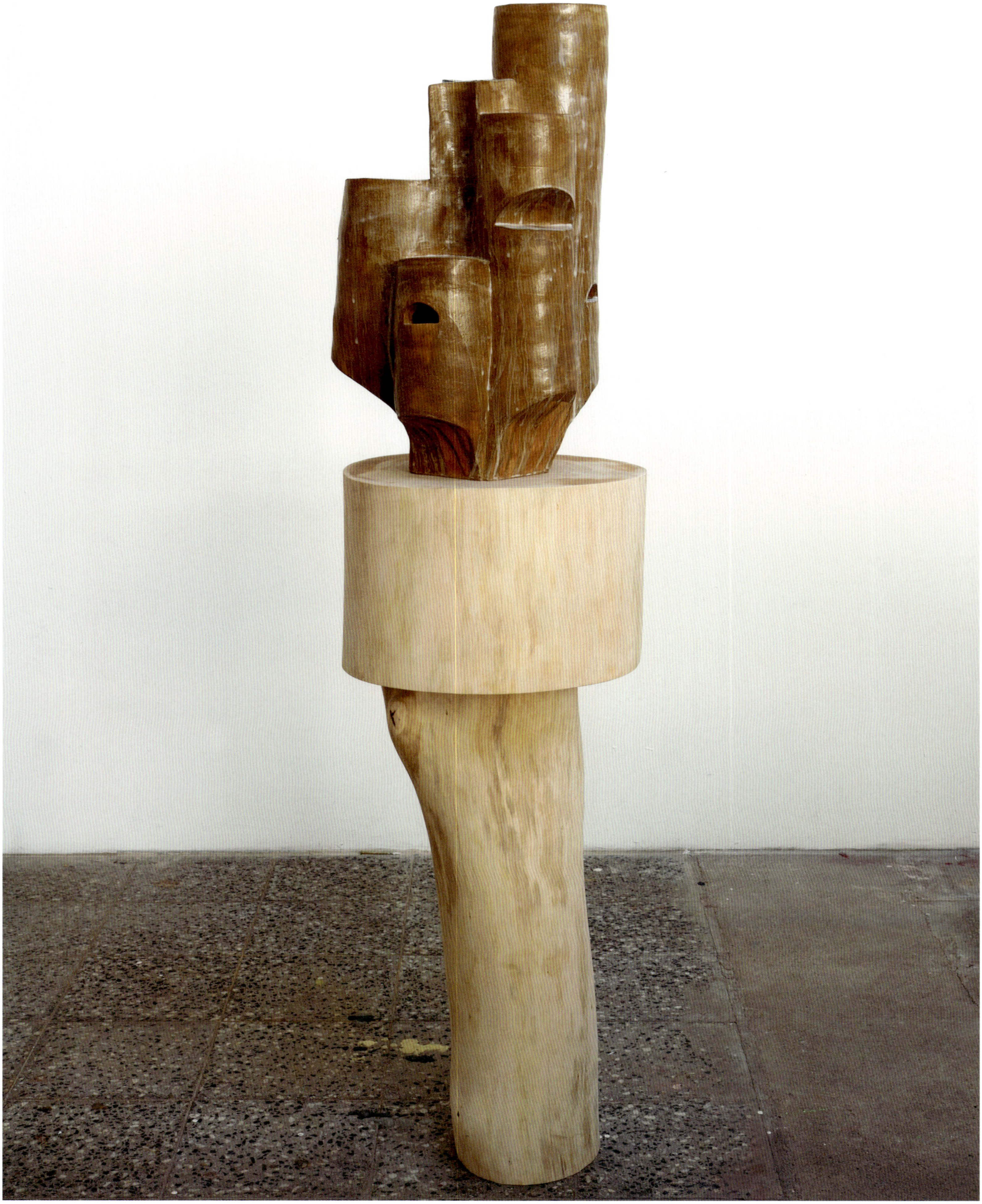

Altenheim für Nationalisten, 2016

Ceramic, glaze, wood / Keramik, Glasur, Holz, 178 × 40 × 44 cm

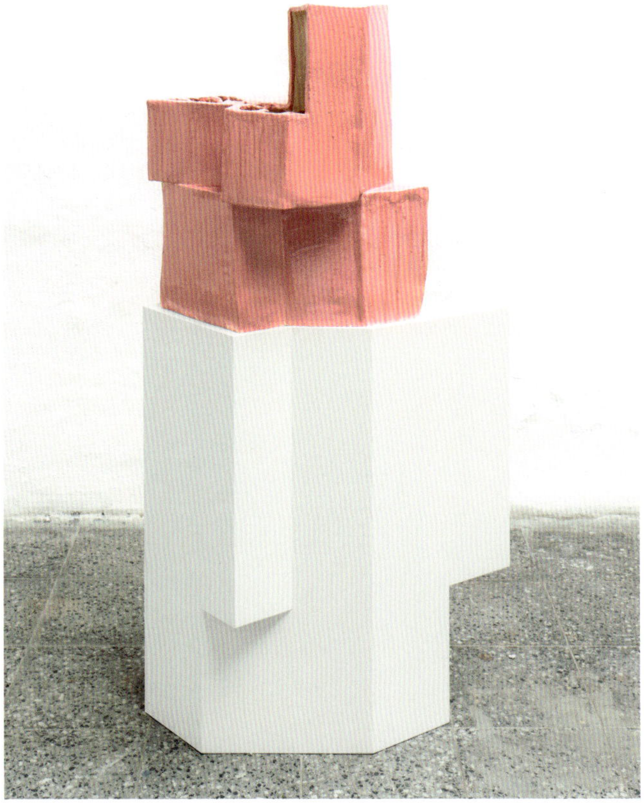

Altenheim für Populisten, 2017
Ceramic, glaze, wood / Keramik, Glasur, Holz, 147 × 74 × 40 cm

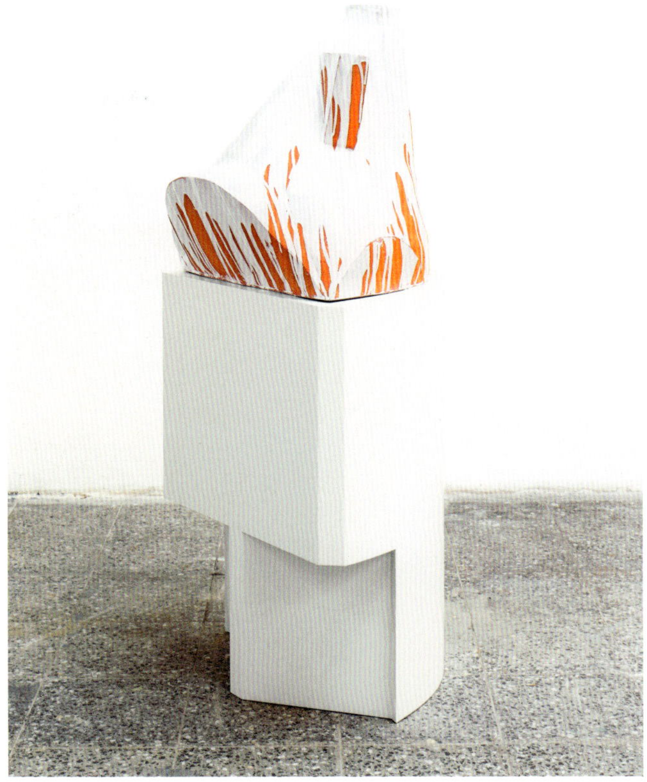

Palast, 2017
Ceramic, glaze, wood / Keramik, Glasur, Holz, 160 × 58 × 54 cm

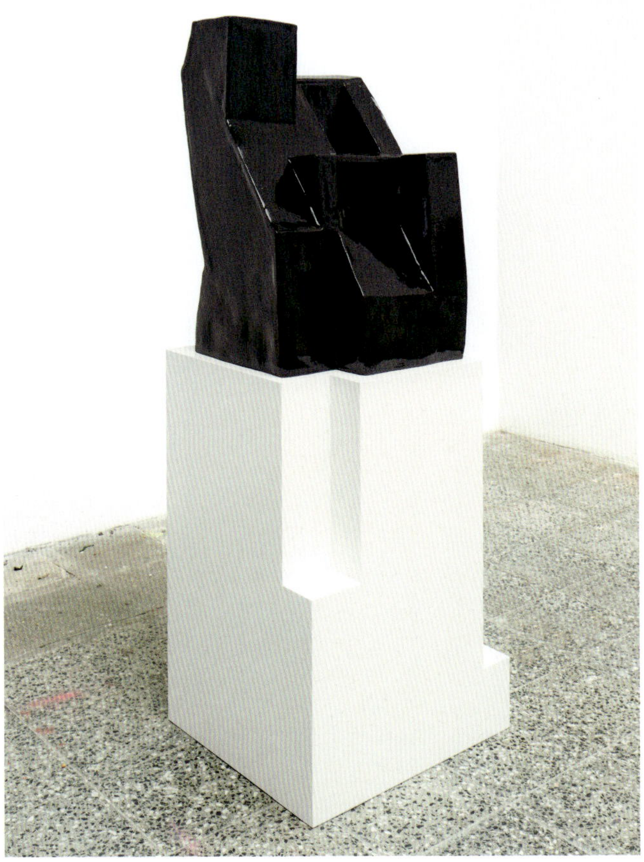

Altenheim für Astronauten, 2017
Ceramic, glaze, wood / Keramik, Glasur, Holz, 142 × 62 × 51 cm

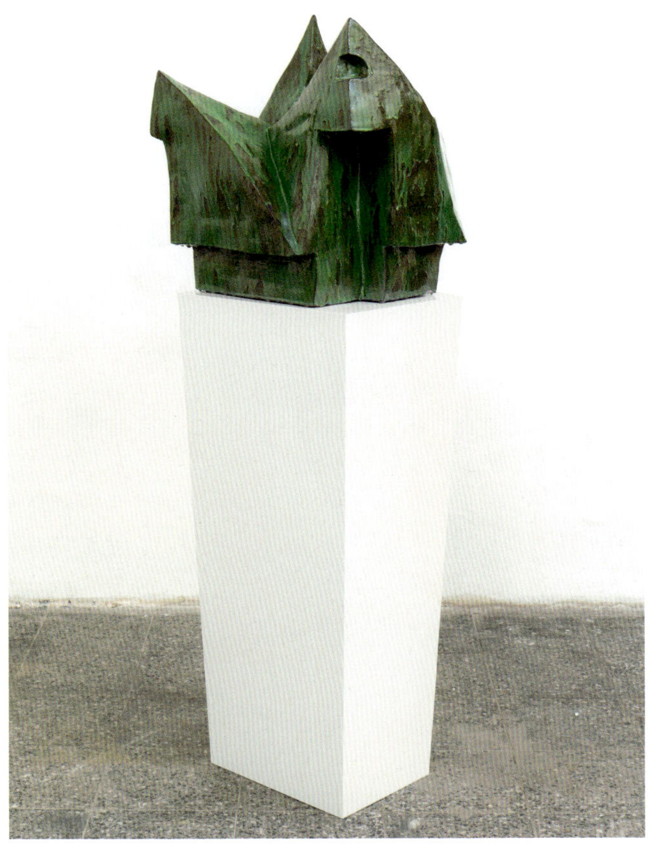

Altenheim für Nationalisten, 2017
Ceramic, glaze, wood / Keramik, Glasur, Holz, 161 × 56 × 55 cm

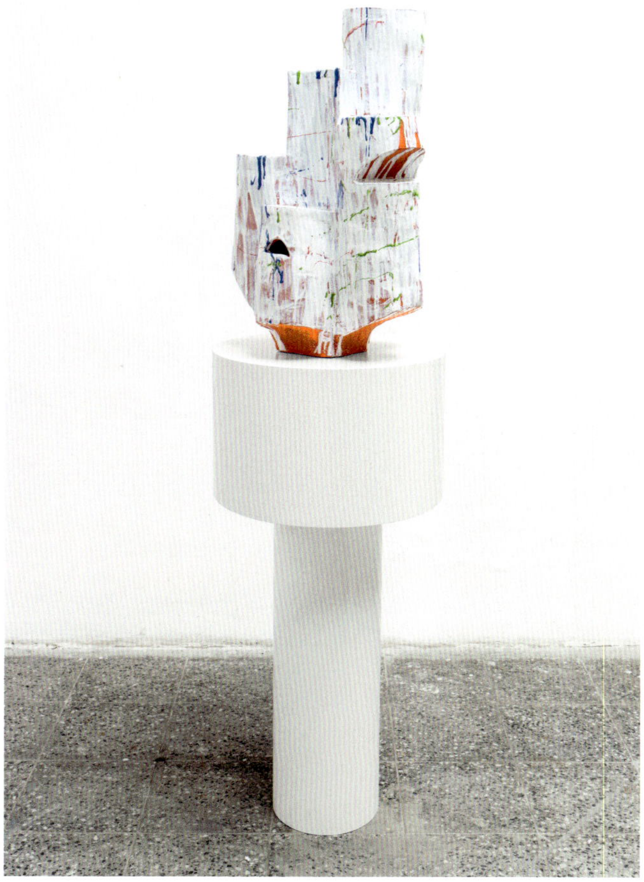

Altenheim für abstrakte Expressionisten, 2017
Ceramic, glaze, wood / Keramik, Glasur, Holz, 176,5 × 52 × 52 cm

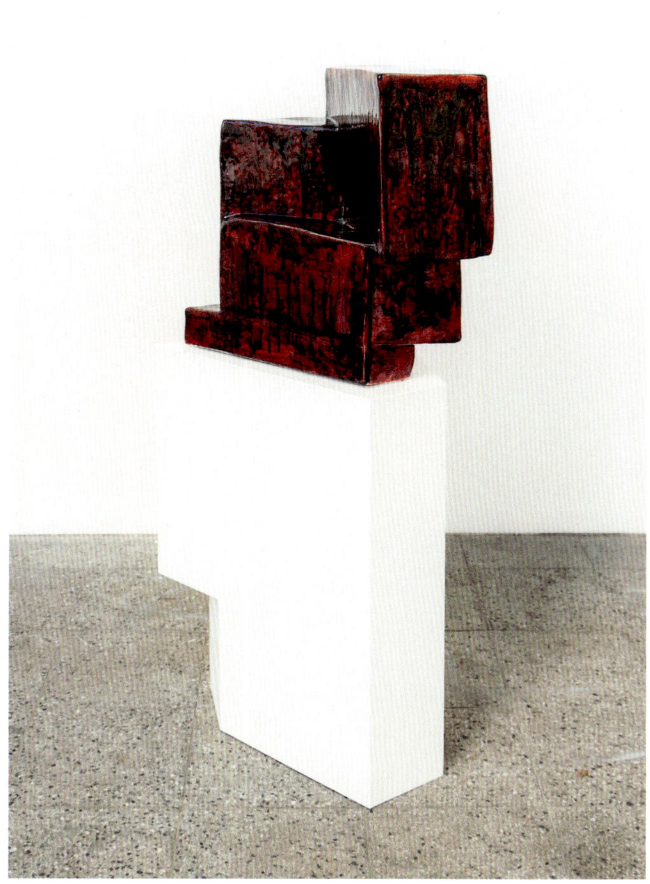

Gefängnis, 2017
Ceramic, glaze, wood / Keramik, Glasur, Holz, 124 × 57 × 47 cm

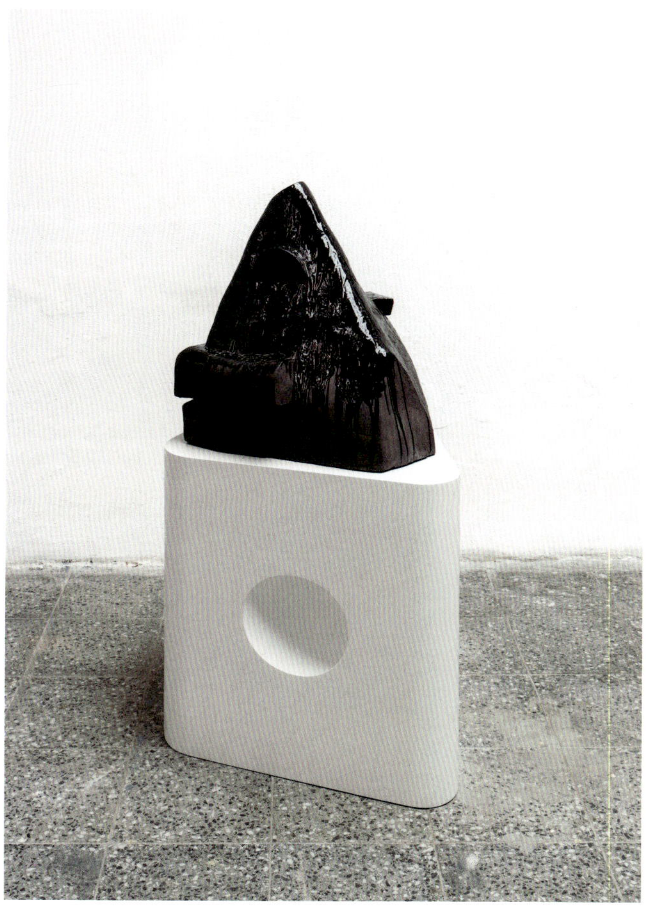

Altenheim für Kosmonauten, 2017
Ceramic, glaze, wood / Keramik, Glasur, Holz, 116 × 76 × 70 cm

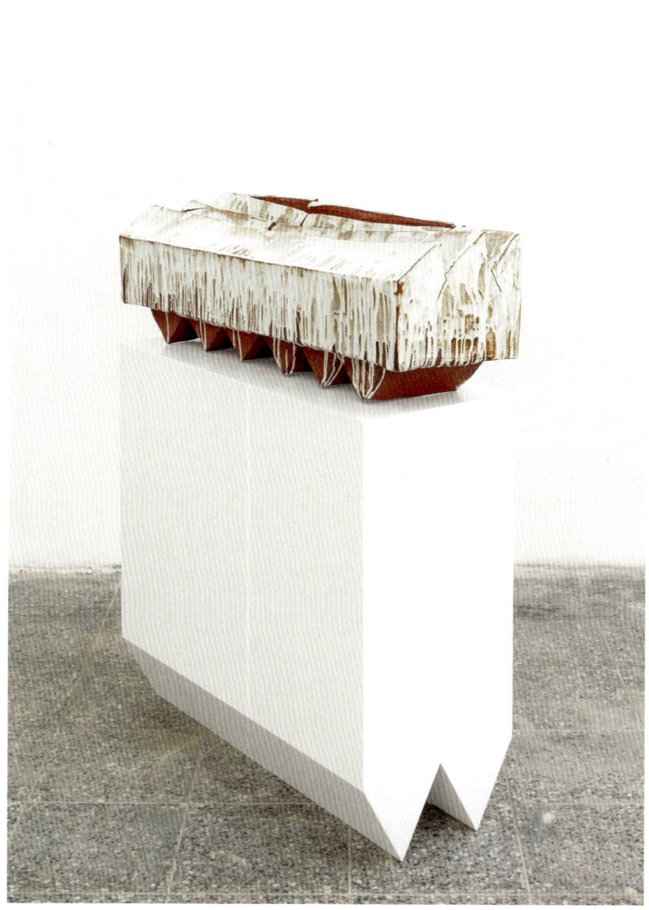

Unterkunft, 2017
Ceramic, glaze, wood / Keramik, Glasur, Holz, 110 × 94 × 35 cm

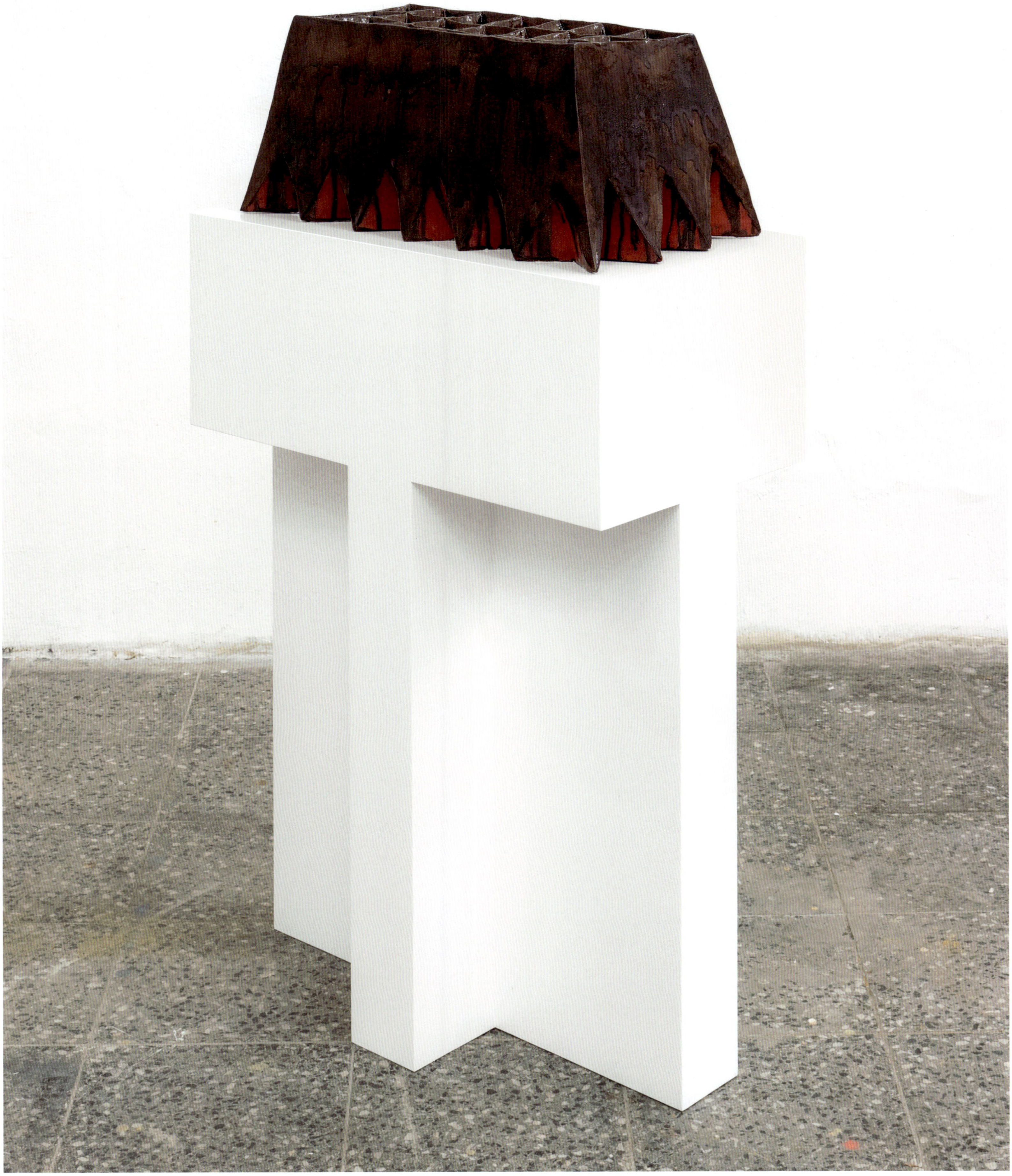

Tresor 2, 2017

Ceramic, glaze, wood / Keramik, Glasur, Holz, 115 × 65 × 36,5 cm

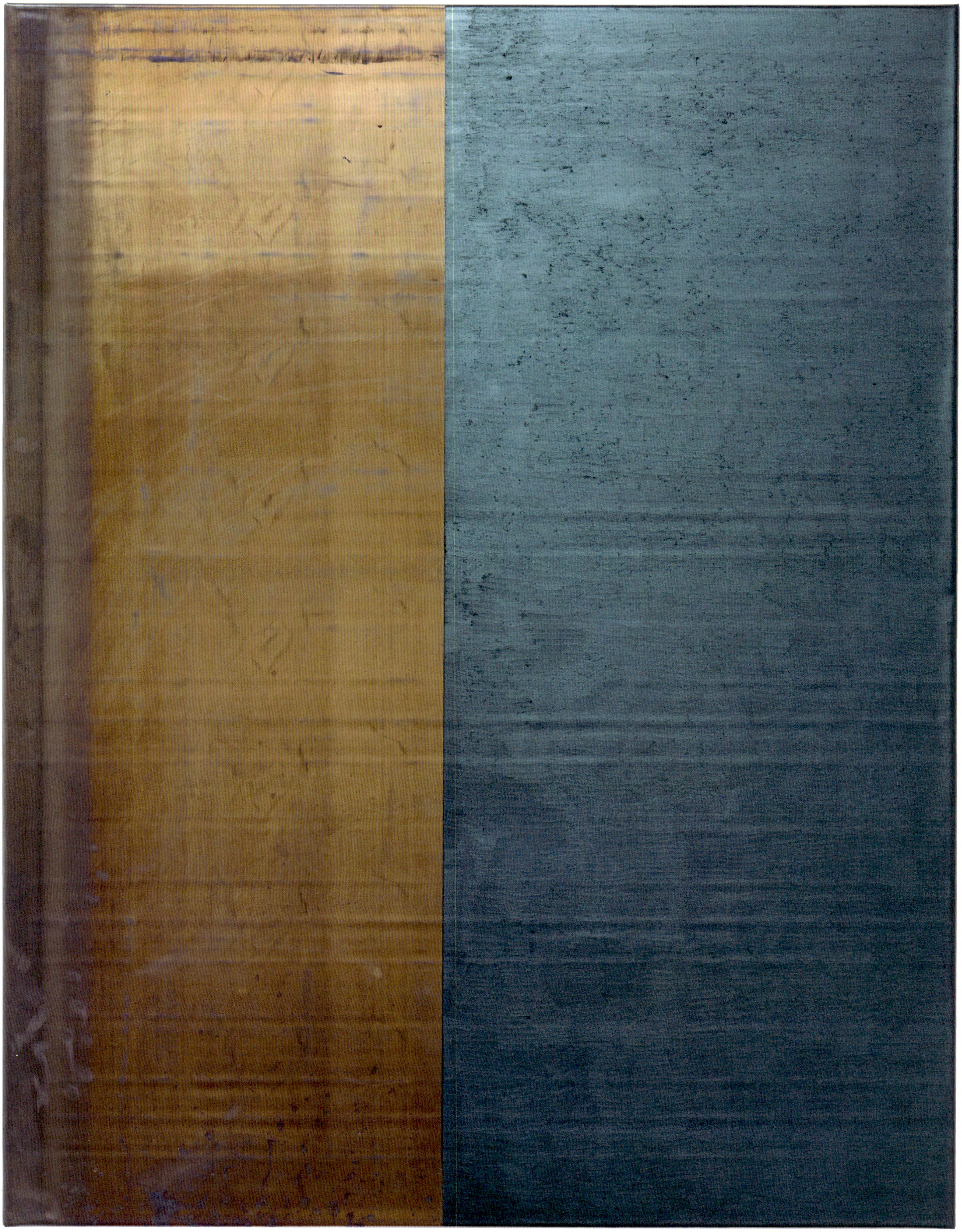

Heavy Eyes 111 DEEP BLUE GREEN, 2022

Lead, eyeshadow / Blei, Lidschatten, 140 × 110 cm

Heavy Eyes 73 BLONDE'S GOLD, 2022

Lead, eyeshadow / Blei, Lidschatten, 140 × 110 cm

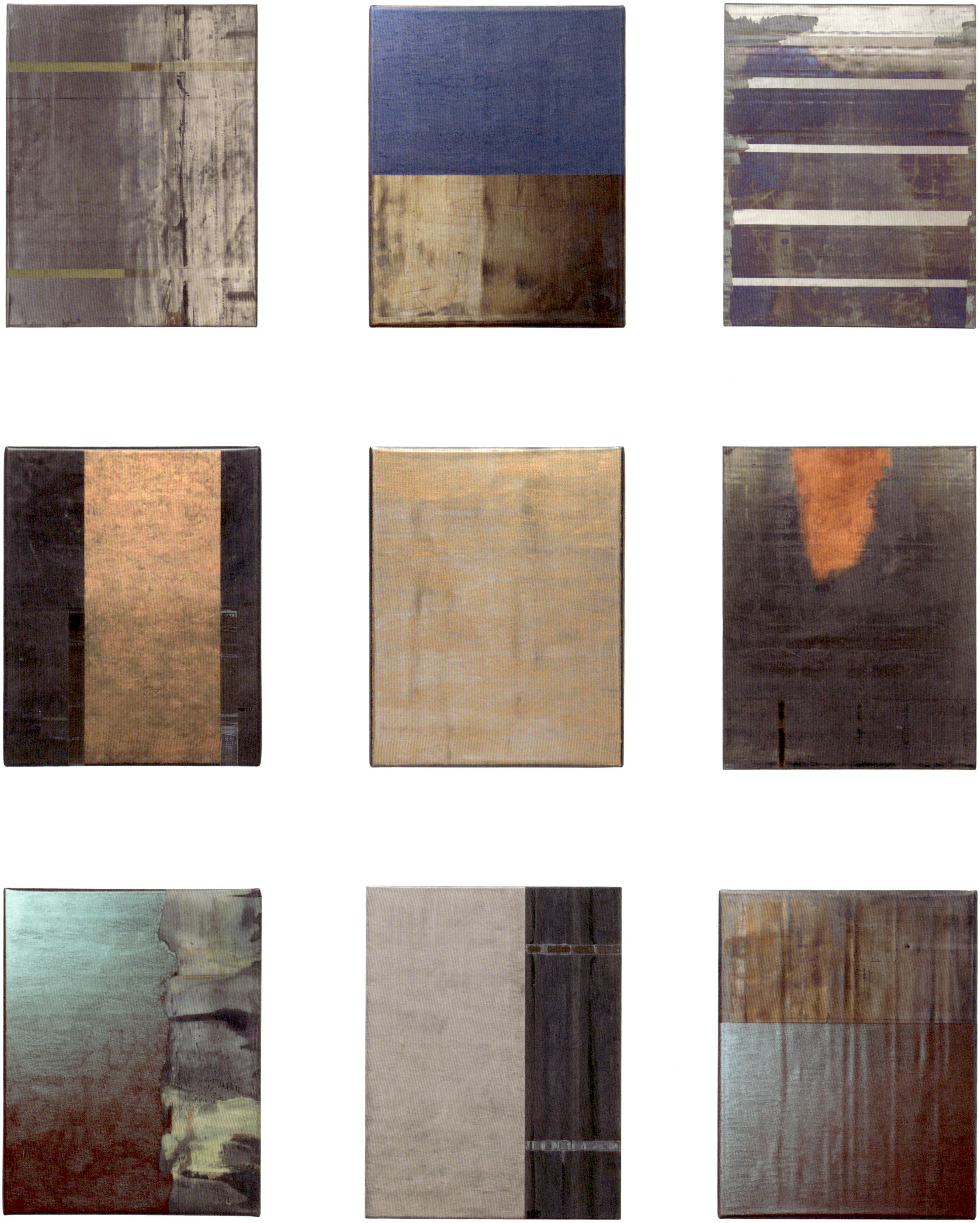

Heavy Eyes, 2020–2022

Lead, eyeshadow / Blei, Lidschatten

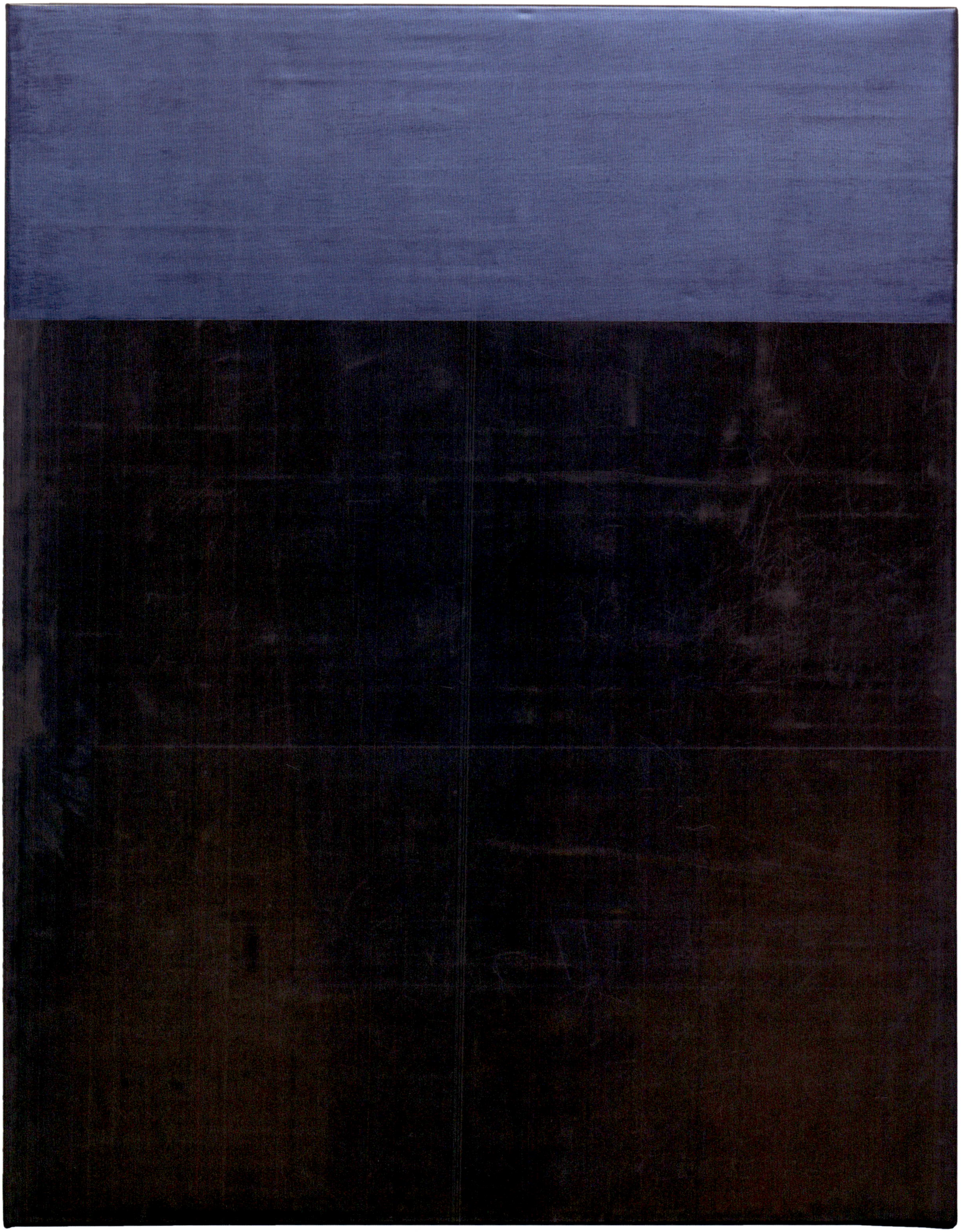

Heavy Eyes 71 NAVAL BLUE, 2021

Lead, eyeshadow / Blei, Lidschatten, 140 × 110 cm

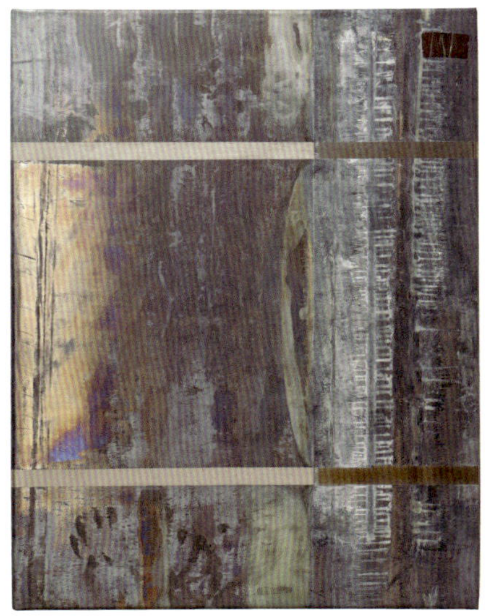

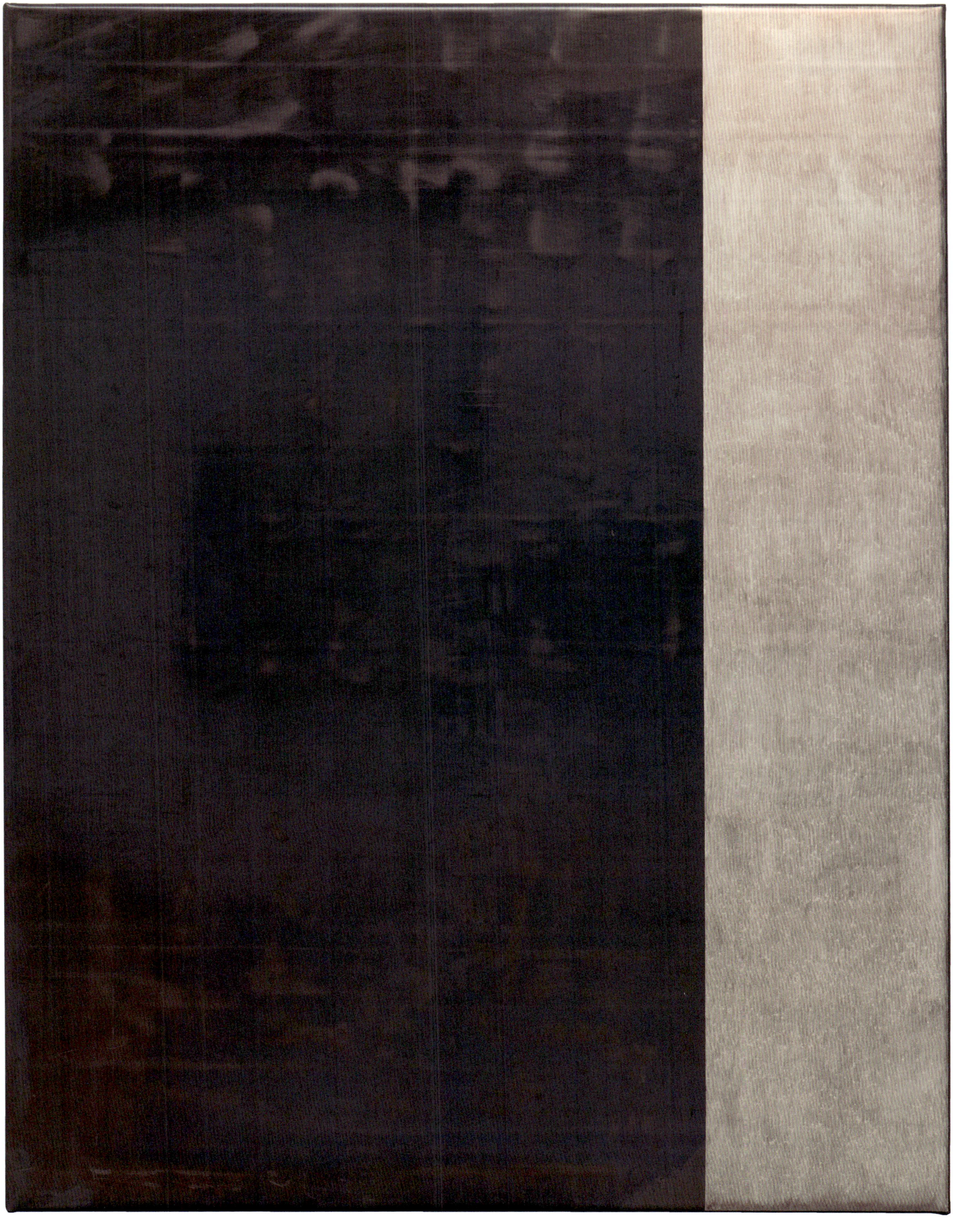

Heavy Eyes 72 VANILLA, 2021

Lead, eyeshadow / Blei, Lidschatten, 140 × 110 cm

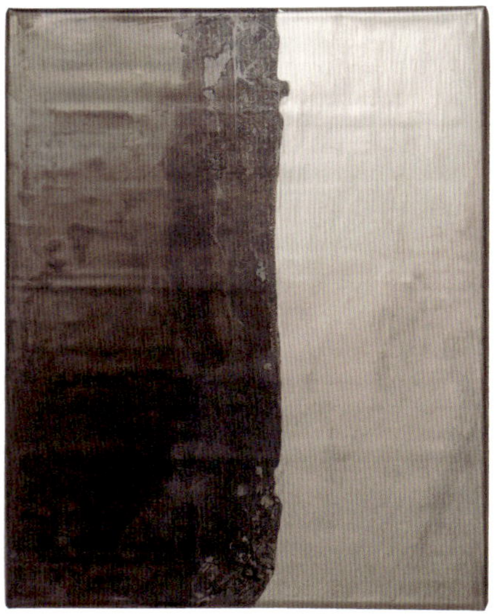

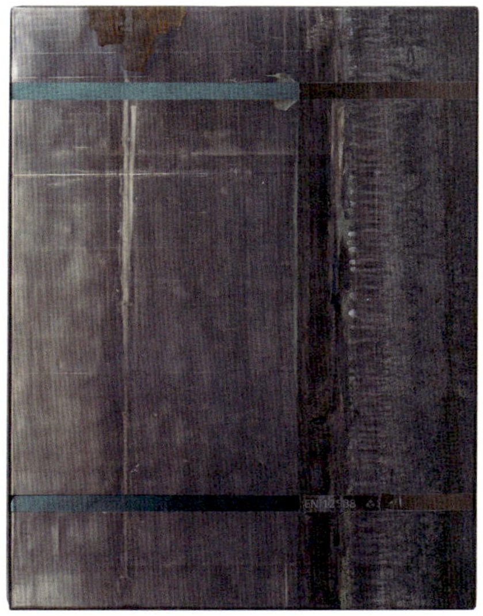

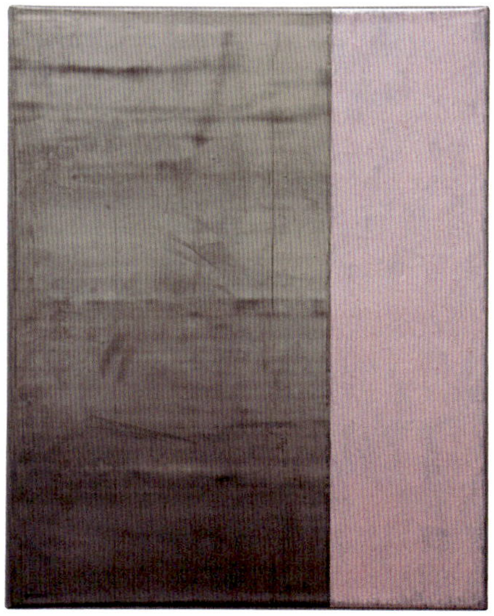
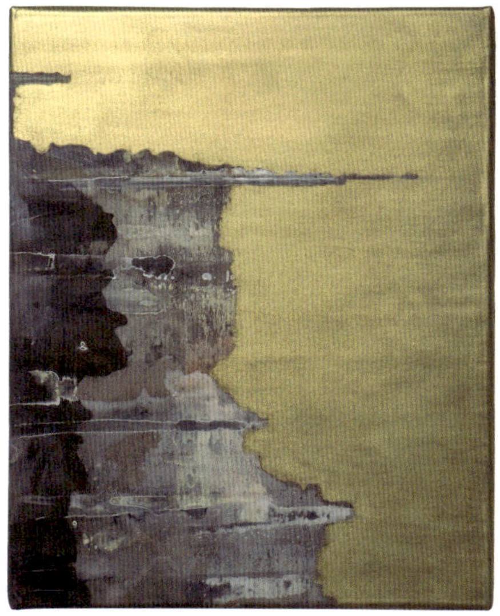
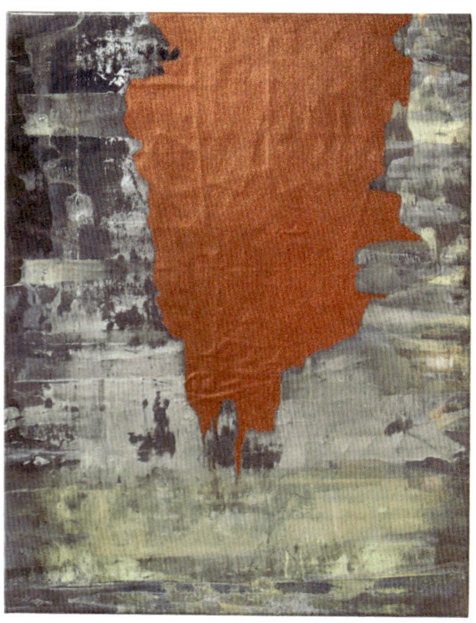

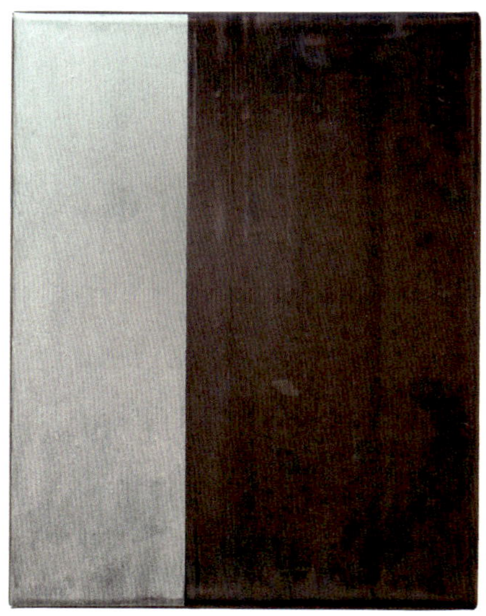

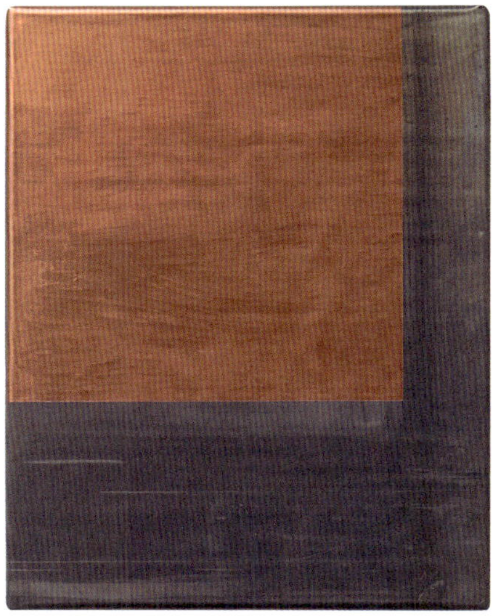

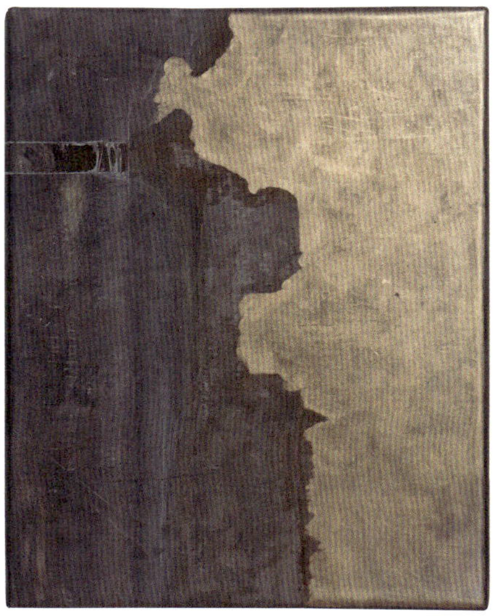

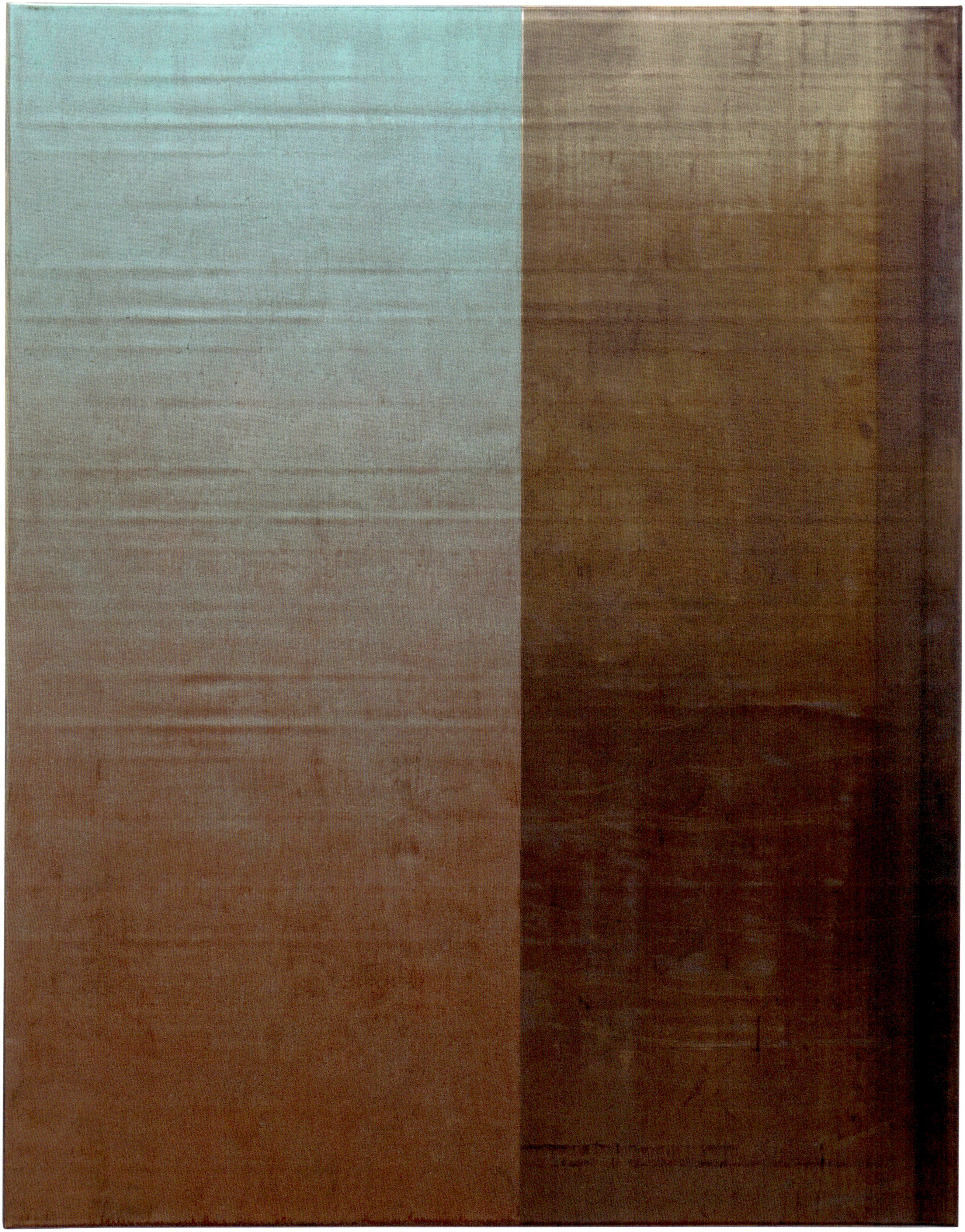

Heavy Eyes 108 BLUE BROWN, 2022

Lead, eyeshadow / Blei, Lidschatten, 140 × 110 cm

Heavy Eyes 10 AMAZE, 2020

Lead, eyeshadow / Blei, Lidschatten, 50 × 40 cm

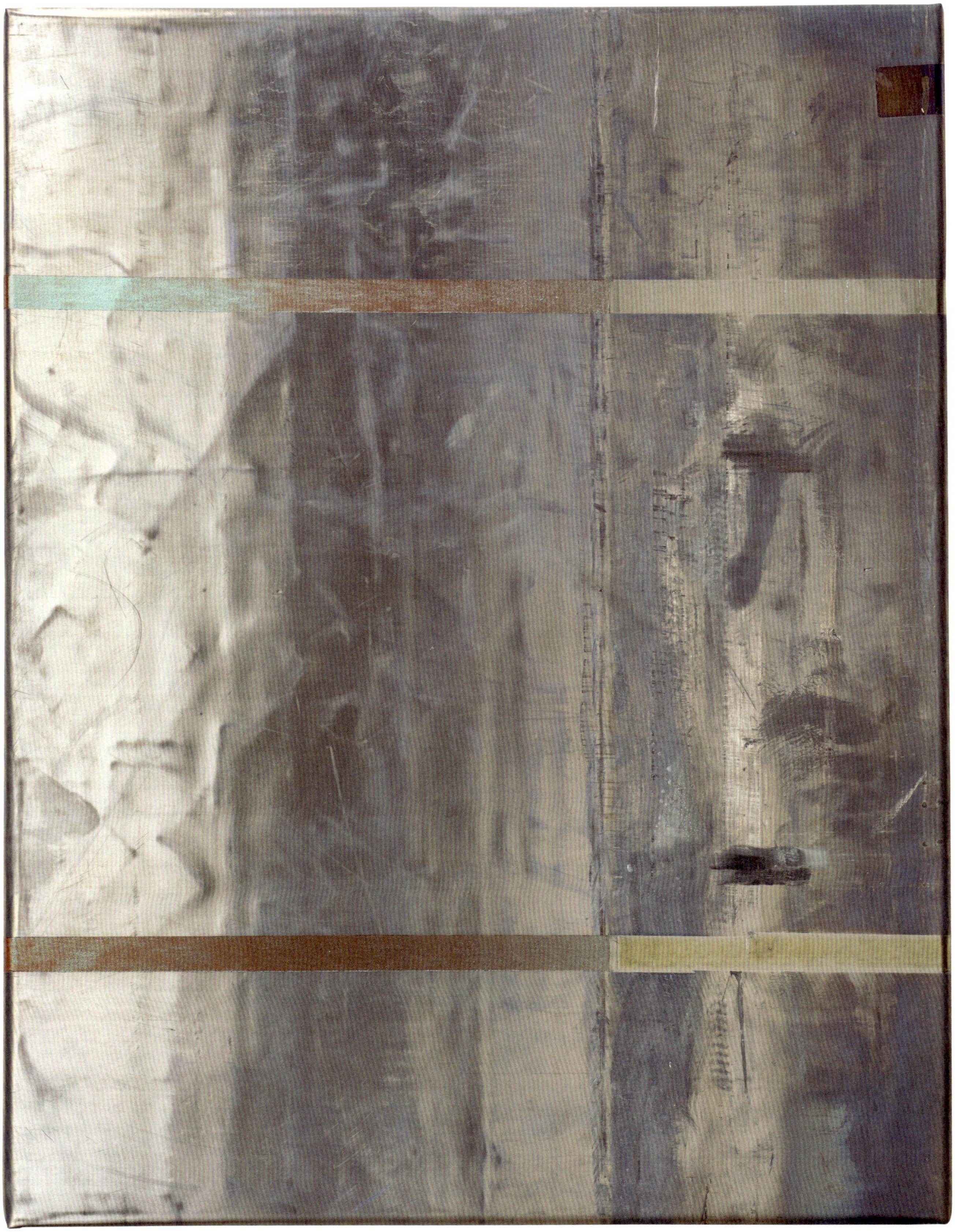

Heavy Eyes 38 BLUE BROWN, 2021

Lead, eyeshadow / Blei, Lidschatten, 90 × 70 cm

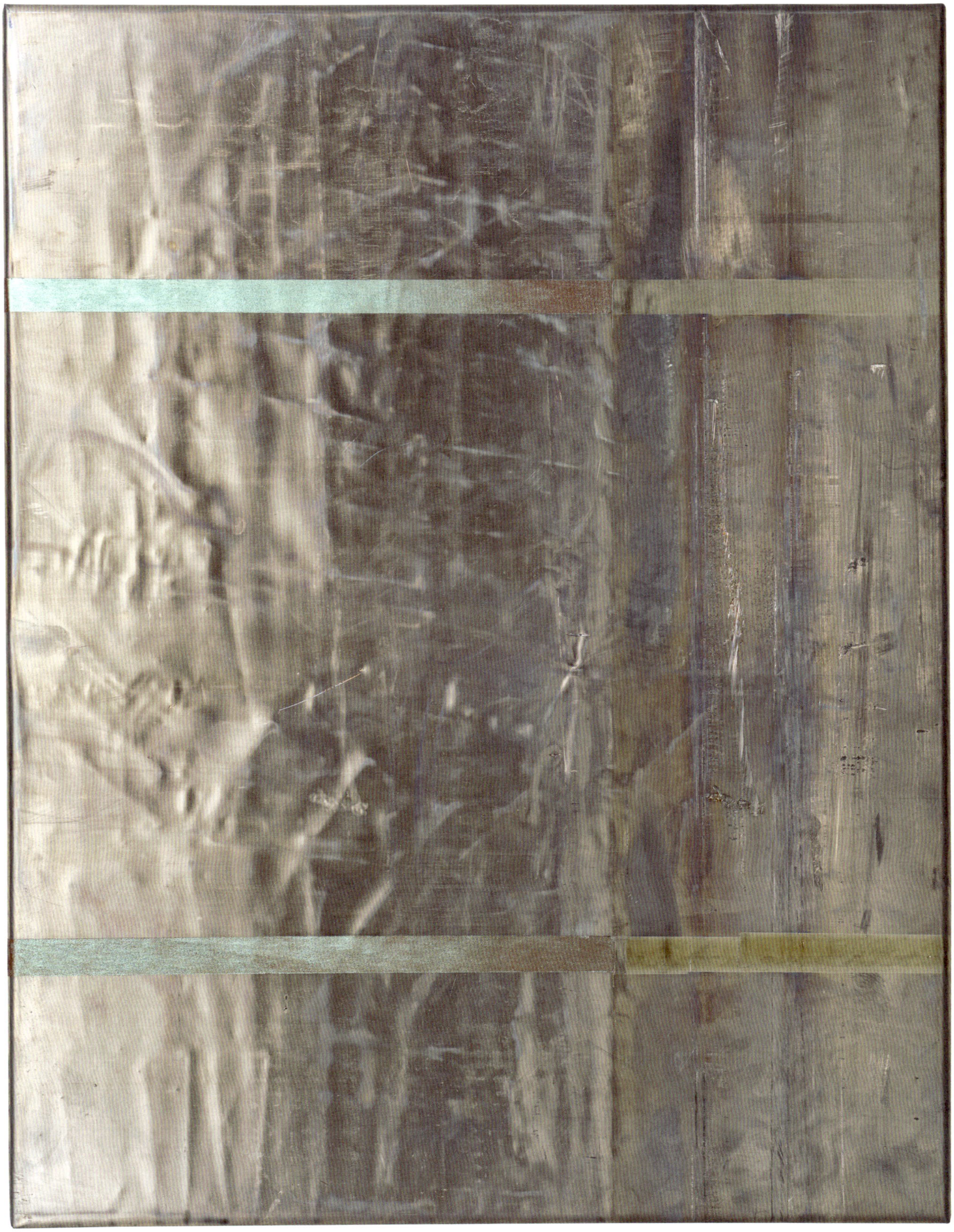

Heavy Eyes 37 BLUE BROWN, 2021

Lead, eyeshadow / Blei, Lidschatten, 90 × 70 cm

HEAVY EYES

In the series *Heavy Eyes* ↗168–179, 182–185, German artist Michael Sailstorfer follows his ongoing investigation into the transformative power of common materials, constructing associations between diverse themes that allow for seamless shifts between conceptual and metaphorical propositions. Here, Sailstorfer explores the notion of "weight" in its many connotations—from the innately material or physical heaviness to the emotions of burden and sadness. In exploring these and other converging histories, we see again how Sailstorfer uniquely reinterprets material, form, and time, simultaneously building and releasing tension through multiple means.

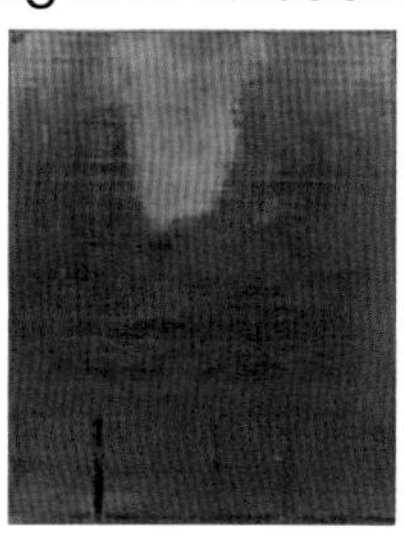

Heavy Eyes 23 Copper Sparkle, 2020

Materially, these works are created with lead sheet and commercially available cosmetics—specifically eyeshadow. The combination of these materials may initially seem in patent opposition, but this is (of course) by design. Presented in a traditionally formal and modernist manner, the works refer to a number of diverse art historical contexts, while simultaneously creating new aesthetic and metaphorical positions. Sailstorfer readily understands the history, implications, and use of lead as a material, not least by a number of his compatriots—Günther Förg, Anselm Kiefer, and Joseph Beuys, to name a few. As these artists focused on contemporary issues and circumstances, so too does Sailstorfer, albeit in his

In der Serie *Heavy Eyes*, 2020–2022 ↗168–179, 182–185, führt Michael Sailstorfer seine fortwährenden Untersuchungen an der transformativen Kraft von alltäglichen Materialien fort, indem er Assoziationen zwischen unterschiedlichen Themen konstruiert, die nahtlose Übergänge von konzeptuellen und metaphorischen Vorschlägen ermöglichen. Hier erforscht Sailstorfer die Vorstellung von „Gewicht" in ihren vielen Konnotationen – von der Perspektive der natürlichen oder physikalischen Schwere bis zu den Empfindungen von Belastung und Schwermut. Daran wie er diese und andere konvergierende Geschichten auslotet, sehen wir einmal mehr, wie Sailstorfer auf einzigartige Weise Material, Form und Zeit reinterpretiert, indem er mit ganz diversen Mitteln Spannung gleichzeitig auf- und abbaut. Im Wesentlichen bestehen diese Arbeiten aus Bleiblech und im Handel erhältlichen Kosmetika – insbesondere Lidschatten. Die Kombination dieser beiden Substanzen mag anfänglich in offensichtlichem Widerspruch stehend erscheinen, aber das ist (natürlich) Absicht. In traditioneller formaler und modernistischer Manier präsentiert, referieren die Arbeiten auf eine Reihe verschiedener historischer Kontexte, während sie zugleich eine neue Ästhetik und übertragene Positionen schaffen. Als deutscher Künstler versteht Sailstorfer sofort die Geschichte und Implikationen, die dem Gebrauch von Blei, insbesondere bei manchen seiner Landsmänner – Günther Förg, Anselm Kiefer und Joseph Beuys, um nur einige zu nennen, innewohnen. Diese Künstler haben sich mit den Problemen und Bedingungen ihrer Zeit beschäftigt und das Gleiche tut auch Sailstorfer, aber auf seine ganz eigene, unverwechselbare und charakteristische Weise. Wenn jemand zu einer bestimmten Art von Humor neigt, dann könnten die Werke der obengenannten

own distinctive and characteristic manner. If one were prone to a certain sense of humor, the work produced by the aforementioned artists could be characterized as quite "heavy" in political, social, historic, or personal terms. In establishing and working within a new tradition of interpretation and production, Sailstorfer both acknowledges and challenges these histories, finding an idiosyncratic balance somewhere between profound seriousness and light-hearted humor.

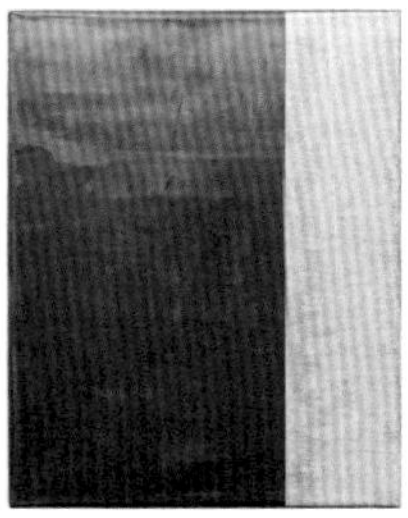

Heavy Eyes 124 White Gold, 2022

In choosing the title for the exhibition, Sailstorfer makes direct reference to his choice of materials for this series, and the physical and metaphorical implications therein. In many respects, the eyes have been a focus for artists over millennia, deployed not only to reference or reinforce understandings of beauty, but also as a perceived door or passageway into the deeper recesses of the soul. As trite or as commonplace as this notion may be, Sailstorfer considers it more deeply, specifically with a combination of materials that provides a unique dichotomy both physically and allegorically. As a base, the use of lead brings many avenues for interpretation—its weight or heaviness, its toxicity, and the various ways it has been utilized throughout history. In striking juxtaposition, the lead is applied with eyeshadow, something soft and feminine, used to create or augment beauty. But in the same way cosmetics can highlight and enhance what is already present, they can also cover or mask the unwanted, providing the user with a means to present a more desired projection of self. We may have tired eyes that we want to conceal, or hide in certain respects behind a "mask". Together, this combination of materials and specific use of color presents the viewer with an object that on the one hand can be interpreted as deeply personal and containing the notion of choice, but on the other broaden to include more collective states of being that may be out of our control. Again, in the alteration and use of these materials, we are given objects that ostensibly present themselves within the boundaries of a known aesthetic. But upon further inspection and consideration of details, we have the capacity to shift our perspective and understand Sailstorfer's compelling objects and their complex personal, social, historic, and conceptual underpinnings.

Künstler im Hinblick auf politische, soziale, historische oder persönliche Belange als ziemlich „schwergewichtig" bezeichnet werden. Während Sailstorfer mit seiner Arbeit eine neue Sichtweise der Interpretation und Produktion etabliert, erkennt er diese Traditionen bereitwillig an und hinterfragt sie trotzdem, wobei er eine eigenwillige Balance aus tiefstem Ernst und unbeschwertem Humor findet. Mit der Wahl des Titels für die Ausstellung nimmt Sailstorfer direkt Bezug auf die Auswahl der Materialien für diese Serie und die physikalischen und metaphorischen Implikationen.

In vielerlei Hinsicht stehen die Augen seit Jahrtausenden im Fokus von Künstler*innen, nicht nur um ein Gefühl für deren Schönheit zu erwecken und dieses zu verdeutlichen, sondern auch um das Auge als eine wahrgenommene Tür oder einen Durchgang in die tieferen Abgründe der Seele zu verstehen. So banal oder weitverbreitet diese Erkenntnis auch sein mag, Sailstorfer geht ihr auf den Grund, indem er eine Kombination von Materialien benutzt, die sowohl physisch als auch allegorisch eine ganz eigene Dichotomie besitzt. Die Verwendung von Blei bietet den Ausgangspunkt für eine Vielzahl von Interpretationsmöglichkeiten, wobei sein Gewicht oder seine Schwere, seine Giftigkeit und die unterschiedlichen Arten, wie das Material in der Geschichte eingesetzt wurden, eine entscheidende Rolle spielen. In besonderem Gegensatz zu dem Blei steht der aufgetragene Lidschatten, irgendwie weich und feminin, um Schönheit zu erzeugen oder zu verstärken. Auf die gleiche Weise kann Kosmetik, das betonen oder unterstreichen, was schon vorhanden ist, aber sie kann auch das Ungewollte verdecken oder maskieren und somit dem Benutzer ein Mittel an die Hand geben, eine vorteilhaftere Projektion von sich selbst zu präsentieren. Vielleicht haben wir müde Augen, die wir kaschieren oder auf gewisse Weise hinter einer „Maske" verstecken wollen. Deshalb zeigt diese Kombination von Material und der ganz spezielle Einsatz von Farbe den Betrachter*innen ein Objekt, das einerseits eine sehr persönliche Wahl und andererseits kollektive Seinszustände außerhalb unserer Kontrolle suggeriert. Oder anders gesagt: Mit der Modifizierung des Gebrauchs dieser Materialien bekommen wir Artefakte vorgeführt, die sich nur vordergründig innerhalb der Grenzen einer bekannten Ästhetik präsentieren. Aber nach eingehender Begutachtung und Überprüfung der Details können wir unsere Sichtweise verändern und Sailstorfers faszinierende Objekte und ihre komplexen persönlichen, sozialen, historischen und konzeptuellen Wurzeln verstehen.

Heavy Eyes 7 GOLDEN OLIVE, 2020

Lead, eyeshadow / Blei, Lidschatten, 50 × 40 cm

Heavy Eyes 53 COPPER SPARKLE, 2021

Lead, eyeshadow / Blei, Lidschatten, 115 × 90 cm

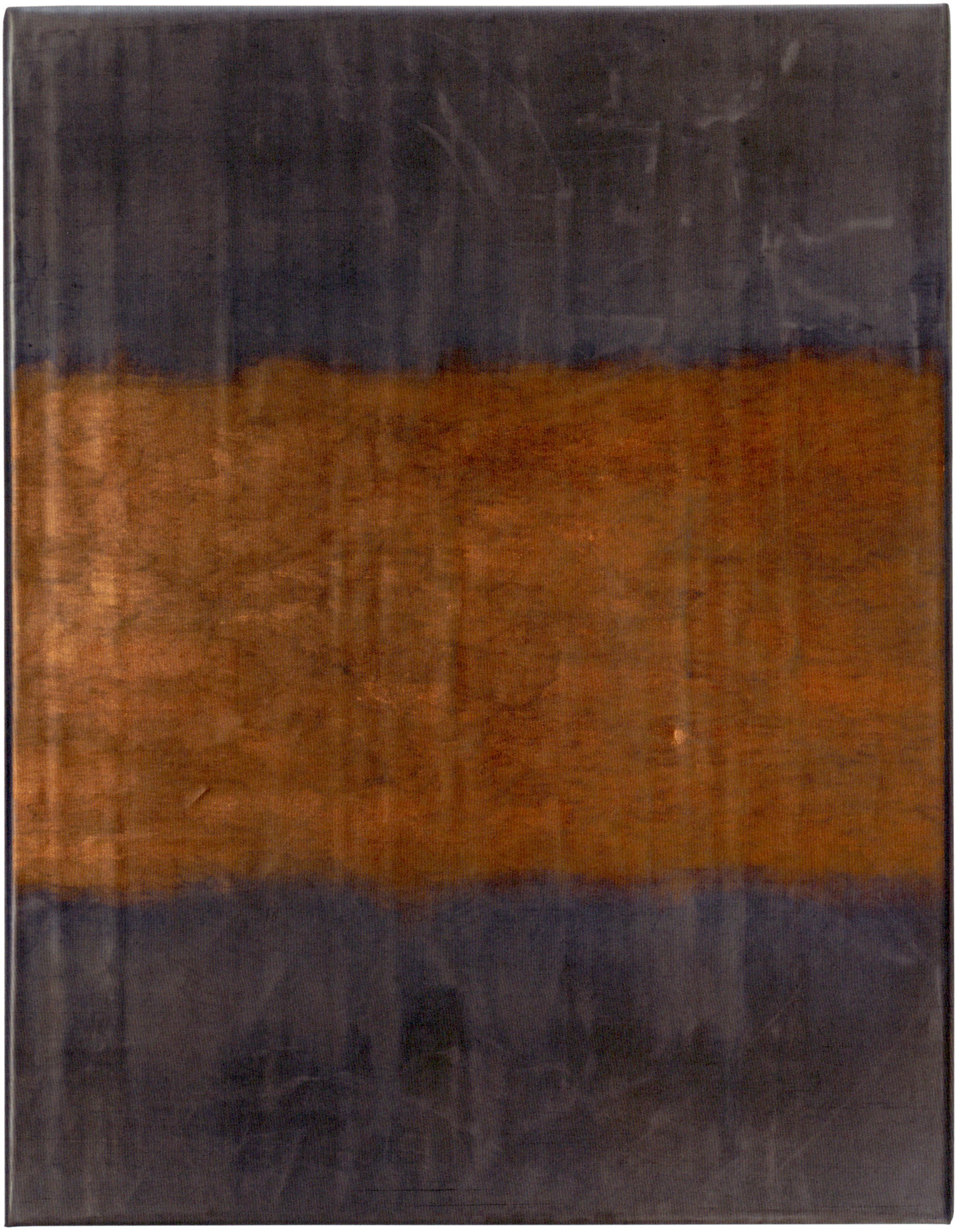

Heavy Eyes 21 COPPER SPARKLE, 2020

Lead, eyeshadow / Blei, Lidschatten, 90 × 70 cm

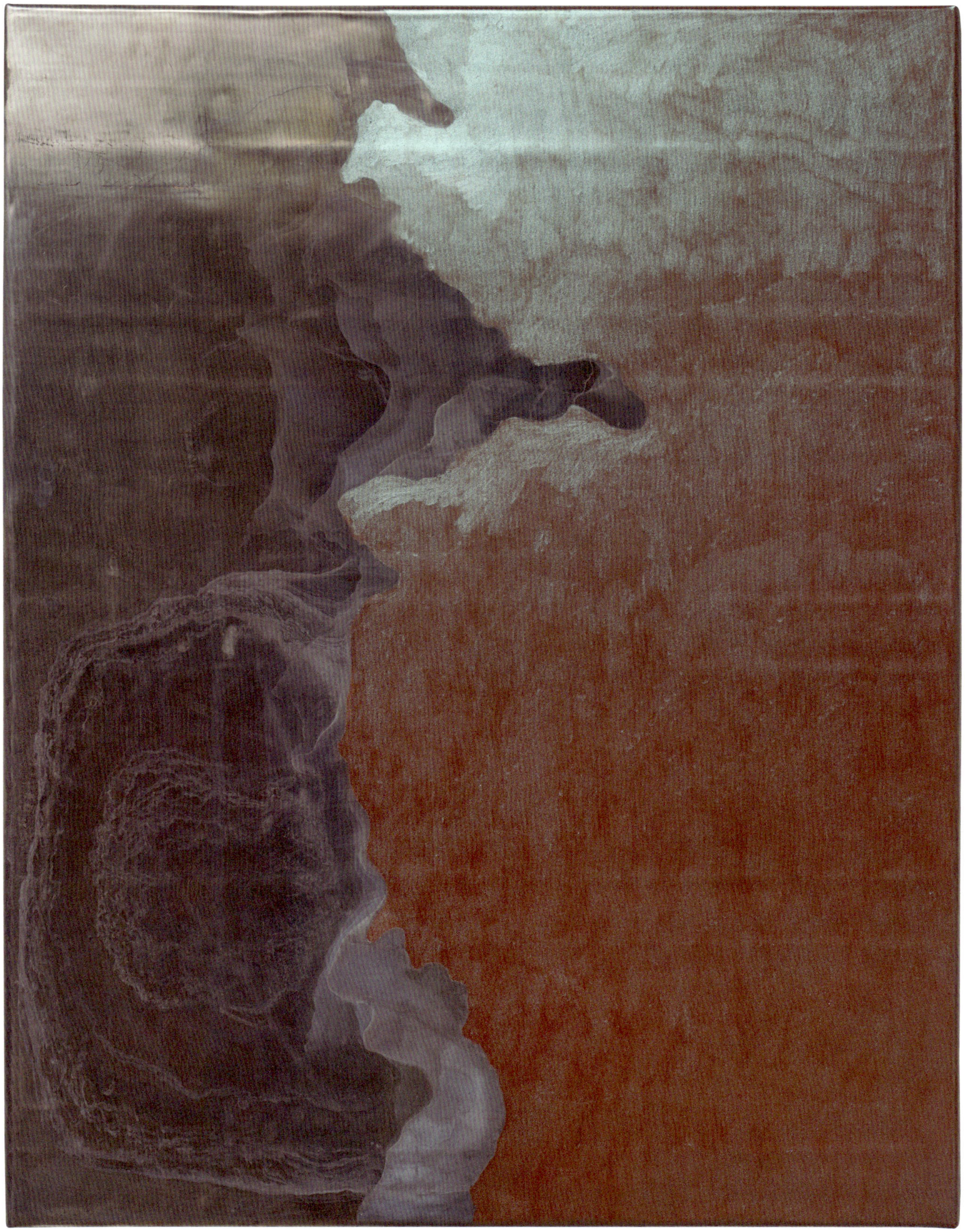

Heavy Eyes 41 BLUE BROWN, 2021

Lead, eyeshadow / Blei, Lidschatten, 115 × 90 cm

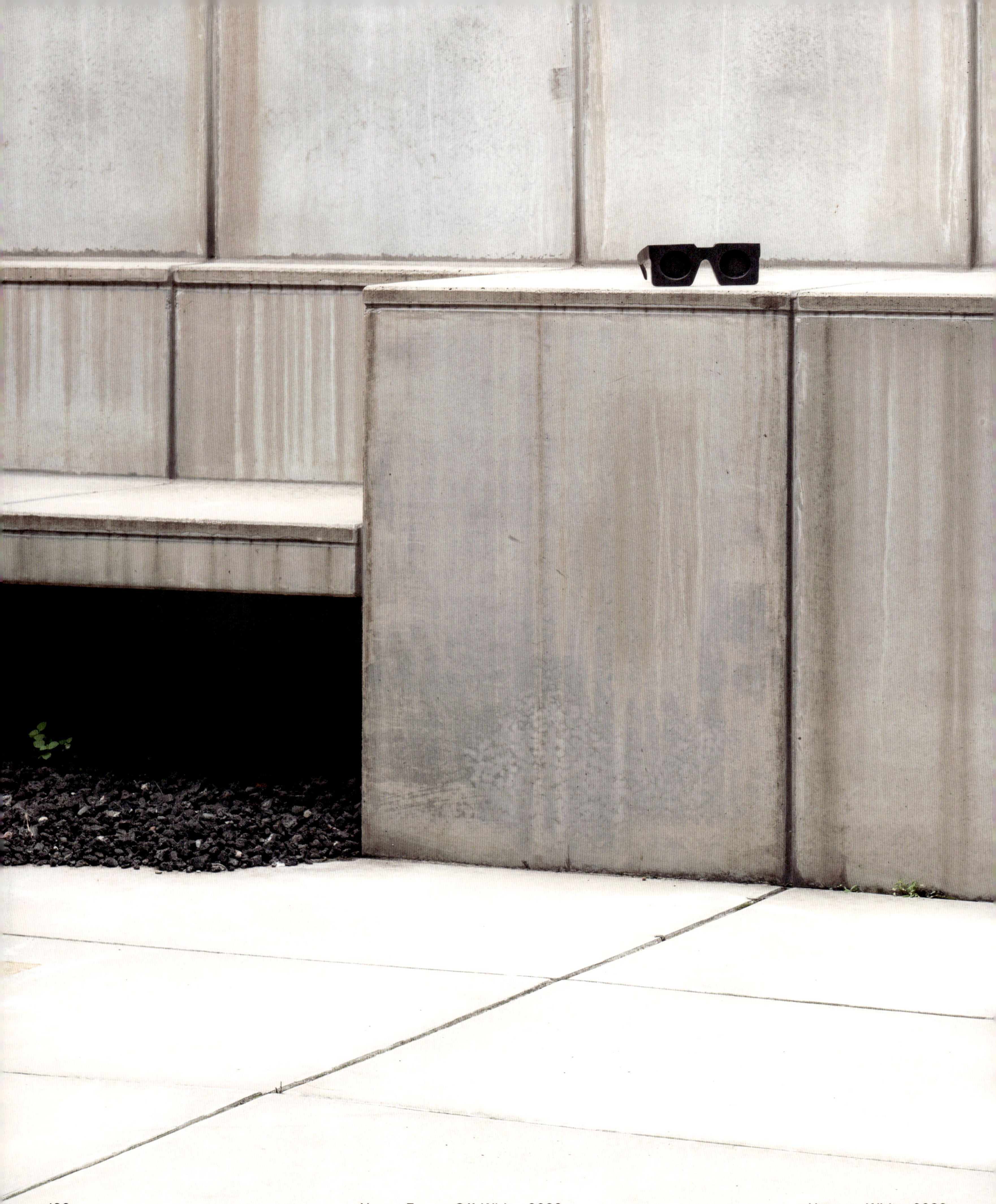

Heavy Eyes – Off-White, 2022

Bronze, 5,5 × 14,5 × 15 cm, Installation view / Installationsansicht
Heavy Eyes, König Galerie, Seoul

Heavy – White, 2022

Bronze, 18 × 30 × 32 cm

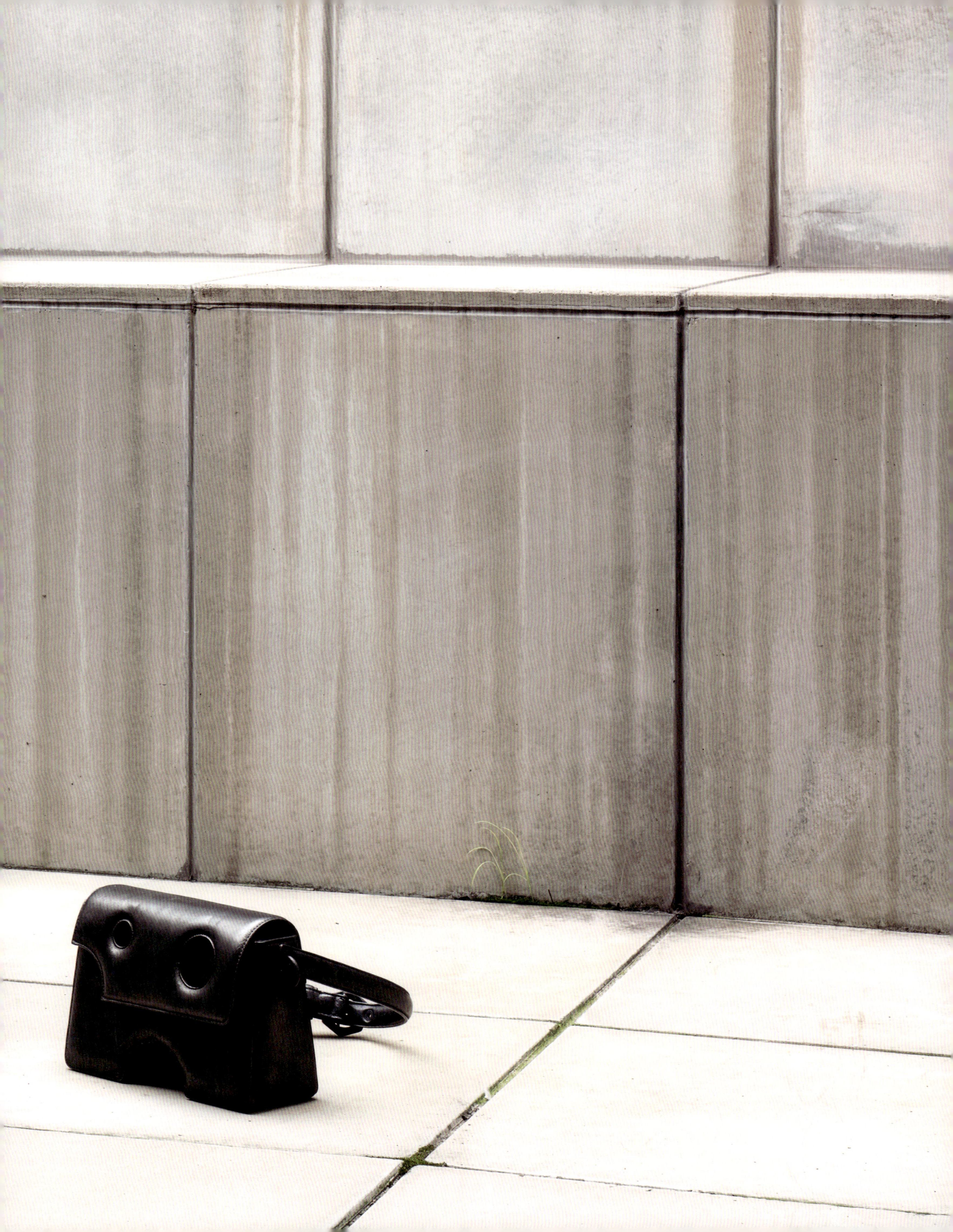

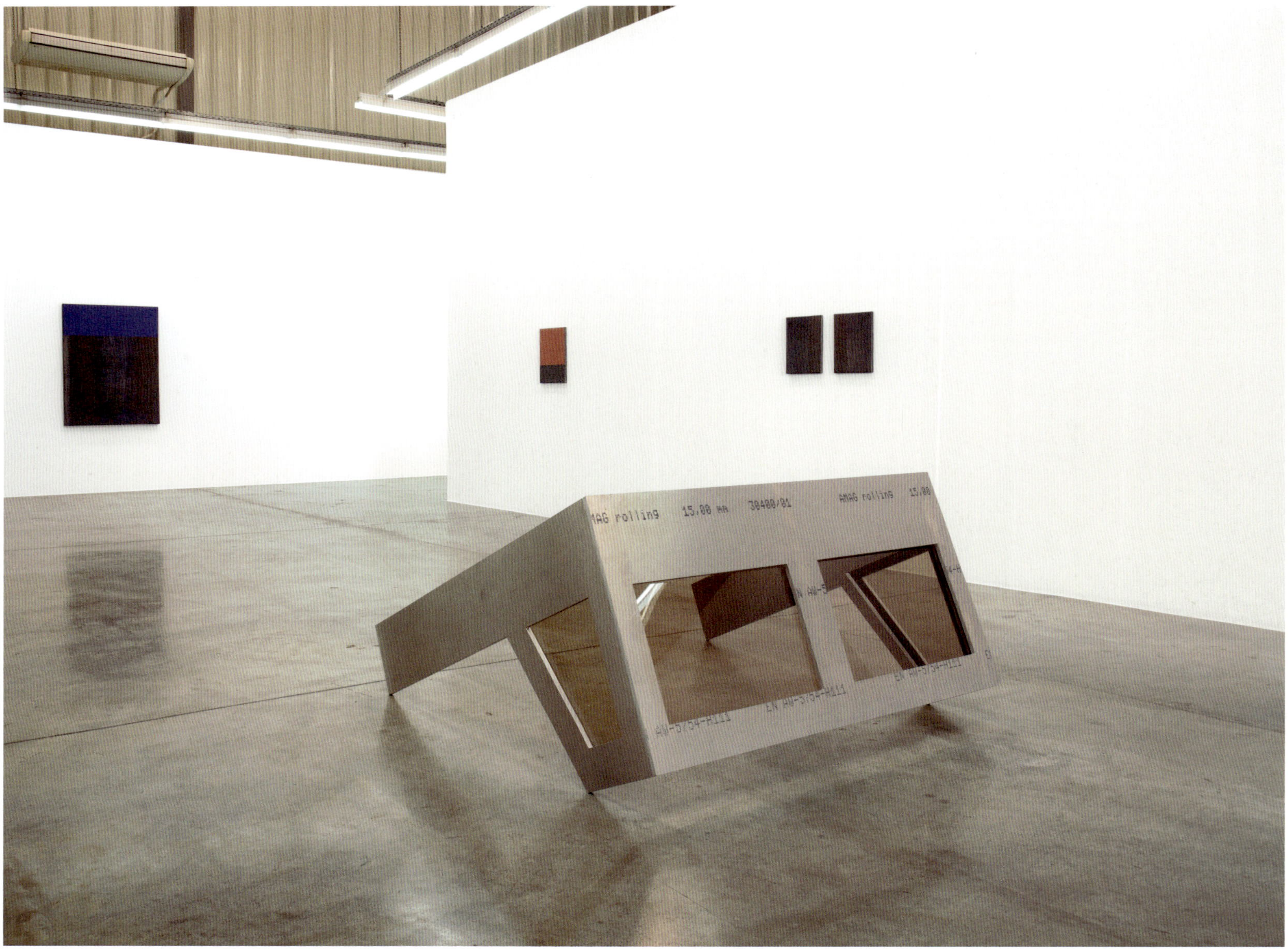

Sunglasses 2, 2022

Acrylic glass, aluminum / Acrylglas, Aluminium, 80 × 160 × 150 cm,
Installation view / Installationsansicht *Heavy Eyes*, Carbon 12, Dubai

Sunglasses 1, 2022

Acrylic glass, steel / Acrylglas, Stahl, 180 × 52,5 × 160 cm,
Installation view / Installationsansicht *Heavy Eyes*, Carbon 12, Dubai

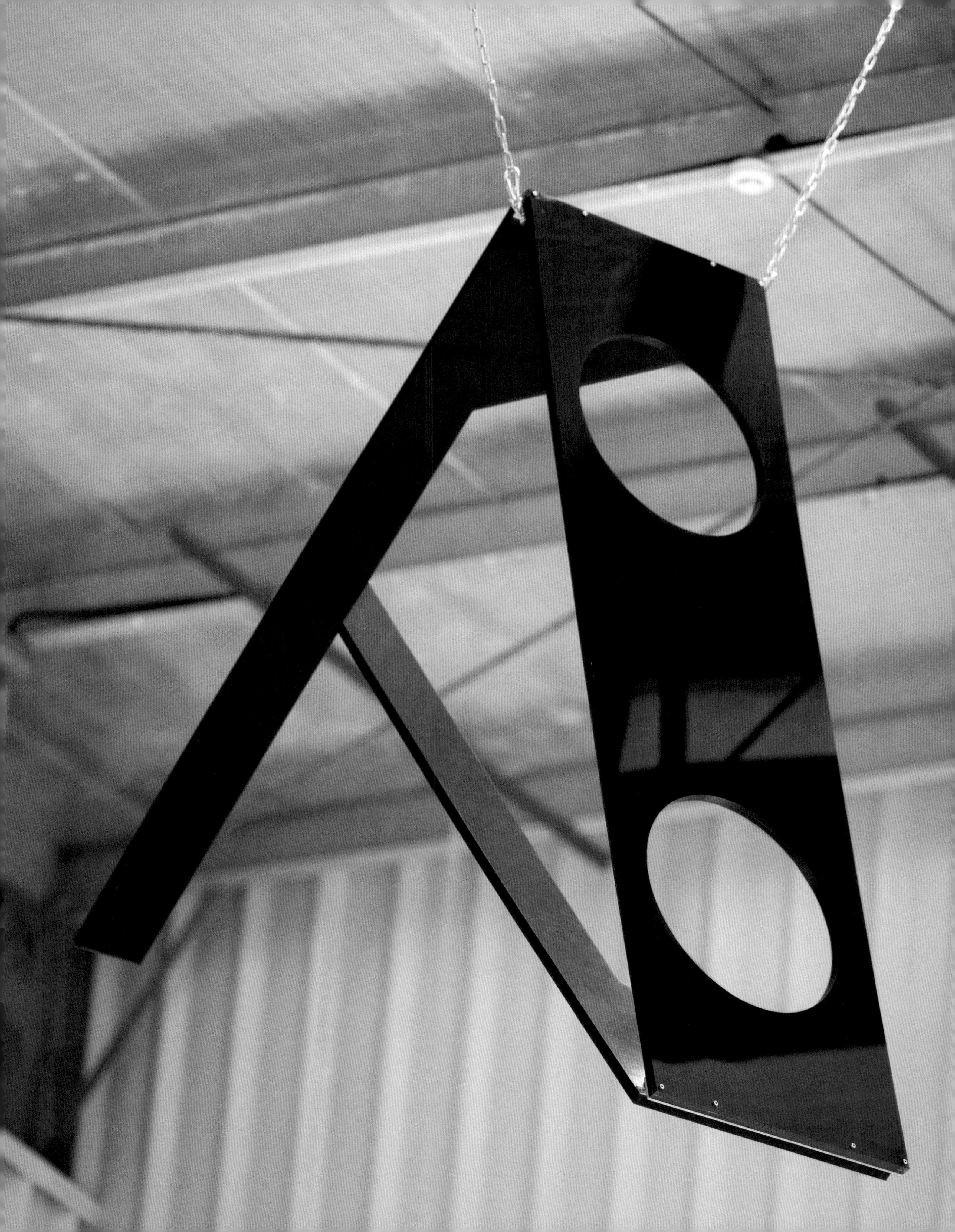

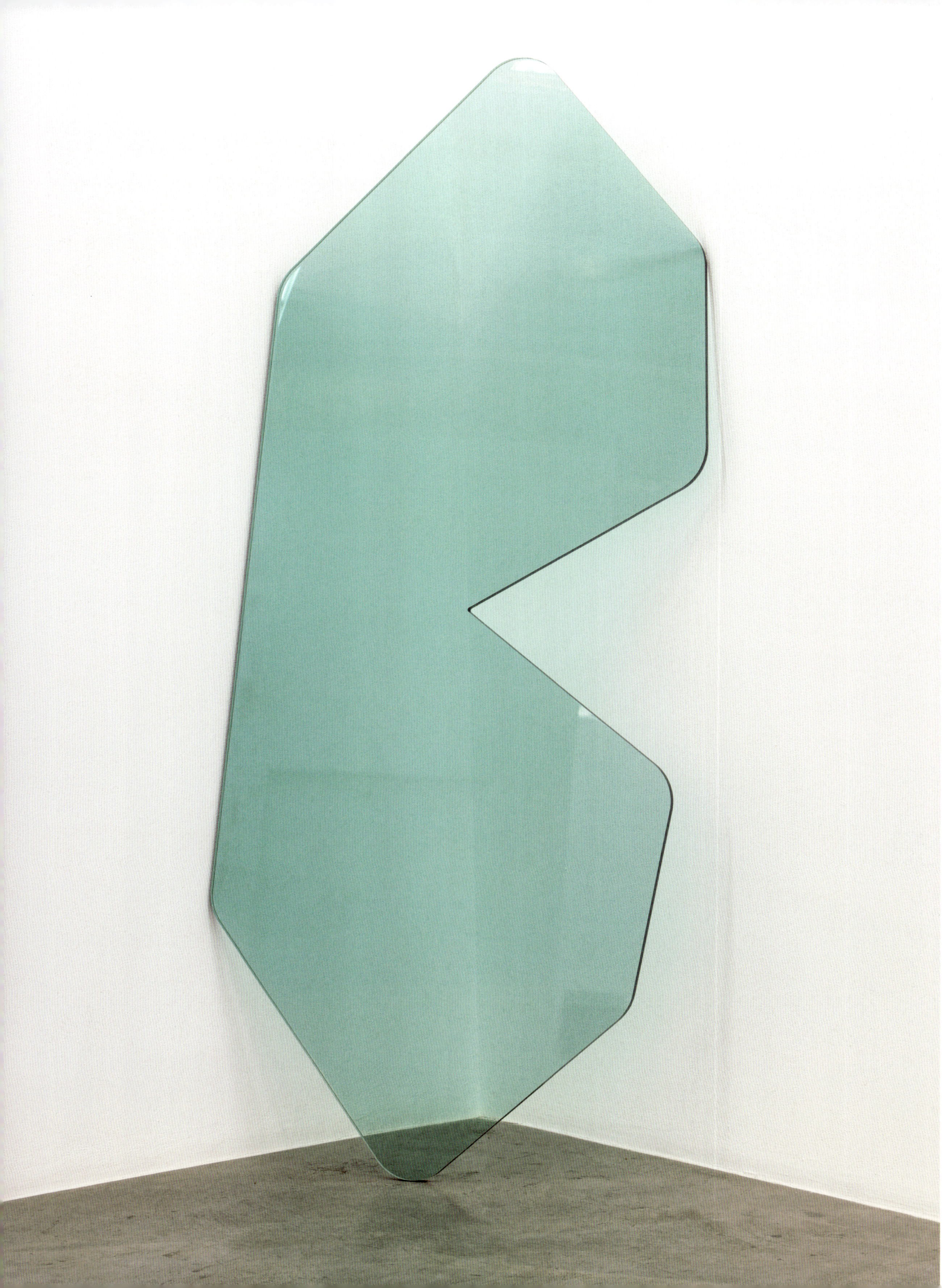

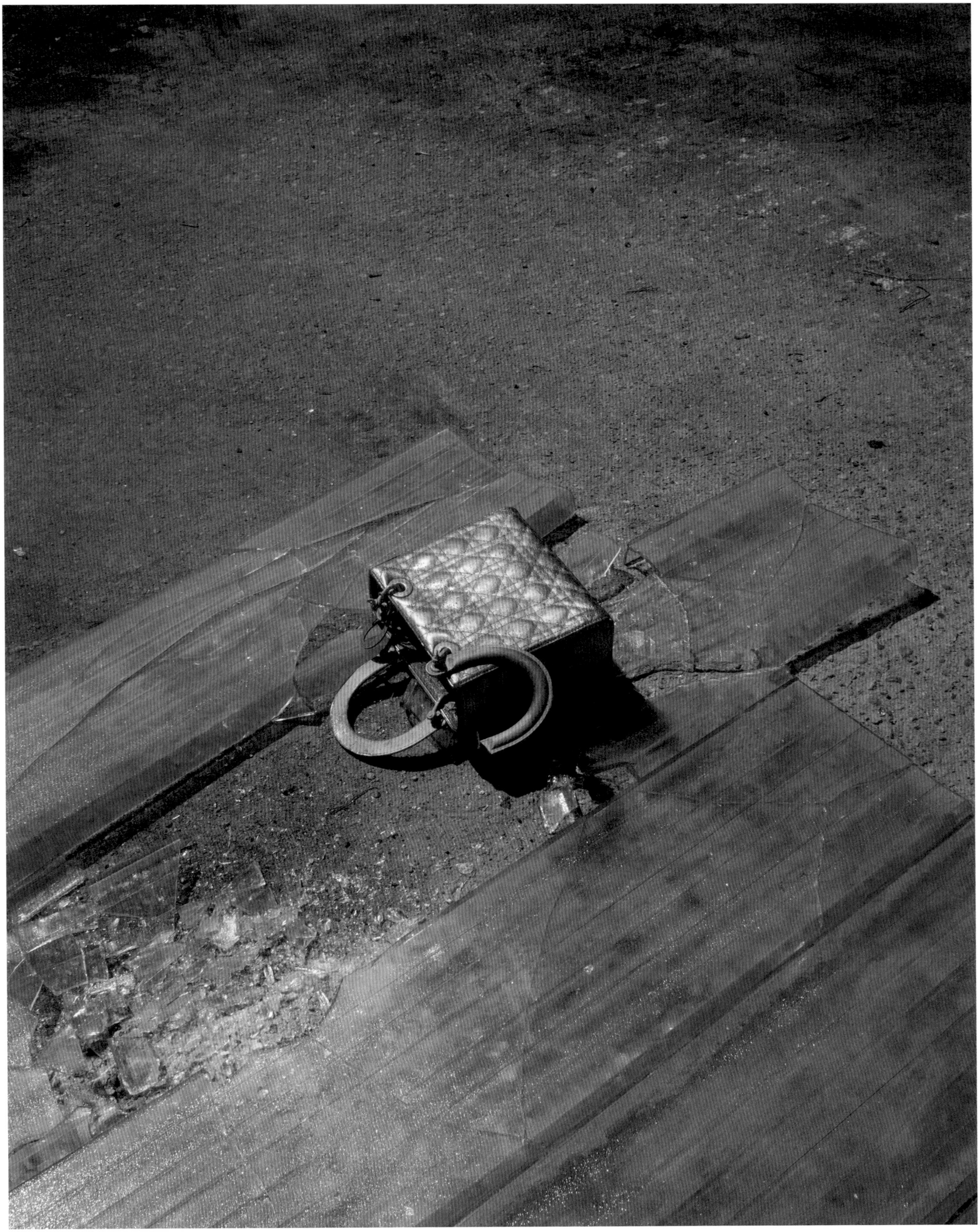

Sunglasses 3, 2022
Acrylic glass / Acrylglas, 230 × 97,5 × 2 cm

Heavy Dior, 2021
Iron / Eisen, 32 × 32 × 12 cm

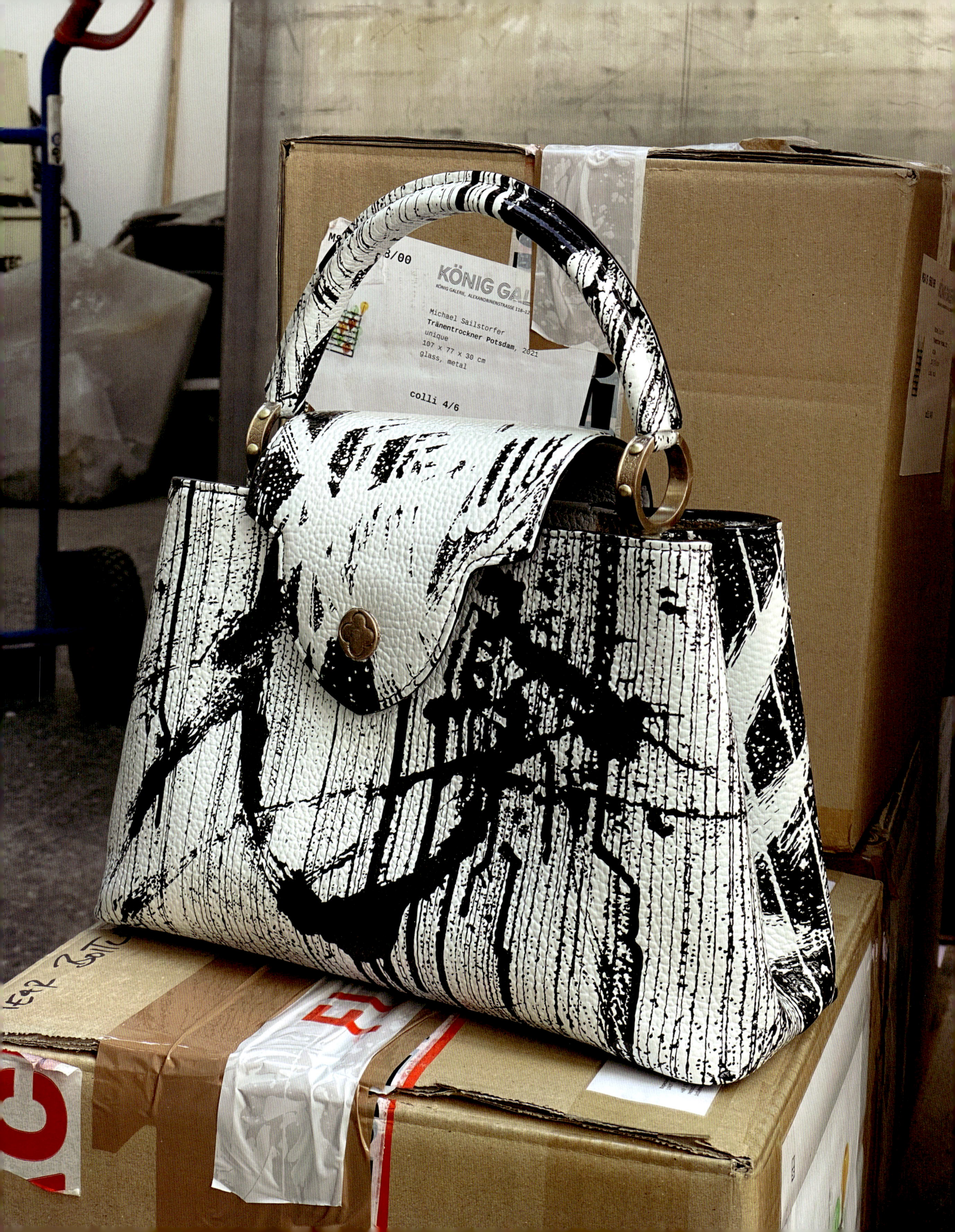
Michael Sailstorfer
Tränentrockner Potsdam, 2021
unique
107 x 77 x 30 cm
glass, metal
colli 4/6

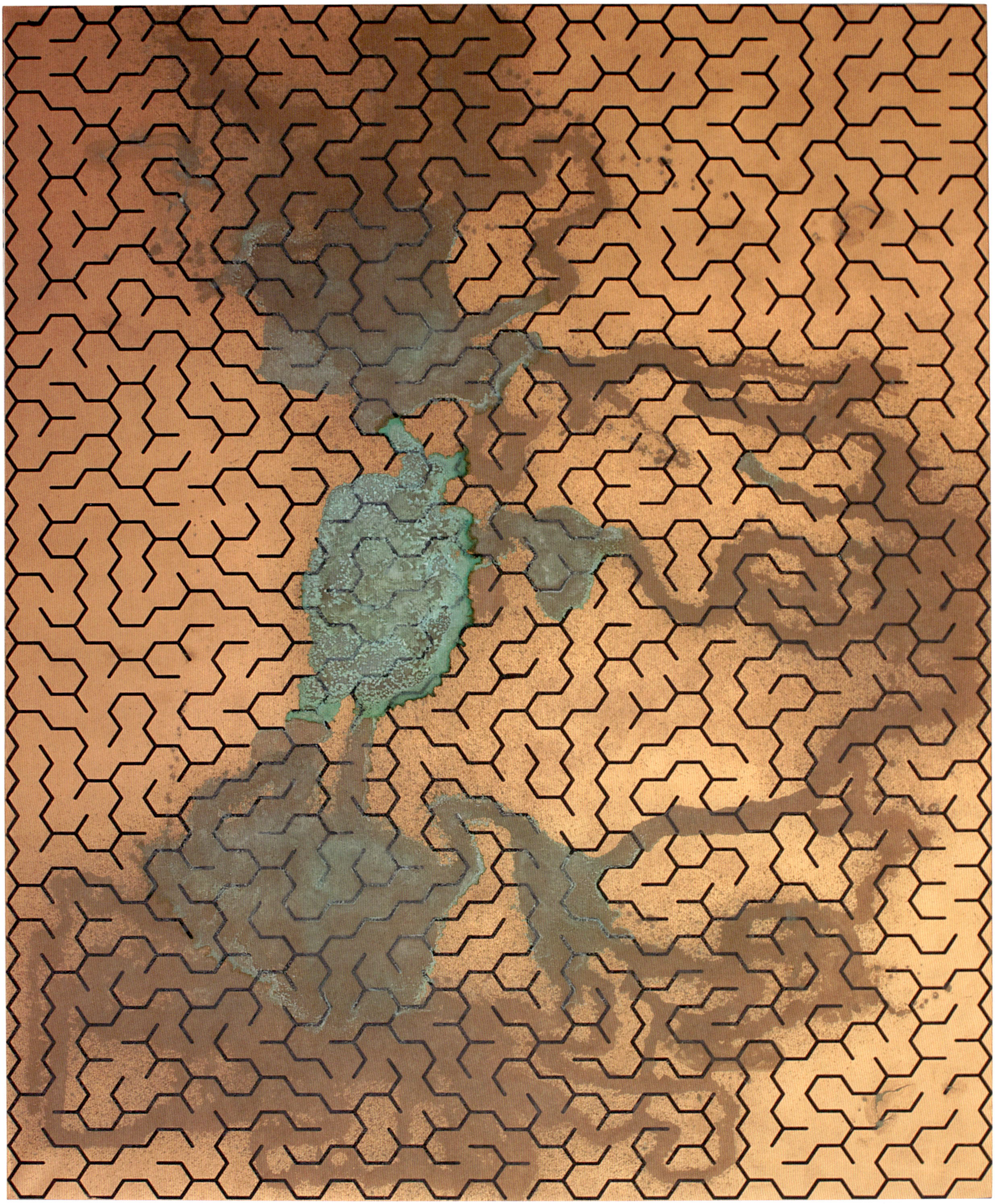

Maze 77, 2013

Screen print and acid on copper primed canvas / Siebdruck und Säure auf mit Kupfer grundierter Leinwand, 230 × 190 cm

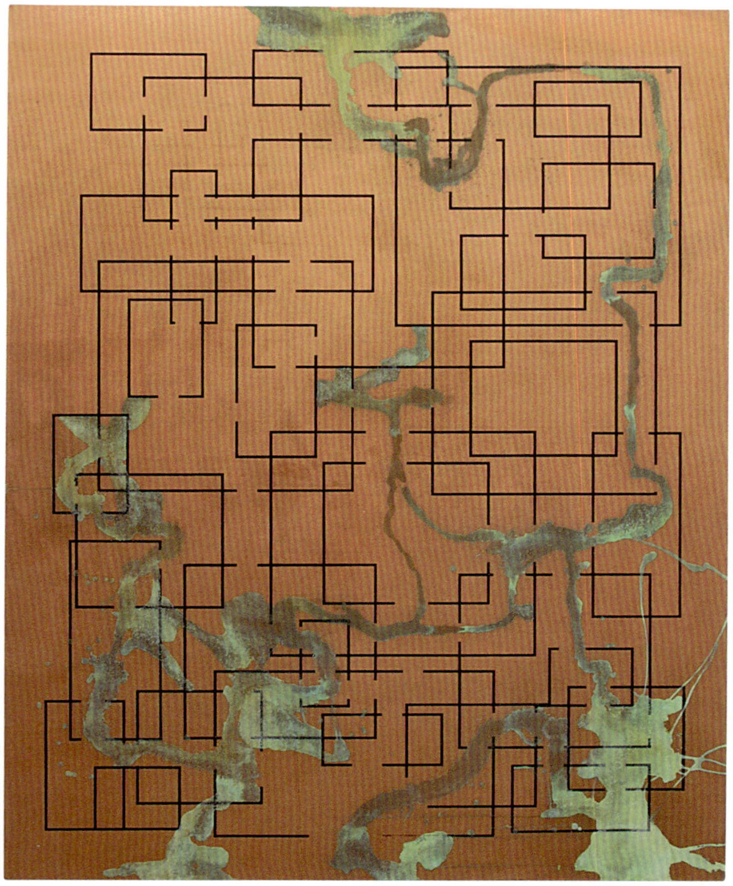

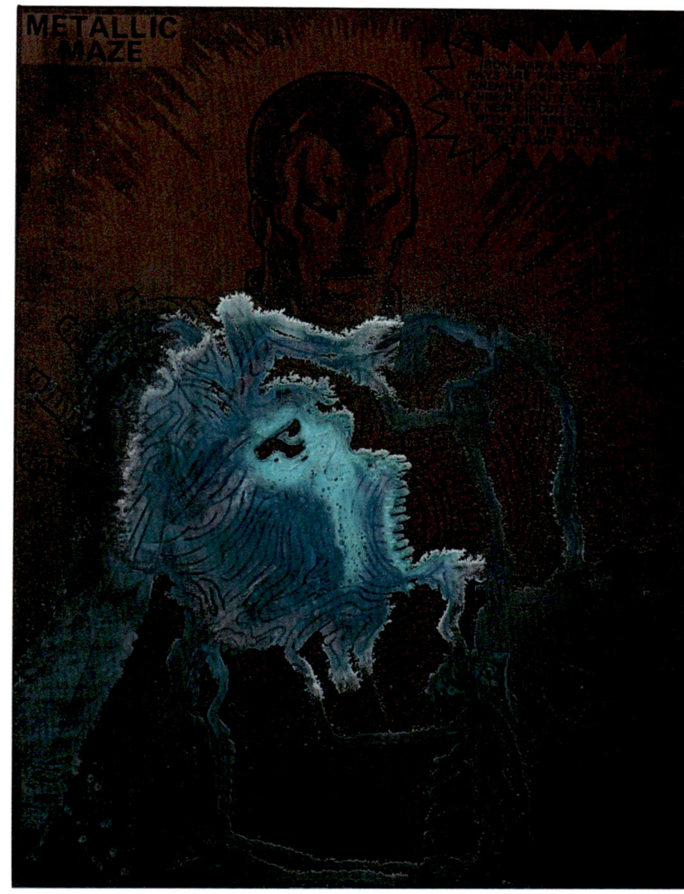
METALLIC
MAZE

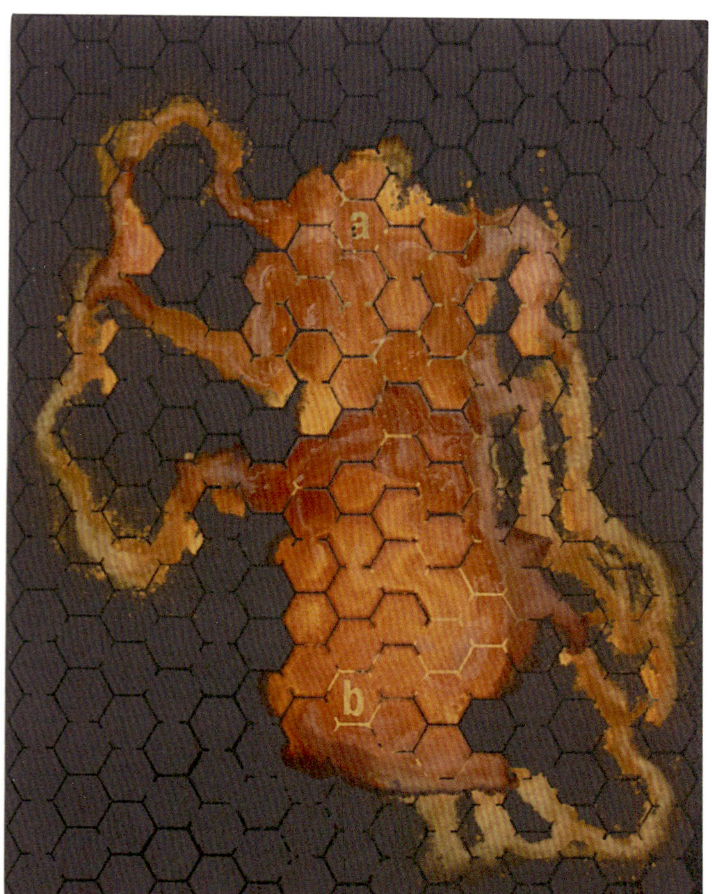
a
b

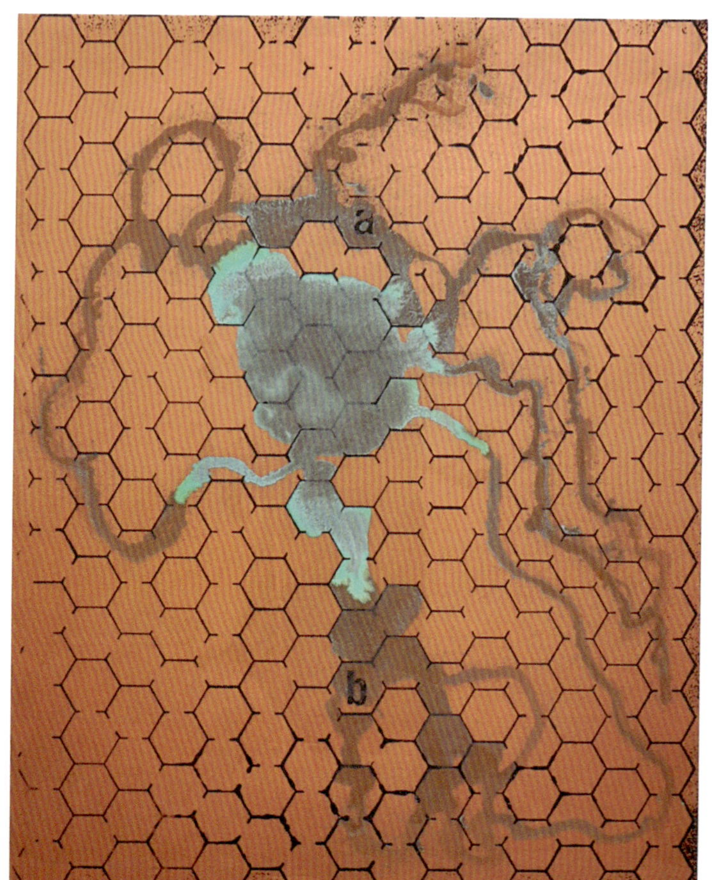
a
b

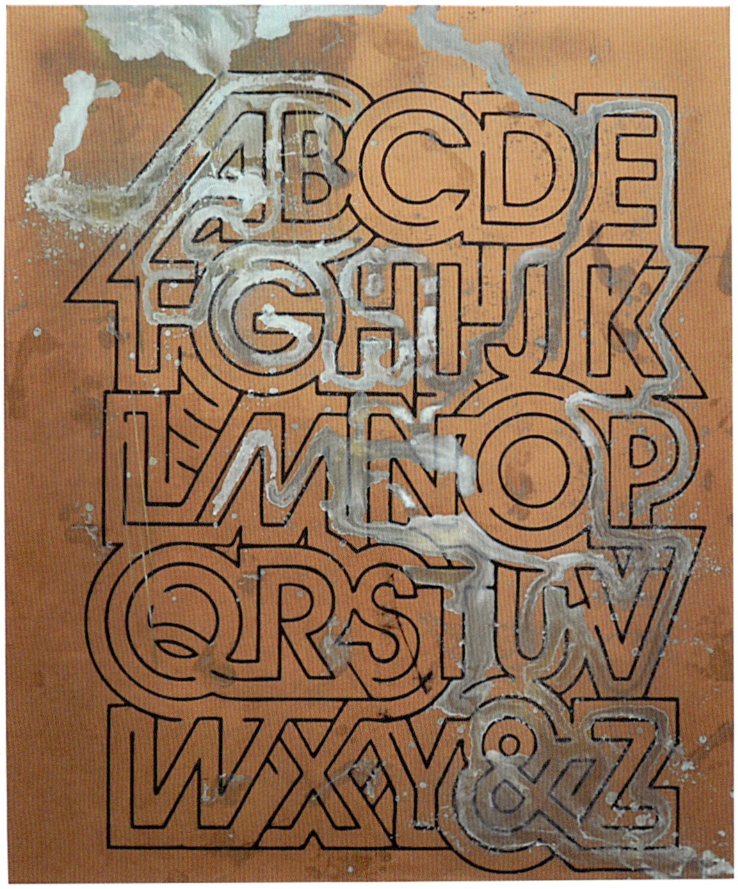
ABCDE
FGHIJK
LMNOP
QRSTUV
WXY&Z

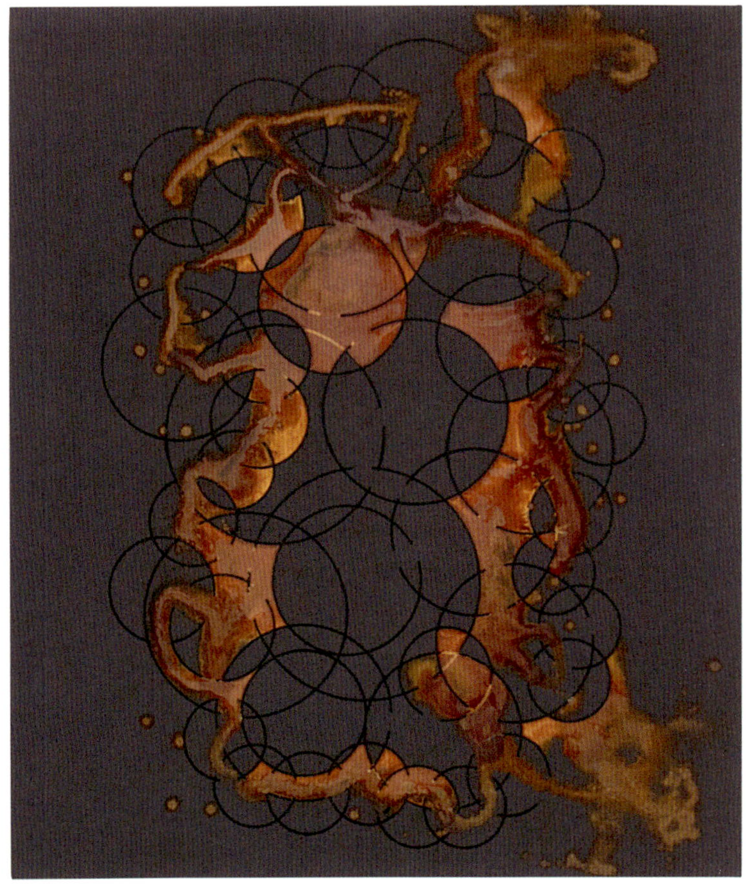

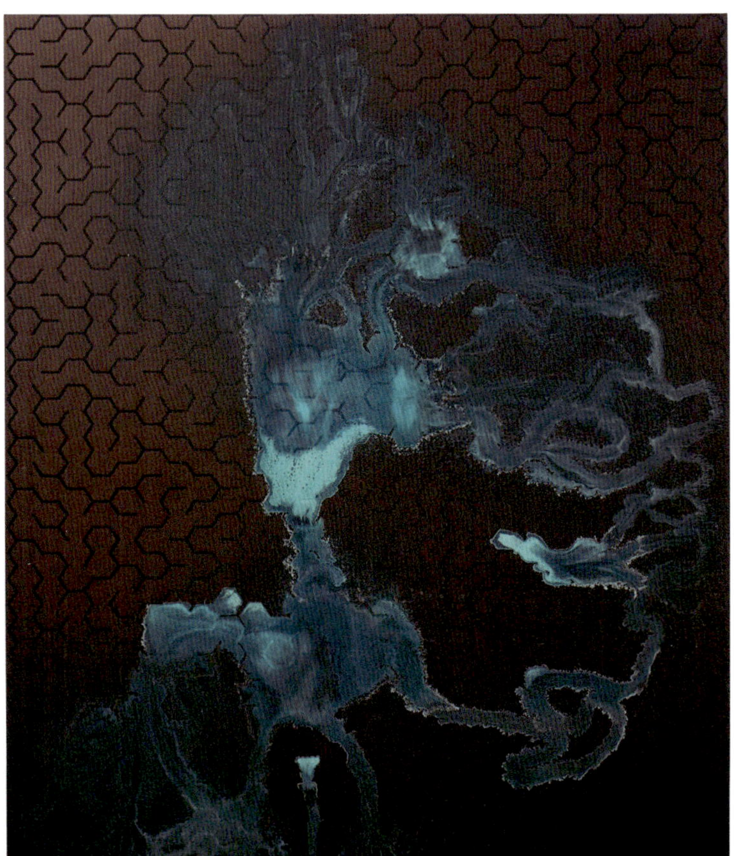

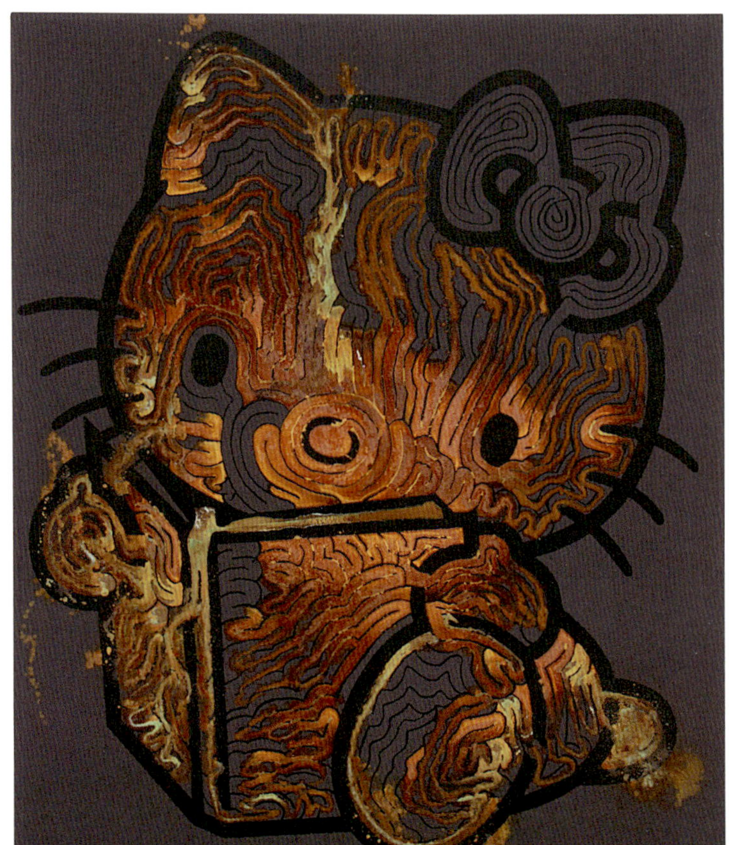

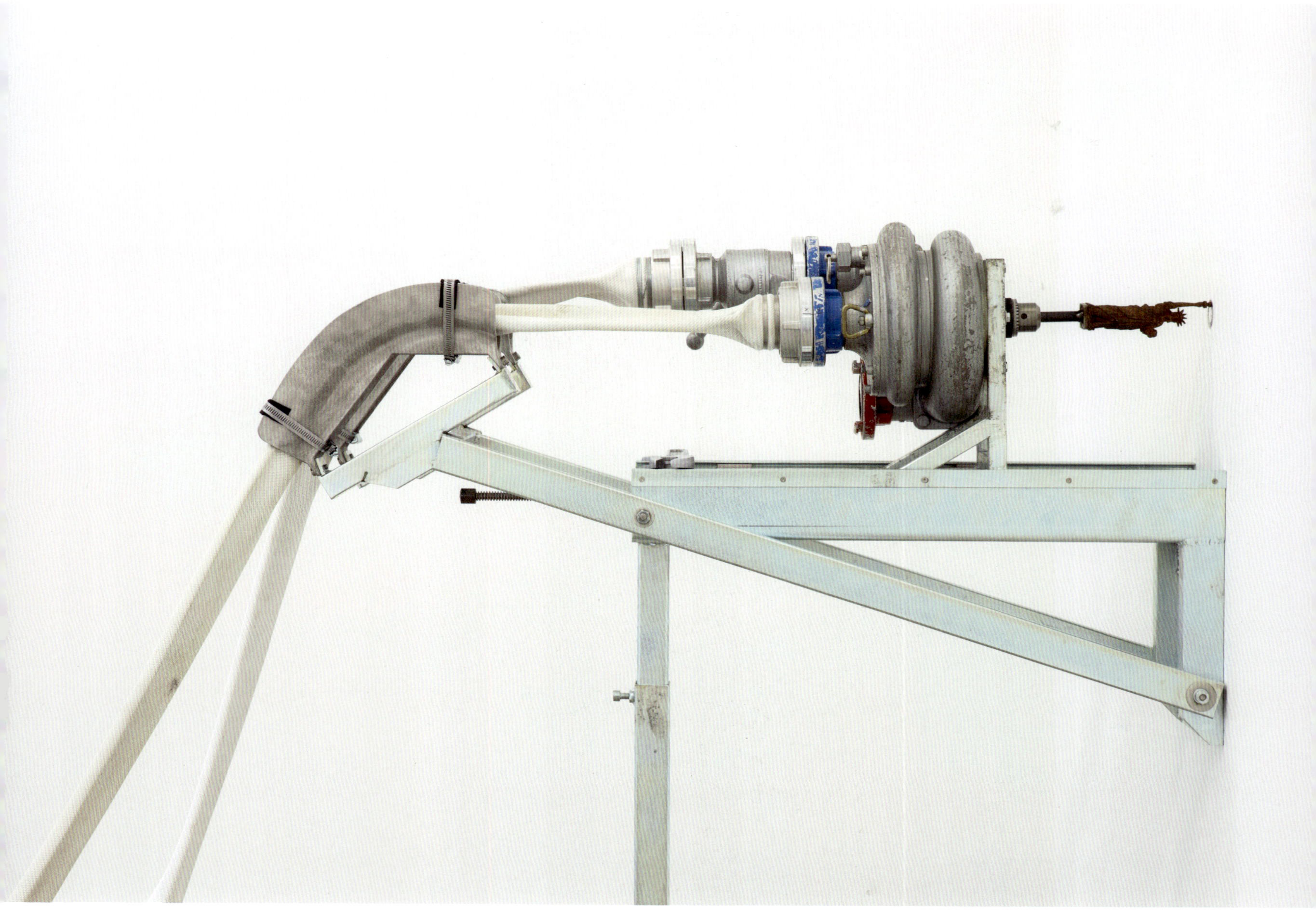

Freedom Fries am Arbeitsplatz, 2013

Barrel, pump, steel, firehoses, water turbine / Fass, Pumpe, Stahl, Feuerwehrschläuche, Wasserturbine, Dimensions variable / Maße variabel

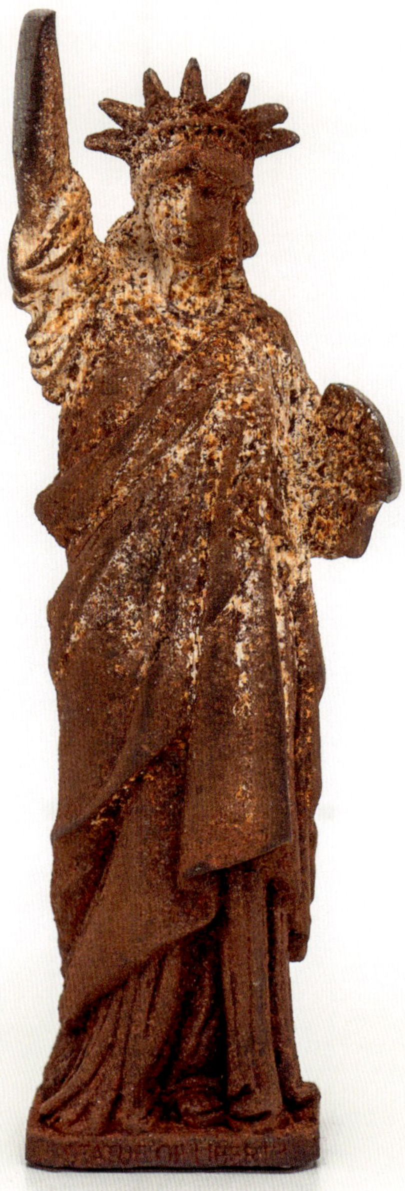

Verlust durch Reibung, 2015

Iron / Eisen, 14,5 × 5 × 4 cm

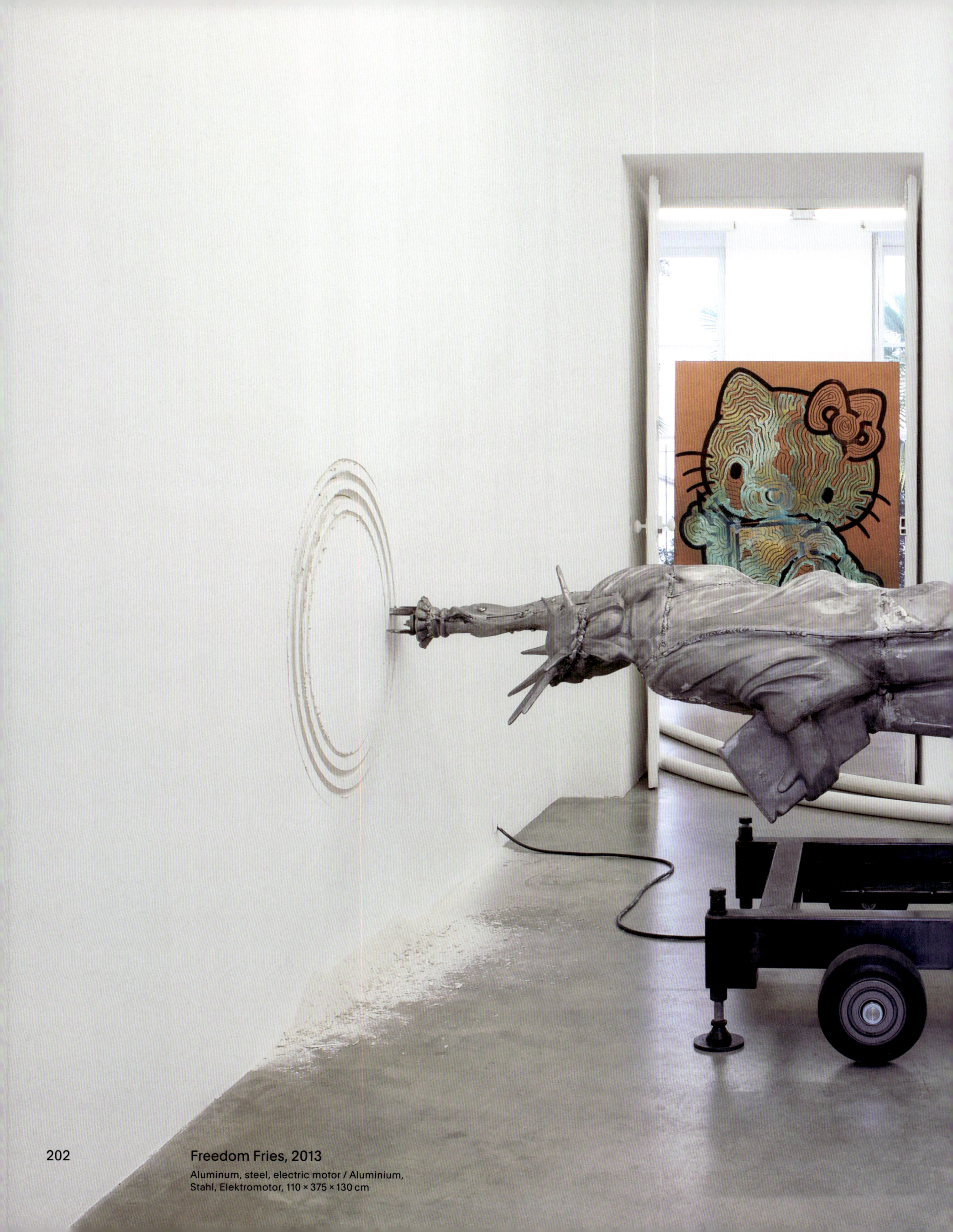

202

Freedom Fries, 2013

Aluminum, steel, electric motor / Aluminium, Stahl, Elektromotor, 110 × 375 × 130 cm

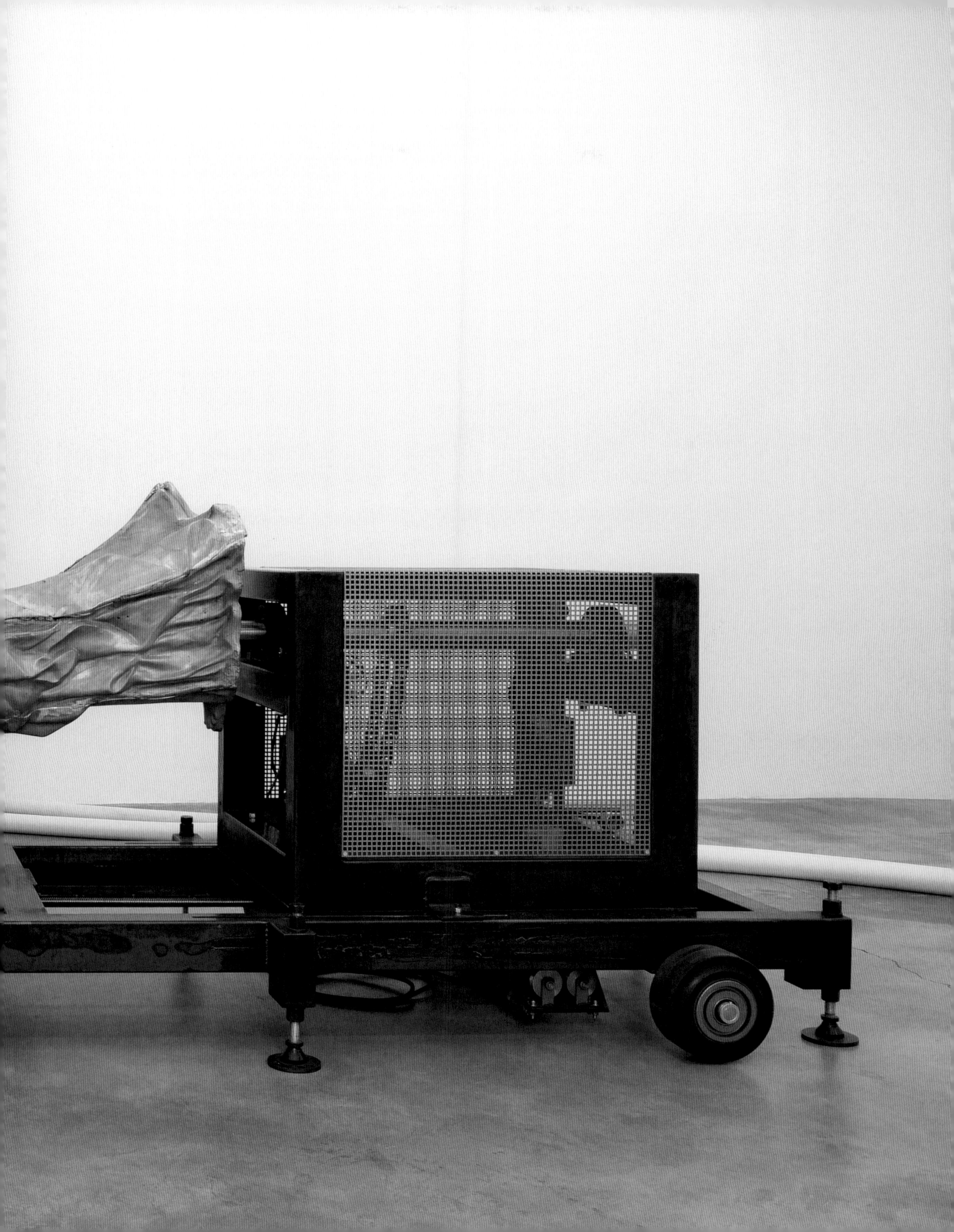

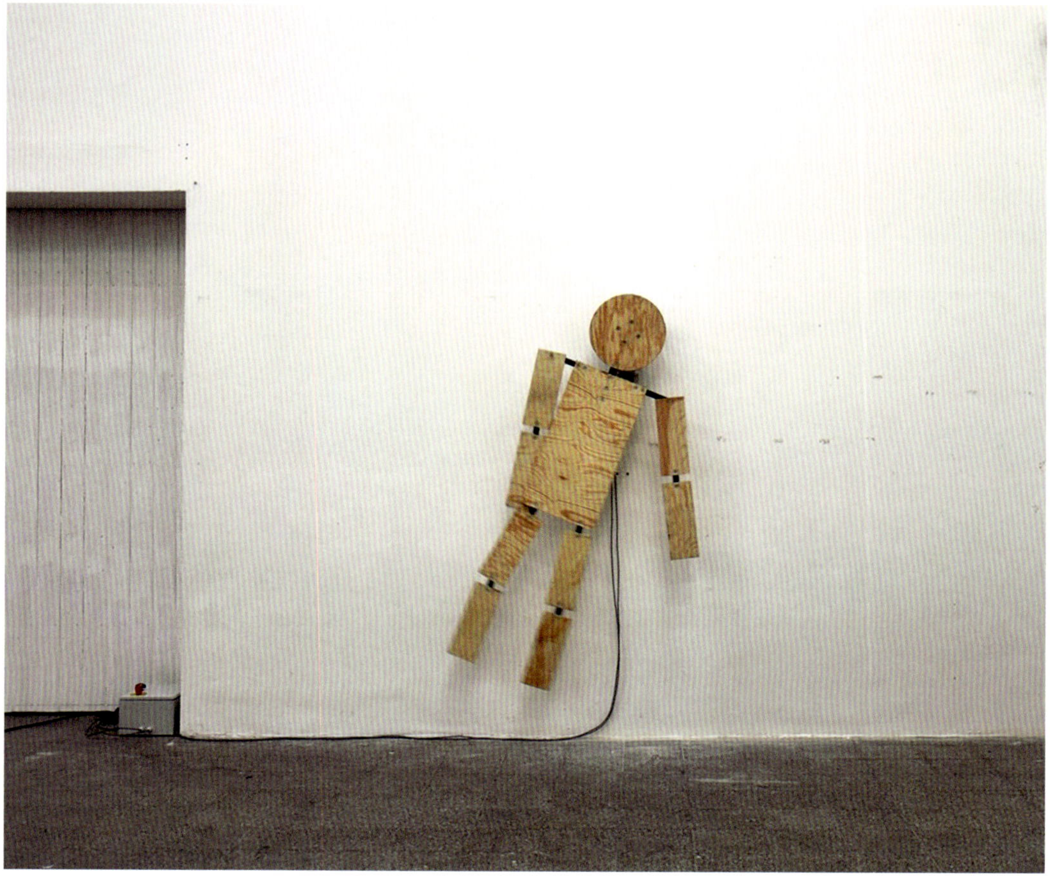

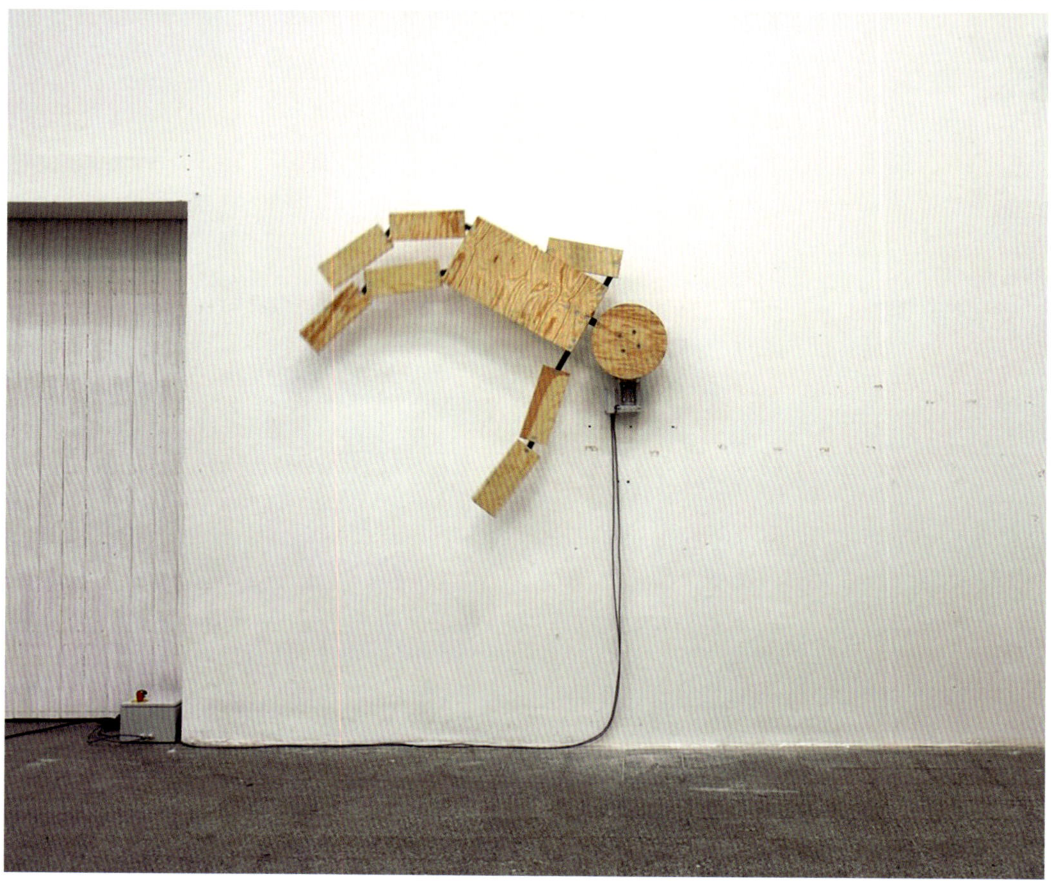

Ragdoll Boss, 2009

Wood, steel, electric motor, controller / Holz, Stahl, Elektromotor, Steuerung, 210 × 85 × 20 cm

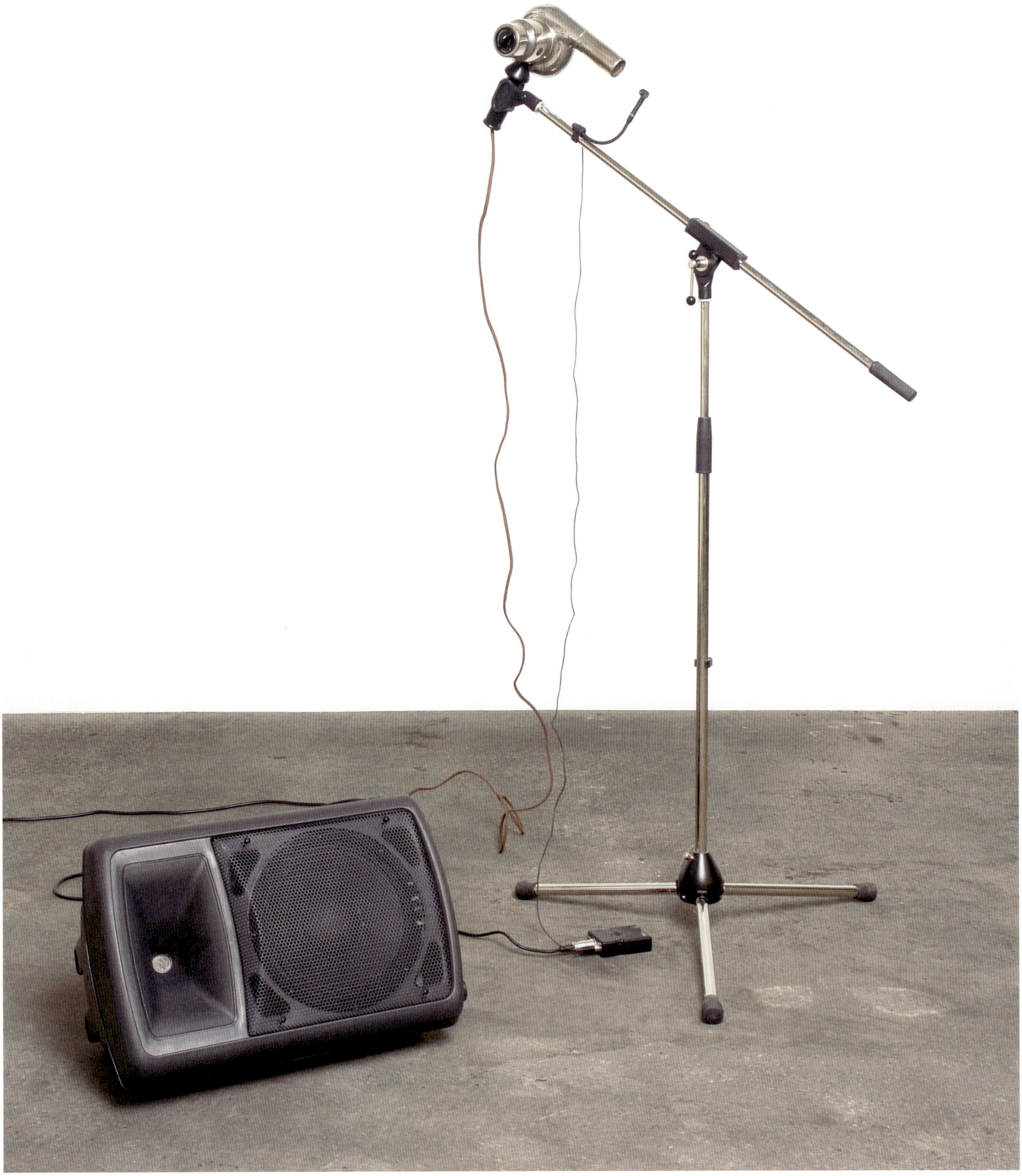

Anna, 2004

Hairdryer, microphone, microphone stand, loudspeaker / Föhn, Mikrofon, Mikrofonständer, Lautsprecher, 165 × 120 × 150 cm

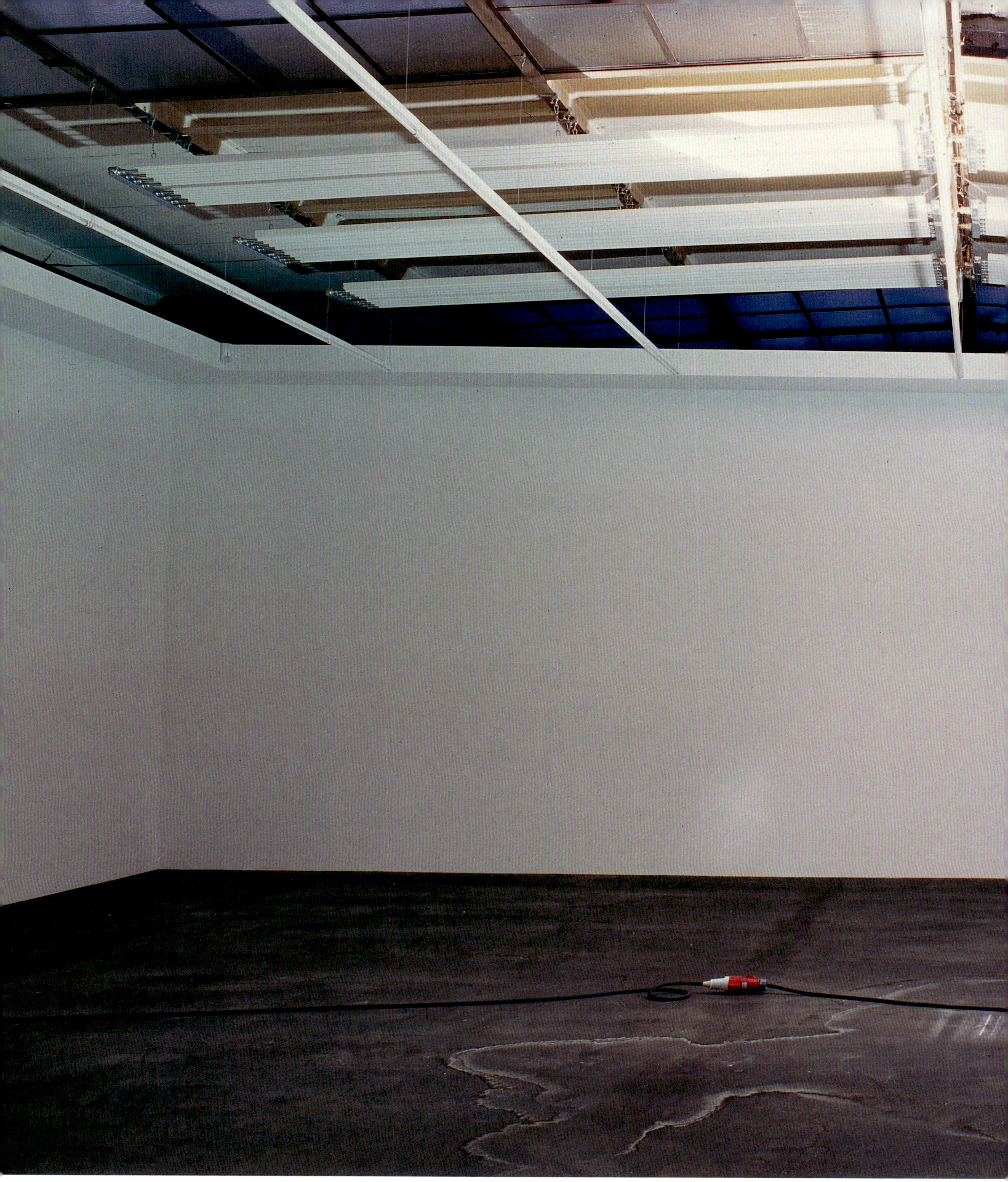

Unendliche Säule, 2006

Searchlight / Scheinwerfer, 500.000 × 100 × 85 cm,
Installation view / Installationsansicht, Galerie Johann König, Berlin

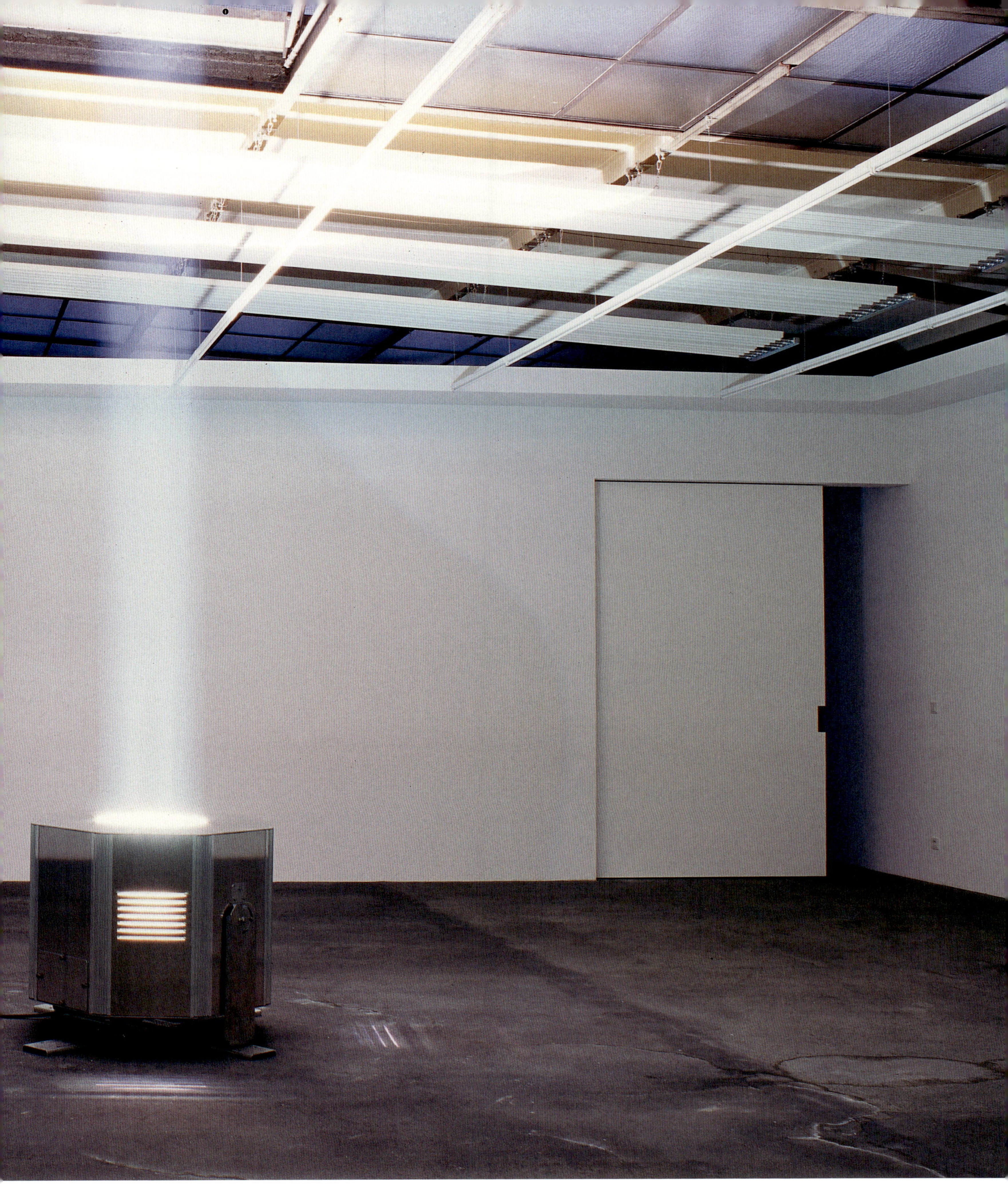

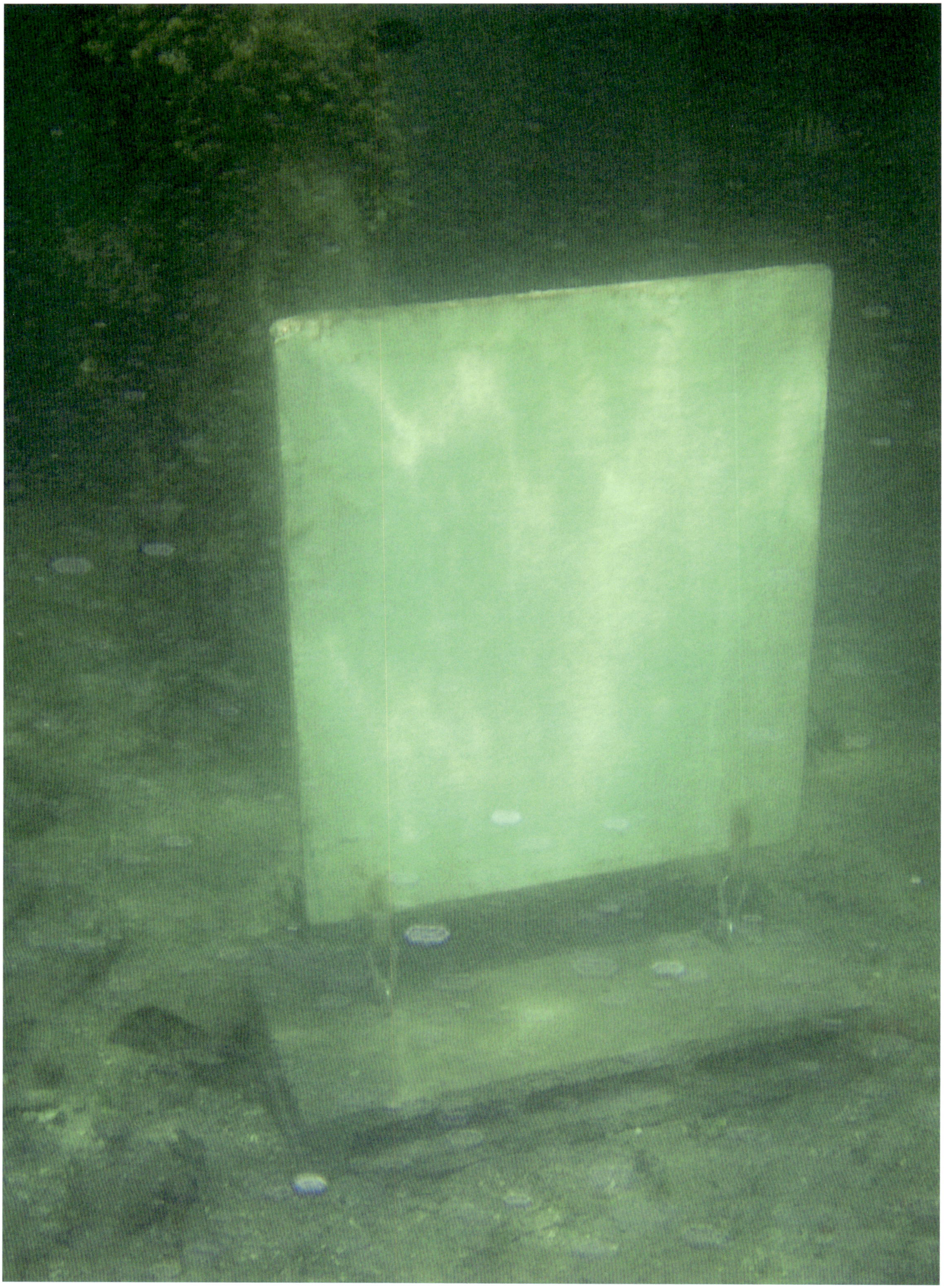

U4, 14° 34' 79,0" N / 60° 50' 69,6" W, 2007
C-print, 75 × 50 cm (framed / gerahmt)

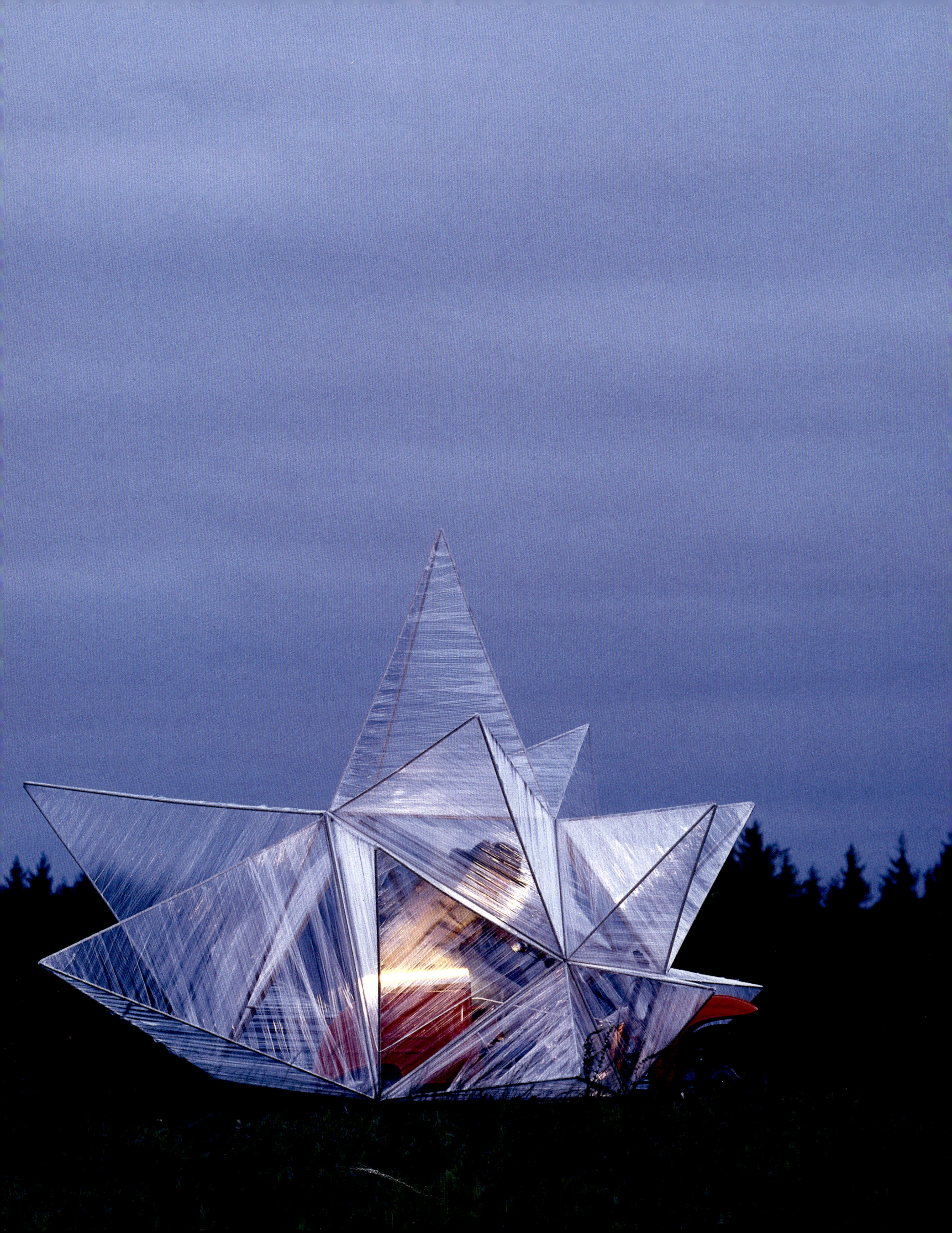

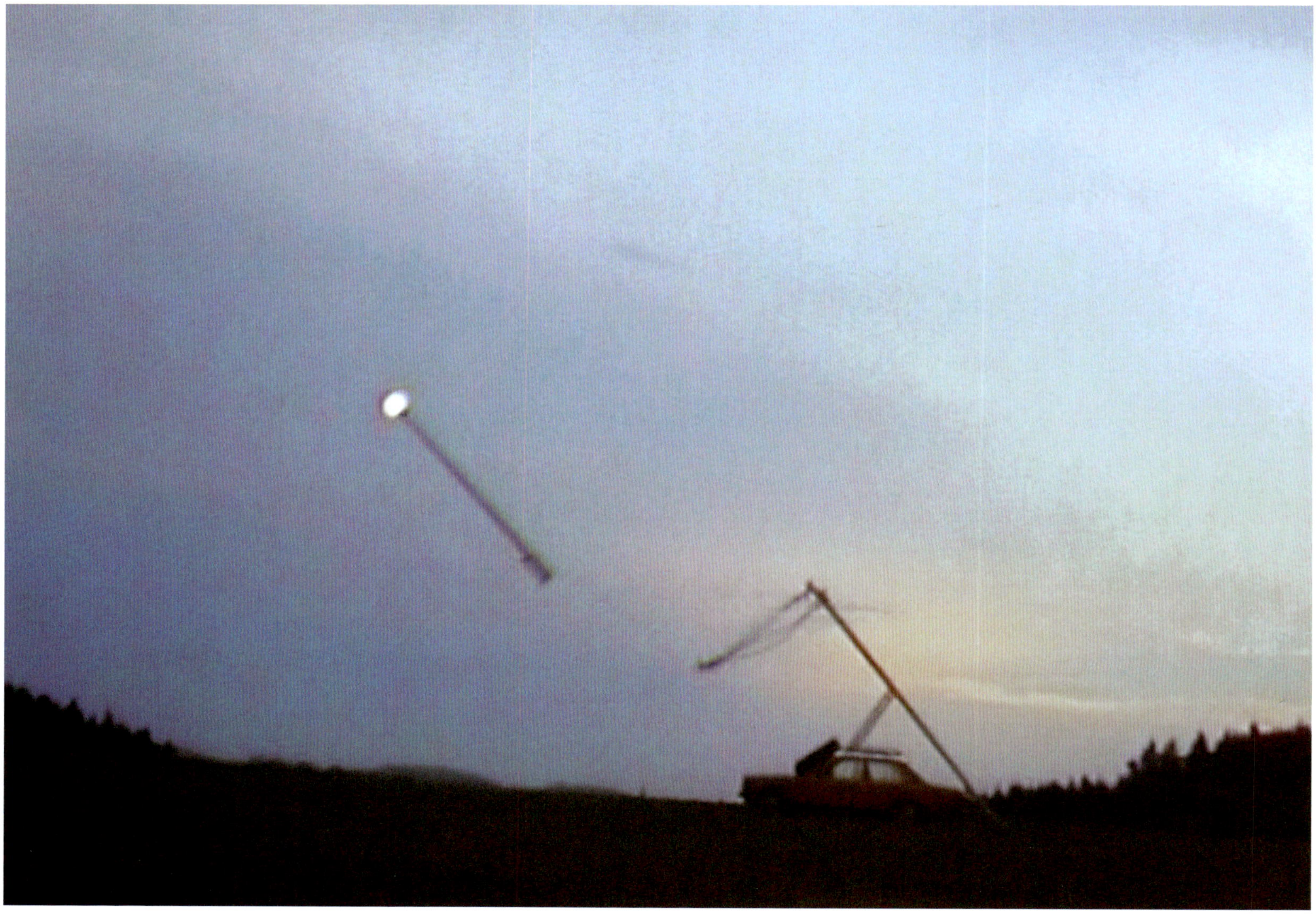

Sternschnuppe, 2002

Mercedes-Benz, street lamp, rubber ropes, steel, winch / Mercedes-Benz, Straßenlaterne, Gummibänder, Stahl, Winde, 500 × 200 × 510 cm

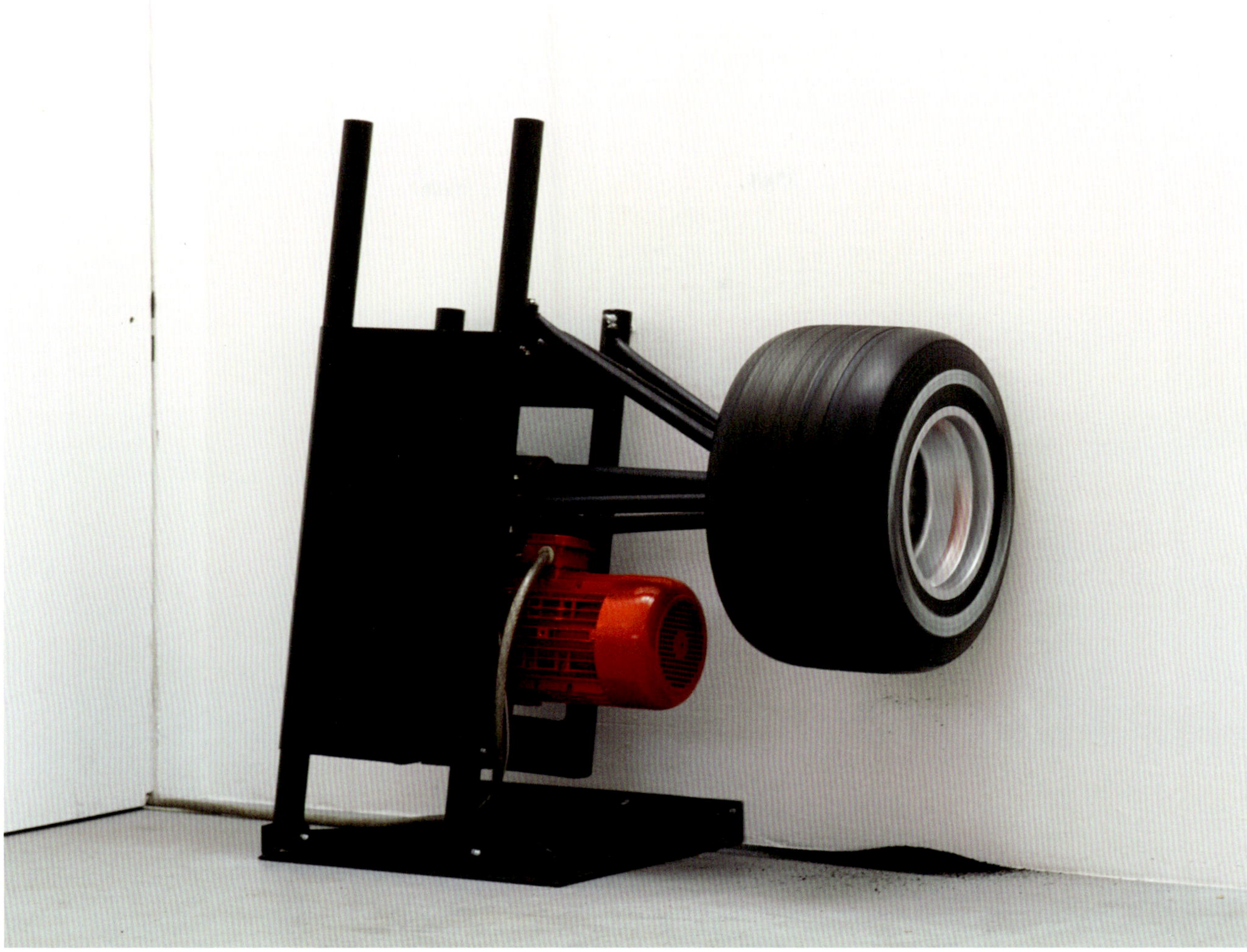

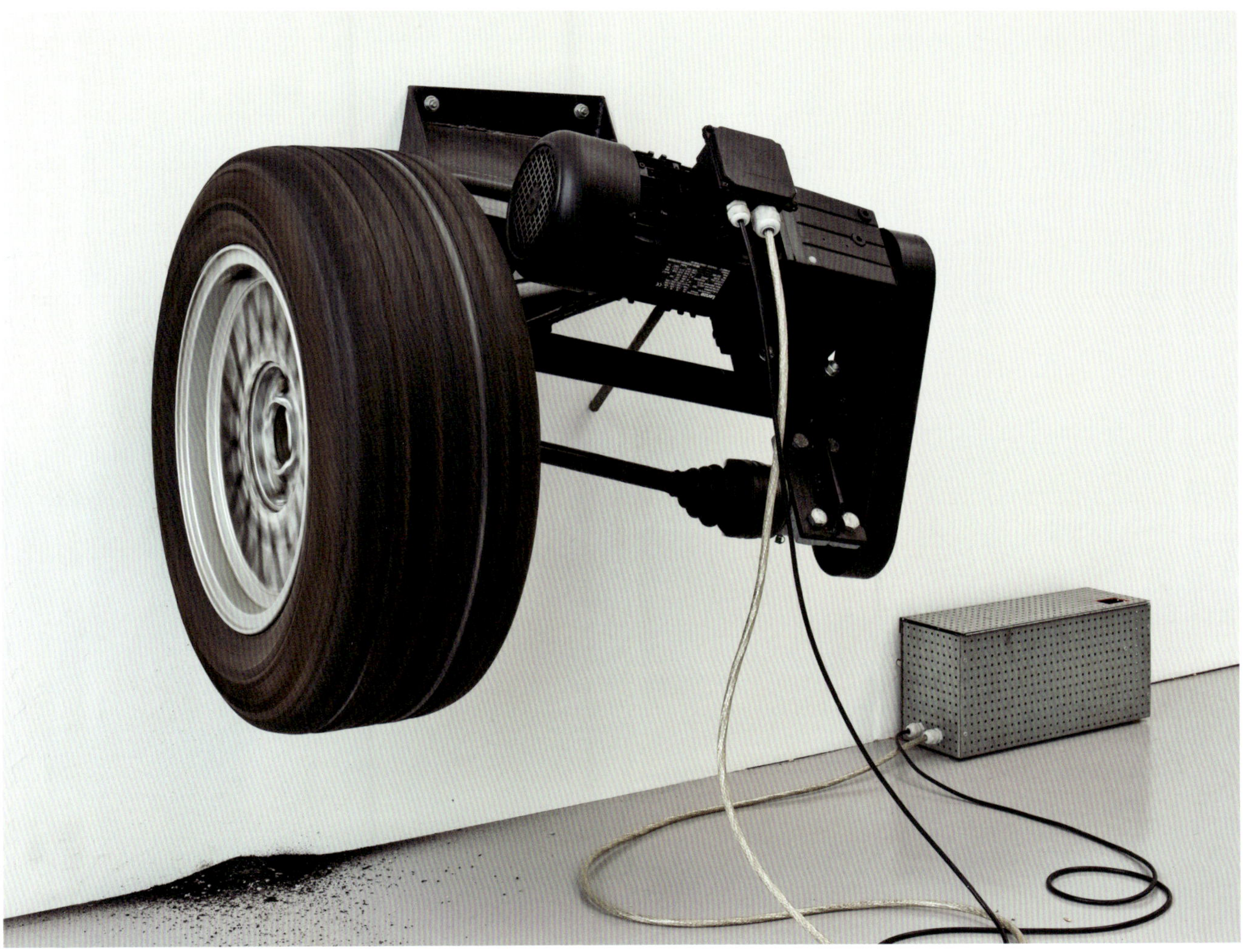

Zeit ist keine Autobahn, 2005–2020

Tire, iron, electric motor / Reifen, Eisen, Elektromotor

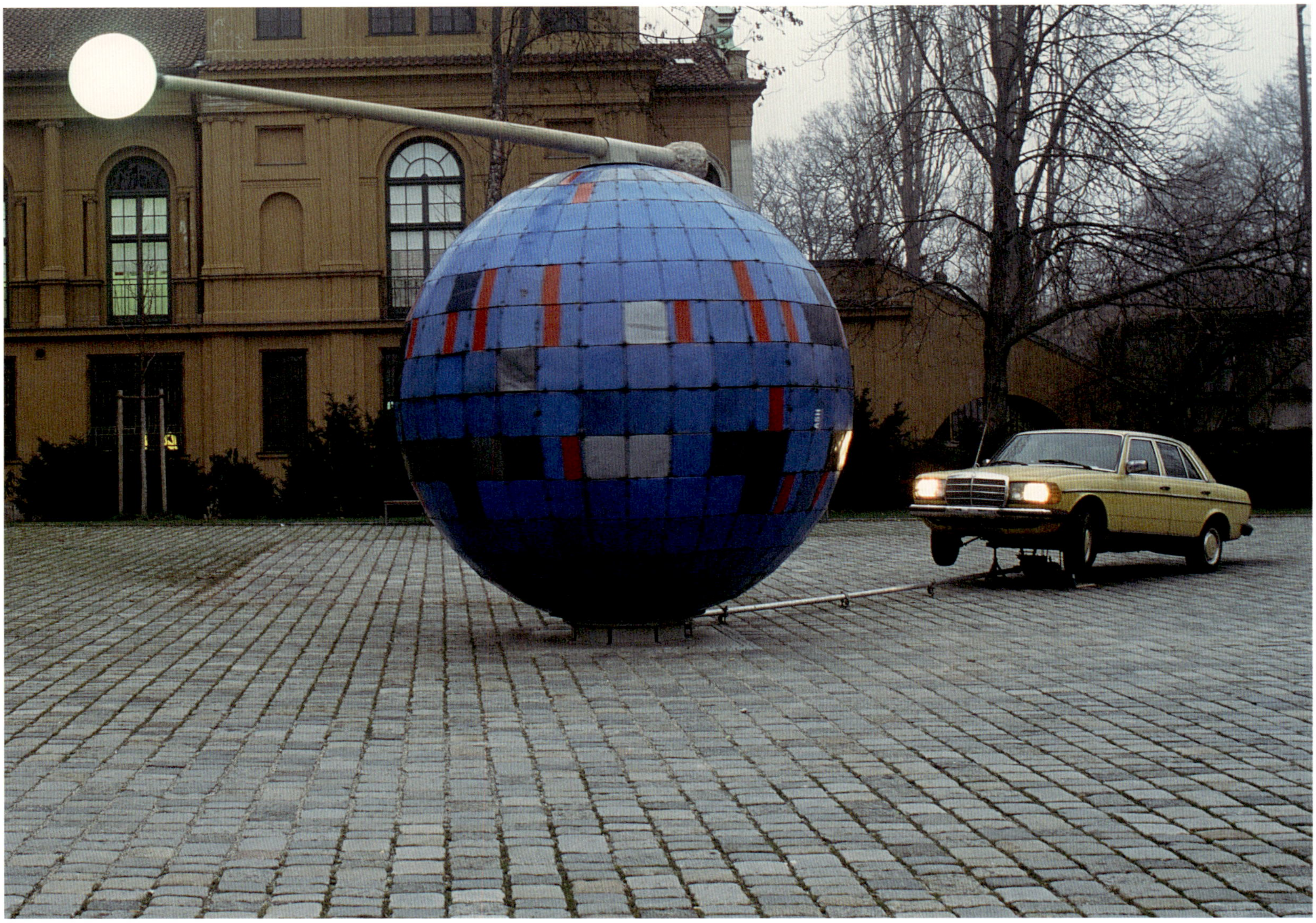

Und sie bewegt sich doch, 2002

Mercedes-Benz, street lamp, sheet metal, steel / Mercedes-Benz, Straßenlaterne, Blech, Stahl, 400 × 1.500 × 500 cm, Installation view / Installationsansicht, Städtische Galerie im Lenbachhaus, Munich / München

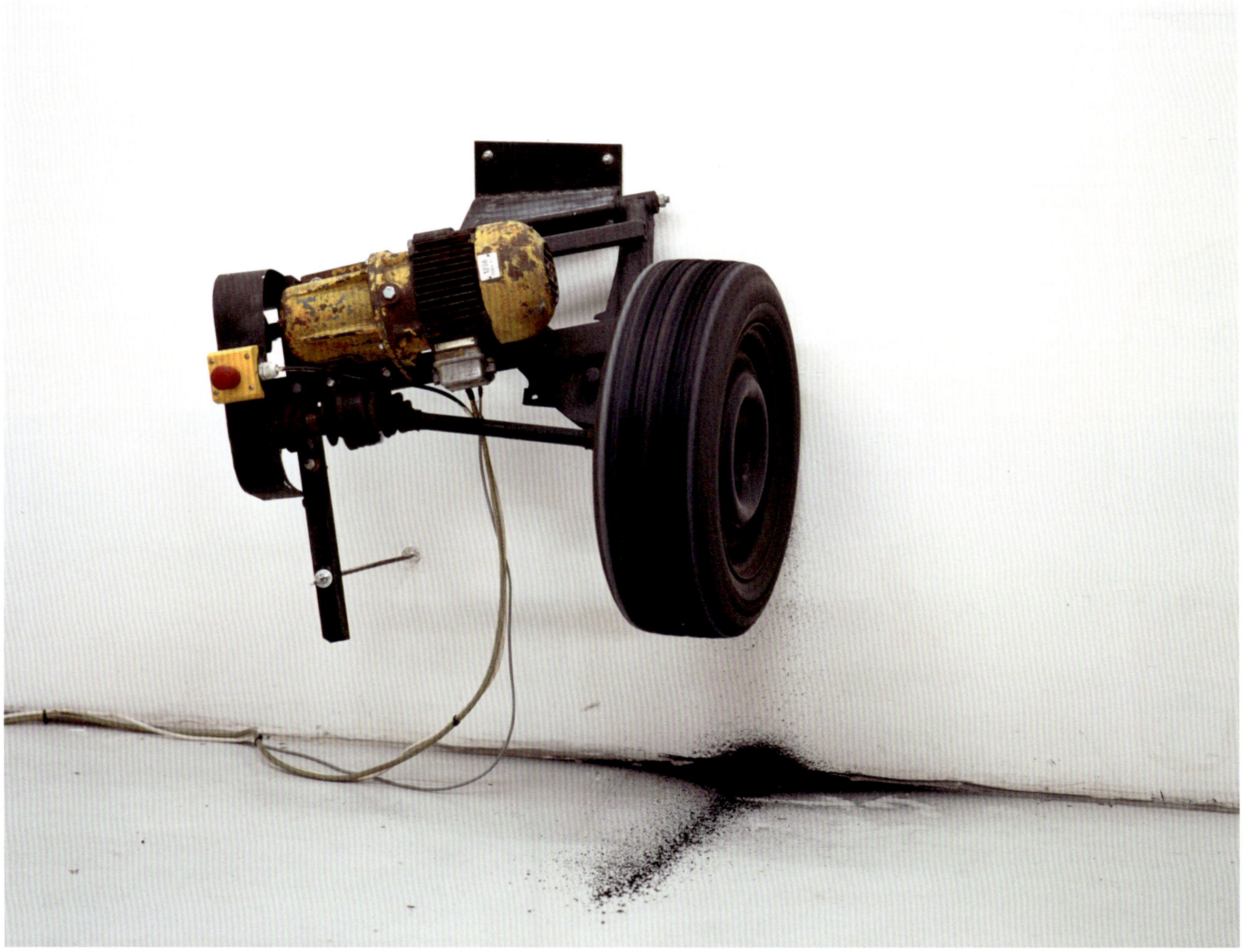

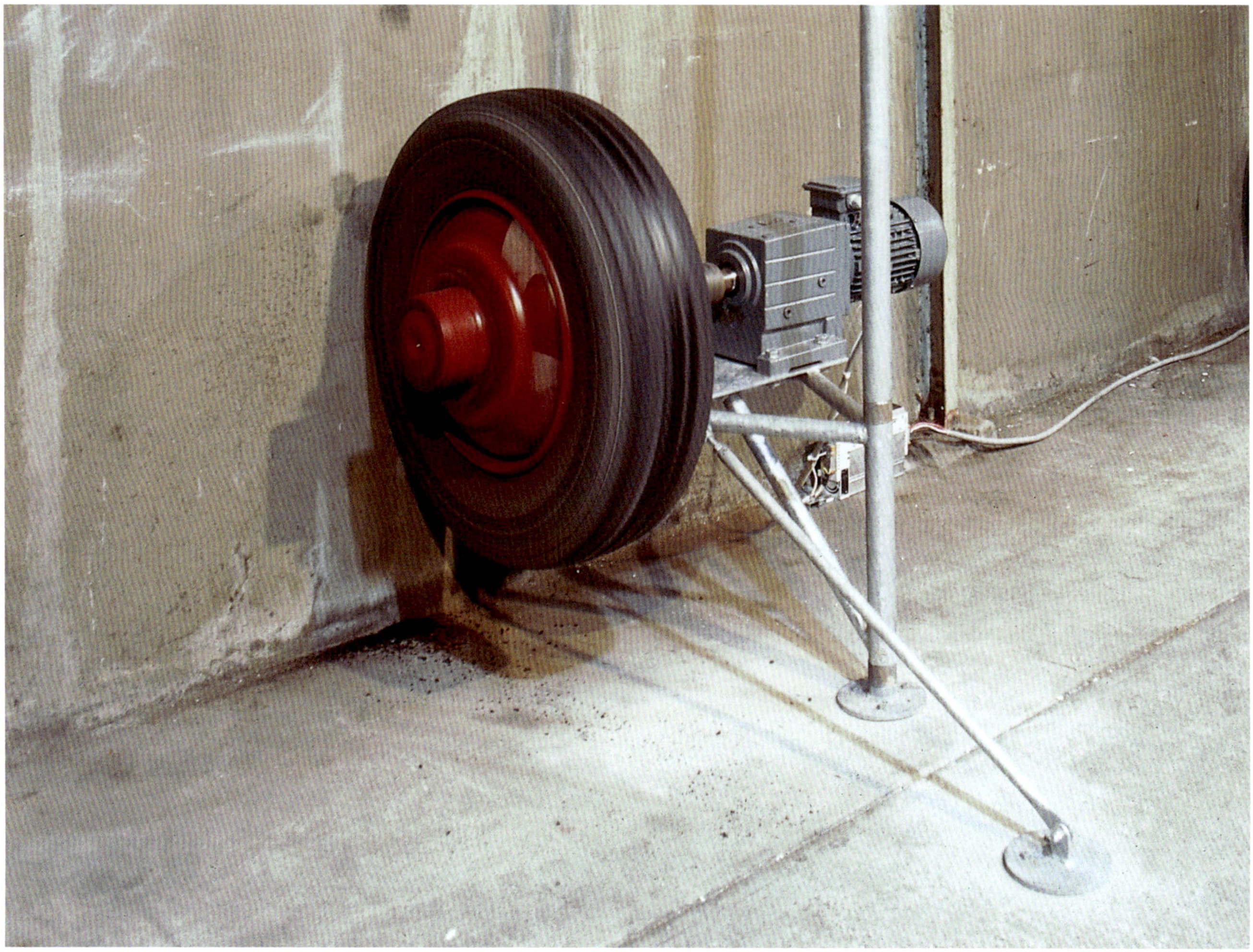

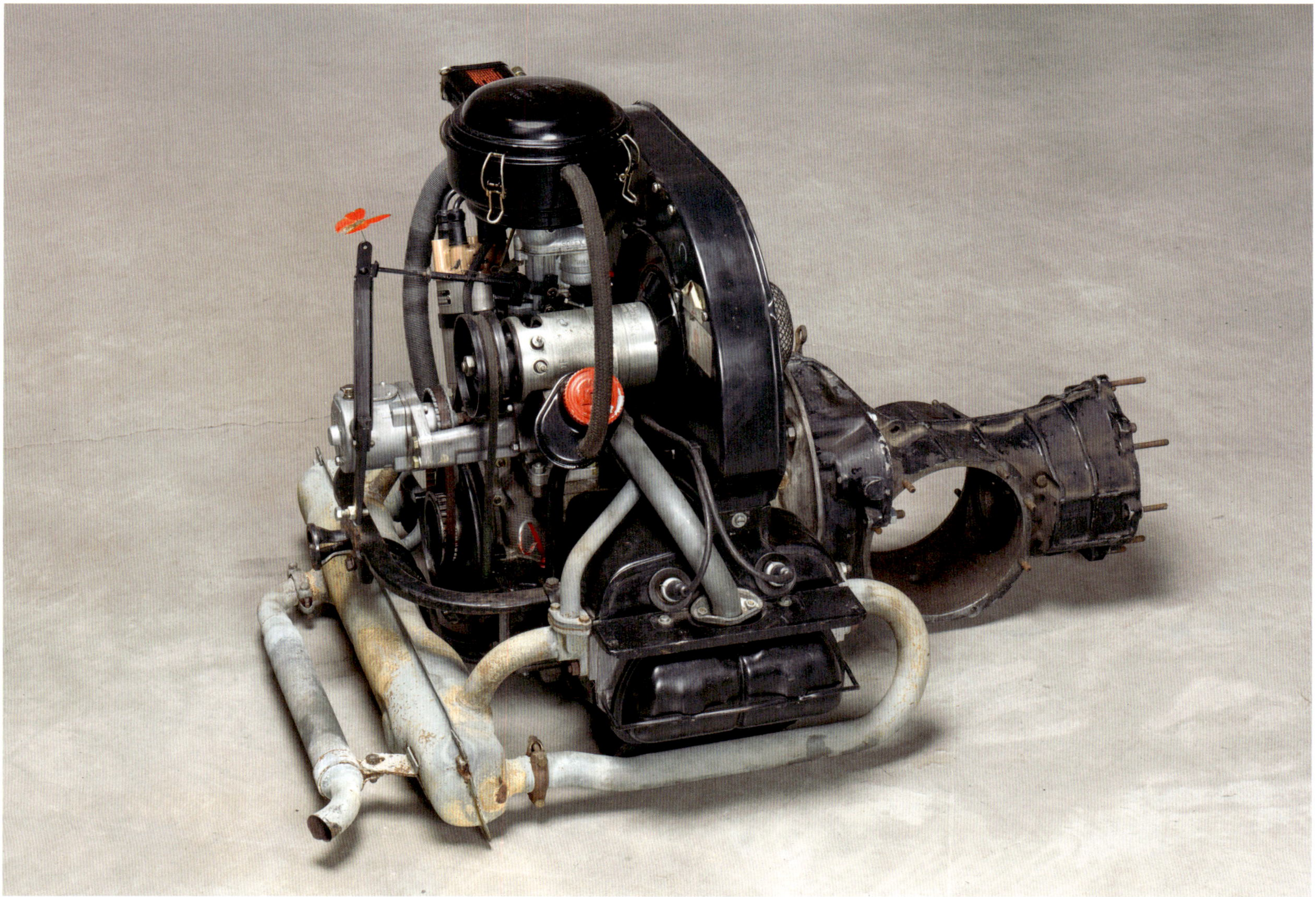

Antrieb, 2019

Gasoline engine, butterfly, fan / Benzinmotor, Schmetterling, Ventilator, 70 × 100 × 80 cm

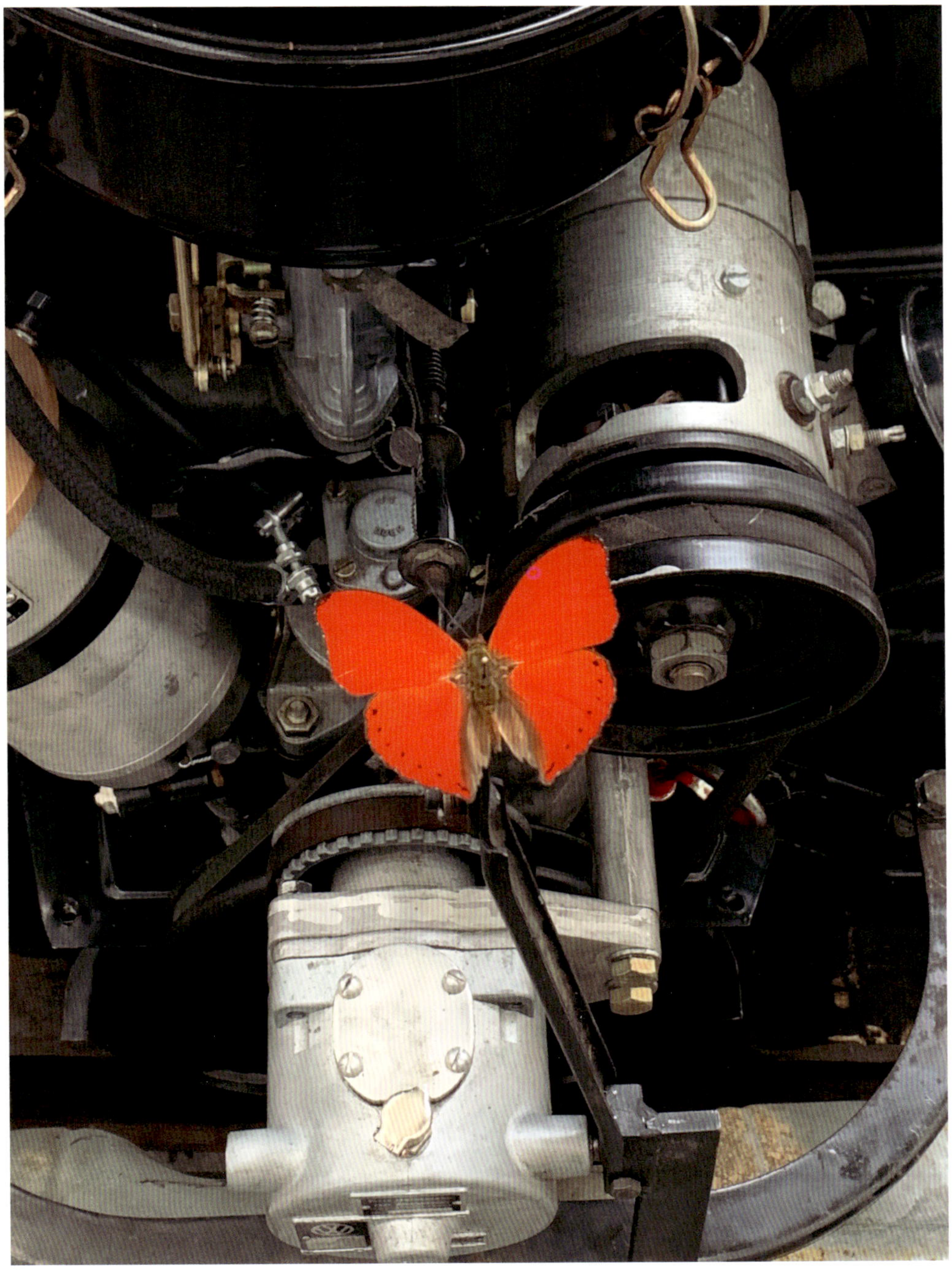

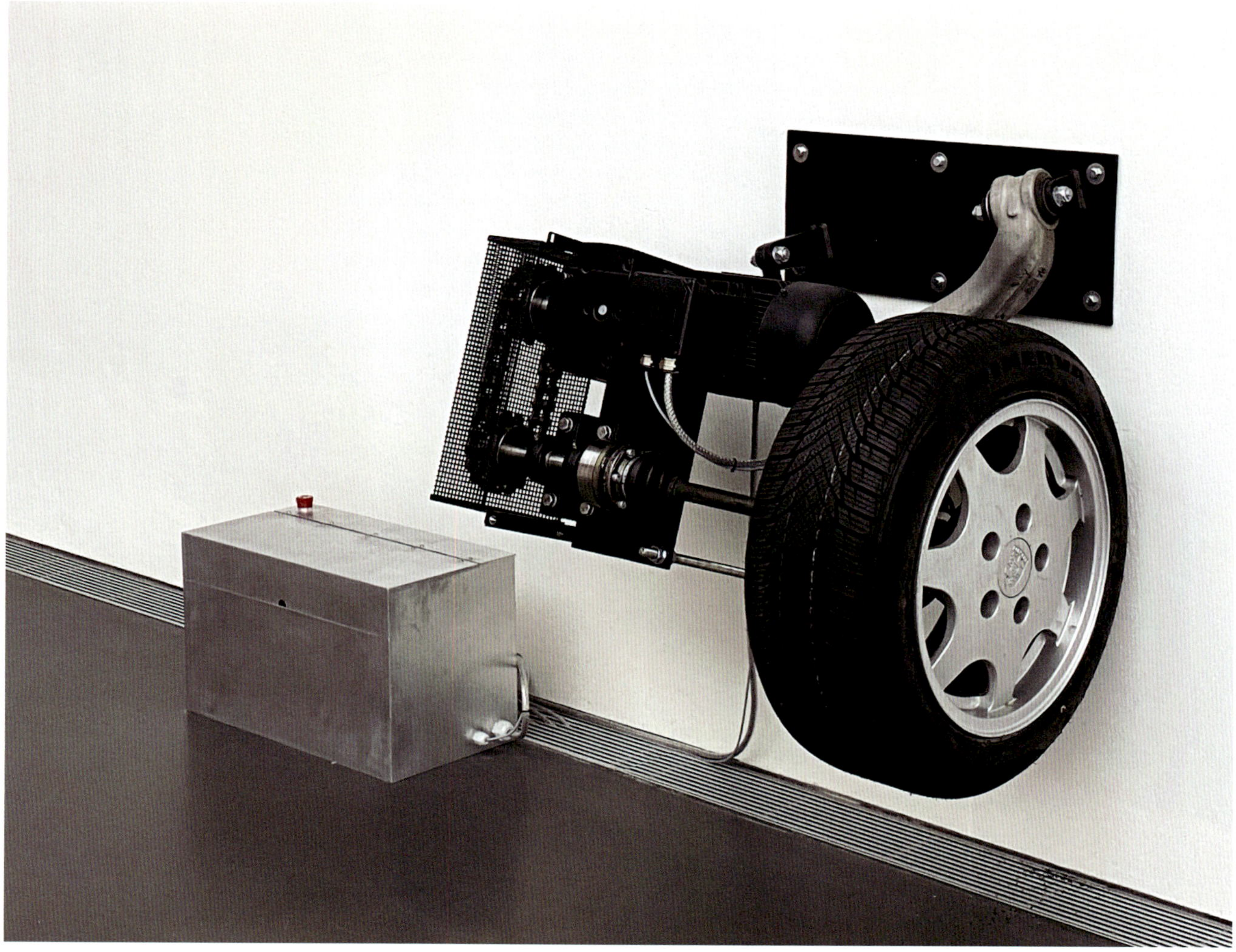

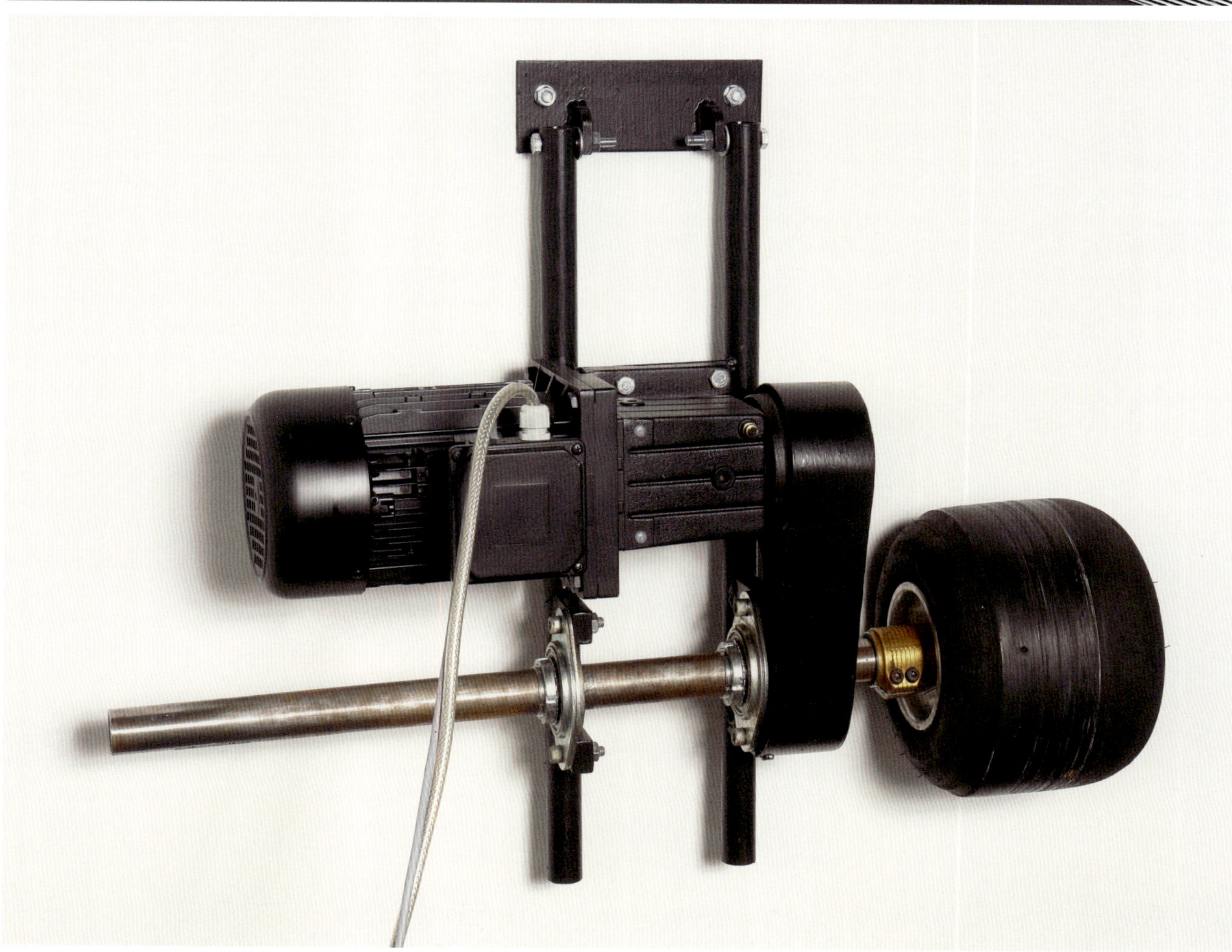

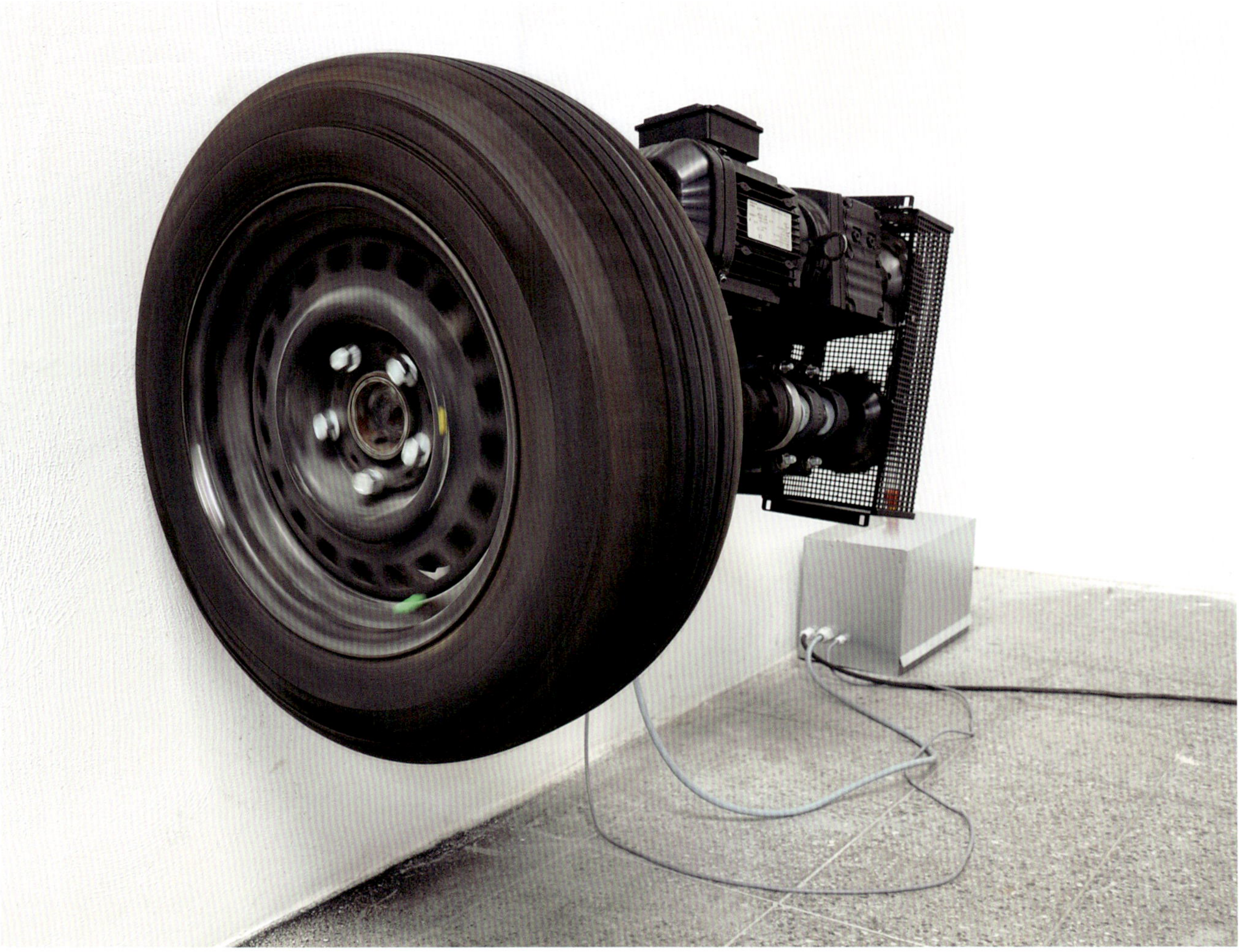

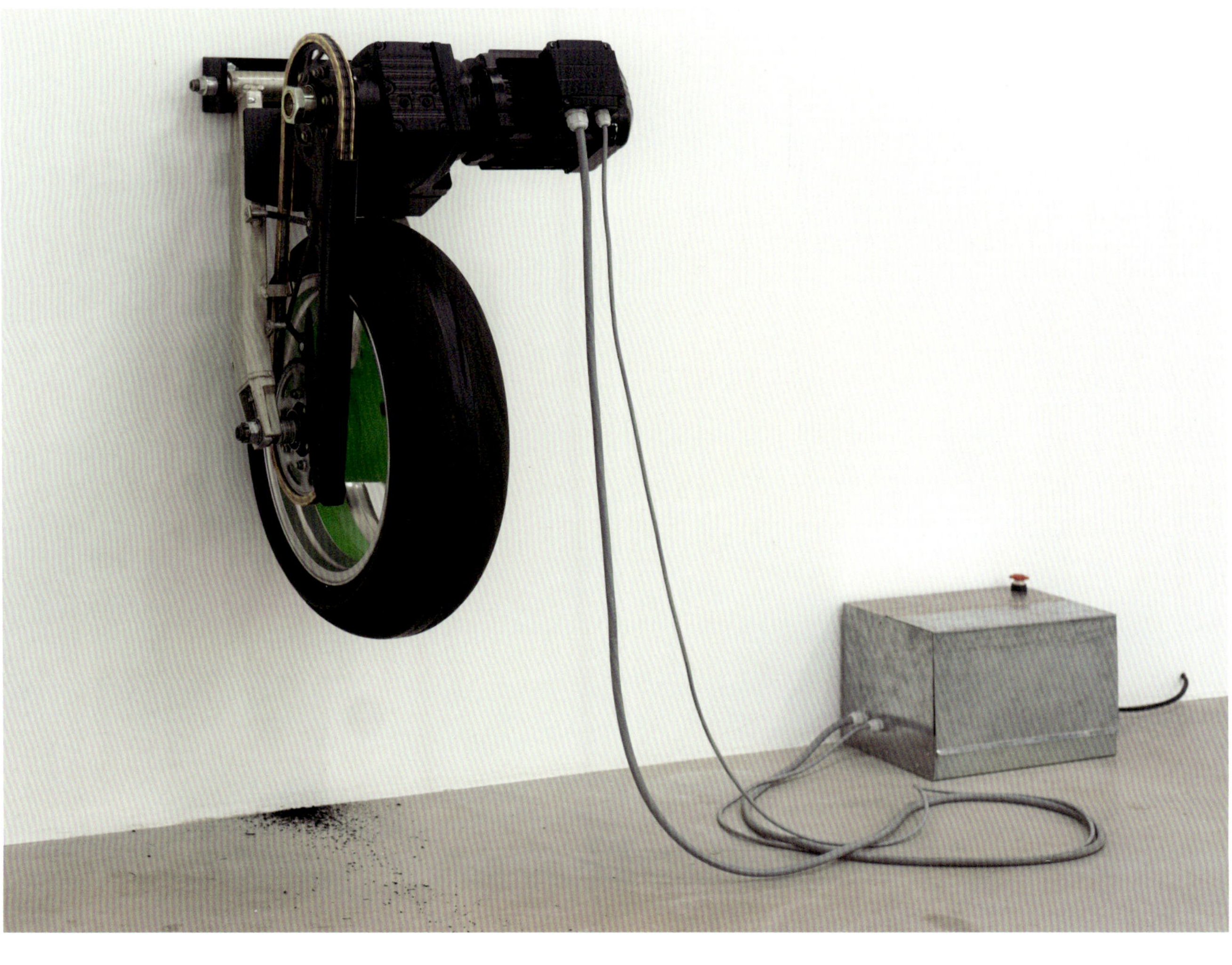

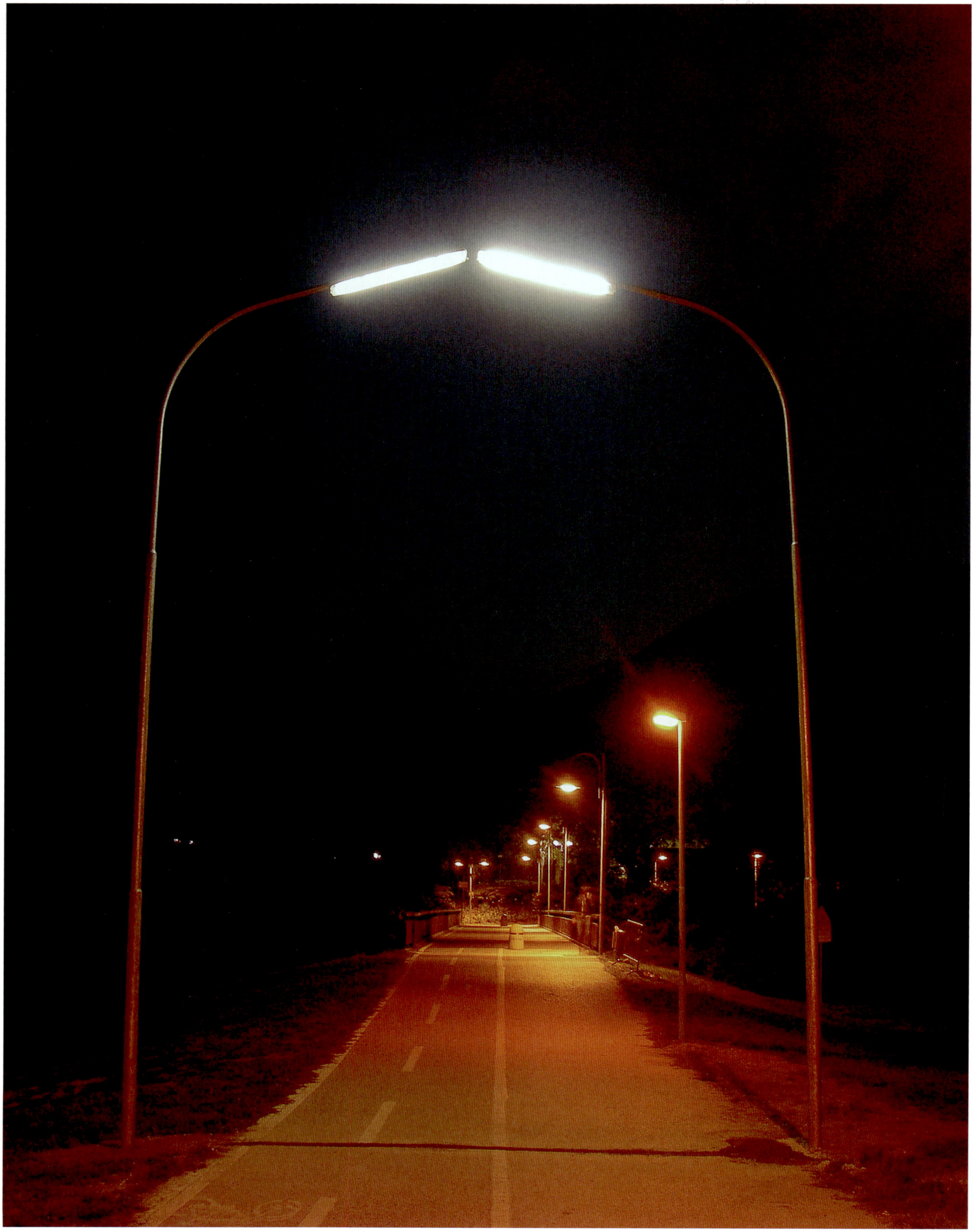

Elektrosex, 2005

Street lamps, electric components / Straßenlaternen, elektrische Komponenten, 700 × 520 × 25 cm, Installation view / Installationsansicht, Museion, Bolzano / Bozen

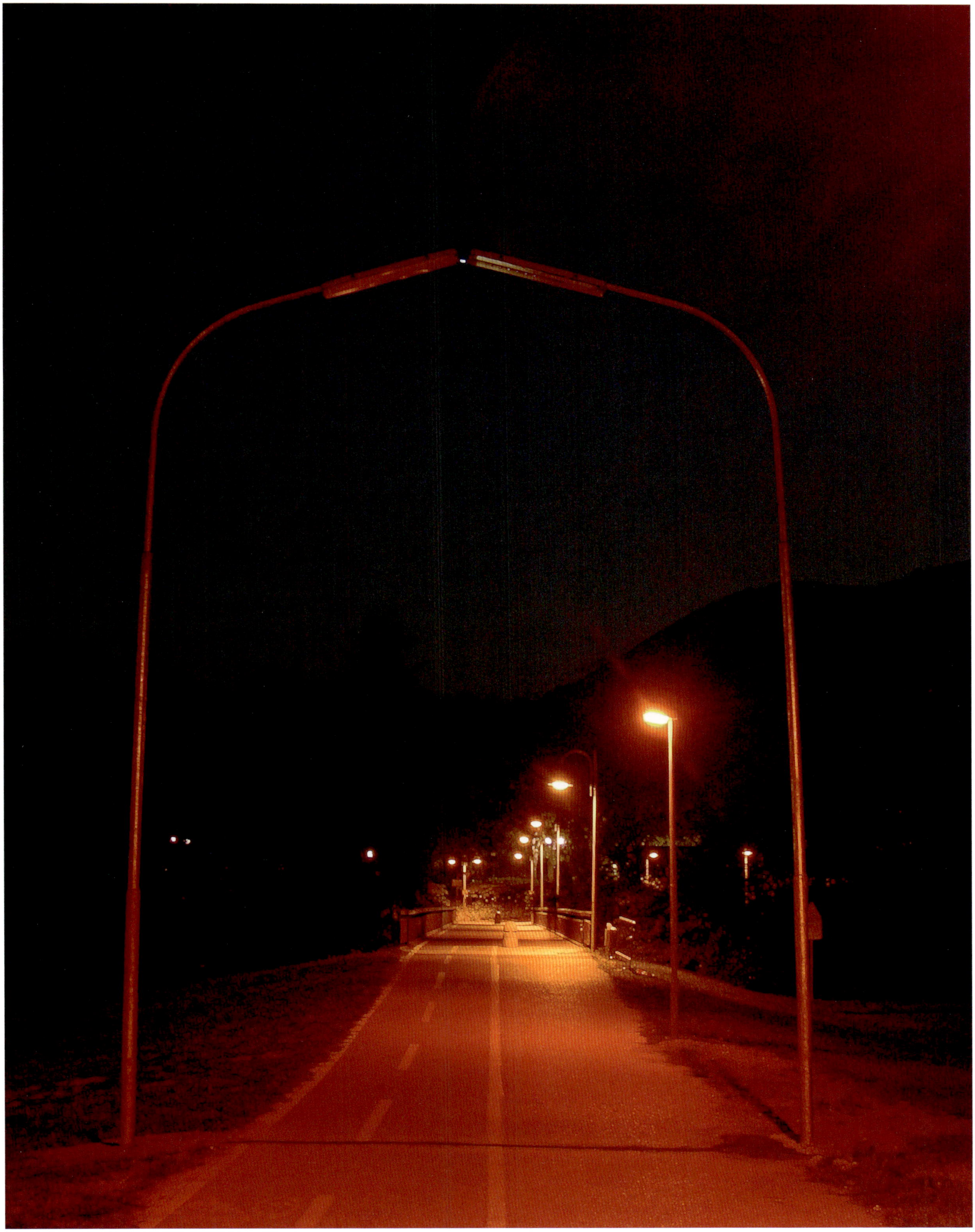

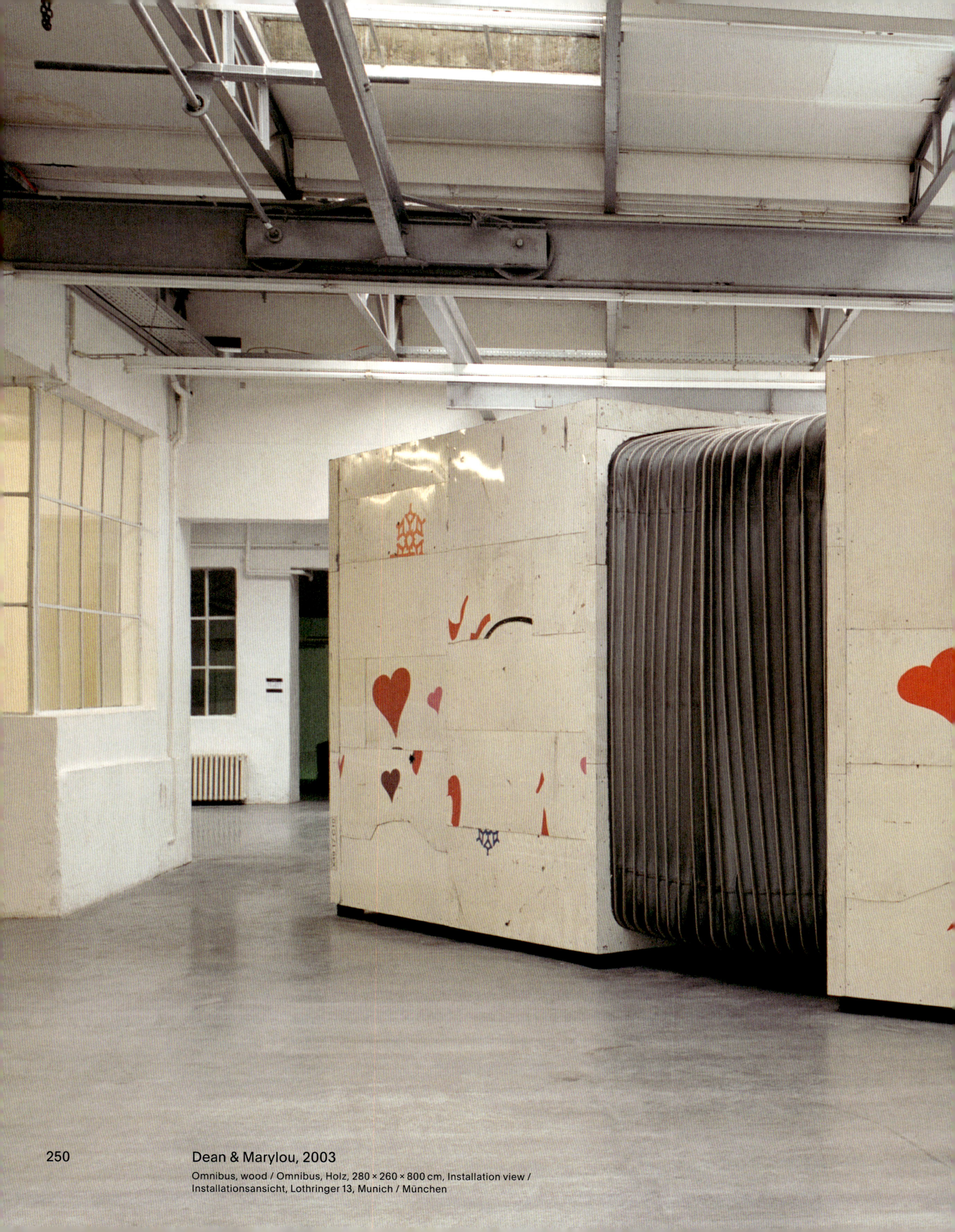

250

Dean & Marylou, 2003

Omnibus, wood / Omnibus, Holz, 280 × 260 × 800 cm, Installation view / Installationsansicht, Lothringer 13, Munich / München

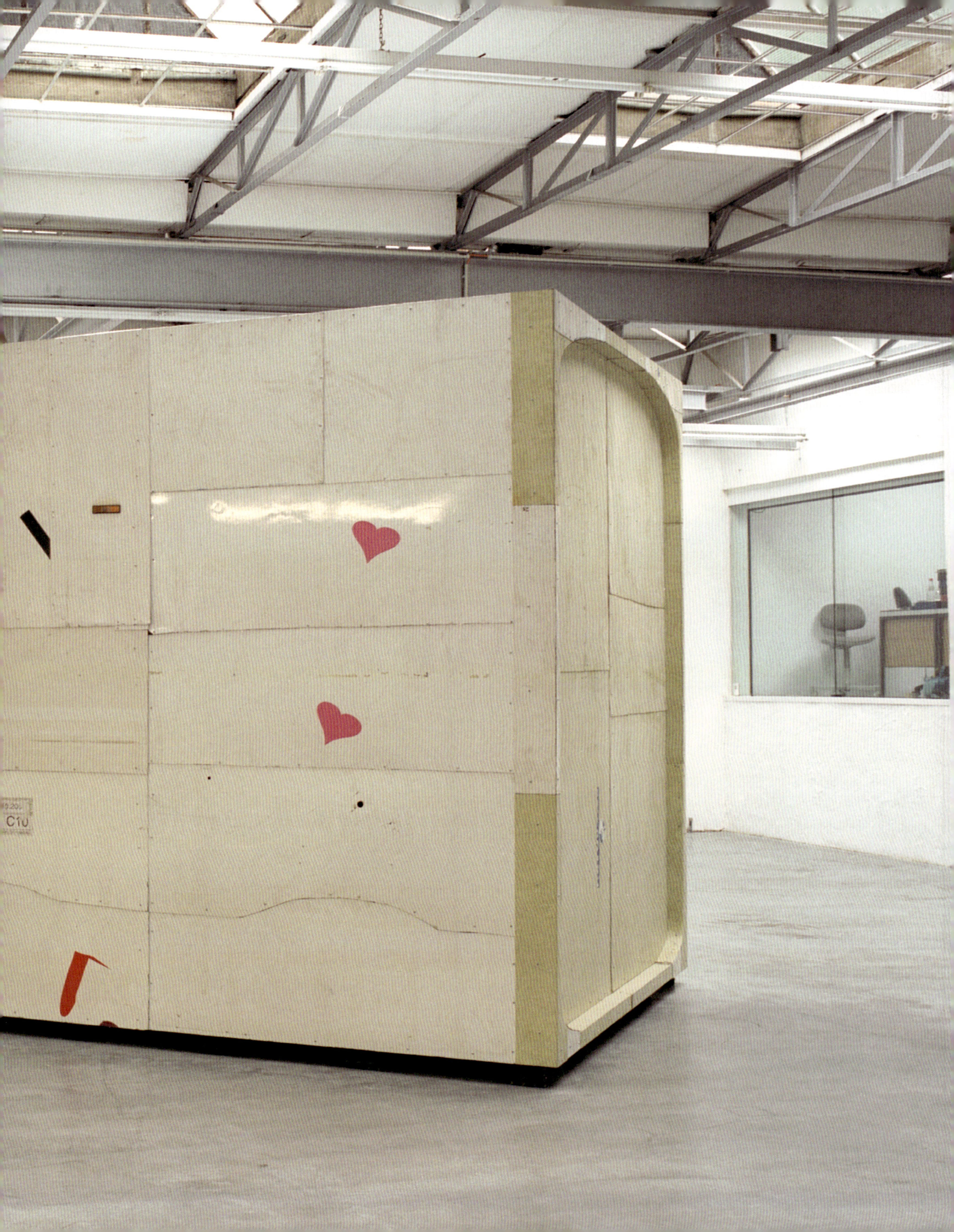

A conversation between
NEVILLE WAKEFIELD
and
MICHAEL SAILSTORFER,
January 16, 2022

NW Let's start with where we left off, which was probably ten years ago.
MS We did an interview for the *Reaktor* book. That's almost fifteen years ago.
NW But then we did the show in São Paolo, which was short time after that.
MS Yeah, it was short time after, but I don't remember the year—it must have been 2007 or 2008.
NW Yeah, that makes sense. Let's start with *Reaktor* ↗231, 233. It's been a while. I'd like to go back to the genesis of that piece, because it appeared in two shows that we did together, in different forms. And this idea of how sound and architecture and internment all come together has obviously been a fascinating one. I think the idea of architectural entropy is an important aspect that runs throughout your work; and I see the beginning of that—or not actually the beginning of that but one manifestation of it—in the *Reaktor* pieces.
MS I think you're right, and it's definitely a starting point. And it's definitely connecting or leading to the pieces I'm doing now. I think, with the *Reaktor* pieces, the important thing was how they react to the space, to people, to the ambience of the space, and how a physically small piece occupies a whole space with another medium, which is sound or smell, and which is bigger than the physical sculpture itself.
NW Is it true that all the sculptural works have a kind of physical nucleus? I don't want to use the word *psychic,* but perhaps *emotional* residue—you know, a psychic half-life that expands beyond them?
MS With most of them, it's a fact. Either they have a life of their own, or they're pretty much connected to my life—and that's the starting point, and I think that's pretty often the connection: what brings them to life, or how they can have a kind of life and spread out in the space and have a presence in the space.
NW Let's talk a little bit about what you're hinting at here: What is the biographical aspect, and how does that affect the making of some of these works? How it operates perhaps as a starting point before they reach out into the world in terms of more universal forms of meaning.
MS Yes, I think it's actually always a starting point. Or most of the time, it's a starting point, and maybe it's even clearer in the more recent pieces. Also, when we talk about the *Reaktor* piece, it's about gaining attention in the space; meaning: You put it there, and then the piece says, "I'm here. Look at me. I'm reacting to the people entering." The piece has a strong physical presence. But maybe it becomes clearer with the more recent pieces. I've done this piece, this whole show in New York with Perrotin, called *Tears* ↗26–30, and the starting point was a video piece called *Tränen* (Tears) ↗34/35, in which you see a house being destroyed by tears, cast-iron tears falling on the house and gradually demolishing it. I think the piece is, of course, about a kind of sadness which is just there, and which is strong enough to destroy your natural surroundings or whatever. I think those pieces came quite naturally. I think it's all very personal work which was important during that time.
NW Also that very early piece that left such an impression on me: *3 Ster mit Ausblick* (3 Cubic Meters of Wood with a View) ↗219–222.
MS Exactly. One "Ster" is one cubic meter of burning wood. It's a Bavarian expression. It's from 2002. I did it when I was still a student at art school. But, of course, there is, on the one hand, a strong connection between the *Tränen* work, the piece with the house being destroyed, and *3 Ster mit Ausblick*, using the material that the house is made of and burning it down and, on the other hand, destroying your environment or your house or whatever that stands for.
NW I remember that, when I first saw that piece, it made me think about the difference between European and American traditions. And I obviously thought about Chris Burden, who I see in some ways in your work and about *Samson*, that piece that was designed to bring the institution down. But I feel that Burden takes on the institutions, and you take on these spaces that are much more personal, that have the imprints of individuals, of history, and I feel that's very different. I guess what I'm trying to get at is that you're creating memories out of these actions on these buildings, which are enclosed and contained, and you're breaking them open. Is there a catharsis in that? Are you letting the memories out? Do you see these architectural forms that you take on as being bodies?
MS Yes, I think they stand for different things. I think they stand for bodies. I think they stand for an environment where you actually live. But I think they stand for something as bodies—and yes, I think they can be seen as being very personal.
NW By bodies I mean containers of memory, so to speak, melodramatic spaces that have this idea of enclosure and containment. A lot of the work plays with the boundaries of that by opening these spaces up to the world, both literally, by destroying the walls in some instances, or the roof, but also metaphorically.
MS Yes, I think, of course, they open up the space; something is destroyed to open up the space and to give another perspective on the thing.
NW Could you tell me a little more about the teeth pieces and how they came about? You know, of course, that this is a transition away from the body.
MS I think a lot of my work is about transformation. When we talked about *3 Ster mit Ausblick*, the house, it's about transformation, and also the *Tränen* piece: the tears destroying the house. At the time, I was looking from the house to the body, and then I realized that the teeth are a very strong symbol of the transformation of the body. When you're born, you have no teeth at all; and then you have the first teeth, and then you lose them, and then you're slowly growing up and have your second teeth. It's also a symbol of decay when your teeth gradually start to not work anymore. I was interested in that. And I was also interested in the subconscious symbolism of the teeth, the surreal part; sometimes, you dream about your teeth. And during that time, I was also talking a lot with my homeopathic doctor, and he said every tooth is connected to some kind of meridian; and when one of your teeth is not working, maybe then you have problems with your heart or whatever. And I think all that stuff came together, and then I started to make those teeth from salt. It's about time and decay. Actually, I made them for the show in Berghain, for the *Studio Berlin* show. I was interested in this space where the subconscious and the night life and the surreal come together. That's where I showed them for the first time. And that's how this piece was born.
NW Interesting! The teeth thing. It's funny you should say that, because I was just listening to someone, a neuroscientist, talk about the effects of a concussion on the brain and more generally about mental health. The bulk of the conversation was about concussions, even very minor ones that we're not even aware of. Then he started talking about the mouth and how the mouth and the teeth actually play an enormous role in not just behavioral health but actually in the way that the brain is configured and significant in

the way that it's cased. So that was interesting.
MS I wasn't aware of that. That's super interesting. I also just started working on a new project. It's called *Minteeth* ↗137. It's small mints. One package contains 32 mints. It's mint bonbons, like lozenges, teeth shaped, so you can actually eat them.
NW The thing that destroys it in the form of the thing it destroys.
MS A vending machine where you can buy mint teeth.
NW And then, while we're sort of exploring this theme with the body, whether it's architectural or physical, it would be good to talk about the two kinds of automotive skeletons that you've made: *Brenner* (Combustor) ↗257–261 and *Ofen Mailand* (Milan Oven) ↗223.
MS There's also a strong link to the *Reaktor* piece. The *Brenner* piece was shown at König Galerie in Berlin. I did those six car bodies or skeletons, and they were all painted in black, heat-resistant paint. Where the engine once was, there was now a wooden oven; and during the exhibition, they were fired constantly, with chimneys going up through the ceiling of the gallery: thirteen meters high. Like a black line drawing in space. And, of course, just as the *Reaktor* piece had the acoustic signal, here you had the heat. It was thus almost like a sauna in the space: it was pretty claustrophobic. And it's reminiscent of a production line, a car factory—the cars rolling through the production line. On another hand, it's almost like a traffic jam, producing heat. Then you almost have this post-apocalyptical image. Those car bodies burning, generating heat, and actually firing up the gallery space which used to be a church years ago. I also liked that the church is actually becoming a factory space, and you have this smoke coming out from the chimney above the church. Actually, the piece was made or designed for the exhibition space. Downstairs, in the entrance, we had a huge pile of wood; on the first floor, you had the cars; and in the bell tower we had the *Tränen* video projected. So almost like the heat condensing and then the water dripping down on the house and then destroying the whole thing, the whole environment in the end.
NW That must have pleased Johann!
MS Not really (laughter). Johann was a little bit nervous; but I think, for both of us, it was an important show in the end.
NW Obviously a lot of the working process is documented. When you're thinking about these pieces, do you see them as process pieces, or do you care about the end result?
MS I think it's a process. Quite often, I don't even know what the end result might look like. So, with this piece, it was also an experiment: how it works or how it looks. You can have an idea, but it's almost pretty much different when you start to work on it and realize it physically. You quite often can't plan it, and that's why you can't animate a piece like the *Tränen* piece, because you would never have been able to do it as it looks for real.
NW And while we're staying on the kind of automotive body, the *Antrieb* (Drive) pieces …
MS That was the show afterwards, a small show at König.
NW What was the origin of those works?
MS It's two pieces actually. One (*Antrieb* ↗242/243) is a car engine, and you see a butterfly on top, and the butterfly is dancing on the car engine. It's slowly rotating.
NW When I saw images of this, it was at a time when I was reading a lot about chaos theory and the butterfly effect and how a small action in one part of the world can be amplified across an ecosystem to a have huge impact somewhere else. I was curious about whether this piece had any environmental message along those lines?
MS Of course. I think that was actually the starting point. There's the engine, which is manmade, and it's fantastic; but on the other hand, you have the butterfly dancing on the top of it. Man will never be able to do something as beautiful as that. It's about the magic and the beauty and the question as to where the power comes from. You can't really tell what moves the butterfly on the engine. It's just a small air stream coming off the ceiling.
NW And, of course, transformation, because the butterfly is the most metamorphic creature, as is the engine.
MS I didn't think about that, but I do like it very much.
NW You know, transforming fossil fuel into movement is just as extraordinary in some ways.
MS You're right! It's about energy and transformation.
NW And the companion piece, which was like a transmission with the salt sculpture kind of emerging from it.
MS It's called *Antrieb 2* ↗130/131. It's a gear box and a salt stone sculpture in the shape of a human heart. The heart is actually powering the human body, and then it's linked to the gear box of a car, and it's about what power is, what provides the energy, what's the motivation. It's stands in one line with the butterfly piece.
NW And there's also that interesting question of about which is driving which.
MS Exactly.
NW I was just thinking about that in terms of that book, *Sapiens: A Brief History of Humankind,* and Yuval Noah Harari describing the agrarian revolution in terms of mankind starting to control nature and mass produced agricultural goods, particularly weeds. But then he reverses that and was like, well, from the point of view of the weed, it's the weed controlling the humans. From the point of view of genetic survival, the weed is the winner. Those reversals become very interesting in terms of your work and what's actually driving what. And particularly, perhaps the other thing that I see running throughout the work is this idea of entropy and how it might be reversed. How we control the flow of energy. And obviously, with the burning pieces, the circle of thermodynamics is actually an effect. But I'm thinking also about emotional entropy and emotional loss.
MS Which pieces are you referring to?
NW Well, I am thinking about the *Tränen* pieces as a literal version of that, but perhaps the tears and these other things being in some ways about emotional entropy, about the dissipation of emotion in the world.

Gespräch zwischen
NEVILLE WAKEFIELD
und
MICHAEL SAILSTORFER
am 16. Januar 2022

NW Lass uns dort beginnen, wo wir vor zehn Jahren aufgehört haben …
MS Wir haben ein Interview für das Buch *Reaktor* gemacht. Das ist wahrscheinlich fünfzehn Jahre her.
NW Und dann haben wir die Ausstellung in São Paulo organisiert.
MS Ja, das war kurz danach, aber ich erinnere mich nicht mehr an das Jahr, das muss 2007 oder 2008 gewesen sein.
NW Ja, das macht Sinn. Also fangen wir mit der Arbeit *Reaktor* ↗231, 233 an. Es ist schon eine Weile her. Ich möchte auf ihre Entstehungsgeschichte zurückkommen, weil sie in unterschiedlichen Formen in zwei Ausstellungen vertreten war, bei denen wir zusammengearbeitet haben. Der Gedanke, wie Sound und Architektur und Eingeschlossenheit zusammenkommen, ist faszinierend. Ich glaube, die Idee von architektonischer Entropie zieht sich durch dein ganzes Werk und ist darin sehr wichtig und ich sehe den Anfang oder eben auch nicht den Anfang, aber eine Manifestation davon in *Reaktor*.
MS Du hast recht, diese Arbeiten waren definitiv ein Startpunkt und stehen in engem Zusammenhang mit dem, was ich jetzt mache. Bei *Reaktor* war das Wichtigste, wie das Werk auf den Raum, auf die Umgebung, auf die Menschen reagiert und wie ein physisch so kleines Teil einen ganzen Raum mit einem anderen Medium, das Geräusch oder Geruch sein kann und das viel größer als die Skulptur an sich ist, füllt.
NW Stimmt es, dass alle skulpturalen Arbeiten eine Art physikalischen Nukleus haben? Ich will nicht den Begriff psychisch gebrauchen, aber vielleicht ist es ein emotionaler Rest, ein seelisches Halbleben, das über sie hinauswächst?
MS Bei den meisten ist das der Fall. Entweder sie haben ein eigenes Leben oder sie sind mit meinem Leben verbunden. Das ist die Ausgangsbasis und eben ganz oft auch der Zusammenhang. Das, was sie zum Leben erweckt oder wie sie ein Eigenleben bekommen und den Raum einnehmen und darin präsent sein.
NW Wenn du schon darauf anspielst, dann lass uns über den biografischen Aspekt sprechen und wie er die Entstehung mancher Arbeiten beeinflusst. Funktioniert er vielleicht als Ausgangspunkt, bevor sie mit einer universelleren Bedeutung hinaus in die Welt gehen?
MS Ja, ich denke eigentlich, dass das immer oder meistens der Startpunkt ist und das wird vielleicht in den neueren Arbeiten auch noch klarer. Wenn wir über *Reaktor* reden, dann geht es darum, Aufmerksamkeit in einem Raum zu erregen. Du stellst ihn hin und dann sagt das Ding: „Hier bin ich. Schau mich an. Ich reagiere auf die Leute, die reinkommen.“ Die Arbeit hat eine starke physische Präsenz. Aber das ist in aktuelleren Werken vielleicht noch deutlicher. Ich habe mit der Serie *Tears* ↗26–30 eine komplette Ausstellung bei Perrotin in New York gemacht und die Ausgangsbasis war ein Video mit dem Titel *Tränen* ↗34/35. Darin sieht man ein Haus, das von Tränen zerstört wird. In Eisen gegossene Tränen fallen auf das Haus und zerstören es langsam. Ich glaube, es geht darin um eine Art Traurigkeit, die einfach da ist und die so stark ist, dass sie deine natürliche Umgebung ruinieren kann. Diese Werke entstanden ganz natürlich. Es sind sehr persönliche Arbeiten, sie stehen für etwas, was für mich zu dieser Zeit sehr wichtig war.
NW Auch diese sehr frühe Arbeit, die mich so beeindruckt hat, *3 Ster mit Ausblick* ↗219–222.
MS Genau. Ein Ster ist ein Kubikmeter Brennholz; das ist ein bayerischer Ausdruck. Die Arbeit ist aus dem Jahr 2002, da war ich noch Student an der Kunstakademie. Selbstverständlich gibt es eine enge Beziehung zwischen dem Video *Tränen*, wo das Haus demoliert wird, und *3 Ster mit Ausblick*, wo das Material, aus dem das Haus ist, verbrannt wird. Damit wird deine Lebenswelt oder dein Haus oder, das wofür es steht, vernichtet.
NW Als ich die Arbeiten zum ersten Mal sah, musste ich an den Unterschied zwischen der europäischen und der amerikanischen Tradition denken, und sie erinnerten mich natürlich an Chris Burden, den ich irgendwie in deinen Werken sehe, und an seine Installation *Samson*, die dazu geschaffen war, die Institution einzureißen. Aber ich habe das Gefühl, dass sich Burden an den Institutionen abarbeitet, während du Orte aussuchst, die viel persönlicher sind, die Spuren von Individuen, von einer Geschichte tragen, und ich meine, das ist etwas Anderes. Was ich sagen will, du lässt Erinnerungen entstehen, aus diesen Aktionen mit den Gebäuden, die Geschlossenheit und Einhegung bedeuten und du brichst sie auf. Liegt darin eine Katharsis? Oder lässt du die Erinnerungen frei? Betrachtest du diese architektonischen Formen, mit denen du dich beschäftigst, als Körper?
MS Ich denke, sie stehen für verschiedene Dinge, wie für die Umgebung, in der man gerade lebt, aber ich glaube schon, dass sie so etwas wie Körper darstellen, und, ja, sie können als etwas sehr Persönliches betrachtet werden.
NW Mit Körpern meine ich Behälter der Erinnerung, wenn du so willst, melodramatische Orte, die diese Idee von Gehäuse und Sicherheit in sich tragen. Viele deiner Arbeiten spielen mit den Begrenzungen davon, indem sie die Räume für die Welt öffnen, sowohl wortwörtlich dadurch, dass in einigen die Wände eingerissen werden, als auch im übertragenen Sinn.
MS Ja natürlich machen sie den Raum auf, etwas wird zerstört, um eine andere Perspektive auf die Sache zu eröffnen.
NW Erzähl mir etwas mehr über die Arbeiten mit den Zähnen. Wie sie entstanden sind. Du weißt sicher, dass sie eine Überleitung zum Körper sind.
MS In vielen meiner Arbeiten geht es um Transformation, in *3 Ster mit Ausblick* und auch in *Tränen*. Die Tränen zerstören das Haus. Dann schaute ich vom Haus auf den Körper und stellte fest, dass die Zähne ein wichtiges Symbol für die Transformation des Körpers sind. Wenn man geboren wird, hat man überhaupt keine Zähne, dann bekommt man die ersten Zähne und verliert sie und dann wird man allmählich älter und bekommt die zweiten Zähne. Es ist auch ein Zeichen für Verfall, wenn die Zähne langsam anfangen, nicht mehr zu funktionieren. Das hat mich interessiert und auch die unterbewusste Bedeutung, die Zähne haben, der surreale Part, manchmal träumt man von seinen Zähnen. Zu der Zeit habe ich oft mit meinem Homöopathen gesprochen und er sagte, dass jeder Zahn in Verbindung mit einem Meridian steht, und wenn ein Zahn nicht in Ordnung ist, dann hat man vielleicht Herzprobleme oder so. Diese Dinge kamen alle zusammen und dann habe ich diese Zähne aus Salz gemacht und natürlich geht es dabei um Zeit und Verfall. Eigentlich habe ich sie für die Ausstellung *Studio Berlin* im Berghain produziert. Mich faszinierte dieser Ort, wo das Unterbewusste und das Nachtleben und das Surreale aufeinandertreffen. Hier habe ich sie zum ersten Mal gezeigt. So ist diese Arbeit entstanden.
NW Das mit den Zähnen ist interessant! Ich habe neulich einen Vortrag von einem Neurowissenschaftler über die Auswirkungen von Erschütterungen auf das Gehirn und die mentale Gesundheit gehört. Der größte Teil der Vorlesung ging über Gehirnerschütterungen, auch ganz geringfügige, die wir gar nicht wahrnehmen. Dann sprach er über den Mund und was für eine enorme Rolle der Mund und die Zähne nicht nur für die verhaltensabhängige Gesundheit spielen, sondern auch dafür, wie das Gehirn konfiguriert

und wie es eingebunden ist. Das war spannend.
MS Das wusste ich nicht, das ist super interessant. Ich arbeite gerade an einem neuen Projekt, das *Minteeth* ↗137 heißt. Eine Packung enthält 32 Stück. Das sind kleine Pfefferminzbonbons, wie Dragees, in Form eines Zahns, die man essen kann.
NW Eine zerstörerische Sache, in Gestalt dessen, was sie zerstört.
MS Man kann sie an einem Automaten kaufen.
NW Wenn wir über das Thema Körper diskutieren, ob er nun architektonisch oder physikalisch ist, sollten wir auch über die Fahrzeugkarosserien sprechen, die du produziert hast, *Brenner* ↗257–261 und *Ofen Mailand* ↗223.
MS Sie stehen auch in direktem Zusammenhang mit der Arbeit *Reaktor*. *Brenner* wurde in der König Galerie gezeigt. Ich habe sechs Autokarosserien mit schwarzer, hitzebeständiger Farbe lackieren lassen. Der Motor wurde durch einen Holzofen ersetzt, der während der Ausstellung durchgehend befeuert wurde und die Abzugsrohre gingen durch die Decke der Galerie, in einer Höhe von dreizehn Metern, nach draußen. Wie eine schwarze Linienzeichnung im Raum. Was bei *Reaktor* die Akustik war, war hier die Hitze. Der Raum wurde zur Sauna, das war ziemlich klaustrophobisch. Es erinnerte an eine Produktionsstraße in einer Autofabrik, wo die Autos über ein Fließband laufen. Und auf der anderen Seite war es wie ein Verkehrsstau, der Hitze freisetzt. Ein postapokalyptisches Bild. Diese brennenden Karosserien, die Hitze erzeugten und den Galerieraum beheizten, der Jahre zuvor eine Kirche war. Ich mochte, dass die Kirche zur Fabrik wurde und dass der Rauch durch die Schornsteine aus der Kirche kam. Das Werk wurde speziell für diesen Ausstellungsraum konzipiert. Unten am Eingang war ein großer Holzhaufen, im ersten Stock die Autos und im Glockenturm wurde das Video *Tränen* gezeigt. Fast als ob die Hitze kondensieren und das Wasser dann auf das Haus heruntertropfen und es am Ende mitsamt der ganzen Umgebung zerstört werden würde.
NW Das muss Johann gefallen haben!
MS Nicht wirklich (Gelächter). Johann war ein bisschen nervös, aber für uns beide war es letztendlich eine wichtige Ausstellung.
NW Offensichtlich wird in diesem Video ein Prozess eines Werkes dokumentiert. Betrachtest du es und ähnliche Videos als „Prozess-Arbeiten" und ist dir das Resultat überhaupt wichtig?
MS Ich sehe es als Prozess. Oft weiß ich gar nicht, wie das Ergebnis am Ende überhaupt aussehen wird. Bei dieser Arbeit war es ein Experiment, wie es funktionieren oder wie es aussehen würde. Ich kann eine Idee haben, aber sie steht in großem Unterschied zu dem, was passiert, wenn man beginnt, sie physisch umzusetzen. Das kann man oft nicht planen, eine Arbeit wie *Tränen* kann man nicht animieren, weil das nie so wie in der Realität aussehen würde.
NW Wo wir gerade bei den „Auto-Arbeiten" sind, was war *Antrieb*?
MS Das war die nächste Show bei König, eine kleinere Ausstellung.
NW Was war der Ursprung dieser Arbeiten?
MS Es sind zwei. Eine (*Antrieb* ↗242/243) ist ein Automotor, auf dem ein Schmetterling tanzt. Er rotiert ganz langsam.
NW Zu der Zeit als ich Bilder davon sah, habe ich eine Menge über Chaostheorie und den Schmetterlingseffekt gelesen, wie eine kleine Handlung in einem Teil der Welt durch ein Ökosystem verstärkt werden und in einem anderen Teil große Auswirkungen haben kann. Ich war neugierig, ob in dieser Arbeit eine Botschaft die Umwelt betreffend mitschwingt.
MS Natürlich, das war eigentlich der Ausgangspunkt. Da ist die Maschine, die der Mensch geschaffen hat und die fantastisch ist und dann tanzt der Schmetterling darauf. Der Mensch wird so etwas Wunderbares wie das nie zustande bringen. Es geht um Magie und um Schönheit und um die Frage, wo die Energie herkommt. Man kann nicht wirklich sagen, was den Schmetterling auf dem Motor in Bewegung setzt. Es ist nur ein schwacher Luftstrom von der Decke.
NW Und es geht um Transformation, weil ein Schmetterling ein sehr wandelbares Wesen ist, wie der Motor auch.
MS Darüber habe ich noch nicht nachgedacht, aber es gefällt mir sehr.
NW Normalen Kraftstoff in Bewegung umzusetzen, ist etwas Außergewöhnliches.
MS Da hast du recht, es geht um Energie und Umwandlung.
NW Und das Zwillingsstück, eine Art Getriebe, aus dem eine Salzskulptur herauskam.
MS Die Skulptur heißt *Antrieb 2* ↗130/131. Es ist ein Getriebegehäuse mit einem menschlichen Herz aus Salzstein. Das Herz treibt den Kreislauf eines Menschen an und es ist mit dem Getriebe eines Fahrzeugs verbunden. Dabei geht es um Kraft, was gibt die Energie, was ist die Motivation. So ähnlich wie bei der Schmetterlingsarbeit.
NW Es gibt noch eine andere interessante Frage: Was treibt was an? Ich frage mich das im Bezug auf das Buch *Eine kurze Geschichte der Menschheit,* in dem Yuval Noah Harari die landwirtschaftliche Revolution beschreibt und wie die Menschheit anfing, die Natur zu kontrollieren und Agrargüter als Massenware zu produzieren, besonders Getreide. Und dann kehrt er es um und sieht es vom Standpunkt des Getreides aus und dann kontrolliert das Getreide die Menschen. Aus der Sicht des genetischen Überlebens ist das Getreide der Gewinner. Solche Umkehrungen werden im Hinblick auf dein Werk sehr interessant und darauf, was was bedingt. Und besonders auf den anderen Gedanken, den ich in deinen Arbeiten sehe, den der Entropie und wie sie umgedreht werden könnte. Wie wir den Fluss der Energie kontrollieren. Und offenbar ist bei den *Brenner*-Skulpturen der Kreislauf der Thermodynamik ein Effekt. Aber ich denke auch an emotionale Entropie und an emotionalen Verlust.
MS Welche Arbeiten meinst du?
NW Ich denke an die Arbeit *Tränen*, als tatsächliche Version davon, aber vielleicht handeln die Tränen und die anderen Dinge von emotionaler Entropie, von der Verschwendung von Gefühlen in der Welt.

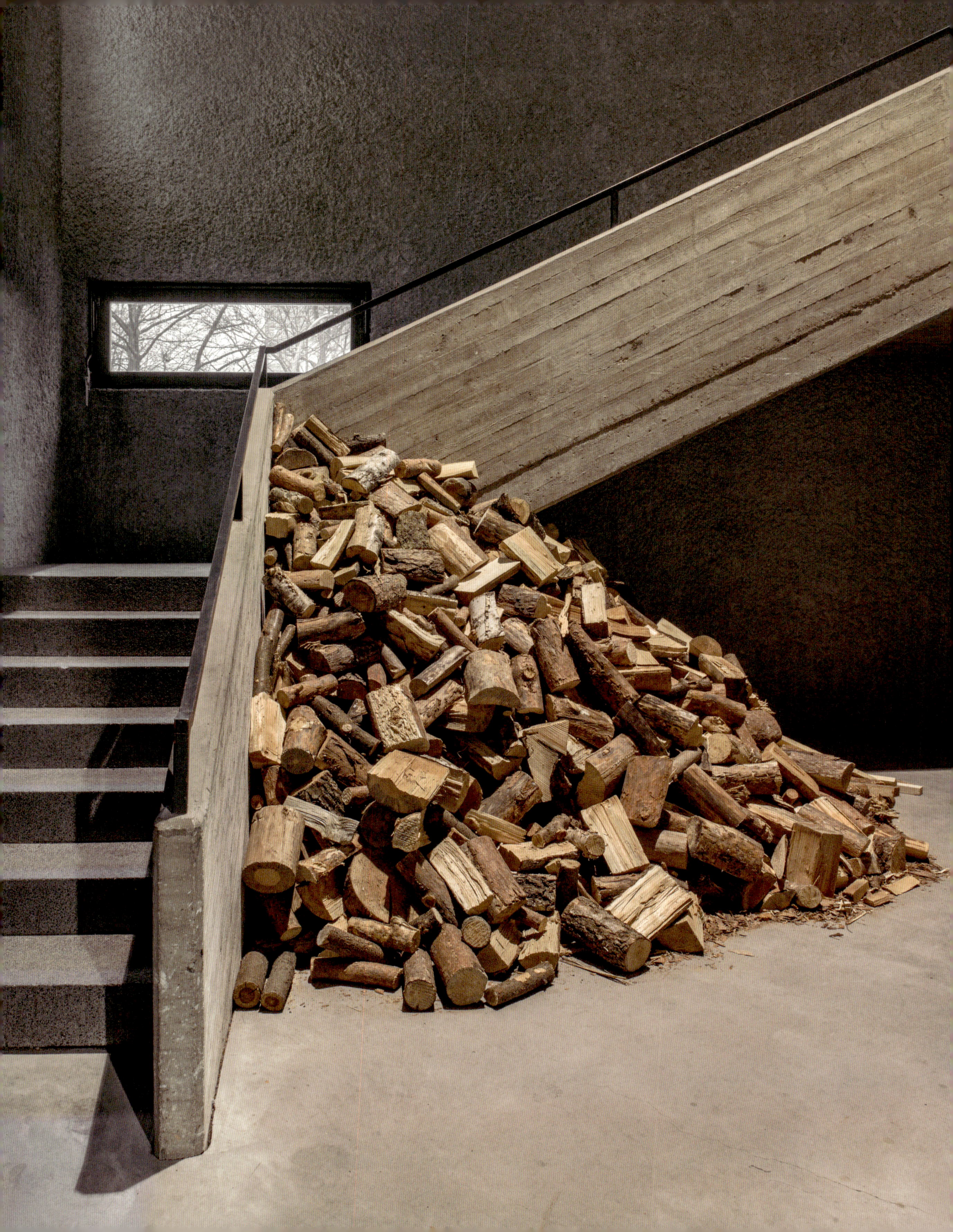

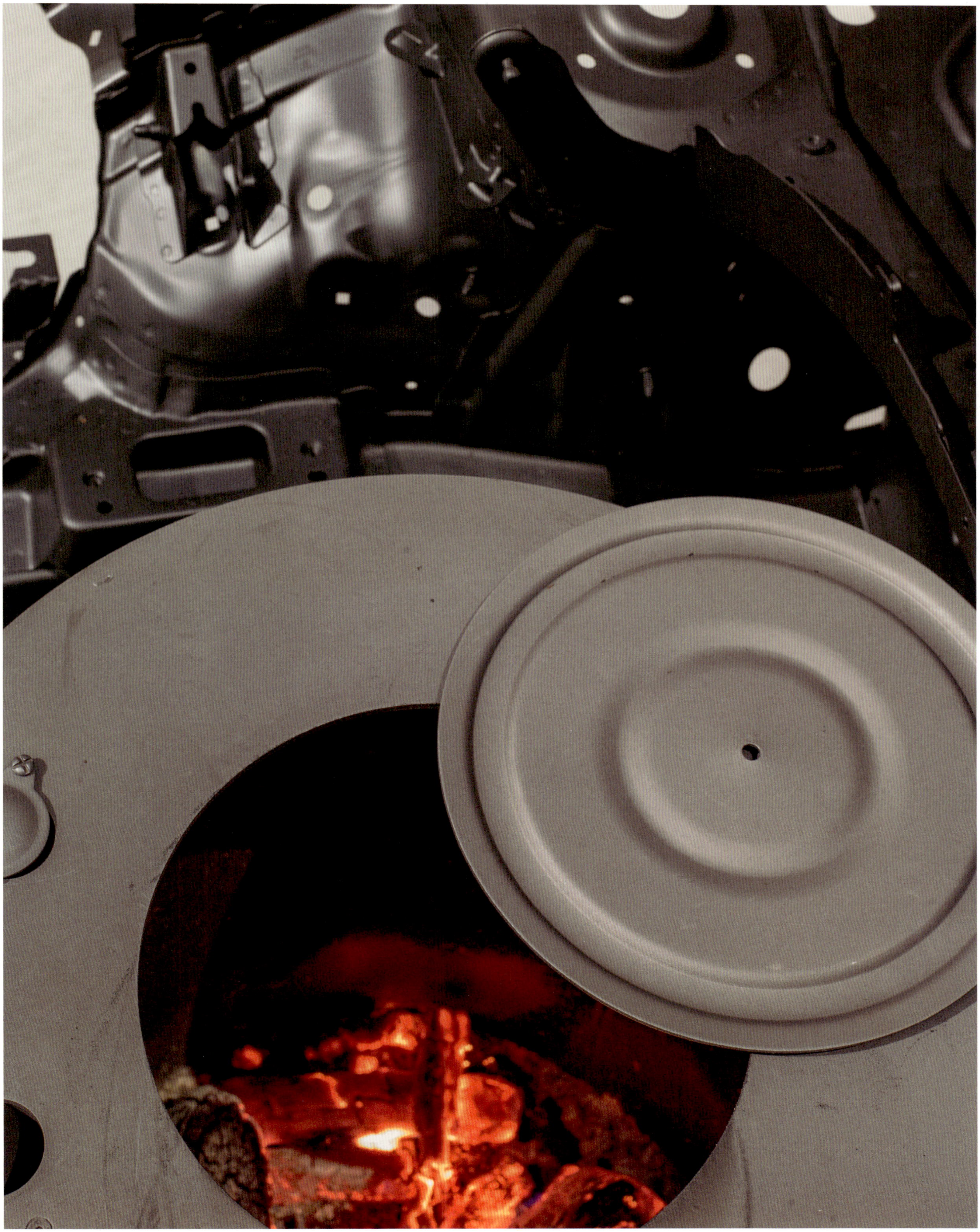

Brenner, 2017

Steel, paint, wood / Stahl, Farbe, Holz,
Dimensions variable / Maße variabel

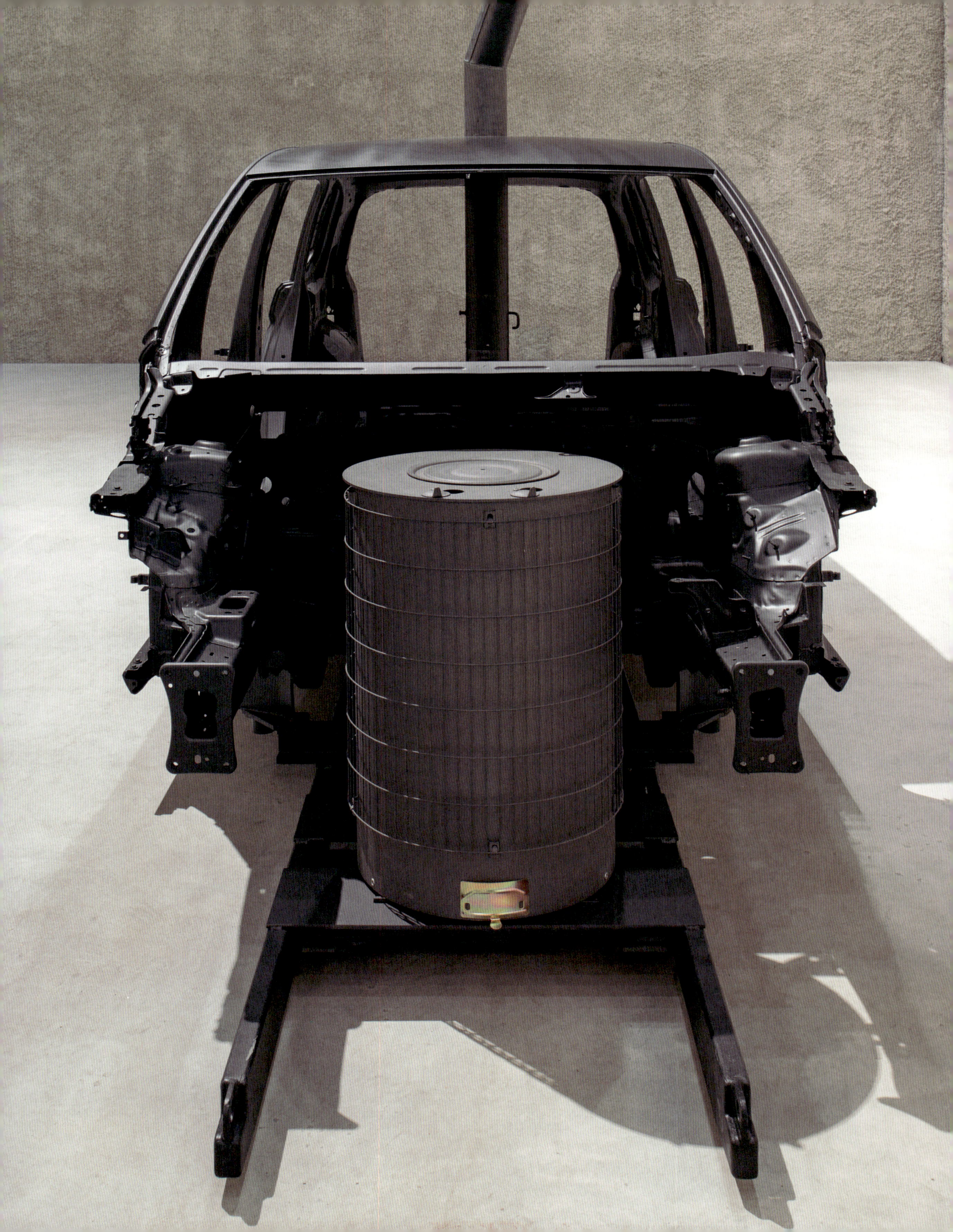

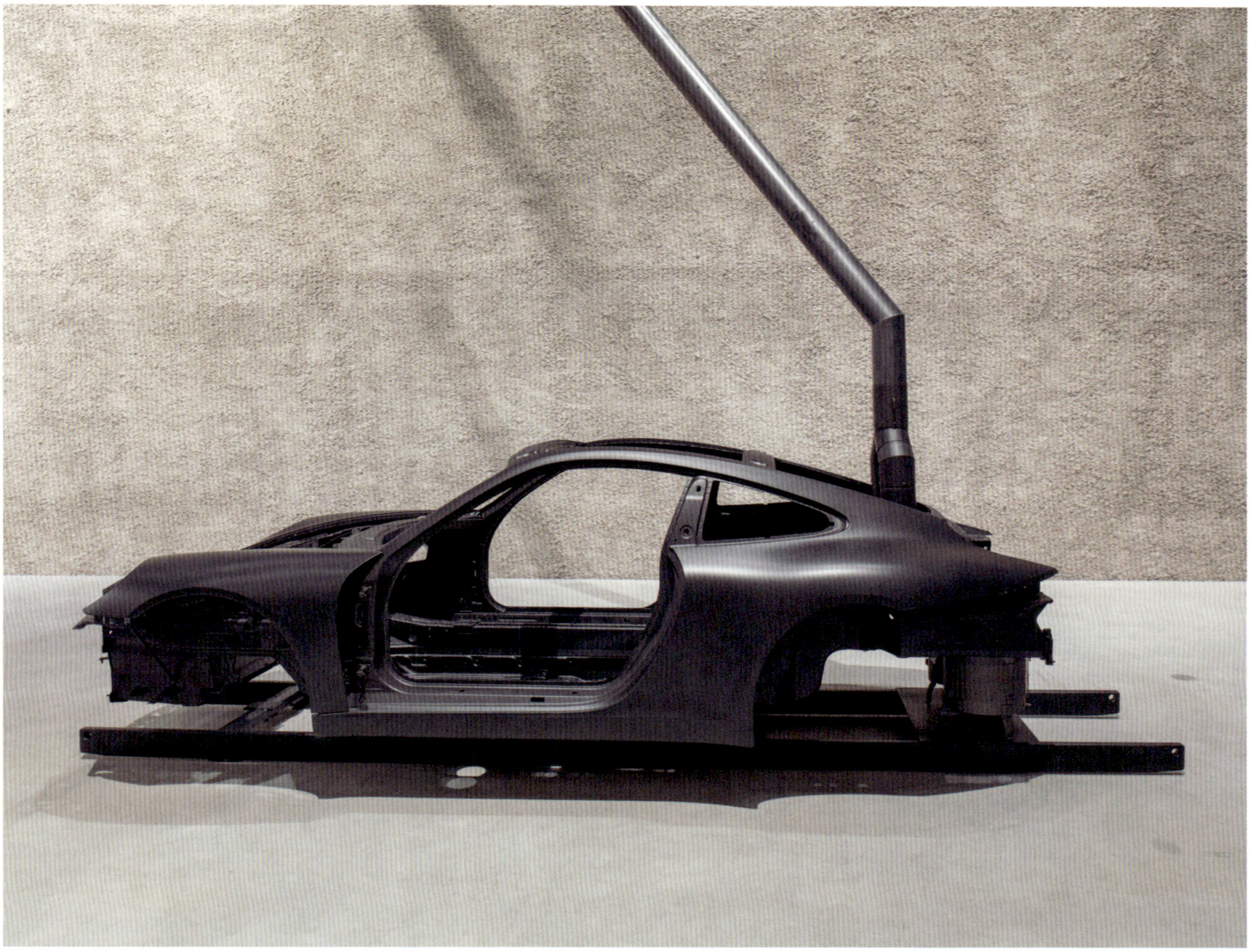

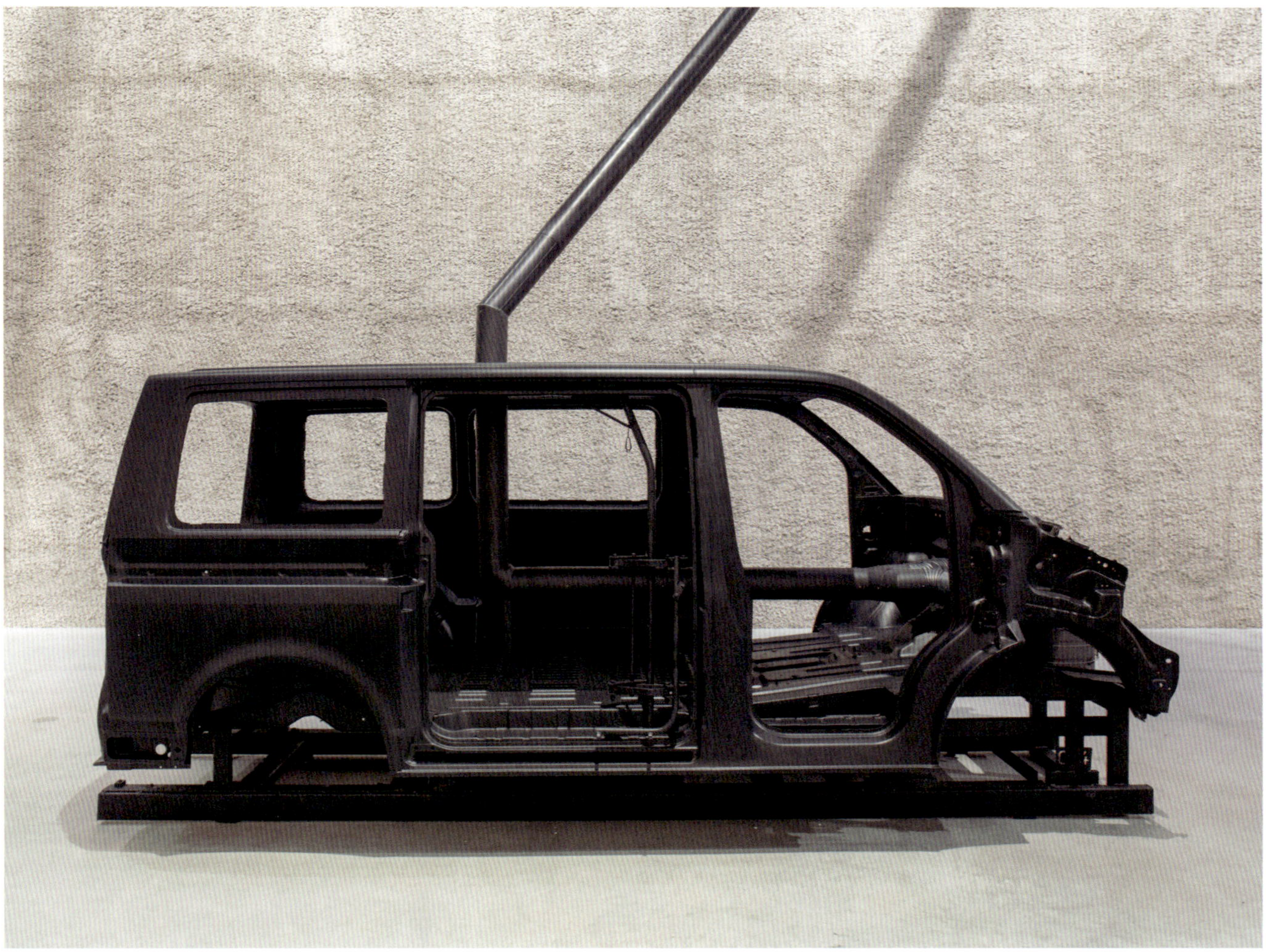

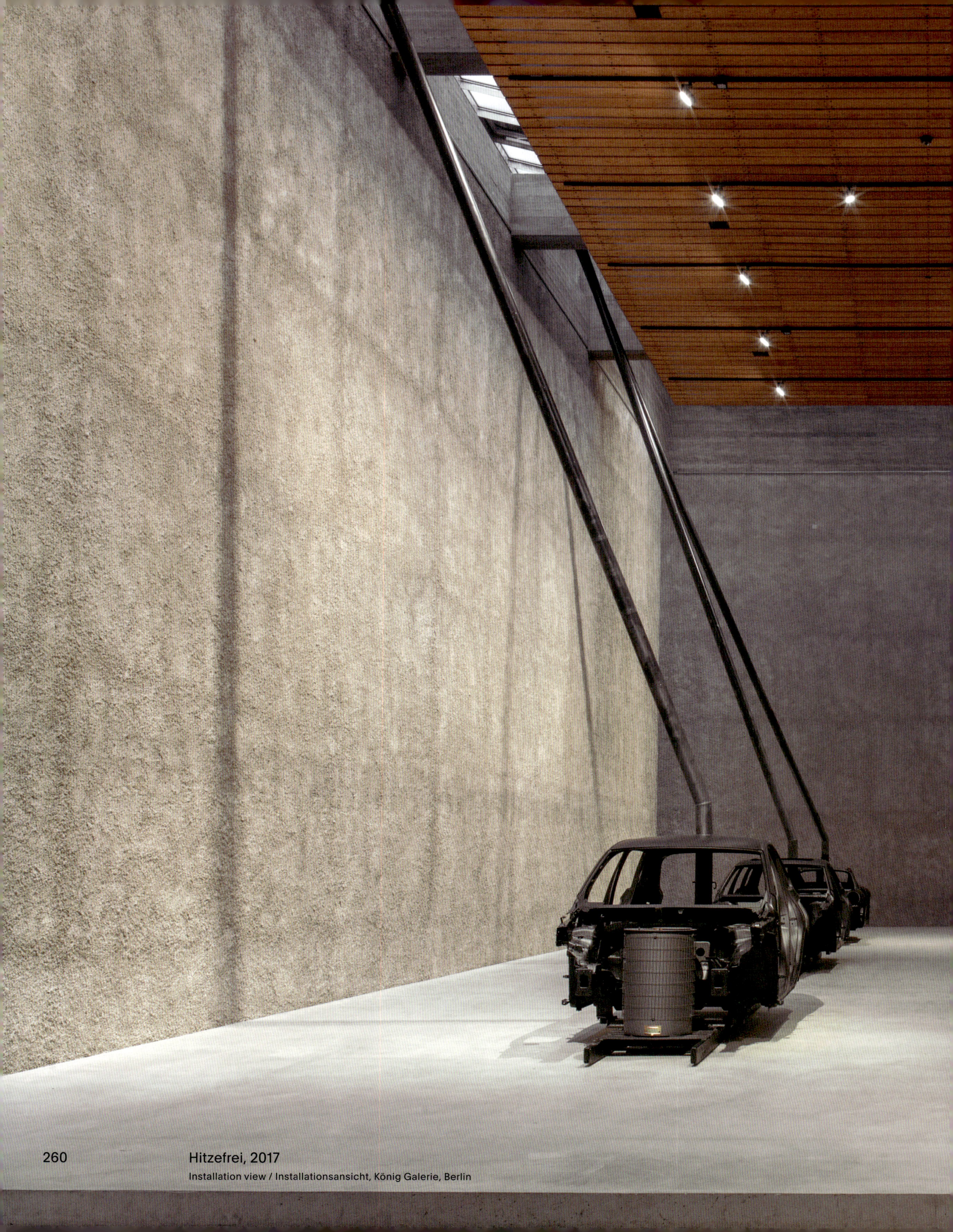

Hitzefrei, 2017
Installation view / Installationsansicht, König Galerie, Berlin

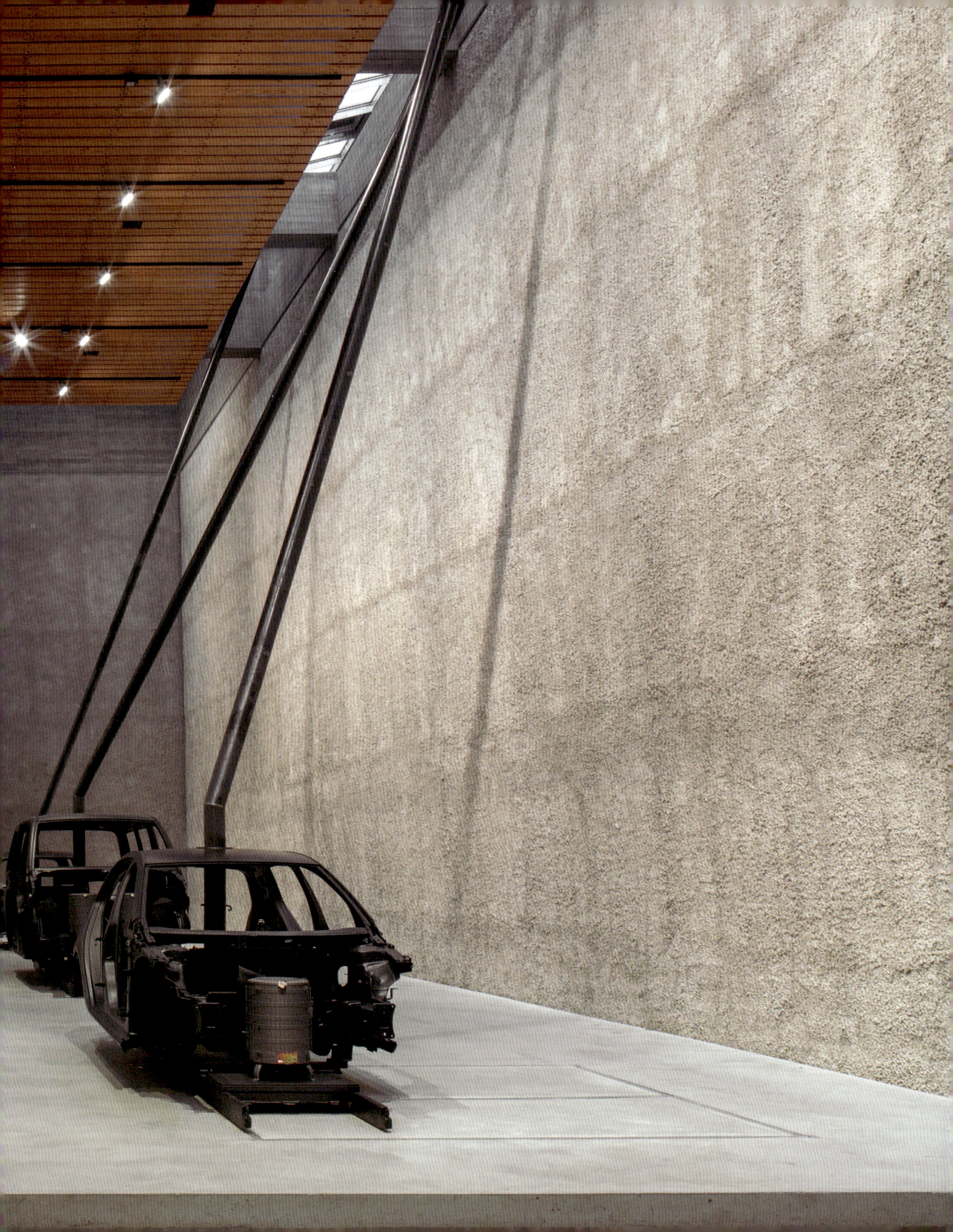

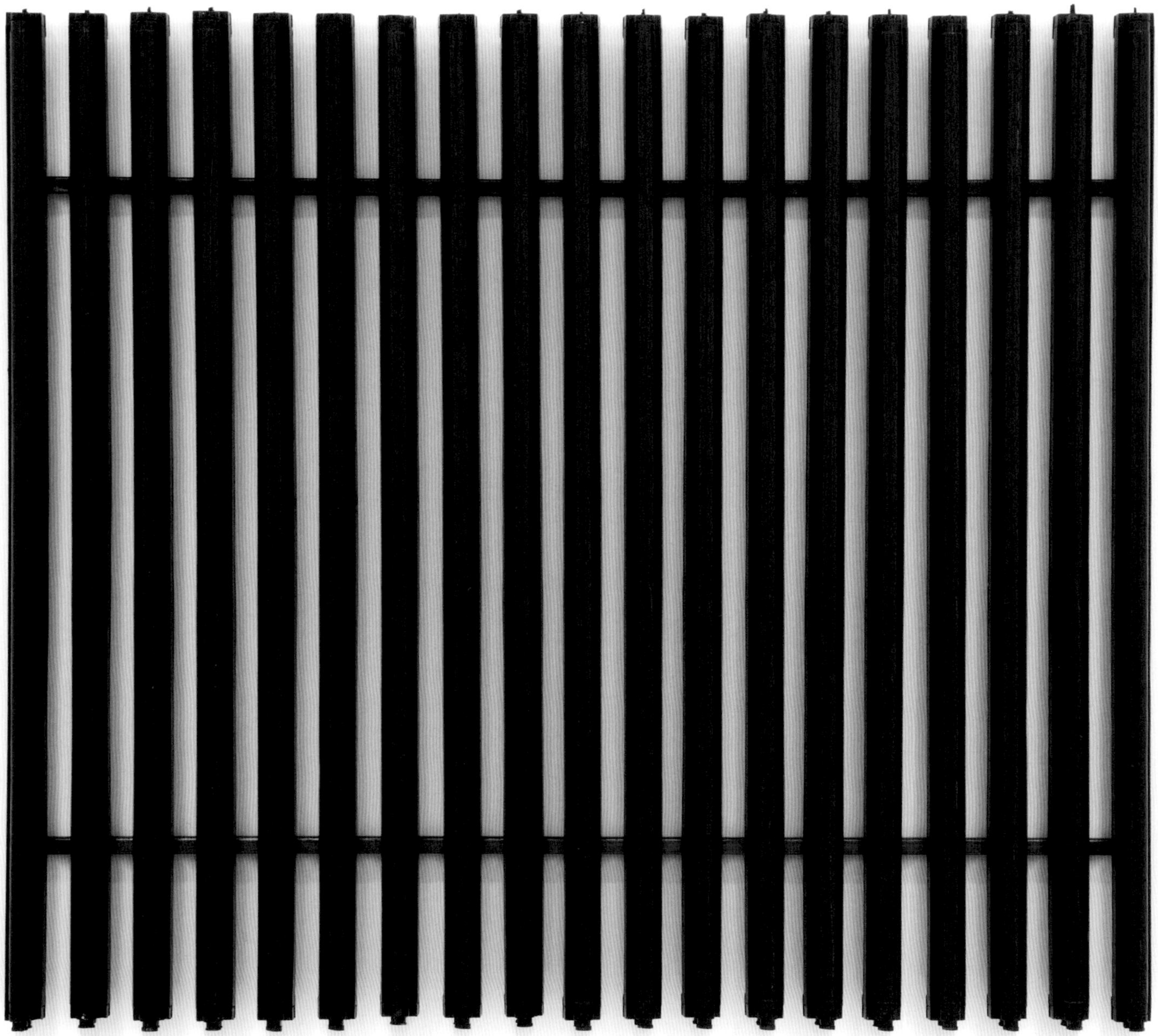

262

No Light (pb), 2009

Polyurethan, steel / Polyurethan, Stahl, 125 × 132 × 10 cm

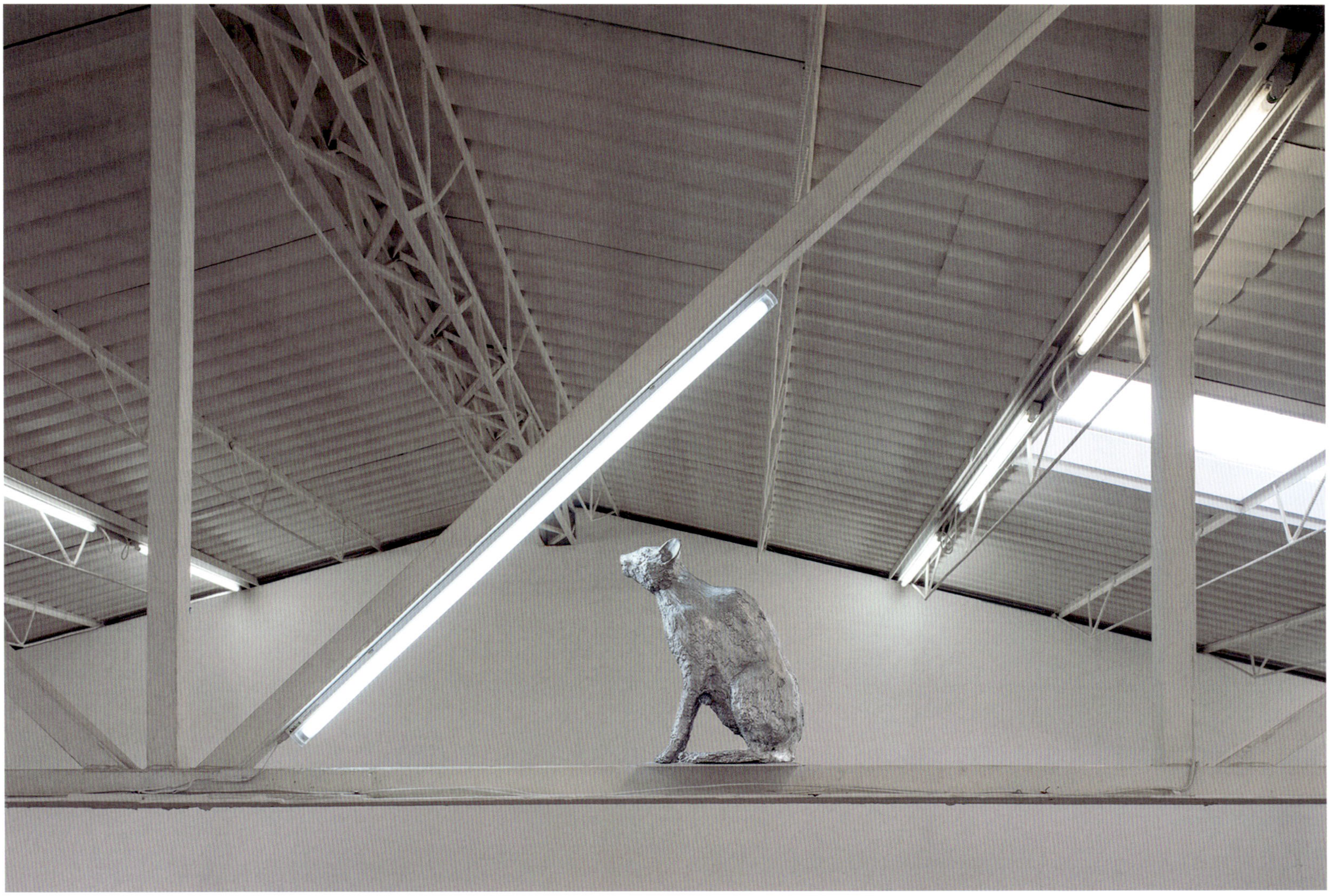

Solarkatze Monclova, 2017

Aluminum, neon tubes / Aluminium, Neonröhren, 40 × 33 × 24 cm

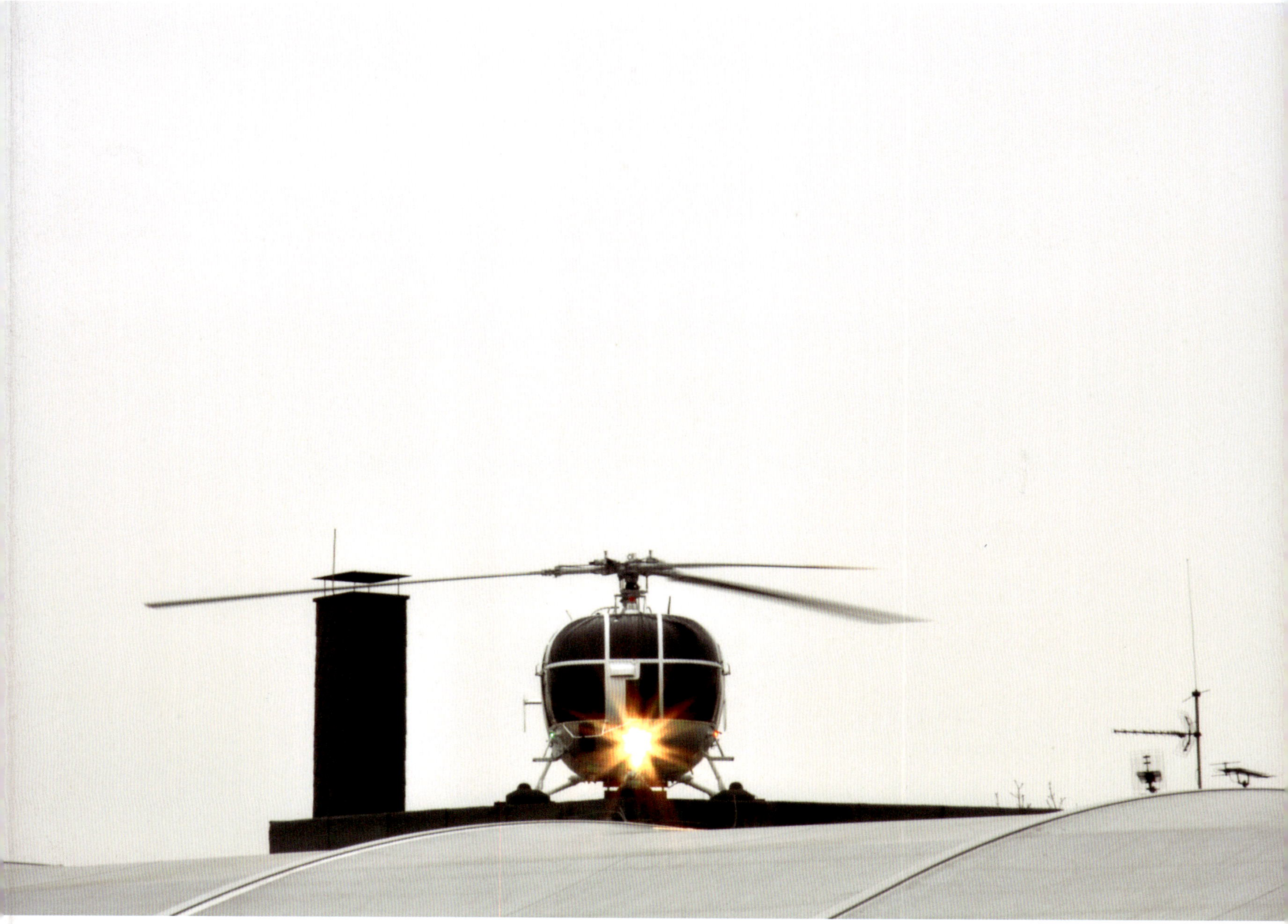

Hoher Besuch, Köln, 2009

Helicopter, electric motor, paint / Hubschrauber, Elektromotor, Farbe,
300 × 960 × 1.290 cm, Installation view / Installationsansicht, Skulpturenpark, Köln

Mückenhaus, 2012

Street lamp, aluminum, mosquito net / Straßenlaterne,
Aluminium, Moskitonetz, 320 × 120 × 280 cm

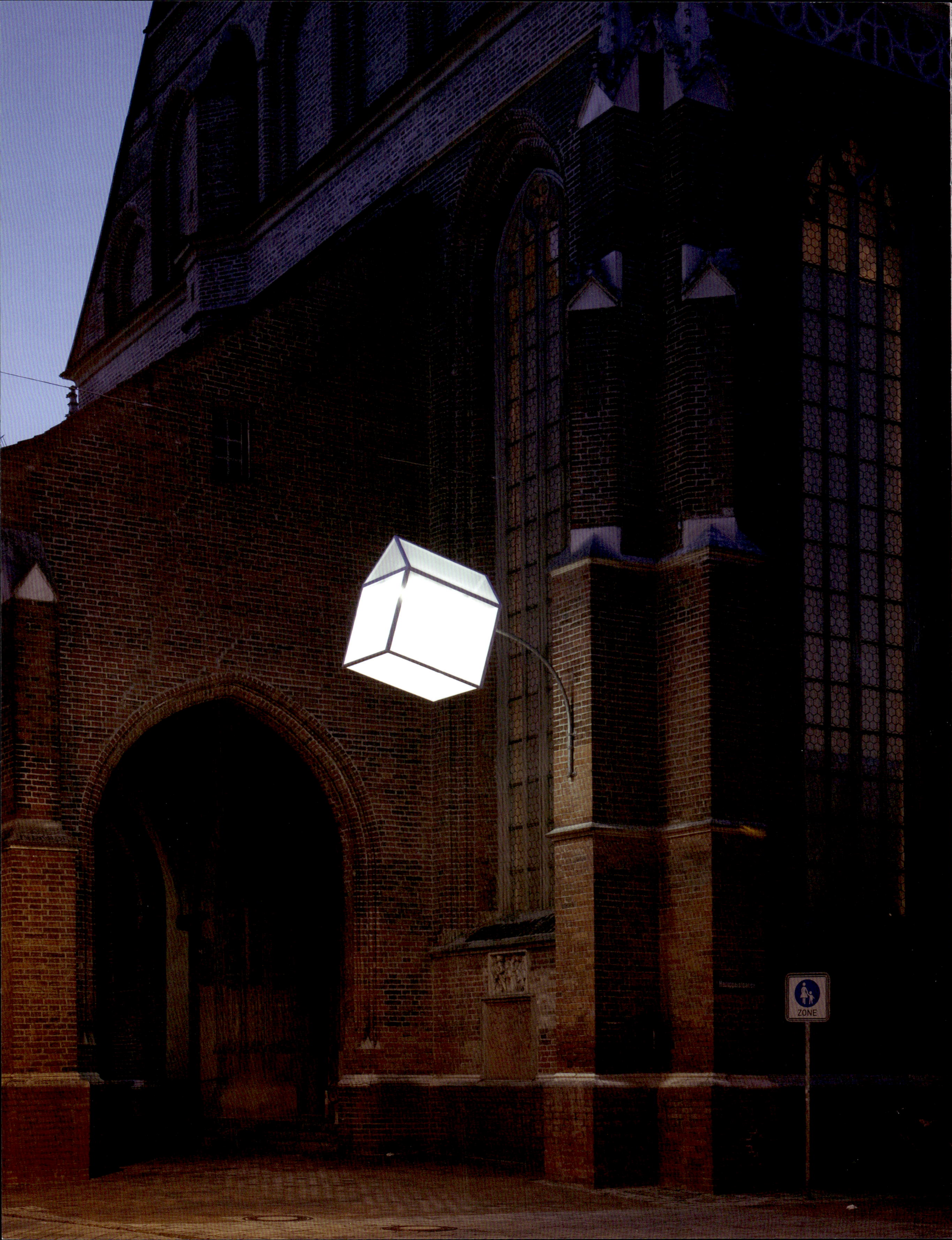
ZONE

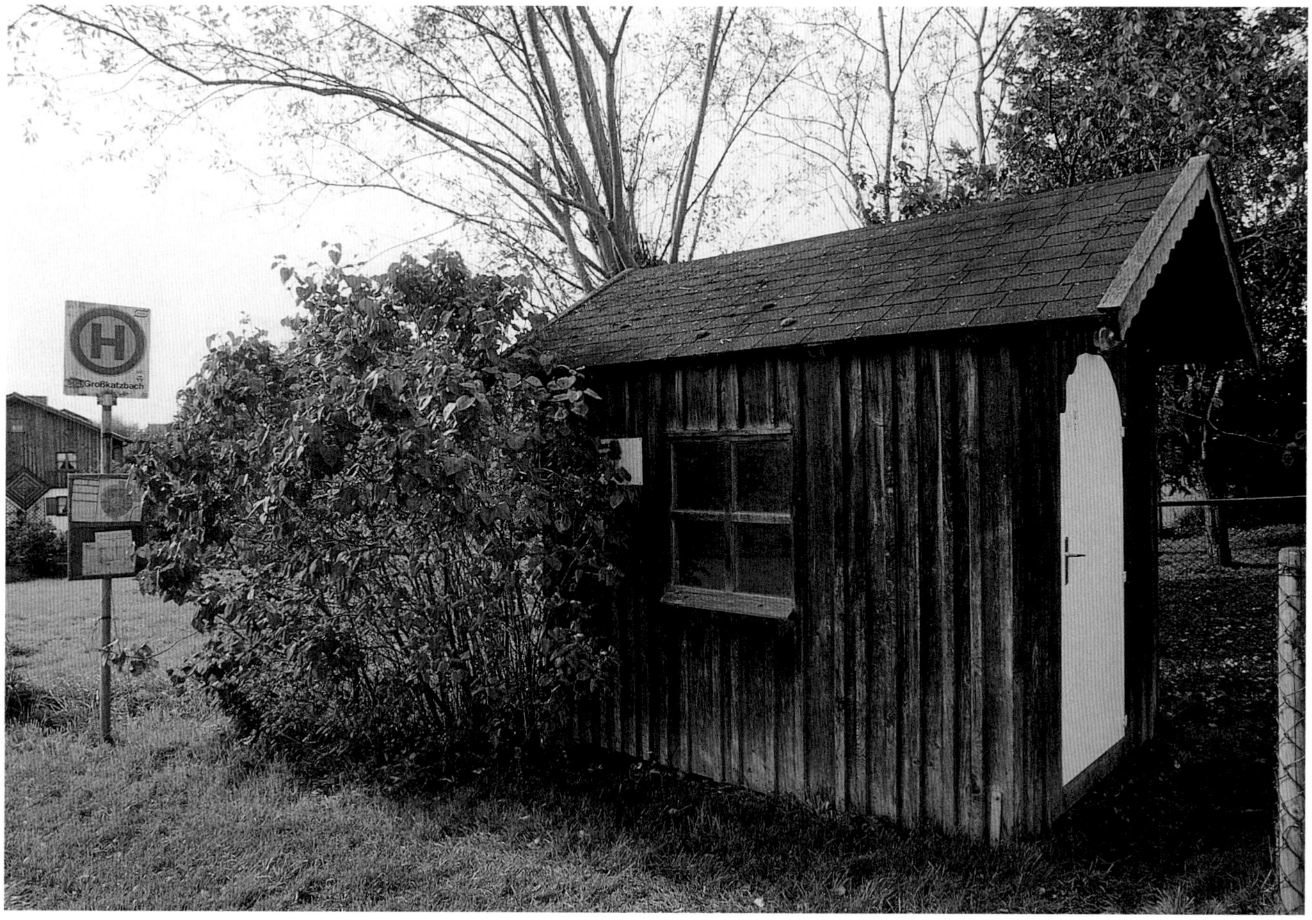

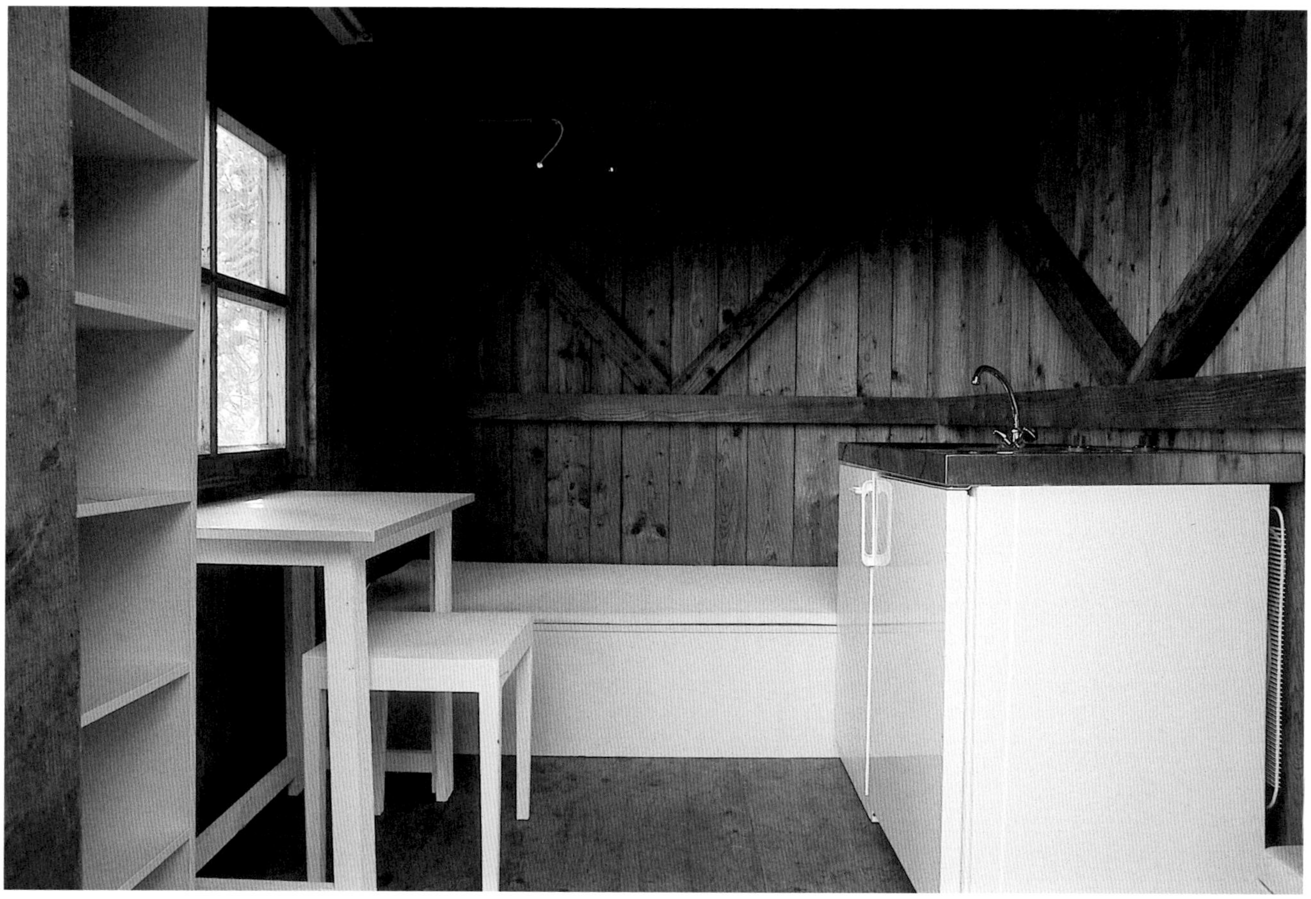

Wohnen mit Verkehrsanbindung, 2001

Bus shelter, bed, kitchen, table, chair, bookcase, toilet, door, light, electricity, water / Bushaltestelle, Bett, Küche, Tisch, Stuhl, Bücherregal, Toilette, Tür, Licht, Elektrizität, Wasser, Dimensions variable / Maße variabel

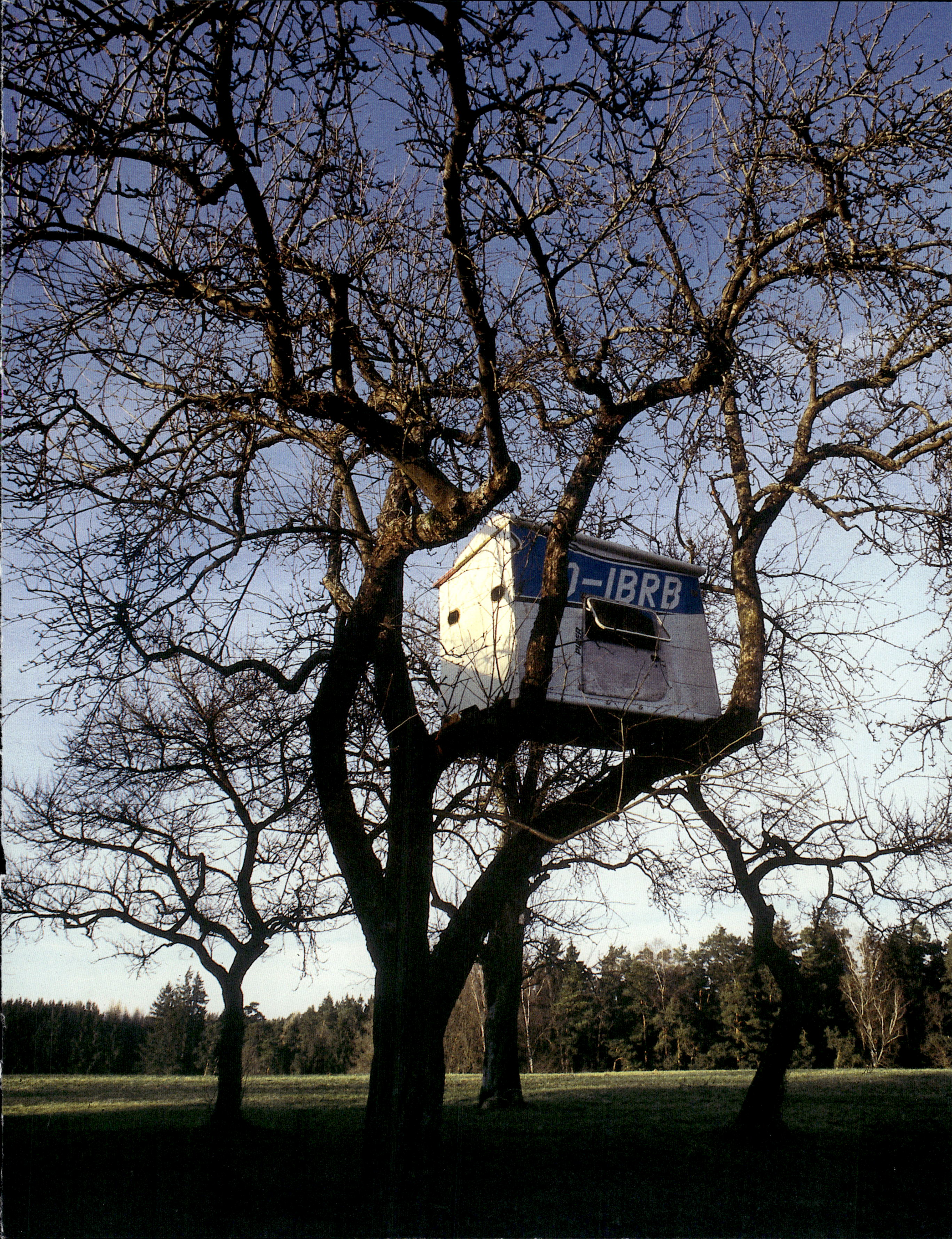
-IBRB

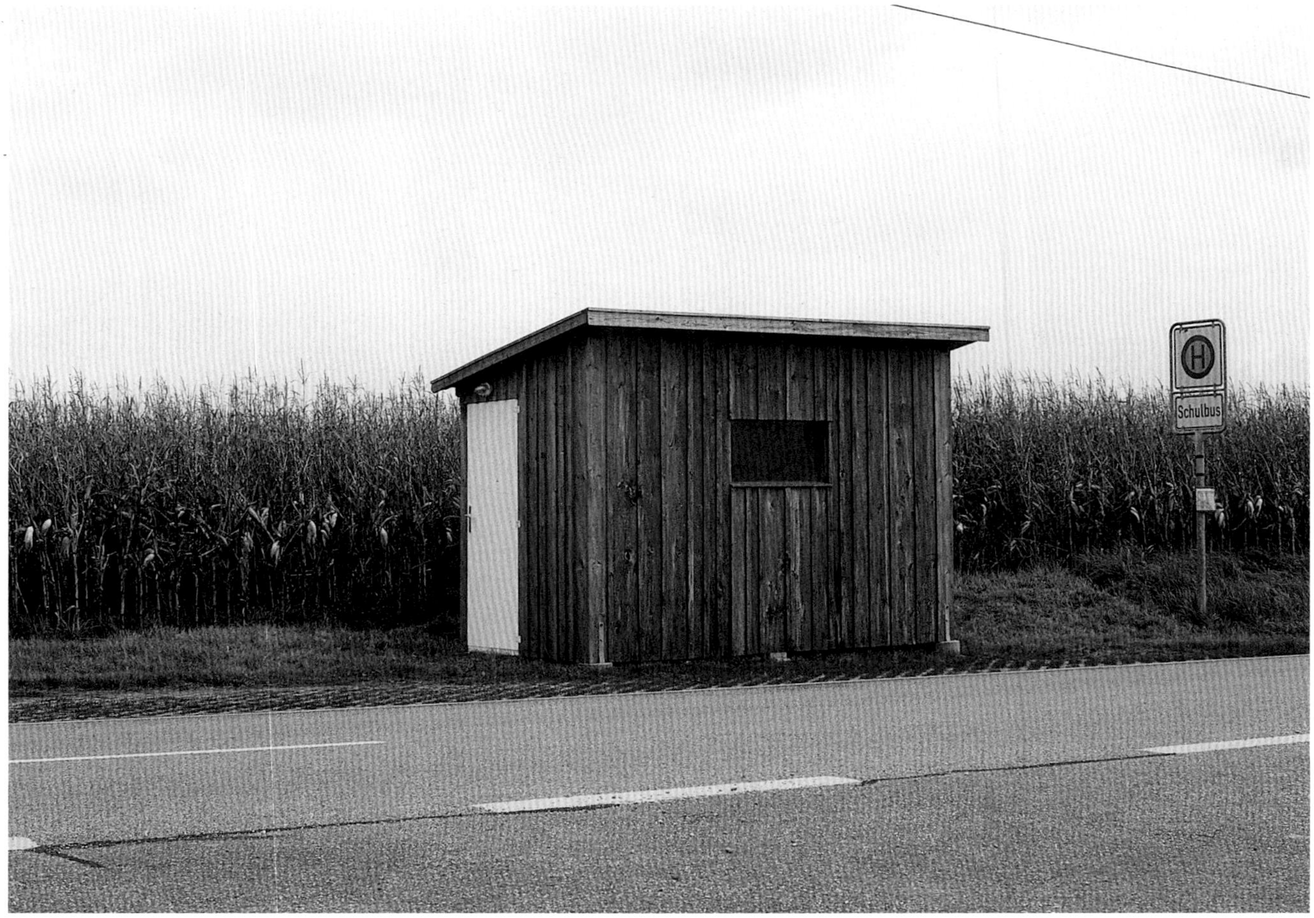
H
Schulbus

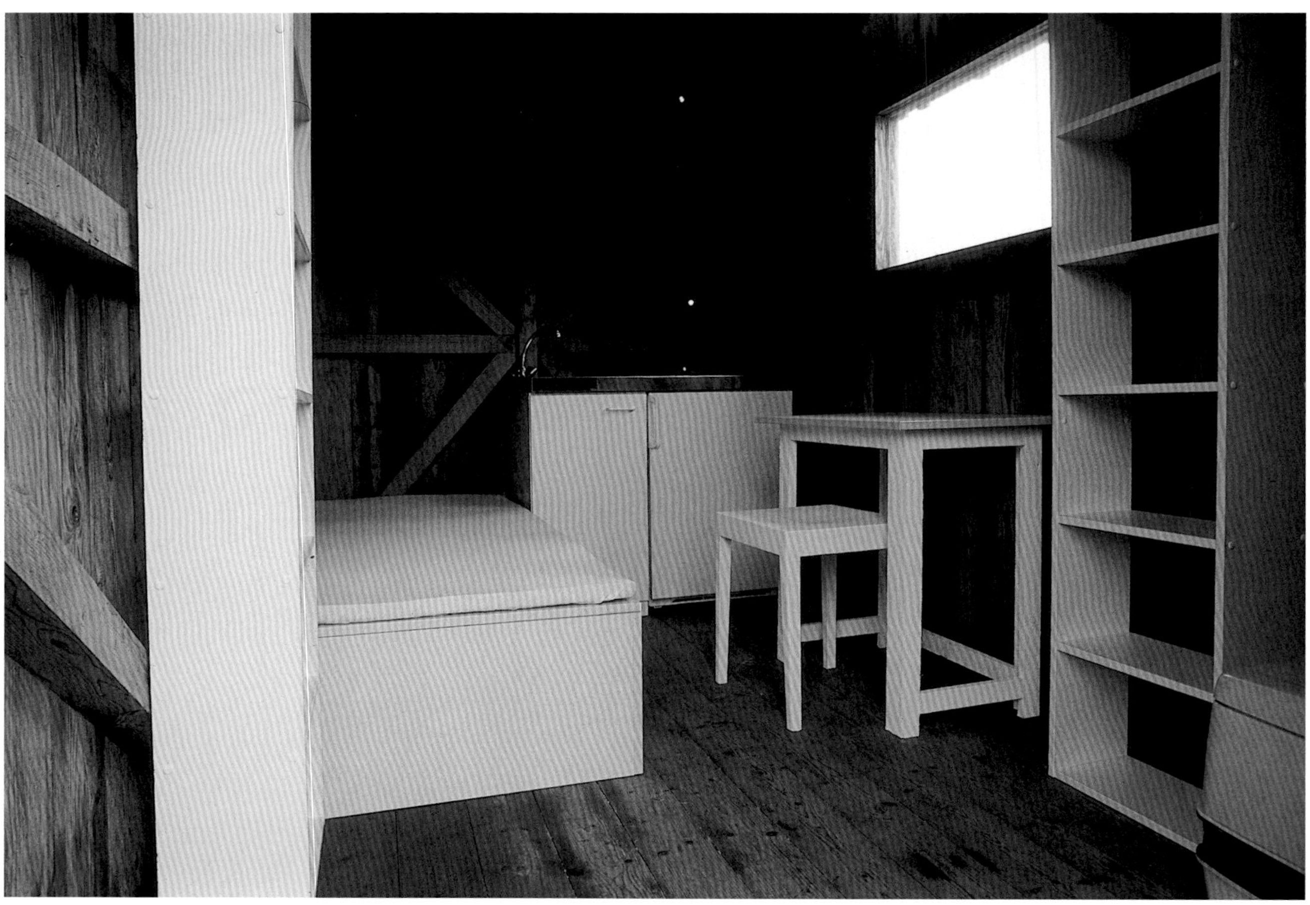

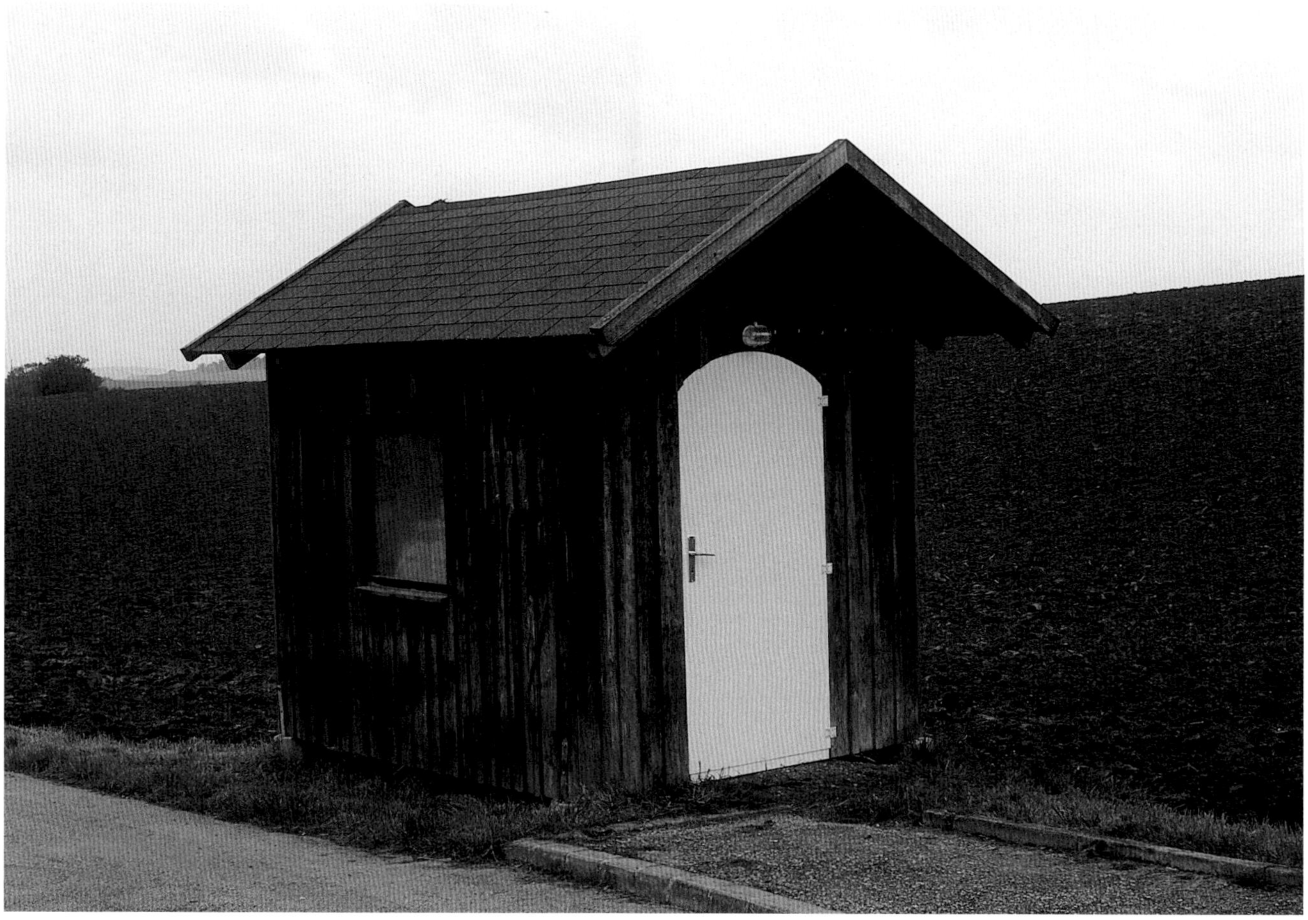

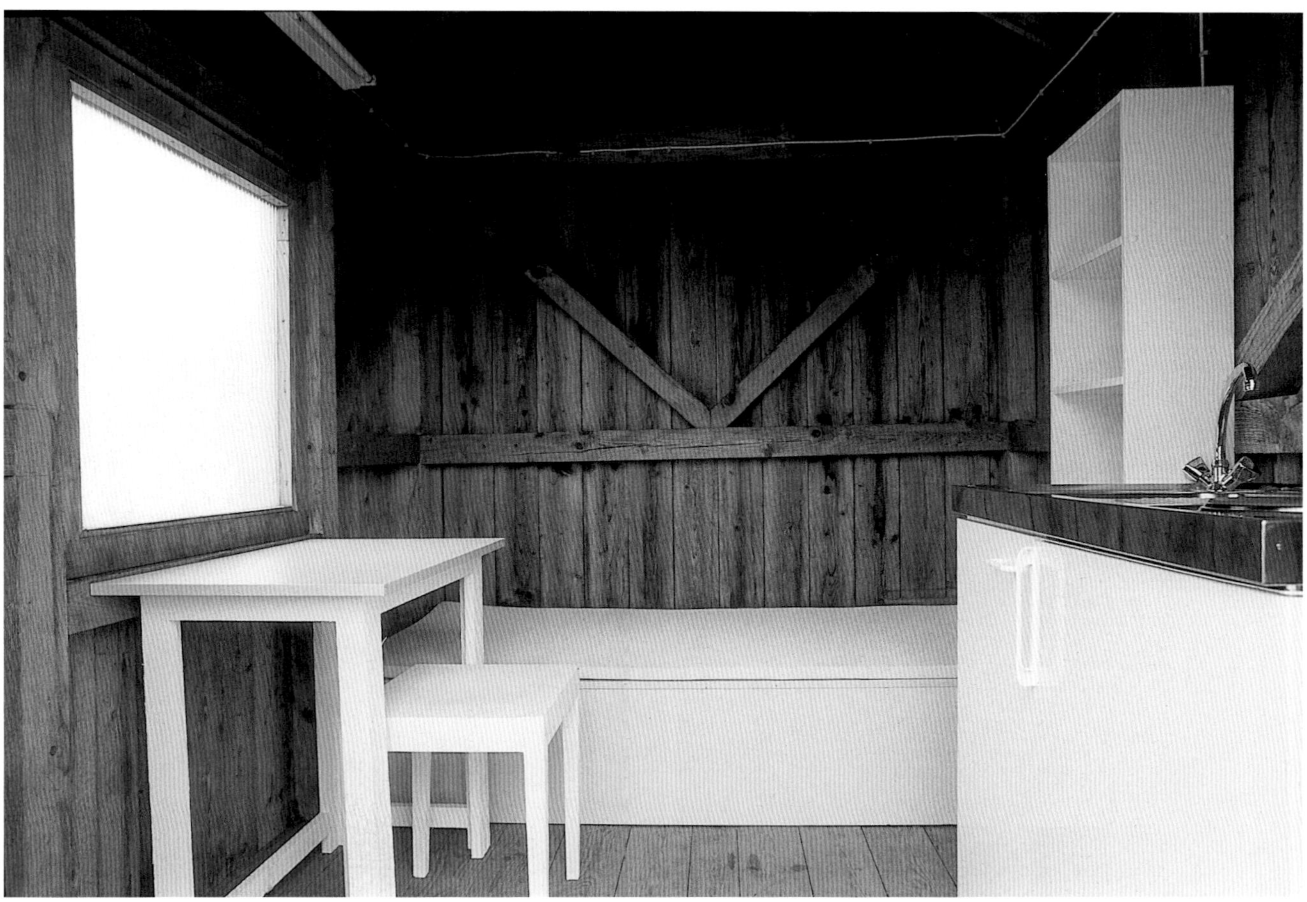

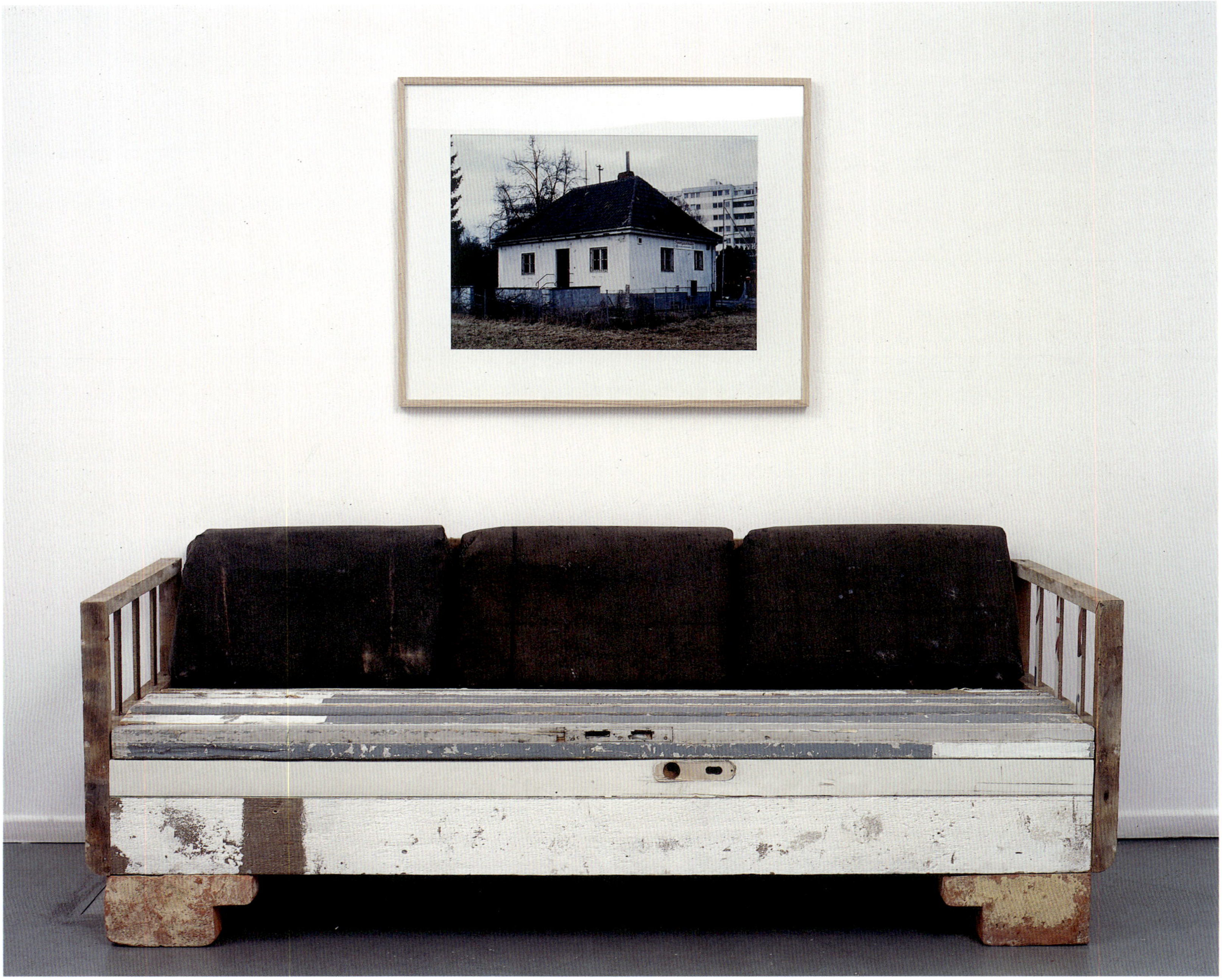

Herterichstraße 119, 2001

Demolition material, photograph, frame / Abbruchmaterial, Fotografie, Rahmen, 175 × 200 × 95 cm

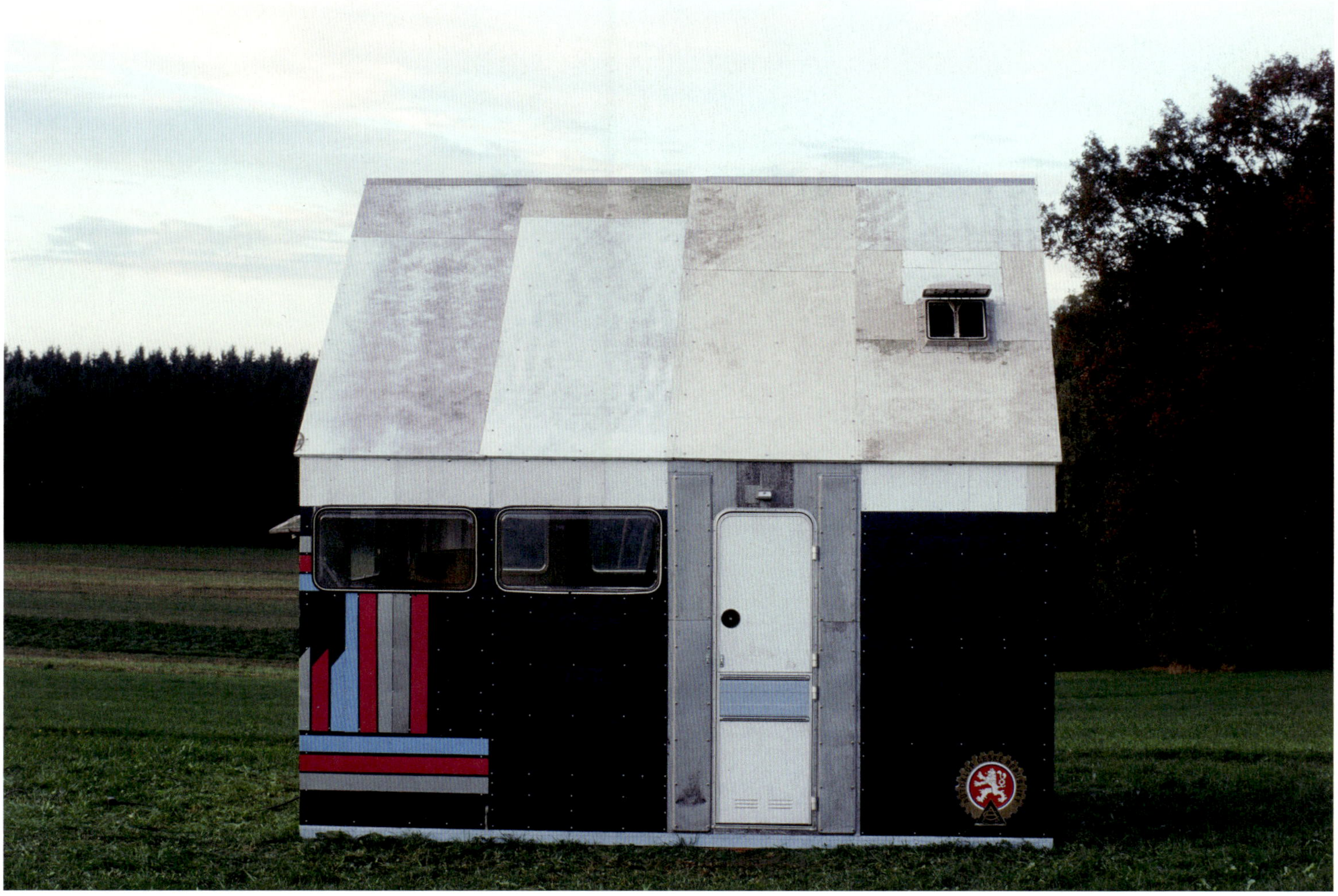

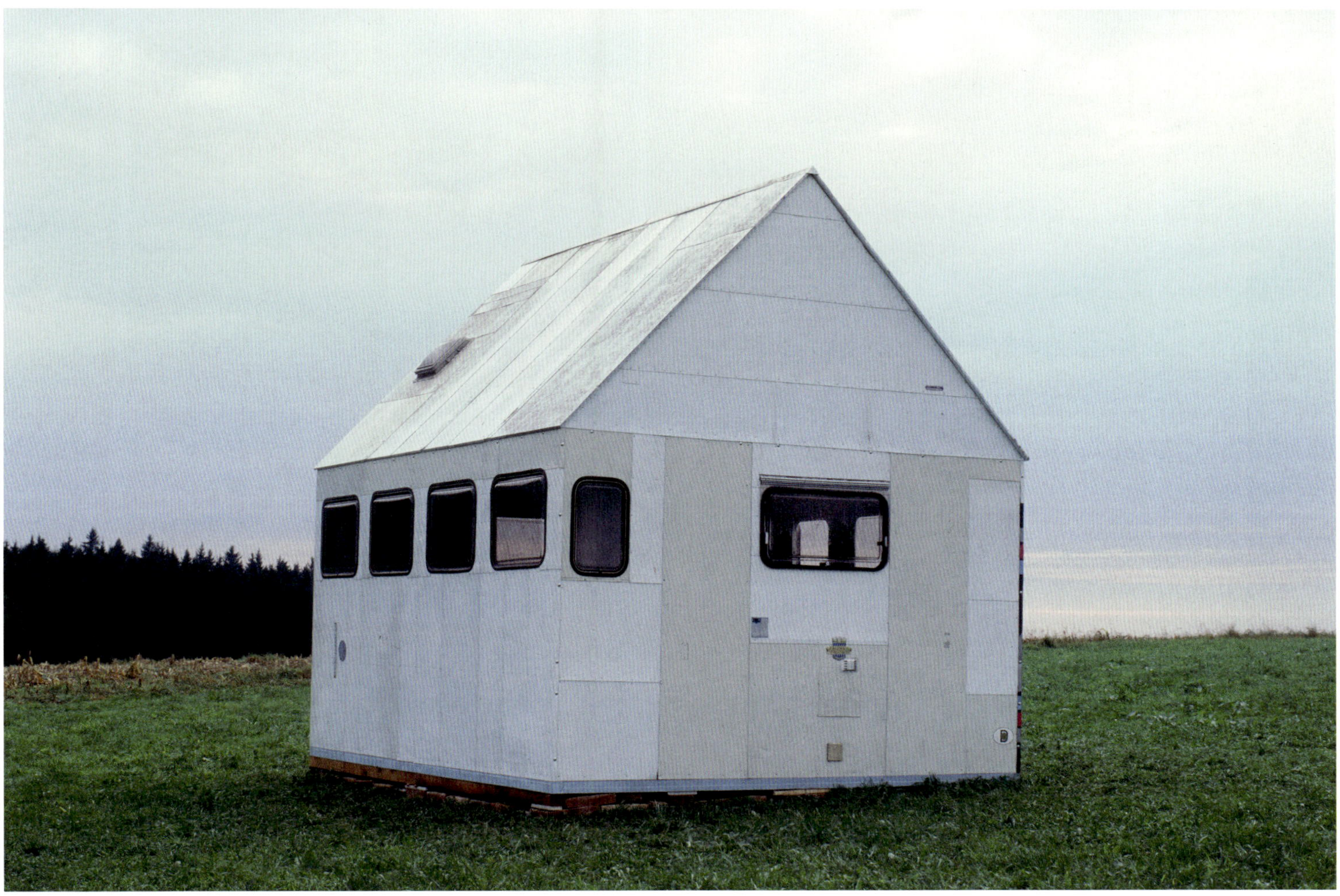

Heimatlied, 2001

4 camper vans, wood, electricity, water / 4 Wohnwagen, Holz, Elektrizität, Wasser, 375 × 360 × 410 cm

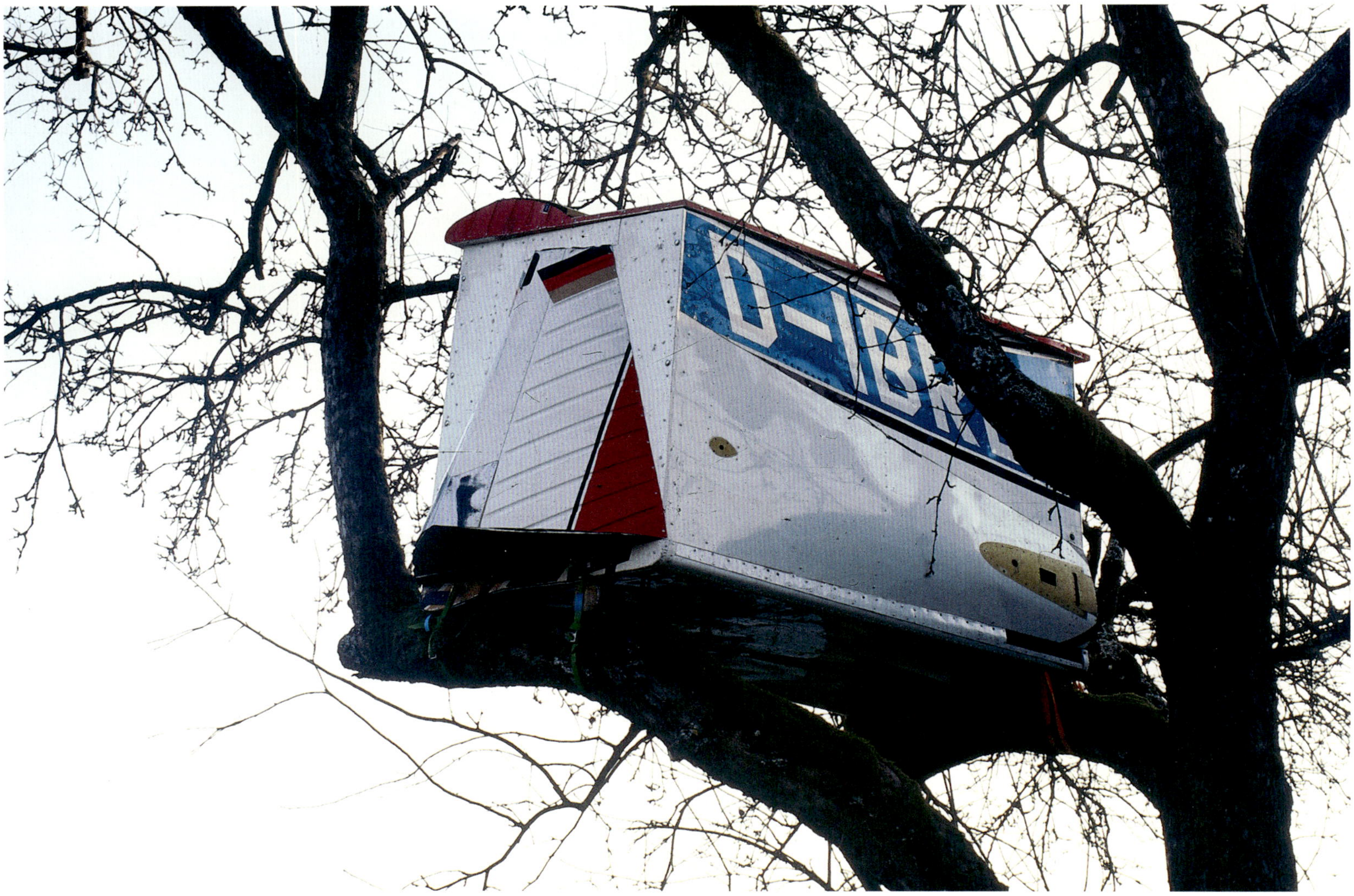

D-IBRB, 2002

Aluminum (airplane), wood / Aluminium (Flugzeug), Holz, 170 × 250 × 120 cm

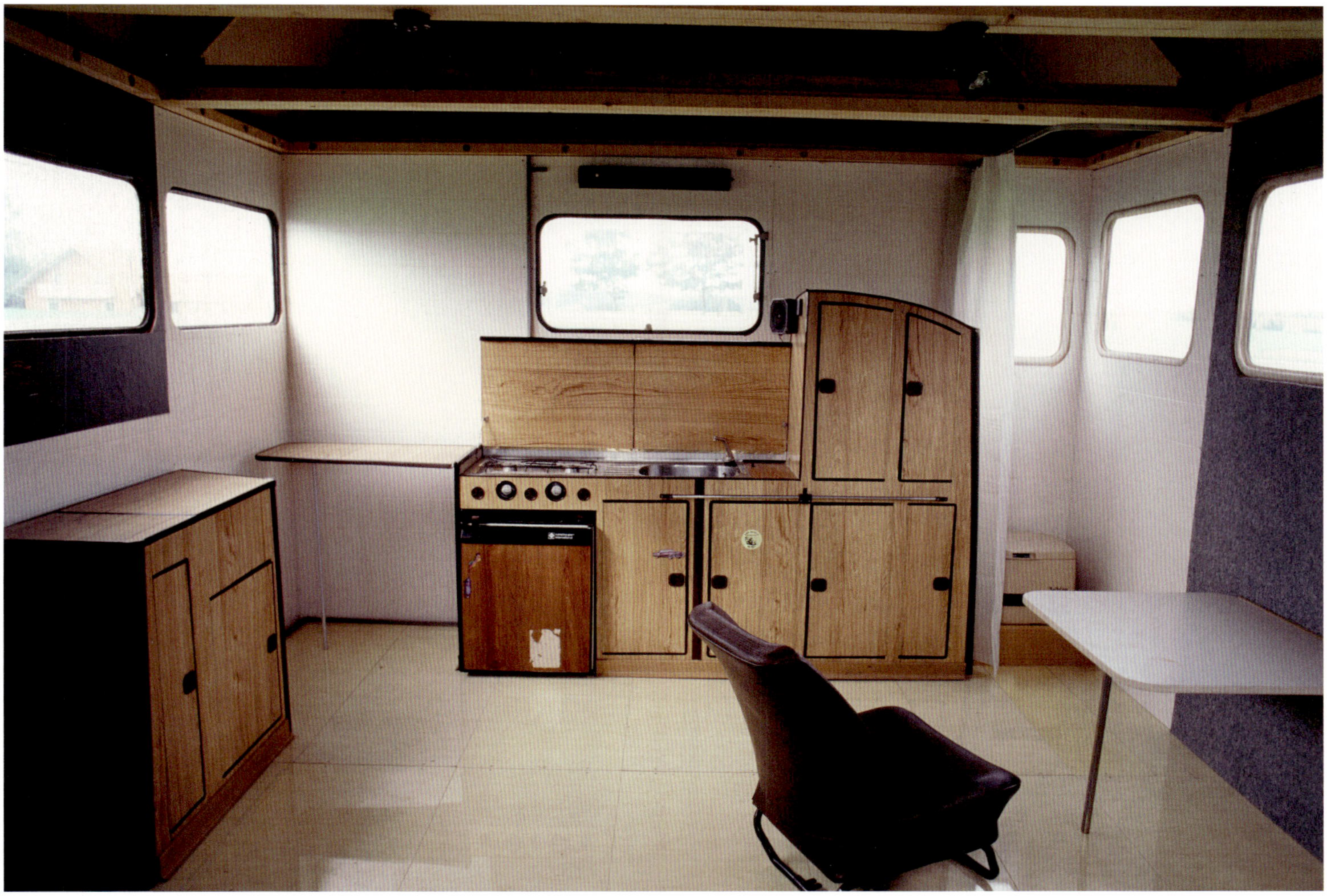

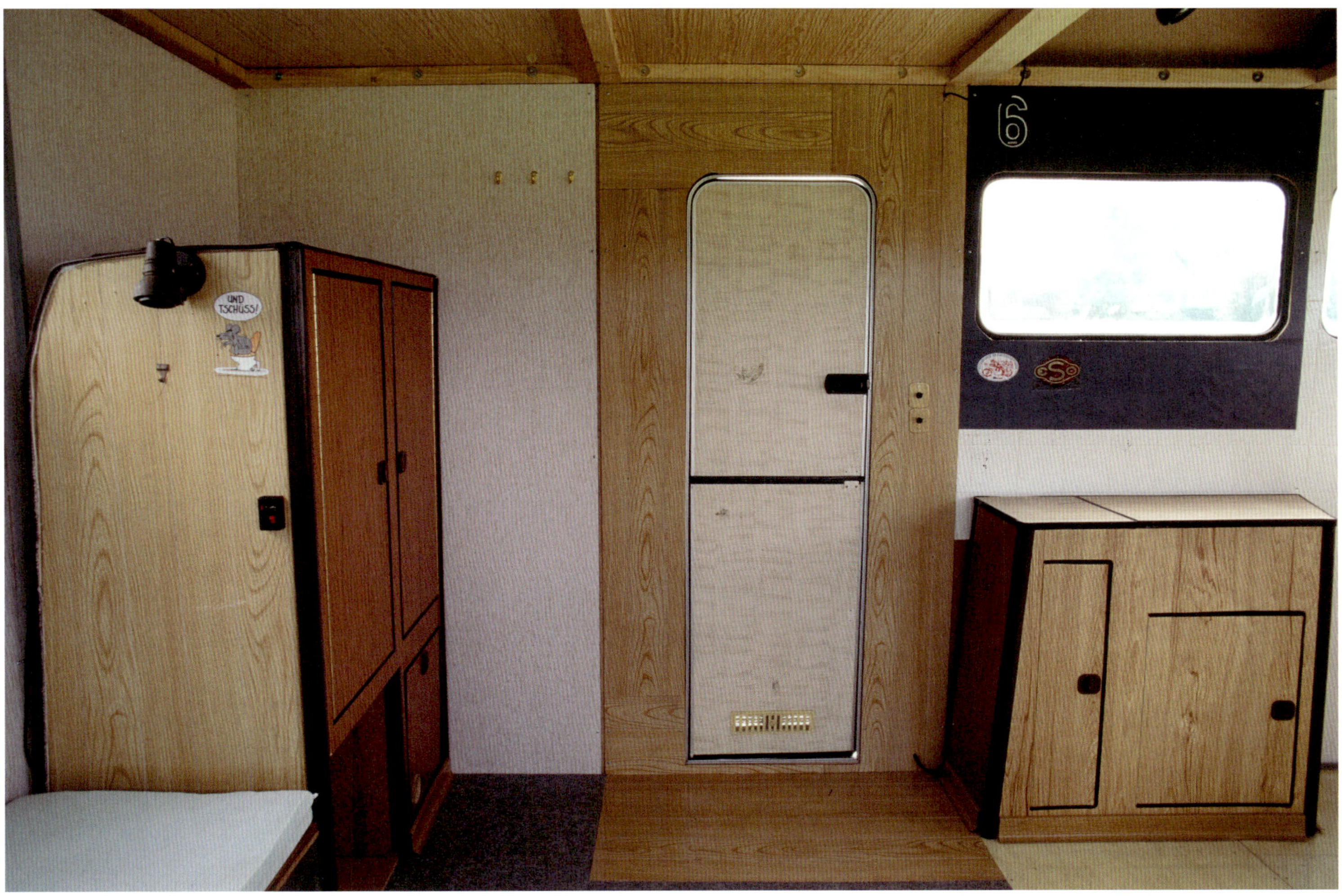
6
UND TSCHÜSS!

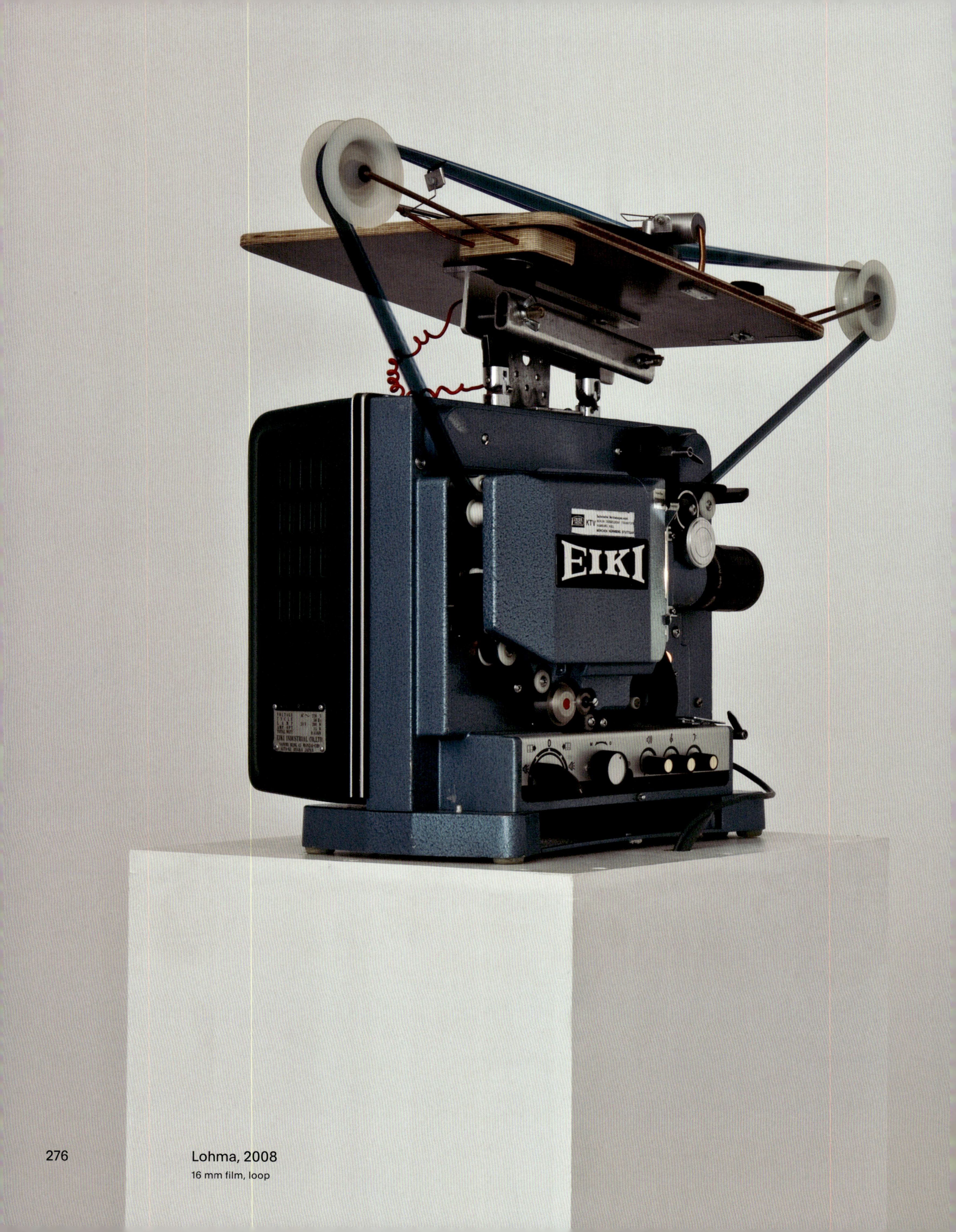

Lohma, 2008
16 mm film, loop

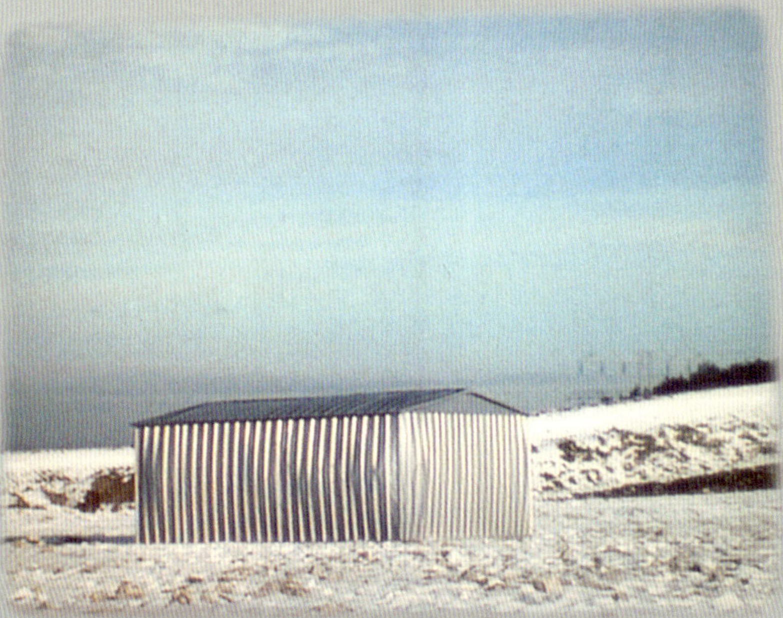

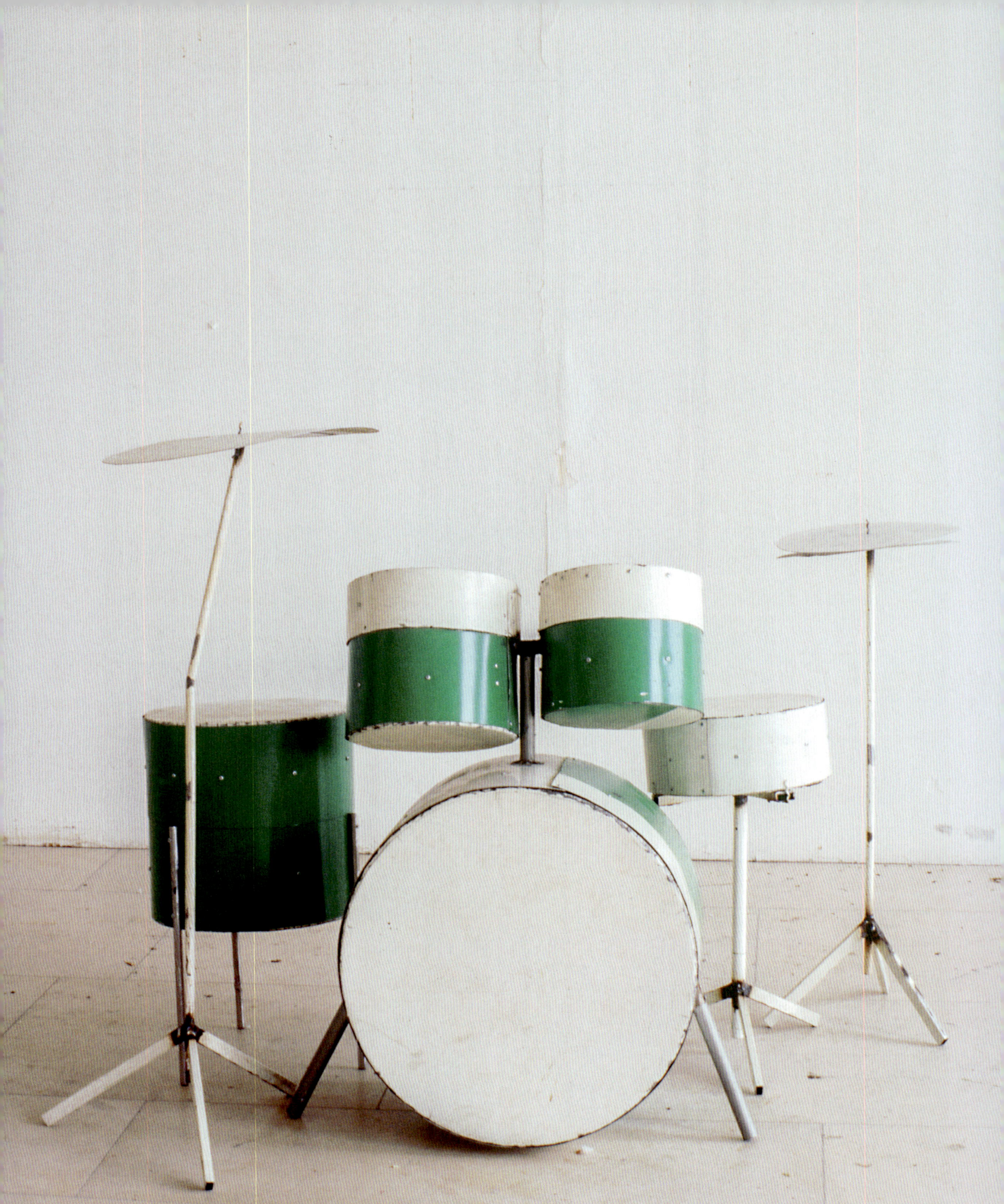

Schlagzeug, 2003

Sheet metal (police bus) / Blech (Polizeibus), 140 × 200 × 135 cm

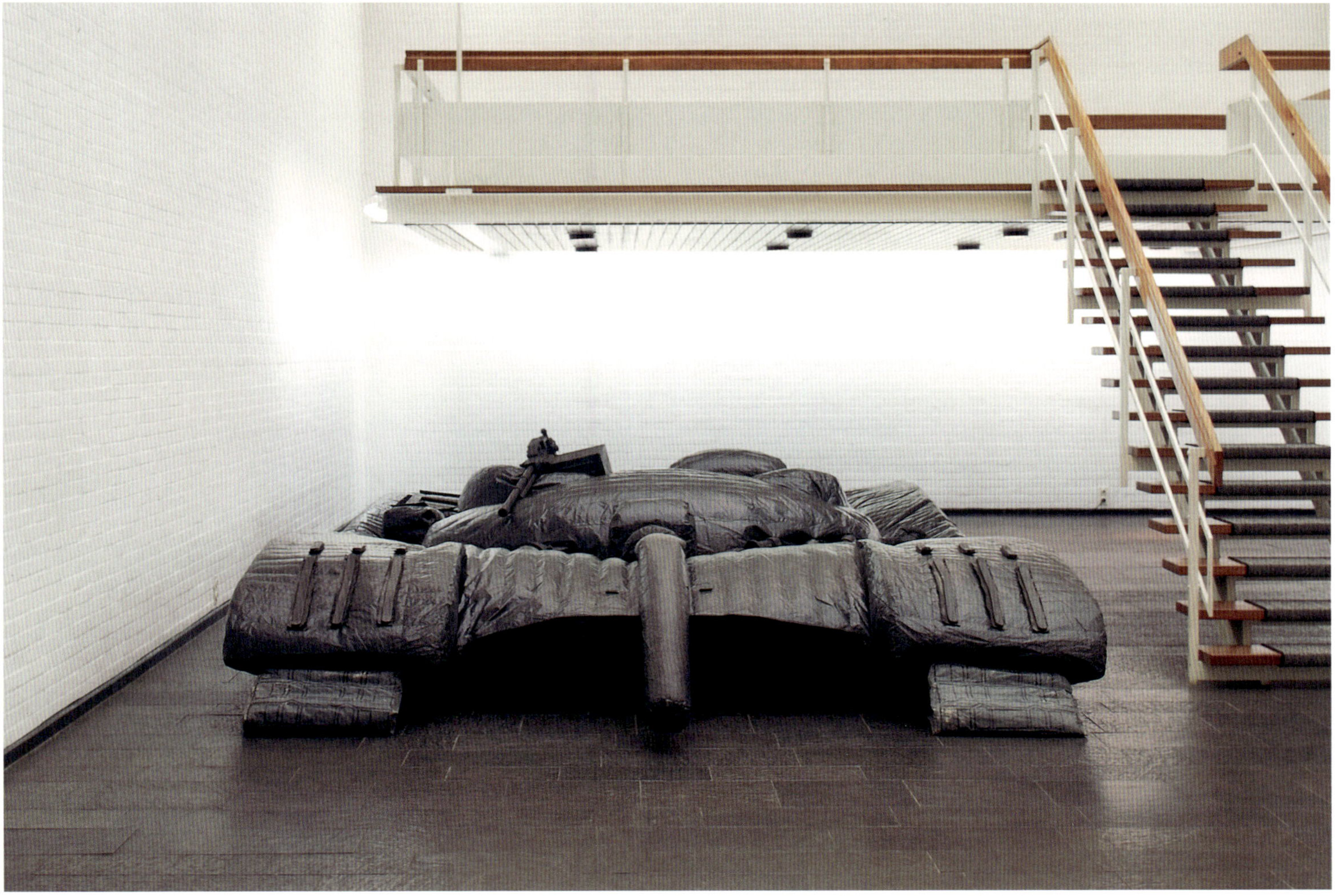

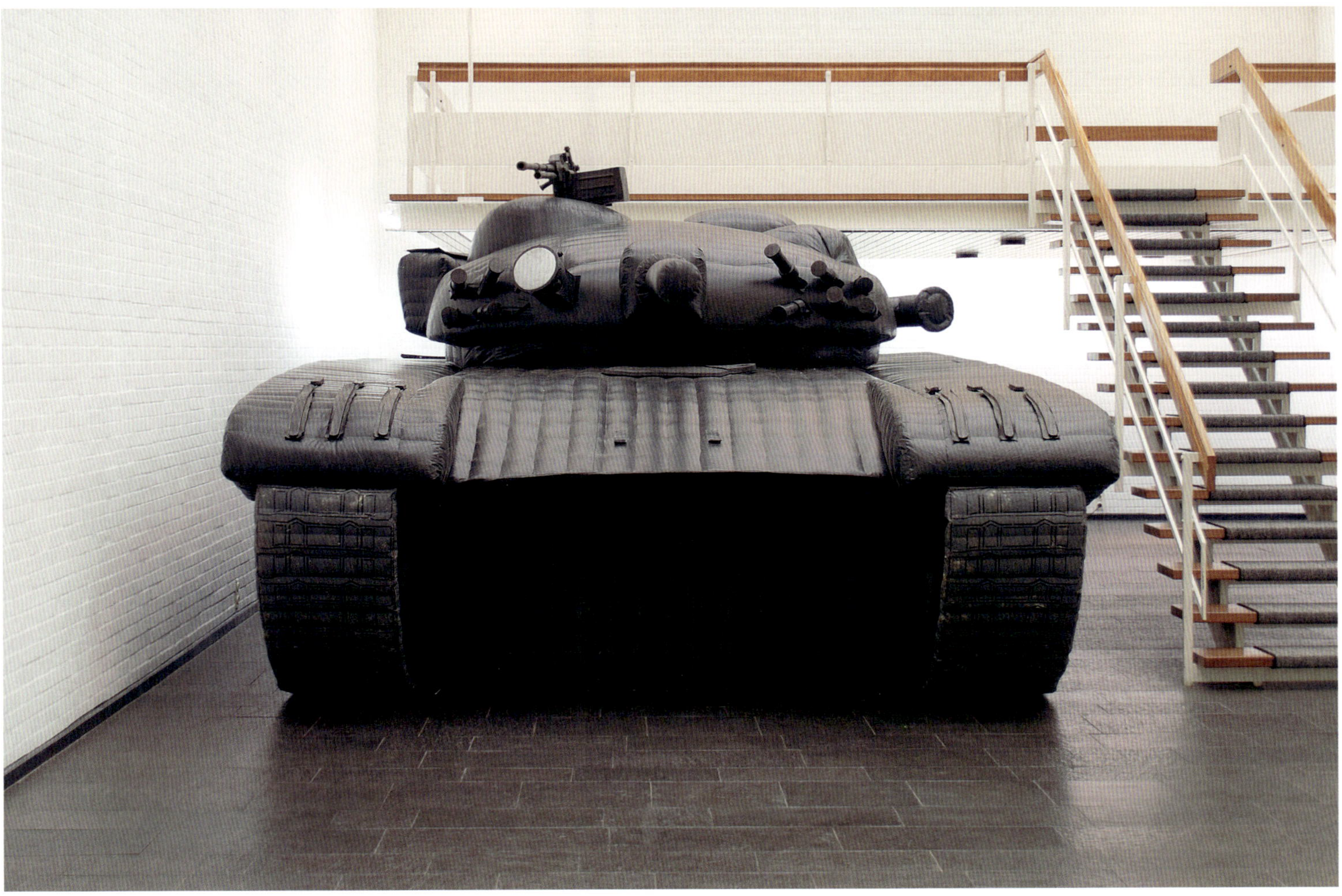

T 72 (black), 2008

Tank dummy, blower, controller / Panzerattrappe, Gebläse, Steuerung, 250 × 270 × 700 cm, Installation view / Installationsansicht, Kunstverein Bremerhaven

DER WASSERFALL stürzte rauschend hinab in ein Becken aus hellem Türkis, das sich in mehreren Stufen tief in die Erde grub. Das sprudelnde Wasser drang über ein eng geführtes Flussbett aus dem Dickicht des Dschungels in die Anlage. Gischt spritzte auf, stob empor und sprühte Viktor einen zarten Film aus feinsten Wassertropfen ins Gesicht. Er stand knietief im Wasser, empfing die Kühle in der Hoffnung, sie könne alle Brände in ihm löschen. Es ist viel passiert in den letzten Wochen, dachte er. Die jüngste Begegnung mit Karla, die Wortmeldung seines Vaters aus dem Jenseits und jetzt die Ermordung von Paco. Die Ereignisse hatten ihn wie eine Sprungfeder auseinandergedehnt, doch statt nach der Anspannung wieder in Position zu schießen, schien seine innere Feder gerissen, endlos entformt. Er sah hinüber zum Urwald und dachte kurz: Hier reift das Ewige. Am Saum zum Wald standen zwei Bäume, deren Geäst ins Blau des Himmels ragten. Zwei Bäume: Dem Urwald entrissen und in riesige Kessel verpflanzt. Zwei Bäume, die sich nun auf Schienen aufeinander zubewegten, wie es die Installation des Künstlers Michael Sailstorfer vorsah. Achtzig Jahre sollte ihr Weg quer über das Terrain andauern. Langsam kamen sie einander näher, würden in der Zukunft an einem genau festgelegten Zeitpunkt aufeinandertreffen, ihr sattes Laubwerk ineinander verweben, ihr Grün vereinen. Danach waren sie bestimmt, ihren vorgebahnten Weg fortsetzen, bis an das Ende der Schiene, um dort wieder ins Erdreich eingepflanzt zu werden und sich ein weiteres Mal im Boden zu verwurzeln. In gegenseitiger Reichweite, doch erneut voneinander getrennt. Die Vorstellung, diese beiden Giganten drifteten aufeinander zu wie zwei Liebende, nur, um sich dann wieder zu verlieren, und dass dies zudem menschengemacht war, brachte eine Unwucht in seine Gedanken.

6

Neben einem mächtigen Sapotenbaum saß Benedetto auf einem Stein am Ufer und las. Als er Viktor bemerkte, legte er sein Buch beiseite und watete durchs Wasser auf ihn zu.

»Grandios, nicht wahr?«, sagte Benedetto und sah auf die Bäume, die noch Hunderte Meter auseinanderstanden.

205

Viktor atmete tief durch: »Ich kann kaum sagen, an welcher Stelle es mir mehr weh tut, wenn ich an das Los der beiden Bäume denke: Die Vorstellung, dass sie sich treffen oder dass sie sich wieder voneinander lösen?«

»Mich fasziniert die Schiene«, sagte Benedetto leise. »Die Illusion der Fügung.«

Ihre Blicke trafen sich, vorsichtig der eine wie der andere. Viktor sah als erster weg: »Nichts ergibt mehr Sinn.«

Benedetto griff nach einem flachen Stein und warf ihn über die Wasseroberfläche. Er versank nach zwei Sprüngen. »Ist es die Abwesenheit von Sinn, die dich kränkt? Oder glaubst du bloß, keinen zu finden?«

»Ich bin es leid, zu suchen«, seufzte Viktor. »An falschen Orten, in mir.«

»Was meinst du?«

»Das Denken macht mich inzwischen müde. Ich will nicht mehr in die eigene Psyche absteigen, um nach irgendwelchen Erklärungen zu suchen«. Er schüttelte mürrisch den Kopf. »Ein dunkles Bergwerk, in dem nichts Kostbares mehr verborgen liegt. Ich empfinde nur Zorn und Verbitterung. Ich habe den Eindruck, es sei ab einem gewissen Punkt nicht mehr wichtig, noch genauer die Motive des eigenen Handelns zu erforschen. Purer Luxus in einer Zeit, die alles ins Belanglose zieht, nichts weiter. Man verebbt schnell an der eigenen Existenz. Ich bin durch damit, alles fühlt sich hier ...«, er klopfte sich mit dem Zeigefinger auf die Brust, »irgendwie eng an, irgendwie bedrückend, was weiß ich ...«

»Ja, ja, düstere Diagnosen, unendlich viele Therapieangebote.«

»Ich meine es ernst.«

»Was genau?«

»Die Frage, was kommt nach dem Ich.«

»Ich verstehe dich nicht.«

Viktor blickte seinem Freund offen in die Augen. »Schau mich an, große Ideale. Ich will etwas schaffen, um die Realität, in der wir leben, zu überwinden. Dabei verleugne ich alles, was ist. Warum

Frank Steinhofer

THE INVENTED NATURE

Ecological readings of
Michael Sailstorfer's work

DIE ERFUNDENE NATUR
Ökologische Lesarten
zu Michael Sailstorfers Werk

Global warming continues unabated. On an almost daily basis, images of destruction circulate in the news. People are afflicted by droughts, species are becoming extinct, and once again the Amazon rainforest is burning. The fire blazes, the wind driving thick smoke into the distance. It happened again in 2019; I still remember it.
An acquaintance's cry for help from São Paulo reached me on my cell phone. "It's raining ash," she wrote agitatedly and sent me, a writer who grew up in Germany and now lives in Mexico, a photo of a darkened sky looming ominously over the Brazilian metropolis. "We can't even breathe anymore. Look at the sky; let the world know what's happening here!" What she meant was: "your world"—that of the Global North.
This world *knows* it, I thought dejectedly, but does it also *feel* it? Questions came to me; they accompany me to this day, every time forests burn again, rivers burst their banks, or plastic waste pollutes the oceans: Has climate change ever reached our hearts? Is the climate crisis not also a crisis of a rationalizing perception that goes hand in hand with a lack of sensitivity? And: Couldn't art, with its specific means, move people to action more effectively than statistics or figures about rising sea levels?

Die Erderwärmung schreitet voran. Nahezu täglich zirkulieren Bilder der Zerstörung in den Nachrichten. Menschen werden von Dürren heimgesucht, Arten sterben, einmal mehr brennt der Regenwald am Amazonas. Das Feuer lodert, der Wind treibt dichten Rauch in die Ferne. So geschah es auch 2019. Ich erinnere mich noch daran.
Der Hilfeschrei einer Bekannten aus São Paulo erreichte mich auf meinem Handy. „Es regnet Asche", schrieb sie aufgeregt und schickte mir, dem in Deutschland aufgewachsenen und in Mexiko lebenden Schriftsteller, das Bild eines verdunkelten Himmels, der bedrohlich über die brasilianische Metropole hinwegzog. „Wir können nicht einmal mehr atmen. Schaut euch den Himmel an, lasst die Welt wissen, was hier passiert!" Sie meinte: deine Welt, diejenige des globalen Nordens.
Diese Welt weiß es, dachte ich niedergeschlagen, aber fühlt sie es auch? Mir drängten sich Fragen auf, sie begleiten mich bis heute, jedes weitere Mal, wenn Wälder brennen, Flüsse über Ufer treten oder Plastikmüll die Ozeane verschmutzt: Hat der Klimawandel unsere Herzen jemals erreicht? Ist die Klimakrise nicht auch die Krise einer rationalisierenden Wahrnehmung, die mit einem Mangel an Empfindsamkeit einhergeht? Und: Könnte die Kunst mit ihren Mitteln

AT THE END OF A MECHANISTIC WORLD VIEW

"One almost never arrives at the reasonable by way of reason," the French philosopher Charles de Montesquieu noted as early as 1721 in his *Persian Letters*, fearing that a mere increase in knowledge could contribute to the destruction of the earth, insofar as a specific emergence of knowledge would blunt empathy.[1]

When it comes to climate issues, knowledge production is running at full speed. Every day, numbers, maps, and graph curves pile up. Science is running out of red when it warns of the consequences of global warming. From the sphere of politics come appeasements, from corporations promises to reduce emissions. 1.5-degree targets are formulated; and, at the same time, the idea of a thermostat that can be regulated hangs in the air. Nature is "suffering," we keep hearing, and it must finally be saved, for example with geoengineering.

All these voices speak with a sense of alarm. An urgency that seems more than warranted: Too many people still deny the consequences of the human-made climate crisis. Nevertheless, the statements of concern resonate with that mechanistic worldview that for centuries has turned humans and nature into abstract objects to be mastered instead of establishing a compassionate relationship, as the German philosopher Grit Fröhlich notes.[2]

This is where, in my view, significant works by Michael Sailstorfer come in, telling of the effects of a mechanistic worldview. They invite us to become aware of an experience of separation "that cuts deeply through our existence," as the biologist Andreas Weber puts it:[3] the separation between nature and culture, which merges into further splits, such as body and mind, subject and object.

NATURE AS A CREATION OF CULTURE

In Western thinking, a distinction is made between nature and culture. This has been a philosophical tradition for centuries. The state of nature is generally imagined as wild and raw, which can be civilized by reason (Thomas Hobbes). The cosmos of trees, plants, and animals surrounding us is downgraded to an inanimate resource space, which can be taken possession of by reason alone (René Descartes). Reality is presented as something external, which we can only experience as a subjective interpretation (Immanuel Kant).

This understanding is absorbed in the idea that nature—and ultimately all beings except humans—are thing-like. Objects. This has an enormous utilitarian effect: Humans can differentiate themselves from nature and dispose of it, distance themselves from it, and in turn idealize it. Nature becomes an invention, a creation of cultural fabrication that becomes controllable through technology.

This reductionist process has its price, as the Brazilian writer Ailton Krenak points out: "It is only possible to

Menschen nicht wirksamer zum Handeln bewegen als Statistiken oder Zahlen über den steigenden Meeresspiegel?

AM ENDE EINES MECHANISTISCHEN WELTBILDES

Fast nie kommt der Mensch mit Vernunft zur Vernunft", hielt der französische Philosoph Montesquieu bereits 1721 in seinen *Persischen Briefen* fest und befürchtete, dass ein bloßer Erkenntniszuwachs zur Zerstörung der Erde beitragen könnte, insofern ein spezifisches Zustandekommen von Wissen das Einfühlungsvermögen abstumpfen ließe.[1]

In Klimafragen läuft die Wissensproduktion auf Hochtouren. Jeden Tag häufen sich Zahlen, Karten und Kurven an. Der Wissenschaft gehen die Rottöne aus, wenn sie vor den Folgen der Erderwärmung warnt. Aus der Sphäre der Politik kommen Beschwichtigungen, von Unternehmen Versprechen, Emissionen zu reduzieren. 1,5-Grad-Ziele werden formuliert und gleichzeitig schwebt die Vorstellung eines Thermostats im Raum, das reguliert werden kann. Die Natur „leide", hört man weiterhin, man müsse sie endlich retten, etwa mit Geoengineering.

Aus all den Stimmen spricht Sorge. Eine Dringlichkeit, die mehr als geboten erscheint: Zu viele Menschen leugnen immer noch die Folgen der menschengemachten Klimakrise. In den besorgten Aussagen schwingt aber gerade jene mechanistische Weltsicht mit, die Mensch und Natur seit Jahrhunderten erst zu abstrakten Objekten gemacht hat, die es zu beherrschen galt, statt einen mitfühlenden Bezug herzustellen, wie die deutsche Philosophin Grit Fröhlich bemerkt.[2]

Hier setzen meines Erachtens bedeutende Werke von Michael Sailstorfer an, die von den Auswirkungen eines mechanistischen Weltbilds erzählen. Sie laden dazu ein, sich einer Trennungserfahrung bewusst zu werden, „die tief durch unsere Existenz schneidet"[3], wie der Biologe Andreas Weber es formuliert hat: der Trennung zwischen Natur und Kultur, die in weiteren Aufspaltungen wie Körper und Geist, Subjekt und Objekt aufgeht.

NATUR ALS KREATION VON KULTUR

Im abendländischen Denken wird zwischen Natur und Kultur unterschieden. Das hat seit Jahrhunderten philosophische Tradition. Der Naturzustand wird meist als wild und roh imaginiert, der mit Vernunft zivilisiert werden kann (Thomas Hobbes). Der uns umgebende Kosmos aus Bäumen, Pflanzen und Tieren wird zum unbelebten Ressourcenraum herabgestuft, dessen sich allein der Verstand bemächtigen kann (René Descartes). Die Wirklichkeit wird als etwas Äußerliches dargestellt, das wir nur als subjektive Interpretation erfahren können (Immanuel Kant).

Dieses Verständnis geht in der Idee auf, dass die Natur – und letztlich alle Wesen außer den Menschen – dinghaft sind. Objekte. Das hat eine enorme utilitaristische Wirkung:

imagine nature if you are outside of it. How could a baby that is inside its mother's uterus imagine the mother?"[4]
To perceive nature merely as an external setting, something that stands outside of the body and feelings—this differentiating view is at odds with the actual, ecological experience. Humans are physical beings; they exist because everything else exists and is based on a plexus of reciprocity. We do not need to go into nature, to understand it as something opposed to us; we are already nature: living organisms, woven from birth into this world that knows no externality.
Works by Michael Sailstorfer map out this tension in a variety of ways. Sailstorfer takes the Western notion of "nature" as his base material, revealing it as an expressive construct, as the image we produce of it. He reveals: Nature in particular is first created in the eye of the person contemplating it.

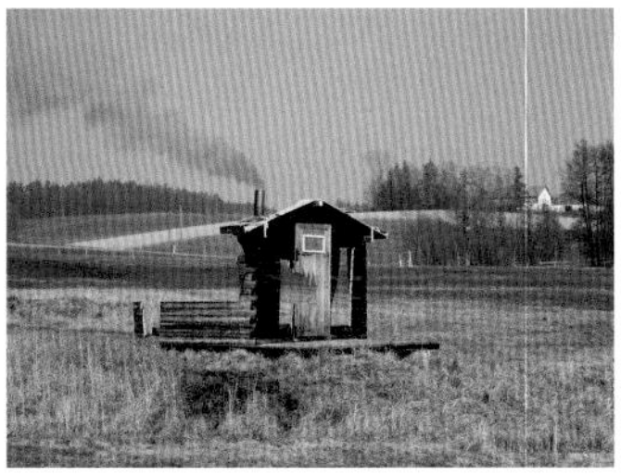

3 Ster mit Ausblick, 2001

For *Waldputz* [Cleaning the Forest, 2000] ↗298/299, Sailstorfer drew a square in the forest, removed the foliage in it, and cleaned trees and stumps with a root brush, thereby ultimately creating an artificial order in the emergence of a forest. The cleaned area seems like a blank space in the rampant greenery. For human perception, mind you. Non-human organisms such as mushrooms or animals in the soil had never disappeared; they continue to exist beyond the directed gaze.
In the short film *3 Ster mit Ausblick* [3 Cubic Meters of Wood with a View, 2002] ↗219–222, Sailstorfer presents an idyllically situated log cabin with a stove pipe protruding from its roof. Thick smoke rises from a chimney. It soon becomes clear that the fire feeds on the wood of the log cabin, which consumes itself bit by bit until, in the end, only a lone stove on a wooden floor protrudes into the landscape. When the floor is also consumed, sparks fly into the night sky for the very last time, and the fire burns out.
A wooden shack incinerating itself. What a fitting allegory for climate change! We are not only sawing off the branch on which we are sitting, we are sawing off the branch that we ourselves are. We are destroying our own livelihoods; and, as the German philosopher Friedrich Schelling put it, the more we cut the relationship between ourselves and countless other sentient beings, we cut the "band of creatureliness", denying our ecological consanguinity and rejecting non-human agency.

Der Mensch kann sich von der Natur abgrenzen und über sie verfügen, sich von ihr distanzieren und sie wiederum idealisieren. Natur wird zu einer Erfindung, eine Kreation kultureller Hervorbringung, die mit Technik beherrschbar wird.
Dieser reduktionistische Vorgang hat seinen Preis, wie der brasilianische Schriftsteller Ailton Krenak pointiert: „Die Natur kann sich nur vorstellen, wer außerhalb von ihr steht. Wie soll ein Baby im Uterus sich seine Mutter vorstellen?"[4]
Die Natur bloß als ein äußeres Setting wahrzunehmen; etwas, das außerhalb von Körper und Gefühlen steht; diese abgrenzende Sichtweise steht im Widerspruch zu der eigentlichen, ökologischen Erfahrung. Menschen sind leibliche Wesen, sie existieren, weil alles andere existiert und auf einem Geflecht von Gegenseitigkeit beruht. Wir brauchen nicht in die Natur zu gehen, sie als etwas Gegensätzliches begreifen, wir sind bereits Natur: lebendige Organismen, von Geburt an eingewoben in diese Welt, die kein Äußerliches kennt.
Werke von Michael Sailstorfer arbeiten auf vielfältige Weise dieses Spannungsverhältnis heraus. Sailstorfer nimmt die abendländische Vorstellung von „der Natur" als Ausgangsmaterial, offenbart sie als expressives Konstrukt, als das Bild, das wir von ihr hervorbringen. Er zeigt: Gerade Natur entsteht erst im Auge der betrachtenden Person.
In *Waldputz*, 2000 ↗298/299, zieht Sailstorfer ein Viereck im Wald, entfernt darin das Laub, reinigt Bäume und Stümpfe mit einer Wurzelbürste, erzeugt dadurch letztlich eine künstliche Ordnung in der Emergenz eines Waldes. Die gesäuberte Fläche wirkt wie eine Leerstelle in dem wuchernden Grün. Für das menschliche Empfinden wohlgemerkt. Nichtmenschliche Lebewesen wie Pilze oder Tiere im Erdreich waren nie verschwunden, sie existieren abseits des gelenkten Blickes fort.
In dem Kurzfilm *3 Ster mit Aussicht*, 2002 ↗219–222, zeigt Sailstorfer eine idyllisch gelegene Blockhütte, aus deren Dach ein Ofenrohr ragt. Dichter Qualm steigt aus einem Schornstein auf. Bald wird deutlich, dass sich das Feuer vom Holz der Blockhütte nährt, die sich Stück für Stück selbst verzehrt, bis am Schluss nur noch ein einsamer Ofen auf einem Holzboden in die Landschaft ragt. Als auch der Fußboden verfeuert ist, stieben ein allerletztes Mal Funken in den Nachthimmel, das Feuer verglüht.
Eine Holzhütte verfeuert sich selbst. Welch passende Allegorie auf den Klimawandel! Wir sägen nicht nur den Ast ab, auf dem wir sitzen. Wir sägen an dem Ast, der wir selbst sind. Wir zerstören die eigenen Lebensgrundlagen und schneiden zudem, wie es der deutsche Philosoph Friedrich Schelling bezeichnet hat, das „Band der Kreatürlichkeit" durch, je mehr wir die Beziehung zwischen uns und unzähligen anderen fühlenden Wesen kappen, unsere ökologische Artverwandtschaft leugnen und nichtmenschliche Handlungsmacht zurückweisen.

With his *Kopf und Körper Marzahn 01–03* [Head and Body Marzahn 01–03] sculptures from 2017 ↗92, 93, Michael Sailstorfer addresses this, showing that the animate world is a world full of creators. For the Italian philosopher Emanuele Coccia, being in the world means already finding a space for every being that has been designed and brought forth by others—and that must constantly be reshaped. He points out that every lizard, every bee designs itself in its relation to the world, changing the environment of the others.[5] Designing in this sense is the epitome of a mutual exchange. This was also the case with *Kopf und Körper Marzahn 01–03*: Michael Sailstorfer installed three concrete beehives at the foot of the Kienberg in Berlin, each containing a sculptural model designed by him. Bee colonies moved into the hives for months. The bees went about their work, building their honeycombs inside and transforming the sculptural models in a natural process. Sailstorfer later cast golden-yellow bronze sculptures from the models and placed them on the concrete beehives, which now served as pedestals.

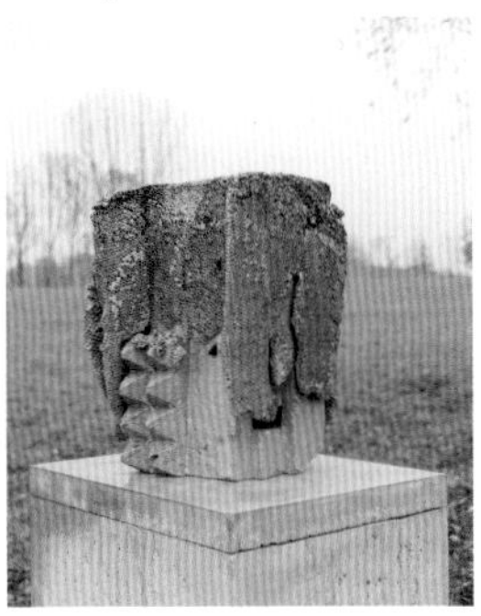

Kopf und Körper Marzahn 01, 2017

The plant sketches *Distel* and *Brennnessel* [Thistle and Nettle, 2019] ↗296, 297 are reminiscent of botanical drawings and the aesthetics of contemplating nature. Sailstorfer chose industrially manufactured sandpaper for the drawings, which deftly resists the movements of the slate stylus used. The act of drawing thus becomes a conflict. When touched, the rough sandpaper "stings," the material friction making drawing difficult—and it seems as if the industrial sandpaper could erase the beauty of the plants. The process of creation thus holds sensual qualities that the plants themselves evoke in the human body; in the act of drawing itself, materiality is discovered through abrasion. In this way, these amazing works of art raise the question of misappropriation and object status. What would be a fitting engagement with the natural world? A painful, possibly destructive appropriation or an even more peaceful form of coexistence? Entirely in the spirit of Christian Morgenstern, who, in his poem, appeals to the abstention of practice: "I haven't picked a few flowers for you, in order to bring you their life."

Mit seinen Skulpturen *Kopf und Körper Marzahn 01–03*, 2017 ↗92, 93, geht Michael Sailstorfer darauf ein und zeigt, dass die belebte Welt eine Welt von lauter Gestaltenden ist. Für den italienischen Philosophen Emanuele Coccia bedeutet auf der Welt zu sein, für jedes Wesen bereits einen Raum vorzufinden, der von anderen entworfen und hervorgebracht wurde – und der immerzu umgestaltet werden muss. Er weist darauf hin, dass sich jede Eidechse, jede Biene in ihrem Bezug zur Welt entwirft und so die Umgebung der anderen verändert.[5] Gestalten ist in diesem Sinne der Inbegriff eines gegenseitigen Austausches. So auch bei *Kopf und Körper Marzahn 01–03*: Michael Sailstorfer installierte am Fuße des Kienbergs drei Bienenstöcke aus Beton, in denen sich jeweils ein Skulpturenmodell von ihm befand. In die Stöcke zogen Bienenvölker für Monate ein. Die Bienen gingen ihrer Arbeit nach, bauten im Innern ihre Waben und wandelten die Skulpturenmodelle in einem natürlichen Prozess um. Sailstorfer goss später aus den Modellen goldgelbe Bronzeskulpturen, die er auf die Bienenstöcke aus Beton setzte, die nun als Sockel dienten.

Die Pflanzenskizzen *Distel* und *Brennnessel*, 2019 ↗296, 297, erinnern wiederum an botanische Zeichnungen und an die Ästhetik von Naturbetrachtungen. Für die Zeichnungen hat Sailstorfer industriell gefertigtes Schleifpapier gewählt, das sich behände den Bewegungen des eingesetzten Schiefergriffels verwehrt. Der Akt des Zeichnens wird so zu einem Widerstreit. Bei Berührung „sticht" das raue Schleifpapier, die materielle Reibung erschwert das Zeichnen – und es wirkt so, als würde das industrielle Schleifpapier die Schönheit der Pflanzen wieder ausradieren können. Der Schöpfungsprozess birgt also sinnliche Qualitäten, welche die Pflanzen selbst im menschlichen Körper hervorrufen, im Zeichnen selbst entdeckt sich Materialität durch Abrieb. Dadurch werfen diese erstaunlichen Kunstwerke die Frage der Zweckentfremdung und des Objektstatus auf. Was wäre eine passende Auseinandersetzung mit der natürlichen Welt? Eine schmerzhafte, womöglich destruktive Aneignung oder gar friedlichere Form der Koexistenz? Ganz im Sinne von Christian Morgenstern, der in seinem Gedicht den Verzicht der Ausübung beschwört: „Ich habe Dir heute ein paar Blumen nicht gepflückt, um Dir ihr Leben zu schenken."

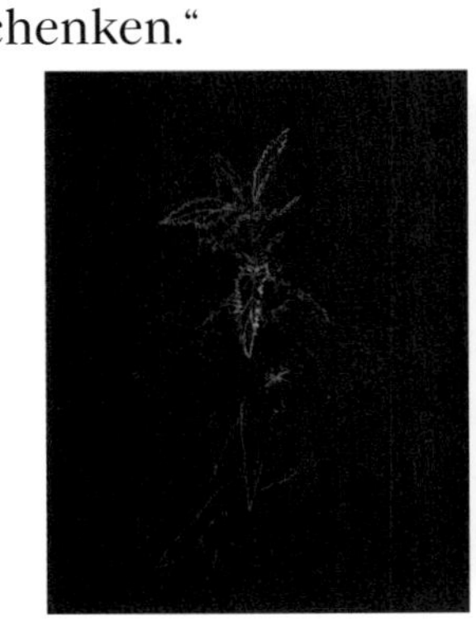

Brennnessel, 2019

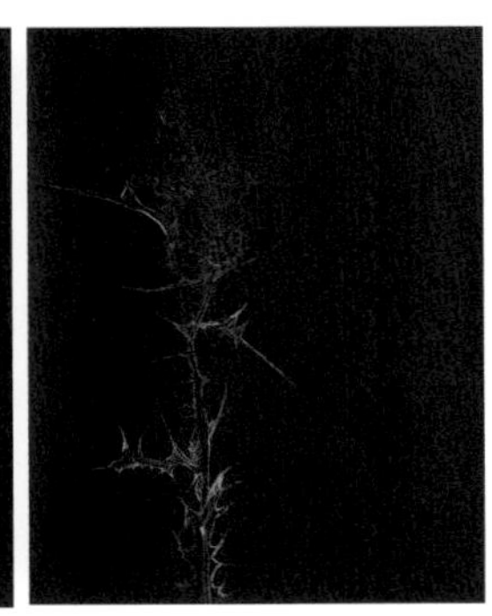

Distel, 2019

THE LONG PATH TO LIVELINESS

The metaphorical quality of Sailstorfer's works is particularly stimulating. As an outstanding sculptor, his material is not only the substance itself; he condenses material, sound, smell, and time—revealing possibilities of transformation, so that his works are surrounded by a semantic limbo that seems to open itself up to a different reading every moment.

For my novel *Das Terrain*, Michael Sailstorfer designed an installation based primarily on one material: Imagination. On the one hand, the book is about a German architect who wants to build close to nature with clay; and, on the other hand, it is about a Mexican art collector who reforests an illegally cleared forest area on the border of the rainforest in order to build the new Xinatli museum there. The museum building grows in her mind to contribute to abating the climate crisis and to fight against a climate of injustice, as well as to advocate for other forms of art and its aesthetics, ecological construction methods, and the coexistence of all species. The name of the museum, Xinatli, is derived from the Nahua word *"xinachtli,"* which describes the moment when a seed germinates and grows into a life-giving plant.

For the fictional museum in the novel, Michael Sailstorfer designed the installation *Zwei Bäume* [Two Trees, 2021], which addresses human intervention in the natural environment. In the process, his sketches and ideas were literarily incorporated into the novel.

For the installation, two trees are planted in round troughs and placed on moving rails. The trees move toward each other. It takes them eighty years to travel the entire distance. In the middle, they meet and connect with each other, until they part from each other again and continue their journey to the end of the track. There, they continue to grow.

In the novel, two protagonists converse about the installation and reflect on their relationship to each other through the artwork. The installation offers a wealth of readings, one of which revolves around the theme of temporality. A connection is established between human sentience and the deep time of a tree. Thus, it is difficult for a human being to perceive the moment of coming together or departing again; one can only imagine the whole process. Gently progressive developments are not seen by humans, whose time and attention span are limited. Are we thus prisoners of our perceptible present? Can we expand our temporal horizons and learn to develop a sense for decades? This is a quality that would be needed to remain effective in the face of climate change. Global warming is progressing without the effects being immediately felt from one day to the next. It seems appropriate that, in relation to the climate crisis, we as humans treat the questions about the future less

DER LANGE WEG ZUR LEBENDIGKEIT

Die metaphorische Qualität von Sailstorfers Werken ist besonders anregend. Als herausragender Bildhauer ist sein Material nicht nur der Werkstoff an sich, er verdichtet Material, Klang, Geruch und Zeit – und zeigt Möglichkeiten der Wandlung auf, sodass seine Arbeiten eine semantische Schwebe umgibt, die sich jeden Augenblick einer anderen Lesart zu öffnen scheint.

Für meinen Roman *Das Terrain* hat Michael Sailstorfer eine Installation entworfen, die vor allem auf einem Werkstoff beruht: Imagination. In dem Buch geht es einerseits um einen deutschen Architekten, der naturnah mit Lehm bauen möchte, und andererseits um eine mexikanische Kunstsammlerin, die an der Grenze zum Regenwald ein illegal gerodetes Waldgebiet wieder aufforstet, um dort das neue Museum Xinatli zu errichten. Der Museumsbau wächst in ihrer Vorstellung, um einen Beitrag zur Klimakrise und gegen ein Klima der Ungerechtigkeit zu leisten und sich für andere Formen der Kunst und ihrer Ästhetik, ökologische Bauweisen und dem Miteinander aller Spezies einzusetzen. Der Name des Museums, Xinatli, stammt von dem Begriff „Xinachtli" aus der Nahua-Sprache und beschreibt den Moment, in dem ein Samen keimt und zu einer lebenspendenden Pflanze heranwächst.

Für das fiktive Museum aus dem Roman hat Michael Sailstorfer die Installation *Zwei Bäume*, 2021, entworfen, die Eingriffe des Menschen in die natürliche Umgebung thematisiert. Dabei wurden seine Skizzen und Ideen literarisch in den Roman eingearbeitet. Bei der Installation werden zwei Bäume in runde Tröge gepflanzt und auf bewegliche Schienen gesetzt. Die Bäume bewegen sich aufeinander zu. Für den gesamten Weg benötigen sie achtzig Jahre. In der Mitte treffen sie sich, verbinden sich miteinander, bis sie sich wieder entzweien und ihre Fahrt zum Ende der Strecke fortsetzen. Dort wachsen sie weiter.

In dem Roman unterhalten sich zwei Protagonisten über die Installation und reflektieren anhand des Kunstwerks ihre Beziehung zueinander. Die Installation bietet eine Fülle von Lesarten, eine davon ist Zeitlichkeit. Menschliches Empfindungsvermögen und die Tiefenzeit eines Baumes werden miteinander in Verbindung gebracht. So ist es für ein menschliches Wesen schwer möglich, den Augenblick des Aufeinandertreffens oder Ablassens wahrzunehmen, es kann sich lediglich den gesamten Vorgang vorstellen. Sanft fortschreitende Entwicklungen werden von Menschen, deren Zeit- und Aufmerksamkeitsspanne begrenzt ist, nicht gesehen. Sind wir also Gefangene unserer empfindbaren Gegenwart? Können wir unseren zeitlichen Horizont erweitern und lernen, ein Gefühl für Jahrzehnte zu entwickeln? Eine Eigenschaft, die für den Klimawandel vonnöten wäre, um handlungsfähig zu bleiben. Die Erderwärmung schreitet voran, ohne dass die Auswirkungen von einem auf den anderen Tag unmittelbar zu

shortsightedly and think beyond our own lifespan; that we perceive long-term movements, changes that we have not felt thus far because of our limited understanding of time.

The installation *Zwei Bäume* is a work of art that inspires a certain "epochal empathy" because it outlasts and reflects on the human lifespan. Furthermore, it raises the question of how the individual phases are to be understood in terms of time and space. Is the planting and setting on rails of the trees merely an anthropocentric metaphorical play before their actual settling in the earth? Does a single moment count or only the constant transition? And who counts at all? At what point can we speak of an artificial or natural state?

The work guides us to stop looking for a relationship to "nature," but instead to let nature take place as a relationship, as a constantly ongoing connection between humans and beings whose boundaries of unfolding are fluid and who resist final categorization. In the end, the expression to life prevails; the trees continue to grow in the soil. Nothing points more to a work of art; only the rails tell of an intervention in the environment. Could we humans therefore not take a shortcut: To immediately value any life without first having to lay hands on it?

Michael Sailstorfer's works challenge us to step out of the destructive zone of division by questioning humankind's purported monopoly on design, taking a closer look at the spatial and temporal constructedness of nature, and holding out the prospect of a round table for the co-creation of all beings. When we change our relationship to each other, we change our understanding of the world—in my opinion, this is the ecological message of his work.

spüren sind. Es erscheint angebracht, dass Menschen in Bezug auf die Klimakrise die Fragen nach der Zukunft weniger kurzsichtig behandeln und über die eigene Lebensspanne hinausdenken; dass wir langfristige Bewegungen, Veränderungen wahrnehmen, die wir bislang aufgrund des begrenzten Zeitverständnisses nicht spüren.

Die Installation *Zwei Bäume* ist ein Kunstwerk, dass zu einer gewissen „Epochenempathie" anregt, weil es die menschliche Lebenszeit überdauert und über sie reflektiert. Darüber hinaus wirft es die Frage auf, wie die einzelnen Abschnitte zeitlich und räumlich zu begreifen sind. Ist das Pflanzen und auf Schienen setzen der Bäume nur ein anthropozentrisches Metaphernspiel vor ihrem eigentlichen Sesshaftwerden in der Erde? Zählt ein einzelner Moment oder nur der stete Übergang? Und wer zählt überhaupt? Ab welchem Zeitpunkt ist von einem künstlichen oder natürlichen Zustand zu sprechen?

Die Arbeit leitet dazu an, nicht mehr nach einem Verhältnis zu „der Natur" zu suchen, sondern stattdessen Natur als Verhältnis stattfinden zu lassen, als ständig währende Beziehung zwischen Menschen und Wesen, deren Grenzen der Entfaltung fließend sind und die sich gegen eine finale Kategorisierung wehren. Am Ende obsiegt der Ausdruck zum Leben, die Bäume wachsen im Erdreich fort. Nichts deutet mehr auf ein Kunstwerk hin, nur noch die Schienen künden von einem Eingriff in die Umgebung. Könnten wir Menschen also nicht eine Abkürzung nehmen: Jegliches Leben unmittelbar wertzuschätzen, ohne vorher Hand an solches anlegen zu müssen?

Michael Sailstorfer fordert uns mit seinen Werken auf, aus der zerstörerischen Zone der Spaltung herauszutreten, indem er das vermeintliche Gestaltungsmonopol des Menschen hinterfragt, die räumliche und zeitliche Konstruiertheit von Natur in Augenschein nimmt und den runden Tisch zur Mitgestaltung aller Wesen in Aussicht stellt. Wenn wir die Beziehung zueinander ändern, wandeln wir das Weltverständnis, darin liegt meines Erachtens die ökologische Botschaft seines Schaffens.

1 Charles de Montesquieu, *Persian Letters* [1721], quoted in: Mark Hulliung, *Montesquieu and the Old Regime* (Berkeley: University of California Press 1976), p. 228.

2 Grit Fröhlich, "Mit Pflanzen denken," in: *Philosophie Magazin* [special edition: *Klimakrise*], 1st ed. (Berlin: Philomagazin Verlag 2020), pp. 29–30.

3 Andreas Weber, *Indigenialität*, 1st ed. (Berlin: Nicolai Publishing & Intelligence 2018) [translated].

4 Ailton Krenak, "Ein Wald, der im Raum schwebt," in: *CULTURESCAPES*, no. 16: *Amazonas* [published on the occasion of the CULTURESCAPES festival dedicated to Amazonia] (Basel 2021), https://culturescapes.ch/en/magazine/ein-wald-der-im-raum-schwebt [last accessed on July 25, 2022].

5 Emanuele Coccia, *Metamorphosen – Das Leben hat viele Formen. Eine Philosophie der Verwandlung* (Munich: Carl Hanser Verlag, 2021).

1 Charles de Montesquieu, *Persische Briefe*, Stuttgart: Reclam 1991.

2 Grit Fröhlich, „Mit Pflanzen denken", in: *Philosophie*, Sonderausgabe „Klimakrise", Berlin 2020, S. 29–30.

3 Andreas Weber, *Indigenialität*, Berlin: Nicolai Publishing & Intelligence 2018.

4 Ailton Krenak, „Ein Wald, der im Raum schwebt", in: *Culturescapes 2021 Amazonas*, Basel, 2021, S. 4–5.

5 Emanuele Coccia, *Metamorphosen – Das Leben hat viele Formen. Eine Philosophie der Verwandlung*, München: Carl Hanser Verlag 2021.

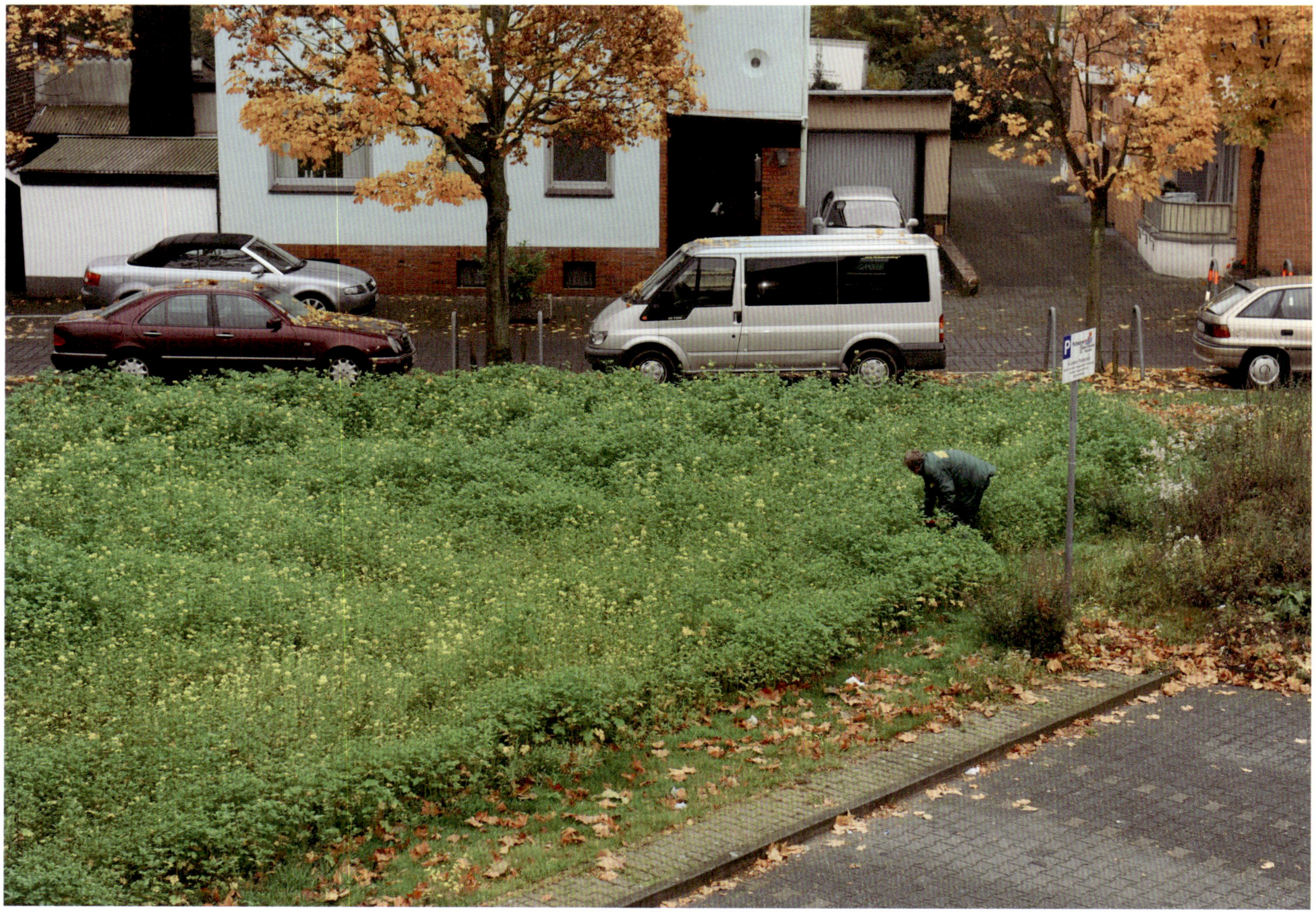

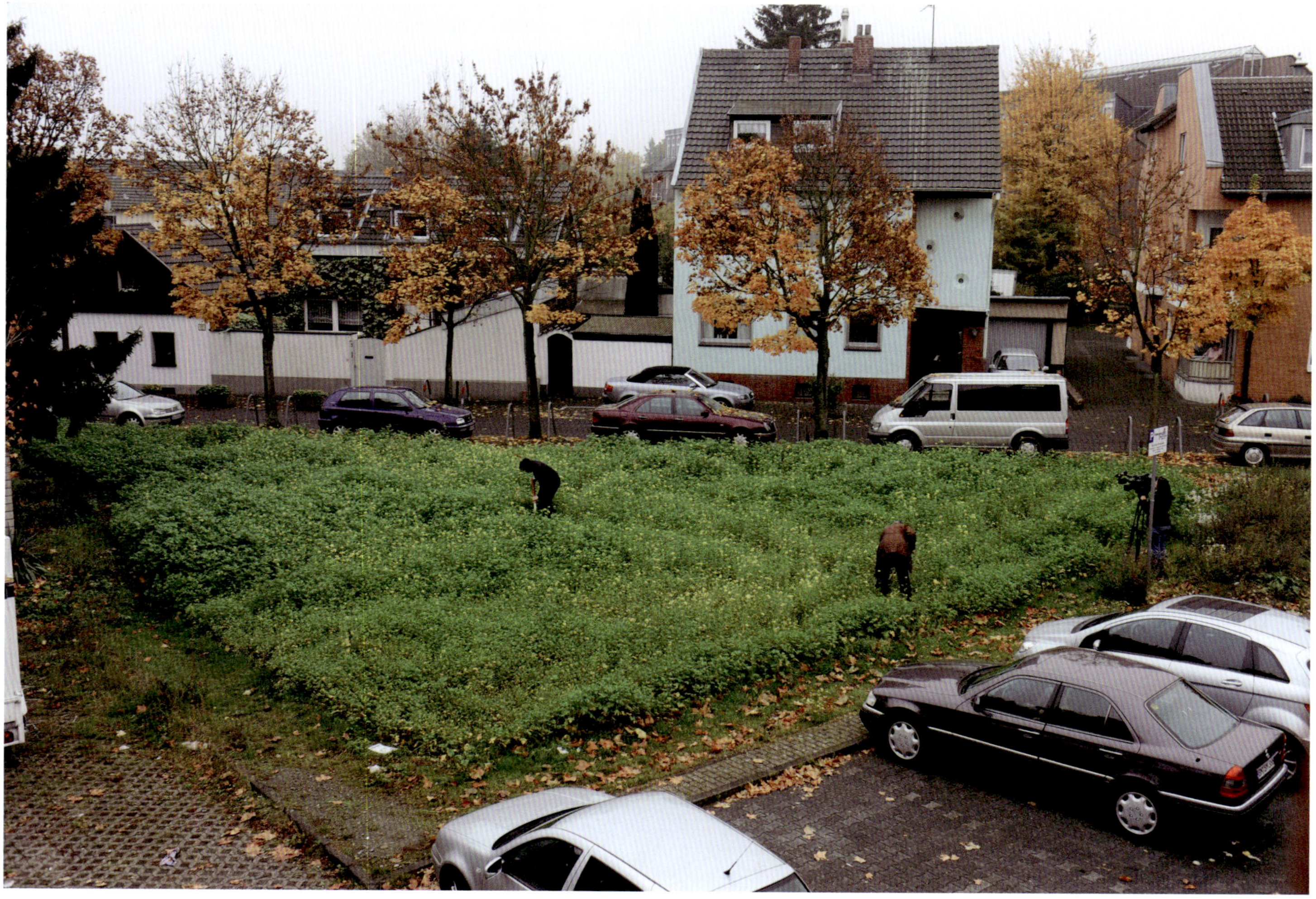

Pulheim gräbt, 2009/2010

Mixed media

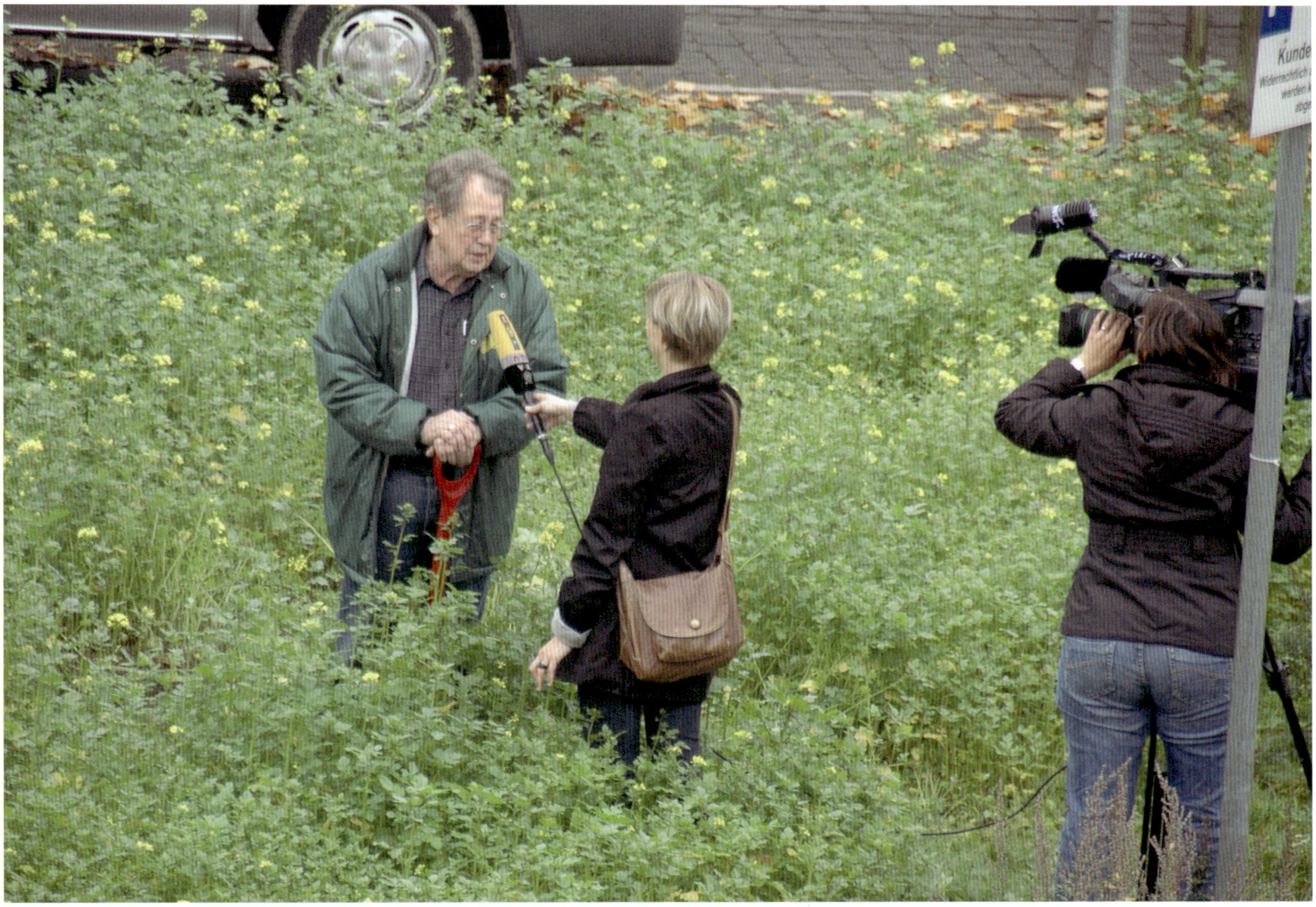

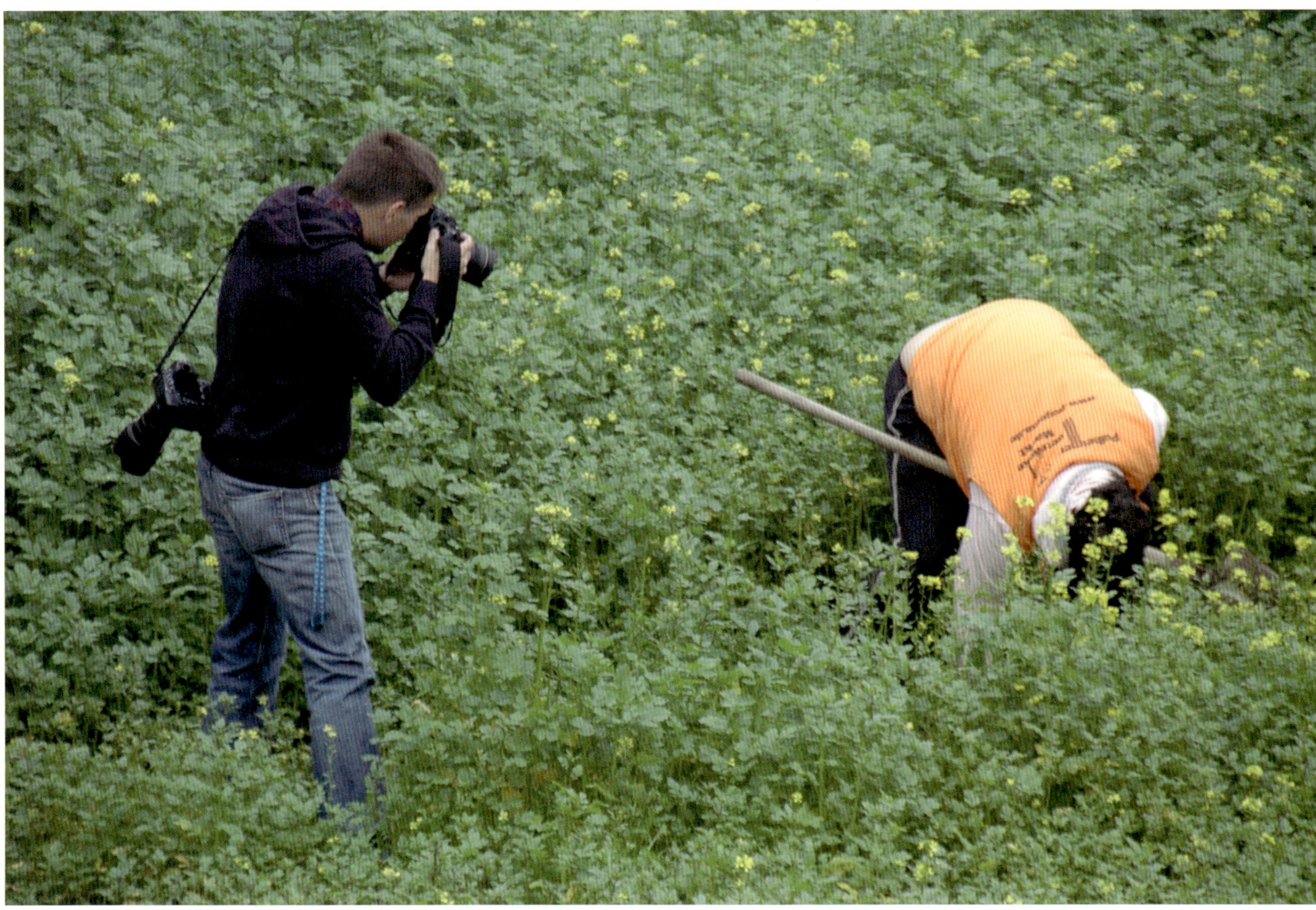

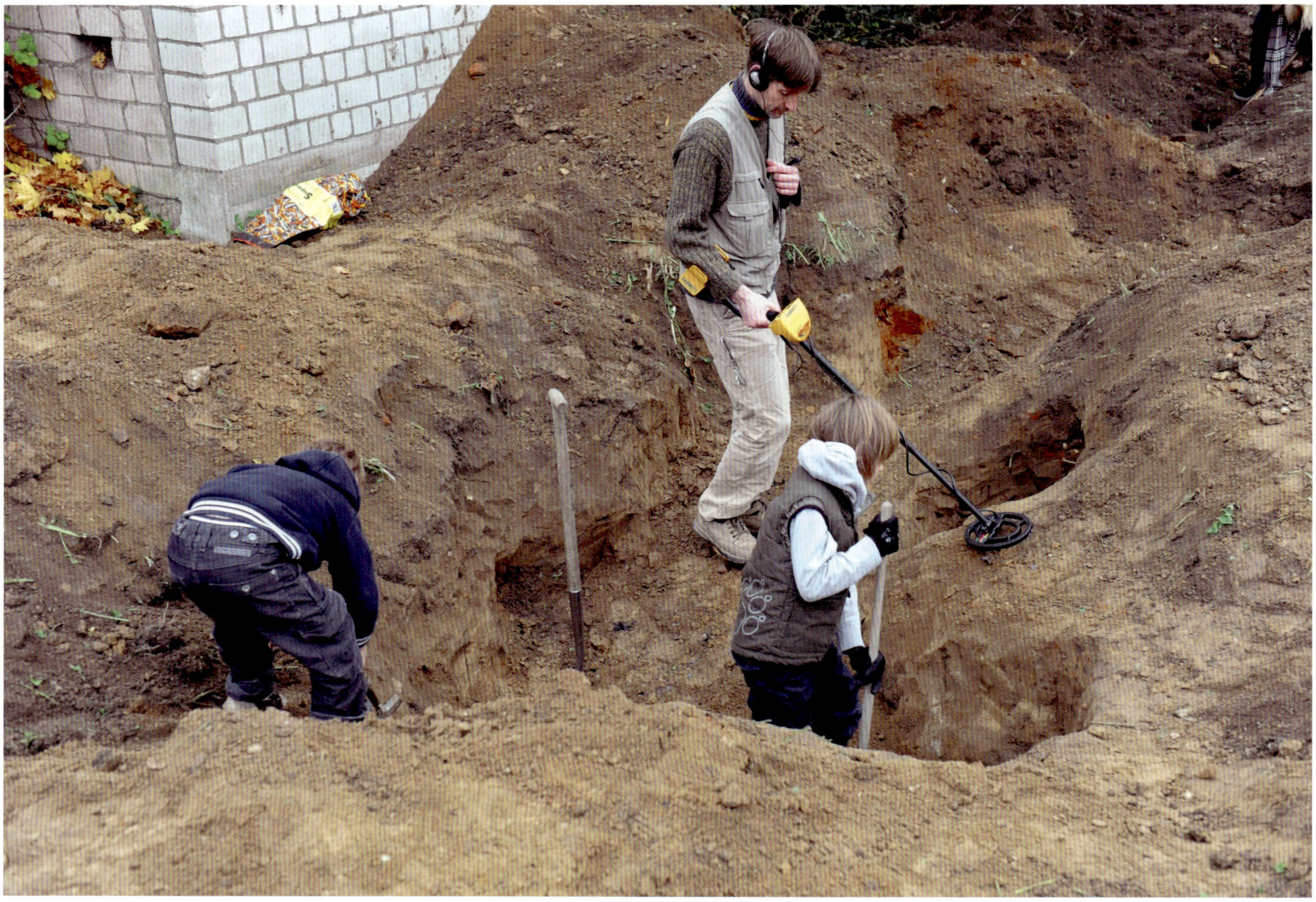

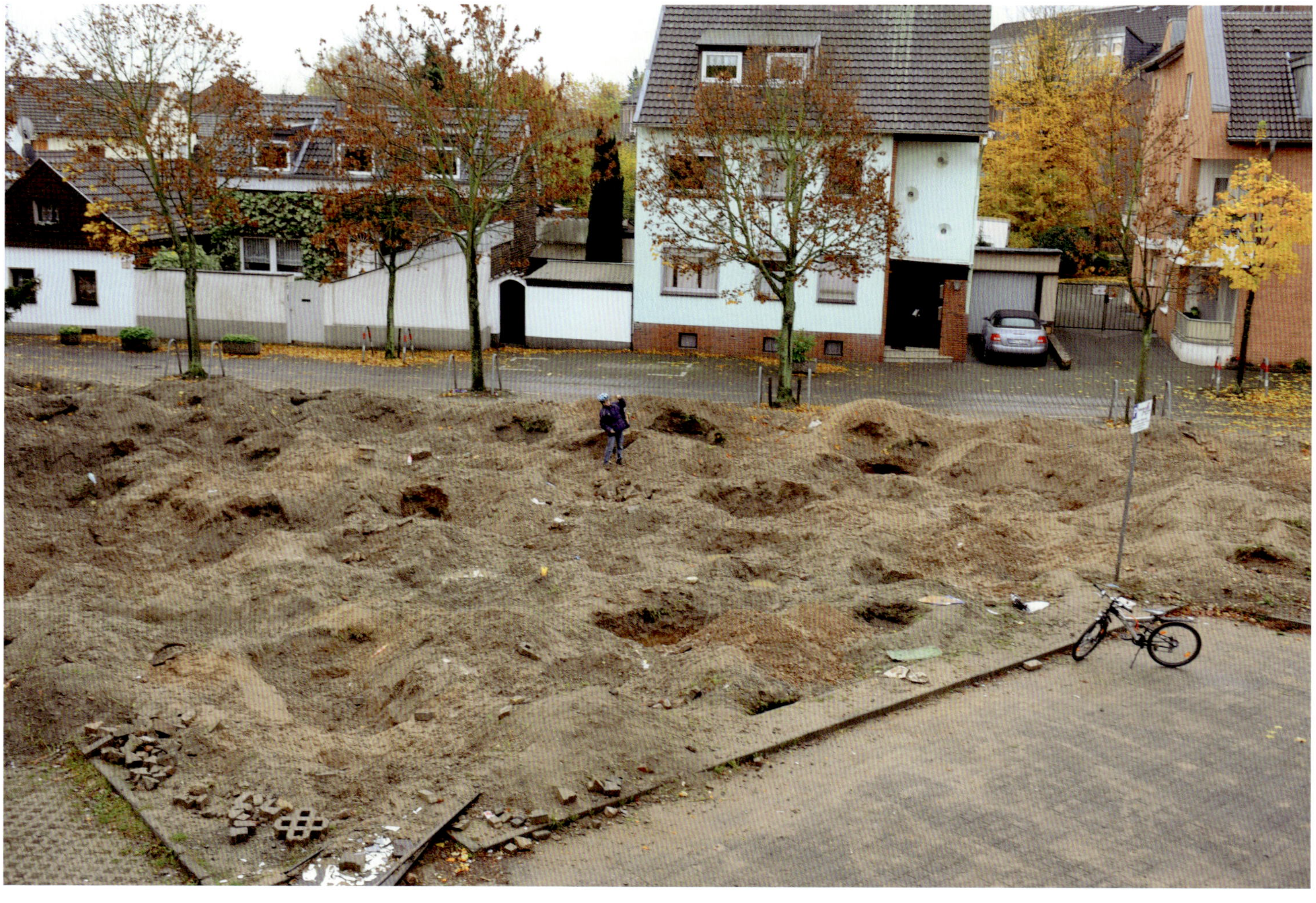

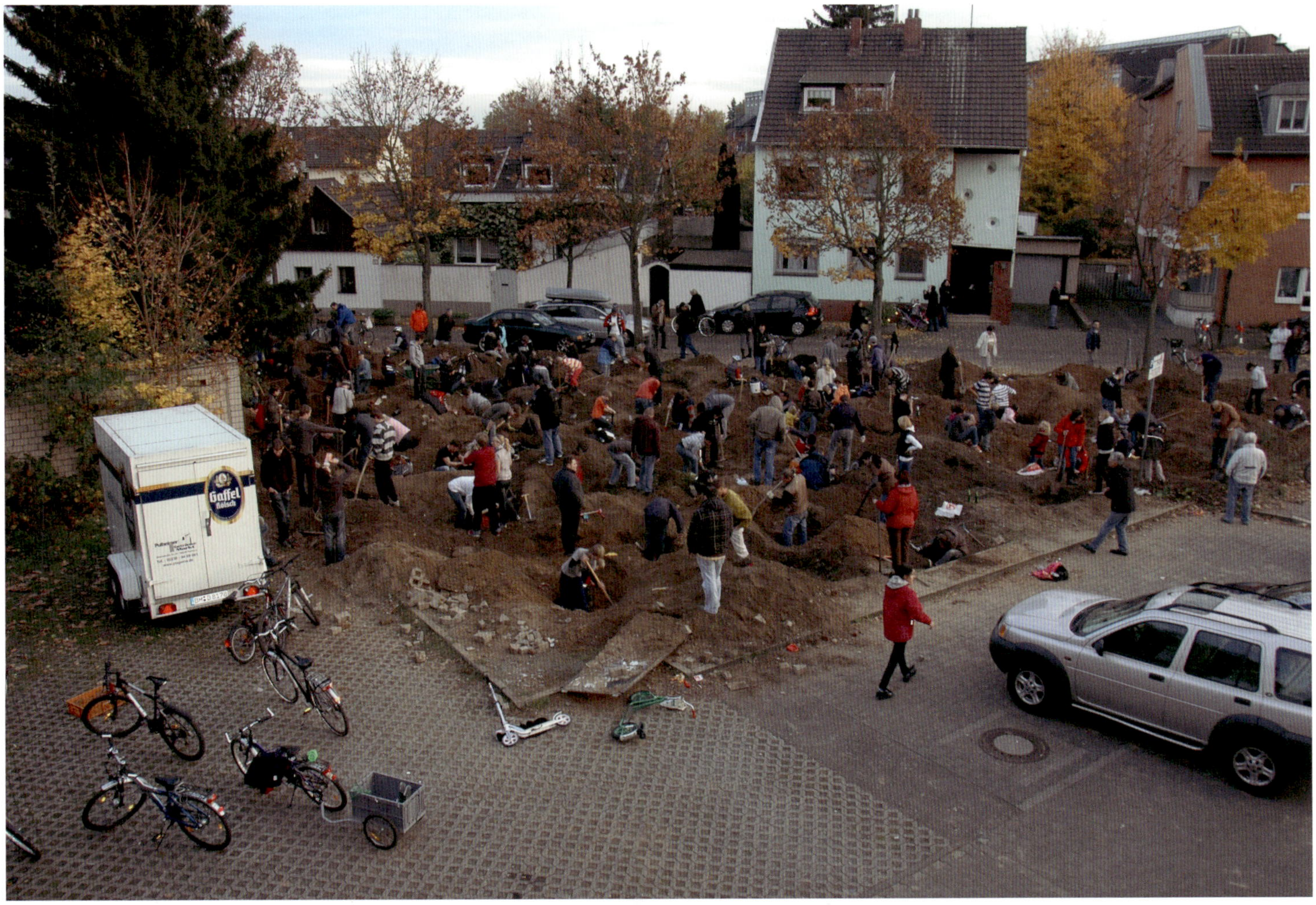

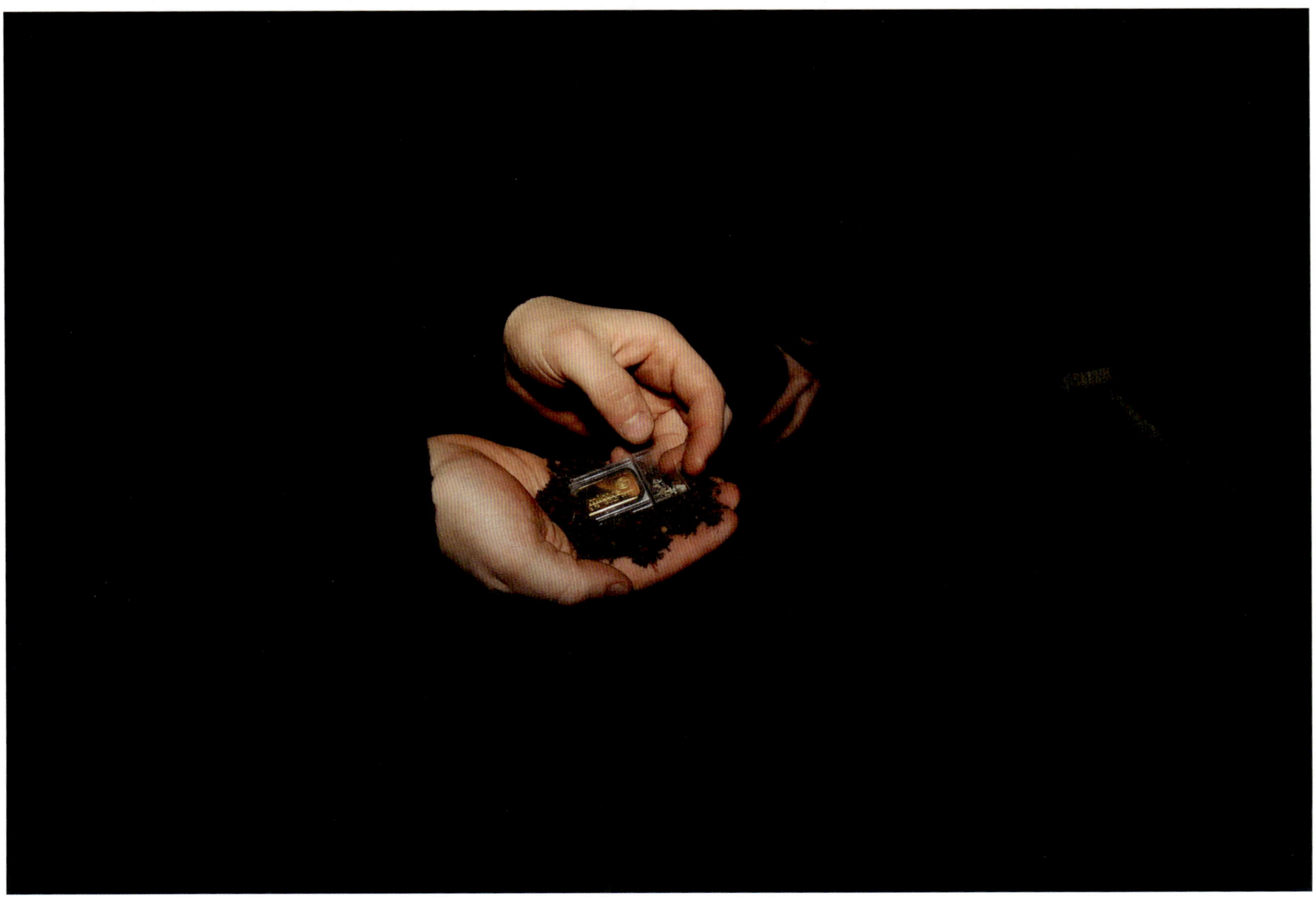

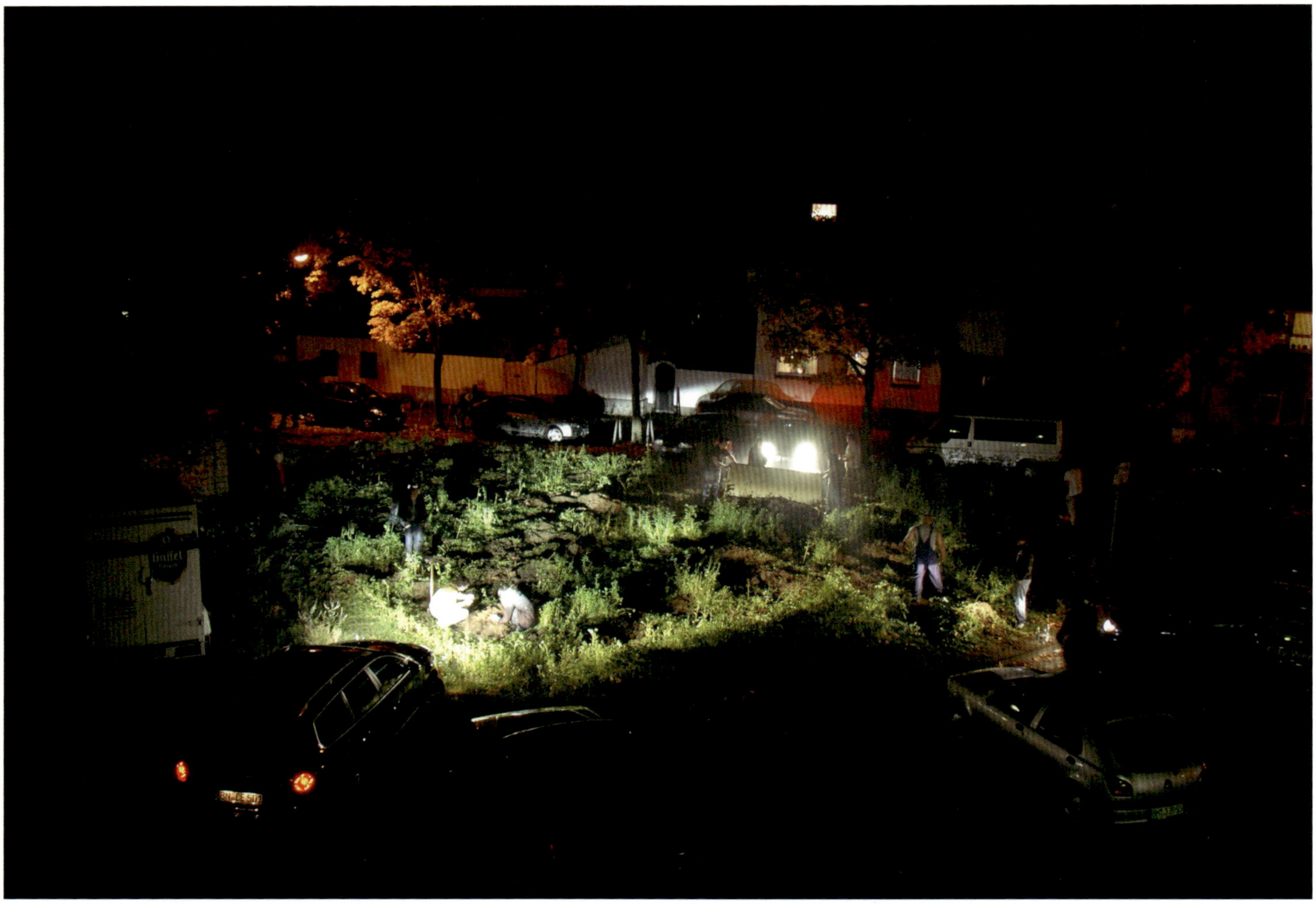

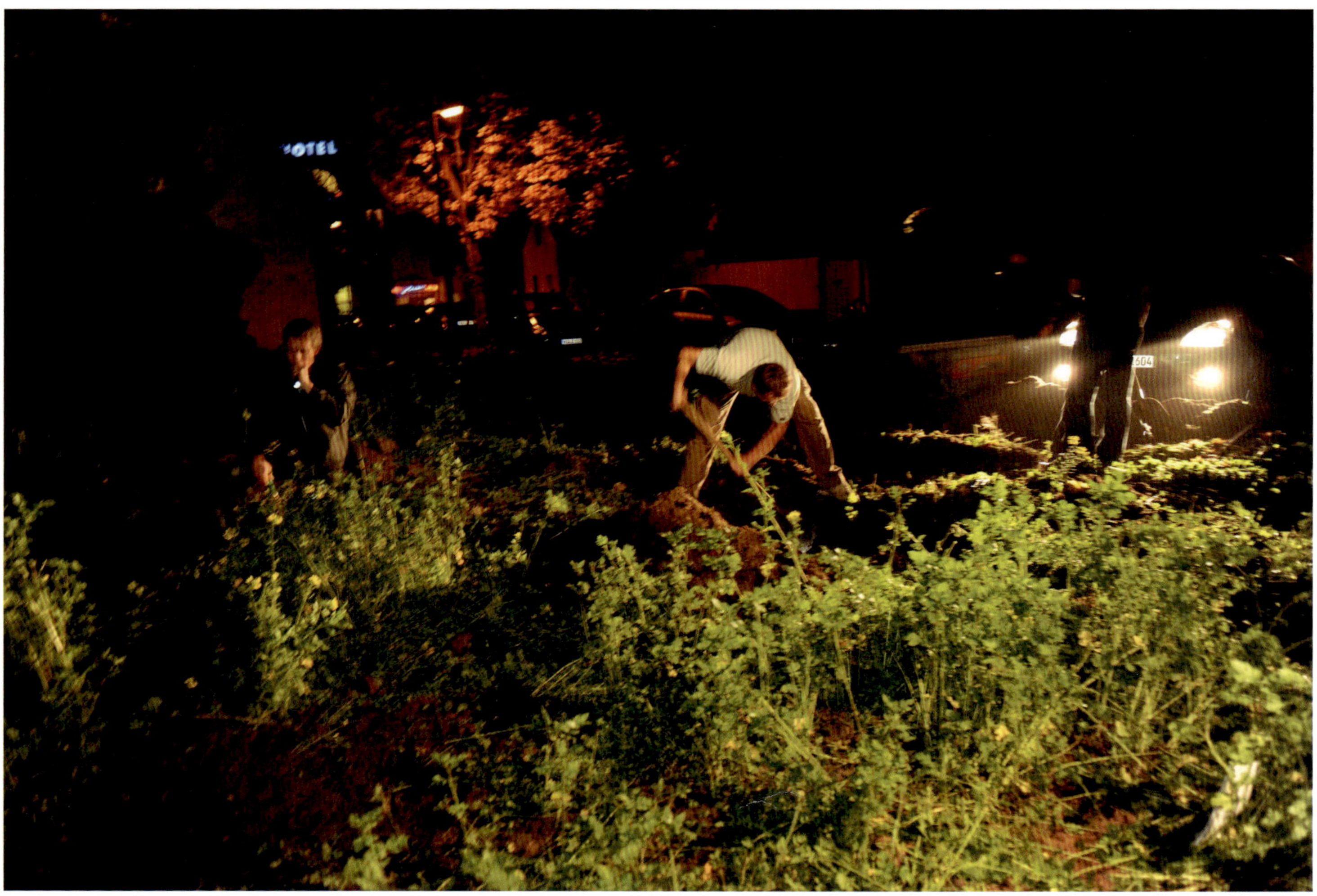

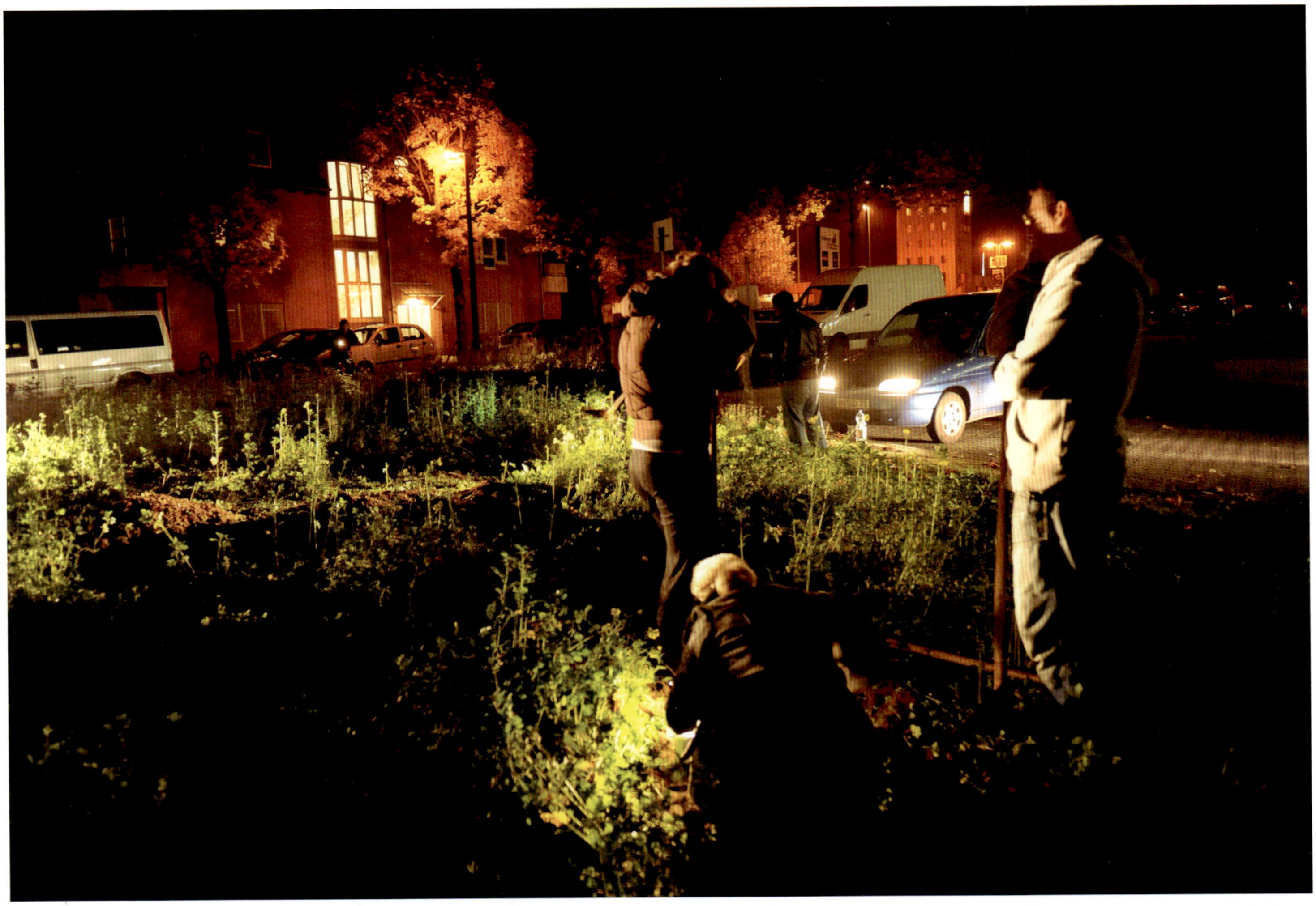

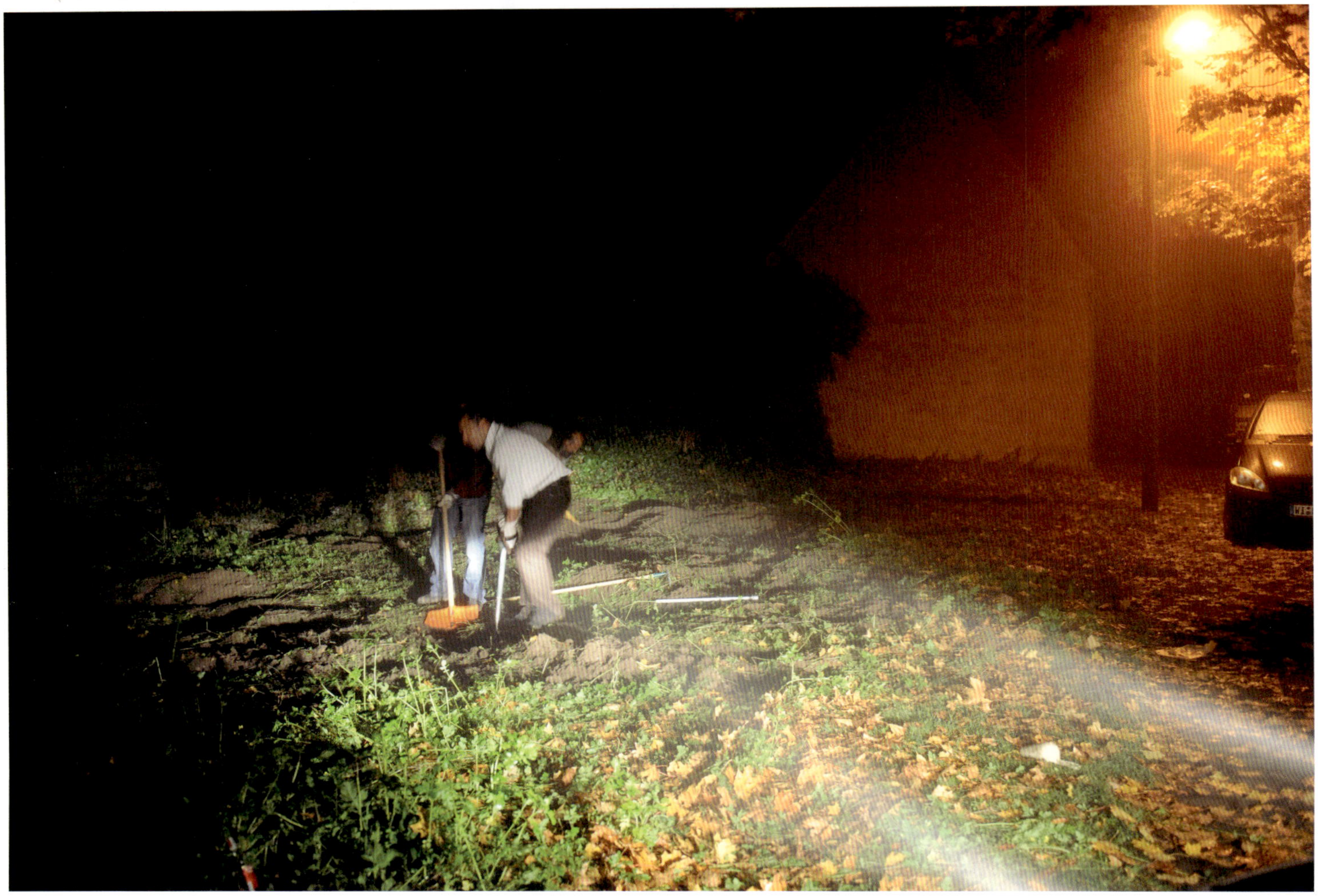

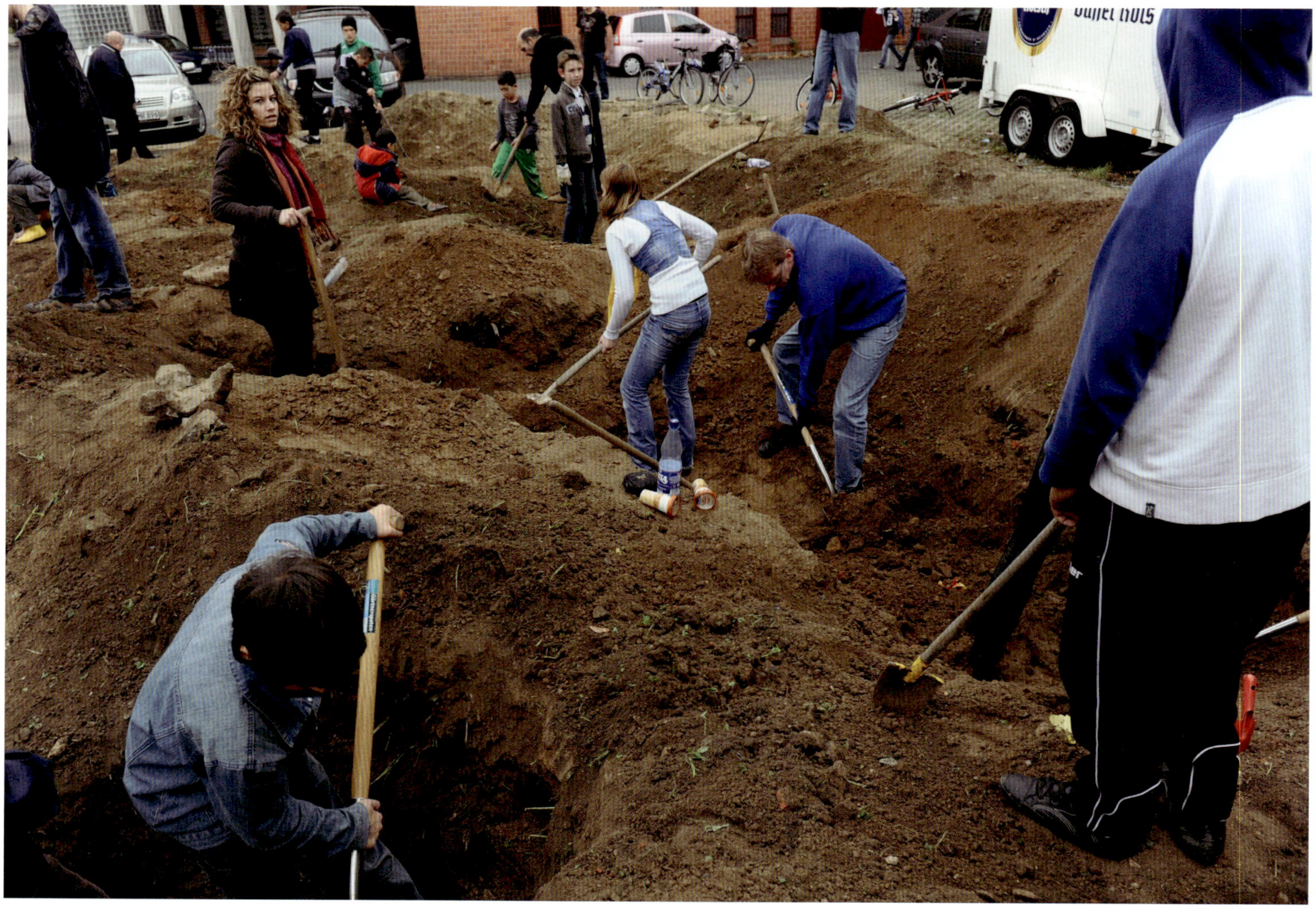

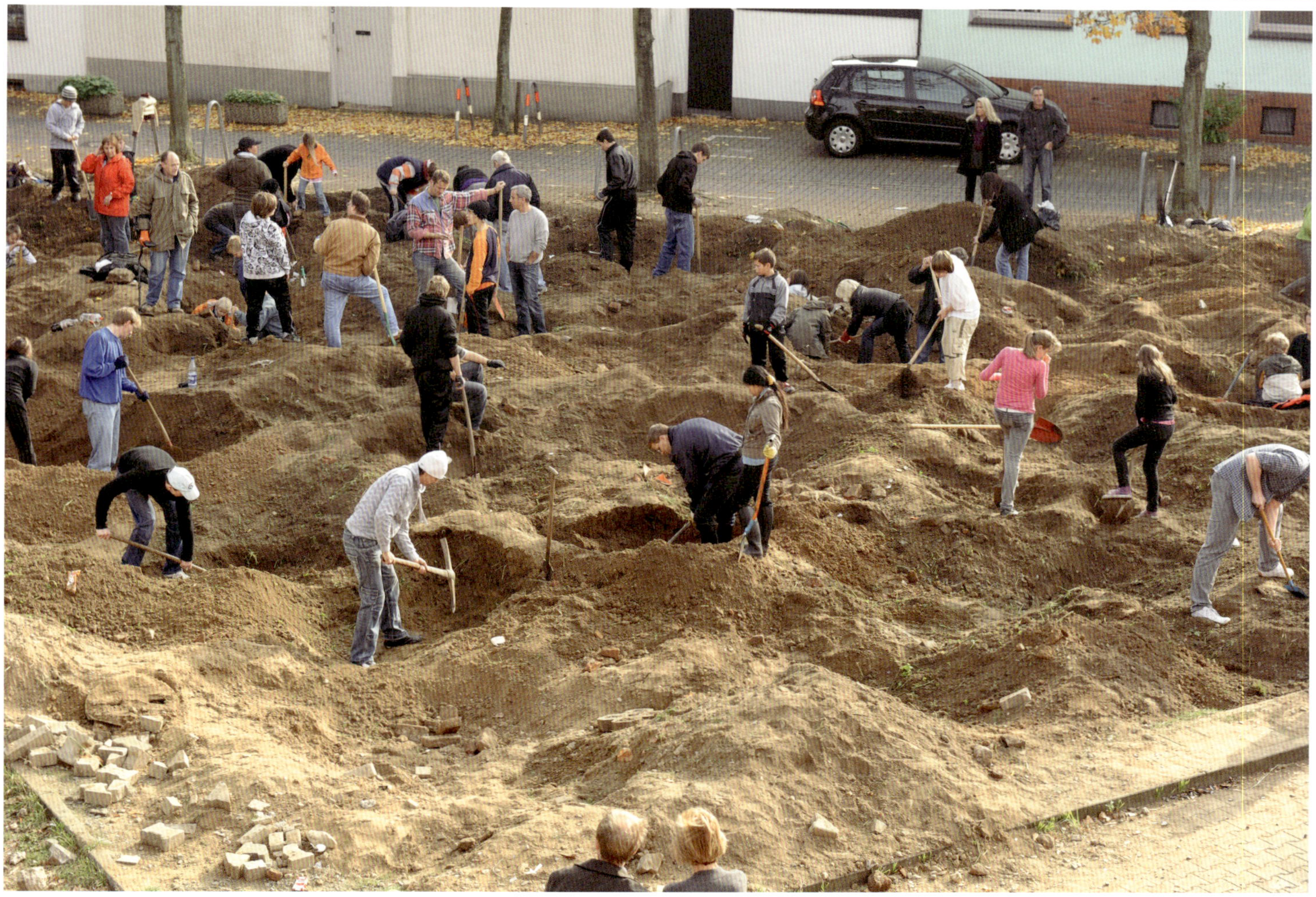

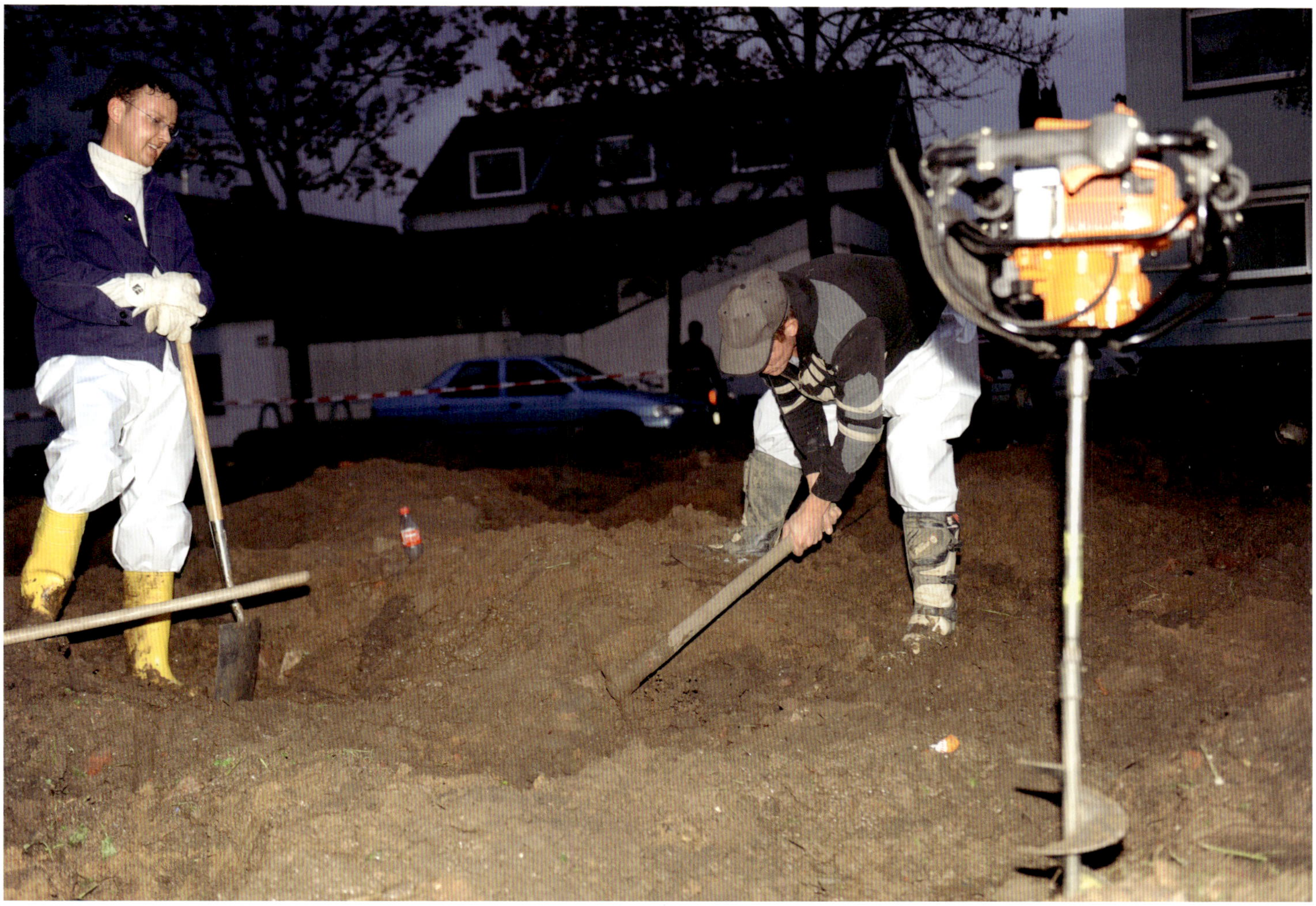

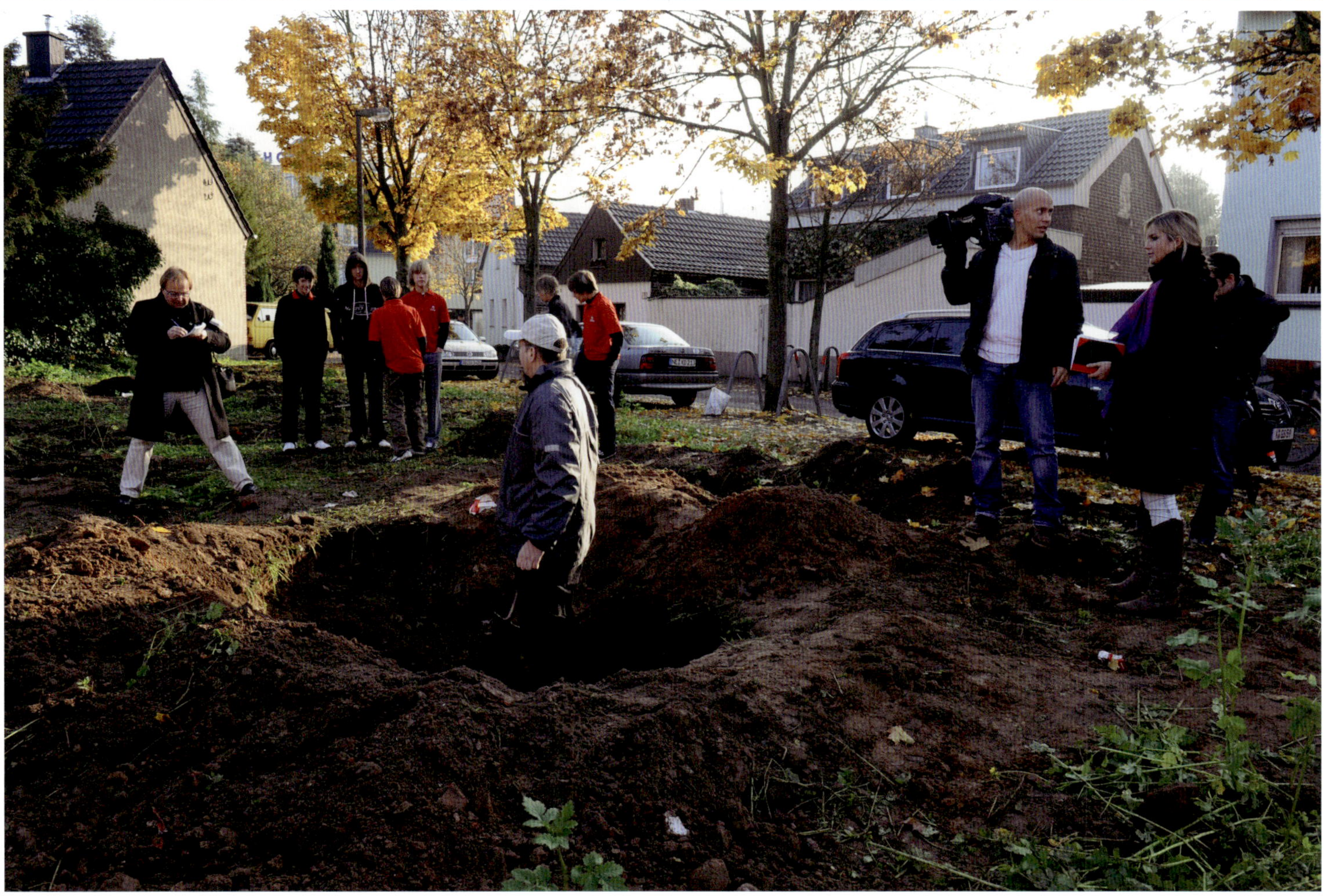

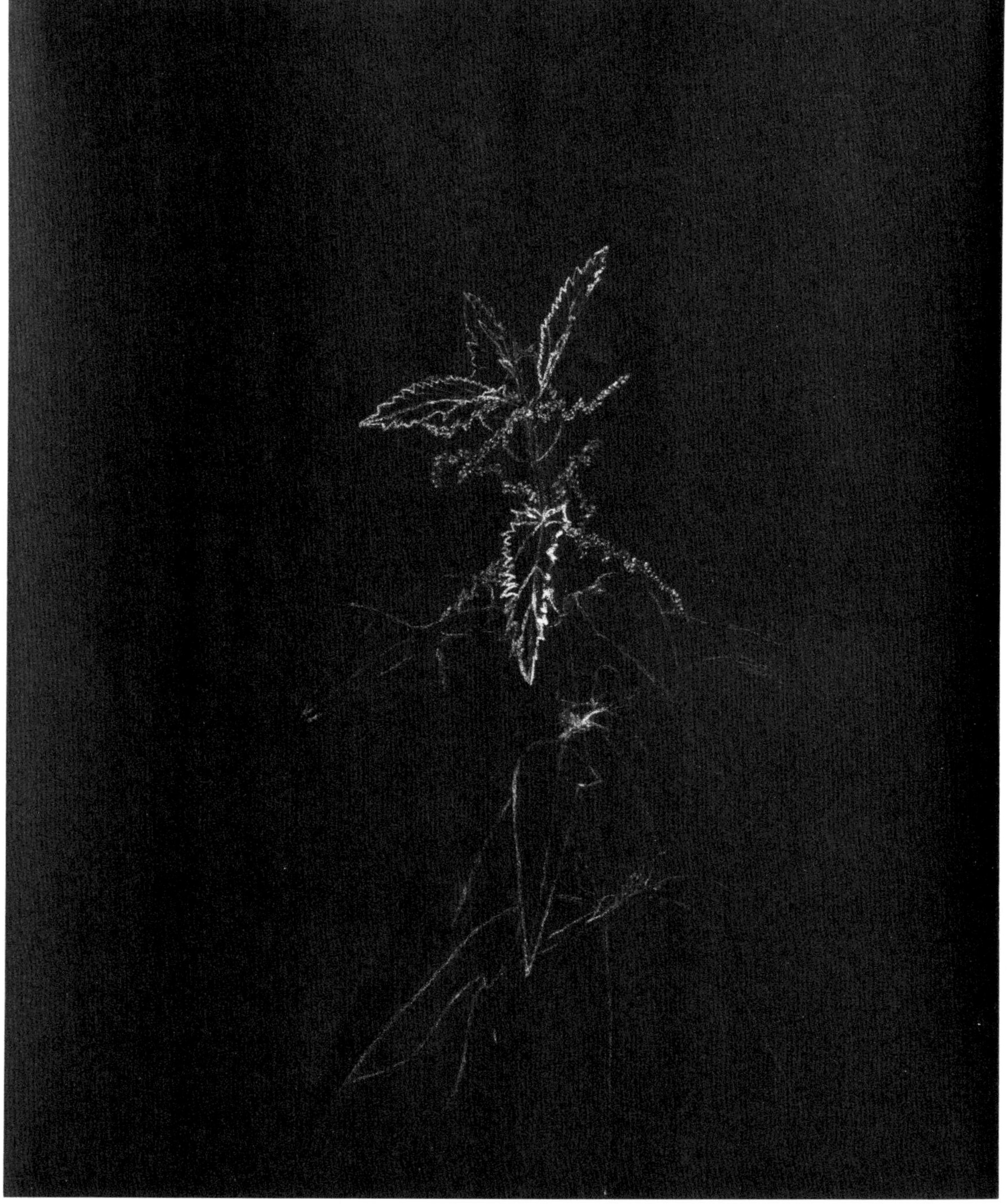

Brennnessel, 2019

Sandpaper, slate pencil / Sandpapier, Schieferstift,
33 × 28 cm (framed / gerahmt)

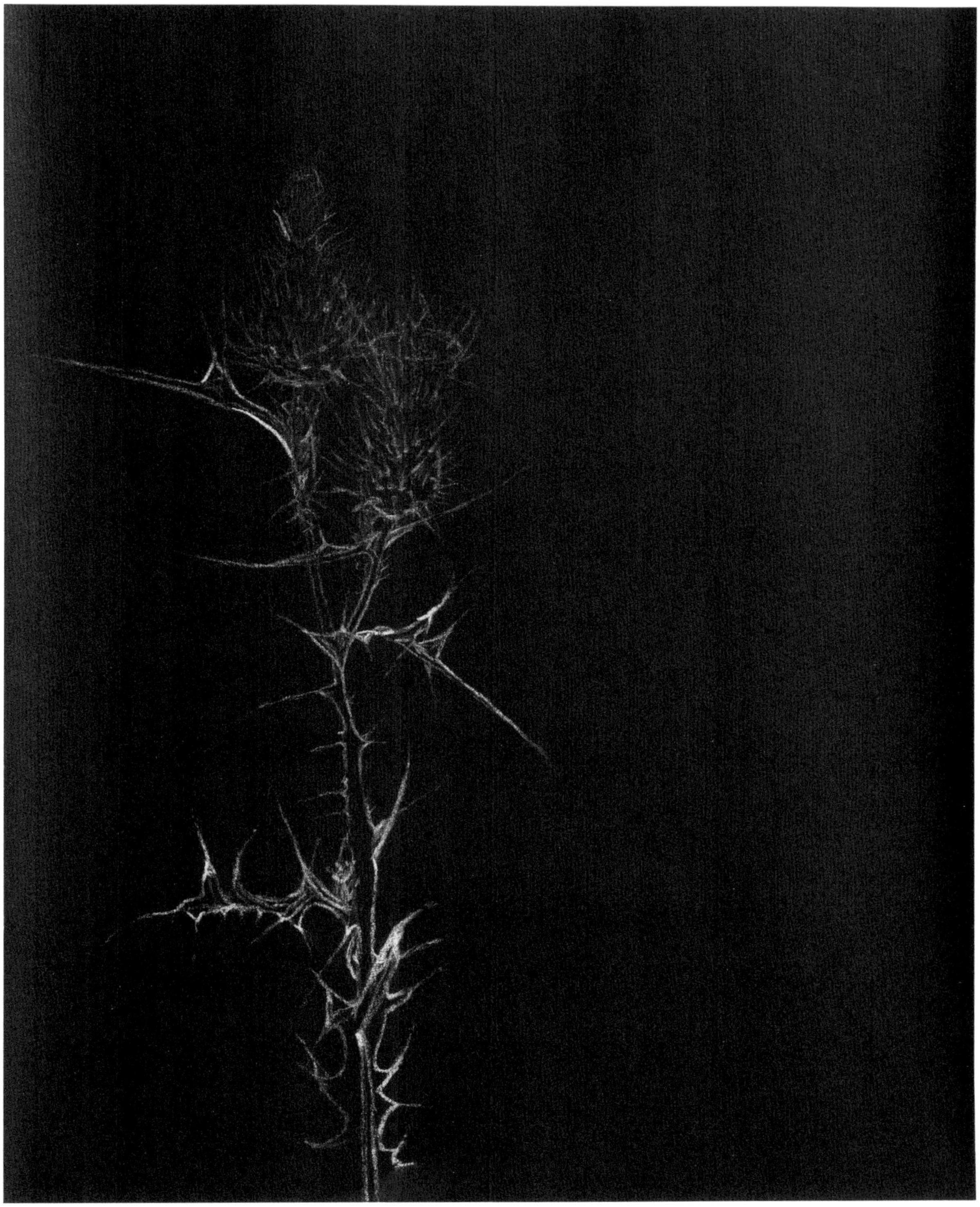

Distel 3, 2019

Sandpaper, slate pencil / Sandpapier, Schieferstift,
33 × 28 cm (framed / gerahmt)

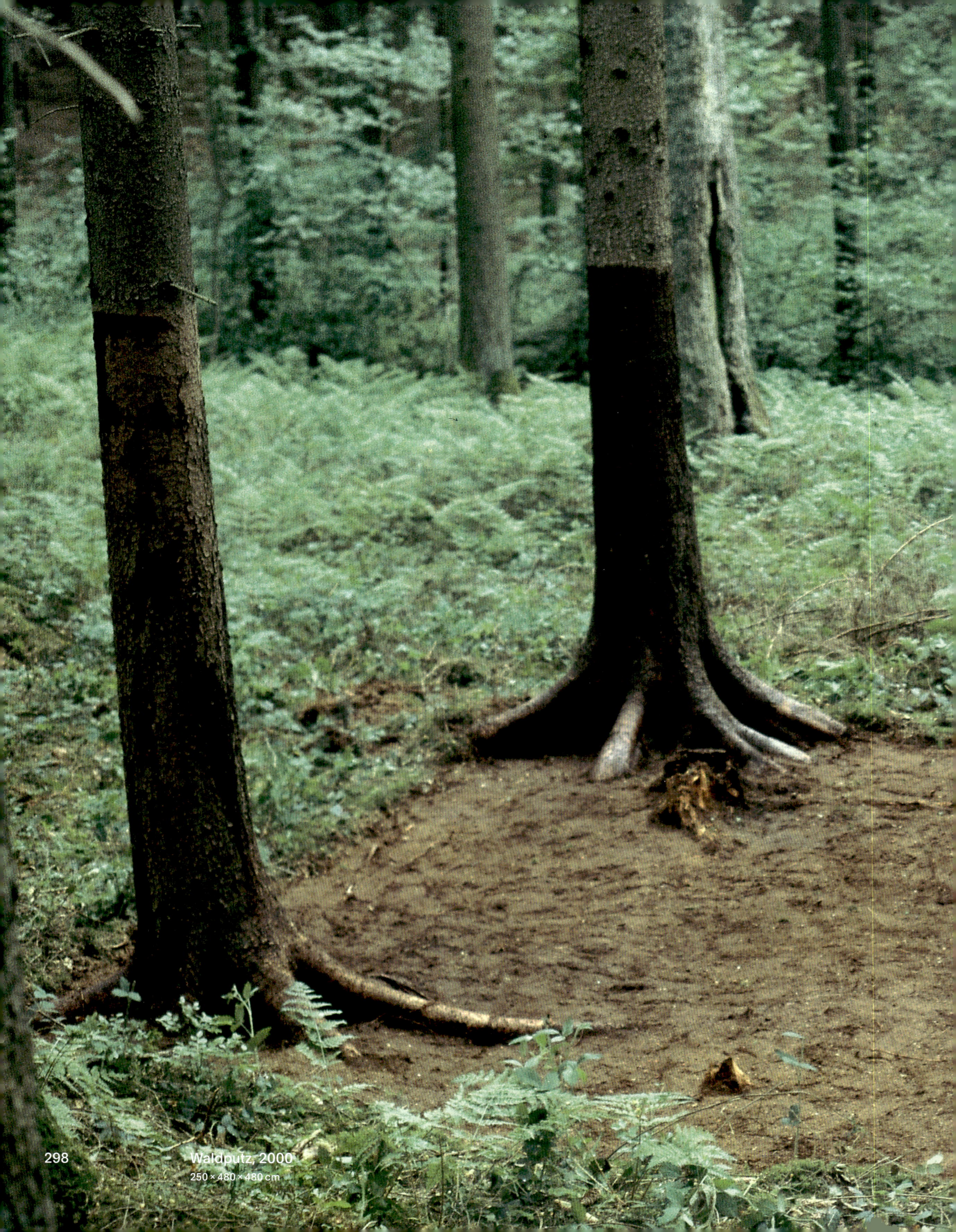

Waldputz, 2000
250 × 480 × 480 cm

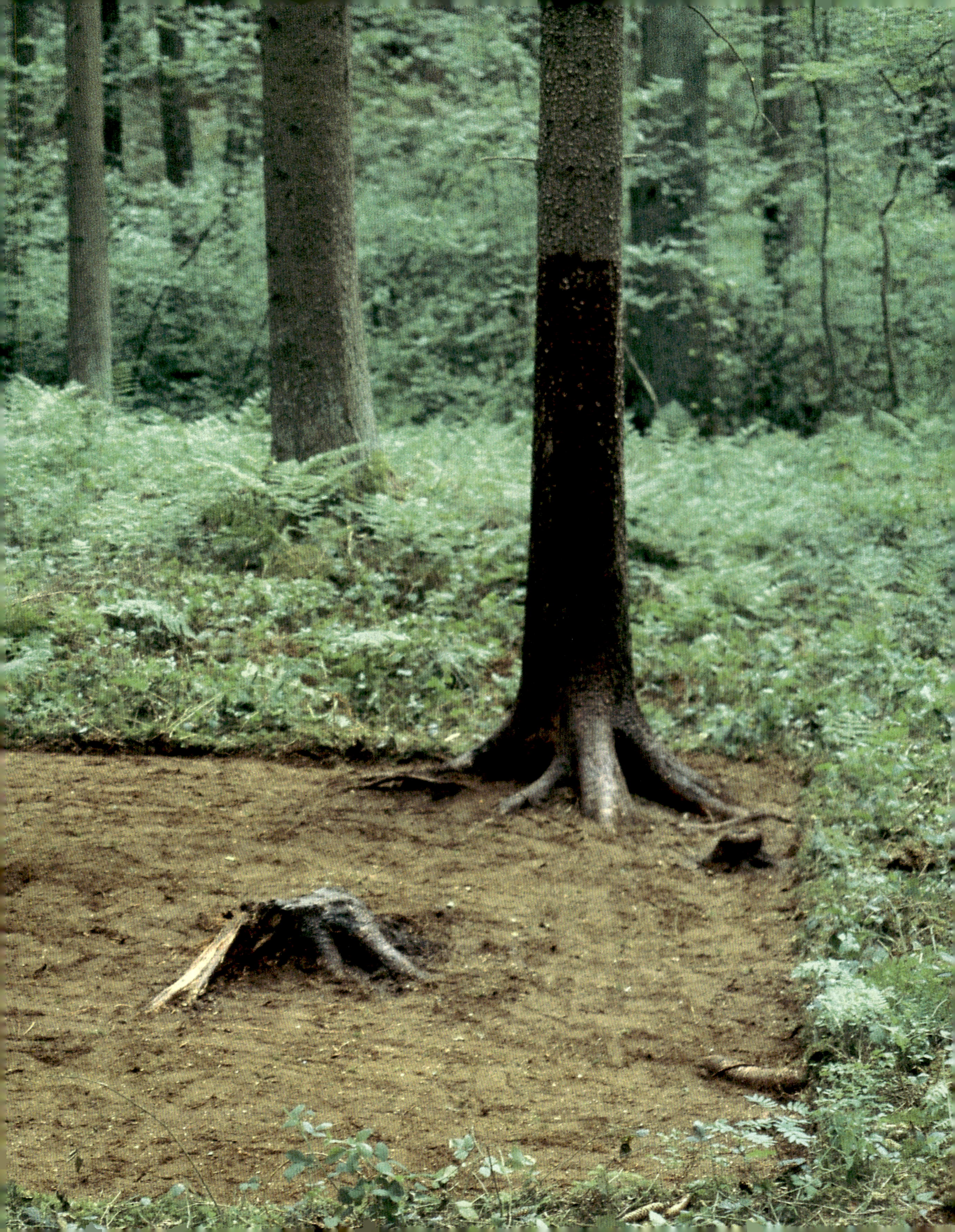

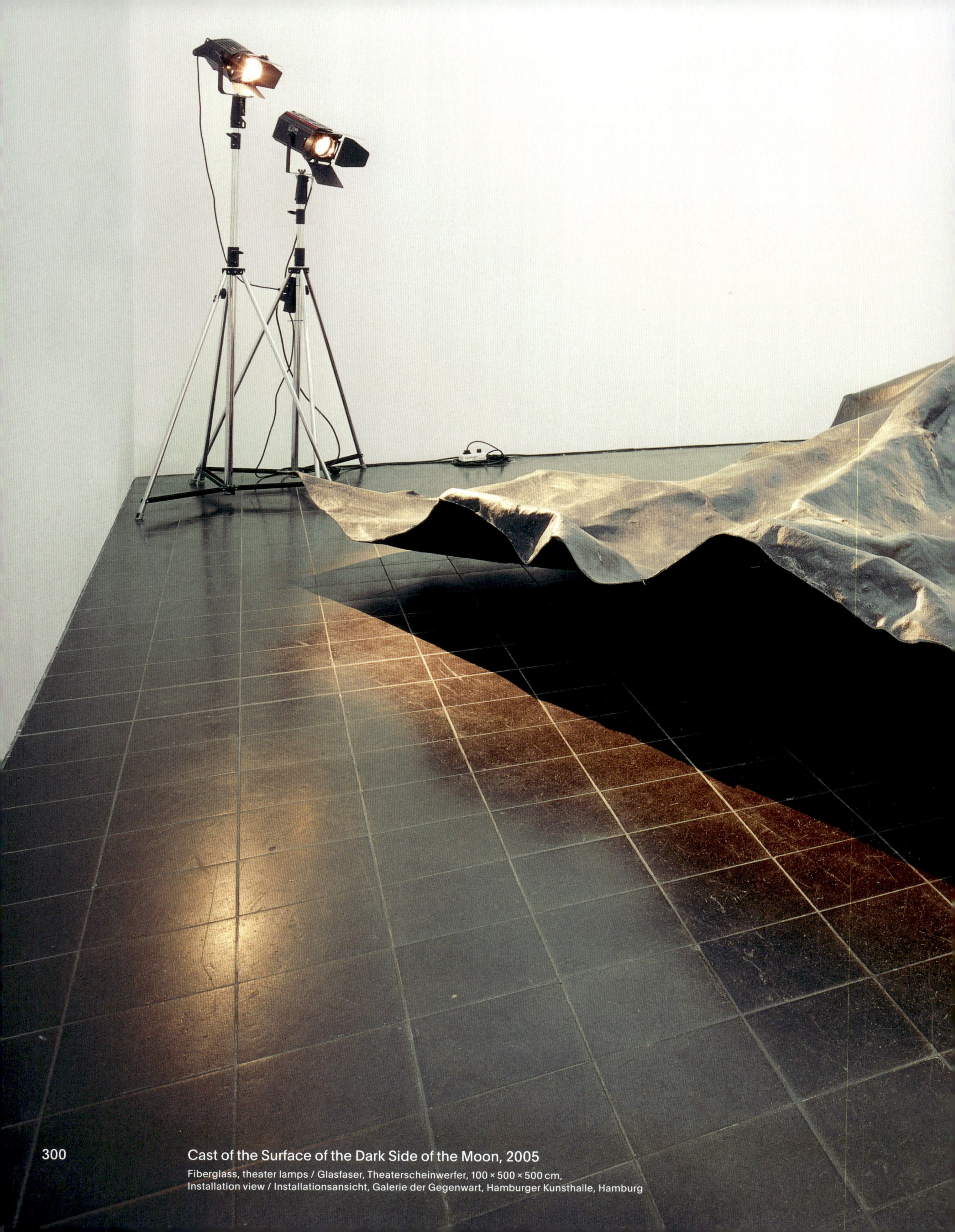

Cast of the Surface of the Dark Side of the Moon, 2005

Fiberglass, theater lamps / Glasfaser, Theaterscheinwerfer, 100 × 500 × 500 cm,
Installation view / Installationsansicht, Galerie der Gegenwart, Hamburger Kunsthalle, Hamburg

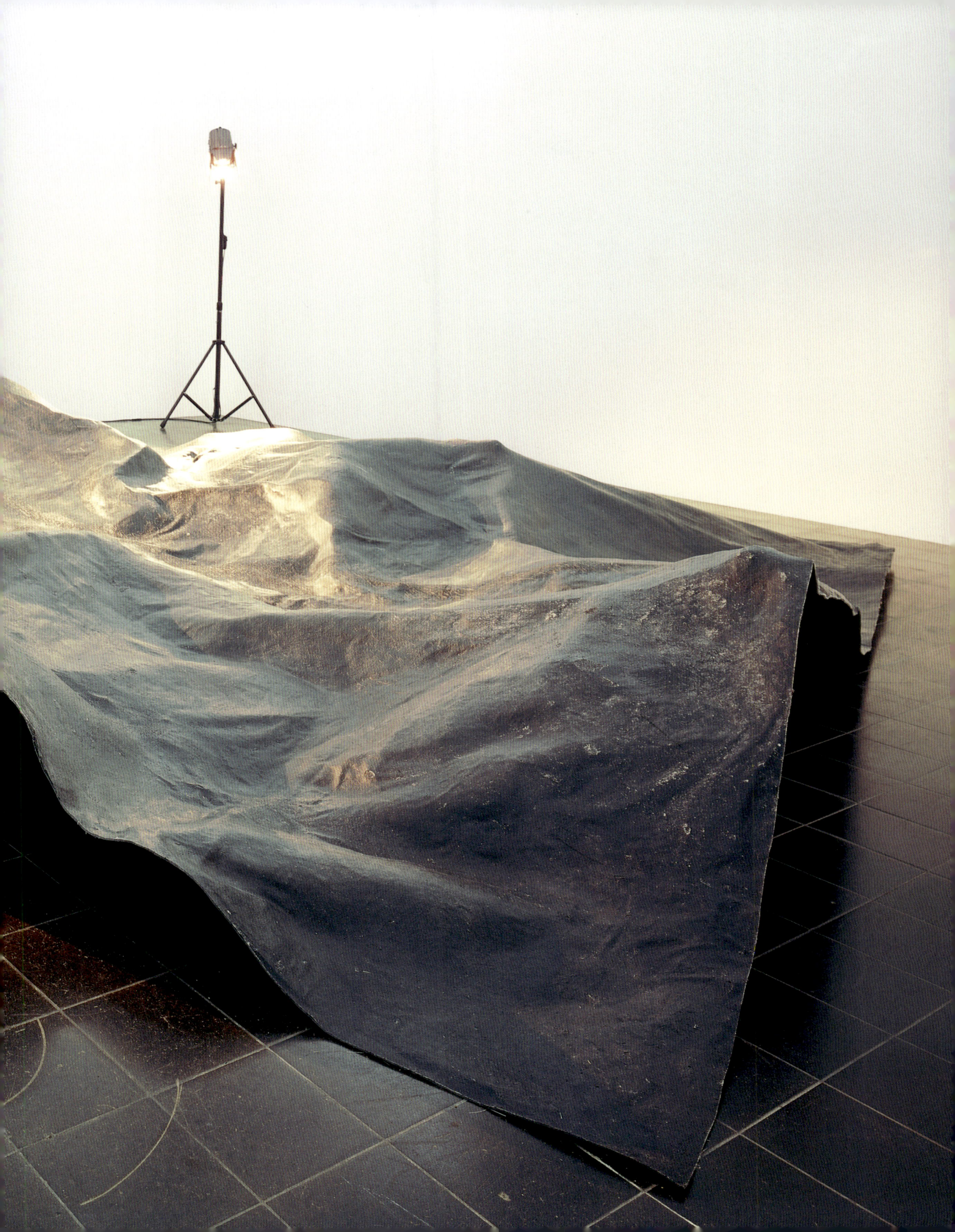

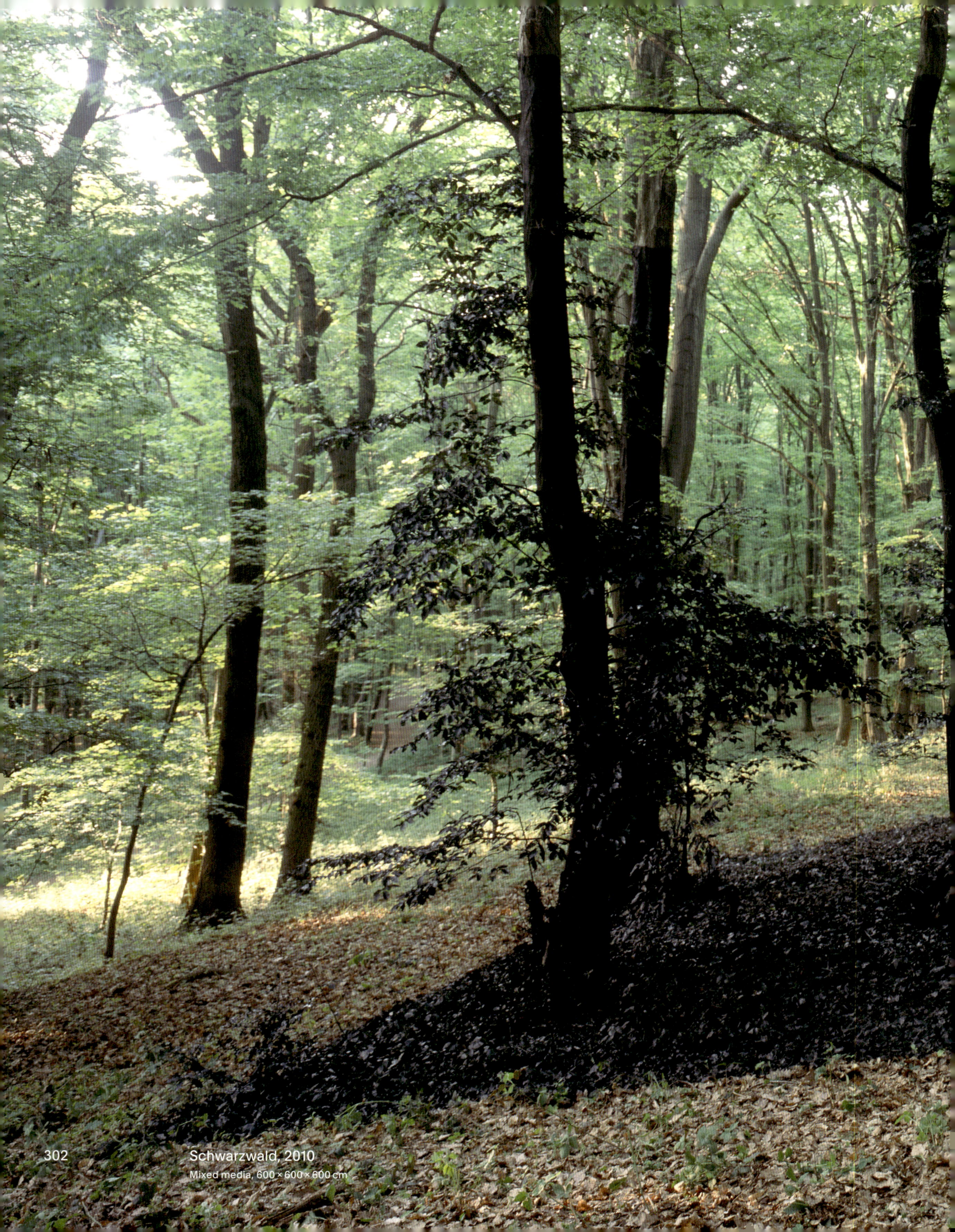

Schwarzwald, 2010
Mixed media, 600 × 600 × 600 cm

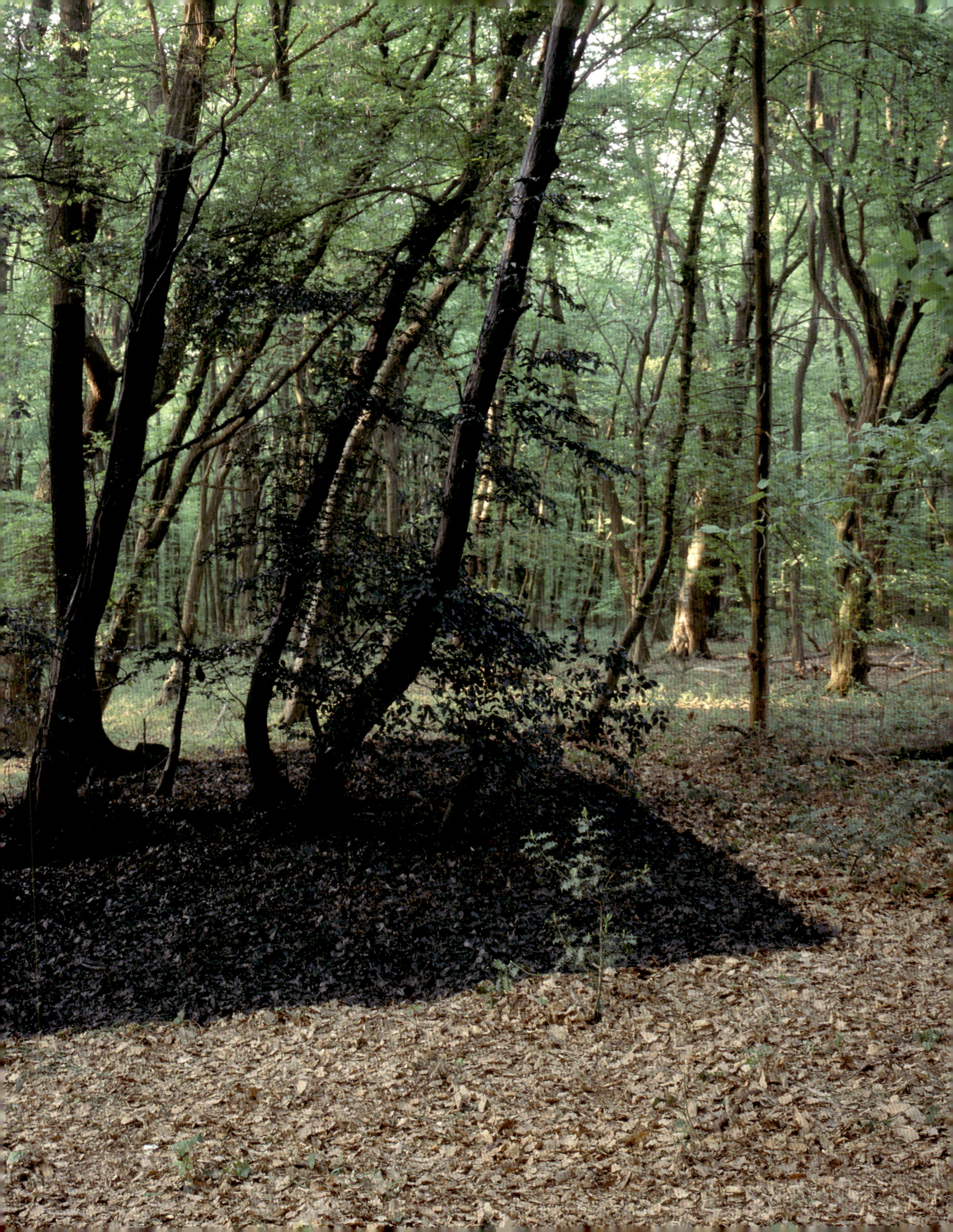

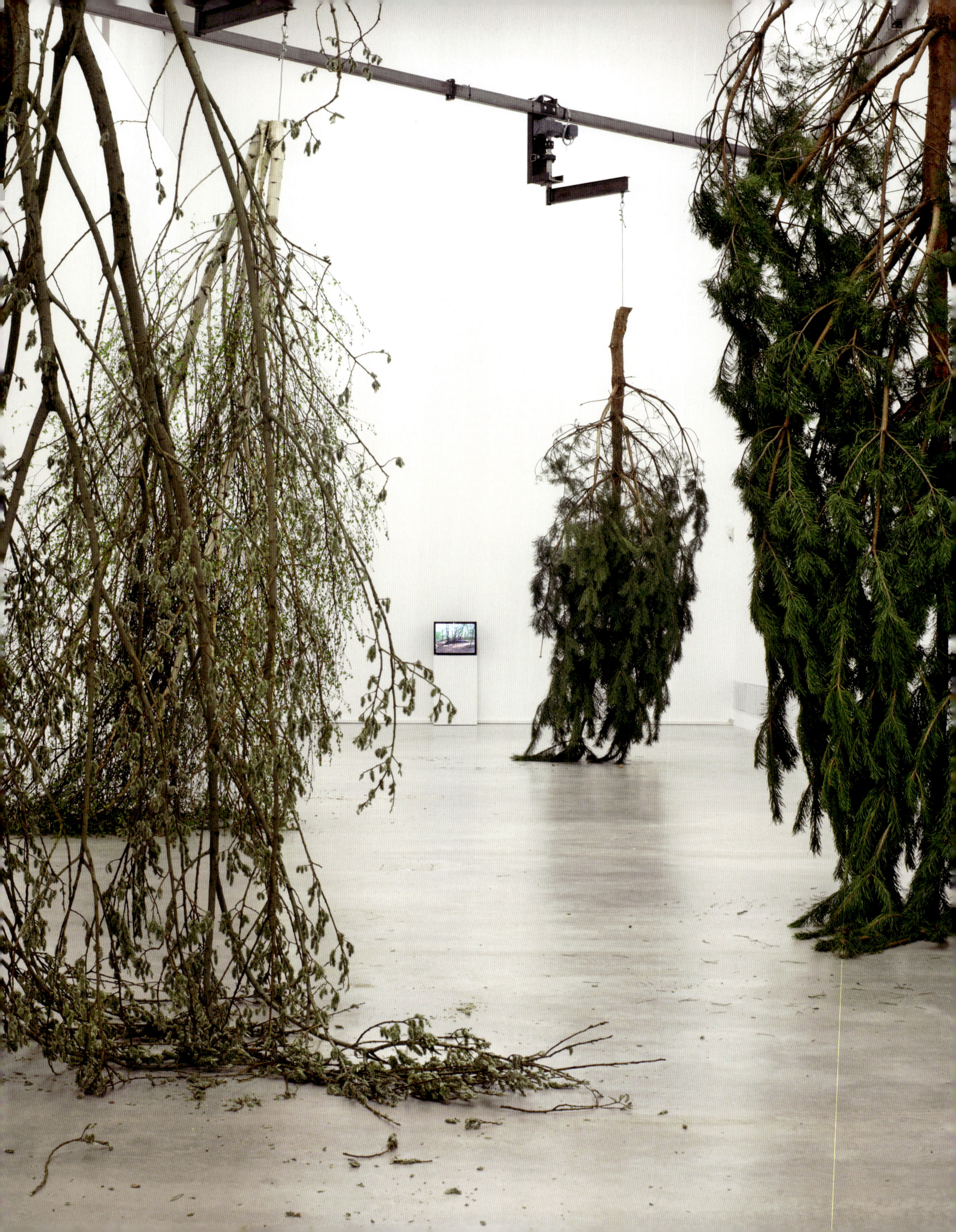

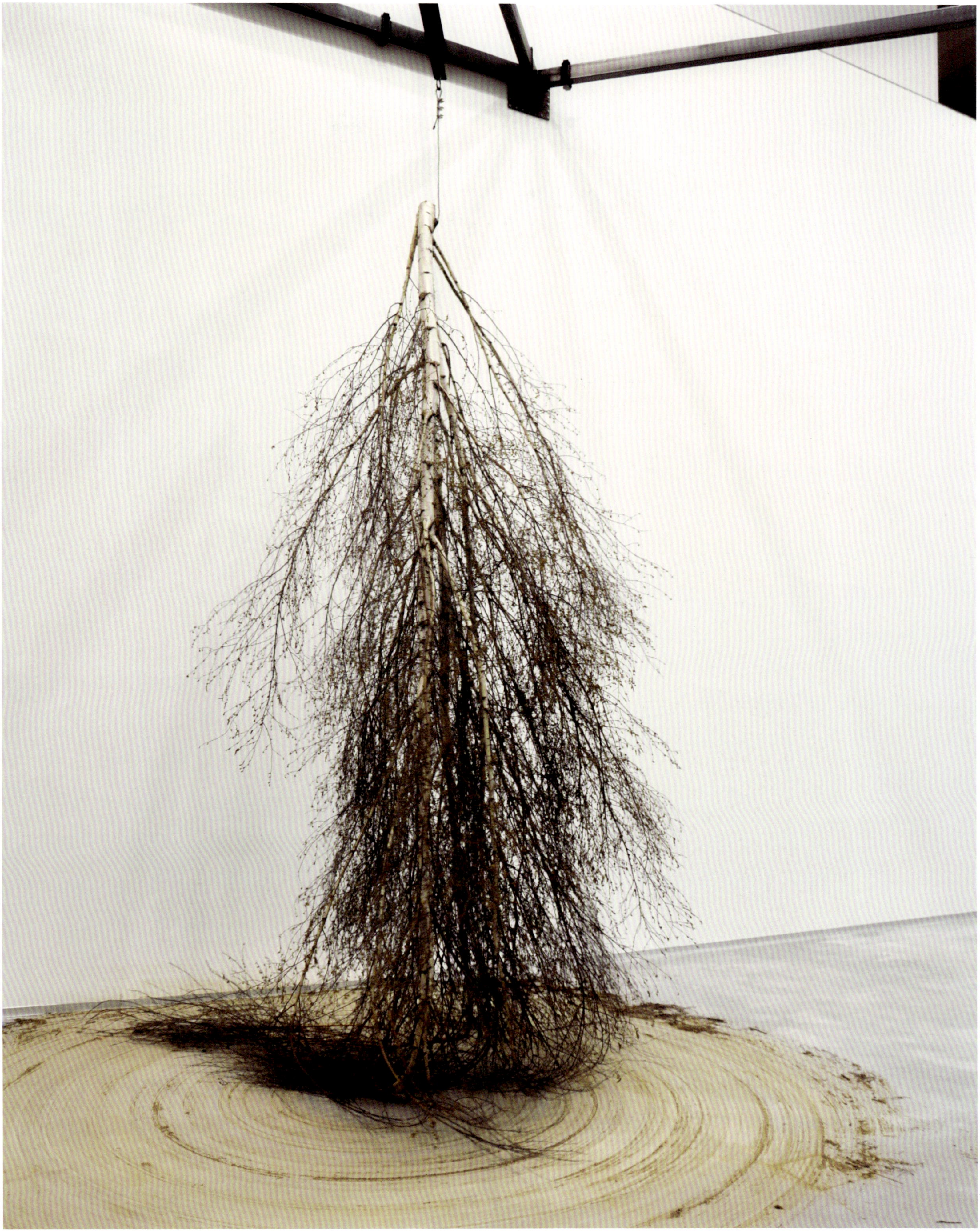

Forst, 2010
Trees, electric motors, steel / Bäume, Elektromotoren, Stahl,
Installation view / Installationsansicht, Berlinische Galerie, Berlin

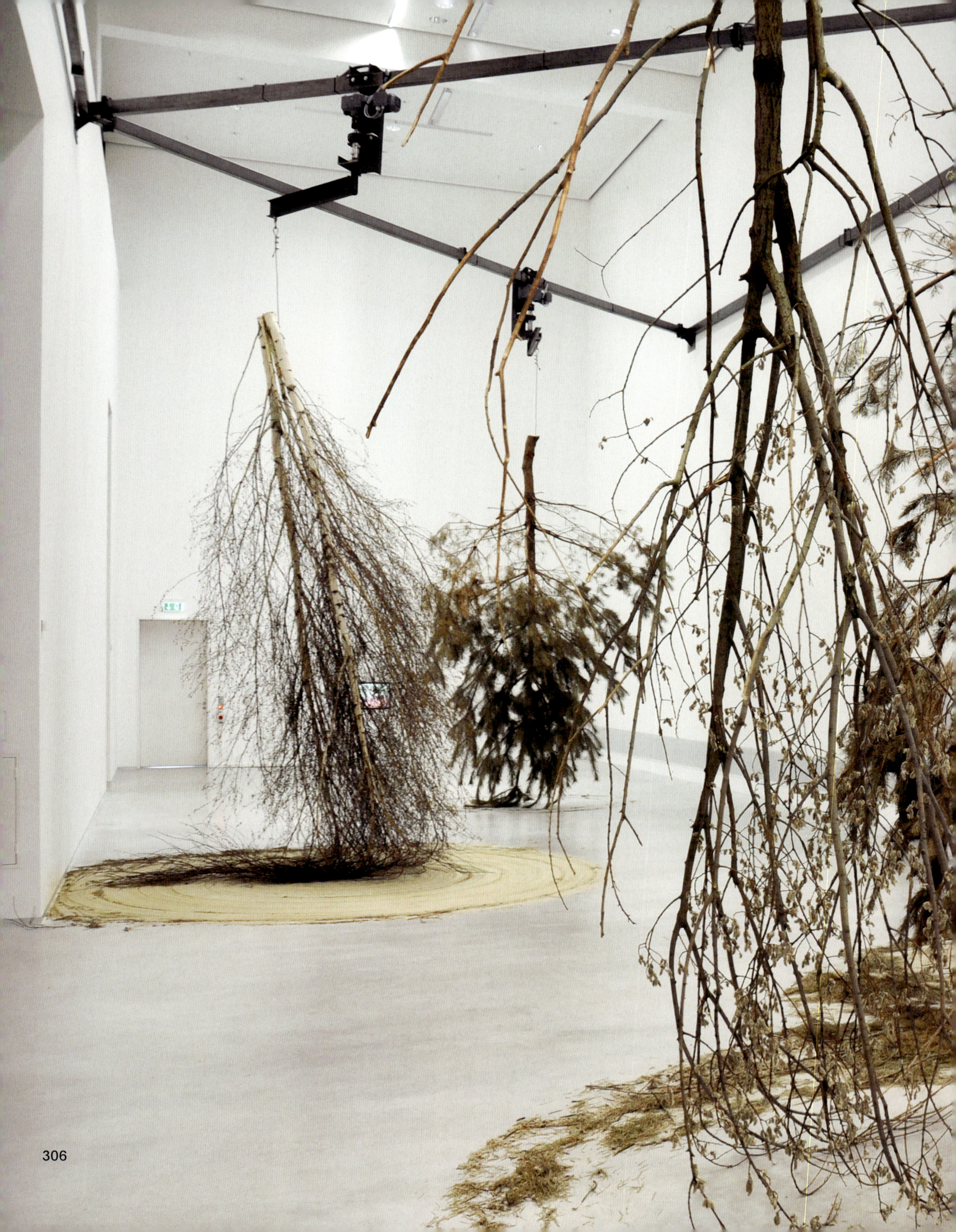

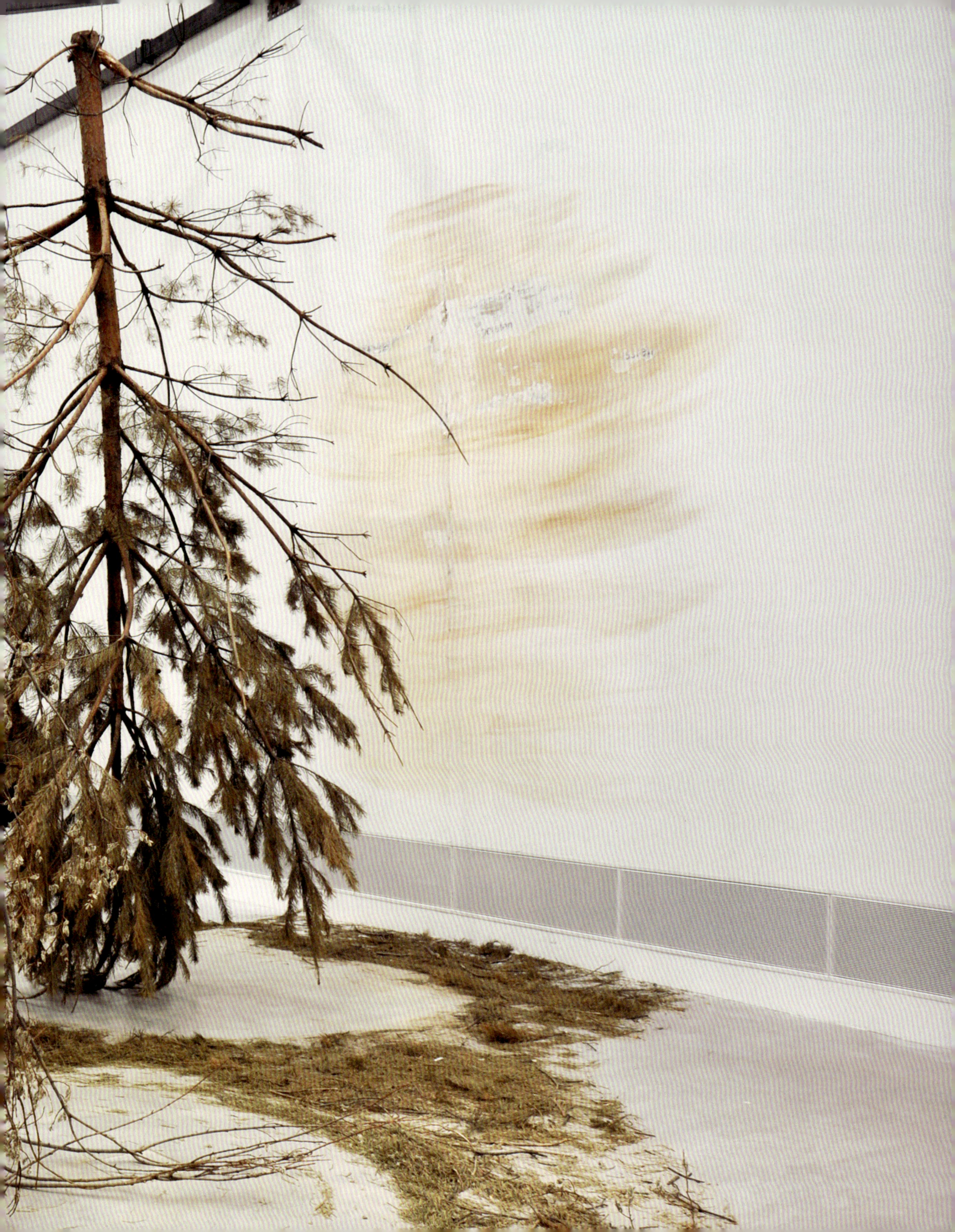

PRODUCTION

ANFERTIGUNG

There are artists who, when they come to us, already have a very precise idea of a form in mind. In our workshop for the production of artworks by contemporary artists, we then have to find solutions for the realization and make the seemingly impossible possible. Often, we invent elaborate techniques so that something like magic can emerge. And then there are artists who have an idea for a sculpture, the final form of which only emerges in the course of the process.

This second version of form-finding clearly describes our work with Michael Sailstorfer. I cannot say, however, that the drawings that Michael makes—often spontaneously in our workshop—and which do not contain any details, are fundamentally different from the result. Somehow, everything is already there, in those first, simple sketches. At that point, I probably do not yet know how the conveyor belt will have to be guided and stored, how the water wheel might be constructed, which steel cable we will need, or what the structural analysis will reveal. Also, I certainly cannot yet say what level of craftsmanship would be appropriate for the job.

But the image is there.

Michael Sailstorfer and we have thus always managed to make decisions around his original idea that do not take themselves too seriously in terms of execution but rather support this.

The magic of Michael Sailstorfer's work emerges on an additional level that is not so easy to describe. Time and again, I was surprised by the result, despite the fact that I was already completely involved in its development.

I experienced this particularly intensively in 2010, when I was working on *Forst* (Forest) ↗304–307. Michael described to me the relatively clear idea: Several trees hang upside down and sweep their own leaves that have fallen onto the ground.

Es gibt Künstler*innen, die schon eine sehr genaue Vorstellung von einer Form haben, wenn sie zu uns kommen. In unserer Werkstatt für die Produktion von Kunstwerken zeitgenössischer Künstler*innen gilt es dann, Lösungen für die Umsetzung zu finden und scheinbar Unmögliches möglich zu machen. Oft erfinden wir dabei handwerklich aufwändige Techniken, damit so etwas wie Magie entstehen kann.

Und dann gibt es Künstler*innen, die eine Idee für eine Skulptur haben, deren Form im Laufe des Prozesses erst entsteht. Diese zweite Version der Formfindung beschreibt eindeutig unsere Arbeit mit Michael Sailstorfer. Es ist nicht so, dass die Zeichnungen, die Michael – oft spontan, bei uns in der Werkstatt – anfertigt und die keine Details enthalten, sich ganz grundsätzlich vom Ergebnis unterscheiden würden. Irgendwie ist alles schon da, in diesen ersten, einfachen Skizzen.

Zu dem Zeitpunkt weiß ich dann wahrscheinlich noch nicht, wie das Förderband geführt und gelagert werden muss, wie das Wasserrad konstruiert werden könnte, welches Stahlseil wir benötigen und was die statische Berechnung ergeben wird. Auch kann ich sicherlich noch nicht sagen, welcher handwerkliche Ausführungsgrad für die Arbeit passend wäre.

Aber das Bild ist da.

Und so haben Michael Sailstorfer und wir es immer geschafft, um seine Ursprungsidee herum Entscheidungen zu treffen, die sich von der Ausführung her nicht zu wichtig nehmen, sondern diese unterstützen.

Die Magie der Arbeiten von Michael Sailstorfer entsteht auf einer zusätzlichen, nicht so leicht zu beschreibenden Ebene. Immer wieder wurde ich vom Ergebnis überrascht, obwohl ich doch schon so involviert in die Entwicklung war.

Besonders intensiv habe ich das 2010 bei der Arbeit *Forst* ↗304–307 miterlebt. Michael beschrieb mir die relativ

I quite freely designed the construction of the suspension; and often, of course, one decision leads to another. The motor was chosen according to the technical requirements, whereby the drive of one manufacturer seemed to be more powerful. A wide U-profile could perfectly accommodate the selected motor base, so that the rest of the casing still protruded above it and floated a bit freely. Certainly, there would have been many other options, but we all ultimately felt it was most coherent this way.

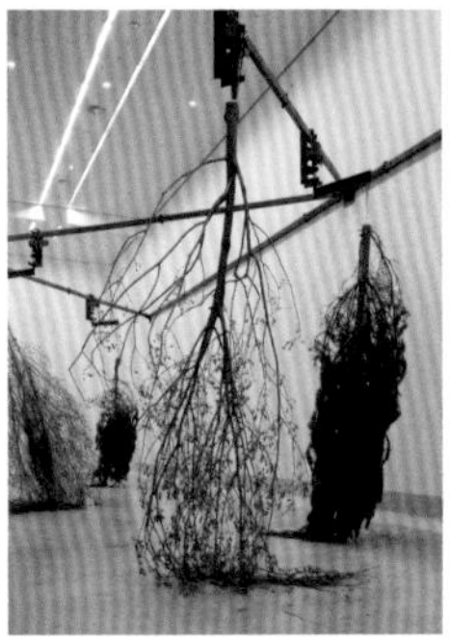

Forst, 2010

During the first test hanging, we noticed that there was a wobble in the movement when we let the trees rest a little more on the ground. It was a really nice moment with a decision in the process, which changed the work a tiny bit. Michael let it evolve.

I was then particularly impressed by the power of the work after it had been installed. It was first shown at the Kestner Gesellschaft in Hanover. When we had finished and had complied with Michael's request to shift the position of one tree, I really understood for the first time how much everything was more than the proverbial sum of its individual parts. For the space had been added as an element. Depending on the line of sight, *Forst* looked like a dense stock of trees; but then we saw individual trunks swaying again. The sounds of cracking branches were realistic and poetic at the same time. The engines on the ceiling hummed distantly. The effect of Michael's work resonated throughout the space and into the adjoining rooms.

The initial idea had taken shape: Several trees hung upside down, sweeping their own leaves that had fallen onto the floor. But it was more than that. Perception was literally turned topsy-turvy: We were standing in the middle of a surreal, magical forest.

eindeutige Idee: Mehrere Bäume hängen mit den Wipfeln nach unten und fegen auf dem Boden ihre herabfallenden Blätter selbst zusammen.

Die Konstruktion der Aufhängung habe ich ziemlich frei gestaltet, oft ergibt ja eine Entscheidung die nächste. Der Motor wurde nach den technischen Anforderungen ausgesucht, eventuell wirkte der Antrieb des einen Herstellers kraftvoller, ein breites U-Profil konnte den ausgewählten Motorfuß perfekt aufnehmen, sodass der Rest des Gehäuses noch darüber hinausragte und ein wenig frei schwebte. Sicherlich hätte es viele andere Möglichkeiten gegeben, aber wir empfanden es alle schließlich so am stimmigsten.

Bei der ersten Probehängung stellten wir fest, dass sich ein Taumeln in der Bewegung einstellt, wenn wir die Bäume etwas mehr auf dem Boden aufliegen lassen. Das war ein wirklich schöner Moment mit einer Entscheidung im Prozess, wodurch sich die Arbeit ein klein wenig veränderte. Michael hat sie sich entwickeln lassen.

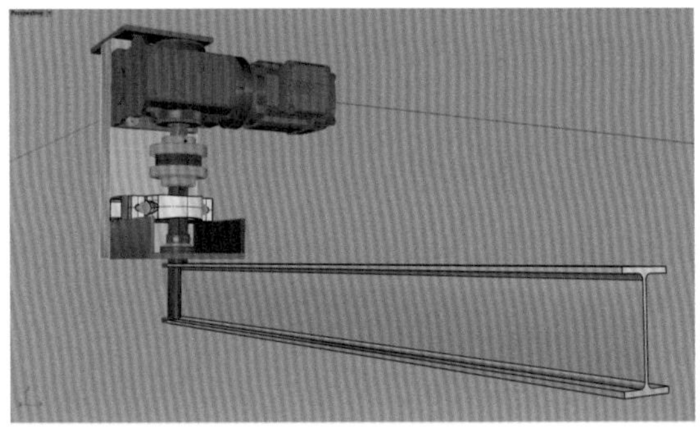

Konstruktionszeichung *Forst*

Beeindruckt war ich dann vor allem von der Kraft der Arbeit nach der Installation. Sie wurde zuerst in der Kestner Gesellschaft in Hannover gezeigt. Als wir fertig waren und noch Michaels Wunsch nach dem Versetzen der Position eines einzelnen Baumes entsprochen hatten, habe ich zum ersten Mal richtig verstanden, wie sehr alles mehr als die sprichwörtliche Summe seiner einzelnen Teile war. Denn der Raum war als Element hinzugekommen. Je nach Sichtachse wirkte *Forst* wie ein dichter Baumbestand, aber dann sahen wir wieder vereinzelt taumelnde Stämme. Die Geräusche der knackenden Äste waren realistisch und poetisch zugleich. Die Motoren an der Decke summten entfernt. Die Wirkung von Michaels Arbeit entfaltete sich im gesamten Raum bis in die Nebenräume hinein.

Die Anfangsidee hatte Gestalt angenommen: Mehrere Bäume hingen mit den Wipfeln nach unten und fegten ihre herabfallenden Blätter auf dem Boden selbst zusammen. Aber es war mehr als das. Die Wahrnehmung war buchstäblich auf den Kopf gestellt: Wir standen mitten in einem surrealen, magischen Wald.

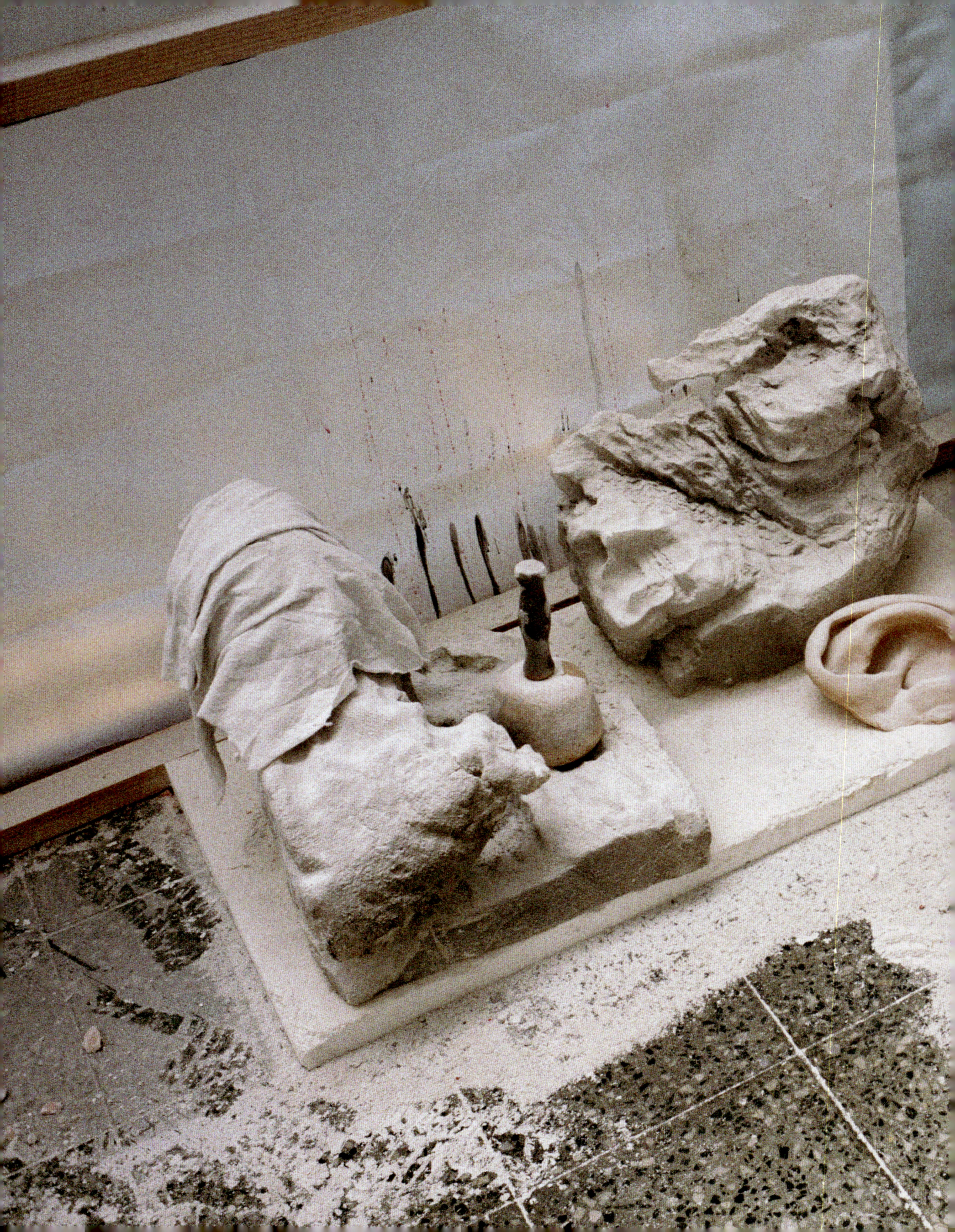

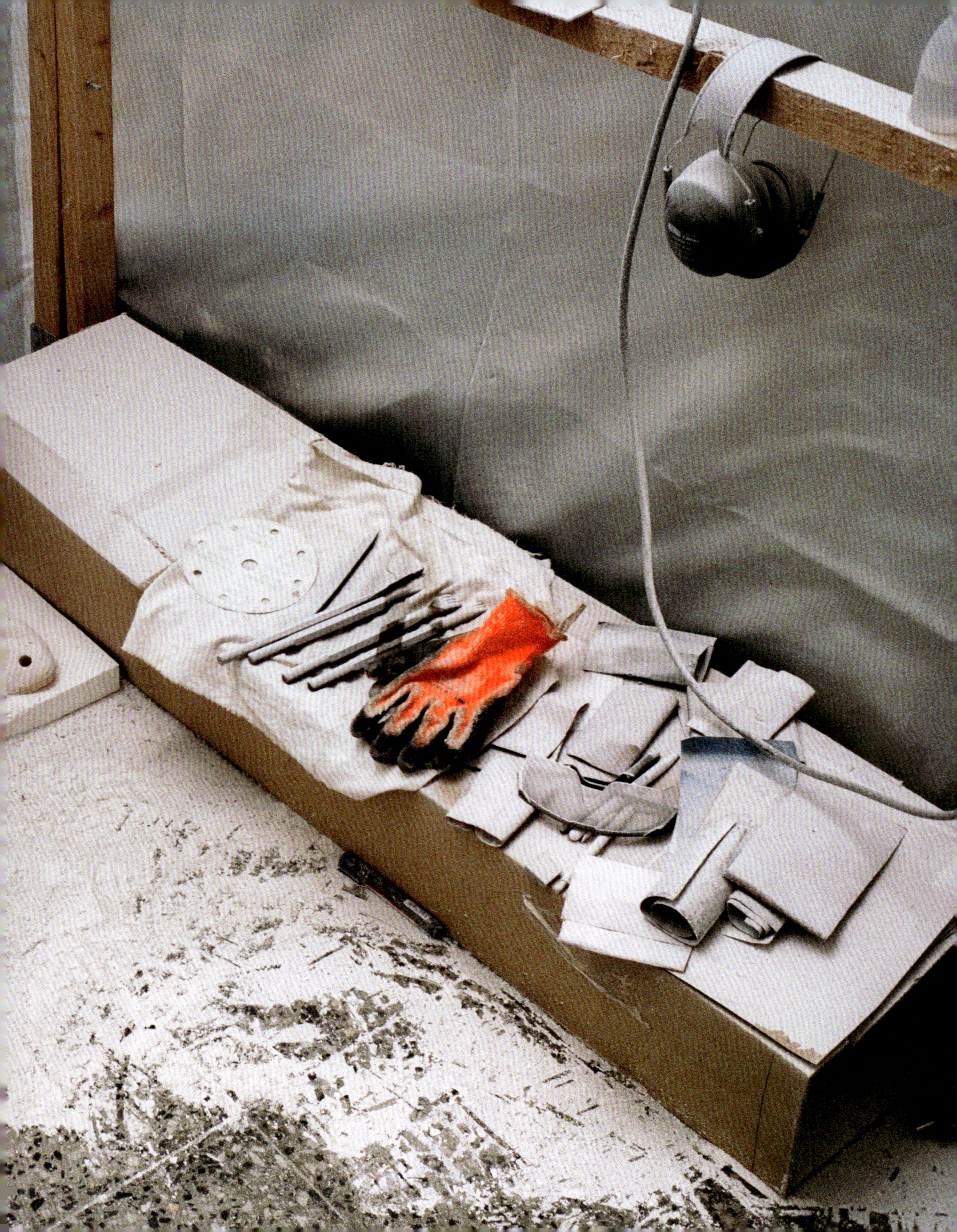

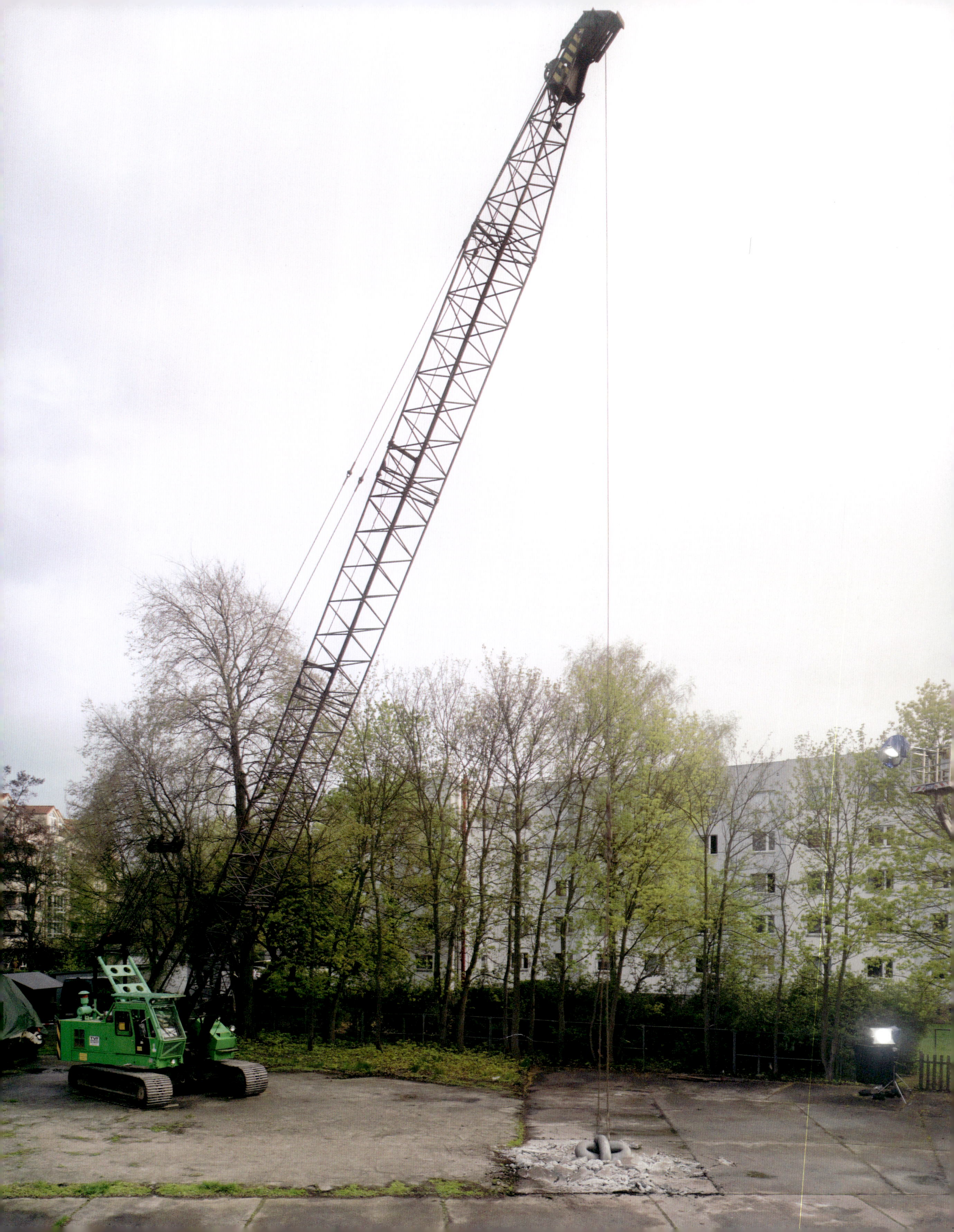

MICHAEL SAILSTORFER

Born / Geboren 1979 in Velden

Lives and works / Lebt und arbeitet in Berlin DE

EDUCATION
AUSBILDUNG

2019
Artist-in-Residence, CCA Andratx, Andratx, Mallorca ES

2008–2010
Grant of / Stipendium der Günther-Peill-Stiftung, Düren DE

2006
International Studio Program, Office for Contemporary Art Norway, Oslo NO

2005
Villa Aurora Residency / Stipendium der Villa Aurora, Los Angeles CA, US

2003–2004
MA Fine Arts, Goldsmiths' College, London GB

2003
Grant of / Stipendium der Studienstiftung des Deutschen Volkes

1999–2005
Studies at / Studium an der Akademie der Bildenden Künste, Munich / München DE (Prof. Olaf Metzel)

TEACHING
LEHRE

2018–2019
Guest Professor / Gastprofessur, Project class for sculpture / Projektklasse Bildhauerei, Akademie der Bildenden Künste Nürnberg DE

2010–2011
Guest Professor / Gastprofessur, Basic class for sculpture / Grundklasse Bildhauerei, Hochschule für Bildende Künste Braunschweig DE

SOLO EXHIBITIONS
EINZELAUSSTELLUNGEN

2022
Heavy Eyes, Carbon 12, Dubai AE
Heavy Eyes, König Galerie, Seoul KR

2021
Plumbum, Livie Fine Art, Zurich / Zürich CH
Ariadne Raum, Museen der Stadt Landshut, Landshut DE
Heavy Eyes, Avlskarl Gallery, Copenhagen / Kopenhagen DK

2020
C'est la vie, Sellerie, Galerie Jahn, Landshut DE
1–32, Galerie Zink, Waldkirchen DE

2019
SINK, SANK, SUNK, König Galerie, Berlin DE
TEAR SHOW, Perrotin, New York NY, US
Michael Sailstorfer, BNKR, Munich / München DE

2018
Tear Show, König London, London GB
Brainspotting, Avlskarl Gallery, Copenhagen / Kopenhagen DK
We Love Them All, Carbon 12, Dubai AE
Troubling Matter II, Galerie Jahn, Landshut DE

2017
Clouds and Tears, Proyectos Monclova, Mexico City MX
Zwei Äpfel, Kunsthaus Alte Mühle & Lenne-Atelier, Schmallenberg DE
Jupiter Artland, Edinburgh GB
Altenheim für Kosmonauten, Kunsthal 44, Møen DK
Altenheim für Populisten, Grieder Contemporary, Zurich / Zürich CH
Hitzefrei, König Galerie, Berlin DE

2016
Maze, Senatsverwaltung für Justiz, Berlin DE
Troubling matter, Galerie Jahn, Landshut DE
Silver Cloud, Studio Michael Sailstorfer, Berlin DE

2015
Freundschaft, Galerie Michael Zink, Waldkirchen DE
Wiesen bei Nacht, Kunstverein Wiesen, Wiesen DE
Michael Sailstorfer, Kunsthaus Pasquart, Bienne /Biel CH

2014
Breakwater, Loushy Art & Projects, Tel Aviv IL
It might as well be spring, Rochester Art Center, Rochester MN, US
Kopf und Körper, Museum Kurhaus Kleve – Ewald Mataré-Sammlung, Kleve DE
B-Seite, Haus am Waldsee, Berlin DE
Every piece is a new problem, CAC Contemporary Arts Center, Cincinnati CH, US
Antiherbst, Johann König, Berlin DE
Reibungsverlust am Arbeitsplatz, Grieder Contemporary, Zurich / Zürich CH

2013
Try to reach the goal without touching the walls, Carbon 12, Dubai AE
Freedom Fries am Arbeitsplatz, Perrotin, Paris FR
Young West, Kunsthalle Recklinghausen, Recklinghausen DE

2012
Hauptweg und Nebenwege, König Galerie, Berlin DE
Solarkatze, Galerie Thaddaeus Ropac, Salzburg AT
Forst, Vattenfall Contemporary, Berlinische Galerie, Berlin DE
Nettoyer La Forêt, FRAC Haute-Normandie, Sotteville-lès-Rouen FR
Solarkatze, Galleria Zero, Milan / Mailand IT

2011
Tornado, Public Art Fund New York, Doris C. Freedman Plaza, Central Park, New York NY, US
Raum und Zeit, S.M.A.K. – Stedelijk Museum voor Actuele Kunst, Ghent / Gent BE
Für immer Strom, Kunsthalle Nürnberg, Nuremberg / Nürnberg DE
Clouds, Modern Art Oxford, Oxford GB
Crash, Zeppelin Museum und Kunstverein, Friedrichshafen DE
Sonar / Implicit Sound, Fundació Joan Miró – Espai 13, Barcelona ES
T-72 Sculpture, Galleri K, Oslo NO

2010
Forst, Kestner Gesellschaft, Hanover / Hannover DE
Michael Sailstorfer, Goethe-Institut Moskau, Moscow / Moskau RU
T-72, Kunsthalle Bremerhaven, Bremerhaven DE
Wolken, K20, Düsseldorf DE
Knoten wie Wolken, Galeria Fortes Vilaça, São Paulo BR
Schwarzwald, Leopold-Hoesch-Museum, Düren DE

2009
backyardoutdoorsculptureseries #2: Wohnen mit Verkehrsanbindung, Johann König, Berlin DE
Pulheim gräbt, Pulheim DE
No Light, Rosa-Luxemburg-Platz, Berlin DE
No Light, Perrotin, Paris FR

2008
Michael Sailstorfer, Johann König, Berlin DE
Kulturpreis der Dr. Franz und Astrid Ritter-Stiftung für Bildende Kunst 2008, Weytterturm, Straubing DE
10 000 Steine, Schirn Kunsthalle, Frankfurt/Main DE
Mollstraße, Galleri K, Oslo NO

2007
Parkhaus zeigt 800 M, Parkhaus im Malkastenpark, Düsseldorf DE
Wand über Kopf, Sorry, we're closed, Sébastien & Rodolphe Janssen Project Space, Brussels / Brüssel BE
U6, 14 Grad 34, 790N / 60 Grad 50, 969W, Kasseler Kunstvereinsheim, Kassel DE
U1-U13, Galleria Zero, Milan / Mailand IT

2006
Michael Sailstorfer, Johann König, Berlin DE
High, Studio im Zumikon, Institut für Moderne Kunst Nürnberg, Nuremberg / Nürnberg DE

2005
Zeit ist keine Autobahn, Rote Zelle, Munich / München DE
U, Galerie Zink & Gegner, Munich / München DE
Michael Sailstorfer – Skulptur, Ursula Blickle Stiftung, Kraichtal DE
Hoher Besuch, Marta Herford, Herford DE
Der Schein trügt, Jack Hanley Gallery, Los Angeles CA, US
Zeit ist keine Autobahn, Galleria Zero, Milan / Mailand IT
My Private, Cernusco sul Naviglio, Milan / Mailand IT

2004
Dämmerung, Attitudes – espace d'art contemporain, Geneva / Genf CH

2003
Welttour, Galerie Markus Richter, Berlin DE
D-IBRB, Transit, Mechelen BE

2002
Und sie bewegt sich doch!, Städtische Galerie im Lenbachhaus, Munich / München DE
Heimatlied, Galerie Markus Richter, Berlin DE

GROUP EXHIBITIONS
GRUPPENAUSSTELLUNGEN

2022
Blanc de Blancs, Villa Schöningen, Potsdam DE
Das Gehirn. In Kunst & Wissenschaft, Bundeskunsthalle, Bonn DE
Haut Kontakt, Smac, Berlin DE
Räume 3, GUT Am Flughafen 1 / Flughafen Tegel, Berlin DE
Schatzhaus & Labor – 25 Jahre Museum Kurhaus Kleve, Kleve DE
Drei Farben: BLAU, WEISS, ROT, Walter Storms Galerie, Munich / München DE

2021
Ende Neu, KINDL – Zentrum für zeitgenössische Kunst, Berlin DE
Interactions 7 mit Alexander Iskin, Sexauer Showroom, Berlin DE
"Good artists copy, great artists steal" (Pablo Picasso), Artcurial Germany, Munich / München DE
Portland, Galerie Jahn, Landshut DE
Bout de souffle, Carbon 12, Dubai AE
Three Connections, Kulturstiftung Basel H. Geiger, Basel CH

2020
Various Others, Munich / München DE
Die Wolken und die Wolke, Museum für Gegenwartskunst, Siegen DE
Studio Berlin, Berghain, Berlin DE
Gasträume Zürich, Zurich / Zürich CH
Wände / Walls, Kunstmuseum Stuttgart, Stuttgart DE
ROHKUNSTBAU XXV, Schloss Lieberose, Potsdam DE
And the FORESTs will echo with laughter…, ERES Stiftung, Munich / München DE
Wolken in der zeitgenössischen Kunst – flüchtig – zeichenhaft – bedrohlich, Oldenburger Kunstverein, Oldenburg DE
Mourning. On loss and change, Hamburger Kunsthalle, Hamburg DE
Nine to know, Ruttkowski 68, Paris FR

2019
Primitive Cool, Sardenhaus, Munich / München DE
Fly me to the Moon. 50 Jahre Mondlandung, Kunsthaus Zürich & Museum der Moderne, Salzburg AT
The Big Sleep, Haus der Kunst, Munich / München DE
The Aerodrome – An exhibition dedicated to the memory of Michael Stanley, Ikon Gallery, Birmingham GB
Remake, Quand la vidéo rejoue le cinéma, FRAC Normandie, Rouen FR
Szene Berlin, Okt. 19, Ketterer Kunst, Munich / München DE
+1, Safe Gallery, Berlin DE

2018
Kunst und Kohle. Hommage an Jannis Kounellis, MKM Museum Küppersmühle für Moderne Kunst, Duisburg DE
Riga International Biennial of Contemporary Art, Riga LV
Eruption from the Surface: The Origami Principle in Art, Marta Herford, Herford DE
Cat scan, Galerie Kornfeld, Berlin DE
Zeitspuren – The Power of Now, Kunsthaus Pasquart, Bienne / Biel CH
Rehearsal, Tai Kwun Contemporary, Hong Kong / Hongkong CN
Ngorongoro II, Berlin DE
Art Biesenthal, Wehrmühle Biesenthal, Biesenthal DE
Art Weekend Bad Gastein, Bad Gastein AT

2017
On with the Show, Kunsthalle Nürnberg, Nuremberg / Nürnberg DE
Deutschland 8 – German Art in Beijing, White Box Museum of Art, Beijing / Peking CN
La lama di Procopio, Nuovo Spazio di Casso, Casso IT
Das Auto in der Kunst. Rasende Leidenschaft, Kunsthalle Emden, Emden DE
Facade, Middelburg NL
Art and Alphabet, Hamburger Kunsthalle, Hamburg DE
Adele, Galerie Zink, Waldkirchen DE
Transaktionen, Haus am Lützowplatz, Berlin DE
Meet me in Heaven, Schloss Tüssling, Tüssling DE
Luther und die Avantgarde, Wittenberg DE
Jupiter Artland, Edinburgh GB
Painting or not, Kaviar Factory, Henningsvær NO
Warum bin ich eigentlich Deutscher?, Kunstverein Wiesen, Wiesen DE
Factories, Außenskulptur, IGA Berlin DE
The act of drinking a Coke by myself is the lowest form of art, Galleria Zero, Milan / Mailand IT
Mexibility, Museum Casa del Lago, Mexico City MX
Warten, Hamburger Kunsthalle, Hamburg DE
SMALL – an exploration of miniature, Sexauer Gallery, Berlin DE
Condo, Emalin, London GB
Under Construction, Schau Fenster, Berlin DE
Attics of My Life, Jack Hanley Gallery, New York NY, US

2016
Jeder sollte in der Lage sein, Kunst zu erwerben, Provinz-Editionen, Kunsthalle Recklinghausen, Recklinghausen DE
Open Windows – Reflections on Beuys, Sexauer Gallery, Berlin DE
Kommt zusammen, Galerie Jahn, Landshut DE
Drama Queens, Museum Morsbroich, Leverkusen DE
ach, die sind ja heut so unpolitisch, Salon Dahlmann, Berlin DE
Head & Shoulders, Michael Sailstorfer & Johannes Wohnseifer, Galleri K, Oslo NO
Auftrag Landschaft, ZKR – Schloss Biesdorf, Berlin DE
Mon art à moi, Kunsthaus Pasquart, Bienne / Biel CH
Lichtparcours Braunschweig 2016, Brunswick / Braunschweig DE
The Difference Between Sunrise and Sunset, Sammlung Wemhöner, Schloss Tüssling, Tüssling DE
About Painting. Positionen der Sammlung Wemhöner, Galerie Judin, Berlin DE
Partoftheprocess7, Galleria Zero, Milan / Mailand IT
K A R L, Parkhaus im Malkastenpark, Düsseldorf DE
Brutal schön – Gewalt und Gegenwartsdesign, Marta Herford, Herford DE
~~ICH~~, Schirn Kunsthalle, Frankfurt/Main DE
Statement 3: New Sculpture from Germany, Goethe-Institut Hongkong, Hong Kong / Hongkong CN

2015
Kunst Bier Alchemie, Dortmunder U – Zentrum für Kunst und Kreativität, Dortmund DE
Small sized, Atelierräume Stefan Lenhart, Munich / München DE
Little is left to tell (Calvino after Calvino), Blue Project Foundation, Barcelona ES
About Trees, Zentrum Paul Klee, Bern CH
Zero: Infinite Possibilities, The Farjam Collection, Dubai AE
Transient Material, Haus am Lützowplatz, Berlin DE
Arcadia Unbound, Funkhaus, Berlin DE
Das Gedächtnis des zukünftigen Materials, Bergakademie Freiberg, Freiberg DE
Paperworlds, Museum Buchheim, Bernried DE
A Focus on Sculpture in the Würth Collection – The Winners of the Robert Jacobsen Prize of the Würth Foundation. Würth Collection and Loans, Museum Würth, Künzelsau DE
Ka-boom, Kunstverein Wiesen, Wiesen DE
Alicja Kwade, Michael Sailstorfer, Thomas Rentmeister, Sprovieri Gallery, London GB
Lichtparcours: Auftakt, Kunstverein Braunschweig, Brunswick / Braunschweig DE
Ngorongoro, Berlin DE
Grand Opening Sankt Agnes, Johann König, Berlin DE
Material, Johann König, Berlin DE
Vom Großen und Ganzen. Die Sammlung Haus N, Villa Wachholtz, Herbert Gerisch-Stiftung, Neumünster DE
F.E.G.L., LYKK zu Faserstein – In Memoriam Peter Lang*, Kosmetiksalon Babette, Berlin DE
Ärger im Paradies, Bundeskunsthalle, Bonn DE
Das Mechanische Corps. Auf den Spuren von Jules Verne, HMKV im Dortmunder U, Dortmund DE
Mainzer Ansichten. 110 Künstler/innen in einem Büro, Kunsthalle Mainz, Mainz DE
Sammeln für morgen. Neue Werke im Museion, Museion, Bolzano / Bozen IT
Artisti per Frescobaldi Award, Fondazione Stelline, Milan / Mailand IT

2014
Folkestone Triennale 2014, Folkestone GB, UK
Ciclo, CCBB SP e BH / Centro Cultural Banco do Brasil, São Paulo BR
WAR, Mostyn, Llandudno GB
Scheinwerfer. Lichtkunst in Deutschland im 21. Jahrhundert Teil 2, Kunstmuseum Celle, Celle DE
Das Mechanische Corps, Auf den Spuren von Jules Verne, Künstlerhaus Bethanien, Berlin DE
A Place Like This – Klöntal Triennale 2014, Kunsthaus Glarus, Glarus CH
Grooving Image, TS art projects, Berlin DE
Arsenale der Gegenwart, Villa Schöningen, Potsdam DE
Garage Paradise, La Tôlerie – Espace d'art contemporain, Clermont-Ferrand FR
Drive the Change, 100plus, Zurich / Zürich CH
Paperworlds. Kinder und Jugendzeichnungen zeitgenössischer Künstler, me collectors room – Stiftung Olbricht, Berlin DE

2013
Transferts, Dernières Acquisitions du FRAC, Maison des Arts Solange-Baudoux and Musée d'Art, Histoire et Archéologie, Évreux FR
Westwärts, Grieder Contemporary, Zurich / Zürich CH
Happy Birthday Galerie Perrotin / 25 ans Perrotin, Paris FR
Risk Society. Individualization in Young Contemporary Art from Germany, MOCA Museum of Contemporary Art, Taipei / Taipeh TW
Back to Earth. Von Picasso bis Ai Weiwei. Die Wiederentdeckung der Keramik in der Kunst, Herbert Gerisch-Stiftung, Neumünster DE
Novecento Mai Visto. Highlights from the Daimler Art Collection. From Albers to Warhol to (now), Museo di Santa Giulia, Brescia IT
Emscherkunst 2013, Essen DE
Köln Skulptur #6, Skulpturenpark Köln, Cologne / Köln DE
Disaster. The End of Days, Galerie Thaddaeus Ropac, Salzburg AT
First |Thirteen, Salon Kennedy, Frankfurt/Main DE
Goldrausch. Gegenwartskunst aus, mit oder über Gold, Villa Merkel, Esslingen DE
Wide As An Illusion – Expansion Dissolves, Setareh Gallery, Düsseldorf DE
The Unanswered Question. Iskele 2, TANAS &

Neuer Berliner Kunstverein, Berlin DE

Grünes Holz, Südtiroler Künstlerbund, Bolzano / Bozen IT

When Now is Minimal. Die unbekannte Seite der Sammlung Goetz, Neues Museum – Staatliches Museum für Kunst und Design, Nuremberg / Nürnberg DE

Sociétés Secrètes, FRAC Haute-Normandie, Sotteville-lès-Rouen FR

Reframing the Ordinary, Lothringer 13, Munich / München DE

Herbert Hinteregger + Michael Sailstorfer, Galerie Georg Kargl, Vienna / Wien AT

Heimat und Utopie / Maze 62, KunstFestSpiele Herrenhausen, Hanover / Hannover DE

Nuage, Musée Réattu, Arles FR

German Art 2013, Galleri K, Oslo NO

2012

Slg. Wilhelm Otto Nachf.: Werkräume von Kai Althoff bis Thomas Zipp, Leopold-Hoesch-Museum & Papiermuseum Düren, Düren DE

My Private Universe, The Schaufler Foundation, Sindelfingen DE

Showroom II, Galerie Mirko Mayer / m-projects, Cologne / Köln DE

I Wish This Was a Song. Music in Contemporary Art, The Museum of Contemporary Art, Oslo NO

Other Voices, Other Rooms, Galerie Wentrup, Berlin DE

Sculpture is Everything. Contemporary Works from the Collection, Gallery of Modern Art, Brisbane QLD, AU

Portfolio Berlin 2, Kunsthalle Rostock, Rostock DE

Wie kommt das Neue in die Welt? Neun internationale Bildhauer in Berlin, Haus am Waldsee, Berlin DE

From A to B, CCA Andratx., Andratx ES

Berlin.Status (1), Künstlerhaus Bethanien, Berlin DE

Mobile immobile, FRAC Picardie, Amiens FR

Die Stadt als Bühne der Bilder, Museen der Stadt Landshut, Landshut DE

Absolute Beginner, Fürstlich Fürstenbergisches Schloss und Sammlungen, Donaueschingen DE

Atelier + Küche = Labore der Sinne, Marta Herford, Herford DE

Group Show, Perrotin, Paris FR

Clegg & Guttmann, Elger Esser, Axel Hütte, Michael Sailstorfer, Galerie Mirko Mayer, Cologne / Köln DE

A Touch of Life, Galerie Anita Beckers, Frankfurt/Main DE

Arrivi e Partenze Europa, Fondo Mole Vanvitelliana, Ancona IT

The Dark Side of the Moon, Carbon12, Dubai AE

Goldrausch, Kunsthalle Nürnberg, Nuremberg / Nürnberg DE

Josef Sailstorfer & Michael Sailstorfer, Galerie Johann König, Berlin DE

Group Exhibition, Paula Cooper Gallery, New York NY, US

2011

Kunstpreis „junger westen" 1948 bis 2011, Kunsthalle Recklinghausen, Recklinghausen DE

Culture.climate, Yaffo 23, Jerusalem IL

Werke aus der Sammlung Marta, Kunst und Kulturzentrum Monschau, Monschau DE

Is that True? Possibilities of (Non-)Knowledge, Kunsthaus Dresden, Dresden DE

KölnSkulptur #6, Skulpturenpark Köln, Cologne / Köln DE

Commercial Break, Garage Moscow, Venice / Venedig IT

The Guerrilla Design Show, Conduits, Milan / Mailand IT

Art & Stars & Cars, Daimler Kunst Sammlung, Stuttgart DE

Involuntary, Ford Projects, New York NY, US

Sculpture, Paula Cooper Gallery, New York NY, US

Light in Darkness, Western Bridge, Seattle WA, US

Car Fetish. I drive, therefore I am., Museum Tinguely, Basel CH

Under Destruction Chapter 1, SI Swiss Institute, New York NY, US

Echoes, Centre Culturel Suisse, Paris FR

Wasser Straße Schiene Luft – Mobilität am Bodensee, Zeppelin Museum, Friedrichshafen DE

Höhenrausch.2, Brücken im Himmel, OK Offenes Kulturhaus OÖ, Linz AT

Unwetter / Thunderstorm, Ayala Museum, Makati City PH

Informell Nature, Galerie Sabine Knust, Munich / München DE

2010

FischGrätenMelkStand, Temporäre Kunsthalle, Berlin DE

Trailer Park, Fondazione Morra Greco, Naples / Neapel IT

Review / Preview II, Grieder Contemporary, Zurich / Zürich CH

Monuments on the Move, Galeria Raster, Warsaw / Warschau PL

The Unbearable Lightness of Being, Carbon 12, Dubai AE

Alter Nature: We Can, Z33, Hasselt NL

6 michael sailstorfer, Villa Reykjavik, Reykjavik IS

Sphères 2010, Galleria Continua, Le Moulins, Boissy-le-Châtel FR

From & T(w)o, Kunst Meran, Merano / Meran IT

Under Destruction, Tinguely Museum, Basel CH

Unsichtbare Schatten – Bilder der Verunsicherung, Marta Herford, Herford DE

About us, Galerie Johann König, Berlin DE

Art Biesenthal 2010, Biesenthal DE

E...R...O...D...E...R...E, Märkisches Museum Witten, Witten DE

To the Elements! Aesthetic Phenomena of Climate Change, Goethe-Institut, New York NY, US

Starter Works from the Vehbi Koç, Arter space for art, Istanbul TR

Unwetter, Akademie der Künste, Berlin DE

Arrivals and Departures, Fondo Mole Vanvitelliana, Ancona IT

De(C)obstruction, Micamoca, Berlin DE

As soon as Possible, Centro di Cultura Contemporanea Strozzina, Florence / Florenz IT

Totem and Taboo, Oratorio Basilica St. Ambrogio, Milan / Mailand IT

2009

The Quick and the Dead, Walker Art Center, Minneapolis MN, US

The Secret Live of Objects, Midway Contemporary Art, Minneapolis MN, US

Inclemencia del Tiempo, Centro de Exposiciones Subte, Montevideo UY

Berlin meets Vienna, Salon Österreich, Vienna / Wien AT

Short Circuits, Peter Blum Gallery, New York NY, US

Circus Hein, FRAC Centre-Val de Loire, Orléans & Atelier Calder, Saché FR

Review / Preview, Grieder Contemporary, Küsnacht CH

Variation time, Galerie der Künstler, BBK München und Oberbayern e. V., Munich / München DE

Can Birds Fly?, Galerie Parisa Kind, Frankfurt/Main DE

Cargo / cargo manifest, cargo vision, Autocenter, Berlin DE

Works from the Franks-Suss Collection, London GB

Cargo manifest, Bayerische Staatsoper, Munich / München DE

Spacioux, Lambretto Art Project, Milan / Mailand DE

Romantische Maschinen – Kinetische Kunst der Gegenwart, Georg Kolbe Museum, Berlin DE

Dank an, Galerie Isabella Czarnowska, Berlin DE

Micro House, Bielefelder Kunstverein, Bielefeld DE

Intemperie, 2nd Bienal del Fin del Mundo, Ushuaia AR

KölnSkulptur #5, Skulpturenpark Köln, Cologne / Köln DE

Paradies – Neue Blicke auf einen alten Traum, Diözesanmuseum, Freising DE

2008

God is Design, Galpão Fortes Vilaça, São Paulo BR

Heavy Metal. Die unerklärliche Leichtigkeit eines Materials, Kunsthalle zu Kiel, Kiel DE

Musical Paintings, Aurel Scheibler, Berlin DE

Archeology of Mind, Kuntsi Museum of Modern Art, Vaasa FI

Malcolm McLaren Musical Painting, Aurel Scheibler, Berlin DE

Zeitblick – Ankäufe aus der Sammlung Zeitgenössischer Kunst der Bundesrepublik Deutschland 1998–2008, Martin-Gropius-Bau, Berlin DE

Disarming Matter, Dunkers Kulturhus, Helsingborg SE

younivers, Bienal de Arte Contemporáneo de Sevilla, Sevilla ES

Leftovers, Mariano Pichler Collection, Berlin DE

Archeology of Mind, Fondazione Morra Greco, Naples / Neapel IT

Archeology of Mind, Malmö Konstmuseum, Malmö SE

Fabricateurs d'espaces, Institut d'art contemporain – Villeurbanne/Rhône-Alpes, Villeurbanne FR

Parkhaus, Kunsthalle Düsseldorf, Düsseldorf DE

L'Art Contemporain en Europe, Experience Pommery #5, Domaine Pommery, Reims FR

Walls in the Street, Siemens Art Program, Museum of Contemporary Art, Belgrade / Belgrad RS

Kabul 3000 (Love among the cabbages), Galleria Zero, Milan / Mailand IT

There is No Story to Tell, Tang Contemporary, Beijing / Peking CN

Ad Absurdum – Zeitgemäße Apparate, Städtische Galerie Nordhorn, Nordhorn DE

Ad Absurdum – Zeitgemäße Apparate, Marta Herford, Herford DE

Merkwürdige Maschinen, Phaenomenale 2008, Kunstverein Wolfsburg, Wolfsburg DE

Pop! Goes the weasel, Badischer Kunstverein, Karlsruhe DE

2007

Made in Germany, Kestner Gesellschaft, Kunstverein, Sprengel Museum, Hanover / Hannover DE

Perspektive 07, Städtische Galerie im Lenbachhaus, Munich / München DE

Rubin – Institut für moderne Kunst Nürnberg 1967–2007, Institut für moderne Kunst Nürnberg, Nuremberg / Nürnberg DE

True Romance – Allegorien der Liebe von der Renaissance bis heute, Kunsthalle Wien, Vienna / Wien AT

Disorder in the House, Vanhaerents Art Collection, Brussels / Brüssel BE

Erasing the edge, Uovo/Miami, Miami FL, US

Michael Sailstorfer, Nathan Hylden, Grieder Contemporary, Zurich / Zürich CH

My sweet sixteen Party, Gallery Rodolphe Janssen, Brussels / Brüssel BE

Neue Heimat – Berlin Contemporary, Berlinische Galerie, Berlin DE

Bodycheck, 10. Triennale Kleinplastik, Fellbach DE

storyboard, Galerie Mirko Mayer / m-projects, Cologne / Köln DE

Ironie der Objekte, Museion, Bolzano / Bozen IT

ars viva – Erzählung/Narration, House of the Lords of Kunštát, Brno / Brünn CZ

ars viva – Erzählung/Narration, Stadtgalerie Saarbrücken, Saarbrücken DE

Absent without Leave, Victoria Miro Gallery, London GB

Still Life: Art, Ecology and the Politics of change, Sharjah Biennial 8, Sharjah / Schardscha AE

Kunstpreis der Schering Stiftung, Berlinische Galerie, Berlin DE

My private escaped from Italy, Centre international d'art et du paysage, Île de Vassivière FR

Footnotes on Geopolitics, Market and Amnesia, 2nd Moscow Biennale, Moscow / Moskau RU

2006

Bucolica, Galerie Thaddaeus Ropac, Salzburg AT

Lichtjaren, Historical Center, Gouda NL

Momentum, Nordic Biennial of Contemporary Art, Moss NO

YBA – Young Bavarian Artists, Gagosian Gallery, Berlin DE

Bühne des Lebens, Rhetorik des Gefühls, Kunstbau, Städtische Galerie im Lenbachhaus, Munich / München DE

The Universe in a Handkerchief, Gallery Yujiro, London GB

ars viva, Hochschule für Bildende Künste, Dresden DE

Villa Holiday Warsaw, Galeria Raster, Warsaw / Warschau PL

Und es bewegt sich doch …, Museum Bochum, Bochum DE

On The Move. Verkehrskultur II, Westfälischer Kunstverein, Münster DE

Kontracom 06, Salzburg AT

Transatlantische Impulse, Martin-Gropius-Bau, Berlin DE

Endless Summer, West London Projects, London GB

Eigenheim, everything but the kitchen sink, Kunstverein Göttingen, Göttingen DE

Inaugural Exhibition, Galerie Johann König, Berlin DE

2005

Favoriten, Neue Kunst in München, Städtische Galerie im Lenbachhaus, Munich / München DE

We Disagree, Andrew Kreps Gallery, New York NY, US

Those who have double parked, Parkhaus im Malkastenpark, Düsseldorf DE

Things Fall Apart All Over Again, Artists Space, New York NY, US

Kunstpreis der Böttcherstraße, Kunsthalle Bremen, Bremen DE

Lichtkunst aus Kunstlicht, ZKM I Zentrum für Kunst und Medien, Karlsruhe DE

Talk to the Land, Andrew Kreps Gallery, New York NY, US

Yokohama 2005 – International Triennale of Contemporary Art, Yokohama JP

Rückkehr ins All, Hamburger Kunsthalle, Hamburg DE

XII. Rohkunstbau, Wasserschloss Groß Leuthen, Groß Leuthen DE

LIGHT LAB. Alltägliche Kurzschlüsse, Museion, Bolzano / Bozen IT

So klappt's – Modelle des Gelingens, Künstlerhaus Mousonturm, Frankfurt/Main DE

Bewegliche Teile. Formen des Kinetischen, Museum Tinguely, Basel CH

Light Sculpture – Scultura Leggera, 503 mulino, Vicenza IT

Window Cleaning Days Are Over, The Empire, London GB

2004

Manifesta 5, Donostia-San Sebastian ES

On Reason and Emotion: 14th Biennale of Sydney, Sydney NSW, AU

Bloomberg New Contemporaries 2004, Barbican Centre, London GB

Bloomberg New Contemporaries 2004, The Coach Shed, Liverpool GB

Rheinschau, Cologne / Köln DE

Bewegliche Teile – Formen des Kinetischen, Kunsthaus Graz, Graz AT

Liverpool Biennial of Contemporary Art, Liverpool GB

Agora, Transition Gallery, London GB

Agora, Transition Gallery, Glasgow GB

XS – An Invitation Exhibition, Fa Projects, London GB

Secret Garden, South London Gallery, London GB

Dedobbeleer, Sailstorfer and Wissel, Galerie Zink & Gegner, Munich / München DE

Xtreme Houses, Stiftung Federkiel – Halle 14, Leipzig DE

Xtreme Houses, Lothringer 13 Halle, Munich / München DE

Climats, cyclothymie des paysages, Centre international d'art et du paysage, Île de Vassivière FR

BHF live set + Sailstorfer, Galleria Zero, Milan / Mailand IT

2003

Wings of Art, Ludwig-Forum für internationale Kunst, Aachen DE

Prototipi.03, Fondazione Adriano Olivetti, Rome / Rom IT

8th Havana Biennial, Havana / Havanna CU

Video Screening 04, Galerie Martin Janda, Vienna / Wien AT

Wir, hier!, Lothringer13 Halle, Munich / München DE

Head on, Homeroom – Projektraum für zeitgenössische Kunst, Munich / München DE

Fuori Uso, Ferrotel, Pescara IT

010203, Galerie Transit, Mechelen BE

2002

At least begin to make an end, w139, Amsterdam NL

3x1, Nusser & Baumgart, Munich / München DE

Mit dem Kopf durch die Wand!, Akademiegalerie, Munich / München DE

Oltre il giardino, Rimini IT

Extra dunkel, Alte Mälzerei, Regensburg DE

2001

Kunstpreis „junger westen", Kunsthalle Recklinghausen, Recklinghausen DE

acht x anders, Centro de Arte Joven, Madrid ES

AWARDS
PREISE

2017	August-Macke-Preis
2014	Premio Artisti per Frescobaldi
2012	Vattenfall Contemporary
2011	Kunstpreis „junger westen", Kunsthalle Recklinghausen
2010	Sparda-Kunstpreis NRW, Essen
2007	Kulturpreis der Dr. Franz und Astrid Ritter-Stiftung für Bildende Kunst
2006	*ars viva* Preis für Bildende Kunst
2002	Preis der Darmstädter Sezession Dena Foundation Art Award Förderpreis der Christian Karl Schmidt Stiftung

ART IN PUBLIC SPACE
KUNST IM ÖFFENTLICHEN RAUM

2020	*3 Farben,* Landtag Rheinland-Pfalz, Mainz DE
2018	*Sonne,* Umweltbundesamt, Dessau DE
2015	*Solarkatze,* 50Hertz, Berlin DE
2014	*Mückenhäuser,* Kunstmeile Recklinghausen, Recklinghausen DE
2012	*Tor de France,* Quartier Eurobahnhof, Saarbrücken DE
2012	*Außenthermometer,* UN-Campus Bonn, Bonn DE
2011	*Tornado,* Doris C. Freedman Plaza, Central Park, New York NY, US
2008	*Raketenbaum,* Forschungszentrum für nachwachsende Rohstoffe, Straubing DE
2008	*Bühne,* Fachhochschule Neu-Ulm, Neu-Ulm DE
2005	*Hoher Besuch,* Marta Herford, Herford DE

COLLECTIONS (SELECTION)
SAMMLUNGEN (AUSWAHL)

About Change Collection, Berlin DE

Berlinische Galerie, Berlin DE

Stiftung Museum Modern Art Hünfeld – Sammlung Jürgen Blum, Hünfeld DE

Sammlung Boros, Berlin DE

Centre Pompidou, Paris FR

Sammlung Fiede, Frankfurt/Main DE

Sammlung Goetz, Munich / München DE

FRAC Normandie Rouen, Rouen FR

Haus N Collection DE

Institut d'art contemporain de Villeurbanne, Villeurbanne FR

Kunsthalle Recklinghausen, Recklinghausen DE

Sammlung Andra Lauffs-Wegner, Bad Honnef DE

Leopold-Hoesch-Museum, Düren DE

Marta Herford, Herford DE

Museion, Bolzano / Bozen IT

Museum Kurhaus Kleve – Ewald Mataré-Sammlung, Kleve DE

My Private, Milan / Mailand IT

S.M.A.K. – Stedelijk Museum voor Actuele Kunst, Ghent / Gent BE

Städel Museum, Frankfurt/Main DE

Städtische Galerie im Lenbachhaus & Kunstbau, Munich / München DE

Vanhaerents Art Collection, Brussels / Brüssel BE

Walker Art Center, Minneapolis MN, US

Sammlung Wemhöner, Berlin DE

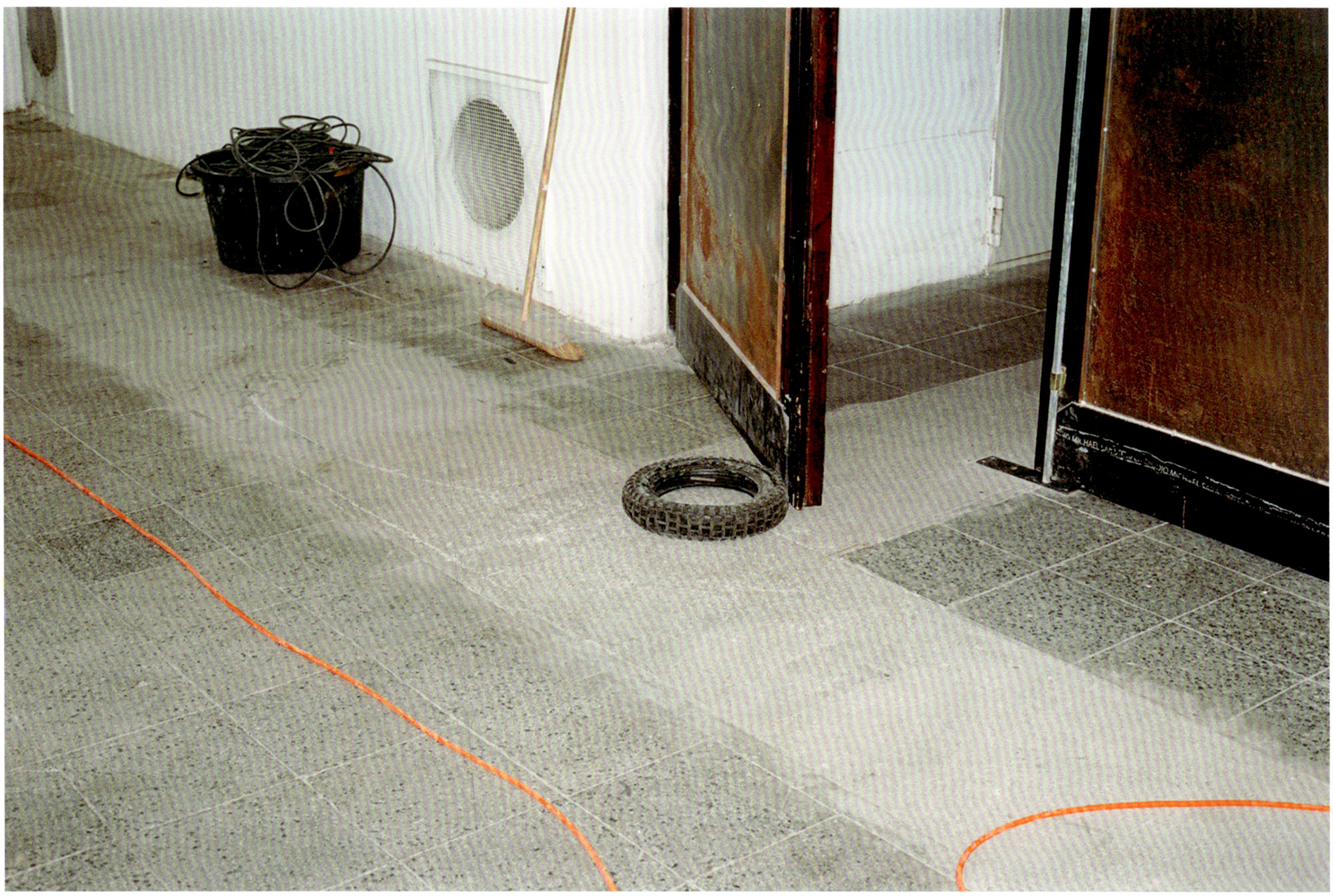

JOHANNA ADAM

is a curator at the Bundeskunsthalle in Bonn where, in addition to exhibitions in the field of modern and contemporary art, she works on interdisciplinary projects between culture and science. Previously, she worked at the Fridericianum in Kassel and for *dOCUMENTA (13)*. She regularly publishes in magazines and exhibition catalogues.

ist Kuratorin an der Kunst- und Ausstellungshalle der Bundesrepublik Deutschland in Bonn, wo sie neben Ausstellungen im Bereich der modernen und zeitgenössischen Kunst an interdisziplinären Projekten zu Kultur und Wissenschaft arbeitet. Zuvor war sie am Fridericianum in Kassel sowie für die dOCUMENTA (13) tätig. Als Autorin publiziert sie regelmäßig in Zeitschriften und Ausstellungskatalogen.

MARIA BREMER

is an art historian based in Berlin. She is currently a postdoctoral academic councilor at the Department of Art History of Ruhr University Bochum. Her field of research includes contemporary art and exhibition history. Previous affiliations include the Bibliotheca Hertziana – Max Planck Institute for Art History in Rome, the Center for Italian Modern Art in New York, and the German Center for Art History (DFK) in Paris.

ist Kunsthistorikerin und lebt in Berlin. Derzeit ist sie als Akademische Rätin a. Z. am Kunstgeschichtlichen Institut der Ruhr-Universität Bochum beschäftigt. Ihr Forschungsbereich umfasst die Kunst- und Ausstellungsgeschichte der Gegenwart. Zuvor war sie unter anderem an der Bibliotheca Hertziana – Max-Planck-Institut für Kunstgeschichte in Rom, am Center for Italian Modern Art in New York und am Centre allemand d'histoire de l'art (DFK) in Paris tätig.

DIANDRA DONECKER

studied art history, modern German literature, and law in Munich. She was a graduate trainee in the Department of Drawings and Prints at The Metropolitan Museum of Art, New York and the British Museum, London. From 2015 to 2017, she worked at Christie's and since 2017 as an expert for works on paper and for photography at Grisebach in Berlin, where she has been Managing Director and partner since 2019.

studierte Kunstgeschichte, Neuere deutsche Literatur und Rechtswissenschaften in München. Sie war Volontärin in der Abteilung für Handzeichnungen und Druckgrafik am Metropolitan Museum of Art, New York, und am British Museum, London. Von 2015 bis 2017 arbeitete sie bei Christie's und seit 2017 als Expertin für Arbeiten auf Papier und für Fotografie bei Grisebach in Berlin, seit 2019 ist sie dort Geschäftsführerin und Partnerin.

KRIS DOUGLAS

is an independent curator based in Berlin. From 2006 until 2015, he served as Chief Curator of the Rochester Art Center, Minnesota, where he organized multiple group exhibitions. In 2004, he initiated the *RAC Emerging Artist Series*, an ongoing exhibition program designed to support artists at the beginning of their careers. As a writer, his essays have been published in various art journals.

lebt als freier Kurator in Berlin. Von 2006 bis 2015 arbeitete er als Chefkurator am Rochester Art Center, Minnesota, wo er zahlreiche Gruppenausstellungen organisierte. 2004 initiierte er das fortlaufende Ausstellungsprogramm *RAC Emerging Artist Series*, das junge Künstler*innen am Anfang ihrer Karriere unterstützen soll. Als Autor hat er Essays in verschiedenen Kunstmagazinen veröffentlicht.

BERND EULER

trained as a metalworker from 1989 to 1991 and passed his master craftsman's examination in 1995. From 1996 to 2003, he studied at the University of Art and Design in Offenbach am Main. In 2003, he wrote his diploma on "Experimental Spatial Concepts" under the supervision of Prof. Heiner Blum. In 2005, he founded Bernd Euler GmbH, specializing in the production of works by contemporary artists.

machte von 1989 bis 1991 eine Ausbildung zum Metallbauer und 1995 seine Meisterprüfung. Von 1996 bis 2003 studierte er an der Hochschule für Gestaltung in Offenbach. 2003 machte er sein Diplom über „Experimentelle Raumkonzepte" bei Prof. Heiner Blum. 2005 gründete er die Bernd Euler GmbH – Werkstatt für Produktion von Arbeiten zeitgenössischer Künstler*innen.

LUKAS FEIREISS

is a curator and author specializing in the international, transdisciplinary mediation of art, culture, and contemporary reflexivity. He is the editor of various books and curator of numerous exhibitions on art, design, and architecture. He teaches at various universities in Germany and abroad and is a visiting professor for transdisciplinary artistic teaching at the Berlin University of the Arts.

arbeitet als Kurator und Autor an der internationalen Vermittlung von Kunst, Kultur und zeitgenössischer Reflexivität jenseits disziplinärer Grenzen. Er ist Herausgeber diverser Bücher und Kurator zahlreicher Ausstellungen zu Kunst, Design und Architektur. Er unterrichtet an verschiedenen Universitäten im In- und Ausland und ist Gastprofessor für transdisziplinäre künstlerische Lehre an der Universität der Künste Berlin.

JOHANNA and/und FRIEDRICH GRÄFLING

build, design, conceive, research, teach, and collect. Together, they run Cultural Avenue, a cultural and design agency for projects in the fields of architecture, interior design, and art. They also run Salon Kennedy, an exhibition space in Frankfurt am Main, and the Kunstverein Wiesen. In parallel, they are continuously expanding their private art collection: the Gräfling Collection.

bauen, gestalten, konzipieren, forschen, lehren und sammeln. Gemeinsam führen sie die Cultural Avenue, eine Kultur- und Gestaltungsagentur für Architektur-, Interior- und Kunstprojekte. Außerdem leiten sie den Salon Kennedy, einen Ausstellungsraum in Frankfurt am Main und den Kunstverein Wiesen e. V. Parallel bauen sie ihre private Kunstsammlung, die Sammlung Gräfling, kontinuierlich aus.

SIGURD LARSEN

is a Danish architect and furniture designer who lives and works in Berlin. After receiving his master's degree from the School of Architecture at the Royal Academy of Fine Arts in Copenhagen, he worked at OMA Rem Koolhaas in New York, MVRDV in Rotterdam, and Topotek1 in Berlin. Since 2016, Sigurd Larsen has been a professor at the Berlin International University of Applied Sciences.

ist ein dänischer Architekt und Möbeldesigner, der in Berlin lebt und arbeitet. Nach seinem Master-Abschluss an der School of Architecture der Royal Academy of Fine Arts in Kopenhagen arbeitete er bei OMA Rem Koolhaas in New York, MVRDV in Rotterdam und Topotek1 in Berlin. Seit 2016 ist Sigurd Larsen als Professor an der Berlin International University of Applied Sciences tätig.

MAGDALENA MAI

is an art historian and curator. After working as a curatorial assistant at KINDL – Centre for Contemporary Art in Berlin on various exhibition and publication projects from 2017 to 2020, she has been working there as a curator and project manager since 2020. She has published numerous texts on various artists and exhibitions.

ist Kunsthistorikerin und Kuratorin. Nachdem sie von 2017 bis 2020 als kuratorische Assistentin im KINDL – Zentrum für zeitgenössische Kunst in Berlin an diversen Ausstellungs- und Publikationsprojekten arbeitete, ist sie dort seit 2020 als Kuratorin und Projektleiterin tätig. Sie veröffentlichte zahlreiche Texte über verschiedene Künstler*innen und zu diversen Ausstellungen.

FRANK STEINHOFER

lives and works as a freelance author of both fiction and nonfiction in Mexico City and Dahn, Rhineland-Palatinate. In his texts, he deals with political ecology, near-natural art, and architecture. His debut novel *Das Terrain* (The Territory) about a new type of museum building near the Mexican rainforest was published in 2021.

lebt und arbeitet als freier Autor und Schriftsteller in Mexiko-Stadt und Dahn, Rheinland-Pfalz. In seinen Texten setzt er sich mit politischer Ökologie, naturnaher Kunst und Architektur auseinander. 2021 erschien sein Romandebüt *Das Terrain* über einen neuartigen Museumsbau in der Nähe des mexikanischen Regenwalds.

NEVILLE WAKEFIELD

is a British writer and curator interested in exploring the ways in which art behaves outside of institutional contexts. He was senior curatorial advisor for MoMA PS1, New York and curator of Frieze Projects and has worked extensively with institutions in the United States and abroad, including the Schaulager in Basel. He is the curator of *Desert X*, an international art biennale in the desert of Southern California.

ist ein britischer Autor und Kurator, dessen Interesse der Kunst außerhalb institutioneller Kontexte gilt. Er war kuratorischer Berater am MoMA PS1, New York, und Kurator der Frieze Projects und hat für zahlreiche Institutionen in den USA und im Ausland gearbeitet, darunter das Schaulager in Basel. Er ist der Kurator von *Desert X*, einer internationalen Kunstbiennale in der südkalifornischen Wüste.

For the generous support of this publication
I would like to thank:

Für die großzügige Unterstützung dieser
Publikation möchte ich danken:
Avlskarl, Copenhagen / Kopenhagen
Carbon 12, Dubai
Max Stepan
Jamil Hallak
Kamil Zniber
Abdelmonem Bin Eisa Alserkal
Ben & Erica Dahl
Magdalena & Thomas Pieper
König Galerie, Berlin, Seoul, Vienna / Wien
Livie Gallery, Zurich / Zürich
Galerie Wolfgang Jahn, Munich / München, Landshut
Proyectos Monclova, Mexico City / Mexiko-Stadt
ZERO…, Milan / Mailand
Galerie Zink, Waldkirchen

I thank the autors for their contributions.

Ich danke den Autor*innen für ihre Beiträge.

Special thanks to all the studio staff, producers, technicians, curators, artist advisors, architects, engineers, perfumers, photographers, consultants and friends who have supported me, the galleries, graphic designers, and DCV publishers.

Besonderer Dank gilt allen Mitarbeiter*innen des Studios, allen Produzent*innen, Techniker*innen, Kurator*innen, Künstlerbetreuer*innen, Architekt*innen, Ingenieur*innen, Parfumeur*innen, Fotograf*innen, Berater*innen und Freund*innen, die mich unterstützt haben, den Galerien, den Grafikern und dem DCV Verlag.

Thanks for great support and commitment:

Dank für die tatkräftige Unterstützung:
Mariona Berenguer, Natalie Brehmer,
Charlotte Spichalsky

Thank you:

Danke:
Liv Andersen, Selma Andersen,
Christine Andersen, Josef Sailstorfer,
Renate Sailstorfer, Anna Wagner-Sailstorfer,
Muk Wagner

Concept / Konzeption
Michael Sailstorfer, Heimann + Schwantes

Design / Gestaltung
Heimann + Schwantes, Berlin

Managing editor / Redaktion
Uta Grosenick

Texts / Texte
Johanna Adam, Maria Bremer, Diandra Donecker, Bernd Euler, Lukas Feireiss, Friedrich Gräfling, Johanna Gräfling, Kris Douglas, Sigurd Larsen, Magdalena Mai, Michael Sailstorfer, Frank Steinhofer, Neville Wakefield

Translation/Übersetzung
Gérard Goodrow, Uta Grosenick

Photo Credits / Bildnachweis
-1/MinusEins, Experimentallabor der Kunsthochschule für Medien Köln: pp. / S. 288–291, 294–295
Cheonho Ahn: pp. / S. 186–187
Thomas Gunnar Bagge: p. / S. 220
Veronika Beckh: p. / S. 7
Benjakon: pp. / S. 310–311
Lea Beyl: p. / S. 191
Helmut Claus: p. / S. 225
Torben Eskerod: pp. / S. 136, 161
James Ewing: p. / S. 73
Johanna & Friedrich Gräfling: pp. / S. 8–9
Damian Griffiths: pp. / S. 20, 40
Pascal Hofmann: pp. / S. 24, 27–30, 145, 156–160, 162
Ulrich Jansen: pp. / S. 300–301
Jörg Koopmann: pp. / S. 250–251
Annette Kradisch: p. / S. 213
Achim Kukulies: pp. / S. 34–35, 42, 44–47, 70–71, 74–81, 302–303, 312
Kultur Ruhr GmbH / Urbane Künste Ruhr: p. / S. 227
Patrick López Jaimes: p. / S. 263
Helmut Mägdefrau: p. / S. 216
Roman März: pp. / S. 10/11, 17, 48, 49, 56, 68–69, 72, 98, 103, 121–135, 137, 139–141, 144, 153, 163, 168–179, 182–185, 215, 234–235, 242, 256–261, 296, 297
Roman März / Torben Eskerod: p. / S. 115
Roberto Marossi: p. / S. 217
Irina Matthes: pp. / S. 12–13
Maren Meier: p. / S. 279
Norbert Miguletz: pp. / S. 276–277
Ina Niehoff: p. / S. 317
Noshe: pp. / S. 218, 304
Toni Ott: p. / S. 265
Ludger Paffrath: pp. / S. 89, 205
Sebastiano Pellion Di Persano: pp. / S. 188–190
Wilfried Petzi: p. / S. 271
Linda Rosa Saal: Portrait Michael Sailstorfer
Studio Sailstorfer: pp. / S.15–16, 18–19, 22, 23, 32, 33, 50–55, 59–67, 90–97, 99–102, 104–105, 120, 142–143, 146–152, 155, 164–167, 192, 195–198, 201, 204, 206–211, 219, 226, 231–233, 236–237, 240, 241, 247–249, 264, 266–270, 272– 275, 278, 298–299, 305–307
Studio Sailstorfer / Roman März: pp. / S. 147–150
Studio Sailstorfer / Gerald Ulmann / Galerie Thaddaeus Ropac / Roman März / Norbert Miguletz: pp. / S. 243 –246
Rolf Sturm: pp. / S. 238–239
Siegfried Wameser: pp. / S. 221–224
Harry Zdera: pp. / S. 43, 57–58, 154
Guillaume Ziccarelli: pp. / S. 14, 25–26, 31, 41, 109, 193–194, 199, 200, 202, 212, 262
Jens Ziehe: p. / S. 214
Erich Spahn: p. / S. 110

Schriften/Typefaces
MS Schrift, Heimann + Schwantes
Plain, Optimo
ES Face, Extraset

Paper/Papier
Condat Matt Perigord, 150 g/qm

Image editing / Lithografie
dpi-factory, Krefeld

Production management / Produktion
DCV

Printing and binding / Gesamtherstellung
Gutenberg Beuys feindruckerei, Langenhagen

This publication is listed in the German National Bibliography by the German National Library. Detailed bibliographic data are available at http://dnb.d-nb.de.
Die Deutsche Nationalbibliothek verzeichnet diese Publikation in der Deutschen Nationalbibliografie; detaillierte bibliografische Daten sind im Internet über http://dnb.dnb.de abrufbar.

Distribution and marketing /
Vertrieb und Marketing DCV
sales@dcv-books.com

ISBN 978-3-96912-106-1

Printed in Germany

Published by / Erschienen bei DCV
www.dcv-books.com

DCV